TIM COOK

THE NECESSARY WAR

CANADIANS FIGHTING THE SECOND WORLD WAR 1939–1943

VOLUME ONE

ALLEN
LANE

ALLEN LANE

an imprint of Penguin Canada Books Inc., a Penguin Random House Company

Published by the Penguin Group

Penguin Canada Books Inc., 90 Eglinton Avenue East, Suite 700, Toronto, Ontario, Canada M4P 2Y3

Penguin Group (USA) LLC, 375 Hudson Street, New York, New York 10014, U.S.A.
Penguin Books Ltd, 80 Strand, London WC2R 0RL, England
Penguin Ireland, 25 St Stephen's Green, Dublin 2, Ireland (a division of Penguin Books Ltd)
Penguin Group (Australia), 707 Collins Street, Melbourne, Victoria 3008, Australia
(a division of Pearson Australia Group Pty Ltd)
Penguin Books India Pvt Ltd, 11 Community Centre, Panchsheel Park, New Delhi – 110 017, India
Penguin Group (NZ), 67 Apollo Drive, Rosedale, Auckland 0632, New Zealand
(a division of Pearson New Zealand Ltd)
Penguin Books (South Africa) (Pty) Ltd, 24 Sturdee Avenue, Rosebank, Johannesburg 2196, South Africa

Penguin Books Ltd, Registered Offices: 80 Strand, London WC2R 0RL, England

First published 2014

1 2 3 4 5 6 7 8 9 10   (RRD)

Copyright © Tim Cook, 2014
Maps and artwork © Crowle Art Group, 2014

The credits on page 519 constitute an extension of the copyright page.

Manufactured in the U.S.A.

Library and Archives Canada Cataloguing in Publication

Cook, Tim, 1971–, author
The necessary war / Tim Cook.

Includes bibliographical references and index.
ISBN 978-0-670-06650-6 (v. 1 : bound)

1. World War, 1939–1945—Canada. 2. Canada. Canadian Army—
History—World War, 1939–1945. 3. World War, 1939–1945—Battlefields.
4. World War, 1939-1945—Campaigns. I. Title.

D768.15.C64 2014   940.54'1271   C2014-902039-2

eBook ISBN 978-0-14-319304-3

Visit the Penguin Canada website at **www.penguin.ca**

Special and corporate bulk purchase rates available; please see
www.penguin.ca/corporatesales or call 1-800-810-3104.

For Dr. Terry Cook,
who taught me how to be
an historian and a man
(1947–2014)

Also by Tim Cook

No Place to Run

Clio's Warriors

At the Sharp End:
Canadians Fighting the Great War,
1914–1916, Volume One

Shock Troops:
Canadians Fighting the Great War,
1917–1918, Volume Two

The Madman and the Butcher:
The Sensational Wars of Sam Hughes
and General Arthur Currie

Warlords: Borden, Mackenzie King,
and Canada's World Wars

CONTENTS

Introduction: The War Against Hitler   *1*

CHAPTER 1   Reluctantly to War   13

CHAPTER 2   The Fall of France   31

CHAPTER 3   The Battle of Britain   45

CHAPTER 4   The War in the Far East   59

CHAPTER 5   The War at Sea   95

CHAPTER 6   Life on a Corvette   133

CHAPTER 7   Bomber Command   153

CHAPTER 8   The Struggle to Survive   173

CHAPTER 9   Striking Back   199

CHAPTER 10   A Sortie Against a City   223

CHAPTER 11   Day of Destruction   251

CHAPTER 12   Backs to the Wall   287

CHAPTER 13   Making an Impact   309

CHAPTER 14   Test of Battle   329

CHAPTER 15   The Italian Campaign   377

Conclusion: The End of the Beginning   419

Endnotes   425

Acknowledgments   471

Bibliography   475

Index   503

Credits   519

MAPS AND DIAGRAMS

Hong Kong, December 18–25, 1941   78

The North Atlantic Air Cover,
    May 1941–February 1942   111

Typical Convoy   115

Usual Sequence of Pilot Training in the BCATP   164

The North Atlantic, 1939–1945   180

The Dieppe Operation, August 19, 1942   261

Sicily, 1943   345

The Adriatic Sector: November 28, 1943–
    January 4, 1944   391

The Crossing of the Moro and the Battle of
    Ortona: December 6, 1943–January 4, 1944   399

THE WAR AGAINST HITLER

The Second World War casts a dark shadow across the twentieth century. The enormous battles that raged from continents to oceans, and in the skies, continue to fascinate and horrify us. Entire societies were transformed into enormous war machines to meet the needs of Allied and Axis air, land, and sea forces. Civilians became as much a part of the war effort as the men and women in uniform and consequently they were, in the minds of all political and military leaders, legitimate targets. Willing war workers and hapless civilians alike were killed by ordnance and weapons that made no distinctions between classes and genders, between the firing line and the home front. The combined death toll of combatants and bystanders was nothing short of staggering: in round terms, some sixty million people were killed. Hundreds of millions more were scarred forever—either physically maimed or psychologically traumatized—by the conflict.

The Second World War was not just one war but a series of campaigns and battles around the world. These campaigns brought together millions of men and women to fight the so-called Thousand Year Reich that Adolf Hitler had created to unleash war and genocide on Europe. The war pitted the Axis powers of Germany, Italy, Japan, and a number of less influential nations against the Allied powers of Britain, its dominions and colonies—primarily Canada, Australia, New Zealand, Newfoundland, South Africa, and India—along with France, the Soviet Union (an antagonist turned unlikely ally in the summer of 1941), the United States (after December 1941), and other nations. It began, arguably, in the Far East, when Japan went to war against China in 1937, and it didn't end until Japan capitulated in August 1945, a few months after Germany was defeated. This worldwide conflagration caused the massive dislocation of populations, set the stage for the postwar decolonization of Asia and Africa, and remade the international order through the toppling of Nazi Germany, the reduction in status of Britain and France, and the creation of two new world leaders: the United States and the Soviet Union. At war's end, with Europe exhausted, those two ideologically opposed superpowers almost immediately plunged into the Cold War, which lasted five decades and brought the divided world to the brink of nuclear annihilation.

The Allied victory was no foregone conclusion. Many people believe that brute force wins wars, that the enemy is driven into defeat by the side with more guns, tanks, planes, and warships. But history is replete with examples of battles, campaigns, and wars in which smaller forces drove their larger, lumbering foes from the field. Achieving victory requires more than blindly battering the enemy into submission. Numerous factors affect the combat performance of armies (and navies and air forces); these range from superior command, to the application of strength against weakness, to the coherence, motivation, and endurance of combatants in battle. Technological advances and new weapon systems can even the odds, reverse defeat, or deliver victory.

Nevertheless, for several decades, most historians have been guided by the belief that the Allied military forces smashed Germany and its co-belligerents into submission by simply overwhelming the opposition's fighting formations. Some raw numbers support this thesis: the Axis powers' gross population of 191 million was dwarfed by the Allies' 345 million, who were further backed by hundreds of millions more citizens in colonies and dominions throughout the British Empire. Similarly, the Allies' production advantage—especially after the industrial and economic might of the United States was added to that of Britain and the dominions—suggests that no outcome was possible except an Allied victory.[1] The Axis powers, according to this argument, were out-produced to death.

And yet, it is one thing to mobilize the industrial capacity of a nation and fully another to apply that might on the battlefield. Material superiority is never decisive in itself. How warriors and weapons systems are wielded in battle through coherent doctrine, ethos, and tactics is crucial. Long wars allow for a constant appreciation of technology and weapons by scientists. War-fighting skills evolve constantly and frequently to make the difference between winning and losing. In this regard, the Allies proved to be more effective than the Axis during the Second World War. In writing this book, rather than embracing the brute force thesis, I have chosen to show how soldiers, airmen, and sailors fought, focusing on the evolving tactics, doctrines, weapons, logistics, and technology they employed. The Canadians, in particular, had to find ways to fight effectively against a skilled enemy in conditions that ranged from the sweltering heat of Sicily to the frigid waters of the North Atlantic, and from the narrow streets of Ortona to the dark skies over Germany. At the same time, I have examined the equally important factors of morale, discipline, and fortitude of the Canadian citizen-soldiers, sailors, and airmen, and have tried to show how these young men coped while under fire. These Canadians would surely have scoffed at the notion that their victory was preordained, especially as they witnessed the death and destruction that was visited upon their comrades and friends.

While the carnage overseas was relentless, Canada was almost entirely spared from the war's ruin. Nevertheless, the country, with its modest population of fewer than 12 million, embraced its role as an arsenal of democracy, exporting war supplies, feeding its allies, and raising a million-strong armed force that served and fought in nearly every theatre of war. Under the steady, if slippery, hand of Prime Minister William Lyon Mackenzie King, the governing Liberal Party kept the national interest as its guiding star in navigating Canada through the Allied war effort. Above all, King sought to avoid a cleavage between English and French Canada. The nation was mobilized as never before in the fight to preserve the liberal, democratic order. At the same time, the six-year-long exertion had lasting effects: it caused widespread disruption to almost everyone's way of life, promoted nation-wide industrialization, ushered in changes to gender roles, exacerbated the tension between English and French, and forged a new sense of Canadian identity. The war led to a decisive break in English Canada's deep and almost sacred economic bond with Britain when the Dominion irrevocably embraced the United States as its largest trading partner. The emotional bond between Canada and Britain lasted longer, though Canada's independent role during the war weakened these intangible links over time, and strengthened the nation's resolve to set off on an increasingly independent course. Shrouding all of these changes was the blood sacrifice of close to 44,000 dead and almost 55,000 wounded that brought an endless grief to families and communities across Canada.[2]

The Second World War changed Canadians forever. Sergeant Barney Danson of the Queen's Own Rifles, who was severely wounded during the war and then came back to Canada to make a successful career in public life, remembered how his experiences in uniform broadened his outlook:

> The Second World War was a defining event for me, as it was for many of my age. For most of us, the war represented our first time away from home and family. It gave us our first experience of travel across Canada and overseas, and our first exposure to a broad cross-section of society: farmers, miners, lumber-jacks, rootless "hoboes," ex-convicts who generally kept their status secret but were known to the other former "cons" among us, "old guys," in their late twenties, or the still older ones we called "Pop," many of whom were trying to disengage themselves from family responsibilities, or failed marriages, or who found in the military something that eluded them in the Depression—the job they needed to support their families. Many of us also encountered, for the first time, the full diversity of Canada's population. We met francophone Canadians, individually and in their regiments, aboriginal Canadians, who were adjusting to us as we were adjusting to them and each of them we almost always called "chief," and others from the whole range of ethnic groups which made Canada their home even in those times.[3]

THE MEN AND WOMEN WHO WENT OVERSEAS endured sometimes horrifying and often miserable conditions, but their letters home mostly played down the danger. Flight Lieutenant Bill Bell, a Royal Canadian Air Force (RCAF) navigator, wrote to his family in July 1942 after harrowing months of front-line service:

> I can't remember when I wrote last, but it must have been awhile back. I'm a lazy devil. And rather busy in spots as you've found out from the local paper. I

was doing very well in keeping deep dark secrets too. I've been trying to keep you people from worrying. But it isn't much use now.... It is rather exciting in spots. But mostly you're too damn busy to think about anything but your work at hand. There isn't much to it tho: you go over there—they shoot at you, you drop bombs on them—then everyone goes back to bed. Terrific isn't it. I haven't developed any operational twitch yet but I suspect my hair is falling out a bit. But anyways, don't worry about me.[4]

Of course his family agonized, and only a month later he had a brush with death when his two-engine Hampden bomber was pounced on by a night fighter and raked with cannon fire, smashing the tail fin, holing the fuselage, riddling the fuel tanks, and shooting away the hydraulics. The crew brought the damaged plane back to England, and Bell and the pilot received the Distinguished Flying Medal. Bill Bell was like most of the warriors in the Canadian forces: he was desperate to keep the uncertainty and terror of combat from his family at home, even as he hinted at the strain as revealed through the likelihood of stress-related tics and falling-out hair. Seventy years later, it is the historian who needs to probe these words and push past the jauntiness of letters to piece together the experience of battle. At times it was, as Bell wrote, terrific and exciting; at other times, it was monotonous and banal. There was no shortage of fear and death.

What was it like to sail in the merchant navy across the Atlantic in ships encrusted with ice while U-boats lurked below? Where did the surgeons and nurses of the Royal Canadian Army Medical Corps find the courage to operate on or ease the pain of broken, twisted bodies of twenty-year-olds who had been mangled by steel and fire? Was it immoral to fly 18,000 feet above German cities and bomb their inhabitants with high explosive and incendiary bombs? How did Canadian infantrymen deal with the grim requirements of close-quarters combat, where the choice was to either kill or be killed? Where did these combatants find the courage and fortitude to face the storm, day after day, through long and costly campaigns? These are some of the questions that must be posed in order to recreate the Canadian combat experience.

The vast majority of Canada's men and women in uniform were not professional soldiers but civilians who put down their ploughs and pens, leaving behind their factories and schools to serve their King and country. They were ordinary men and women thrust into extraordinary circumstances. They sought simple pleasures, they chafed against the military system, and they felt anxiety. On the battlefield, some chose self-preservation over completing the mission, by dropping bomb loads short to deliberately avoid anti-aircraft (flak) fire, or by diving for cover in a shell crater and staying there, head down, until the battle was over. Body-immobilizing terror and even cowardice are part of the Canadian war effort, no less than jaw-dropping heroics and tear-inducing sacrifice. This book, then, is an intimate history of Canadians in combat, set against the backdrop of the national war effort and mapped against a worldwide war.

CANADIAN WOMEN PLAYED AN ENORMOUS PART in winning the war. Tens of thousands filled the jobs left vacant when men enlisted and were sent overseas, and thousands more were themselves enlisted in newly created branches of the three services. Their work helped the war effort. It also had a lasting effect on women themselves, both on what was expected of them and how they saw themselves.

On July 31, 1942, the navy established the Women's Royal Canadian Naval Service, and the women who served in uniform were widely and affectionately known as Wrens. "Carry On! Carry On! Sailor boys must sail!" went the Wrens' song, and 6,781 women served in shore stations during the course of the war. The Wrens constituted a service within a service, but they generally worked in mixed-gendered environments. The systemic inequality of the civilian workplace was replicated in the naval service, with female service personnel being paid 60 percent of what a male would be paid. Audrey Hill remarked, "At no time did I think of myself as a second class citizen in the Navy.... I was glad to be able to be there, doing whatever I could to help, which was what most of us were seeking. There was never any discussion about only being paid three-quarters [sic] of what the sailor got. We didn't go to sea, so it just never entered our discussions.... We were so fired up that we could do something to help end the terrible war that had been going on forever by 1943."[5] Other service women were not so sanguine and complained about the unfairness. In July 1943, pay was raised to 80 percent of a male service salary.[6]

The other two services also created women's formations. On July 2, 1941, the Women's Auxiliary Air Force was established—a formation later redesignated as the RCAF's Women's Division (WD). Some 17,000 Canadian women would eventually serve as WDs. The first designated positions were an extension of traditionally female jobs, such as cooking and secretarial work, but wartime trades were added as of early 1942, when the WDs arrived at RCAF stations and at air training schools. Women in uniform served as meteorological observers, radio operators, and cypher clerks, and later that year, jobs were opened up as pharmacists, parachute riggers, and lab assistants. The first women went overseas in the summer of 1942, and two years later about 1,500 served in RCAF commands and headquarters.

The Canadian Women's Army Corps was established in August 1941 to free up male volunteers for overseas service, and it was incorporated into the army in March 1942. The CWACs, as they were known, adopted army rank structures and served in all manner of trades, although not in combat roles.[7] Its 21,264 members wore collar badges bearing an image of Athena, the Greek goddess of war, along with a uniform of khaki that included four-buckle cloth overshoes that quickly became known, with thick sarcasm, as "glamour boots."

Women enlisted for a number of reasons. Many were driven by a patriotic urge, or else they sought adventure or something different to do. Yvonne Jukes served overseas with the Women's Division, working in intelligence and studying the aerial photographs from bomber raids to assess accuracy and damage. She enlisted because of the Nazi threat: "You looked at what was going on, a blitzkrieg going through Europe, just going into every country and menacing people that stood in your way. How could you sit back?"[8]

Serving in bases and commands across the Dominion and overseas, women in uniform had a chance to see their own country and meet other Canadians. As one CWAC officer remembered, she trained with a French-Canadian comrade and her bigotry did not stand the test of meeting the smart, personable, and patriotic Quebecker: "That's where I gained respect for the French Canadians ... it was from her."[9] These women were brought together during the war years and were exposed to new experiences.

One of the cruel ironies of the war was that, despite their important work, many of the tens of thousands of patriotic women in uniform were subject to a mean-spirited rumour campaign. These sexist attacks—"malicious propaganda, gossip and careless talk," in the words of one male RCAF officer—made no sense: after all, the armed forces had turned to women for their assistance. Nevertheless, early in the war, these female service personnel were sometimes labelled degenerates or prostitutes, occasionally spat on and intimidated in the streets, and accused of having sacrificed their femininity for military service.[10] To some civilian onlookers, seeing women in uniform came as a shock. Margaret Fleming recounted one of her first parades as a WD: "I can remember people booing us because they thought that women who joined up [had] loose morals."[11]

Fleming believed that the prejudice lessened as the forces recruited more women. Kitty Hawker enlisted in the WDs after seeing men and women "crying openly" in the streets of Windsor after the disaster of the Canadian raid on Dieppe in August 1942. Hawker's family was proud of her decision to serve, but "some of my mother's friends were horrified, because there were many false stories going around about the 'looseness' of women in the services."[12] Her mother thought that such talk was nonsense, and so did Hawker. She served during the war and then took advantage of the benefits of the Veterans Charter after the cessation of hostilities to go to university. In looking back on her experience, she testified, "Though we were young and inexperienced, we gained a confidence in ourselves which, I am proud to say, has stayed with us."[13] The rumours and accusations became more muted with time. The status of the women's corps was enhanced by the release of official posters and National Film Board documentaries with titles such as *Proudly She Marches* and *Wings on Her Shoulders.* Advertisements that showed women in uniform with taglines such as "This is our battle too!" or proclaimed that women were needed to "Back the Attack" helped as well.

Another 4,400 Canadian women served as nurses during the war, with the rank of lieutenant or higher. Military nurses had long proved their important role in saving lives and comforting the wounded, and their service did much to reverse the trend of the Depression years that had seen female nurses suffer wage cuts and attacks to their professionalism.[14] While some critics suggest that women made no progress in accruing significant rights in Canadian society through their war service, there were very few women who served in uniform who did not look back positively on their challenging and satisfying work in supporting the Canadian war effort.[15] Almost none of them set out to be feminist trail-blazers, but nearly all were content in having served their country and were enriched by their experiences. One wonders about how many of these proud women passed on the stories of their service and pride in achievements to their daughters, who, as part of the next generation that came of age in the 1960s, demanded substantial change to society and the equality of women within it. Important though these stories are, this is a book about combat. Canadian women in uniform were not in combat and their contributions to victory must be told, for the most part, elsewhere.

BATTLES ARE COMPLEX AND CONFUSING. They involve thousands of individuals, and are conducted with limited communication and with both sides reacting to shifting circumstances. Canadian infantryman Stanley Scislowski of the Perth Regiment described the difficulty of remembering the sequence of events in a military confrontation: "You could talk to five men who were in a certain battle and invariably you would hear five different versions of what happened.... Everyone sees a battle in a different way and from a different perspective, depending on the ferocity of what is going on around them."[16] Battle involves men, in close contact, attempting to kill other men while finding ways to keep themselves alive. Warriors who have been under fire provide the most vivid narratives, even if they often have little understanding of the wider battle or campaign. Official records such as maps, intelligence reports, summaries of action, and casualty compilations contextualize the eyewitness accounts. The historian tries to draw together these multiple perspectives, with the benefit, in this case, of generations of studies. The historian's task is always undertaken after the fact, sometimes years or decades later, and one must guard against the unwitting clarity of hindsight. Views and opinions that have developed over decades and in countless books were not available to the combatants at the front, or even to their commanders in the rear echelons. We must remember that all decisions made before battle or in the heat of it were based on partial appreciations of the enemy and limited intelligence, and conducted while under tremendous pressure. The past we read about today, from the soldiers, sailors, nurses, and airmen, was once the participants' uncertain present. To understand their decisions, we need to try to put ourselves in their place and judge them on the basis of what they could conceivably know, rather than through the lens of our more complete knowledge. This does not mean we cannot pass critical judgment—only that the context surrounding a battle is as important as what may have occurred in the conflict itself.

Battle is a lunatic landscape seen only by the dead, the damned, and the survivors. It changes forever those who pass through it. We cannot experience what the Canadian combatants went through during the Second World War, but their recollections, in the form of memoirs and oral histories, illuminate what would otherwise remain obscure. In this book, new stories have been dug out of the archives. But this is also a work that builds upon three generations of scholarship. I am indebted to those who cleared the terrain first, and to those who continue to do so now. This book and its successor to follow are works of synthesis, and the endnotes draw upon hundreds of published and unpublished sources that provide evidence of claims and point to further reading on the subject. To meet the challenge of telling the story of Canadians fighting across the world, I have delved into the newest scholarship and the oldest archives, and I remain guided by the voices of Canadians who were there.

This is a collective biography of more than a million Canadians at war. It is weighted towards the fighting arms and those who took part in combat rather than those in logistical or administrative positions. The tens of thousands of Canadians who served with units other than Canadian ones, usually in British formations, sometimes fall outside the scope of this book. In this global war, Canadians fought in worldwide campaigns, but the emphasis is on those battlegrounds where the majority of Canadians served: the Atlantic rather than the Pacific Ocean, the Sicilian and Italian campaign rather than the Middle East or Burma, and Northwest Europe rather than the Eastern Front.

THE SECOND WORLD WAR was a war of good against evil. It has been called, perhaps accurately, the last "good war." It was fought against a repulsive tyranny, among the worst ever to inflict a violent ideology on oppressed peoples. It was a war of immense savagery that included the unspeakable horror of the Holocaust; remorseless and bestial cruelty both on the Eastern Front and in the Pacific campaign; and the killing of hundreds of thousands of civilians through relentless bombing campaigns. The war demanded that the desperate Western nations, including Canada, make an alliance with Stalin—a figure as repulsive as Hitler, and the murderer of millions in the Soviet Union, Poland, and the Ukraine. Allied leaders were forced to make horrible choices. There was no easy way to win. The "good war" epithet may be too self-congratulatory in the face of such trauma, villainy, and violence. If that is the case, the war was, without a doubt, a war of necessity. Hitler and his malevolent Nazi regime had to be stopped. Most Canadians believed that at the time, and they made the coalition war effort against Hitler Canada's war too. In this necessary war, Canadians were willing to bear almost any burden and pay the ultimate price in the pursuit of victory. This is their epic story of heroism and horror, of loss and longing, and of sacrifice and endurance.

CHAPTER 1

RELUCTANTLY TO WAR

Adolf Hitler wanted war. He made no secret of his plan to attack his neighbours in Europe and then to take on the world. Both his bellicosity and his virulent racism were evident in his speeches and publications. He did exactly what he set out to do. The origins of the Great War may be mired in controversy, but the cause of the Second World War is clear.[1] This was Hitler's war.

The German dictator's career was a long one. It began in the early 1920s when he met with other disaffected outsiders in Munich's beer halls, and ended a quarter century later in a bunker in Berlin. As a young man who had served in the trenches of the Western Front during the Great War, he had grown up in war. And it had damaged him. Germany's defeat left him reeling and searching for the enemies who had defeated his country and his comrades. Even as Hitler aged, he had a feral, frenzied look about him, with his black hair parted sharply to one side and his bared teeth flashing white in contrast to his toothbrush moustache. But it was his oratory that set him apart. It was the rage and rapture of his speeches that inspired his listeners, convincing them to rise up against multiple imagined enemies of the German state.

The German people were anxious to reverse the humiliations of the Great War of 1914 to 1918. During those four long years, Germany had been strangled by a naval blockade and crushed on the battlefield. In defeat, the German people had been forced to pay billions in reparations, and on top of all this, they were made to accept blame for starting the conflict. The punishments inflicted by France, Britain, the United States, and their allies through the 1919 Treaty of Versailles were seen by most

Germans as a victor's vindictive revenge, even though Germany itself had invoked harsher penalties on Russia in early 1918 when it had driven that revolution-riven Communist state to defeat. The Great War's sickening battlefield toll of nine million dead worldwide had left few opportunities for reconciliation or a lasting peace.

The fledgling democratic Weimar Republic, set in place after the German emperor, Kaiser Wilhelm II, was forced to abdicate in 1918, was bankrupt and broken from the beginning. The wanton printing of money to pay Germany's crippling debts drastically devalued the Reichsmark (RM). In October 1923, for example, hyper-inflation had escalated to the point that one US dollar cost 25 billion RM.[2] The German state could no longer afford to pay for veterans' medical treatment or pensions, leaving millions of demobilized men disillusioned and abandoned.[3] Hitler's National Socialist Party fed off the veterans' resentment, and then channelled this anger into wider components of society. A fringe party through the 1920s, it slowly clawed its way into power as the economically devastating Depression of the early 1930s left one third of all Germans out of work.

As a consummate and charismatic manipulator, Adolf Hitler was able to conjure up imagined enemies within the state to mobilize support for his cause. He claimed that Communist agitators and Jewish socialists had stabbed the nation's army in the back during the Great War, with their active undermining of the economy through exploitation, leading to Germany's unwarranted defeat. Even in the aftermath of war, he contended, these alien elements conspired to keep the nation down through nefarious means, even though Jews made up less than 1 percent of the population.[4] It did not matter that the conspiracy was a dark fantasy conjured up in Hitler's mind: these Jewish and Communist elements would be made to pay for their treachery. Hitler's thundering, furious speeches resonated with many Germans and when the forty-three-year-old Austrian-born Hitler was democratically elected as Germany's chancellor in January 1933, he quickly consolidated his gains through trickery, intimidation, and the murder of his opponents.[5] The Weimar Republic's unhappy existence became history that March as Hitler took power in an increasingly totalitarian state. Opposition went to ground and was soon wiped out by the National Socialists, known widely as the Nazis. The cheering German people marched behind Hitler into the waiting abyss.

Once his position was secure, Hitler set out to restore Germany's status within Europe, regain lost territory, and eradicate the Jews and other "undesirables" who had no place in his conception of an Aryan society; his was a vision where whites were the masters and all others were to be removed or enslaved. To these ends, the German dictator first circumvented and then openly flouted the terms of the Versailles treaty.

Bred to believe that military might was the only way to restore what was lost, Hitler rebuilt the German military that had been all but banned since 1919. He also encouraged its leaders to find ways to win a new war. From 1914 to 1916, the deep trench systems of the Western Front—protected by barbed wire, defended by nearly limitless reinforcements, and backed by shattering firepower in the form of machine guns and artillery—had blunted most attacks. By 1917, thousands of heavy artillery pieces firing millions of shells could blast a hole through a trench line, but no army could follow through with an infantry attack because the advancing riflemen soon outdistanced their fire and logistical support, and were forced to face the enemy guns without artillery cover or adequate ammunition.[6] The Germans nearly broke the stalemate in early 1918 with aggressive infantry tactics that saw them attacking around Allied strongpoints, but the offensive was unsustainable and led to crippling casualties. With the Germans spent, the Allies were on the verge of a breakthrough in the final months of the war, employing a sophisticated combined-arms doctrine of infantry, tanks, and artillery, but

The German dictator Adolf Hitler was responsible for starting the Second World War in Europe. This signed portrait by Hitler was given to Canadian prime minister William Lyon Mackenzie King during his June 1937 visit to Berlin, when he unsuccessfully attempted to convince the Führer to pursue peaceful diplomacy rather than mount aggressive manoeuvres against his neighbours.

the Kaiser's armies capitulated before the Allied victory was realized. When the war ground to halt with the armistice on November 11, 1918, the civilian armies were demobilized and the men returned to their now impoverished nations. The German military, much reduced in the postwar years, nonetheless studied its defeat, sought new tactics and weapons, and developed doctrines (the means of wielding tactics and weapons together) to avoid a repetition of its humiliating loss. The remaining small cadre of professional soldiers would find the answer in the application of surprise, speed, and shock.

Throughout the 1930s, Hitler positioned Germany for war. Rebuilding the military was the first imperative, but he was also driven by his obsessions with racial purity, the restoration of lost territory, and the desire for revenge. The issue of racial

Nazi soldiers displaying force, might, and willpower at the annual Nuremburg Rally.

purity led him to systematically hunt down Jews and other supposedly inferior peoples. The territory he coveted was to the east, in the Soviet Union, which he planned to exploit for Germany's economic renewal and expansion. Revenge would come with retaliation against all those powers, real and imagined, who had subjugated Germany. By the mid-1930s, Hitler's Fascist regime had the prosecution of war as its reason for being.

Hitler gambled that neither the Soviet Union nor the West would resist his aggressive actions. France and Britain had been badly traumatized by the Great War, with their millions of dead and maimed veterans, and during the 1930s they had within them vocal antiwar factions that demanded peace at almost any cost. The United States, meanwhile, had embraced a policy of isolation and was, in any case, far away, across the Atlantic Ocean. The Soviet Union was even less interested in a war. The paranoid and psychotic Soviet dictator Joseph Stalin was implementing his own genocidal vision within this sphere of influence—ultimately murdering about four million citizens, largely in the Ukraine, through starvation, execution, and widespread imprisonment in gulags. Stalin preferred to see the Western allies in disarray, as it left him a free hand to put in place the structures to export Communism throughout Europe.[7]

The League of Nations, an international organization set up in the aftermath of the Great War with the goal of preventing future conflicts, was no more effective than any individual state at imposing limits on the dictators' ambitions. Lacking any military backing to enforce its resolutions, the League's successive diplomatic failures led to a growing sense of impotence and despair among Western observers. In East Asia, the Japanese incursion into Manchuria in 1931 was followed in Africa by the brazen invasion by Fascist Italy of Abyssinia (now Ethiopia) in late 1935. In both cases, the League was little better than a talking shop. The major powers did nothing. Canada, at best a minor player, chose to back away from any commitment.[8] Though few cared what Canada thought or did, when France and Britain abandoned Abyssinia and refused to go to war to save its people, both the Italian leader, Benito Mussolini, and Hitler were emboldened. The German dictator continued to consolidate power, rebuild his military, and persecute the Jews. The Fascist states were embarked upon a steady march to a wider European war.

IN REBUILDING HIS MILITARY, Hitler paid particular attention to the development of an effective air force and armoured corps.[9] Despite massive rearmament, however, the German military was not ready for war in 1936. But in March of that year, Hitler engaged in an act of naked provocation by ordering the remilitarization of the Rhineland, a buffer zone the Versailles treaty had created between Germany and France. The German high command waited uncertainly, knowing it likely could not withstand a joint Franco-British assault. France quivered at Germany's brazen action, but did little more than bark impotently. Britain found excuses not to act. The democratic Western powers folded again.

For Hitler, every aggressive action on Germany's part was a defensive and pre-emptive manoeuvre against the vast, international, and shadowy Jewish conspiracy that controlled world markets, or else it was intended to fend off the future war that was to be unleashed by the Communists in the Soviet Union. Diplomacy, he was convinced, would never be enough to hold back his enemies. And, indeed, neither Hitler nor the leaders of rising totalitarian regimes in Italy and Japan were intimidated by diplomatic initiatives meant to curb their aggression. They saw it rather as weakness to be exploited through threats and war. Hitler calculated that with German rearmament in full swing, and the Allies stymied by apathy, pacifism, and fear, he must attack sooner rather than later.

By the late 1930s, "the war to end all wars"—the phrase used to describe the Great War—had become a cruel joke. The Fascists had spent much of the decade honing new weapons and tactics, and benefited from an opportunity to test them in the Spanish Civil War, which raged from 1936 to 1939. In particular, they experimented with the use of light bombers in supporting ground troops.[10] The Spanish conflict also served to distract the Allies from Hitler's aggression closer to home. After menacing Austria, and forcing its political leaders to accede to a union with Germany, he annexed that country in early 1938. Hitler then looked for new victims, turning his sights on the Sudetenland, a predominately German-speaking enclave within Czechoslovakia. France and Britain lurched from bellicosity to appeasement. British Prime Minister Neville Chamberlain, as anxious to avoid war as most of his fellow citizens, conceded to Hitler the part of Czechoslovakia he claimed as his due during the Munich Crisis of September 1938. Even as Austrian, and soon Czechoslovakian, factories were turning out weapons of war for their new Nazi masters, the appeasers hoped that Hitler's appetite for new conquests would be satiated. It was not. What remained of Czechoslovakia and all of Poland, a historic enemy of Germany, trembled as they appeared to be next on Hitler's hit list.

Europe's nations gulped at the thought of war, but slowly began to revitalize their military forces, aware in this eleventh hour that conflict was almost certainly unavoidable. There was never any doubt that "the annihilation of the Jewish race in Europe" remained Hitler's underlying objective.[11] He had harassed, persecuted, and murdered Jews in Germany since 1933, but his plan to eliminate European Jewry could only be achieved by conquering and occupying all those nations where Jews lived. In the process, he intended also to enslave Slavic peoples, wipe out Communism, and remake the world order.

In March 1939, Hitler broke his promise to Britain and France that he was done threatening his neighbours when the German army marched on Czechoslovakia, occupying the nation, seizing its resources, and plundering its military. The booty included 4,000 field guns, 57,000 machine guns, 810 tanks, and more than 1,200 aircraft.[12] With this massive addition to Germany's arsenal, few in the West could doubt that a new war was imminent. Nonetheless, when Hitler and his ideological arch-enemy, Stalin, signed a non-aggression pact on August 23, 1939, the world was stunned, and only too aware that the agreement cleared the way for Germany to invade Poland.

The attack was launched on September 1. In preparing for the campaign, Hitler urged his generals to "kill without mercy men, women and children of the Polish race or language."[13] This was to be warfare unlike anything Europe had witnessed for centuries. The Polish military, despite appearing strong on paper, were quickly overrun by the rapidly moving Wehrmacht, sixty divisions strong, which knifed through their country with tanks, tactical bombers, and infantry. Chamberlain's government, having guaranteed to protect Poland in a last-ditch effort to dissuade Germany from carrying out its invasion, declared war on September 3. France, too, realized the time to fight had finally come. Unfortunately, neither of the Great Powers had an effective means of coming to Poland's aid, and France made only a few half-hearted probing attacks along Germany's western frontier before retreating. As Europe went to war for the second time in as many generations, Poland died alone.

"THE FIRST HORRORS OF HUN WARFARE were brought home less than 24 hours after Great Britain's declaration of war," lamented one Canadian newspaper, the *Hamilton Spectator*.[14] On the first day of Britain's war with Germany, September 3, 1939, the unescorted British passenger liner, *Athenia*, was on a westward route to Montreal. Hitler and Admiral Karl Dönitz, commander of the U-boat arm, well remembered the international outrage provoked by unrestricted submarine warfare in the Great War, which had seen U-boats sink any and all ships on the high seas, including neutral and hospital ships, and so they had ordered their U-boats to avoid attacking civilian ships. But the captain of submarine *U-30* mistook the defence-less *Athenia* for an armed merchant cruiser and torpedoed it without warning. Hit northwest of Ireland, *Athenia* took 118 of its 1,000 passengers, including several

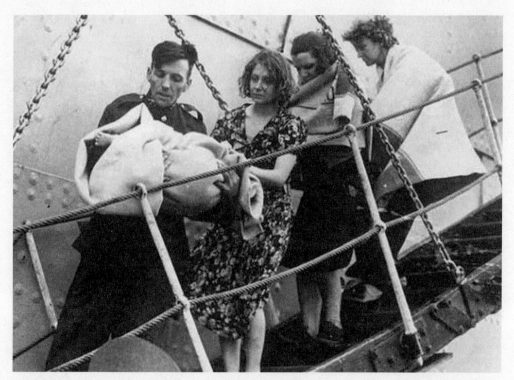

Survivors of Athenia, *the unescorted passenger liner sunk by German U-boat U-30 on September 3, 1939. The shock of the attack on civilians seemed to signal to the Western Allies that Hitler planned an unrestrained war against women and children as well as combatants.*

Canadians, to their doom. The attack, mounted only a few hours after the declaration of war, stoked the fires of fear and anger in the Western world. The sinking of *Athenia* surely was clear evidence of Hitler's mad desire to take war to a new level of savagery. However, this outrage soon gave way to the alarming realization that the war would be fought without restraint.

Poland was lost, Britain committed, and a civilian ship had been sunk. Canada, witnessing these events from afar, again had to make a gut-wrenching decision: whether or not to enter a European war. As unpalatable as this prospect was, however, few Canadians could stomach the idea of abandoning Britain in its time of need. The Dominion girded itself for the coming struggle. Canada had been bloodied by its exertions during the Great War, when the nation of 8 million had put an astonishing 630,000 citizens into uniform, and had grieved for more than 66,000 dead.[15] That war had created a pantheon of heroes, from Corps Commander Sir Arthur Currie to air ace Billy Bishop. It also had allowed Canada to distinguish itself within the British war effort, and its wartime exertions were regarded by many as the crucible within which the young nation had been forged. But the Great War also left deep divisions in Canadian society. Young men had been conscripted for military service against their will; Ukrainian and German Canadians deemed a threat to internal security had been locked up; city dwellers had accused farmers of raking in profits while they paid high prices for food; workers had felt exploited by owners who shared few of the wartime profits.[16] Most significantly, perhaps, relations between English and French Canada had been strained nearly to the breaking point over the conscription crisis. The country was forever changed, and the spectre of war, with its legions of dead and its legacy of disunity, loomed large in Canadians' memory.

Canada's prime minister in 1939, William Lyon Mackenzie King, had also been scarred by the war in which he did not fight. King was a political survivor. Now sixty-four years old, his once handsome features had run to fat, but he had lost none of his shrewdness. He abhorred war but, like most Canadians, believed in the British Empire, revelling in its culture, its political institutions, and its history, even as he struggled to guide Canada along its own independent path. Prime minister since 1921, save for a five-year sojourn out of power during the worst of the Depression, King had acquired the habit of going slowly, weighing his options, and calculating his every move. In his mind, Canada could not avoid supporting Britain in a major European war, and he had written a year earlier that it was a "self-evident national duty" to stand by the Empire, a conviction he had formed as early as 1923.[17] At the same time, King believed that Canada could not endure another slaughter like the Great War. And he especially intended to avoid another divisive debate over conscription, such as the one that had erupted in 1917. He planned for a modest war effort, which others have since labelled a war of limited liability. His nation of fewer than twelve million Canadians would be suppliers of munitions and food, sustaining Canada's allies so that they might better bear the brunt of the Nazi attack. War on the cheap, in terms of lives expended, was King's goal. This inglorious if practical objective was in line with the limitations of his poor and dispirited country, which was still in the throes of the decade-long Depression. It was a policy that accurately reflected Canada's national interests, but, as King was soon to find, not that of Canadians.

William Lyon Mackenzie King had been prime minister for most of the period since 1921. He would be Canada's war leader throughout the Second World War.

King had tried to walk a fine line throughout the late 1930s, seemingly providing contradictory statements—offering support for Britain on the one hand while claiming the right for independent action on the other—to the point that the British hardly knew where Canada stood. The Canadian prime minister knew that in the event of war, English Canada, with its close ties to the British Empire, was bound to demand that an expeditionary force be sent overseas, and King was determined to dampen that urge. As every major nation had rearmed in the late 1930s, and with war all but assured because of Hitler's ravenous desire for land and conquest, it was folly not to prepare for the worst. And yet King had refused to join the rush to remilitarization for fear of alienating Quebec, which formed a vital part of his political power base and which would construe any such policy as a commitment to engage in another European war. It wasn't that Quebec was pro-Hitler, only that it was not particularly pro-British Empire. Although a distressingly significant segment of the French-Canadian elite admired the Nazis, the province for the most part opposed them. But going to war was another matter. War led inexorably to conscription, or such was the unshakeable belief among many Quebeckers. Besides, hadn't the popular US president, Franklin Roosevelt, promised as recently as 1938 in a speech in Kingston, that the United States would never allow Canada to be threatened?[18]

A pacifist sentiment also held sway among many Canadians, both English and French, and this sizable faction wanted nothing to do with another war among European states. This element opposed spending the nation's limited wealth on arms and munitions, especially when the widespread effects of the Depression were still hurting so many industries, communities, and families. F.R. Scott, an influential Montreal poet and lawyer, and the son of a Canadian Great War veteran, summed up succinctly, if viciously, another point of view: "Elderly sadists of the last war are emerging from their obscurity to join the war-dance again, their eyes glistening and their mouths watering as they think of the young men whom they will send to the slaughter."[19] And so King allowed only a pittance for rearmament in the late 1930s, and that only in the cause of defending Canada. That much he could sell to Quebec while, at the same time, holding off the English-Canadian imperialists by making increasingly firm promises that Canada would not let Britain face the enemy alone.

From 1936 onward, defences and naval guns on the country's east and west coasts were upgraded and the Royal Canadian Navy was allowed to purchase a handful of modern destroyers.[20] But even as late as 1938, when King admitted to himself and told his cabinet that war was unavoidable, the nation's coffers were opened only with much hesitation.[21] It was not enough. All branches of the Canadian military were woefully under-equipped. The roughly 3,000 Royal Canadian Air Force members were left flying ludicrously obsolete machines—a hotchpotch of 270 aircraft, of which fewer than 20 were modern Hurricane fighters. The army was even worse off, with little to show in any category of weapon, from mortar to anti-aircraft gun.

Across the entire Dominion, the army possessed only a handful of machine guns and sixteen outdated tanks (or machines that resembled a tank).[22] And so, in September 1939, King was probably right to plan for a limited war, since the nation's desiccated armed forces would never stand a chance on the modern battlefield.

IN AUGUST 1914, Canadians had no influence over the decisions made in London. They were, in international affairs, little more than an appendage of the Empire. The situation was different twenty-five years later, partially as a result of the autonomy won on the killing fields of Europe during the Great War. The 1931 Statute of Westminster made Canada a self-governing nation in the British Commonwealth, empowered to decide its own foreign policy and matters of war and peace. While King hated war, and felt trapped by the "sheer madness" of being dragged into another conflagration, he guided Canada into this new conflict as Britain's ally, skilfully urging on his cabinet while calming the Quebec wing of his party.[23] It was unthinkable to him that Canada would not support Britain in a major war, but he understood the need for political cover: his mantra, accordingly, was that "Parliament would decide." The King government recalled Parliament on September 7, 1939.

Canada would never have gone to war unless Britain was threatened; nor was it able—even with control over its foreign policy—to stay out of the conflict, so deep were its ties to the British Empire. Yet many Canadians also saw the defence of Western values and liberal democracy as part of their wider duty beyond the Dominion's shores. In this sense, Member of Parliament H.S. Hamilton, a Great War veteran, seemed correct when he claimed in the House that Hitler threatened more than just Europe, declaring, "This is Canada's war. The effective defence of Canada consists in the utilization of the organized and united power and strength of this Dominion however, wherever and whenever it can best be used to defeat Germany's armed forces and to destroy the philosophy on which they are based."[24] The Canadian Parliament, led by King and his Quebec lieutenant, Ernest Lapointe, brought Canada into the war on September 10. To calm Quebec, the uncommitted, and the fearful, they promised faithfully that this would be a voluntary war.[25] There would be no conscription.

Everyone remembered or had heard stories of the crowds that enthusiastically cheered the declaration of war in 1914. Canadians in the major cities, and to a lesser extent in the countryside, had greeted the news with wild, naive excitement. The reaction was different this time. A grim stoicism prevailed among Canadians who did not relish the thought of hurling themselves headlong into harm's way. Nonetheless, tens of thousands of young men queued up at recruiting centres and armouries to enlist in the ill-prepared army, air force, and navy. They recognized that Hitler represented a malignant force that had to be stopped and were motivated mainly by the military threat he posed to Britain and Europe. Indeed, few Canadians paid much attention to the plight of European Jews under the Nazis. Canada's record with respect to Jews was hardly a noble one: the country had even turned away

New recruits of the Black Watch of Canada marching in Montreal in 1939.
Note the mixture of civilian clothing and military uniforms.

asylum-seeking Jewish refugees in the 1930s.[26] It was not abhorrence of racial persecution that prompted many Canadians to act. Nor can it be said that it was a principled defence of democracy, at least in the case of supporting Poland, which was no bastion of democratic values. Moreover, many Canadians, including King, believed that Polish intransigence was partly responsible for provoking the war. The suspicion was unfounded: both Germany and the Soviet Union sought to annihilate the state of Poland—which had been formed largely out of their territory after the Great War—and in the process to annex its land and people. But Poland's relative innocence was irrelevant as far as Canada was concerned. It was, above all, because Britain was threatened that Parliament voted for war and Canadians volunteered to fight. In the eyes of most Canadians, Britain was the liberal democracy that had to be defended. J.K. Chapman, a married New Brunswicker who enlisted in November 1940 at age twenty, summed up the feelings of many when he wrote that he and his friends were "proud of being Canadians, [but] we were prouder still to belong to something greater: The British Empire upon which the sun never set."[27]

Other factors were at play as well. There can be no doubt that the brutal Depression compelled some men to join the forces. Canadians had been savaged during the locust years, as jobs disappeared, crops dried up and blew away, and desperate families were reduced to seeking social assistance, meagre as it then was. The very foundations of capitalist society were shaken, and some Canadians naturally drifted to socialism and Communism, although they did not grasp the horror of its implementation in the Soviet Union. Robert Crozier, who had graduated from Queen's University in 1940 and served with the Irish Regiment of Canada during the war, wrote that "The Depression was a total preoccupation for most people—those who had jobs feared losing them, and those who had no jobs watched helplessly while their families slowly starved, their homes were taken from them, their children went unclothed and uneducated, their hopes ground into dust.... During that ten-year period, life for millions of people was a struggle simply to survive."[28] In uniform, a man received regular meals, $1.30 a day for privates and $35 a month for his wife, plus another $12 per child (to a maximum of two).[29] It was enough money to support a family, and much more than most Canadians had lived on in the past few years.

Though the Depression's effects pushed some men into uniform, of those who enlisted in the first three months, 89 percent left jobs.[30] Even if some might have lied about having an occupation in order to better their chances of being taken on, "hungerscription" was not the driving force for most. There was, of course, the lure of adventure. Issues of masculinity—serving in uniform and impressing girls—motivated others.[31] Some drifted into the service, inspired by a speech, urged on by mates, or fortified by drink. Others sought escape from a bad job, a dull life on the farm, or an unhappy marriage. The air force and the navy—although not the army—had exclusionary racial policies, denying enlistment to most identifiable minorities, although the occasional Japanese, black, or Chinese Canadian was accepted. The formal racist policy was rescinded in March 1942.[32] First Nations recruits, as in the Great War, were embraced for their supposed warrior skills. Some 4,300 First Nations men enlisted during the Second World War, serving with more rights in the overseas forces than those who stayed in Canada enjoyed. These soldiers served largely in the army, though the numbers were not high: the percentage of the total indigenous male population was about half of that derived from white Canada, which may have betrayed hidden prejudices in the recruitment process or lack of interest on the part of First Nations.[33] Tommy Prince, from the Ojibwe Nation, volunteered early in the war, and would later be decorated for his service both during the war and later in Korea. He enlisted, he said, to show that First Nations recruits "were as good as any white man."[34]

Underage soldiers were turned away and told to come back when they were eighteen. Many adolescents returned within days with lies on their lips or forged papers in their hands. Multiple attempts usually brought success.[35] Six-foot, four-inches-tall George MacDonell, who enlisted in September 1939 at age fifteen by claiming to be eighteen, wrote later that he took pride in being able to "strike out on my own … and serve my country at the same time … in this vital struggle with the forces of darkness."[36] Thousands of greybeards, many of them Great War veterans, also sought service, some sneaking through the rather cursory inspection with gruff and growl—and not a little bit of black shoe polish in their hair. Others who were refused left in tears. Initially, the rate of rejection for medical ailments was high, and rotting teeth kept many men from the army, few scarcely believing that modern warfare required a working set of chompers.[37]

One Princess Patricia Canadian Light Infantry recruiting officer reported a "complete absence of jingoism and war excitement" among the long lines of recruits. He said these men were enlisting with a "full realization of their responsibilities."[38] The recruits had a strong desire to stop Hitler, no matter if it was mixed with a feeling of duty to defend Britain, a patriotic feeling for Canada, or some other motivation. One French Canadian, Lieutenant Claude Chatillon, remembered that even though he felt no kinship with England and had experienced prejudice in Canada, "Something is happening over there [in Europe] that has profoundly touched me, my convictions and my principles.... Above all, it's a war of ideas ... of freedom, of rights."[39] Both public pronouncements and private decisions demonstrated that this was Canada's war.

THE PERMANENT FORCE (the army) had a strength of 4,261 officers and men in the summer of 1939. They were backed by around 46,500 militia soldiers who trained part-time at night and on weekends across the Dominion.[40] While the total permanent and militia force of 50,000 or so consisted of military-minded men and boys, they had never trained together en masse. At the higher ranks, only a few dozen officers, nearly all Permanent Force members, had attended the two-year British Army Staff College course that exposed them to issues of strategy, logistics, and mechanization and so prepared them for a senior command position.[41] There had been some intellectual debates in the service journal, *Canadian Defence Quarterly*, about how to fight on the modern battlefield—especially about the proper use of the tank in the attack—but all of this was academic due to the chronic shortage of equipment. The infantry soon found that

A Canadian war poster that proclaims "IT'S OUR WAR."

they would be issued the Lee-Enfield No. 4 Mk I rifle and the Lewis machine gun, similar weapons, with minor variations, to those used by their fathers in the Great War. Even battle dress, webbing, and boots were in embarrassingly limited supply. Entrepreneurial units went shopping for equipment at department stores such as Eaton's to clothe the new recruits. However, no off-the-shelf solution could alleviate the shortage of artillery, mortars, light machine guns, and vehicles. The army, virtually naked and unarmed, would have to beg for assistance from the British.

Despite these setbacks, the army high command was pleased to find in September 1939 that more than 58,000 men had enlisted, about half of them drawn from the Permanent Force and militia. The number included about 4,000 Great War veterans as well as several thousand French Canadians—which eased the fears of those who suspected that Quebec was ambivalent about the war.[42] This new army, initially called the Canadian Active Service Force, and later the Canadian Army Overseas, would be the basis for a large expeditionary force that the senior army command had secretly planned for in the form of a corps of two divisions and supporting troops.

King's cabinet was horrified by the plan. Outfitting and paying for such a large overseas force flew in the face of the government's policy of limited engagement and home defence. In late September 1939, King and his minister of finance, the Great War veteran J.L. Ralston, cut in half the military's request for $500 million in funds, but it was evident to the politicians that Canadians still wished to see an overseas division.[43] The government relented.

The 1st Canadian Infantry Division, 18,376 strong, would go to England under the command of the charismatic Major-General Andrew McNaughton. The fifty-two-year-old soldier and scientist had

Andrew McNaughton, Canada's most respected soldier, was given command of the 1st Canadian Infantry Division, which sailed for Britain late in 1939.

proven himself as an innovative leader in the previous war, had been chief of defence staff in the early 1930s, and had served as head of the National Research Council. "Andy" was a powerful orator and undeniably brilliant, but it had been close to five years since he had commanded Canadians in uniform. Such was the threadbare nature of the Canadian army. It would take time to train a division for overseas service (and a second division to defend the Dominion), and so initially Canada's primary contribution would be its navy, a few RCAF squadrons, and Canadians flying in the British Royal Air Force.

CHAPTER 2

THE FALL OF FRANCE

The war with Poland was over almost before it started. Hitler's armoured formations rolled through the countryside, tearing apart Polish cavalry, infantry, and tank
formations, while dive-bombing Stukas machine-gunned and bombed anything and
anyone in their path. Still, it was not as stunning or as complete a victory as is
sometimes suggested in the history books. Some 14,000 Germans were killed and
another 30,322 wounded in battle.[1] After the campaign, studies revealed problems
with coordinating the attacking forces and numerous communication breakdowns,
but the German high command had time to address many of these issues before
facing new adversaries.

The Russians entered the battle on September 17, when the Polish were in their
death throes; their unambiguous objective was to carve up the corpse of their historic
enemy. The non-aggression pact between Germany and the Soviet Union, as unlikely
as it was from an ideological standpoint, forged a powerful alliance. As a harbinger
of things to come, thousands of Polish officers and intellectuals were rounded up
and executed by the occupiers, while 1.3 million others were sent into exile. Tens of
thousands of Polish citizens died of starvation or disease in Soviet gulags.[2] Hitler and
Stalin never blinked an eye at the slaughter, having long perfected the butchering of
their own people before taking their terror to others.

Even as British forces were rushed to defend France, the French prepared for the
German onslaught against the 700-kilometre-long defensive fortifications they called
the Maginot Line. It consisted of dozens of concrete forts and underground tunnels

protected by casements, armoured structures, deep pockets of barbed wire, inter-locking machine guns, anti-tank trenches, and artillery. The French, having suffered grievously when they sought to regain German-occupied French territory during the Great War, were determined to make their opponents pay a similar blood debt in this war. The Maginot Line was not impregnable—there were significant gaps between the concrete forts—but the German generals were mystified as to how to break it without taking crippling casualties. Hitler's high command set about finding an audacious solution to the problem, but for months the two opposing sides faced each other in a stalemate that was soon dubbed the Phoney War. The long delay, as Allied soldiers dug in and the Germans brought up reinforcements, bred discourage-ment and passivity in many of the British and French soldiers who had been rushed to the front only to find that boredom awaited them. The German soldiers, however, were motivated by their nation's recent victory over Poland, were more thoroughly indoctrinated, and were anxious to reverse the Great War's humiliating defeat.

In Canada, the Phoney War brought a much-needed respite to allow the nation to build up its military capabilities. Factories retooled and upped their rate of pro-duction, but their pace was well short of frenzied, at least partly because Britain was stingy when it came to placing contracts in Canada. Nonetheless, industry picked up steam in late 1939 and early 1940, producing all manner of war materiel—and the rising demand for these goods was putting Canadians back to work. King was also shoring up control, making strong appointments to his cabinet and handing out new responsibilities to his proven political lieutenants. While few envisioned the prime minister as a war leader, he had expertly guided a united country into the war, firm in its support for Britain and France. His minister of finance, J.L. Ralston, was much respected across the country, as was C.D. Howe, who would take con-trol of all war supplies and manufacturing, and would soon be dubbed "minister of everything." Norman Rogers was a hard-working minister of defence; when he died in an aircraft accident in June 1940, he was replaced by Ralston. The gregarious and bibulous Charles "Chubby" Power, a Great War veteran and efficient party organ-izer, became minister of defence for air, while Angus Macdonald was plucked from Nova Scotia, where he had been premier, to oversee the navy. J.L. Ilsley, another stern Nova Scotian, would work heroics in finance after Ralston moved to defence.

It would be Ilsley who introduced new taxes and war bonds to help pay for the war. Most influential in the cabinet was King's right-hand man from Quebec, Ernest Lapointe, who served as minister of justice and controlled the Quebec wing of the party.[3] King led his cabinet but provided his able ministers with the room to develop their own agendas and find solutions to the complex challenges of the war. While King rarely interfered, he remained aware of nearly everything related to the home front. Cabinet ministers would come and go, exchanging portfolios or resigning under duress, but King remained constant. He grew into the role of Canada's warlord.

Meanwhile, politics and the manoeuvring for power within and among the provinces never stopped. Only days into the war in September 1939, Quebec premier

Prime Minister William Lyon Mackenzie King shored up his power by forging a talented cabinet and by winning the March 1940 federal election.

Maurice Duplessis charged that the King government would bring in conscription and called a snap election. Duplessis was hoping to secure power early in the conflict by inciting deep fears in Quebeckers. Only his government, claimed Duplessis, would prevent King from forcing French-Canadian youngsters against their will into a European war. King was horrified by Duplessis's lies, and he believed that if the premier won on the strength of his fear-mongering, then Ottawa could never mount an all-out war effort for worry of alienating Quebec and tearing the country apart along linguistic lines. This was political war. King's Quebec ministers—in particular Lapointe and Power—led the charge against Duplessis. By hook and by crook, the federal party poured money into swing ridings and threatened openly that if Duplessis was re-elected, the French-Canadian ministers in Ottawa would resign, thereby leaving Quebec without representation in an anglophone cabinet. An outmanoeuvred Duplessis was stunned by the federal intervention. He also underestimated the support among Quebeckers for the just war against Hitler. Quebec opted for the Liberal Party and Duplessis was voted out.

King also politically manhandled a long-time enemy in Ontario. The unstable premier, Mitchell Hepburn, launched an imprudent personal attack on King with the passage in the Ontario legislature, on January 18, 1940, of a resolution that said King had not "done his duty by his country and he never will."[4] A wounded but wily King, who had last faced the voters five years previously, called an election and ran on a war record that, although brief, was quite strong. He guessed that the Phoney War in Europe could not last much longer and sought to win a new mandate before the shooting war resumed. With the Conservatives demanding a more committed war effort, which was interpreted in Quebec as a call for conscription, and the Co-operative Commonwealth Federation (CCF) labelled as a party of pacifists and socialists, King guided the Liberals down the centre. In the March 1940 election, he won a majority of seats in the House of Commons and so ensured that he would remain prime minister for the duration of the war.[5]

THE CANADIAN GOVERNMENT actively discouraged enlistment in late 1939 for fear of the army dragging the nation into greater and uncontrollable war commitments. Major-General Andrew McNaughton nonetheless breathed much vigour into the mobilization. Combining both professional and volunteer soldiers, his 1st Canadian Infantry Division included, on the one hand, recognizable Permanent Force infantry formations such as the Royal Canadian Regiment (RCR), the Princess Patricia's Canadian Light Infantry (PPCLI), and the Royal 22e Régiment, and, on the other hand, historic militia units such as Vancouver's Seaforth Highlanders, the West Nova Scotia Regiment, and the Hastings and Prince Edward Regiment. As in the previous war, the first contingent of soldiers sent overseas was mainly white and Anglo-Saxon: there were few francophones other than those in the Royal 22e Régiment, and almost no First Nations or ethnic Canadians. With thousands aching to enlist, recruiters were able to take their pick. The average rifleman sent overseas was twenty-three years old, stood about five foot seven, and weighed less than 140 pounds (although all men later put on considerable weight in training), and more than half had left school before grade seven.[6]

Tens of thousands of Canadians enlisted for overseas service in 1939.
Some were away for six years; others never returned to their loved ones.

"The reputation Canadians earned in the last war has not been forgotten," intoned the British War Office, as the first of the Canadians arrived in England in December 1939.[7] The 20,000 servicemen who landed in England personified Canada's commitment to mother Britain, and their arrival was seen as an important boost for morale—though it was understood that the newly raised division would not immediately have a military impact. Felix Carrière of the PPCLI remembered that the British people were "good to us because here we were, the heroic Canadians ... back again after twenty years."[8] But gratitude did not always equate with understanding, and some popular misconceptions about Canadian soldiers were carried forward from the Great War. It was widely believed, for instance, that the Canadians were a martial race drawn from the outer reaches of the frozen Dominion. Canucks were born in snow banks and lived in igloos, or were raised in the bush to become voyageurs. One English paper gushed, "The [Canadian] contingent as a whole has been selected in proportion from every Canadian district: lumbermen from up-country, fishermen and farmers from the Maritime Provinces, artificers and drivers from the cities, large numbers of French-Canadians from Quebec. A negro sergeant led the band. There were fair heads, black heads, brown heads, red heads—and Red Indians too; one of them from Aklavik in the Arctic Circle."[9] The Canadians were pictured as a different, exotic breed of warrior, despite the fact that most volunteers came initially from urban centres where the majority of Canadians lived, and where the militia and regular units were established. In fact, the "hearty men of the north" found the English winter damp and miserable. At Aldershot camp, the Canadians huddled together for warmth, swore at the slush that emerged from the taps (when they weren't plugged), and devoted time and energy to liberating coal or clandestinely converting park benches into kindling.

The popular song "Roll Out the Barrel" was sung with gusto by the Canadians wherever they went during the fall, but as winter settled in, the glamour turned to gloom and the choristers complained. The food was gruel-like and Canadians grumbled that they would starve to death before they ever met the enemy. The Dominion's soldiers revealed in letters home that they were homesick, and one Canadian military headquarters report based on intercepted and read mail observed that a high proportion of soldiers "warn their friends and family not to join the army."[10] A bright

THE FALL OF FRANCE 37

spot was the comfort offered by the British people, especially the women. The first marriage between a Canadian soldier and a British bride took place on January 28, 1940, a mere five weeks after the 1st Division arrived.[11] With close to half a million Canadians eventually "invading" Britain, nearly 48,000 marriages would follow in the coming six years.

Even in early 1940, after the world had witnessed the successful German blitzkrieg tactics in Poland, much of infantry training drew on what had been learned in the Great War, with emphasis on marching, bayonet work, and digging trenches. Shortages of small arms ammunition made rifle firing a rare occurrence. Brigadier E.W. Sansom wrote in January 1940, "We have so many visits to arrange programmes for that it is very difficult to get down to the real work of organizing and training the Division."[12] It was not until mid-March that the division began collective training, with night-time and tactical exercises, and even then it was rare for the infantry to work with artillery, armour, and engineers. Few Canadians saw a tank, much less learned how to fight alongside the lumbering beasts or to stop one in battle. Sergeant F.D. Thompson of the Seaforth Highlanders of Canada recounted, "We have learned more than we knew there was, but principally we have learned how little we first knew."[13]

THE PHONEY WAR CAME TO AN END ON APRIL 9, when Germany invaded Denmark and Norway. Hitler struck because he coveted those countries' natural resources and because he needed to control vital trade routes. Both over-matched nations fell quickly, although again the German generals gnashed their teeth at logistical breakdowns and at the challenge of coordinating their fighting forces. There were also painful defeats. In the Norway campaign, the German navy provided fire support to amphibious forces and paratroopers who quickly overran key objectives, but the powerful Royal Navy, with Norwegian assistance, was murderously effective as it sank three German cruisers and ten destroyers. While the British army sent to throw back the enemy bungled its operations, the German high command was shocked at the decimation of its navy, the Kriegsmarine. Going forward, the Germans were increasingly cautious about engaging in offensive naval operations.

The Royal Navy still had teeth, but the German army now demonstrated that it was the hardest-hitting in the world. For the main assault against Britain and France, the German high command had initially planned to sweep through Belgium and northern France, and then drive southward behind the Maginot Line, smashing it from north to south, while other forces moved from west to east in a giant pincer operation. But this was exactly what the French, Belgians, and British expected, and it was similar to the sweeping Schlieffen Plan of the Great War that had failed to deliver victory. A rerun of 1914 seemed to offer little hope for a rapid end to the battle, especially as the bulk of the French divisions already were committed to the northern border. Hitler sought a more daring plan and was persuaded to adopt a

The Nazi forces marched on the West in April 1940. Through a series of stunning victories, France was driven from the war in June 1940, and most of Western Europe occupied.

proposal put forward by a handful of his generals, notably commander of Army Group A, General Gerd von Rundstedt, and his chief of staff, Erich von Manstein. Instead of a northern sweep, von Rundstedt suggested, the panzer divisions should strike through the Ardennes Forest. The notion initially horrified much of the German high command, who feared that the dense terrain would be impassable for German tanks and vehicles. But because the French thought the same, they guarded the area only lightly.

On May 10, aggressive German formations spearheaded by tanks manoeuvred through the forest, while strong attacks launched to the north convinced the French that the primary blow would fall on Belgium. Panzer generals such as Erwin Rommel, a decorated Great War veteran, epitomized the fervour of the hard-driving armoured divisional commanders as he personally led his men across the Meuse River under heavy fire. The French defenders in the Meuse and Somme region were overrun. It was no rout, however, and at several positions along the front, outnumbered French garrisons made the Germans pay dearly for their advance.

Notwithstanding the myth of German blitzkrieg, and our tendency to view history with hindsight, France's defeat was neither preordained nor inevitable. The German tanks were far from unstoppable, and their French counterpart—the Char B, a 32-ton behemoth (then the heaviest in the world)—was as good as the German, if not better. The French, moreover, had more tanks, about 3,200 to the Germans' 2,500.[14] The difference in armies—and in combat effectiveness on the battlefield— was that the French defenders lacked a suitable doctrine for absorbing blows and then counterattacking aggressively.[15] At the same time, as the Germans massed their forces against Allied weakness, the French generals had thirty-six divisions entombed in the Maginot Line: they were unable to wield effectively what was left of their army in the south.[16]

Attackers have the advantage of choosing the time and place of battle and of being able to concentrate their forces; defenders are almost always numerically inferior, but they fight with the benefit of prepared positions that use terrain and firepower to maximize destruction. Germany's army tipped the balance of battle by hurling itself forward relentlessly, refusing to be slowed when confronted by dug-in defenders, which were soon screened and bypassed, to be dealt with later by follow-on units. At the front, the German infantry, down to the section level of a dozen or so soldiers, showed initiative and resourcefulness, finding ways to overcome resistance, slip through weak points in defences, and attack from the vulnerable rear—or simply to keep driving forward. Above the battlefield, dive-bombing Junker Ju 87s unleashed high explosives on French strongpoints and closely supported the ground forces. Soon the French defenders and their vaunted forts were behind enemy lines, communication was cut to the rear, and panic set in. The French commanders were particularly inept at responding to the battle that unfolded before them, ponderously giving orders to units that were already overrun, captured, or surrendered, and proving consistently unable to match the Germans' decision cycle.

The French nation stared uncomprehendingly and impotently as the defeat was transformed into a monumental debacle. A nation that had fought so long, so tenaciously, and so proudly during the four long years of the Great War, and then spent the better part of two decades preparing for the battle on its frontier, collapsed within a fortnight. By May 20, the Germans had occupied the ancient town of Amiens, a logistical hub for rail-lines and roads, which allowed them to mass their formations even more swiftly for disruptive attacks and to launch pre-emptive strikes against slow-forming French counterattacks.[17] Despite fatigue and shortages of food and fuel, the Wehrmacht kept on going, cleaving and hacking its way north towards the English Channel to cut the country in half, aiming either to kill or compel the surrender of the 1.7 million defenders in the north before turning southward for the final blow.

Lieutenant Patrick Nixon, serving at this time on board the destroyer HMCS *St. Laurent*, remembered that when the message arrived that Germany had invaded France, his captain, Lieutenant-Commander Harry DeWolf, remarked with casual gravitas, "Now, we got a war on our hands."[18] The *St. Laurent* was one of three Canadian destroyers sent by Mackenzie King in response to a plea made by the British on May 23 for all possible contributions to a defence against a cross-Channel invasion. In an act that signalled the British army's desperation, the Dominion also sent 75,000 Ross rifles—the Canadian-made rifle that had failed miserably in battlefield conditions in the Great War—for use by the Home Guard. A gravely concerned King felt he had to come to Britain's aid, but he was aware that in doing so he would leave Canada vulnerable to attack.[19] He sent the destroyers. Three others, then undergoing refit, would follow, as well as most of the nation's modern aircraft and trained pilots. Canada denuded itself of its most effective forces to protect Britain.

On land, the defeat achieved monumental proportions. In late May, the British and French armies retreated to Dunkirk, a town on the Channel coast in northwestern France, and held off the Germans in a shallow perimeter. The Allied armies were bombed from the air relentlessly by the Luftwaffe, and seemed ripe for one final armoured thrust by panzer divisions. But now, two and a half weeks into the campaign, the panzer divisions—tank-heavy formations with supporting infantry that were mechanized to move with speed—were slowed by fatigue, weakened by casualties, and in need of a respite. Hitler ordered a temporary stop as he believed that the British and French were cornered and he sought to marshal his forces for future battles. The Luftwaffe could pummel the cornered army until it surrendered. To the Germans' detriment, it was a grave error that allowed the Royal Navy to organize a mass evacuation beginning on May 27. Warships, merchant and pleasure vessels, and almost anything that could float, made the trip across the Channel. The resilience of the sailors and soldiers on the beaches was remarkable, but wars are not won by evacuations. Six British destroyers were lost, several more were damaged beyond repair, and some 200 smaller vessels were sunk. And yet, when the perimeter finally collapsed on June 4, some 224,686 British and 129,942 French had been pulled off the beaches.[20] Hitler might have ended the war had he pushed his panzers a little harder. Instead, the battered British army lived to fight another day.

EVEN AS THE BRITISH RETREATED FROM DUNKIRK, the French fought on in the south. Sometimes they showed an unexpected tenacity and inflicted local defeats on the Germans, who took casualties at a rate of around 5,000 per day—double the numbers of the previous month.[21] But the French defence fell somewhere between a glorious last-ditch stand and a spasmodic death rattle. In the vain hope of shoring up the French defences, the British ordered the Canadians across the Channel in early June. General Andrew McNaughton must have been nervous at his division's prospects against the battle-hardened Nazis, for he told at least one group of officers, "it's going to be a sticky business, you must be absolutely ruthless ... tell the men we are not particularly interested in prisoners."[22] The 1st Canadian Infantry Brigade, around 4,000 soldiers and gunners, landed in Brest on June 8. One Canadian eyewitness observed that the French soldiers were elated to see the Canadians, and were soon passing out wine and "singing French songs" in appreciation.[23]

But less than a week after landing, the Canadian brigade was ordered to return to England; they hadn't fired so much as a single shot. Rumours of approaching panzers led to orders from the British high command that all guns, trucks, and supporting equipment were to be left behind. This was lunacy, as the Germans were more than 250 kilometres away—but panic had set in. One commander in the Royal Canadian Horse Artillery, Lieutenant-Colonel J. Hamilton Roberts, disobeyed the order and managed to save two dozen of its newly issued 25-pounder artillery pieces. Others, however, obediently burned and destroyed their new equipment, and heaps of abandoned kit littered the disembarkation zone, including 217 vehicles—signalling the start of what Private Arthur Wilkinson described as a "run for our lives."[24] Upon their return to England, investigations were mounted into lost payroll funds, breakdowns in discipline, the scuttling of trucks, and even a newspaper account that claimed the Canadians had "fled" from France, all of which amounted to little more than whistling in the wind while a hurricane was gathering on the horizon.[25]

Yet even with one brigade gutted of most of its equipment, the Canadian division in England was

A triumphant Hitler stands as the occupier of Paris, France, and all of Western Europe.

one of the few formations left to defend Britain against the expected coming invasion. It was designated as a mobile strike force to be thrown against any German landing. Winston Churchill's famous fighting speech of June 4 promised that the British people would "fight on the beaches, we shall fight on the landing grounds.... we shall never surrender," but it was the 1st Canadian Division and a handful of other formations, including the soon-to-arrive 2nd Infantry Division, that prepared to defend southern England behind anti-tank ditches, machine-gun nests, and barbed wire obstacles. That summer, the Canadians were moved so many times in response to invasion alarms that one wit labelled the Canadians "McNaughton's Travelling Circus."[26]

The Western world reeled at France's humiliating capitulation on June 22. The Nazis, incredibly, now occupied much of Central and Western Europe. A bloodied Britain was threatened with invasion by a seemingly unstoppable military power. The British people saw themselves as standing alone against the Nazi tide, but they were, of course, backed by the British Empire, covering one quarter of the world and standing 500-million strong.[27] Britain was battered but not broken, and it had a new, inspiring leader. Neville Chamberlain, who had tried to appease Hitler in the late 1930s, had stepped aside on May 10 to allow for the pugnacious sixty-five-year-old Winston Churchill to take the reins. Soldier, adventurer, journalist, best-selling author, and experienced politician, the cigar-chomping Churchill growled heroic words of defiance. There would be no talk, no compromise, and no surrender. Even as Hitler believed that Britain was broken, Churchill stiffened the backbone of the British people, on the island and throughout the Empire.

Much to Canada's shock, the Dominion was now Britain's ranking ally, since the United States remained neutral. Without the backing of the powerful US economy, Britain's defeat seemed not only possible but perhaps inevitable. King's cabinet, up to this point adamantly committed to a limited commitment, almost immediately passed the National Resources Mobilization Act that gave sweeping powers to the government, including the conscription of manpower for home defence and even the imprisonment of suspected seditious troublemakers without trial.[28] A desperate and scared citizenry accepted such intrusions on their civil rights virtually without protest. Canada was now on the front lines, separated from them only by the Atlantic Ocean. To keep Britain in the war, the lifeline from North America had to be kept open. Soon everything would depend on the Allies winning the Battle of the Atlantic. First, however, the British people would have to survive a Nazi invasion from the air.

CHAPTER 3

THE BATTLE OF BRITAIN

The Royal Canadian Air Force was woefully underequipped. Hundreds of eager Canadians joined the ranks in 1939, but aircraft shortages resulted in so few openings that most young men who were anxious to fly went overseas to join Britain's Royal Air Force. About 1,000 Canadians served in RAF formations or were undergoing aircrew training at the start of the war, and almost all were drawn to the dashing fighters, attempting to emulate their heroes from the Great War who had been portrayed as "knights of the sky." The RAF's Fighter Command soon held so many Canadians that the British authorities acceded to the King government's request that they form an independent Canadian fighter formation. The No. 242 (Canadian) Squadron flew Hawker Hurricanes, a closed cockpit monoplane, part metal and part fabric, with a top speed of 530 kilometres per hour. It was well armed with eight Browning 303 machine guns, but outmatched by the Luftwaffe's front-line fighter, the Messerschmitt Bf 109, which could out-dive and out-climb the Hurricanes and was equipped with 20mm cannons.

The original pilots of 242 came from all walks of Canadian life. The average age was about twenty-three, slightly older than fighter pilots later in the war. A sampling of prewar occupations reveals an RCMP special constable, an ex-salmon fisherman, a bank clerk, an employee in a hardware store, a semi-professional hockey player, a lifeguard, a gold miner, a dairyman, and a civil engineer.[1] Most of the pilots had flying experience, having paid for private lessons, although some had simply enlisted in the RAF and gained flight time through training. The fighter pilots were bound together by service and country, and they proudly wore the "Canada" badges sewn onto their tunic shoulders.

Neither of the two Canadian overseas formations—No. 242 or No. 110 "City of Toronto" Squadron (which crossed to Britain with the 1st Canadian Infantry Division as a reconnaissance squadron flying slow Lysanders)—was ready for battle. While the two squadrons were kept in England, a number of the 242 Squadron Canadian flyers went to France to shore up depleted RAF formations. RAF squadrons—flying Hurricanes and Spitfires—fought relentlessly against the Luftwaffe in the swirling air battles and tried to slow or hinder the rapid armoured advance, even destroying key bridges behind the lines. But losses were heavy. Many airmen were killed, not having had the chance to learn their dangerous trade. Instinct and experience saved lives, and it also helped to know when to break and run. Canadian Hurricane pilot William McKnight scored his first kill on May 19; he would amass a total of fourteen by the end of the battle and be awarded the Distinguished Flying Cross. The tough, diminutive McKnight, who unwound at night by listening to Bing Crosby records, wrote of his harrowing experiences during the relentless combat where he lost twenty-seven pounds from sheer stress and overwork: "We've only got five of the original twenty-two pilots in the squadron left now and those of us who are left aren't quite the same blokes as before."[2] The aerial sharpshooter had been a medical student in Edmonton before the war and vowed to return to his studies. He was not able to keep the promise, being killed over France in January 1941.

R.H. Wiens, from Jansen, Saskatchewan, wrote of one offensive patrol in the Le Cateau quadrant:

> I was shot down by a Messerschmitt 110 or rather by about four of them.... It wasn't my first scrap but previous to that we never had such odds against us. We saw them first and went right in on their tail. I got one with my first burst and then followed a general melee. I was trying to manoeuvre for another one when a 110 nearly collided with me. The rear gunner and I had an argument, however. I gave him about 500 rounds and could see him fold up. I don't know whether the plane crashed or not, but if it did I have three.[3]

In the confusing battle, Wiens's engine was riddled with cannon fire and he was losing altitude rapidly. He considered bailing out, but the French army had a reputation for shooting at pilots descending in parachutes, fearing they were airborne enemy troops. He decided to ride it out and, despite crashing into some trees, brought his Hurricane down, surviving with a concussion, a bad leg contusion, and a gash to his face. Wiens eventually made it back to England, and then to Canada, where he died on May 21, 1941, at the controls of a burning Anson while training a new generation of flyers.

The battles over France were intense and frightening. Fighter pilots climbed and dove, searched for prey, and snapped off bursts of fire when they saw it, while always scanning the skies for more enemy aircraft that sought to "bounce" them—or surprise them by swooping out of the blinding sun. The intensity of combat was exhausting: most fighters engaged in three or four two-hour patrols a day, and several pilots testified to falling asleep while flying over enemy territory. Relentless combat dulled the edge. The RAF held its own against the more experienced Luftwaffe in the aerial

Hurricanes of No. 242 Squadron set to engage the enemy.

battles over France, but had little impact on the losing ground war.[4] Flying Officer Stan Turner of Toronto, who flew with No. 242 Squadron, wrote of the retreat from France after the battle was over, "We were a wild-looking bunch, unshaven, scruffily dressed, exhausted, grimed with dirt and smoke.... After weeks of fighting we were all keyed up.... As we headed for England we felt not so much relief as anger. We wanted to hit something.... But we knew that the real war had only just begun."[5]

GERMANY OVERRAN WESTERN EUROPE in less than three months, and in the process drove France to her knees and forced back the British in a humiliating rout. The Battle for Western Europe had cost the Germans 43,000 killed and 117,000 wounded. France lost 50,000 dead but saw 1.5 million soldiers become prisoners and the nation fall under brutal occupation. The British had suffered 11,000 dead and its army was tattered in spirit; no one had any illusions that it could stand for long in a sustained ground war against the Nazis.[6] The neutral Roosevelt administration in Washington privately gave Britain little hope of withstanding the Fascist onslaught, even with the pugnacious and charismatic Churchill at the helm, but if Britain was to have any chance of fighting on, it had to be supported with munitions and materiel. The Americans backed Britain, choosing democracy over fascism, although they were also driven by a healthy dose of self-serving pragmatism, for if Britain fell, Germany, with the potential for acquiring France's navy, might soon swallow up the Royal Navy and bring the war to North America.[7]

Hitler's general staff, meanwhile, was stymied by its own success. German military forces had won a lopsided and improbable victory over France, but their commanders had no plan for taking the war to Britain. The Führer, having gambled and won, rolled the dice again. When Churchill's government ignored Hitler's half-hearted peace offering—which required Britain's acceptance of German dominion over Europe—the German senior air force, navy, and army staffs drew up invasion plans, hoping to set foot on English soil by September 16.[8] Even as friction, discord, and rivalry existed among the German service arms, all agreed that while the British army was still punch-drunk from its recent defeat, the Royal Navy would have to be knocked out before an invasion could succeed, or the 2,000 slow, flat-bottomed river barges transporting the Werhmacht would be slaughtered in the English Channel by

Britain's warships.[9] When Churchill ordered the ruthless but necessary attack on the French navy at Oran on July 3, he enraged his former allies by sinking the battleship *Bretagne*, damaging several other ships, and sending the rest to steam to safety, but he made sure that the German navy was not able to gather more ships under its flag. Without France's navy to augment its own wasted fleet after the Norway disaster, the only way for the Germans to destroy the Royal Navy was to gain command of the air and rain bombs down on the warships, and so the first step to invasion was for the Luftwaffe to grind out the Royal Air Force in a series of battles that would eventually give them command of the skies.

The Battle of Britain was recognized at the time as a fight for Britain's very survival. No one in London was confident of success. The destruction of 1,029 aircraft during the Battle of France left the RAF significantly weakened against the overwhelming German air force.[10] Even though the Luftwaffe had lost about a quarter of its strength in the same battle, it still had more than 2,400 aircraft, including 864 Messerschmitt Bf 109s, their best single-engine fighter.[11] The RAF was deeply outnumbered with only 226 Spitfires and 353 Hurricanes, but it had tactical advantages. The fighter pilots—including British and Canadian flyers, as well as those from the defeated nations of Poland and France—were defending Britain and well aware that their backs were to the wall. Britain would fall if they faltered. Because they were fighting over British territory, these same pilots knew that if their planes were shot down, they could parachute to safety, while the Germans would become prisoners of war. Most importantly, the British had invested during the interwar years in a sophisticated ground-based fighter control system. The triffid-like pylons that dotted the east and south coasts of England picked up the direction and range of incoming German bombers and fighters through advance radar, and the control system allowed the limited resources of the RAF to be vectored to the enemy. Though the integrated radar and control system reduced the likelihood of surprise and saved fuel and wear and tear on the fighter pilots, there would still be a battle royal above British soil.

Two Royal Canadian Air Force squadrons, plus No. 242 Squadron, were in England for the battle. The Westland Lysander—a two-seat, lightly armed and slow aircraft built for reconnaissance—was used by No. 110 Squadron but would play no more than a marginal role. However, the second RCAF formation, No. 1 Squadron (later renamed No. 401 Squadron), which arrived in August, was soon thrown into the defence of Britain with its sixteen Hawker Hurricanes. The Hurricanes were sturdy craft, but the Messerschmitt Bf 109s were faster and had a better rate of climb and deadlier weapons in the form of cannons. The Bf 109 was a high-performance day-fighter but it had a short range, with fuel enough for only about seventy-five minutes in the air. (For both German and British pilots, fuel-tank capacity shaped the nature of aerial combat during the war, now over England and later when the Allies took the battle to Germany.) The RAF's Spitfire was similar to the Hurricane but faster and more nimble, and on par with the 109s. The Spitfires, with their eight Browning .303 machine guns, tended to seek out the Messerschmitts, while the heavier Hurricanes went screaming for the German bombers.

In a multi-pronged attack, the Luftwaffe hoped to both shoot down the RAF's fighters and bomb critical strongpoints—from naval docks to air fields—which they targeted throughout July. But the Luftwaffe did not have an effective heavy bomber and so it relied on a handful of light and medium bombers, the Dornier 17, the Junkers 88, and the Heinkel 111, as well as the twin-engine fighter, the Messerschmitt Bf 110. The Bf 110 had a greater range than the Bf 109, but it was little more than fodder for fast-moving Hurricanes and Spitfires. The shoehorning of the German tactical bombers into a strategic bomber role that could target infrastructure, factories, and key logistical structures revealed that that the German Luftwaffe was ill prepared for the coming battle. German planners had conceived and forged their close tactical air support for ground forces, and not for depositing large bomb loads on cities.

The Battle of Britain raged from July 10 to October 31, 1940, with the most intense fighting in August and September. The Luftwaffe first tried to inflict as much damage as possible on the Admiralty's capacity to wage war, targeting dockyards and ships. When this failed, the Luftwaffe switched its sights onto the RAF. This second aerial campaign was unleashed on August 13 against RAF fighter bases and airfields. Within days, the RAF had thrown back its opponents. On August 15, for instance, the Luftwaffe lost 76 planes, and the losses piled up, with another hundred more shot out of the sky over the next three days. Again and again, the Luftwaffe's bombers proved to be ponderous targets for the agile Hurricanes and Spitfires. The bombers' escorts, the independently effective Bf 109s, were ordered to stay close to the bomber stream and therefore were unable to manoeuvre for full opportunity.[12] Against the desperate British and Allied flyers, who were fighting for national survival, a German victory would have been a triumph against the odds, but the balance hung in the Luftwaffe's choice of targets.

Throughout the early part of the battle, the Germans attacked RAF airfields and radar sites, and in so doing, pushed the RAF to the brink of defeat. But the German high command never understood the importance of the radar chains. Had the Luftwaffe razed those sites, the outcome might have been different.[13] The Luftwaffe's lamentable intelligence section also overestimated the damage that their fighters were inflicting on the RAF and underestimated Britain's ability to compensate, continually predicting that the RAF was on the verge of destruction and that one more assault might finally deliver the death blow. In fact, the British manufacturing sector's ramped-up aircraft production, with its manufacturing of hundreds of new fighters per month, matched and then surpassed the withering rate at which Spitfires and Hurricanes were lost. But there was no easy method of replacing the pilots. Canadian Spitfire pilot Keith Ogilvie, who shot down four enemy aircraft during the Battle of Britain and flew 300 sorties before he was wounded in July 1941, recounted, "The Battle of Britain was a very intense time—people came and went.... You'd get to know a guy pretty well, then all of a sudden he wasn't there anymore. You just sort of got used to it. We had some guys who came to the squadron and went missing on your first trip. You just didn't know—if your luck ran out, it ran out."[14]

In the end, the Luftwaffe required a victory to achieve its strategic goals. The RAF needed only a draw. The Luftwaffe's failure to follow a coherent policy and apply its overwhelming strength to concentrated objectives meant that the field was more level than it might otherwise have been. But even allowing for the Luftwaffe's missteps, the Allied flying forces—despite the steady production of aircraft and trained flyers—were still outnumbered. With every squadron needed to defend against the onslaught, the Canadians were ordered into the air.

THE RCAF'S NO. 1 SQUADRON appeared on the order of battle on August 17. The squadron's first day of combat, August 24, was an embarrassing affair in which three four-plane sections were providing cover for Spitfires patrolling at lower heights. Near Portsmouth, the inexperienced Canadians spotted three twin-engine planes and gunned towards them. Squadron Leader Ernie McNab, who had joined the RCAF in 1928 and had cut his teeth on all manner of aircraft, recognized them as RAF Bristol Blenheim light bombers and called off the engagement, but in the excitement several of the Hurricanes misunderstood and swooped on their unsuspecting prey, even as the startled British flyers fired off recognition flares.[15] In the ensuing melee, one of the Blenheims crash landed and another was shot down in flames. McNab later described the ghastly affair as the "the lowest point in my life."[16] A mortified yet gutsy McNab made a visit to No. 235 Squadron, which had lost the Blenheims, to make a personal apology and offer his condolences.[17] The British flyers, who had

Hurricanes piloted by Canadians in battle over Britain.

seen their fair share of war and, like all experienced airmen, untold numbers of fatal accidents, accepted the apology and got on with the battle.

The second combat operation on August 26 was more successful, as McNab led his twelve Hurricanes into the sun and then dived from 16,000 feet on a Luftwaffe bomber stream. The Canadians knifed through the German formation and McNab shot down a Dornier bomber. Fighter tactics usually involved getting the drop on your enemy by flying high, masking your approach through clouds, and having the sun at your back. In most air battles, the experienced leader took charge, with his wingman keeping close, guarding both of their flanks. The leader engaged the "bandit," firing short bursts slightly ahead of the target (unless he was approaching from directly behind or below). This was known as deflection shooting, aiming fire so that the enemy aircraft flew into the bullet stream. On that day, the Canadians took down three bombers, damaged four more, and lost one RCAF pilot, R.L. Edwards, in return.

From the ground, the white vapour trails scarred the sky in lazy criss-crossing designs, but the middle of a dogfight was fast and deadly. With blood pumping and adrenaline coursing through their veins, the Canadians learned quickly how to survive or face death. Blair Russel of Montreal, nicknamed "Deadeye Dick" in the squadron, described the chaos of an early September battle when he and his comrades in No. 1 Squadron intercepted a German bomber stream:

> As we attacked, we were harried by Me 109s from starboard and above, and as I broke away, I came up under three 109s flying line astern. I gave the last 109 a 3-second burst at about 70 yards, noting strikes on his belly, and he soon bailed out. His leader and No. 2 took violent evasive action and I eventually lost them. Shortly after I climbed to attack a gaggle of Me 110s, and fired from above and behind at the last fighter. I gave him a 10-sec burst which set his starboard engine on fire, and he rolled over, one parachute came out and he crashed just south of Biggin Hill. Still above the 110s, I attacked another and saw strikes on his cockpit before my ammo ran out. The 110 went into a lazy spiral and crashed several miles from the first.[18]

Russel survived his first tour of seventy-eight sorties in Hurricanes and would rise to become a multi-decorated wing commander, serving in seven RCAF squadrons.

He ended the war commanding No. 126 Wing, although he grieved the loss of his younger brother, who was killed in a dogfight over France in June 1944.

"The ideal age for a fighter pilot in the Battle of Britain was nineteen years," wrote Paul Pitcher of No. 1 RCAF Squadron. "After that, you had more sense."[19] Bold leaders were needed to guide these aggressive fighters, and the Canadians were lucky to have McNab. No. 242 Squadron also had a charismatic commander in British ace Douglas Bader, who had lost his legs in a crash before the war. Bader epitomized the relentless spirit of the elite airman by continuing to fly after his terrible injury, although his heroic status, ratified by his twenty-two and a half confirmed victories (with the half being a shared kill), made him a difficult subordinate. But in 1940, Bader and other veterans of the Battle of France passed on the lessons of those aerial battles, and the Canadians learned quickly. Over time, however, the remorseless grind of combat killed or wounded so many Canadians flyers, most of whom were replaced by Brits, that 242 lost its distinctly Canadian character.

The enemy raids continued into September. On the 15th, known subsequently as Battle of Britain Sunday, the Luftwaffe attacked London with 123 bombers and 650 fighters; they lost a crippling 61 aircraft. However, the red-letter day for the RCAF's No. 1 Squadron was September 27, which saw the Luftwaffe's last daylight attack. Along with No. 303 Squadron, the Canadians "scrambled" rapidly and were in the vanguard to intercept the raiders. The RAF and RCAF pilots sawed through the bomber stream, sending seven smoking into the dirt and damaging seven more. They won that day; other days they lost. Of the 21 pilots in No. 1 Squadron, 3 were killed and 10 were wounded. One of the wounded, thirty-two-year-old Hartland Molson, a member of the famous Montreal brewing family, remembered being shot down on October 5. He had been, in the flyer's phrase, "fucked by the five fickle fingers of fate, dashed by the deadly digits of destiny, screwed, blued, and tattooed, all in one go."[20] Canada's No. 1 Squadron claimed 30 enemy aircraft, 8 more "probable" destructions, and 35 damaged. From August 8 to September 6, the most intense period of battle, the RAF and RCAF suffered 186 men killed and another 163 wounded, but the Luftwaffe lost even more with 1,367 killed and 281 wounded.[21] The Luftwaffe was handed a decisive defeat, the first for the Germans in the war.

The battle for supremacy in the air continued into late October, but the Canadians of No. 1 Squadron were rotated out of the line to recuperate in Scotland. Of the

3,000 or so combat flyers who served with the RAF, some 105 Canadians qualified to attach the coveted Battle of Britain clasp to their Air Crew Europe Star.[22] "Never in the field of human conflict was so much owed by so many to so few," intoned Churchill in one of his most famous speeches. While the radar technicians, the Royal Navy, Bomber Command (which kept up steady raids on German airfields and paid a steep price), and multiple other arms helped to win the Battle of Britain, it remained the "few" who were lionized by the desperate British people in need of heroes.[23]

The Battle of Britain lumbered to an official conclusion on October 31. By then the Luftwaffe had realized that its daylight raids were too costly and had turned more aggressively to the night bombing of British cities—particularly London. Before this, a frustrated Hitler had postponed the invasion of Britain and turned his eyes to the east and the Soviet Union. An invasion of Russia had always been part of Hitler's strategy, both to annihilate the threat of Communism and to expand his Germanic empire into the rich, agricultural lands of the east. Nonetheless, to keep Britain occupied and to mask his planned invasion, the Nazi aerial onslaught against Britain's cities continued well into 1941. It would be known as the Blitz.

THE RAF'S VALIANT STAND during the Battle of Britain had shown the British people, their empire, and the pessimistic Roosevelt administration in Washington that Britain would not easily surrender to German aggression.[24] The Americans love an underdog, and the RAF victory shifted opinion in the United States from isolationism towards increased support for Britain with more war supplies.[25]

Yet even as the victory's impact was being felt across the Atlantic, the Luftwaffe made the island people pay for their refusal to bend a knee. The superiority of the Luftwaffe was in evidence from September 1940 until May 1941, as night after night the bombers pounded Britain's urban centres. This looked like the Armageddon many had imagined in the interwar years, in which bombers carrying high explosives and lethal gas bombs had been prophesized to break the will of terrified city-dwellers. The vision became a grim reality when the Germans bombed Rotterdam in May 1940, killing a thousand civilians and leading the Dutch to concede defeat. With such grisly foreshadowing, some believed that the British would fold rapidly under the fiery bombardment.[26] But the British people proved they were made of sterner stuff. They had been emboldened by the "few" fighter pilots who had faced long odds and won; now it was time for the "many" to make a stand.

The Luftwaffe initially tried to strike at factories or industrial sites, as they recognized these were higher-value targets and their damage or destruction was more likely to hurt the British war effort. But, like the Allied bombers later in the war, the German air force had little success at precisely targeting structures on the ground from darkened skies. The Luftwaffe rapidly changed its tactics from precision to carpet bombing, with the hope of hitting factories and everything else beneath the rain of their bombs. Hitler and his air marshals had few qualms about unleashing terror bombing: they viewed it as method of breaking the will of the British and so ending the war more rapidly. In London, from mid-August, and then growing in

The German Blitz of 1940–1941 against the British people killed more than 43,000 in an unceasing aerial assault. The British people were tested but not found wanting.

intensity after September 7, the bombs hit churches and schools, theatres and zoos, palaces and workers' flats. Civilians clutched the respirators they had been issued, hoping that they recalled how to identify deadly gases and could put on their masks before they were asphyxiated. The chemical agents were never sprayed—for lack of an effective delivery system and fear of retaliation rather than for humane reasons—but the fear remained. Air raid wardens kept watch and alerted the always anxious citizens to run to their reinforced shelters or the safety of the deep subway lines. Even with these precautions, lives were ended by the hundreds.

The Blitz was later overshadowed by the Allied bombing campaign against German cities, but it was, at the time, a total assault intended to kill as many British civilians as possible. The 17 attacks on Coventry, a city of 240,000, were a graphic reminder that Hitler planned to take the war to all cities within reach of his Luftwaffe. A big raid on November 14 saw more than 500 bombers blitz Coventry. The air raid sirens howled in advance, providing about ten minutes warning before the bombs and incendiaries rained down. High explosives burst water lines, the fire hoses ran dry, and then thousands of tiny fires ignited by the incendiaries burned unchecked. The majestic cathedral and old city centre were still ablaze when the survivors stumbled out of the fire-proof shelters to look at the twisted metal and rubble that were once their schools, apartments, and factories. Streets were left with gaping holes, blocks of houses burned uncontrollably, landmarks were gutted. The homeless looked for the lifeless. Mass burial sites were dug for the 550 dead. The 863 injured—many hideously burned and suffering compression fractures—were cared for, although two hospitals had been hit in the raid.

The Luftwaffe was not able to replicate the terror of Coventry on massive London, which spanned dozens of square kilometres and was able to absorb the avalanche of bombs. While London was too big to be entirely destroyed by aerial bombardment, for fifty-seven consecutive nights, Londoners were blasted into unrecognizably shattered corpses, buried under buildings, and burned to charred remains. The great city was last struck on May 10, 1941, by more than 500 German bombers; their payload killed and wounded some 3,200. After this horrendous night, Hitler called off the long assault and diverted most of his air force to the soon-to-be-opened Eastern Front.

The aerial attacks on Britain in 1940 and 1941 killed more than 43,000 people, nearly half of them in London. Another 137,000 were wounded and three quarters of a million left homeless.[27] If Hitler had not been diverted by his new war against the Soviets, he would have continued the relentless attacks. Not all civilians who faced the aerial bloodbath had been heroic or steeped themselves in glory, but most stood up to the terror without breaking. They would soon face another test: starvation by the U-boat blockade. But before that, the British Empire would be attacked in the Far East.

CHAPTER 4

THE WAR IN THE FAR EAST

Patriotism was profitable for Canadians. Even though British arms and munitions contracts came slowly in 1939, by spring of 1940 war production in Canada was expanding rapidly, and by the following year the economy was on a full war footing. By the end of the war, Canada had produced millions of shells, thousands of airplanes, hundreds of warships, and hundreds of thousands of trucks—more than Germany, Italy, and Japan combined—for the Allied nations at war.[1] The minister of munitions and supply, C.D. Howe, ran business hard, but he coordinated his home front industrial empire with remarkable efficiency.[2] The government intervened in almost every sector of the economy. Nearly thirty Crown corporations were established to manufacture everything from war-related polymers to weapons of war, and to streamline the extraction and production of raw materials. When the price of everyday goods rose because of inflation, King's government intervened and froze salaries and prices, a measure that proved to be as successful as it was bold. As in the Great War, Canadian farmers continued to produce enormous surpluses of wheat and food supplies to feed Britain. Much of the Canadian economy was being geared towards the war and towards creating a new consumer culture to provide a commercial outlet for rising wealth. By 1941, jobs were available for nearly everyone, and women entered the workforce in significant numbers.[3] Canada had become a warfare state.

In early 1940, King was advised by his military staff that Canada was vulnerable to attack. The country's military might was far away: most of the modern destroyers were overseas, as were two divisions of infantry, with a third and fourth almost ready for overseas service. King yearned to assist Britain, but his duty was also to protect Canada. He turned southward to his friend, President Franklin Roosevelt. Even though King believed that Roosevelt had shirked his duty to democracy by declaring neutrality in September 1939, he was encouraged that the United States had continued to assist the Allies. The Americans had provided war supplies, had agreed to the destroyers-for-bases deal, and had even given direct naval support. King also hoped that Roosevelt would remember the promise made in his speech

Canada was a major producer of food, munitions, and weapons of war.
This image illustrates Bren guns made for the British and Canadian land forces.

at Kingston in 1938 to protect the Dominion should it be attacked.[4] Defending Canada was King's first priority, but not far behind was the question of how to pay for the war. His ministers—in particular James Ilsley in finance and C.D. Howe in munitions and supply—were nervous about the growing trade imbalance with the United States, as Canada paid for raw materials from the Americans but sold its finished goods to the British.

In August 1940, King drove south to Ogdensburg, New York, to meet Roosevelt while he was campaigning for an unprecedented third term as president. King and Roosevelt made an unlikely pair—the gregarious president relished a life of wealth and enormous power, while the prime minister was stuffy, guilt-ridden, and cautious—though they liked each other's company. King listened and empathized with Roosevelt's challenges, but he found time to explain Canada's concerns. Britain was on the ropes, and King was anxious to lay the groundwork for the defence of North America should the unthinkable happen. On August 18, the prime minister and the president agreed to establish the Permanent Joint Board on Defence (PJBD). This allowed Americans and Canadians to share ideas and suggest mutually supporting defence plans, ostensibly on equal terms. Over time, the PJBD bound the two nations together and provided security measures for the vulnerable Dominion.

King returned to the United States in the spring of 1941 to plead for cooperation that would help Canada meet its increasing financial challenges. While the Canadian economy was booming, Britain was all but broke and unable to pay for the Dominion's goods. If Britain faltered financially, it would not only stumble badly in prosecuting the war but would also drag down the Canadian economy. In a meeting at Roosevelt's Hyde Park estate, King used his considerable political skills and solid relationship with Roosevelt to propose a barter system. After some delicate discussions, Roosevelt agreed on April 20, 1941, that the Americans would purchase the same quantity of goods in Canada as Canada was purchasing in the United States, thereby balancing the books and, incidentally, considerably boosting sales for Canadian-made products and equipment. With this agreement in place, King returned to Ottawa a conquering hero: he had solved a difficult financial problem and made it possible for Canada to continue supporting Britain in the dark days of 1941. The strengthened financial and defence links to the United States came at a cost—no one was sure if the links would become shackles, leaving Canada tied to the

United States and dragged out of the British orbit—but the desperation of the war had demanded a radical new relationship to the American powerhouse to the south.[5]

HITLER MADE NO SECRET OF HIS DESIRE to annex large parts of the Soviet Union. He had ranted for the better part of two decades about the abhorrent, subhuman Slavic people, and his Thousand Year Reich needed land in which to expand and resources to exploit. Having failed to knock Britain out of the war, and with the powerful Royal Navy remaining intact, Hitler looked eastward. While some of the German general staff warned against the strength of the Soviet armed forces, the yawning depth of the Russian terrain, and the danger of fighting a two-front war, the victory over France had left Hitler convinced that he was a military genius—"the greatest commander of all time," as his own propaganda claimed.[6] His senior military officers—cowed into submission and having sworn an oath of fealty to Hitler personally—offered little counterweight to his wild visions. Germany had looted enormous stores of war materiel from occupied France, including thousands of armaments, locomotives, raw materials, art, and treasure, but Hitler's war machine needed more food, iron, and steel. A victory in the east would allow Teutonic warlords to enslave Slavic serfs who would work farms and factories for the greater good of Germany. Moreover, by driving the Soviet Union out of the war, Germany would also free Japan to turn its full military might against the United States.[7] Although still officially neutral, President Roosevelt was, in Hitler's mind, a puppet in the vast Jewish conspiracy, and the Führer viewed war with the United States as inevitable. And so he needed another war, against the Soviet Union, to provide the materiel to win the future war with his enemy across the Atlantic—what Hitler dubbed on January 9, 1941, the "war against continents."[8]

Stalin had his own plans to take the Communist revolution to other nations, but the paranoid and ruthless dictator had done his best to ruin his military forces throughout the late 1930s, executing up to 25,000 senior officers—and 650,000 other citizens—in blood-dimmed purges later known as the Great Terror.[9] While neither the British nor the Americans believed the Soviet army could withstand a German invasion, Hitler's generals had dangerously underestimated their enemy's strength. They had pegged Stalin's terrestrial forces at two million, when the figure was in fact closer to five million.[10] There would be other nasty surprises for the invaders.

The Soviet Union had been no mere silent partner of Germany. Stalin used the August 1939 non-aggression pact between the two nations to consolidate his grip over Eastern Europe while waiting in hope of seeing the Western capitalist states—Britain, France, Germany—destroy one another. Soviet troops occupied half of Poland and the Baltic states of Lithuania, Latvia, and Estonia.[11] Finland, which had achieved independence from Russia in 1917, was given an ultimatum whose terms required handing over about 10 percent of the nation's territory. When the Finns refused, the Russians invaded on November 30, 1939, beginning what was dubbed the Winter War. The Finnish forces were vastly outnumbered but made an effective fighting retreat. They used the terrain they knew to their advantage, and launched periodic attacks against bumbling Soviet armies that were incompetently led and ill-equipped. Thousands of Soviet soldiers froze to death in the winter wasteland, their casualties eventually rising to some 126,000 killed and another 300,000 wounded, sick, or frost-bitten.[12] Stalin, undeterred by the losses, renewed the offensive in early 1940, broke through the Finnish lines, and imposed a peace treaty on them in March. The Soviets continued to build up their military capabilities, but they remained deeply unready for a war against the battle-hardened German forces.

Hitler's hand was further strengthened when the Italian Fascist dictator, Benito Mussolini, declared war on June 10 against France and Britain. The Italian Fascists resembled the Nazis, at least outwardly. They favoured similarly elaborate uniforms and goose-stepping displays of power, but they fielded a far inferior fighting force. Hampered by bungling generals and poorly trained soldiers, the Italians soon proved utterly incapable of conducting a modern military campaign.

The British were quick to respond to Italy's declaration of war. They punched back in mid-June 1940, using their garrison in Egypt to attack the unprepared Italian forces in Libya, and destroying much of the enemy's air force on the ground. The Italian generals, who made an art of operational passivity, folded in the face of aggressive action and, in December, provided the British, who were outnumbered about four to one by the Italians, with additional morale-raising victories. Mussolini turned to his new German ally and begged for aid, munitions, and soldiers. A disgusted Hitler ordered the decorated panzer general, Erwin Rommel, to the Africa theatre in February 1941 and, with a handful of German divisions, energized the Axis forces. Lauded as the Desert Fox, Rommel would become a hero as his Afrika

Korps inflicted a series of defeats on the British. The Luftwaffe remained a feared striking arm, but after the victories of the first half of 1941, Hitler pulled back many of Rommel's warplanes to support the invasion of Russia.[13] This gave the British time to recover, and the next year would see shifting campaigns fought over Libya, Egypt, Morocco, Algeria, and Tunisia, with few decisive victories for either side.

HITLER'S CAMPAIGN AGAINST SOVIET RUSSIA was intended to be the largest military offensive in human history. The Germans massed more than 3 million soldiers, 3,500 tanks, and 2,700 planes for their campaign. If the Soviet Union could be conquered rapidly, Hitler believed, "Britain's last hope would be shattered."[14] This was a strange rationale for a dangerous initiative, not least because it overlooked the fact that Stalin was Germany's, and not Britain's, ally. If Hitler had kept faith with Stalin, the British would almost certainly have been defeated in the Middle East and throughout their far-flung empire. Nonetheless, it was undoubtedly true that if Stalin was beaten, then Hitler would be master of all of Europe.

Moving millions of men to the Eastern Front took time, and the British, intercepting reports of this action, became aware of what was happening. They warned their enemy, Stalin, that his ally was turning on him. For a man who had spent much of his political career butchering tens of thousands to protect himself from imagined threats, Stalin remained remarkably passive when he received this news. The Russian dictator was paralyzed by the thought of resisting the seemingly unstoppable German forces, and instead of preparing for the contest, told himself that the desperate British, imperialists to the core, were simply drawing him into a war he was not ready to fight.

The German campaign in the east began with the invasion of Yugoslavia in April, and soon thereafter, Greece and the Mediterranean island of Crete fell. These successful operations allowed Hitler to unleash Operation Barbarossa against the Soviet Union on June 22. Hitler had told his senior generals that this war against Communism would be "very different from the conflict in the west." "This," he said, "is a war of annihilation."[15]

The rapid and deep advance of the Wehrmacht soon enveloped and destroyed much of the Soviet army, which Stalin had incompetently ordered into forward positions instead of a defence-in-depth that might have absorbed the crushing onslaught. It appeared that the Communists were doomed as the three-pronged German assault pierced deep into Russia: one army group moving towards Leningrad, another towards Moscow, and a southern one towards Kiev to occupy the Ukraine. Cut off from their logistical lines and seemingly abandoned by their commanders, some two million Russians were killed or surrendered in the first months of the campaign.

While the opening moves of Barbarossa seemed to represent an even grander evolution of the Blitzkrieg tactics unleashed in Poland and against the Franco-Anglo forces, the Russian steppes were not France. Soon the hot pursuit to victory was reduced to a cold crawl. The roads, many of them virtually medieval in terms of quality, were reduced to mush by the thousands of vehicles that passed over them. Hitler's panzer divisions churned on, but much of the army was not mechanized and instead relied on horses, numbered at around 600,000 at the start of the offensive.[16] With every step they took towards the east, the German logistical lines—the system for conveying fuel, food, men, and munitions to the front—became a little longer. Each victory made it harder to sustain the driving momentum, and while the Germans were nearly unstoppable in combat, they did not properly heed the limitations imposed by strained logistics.[17] Most astonishingly, the Soviet soldiers, though callously treated, poorly led, and almost always horrendously ill-equipped, proved far more resilient than the Germans could have anticipated, and millions more were conscripted into service to replace the summer's losses. The gritty Soviet rank and file risked summary execution by political officers to the rear, and often faced hopeless situations at the front, but they found ways to steel themselves for the coming horror.

The German army achieved rapid and monumental victories in the late summer and fall of 1941, but it also failed to take advantage of the goodwill it might have accrued by rescuing peasants from Stalin's iron grip.[18] Much of the Ukraine had suffered through terrible starvation years under Stalin's wicked rule and might have been expected to greet the Germans as liberators. But in a heinous foreshadowing of the industrialized murder to follow, behind the advancing German armies crept the murderers: special extermination squads that executed all Jews in their path—men, women, children, and the elderly—as well as other enemies and supposed undesirables, such as committed Communists, gypsies, and partisan fighters. Those who were captured were shot or asphyxiated by carbon monoxide in mobile vans, and then dumped in mass graves. In Belorussia, by war's end, 5,454 settlements had been destroyed and more than a quarter of the population killed. Some 2.2 million people were murdered, including 99 percent of the Jews.[19] Even as the Einsatzgruppen units—mobile killing squads composed primarily of German SS troops and police—murdered civilians by the tens of thousands (one of the four units executed more than 270,000 victims by spring of 1942), the pace was not fast enough for Hitler and his minions. In late 1941, Hitler set in motion a system later formalized at the notorious January 1942 Wannsee Conference: the Final Solution, a killing scheme by which millions were transported by rail to concentration camps where gas chambers killed thousands daily. This horrific policy, which would eventually claim some six million victims, would later be labelled the Holocaust.[20]

It was not only the Jewish people that Hitler sought to wipe from Europe. Nazi leaders calculated that thirty million inhabitants of the northern half of Russia—considered by Hitler as "superfluous eaters"—would likely die through starvation.[21] Hitler had given ample evidence of his disregard for humanity when he ordered the murder of the mentally challenged, including children, in Germany, in the interests of protecting the racial purity and health of the Aryan regime. Now the Nazis' brutality and callous disregard for lives was raised to another level with their treatment of Russian prisoners of war.[22] By December 1941, the capture of more than 3.3 million prisoners had been recorded by the Wehrmacht, but only 1.1 million were still alive. More than 2.2 million soldiers had been starved to death, left to freeze, or executed outright. It was German policy to deliberately inflict suffering on prisoners, and even to encourage cannibalism among them. Another million Soviet prisoners would perish under German control by the end of the war.[23] This depraved behaviour by the invaders strengthened the resolve of Soviet soldiers to keep fighting, no matter what hardships they endured, and of partisans caught behind German lines to battle to the end.

Though the Germans made enormous gains in the summer and autumn of 1941, the rain, driving wind, and snow of October and November transformed the campaign. With the prize of Moscow in sight—and a chance to deliver a death blow to Stalin—the Germans were soundly beaten by a renewed Soviet offensive in early

December.[24] Unable to capture Moscow, and with nowhere to shelter from plummeting winter temperatures, disaster loomed for the German soldiers. In their headlong pursuit of a knockout blow, few in the army had prepared for a winter in Russia. Now, at the end of 1941, with the Ostheer (the German Army in the East) thrown back at the end of its 1,000 kilometre advance, the frontsoldaten endured agonies through a freezing winter, wrapped in layers of blankets stolen from civilians and uniforms taken from the dead, crawling with lice, suffering bleeding gums, and clenching blackened, frost-bitten extremities. Tens of thousands died of extreme cold and were left frozen by the side of the road as ghastly sign posts. In 1941, 357,000 German troops were reported killed or missing in action; of those, more than 300,000 perished on the Eastern Front.[25] There would be no German victory in 1941. Instead the Eastern Front became an endlessly bleeding wound.

HALFWAY AROUND THE WORLD, Japan had been bullying its neighbours since the early 1930s as it expanded its influence and sought to forge an empire. Though the Japanese emperor remained the sacred head of state, a powerful military class of expansionist-minded officers positioned the nation for war, murdering political opponents and senior officials in the country, fomenting chaos outside its borders, and pursuing zealously a policy of empire building and economic self-sufficiency through a Japan-controlled trading bloc in Southeast Asia. China became a primary target of Japanese expansionism, and a series of Japanese incursions orchestrated by military officers since the fall of 1931 led finally, in 1937, to full-scale war. Japanese troops, equally adept at combined-arms warfare and close-quarter fighting, surged forward in wide-ranging offensives.[26] Victorious on the battlefield, they were utterly brutal in the aftermath. Japanese forces put Nanjing to the sword in December 1937: more than 200,000 civilians were raped, tortured, or murdered. The Japanese military followed this horror by using biological and chemical weapons on civilians.[27] For East Asia, this was when the Second World War began. Washington carefully monitored Japan's aggression from the outset and slowly enacted embargos on fuel to punish the regime and preserve its own economic interests.

Japan was only loosely aligned with Nazi Germany and Fascist Italy through the September 1940 Tripartite Pact, but the Asian nation was part of the Axis. As Europe toppled to Hitler and his minions, the Western colonial powers—France, Britain, and the Dutch—were vulnerable in their lands in the Far East. A defeated France was the first to find that its weakness left it prey to stronger nations when Japan occupied Indochina in July 1941. After General Hideki Tojo became prime minister in October, few Japanese voices were arguing for peace. The Americans offered them trade incentives to withdraw from Indochina and were rebuffed. The two nations were on a collision course to war.

The Japanese high command knew that their small island kingdom could not match the United States in terms of economy and productivity, or win a prolonged conflict against the 130-million-strong nation, which was essentially impervious to attack. Accordingly, it planned to strike a blow that would end the war decisively, much as Germany had done with its rival, France. In developing this plan, the Japanese wildly misread US strength. They believed the American people were soft, decadent, and unwarlike. Japan would attack, win rapidly, and then dictate a victor's peace.

Months earlier, however, senior British and US commanders had studied the likelihood of a Japanese offensive against their colonies and protectorates in the Far East. President Roosevelt had been told that the American garrison in the Philippines would likely fall quickly. His senior generals and admirals were confident, however, that the United States would win a protracted war against Japan. The British were less certain of their own success. They had been driven from Europe and defeated in a series of battles in North Africa. Loath to lose more of the Empire, the pugnacious Churchill lamented that he had few military and naval assets to spare to strengthen his hand in Asia. The British fortress at Singapore, with its powerful naval guns, was expected to withstand any attack, but isolated colonies such as Hong Kong—a strategically important island on the south coast of mainland China—had to be either abandoned or bolstered with reinforcements.[28]

Hong Kong was an especially hopeless cause. Military appreciations from the late 1930s painted a bleak picture of the decrepit defences there, and Churchill himself had said, in January 1941, "If Japan goes to war there is not the slightest chance of holding Hong Kong or relieving it." But he changed his mind only a few months later.[29] His military advisors—men who were disinclined to accept failure—recommended that extra troops be sent to Hong Kong as a show of force to deter the Japanese and support their ally in the region, Chinese leader Chiang Kai-Shek. Strengthening the garrison at Hong Kong would also offer moral support to Stalin, who worried about the Japanese attacking from the east. Moreover, Hong Kong, an overcrowded, dirty port city that had long been a central supply route for China's nationalist army's fight against the Japanese, was a critical strategic outpost of the British Empire, from which Japanese actions could be monitored and contained.[30] In a show of resolve and sabre-rattling, the Admiralty sent to the Far East two of its most prized capital ships, the battleship *Prince of Wales* and the battle cruiser *Repulse*. The Americans reinforced the effect by transferring B-17 bombers and infantry formations to the Philippines, and Canada joined in by offering modest, incremental

This November 18, 1941, cartoon from the Winnipeg Free Press *starkly illustrates the hubris and confidence that many Canadians had in sending a garrison to Hong Kong.*

support for Washington's hard stance, and particularly by backing the oil embargo and freezing of Japanese finance. Perhaps, mused Churchill, the Canadians might be asked to give further support to the Empire in its bold bluff.[31]

The British request that Canada reinforce Hong Kong came to King's cabinet on September 23. King was dead set against sending any Canadians to an area where the Dominion had little historic interest. However, the minister of national defence, J.L. Ralston, had long advocated an increased role for the Canadian army. The navy was fighting the convoy battles of the Atlantic, and Canadian flyers were involved in the air war against Germany, but the ground forces—which had swelled to three divisions and a tank brigade—seemed to be playing Dad's Army in England, where they did little more than march about the countryside and into the nation's pubs. The chief of the general staff, Major-General Harry Crerar, also prodded his minister to send the available troops to Hong Kong, while downplaying the risks, and soon the influential ministers of defence for the navy and air, Macdonald and Power, supported the operation.[32] Many of the English-Canadian newspapers, urged on by the opposition Conservative Party, also demanded that troops be sent. An outmanoeuvred King, who was always wary of being painted as timid and unmilitaristic (especially in relation to Churchill), agreed reluctantly to send two battalions to Hong Kong.

For decades after the war, historians and filmmakers would suggest that the British conspired to hoodwink the Canadians into sending troops to the garrison, but that is simply incorrect. While it is beyond doubt that the British underestimated the Japanese military's strength and the conviction of its leaders, no imperial conspiracy endeavoured to draw Canada further into the war or send its troops to slaughter. As it happened, the British had more troops in the garrison than the Canadians sent, and had ordered some of their most prized warships to the region as a show of force.[33]

TWO CANADIAN BATTALIONS were needed for this tropical posting. Quebec's Royal Rifles of Canada and the Winnipeg Grenadiers had recently returned from quiet garrison duty in Newfoundland and Jamaica. The Rifles were known informally as the "million dollar" regiment, because the regiment included within its ranks the sons of several wealthy Anglo-Quebeckers, including the minister of air, Chubby Power. But neither the Rifles nor the Grenadiers were fully equipped with modern weapons, and many of the soldiers had not finished their training. In fact, some of the infantrymen had barely fired their rifles, most claimed little experience with anti-tank weapons, and a few did not even know how to arm their grenades. The battalion's 3-inch mortars were a good infantry-support weapon, able to hurl bombs at the enemy, but the battalion was short of rounds for both training and the forthcoming battle. Better-trained soldiers might have been sent, but Crerar did not want to break up the 4th Division that was then being raised in Canada.[34]

Despite these limitations, most of the Canadian infantrymen were aching to serve. Rifleman Vince Calder, who had enlisted only a few months earlier after being turned down ten times, wrote that 150 men who had been left off the initial list bribed comrades with gifts and cash to switch places and ensure that they could go

A candid photograph of the Winnipeg Grenadiers
departing for Hong Kong aboard HMCS Prince Rupert.

overseas.[35] With unbounded optimism, military assessors suggested that the two battalions' unfinished training might be completed at a later date.

C Force, consisting of 1,973 soldiers and two Canadian army Nursing Sisters, left from Vancouver on October 27, arriving at Hong Kong on November 16. The Canadians landed ahead of their trucks and Universal Carriers, which had been loaded on slower transports. The vehicles never arrived, having been diverted to the Philippines after the Japanese attacked the colony. The commanding officer, Brigadier J.L. Lawson, a Great War veteran and admired Permanent Force soldier, tried to prepare his men for battle. One of the Royal Rifles sergeants, George MacDonell, was of the opinion that even with the lack of training, many of his comrades came from hunting, fishing, lumberjack, and farming backgrounds, and were "tough as nails."[36] The northern warriors were pleasantly surprised by the warm climate and the readily available servants to do washing and serve food for mere pennies, but all of the Canucks winced at the heat, the mosquitoes, the abject poverty, and the noxious smells of a city swollen with nearly 1.5 million people. The Canadians were also soon to discover that the military garrison's defensive positions were poorly maintained, with outdated guns, no radar equipment, and a slew of other deficiencies. After surveying the isolated outpost, William Allister, an artist who had studied at McGill, remarked, "My God, another Dunkirk!" to which one dour comrade responded, "No, fella, at Dunkirk they had somewhere to go."[37]

THE BRITISH COLONY consisted of the island of Hong Kong and the New Territories on the Chinese mainland, with the core of the population in the port city of Kowloon. The island and mainland were separated by the Lye Mun Passage, which was a little less than a kilometre wide at its narrowest point. The British plan of defence was to meet the enemy on the mainland, fight a delaying action of about two weeks, and then fall back slowly to the island, where the troops would hold out until reinforcements arrived.

On the mainland, the primary defensive position was the Gin Drinkers Line, a loose series of pillboxes situated in a rugged, hilly region north of the port. It seemed ideally suited for defenders, who could hold high hilltops while sweeping the advancing forces with deadly fire; but a resolute enemy might also be able to use the broken terrain to drive quickly through the defenders, who were isolated in garrisons and unable to support one another. The British commander, Major-General Christopher Maltby, had a garrison of six battalions (two Indian battalions—the 5/7 Rajputs and 2/14th Punjabis—as well as the 1st Middlesex and 2nd Royal Scots, along with the two Canadian battalions), coastal artillery regiments, and the Hong Kong Defence Corps (about 2,000 strong), for a total of about 14,000 troops. In the forward defence, Maltby placed much of his strength in the front-line perimeter or much further to the rear in the port. He had, for instance, only a single company in brigade reserve—far too weak a force to throw back any sort of sustained assault should the enemy break through the Gin Drinkers Line.[38] Maltby situated his two Canadian battalions on the island, anticipating an attack from the sea, which was a possibility, but since all of the island's modern guns and defences were sited outward to protect against such an operation, he would have been better served to place at least one of these battalions on the mainland. One is not relying entirely on hindsight in suggesting that any competent commander would have strengthened the single company he had acting as a mobile reserve with at least one of those Canadian battalions. The Canadians were not happy with their role in guarding against a seaward attack, and at least one British officer was impressed by the ardour of the aggressive Canadians, overhearing one to demand, "When do we get to grips with the Goddamned little yellow bastards?"[39]

AGAINST THE HONG KONG GARRISON was the 38th Division, a battle-hardened Japanese formation of about 7,000 infantrymen, but augmented with thousands of additional troops from the 23rd Army, including artillery, signals, and engineer units.[40] The British had long clung to a racist belief that the Japanese were poor warriors, possessing eyesight so bad that they could not fight at night, and barely simian intelligence. Maltby shared this flawed racism, lecturing fervently to the Canadians that they had little to worry about if Japan should be so reckless as to declare war.[41] In one graphic depiction of the type of lecture the Canadians received, Major Maurice Parker of the Royal Rifles of Canada recorded the message in a postwar memoir, noting that the Japanese "are badly trained, badly equipped, and physiologically unfit to fight. They are buck-toothed, slant-eyed, near-sighted, scrawny little people. Their slanted eyes make them poor night fighters, and prone to sea-sickness. Most of them have to wear thick corrective glasses. Because their diet consists mostly of rice and fish they are weak from malnutrition, and their stamina is poor."[42] In reality, many of the Japanese troops had gained years of combat experience against the Chinese, had learned the art of advancing rapidly under fire, were willing to fight with little logistical support, and were well trained to conduct difficult night manoeuvres.

The Japanese unleashed their spectacular surprise attack against the US navy at Pearl Harbor, Hawaii, on December 7, 1941. The goal of the operation was to sink the United States Pacific Fleet and so give the Japanese military forces a free hand in attacking British, Dutch, and American colonies and outposts in the Pacific. Two waves of fighters, dive-bombers, and torpedo planes launched from six aircraft carriers projected power deep into US territory, with the first bombs dropping a little before 8 A.M. on the unprepared Americans. Intelligence failures, a dereliction of duty, and poor tactical preparation had left the US battleships, cruisers, and destroyers lined up as easy targets.[43] Direct hits from the bombers sank four of the giant battleships and six additional destroyers and cruisers. A significant part of the American fleet went down in flames, with 2,402 killed and 1,282 wounded, although many of the warships were later raised from their temporary graves. The attack left the Americans reeling, but soon the grief was channelled into anger.

The first waves of Japanese bombers struck Hong Kong at 8 A.M. on December 8 (coordinated with Pearl Harbor but a day later because of the time-zone difference), killing civilians, military personnel, and destroying five obsolete aircraft that the British had unfortunately left on the runway. The aircraft were not of much use, but they could have offered crucial intelligence on the advancing Japanese infantry that soon crashed against the Gin Drinkers Line. General Maltby was left largely blind in the face of the enemy offensive. Rifleman Alfred Babin remembered, "I saw the planes flying overhead ... saw and heard them drop their bombs and knew the war was on. That was just about it. The war just seemed to begin. From that date on I can't remember where I ate, where I slept or put any of the events in a chronological order."[44]

The aggressive Japanese forces closed to the Gin Drinkers Line on December 9, and probed the Allied positions. Despite the advantages afforded the British, Scottish, and Indian troops in fighting on the defensive, that night the Japanese bypassed strongpoints and infiltrated through the gaps in the line, capturing a key position, the Shing Mun Redoubt. Maltby had planned for the enemy to fruitlessly attack his fortresses in frontal attacks against concrete bunkers. Inconveniently for him, the experienced Japanese had done no such thing, and, because of Maltby's failure in deployment, when the Japanese breached the lines, few mobile reinforcements were in place to counterattack.

The Japanese were cautious in their advance, and were turned back by the 5/7 Rajput Regiment at points along the line, but the Allied forces were dislodged rapidly from their positions and sent into a headlong retreat back to the port on December 11. The defenders crossed to the island just off the mainland early on the 13th. By all accounts, the evacuation was premature, and it gave up important terrain to the Japanese.[45] The campaign started with defeat and retreat, and would only get worse.

The defenders, already shaken, were further distressed by the news that the two British capital ships, *Prince of Wales* and *Repulse*, had been sunk off Malaya (modern-day Malaysia) by Japanese dive- and torpedo-bombers on December 10, and that the American fleet at Pearl Harbor was in ruins. Reinforcements and rescue were now likely impossible.[46] At Kowloon, on the mainland, Japanese fifth columnists in civilian clothing blew up buildings and sowed confusion; looters ransacked businesses and warehouses; and lawless gangs harassed, robbed, and murdered terrified refugees. As the Japanese troops entered the city, further hysteria erupted among the citizens, especially as the soldiers began to loot and kill. With power out and refrigeration off, the bodies of the rotting dead soon corrupted the air. Excreta and garbage were mixed into the awful swill as more than a million and a half civilians contended with the rampaging army. The Allied garrison troops watched the doomed city go up in flames from their island. Twenty-year-old Sergeant Bob Clayton of the Royal Rifles wrote, "It was one massive scream all night long ... it made your hair stand on end."[47]

MAJOR-GENERAL MALTBY followed up his inept stand on the mainland with an equally questionable defence of the island. He divided his six battalions into four sectors, with an eastern and western brigade command structure. Yet again, bizarrely, he planned for almost no central reserve. While it was expected that the Japanese amphibious invasion would crash against the narrowest point of crossing in the northeast sector, defended by the Indian 5/7 Rajput Regiment, Maltby had no rapid counterattack force there to repel the invaders when they were at their most vulnerable. He split the Canadian brigade, putting one battalion on each side of the island, in the south, where because of their lack of vehicles they would have grave difficulty in striking hard and fast. Brigadier J.K. Lawson commanded the west side of the island, while the forces in the east were commanded by Brigadier Cedric Wallis, who would play a key role in ordering the Royal Rifles of Canada into numerous battles. Maltby's inexcusable errors complicated command and control functions of senior officers and of units working smoothly together in unison.

This propaganda leaflet was dropped on the British and Canadian troops on Hong Kong Island. The text reads: "We want you to know one thing. The very day when Japan makes its furious attacks on Hongkong and Malay, it is also the day that Germany makes its long planned landing in British Isles. The end of Britain has come!"

"We were assured that the demolitions on the mainland had been so extensive that it would take many weeks before the Japanese could bring up their artillery," wrote Major Maurice Parker, the D Company commander of the Royal Rifles of Canada. "The next day the first heavy shells began exploding on Hong Kong Island."[48] The island's defenders found little rest as the Japanese steadily bombarded their positions. Rumours of Japanese atrocities on the mainland further unhinged some men. Sergeant Leo Berard of the Winnipeg Grenadiers described one private who was thoughtfully cleaning his weapon when he "put the muzzle of the rifle underneath his chin and reached down and pressed the trigger. Split his head in half." His suicide left the survivors shaken. As they buried the unfortunate soldier, Berard reflected, "The stress and anxiety caused by our position and the fear of capture by the Japanese were more than some men could tolerate."[49]

For days, Japanese artillery shelled pillboxes in the Rajput sector in the northeast of the island, which seemed to telegraph the location of the enemy's intended invasion point. A commander shrewder than Maltby might have rushed forward additional reserves to meet the attack. This came on the night of December 18, when the Japanese 38th Division crossed the Lye Mun Passage in boats, sampans, and rafts under an oily sky discoloured by the burning city. Indian sentries fired upon the advancing Japanese, who were partially masked by rain and darkness, but the defenders' situation was perilous: they were only about 700 strong and spread over 4 kilometres. One Japanese officer later wrote, "It was a spectacular and grim crossing," but the tenacious Japanese troops, taking fire in the open water, moved forward in sheer numbers, with six battalions of some 4,000 light infantry converging on the tiny garrison.[50] The Rajputs fought hard but were overwhelmed, although not before signalling to Maltby's headquarters that the invasion was on.

BY THE EARLY HOURS OF THE 19TH, the Japanese pushed on from their vulnerable beachhead to advance on a number of high points on the island: from east to west, these were Mount Parker, Mount Butler, and Jardine's Lookout, all in the northeastern quadrant of the island. This high ground was only lightly held by the Allied forces because Maltby had ordered his troops to dig in along the low valleys. In a postwar interview, a senior decorated British gunner, Colonel H.B. Rose, revealed

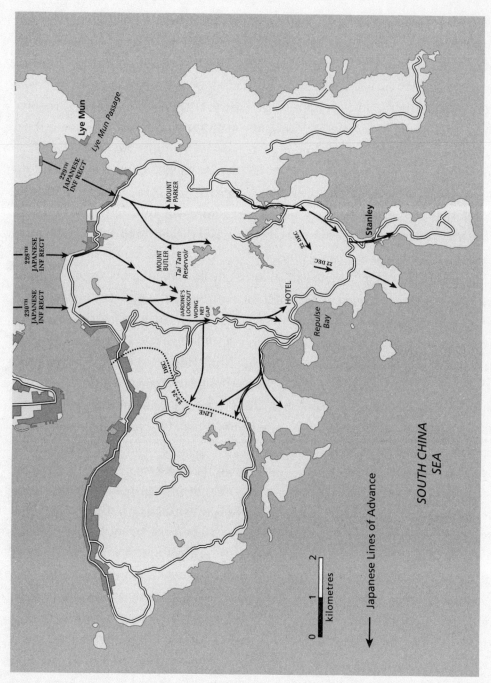

Lye Mun

Lye Mun Passage

229TH JAPANESE INF REGT

228TH JAPANESE INF REGT

230TH JAPANESE INF REGT

MOUNT PARKER

MOUNT BUTLER

Tai Tam Reservoir

JARDINE'S LOOKOUT

WONG NEI GAP

21 DEC

22 DEC

Stanley

HOTEL

Repulse Bay

25 DEC

23-24 DEC

LINE

SOUTH CHINA SEA

0   1   2
kilometres

Japanese Lines of Advance

HONG KONG, DECEMBER 18–25, 1941

that Maltby had told his staff that they did not need to hold the high ground because the "Japs will not attack over hilltops and mountain tops."[51] Since even a first-year cadet knows that the high ground is fundamental to a robust defence—as it forces the enemy to attack upward while allowing for forward artillery observers to call down accurate fire—it is not surprising that the Japanese surged up the hills and ridges, garrisoned the tops, and soon used them to rain down mortar fire on the defenders laid out before them. Major Kenneth Baird, a fifty-two-year-old veteran of the Great War and an officer in the Winnipeg Grenadiers, wrote that his regiment soon caught "merry hell from all angles."[52]

Communication was sporadic from the front, especially after the Rajputs were put to flight, but elements from both the Royal Rifles in the northeast and the Winnipeg Grenadiers, who shifted over from the west towards the sound of fighting, engaged the enemy. Despite being handcuffed by a poor tactical deployment, the Royal Rifles, as the next line of defence behind the Rajputs, fought aggressively. Major W.A. Bishop's C Company was in the firing line and its riflemen and Vickers machine gunners forced advancing Japanese troops to ground in a hail of fire. Rifleman E.I. Bennett was just one of the Canadian defenders. According to an official citation, as the invaders pressed in on his position, Bennett "attacked this enemy post alone, on his own initiative."[53] His counterattack drove back the Japanese and he was awarded the Military Medal for his bravery. Japanese reports later admitted a crippling 65 percent loss to lead units.[54]

With neither Maltby nor his brigadiers basing orders on reliable information about the extent of the enemy incursion, at 2 A.M. Brigadier Lawson ordered four of the Winnipeg Grenadiers' platoons of about thirty-five men each to climb and hold the 1,411-foot-high Jardine's Lookout, in a race to beat the Japanese. Sergeant Tom Marsh of the Grenadiers later wrote, "This was going to war with a vengeance."[55] But the entire Japanese 2nd Battalion of the 229th Regiment, numbering around 500 infantrymen, was already dug in on the mountain. The Canadians came under fire as they wound their way forward up the steep incline, with most soon left bleeding on the slopes. It is difficult to reconstruct these battles, and all the others fought over the following week, because few records were created and most were later burned to prevent them falling into the enemy's hands. Moreover, many Canadian officers and

NCOs were killed and their experiences were lost with them.[56] But the surviving eyewitnesses recounted a fierce battle at Jardine's Lookout. Sergeant Ed Schayler of the Grenadiers remembered his first time in combat: "I heard this crackling sound, and for a little while I couldn't understand what it was. Then it dawned on me. It was bullets going past my ear. If they come close to you, you won't hear the ping like they make in the movies. You just hear a little crackle.... I knew what fear was. I often wondered how I would react, and I shocked myself because I became quiet. I didn't shake, my mind worked well. I didn't shake until I got out of that place."[57] Schayler survived and the Grenadiers demonstrated their grit and determination, as some of them fought to the top. They did not last long and were destroyed by the much larger force. Almost all of the Canadians from the four platoons were killed, wounded, or taken prisoner in the lopsided battle, and the Japanese now overlooked much of the island. This also put them in position to threaten the Tai Tam reservoirs that held about 90 percent of the island's water supply.

Brigadier Lawson, aware that the Japanese were also likely to occupy Mount Butler, which overlooked much of the eastern part of the island, ordered an attack to take it using half of A Company of the Winnipeg Grenadiers, plus a D Company platoon. This is one of the few battles that is known through survivors' accounts. Major A.B. Gresham led a 7 A.M. bayonet assault, supported by Company Sergeant-Major John Osborn. Three platoons advanced up the mountain, shooting, throwing grenades, and driving the enemy back with the business end of a bayonet. Throughout the firefight and bayonet charge, an outwardly calm Osborn organized the attack and then, when the Japanese struck back, the defence. After three hours of battle, the Canadians took the mountain but were soon overwhelmed by a series of Japanese counterattacks. The Canadians were forced to retreat back down Butler's slope, with a number of officers and NCOs killed. Osborn—bleeding freely from a wound to his arm—again took over the fight, placing his surviving Bren gunners to provide a crossfire to keep the enemy from driving forward and cutting off the vulnerable force.

At forty-two years old, Osborn had served in the Great War, been gassed, and lived with little means and wealth near Winnipeg during the 1930s. He was a gruff disciplinarian with five children, whose booming square-bashing voice could be softened for nightly singalongs at the piano with his family. Now, on the 19th, his voice rose above the din of battle to coordinate the desperate defence. By mid-afternoon, the Canadians had been driven into the foot of Jardine's Lookout and were trapped. The Japanese advanced again, firing and throwing grenades. Steel and shrapnel whirled over the battlefield. Canadian eyewitnesses swore that Osborn several times picked up Japanese grenades and threw them back at the enemy in a deadly game of hot potato.

Around 3:15 P.M., Major Gresham concluded that his decimated company was in an untenable position and tried to surrender. As he stood up with a white flag, Japanese machine-gun fire cut him down, nearly tearing his upper torso apart. The desperate fighting continued. Private William Bell, who was wounded in the hip but still firing at the enemy as he bled fiercely, recalled, "The Japanese made numerous attempts to attack us waving swords in the air. At one point, I remember shooting one Japanese officer in the pit of the stomach. I then lifted another one into the air with a burst from my Tommy gun just as he was about to bayonet one of my comrades, Roy Stodgell."[58] The Canadian perimeter slowly shrank as their ranks were cut down. At one point in the battle, an enemy grenade landed amid a group of Canadians that included Bell. With no time to pick it up and throw it back, Osborn gave a shout of warning and threw himself on the grenade, absorbing the fatal blast with his body to save his comrades. "It was the bravest thing we had ever seen," wrote Bell, who owed his life to the regimental sergeant major. A little while after Osborn's death, the

Company Sergeant Major John Osborn of the Winnipeg Grenadiers was an inspiration to his fellow soldiers, and eventually sacrificed his life to save his comrades. He was awarded the Victoria Cross for his gallantry.

Japanese accepted the surrender of the remaining band of wounded and exhausted Grenadiers. Osborn's body was never recovered and he has no known grave, but for his leadership and self-sacrifice during the battle, he was awarded a posthumous Victoria Cross, the first to go to the Canadians during the Second World War.[59]

OTHER JAPANESE FORCES continued to swarm southward throughout the morning of December 19. The Japanese suffered their own breakdown in communication, but in attacking they took the initiative and sowed further confusion in the Allied lines. While the Canadian Bren gunners were especially effective in laying down a punishing sweep of bullets, the Japanese infantry had been trained to drive forward around areas of resistance. As the Royal Rifles' Sergeant Macdonell observed, "When we stopped them [the Japanese] in some position, they would immediately and skilfully begin to slip around us to turn our flanks," thus forcing the Canadians' retreat.[60] Maltby's headquarters, and that of his brigadiers, attempted to react to the slashing Japanese attacks, but they were often working with outdated information, and so most of the Allied companies and platoons fought piecemeal battles with little direction from rear headquarters.

By late morning, a Japanese column of troops advanced southward from Jardine's Lookout, overlooking Brigadier Lawson's headquarters at the Wong Nei Chong Gap in the centre of the island. With the front collapsing, Lawson's brigade headquarters was now a forward outpost. It did not last long. Two platoons of Grenadiers from D Company—no more than 80 men—sought to block some 800 Japanese infantrymen.[61] But though the Canadians slowed the tide, Signaller Georges Verreault, who had earlier boasted that he would be "good for 15 Nips myself," wrote in his diary, "We're trapped like rats without any hope of escape."[62] Around 10 A.M., Lawson's last communiqué to Maltby was that he and his staff were "going outside to fight it out." The slain Lawson was found among Japanese and Canadian corpses.[63]

THE CANADIANS MADE THE JAPANESE PAY for their advance, but thousands of invading troops continued to cross from the mainland to hammer home the final nails in the garrison's coffin.[64] The Japanese first waves numbered around 4,000, but they were concentrated against the scattered Allied defenders, whose numerical superiority of close to 14,000 was frittered away by poor generalship. Though the written record of battle for this period is sporadic, when the Japanese commanders recorded "strong opposition," "fierce fighting," and "heavy casualties," they were almost always referring to fighting against Canadians.[65] A Japanese official report noted clinically, "The advance of our assault troops met with many setbacks.... The enemy fire from these positions was so heavy that not only was the advance balked, but our troops were thrown into confusion."[66]

Aggressive Japanese infantry infiltrated steadily southward on December 20 until they reached Repulse Bay Hotel, which was guarded by a mixed force of British troops and A and C Companies of the Royal Rifles. The Japanese drive was stopped short of the opulent hotel by Canadian and British counterattacks and concentrated fire, but it penetrated enough to allow the invaders to sweep the main road with sniper and artillery shellfire, all but cutting the island in half and severing communication between the eastern and western defenders. The Anglo-Canadian garrison at the hotel was under continuous bombardment but held out for two days. Terrified civilians crouched in the cellars and in makeshift shelters, using fine linen to stop the flow from bleeding wounds and crawling amid the shards of once-fine china as Japanese artillery reduced the hotel to rubble. The building was partially evacuated on December 22, and most of the Canadians escaped westward that night. A number of British soldiers were not so fortunate. They were captured, bound, and tortured, with ropes tied around their arms and between clenched teeth, so that if they fell forward the twine cut deeply into their mouths. After systematic beatings, a number of the captives were lined up and shot. The Japanese commander responsible was convicted of war crimes in 1946; according to the judgment, "the whole route of this man's battalion was littered with the corpses of murdered men."[67]

By the fifth day of the battle, the island was split, the water reserves were lost, and the defenders had endured much of that time with little food, water, or sleep. The Canadians continued to hold out with uncounted acts of heroism and sacrifice. There were few places of safety for the wounded, but the Canadians exhibited enormous bravery in dragging their wounded comrades from the battlefield and in carrying them over the rough ground. They knew that anyone left behind would likely be executed. Corporal Bud Dicks fell into Japanese hands after an ambush. He and a few comrades were tied up roughly and lined up overlooking a cliff. The doomed men stared at one another as the seconds ticked by to their grim fate. A Japanese officer shot one of the sergeants in the back, and the other Canadians jumped to their deaths, choosing action over execution. "I smashed my face on a rock and lost consciousness," remembered Dicks. "When I woke I thought I was dying but I found out that you don't die that easily."[68]

THE ROYAL RIFLES' COMMANDER, LIEUTENANT-COLONEL W.J. HOME, took over command of C Force when Lawson was killed. Though Home, a decorated Great War veteran, reported to the British brigadier, Cedric Wallis, as the senior Canadian officer he also had a responsibility to the Canadian government. Major Maurice Parker of the Rifles wrote that relations, which were strained from the start, soon degenerated during the stress of the losing battle: "The British thought the Canadians were a rag-tag bunch of rowdy, cowardly colonists, not good for very much.... The Canadians thought of the British as arrogant, condescending prigs."[69] In a stormy meeting on the morning of December 21, an exhausted and dispirited Home told Wallis that his soldiers needed a rest, as they had lost more than half of their officers and fought several days and nights with little food or water.[70] It was, he noted, not uncommon for the riflemen on the march to drop from exhaustion, collapsing into a coma-like sleep that resembled death. Wallis was aghast at the suggestion of a pause, even though the battle was clearly lost, the Canadians had been engaged more fiercely than the other units, and the British brigadier had units that had barely been committed to battle. While Home, as senior Canadian, had a right to speak to Major-General Maltby, Wallis refused to allow Home to bypass him, and the British brigadier considered having the Canadian commander shot for defeatism. He did not act on this draconian notion, but Wallis's mind was poisoned towards the Canadians and their commitment to battle.[71] For those Canadians closer to the front, there was no let-up. Home knew the battle was now unwinnable, and twice more he pressed his case over the coming days, arguing that continuing the contest was "a useless waste of lives."[72] Neither Wallis nor Maltby entertained surrender, and both were urged to keep up the struggle by Sir Mark Young, the governor of Hong Kong. A spine-straightener of a telegram by Churchill on December 21, demanding the garrison hold out to the bitter end—"fighting in the inner defences, and, if need be, from house to house"—no doubt also had an impact on the British generals.[73]

The close-quarters combat continued up until the final day of battle, on December 25. Dog Company of the Royal Rifles was ordered to attack against dug-in defenders at Stanley Village in broad daylight—a nearly hopeless task. When Home protested the attack, Wallis promised massive artillery and machine-gun support. With few guns in the area, this was a boldfaced lie. Home must have known this and was nearly ready to mutiny against the callous order. Yet he relented once again when Wallis insisted on the attack, and the Rifles carried out their orders. A little after 12:30 P.M., under a beating sun, about 110 of the Royal Rifles scrambled forward, even though all their officers considered the plan to be "madness."[74] They moved from rock to rock and bush to bush, but soon, according to Rifleman Raymond Elliot, the "enemy spotted us and started shelling and firing."[75] The Rifles took grave casualties but regrouped. They had come too far to retreat, and any reversal would likely see them shot down as they scrambled away from the battlefield to a false safety. The only way was forward.

The survivors readied themselves, fixed bayonets, and charged the final 40 metres. Shouting war cries and brandishing cold steel, they drove back the shocked Japanese, who were backstopped by artillery and machine guns. One of the Rifles later wrote, mincing no words, "The morale was very high, being backed up by hatred, contempt and disgust for those wanton, raping, sadistic, cold blooded murderers from Japan."[76] The Canadians carried the battle but left behind twenty-six dead comrades, while another seventy-five were wounded.[77] No more than a dozen of the Rifles emerged unscathed. Later on that Christmas Day, at 3 P.M., Maltby's forces surrendered.

"I AM VERY FORTUNATE TO BE ALIVE DARLING," wrote signaller Ray Squires a few months after the battle.[78] With the surrender of the entire garrison, the Hong Kong campaign was the only significant action in Canadian military history in which 100 percent losses were inflicted. Not a man escaped either capture or a grave. For those who had fought for their lives, and seen comrades give theirs in battle, it was a crushing defeat. "I saw some men break down and cry like children, 'What, surrender now?' they sobbed," recounted Private Tom Forsyth of the Winnipeg Grenadiers. "'After all the good men we lost?'... I never dreamed it could happen."[79]

The victorious Japanese soldiers had every right to crow about defeating the Allied troops who had held them in contempt, but then they squandered the victory by engaging in acts of outrageous sadism. The Canadians, British, and Indians who had fought gallantly against the Japanese were now treated to horrendous beatings and outright murder.[80] Injured men were routinely executed. Alfred Babin of the Royal Rifles remembered the massacre at St. Stephen's Hospital: "The Japanese who bayoneted those helpless people in their beds just did it. They showed no emotion afterwards.... The slaughter had been done so efficiently that it was impossible to believe that one human being could do such savage things to another human being.... Ears were cut off, tongues cut out and eyes gouged from their sockets hanging on their cheeks.... It was a horrible scene."[81]

Along with the wanton murder, the Japanese soldiers raped women and girls. Canadian Nursing Sister Lieutenant Kay Christie testified that Japanese soldiers rounded up all of the women from one hospital, including secretaries, nurses, and teachers. "As one of the soldiers stood in the doorway with a machine gun, the others took the younger girls, laid them on the floor and raped them while the mothers could do nothing but stand by helplessly and watch."[82] Another Canadian, Private Sid Vale, who was immobilized with injuries, shuddered at the "screams of a nurse getting raped in the room next to us.... I couldn't walk or do anything at that time. I don't know whether I would have had the guts to do anything had I been able to walk. But that's something I'll never forget."[83] There were other horrors and outrages, but all were common for the Japanese army that had repeatedly indulged in similarly barbaric behaviour in their pitiless war against the Chinese over the previous five years.

When the rampant murder subsided, the survivors were finally accounted for by their officers. The Canadians had lost 290 killed, while 493 were wounded. Maltby's entire force suffered 955 killed. Another 659 were recorded as missing, all of whom were presumed dead.[84] The Hong Kong garrison had fought well, with the fallen selling their lives dearly despite poor tactical coordination and planning from Maltby. In relation to other British battles of the time—notably the failed defence of Crete and the lamentable collapse at Singapore—the Hong Kong force endured relatively high combat casualties and held out for seventeen days.[85] Despite their victory, the

Japanese were also bloodied, taking 2,096 casualties, including 683 killed.[86] While the Canadians had not been fully trained for battle, by Japanese accounts they fought tenaciously, with skill, and went to the wall in a lost cause.

WHILE THE DEAD WERE BURNED OR BURIED, the remaining 13,000 or so former combatants and thousands of British civilians were marched into captivity. What lay ahead was a period of grim imprisonment, "a new living hell," according to William Bell, most of whose closest friends had been killed during the battle.[87] Canadian prisoners were put in camps in Hong Kong—at North Point or Shamshuipo—and, later, a group was sent to Japan as slave labour. Though the Japanese had never signed the Geneva Convention and therefore had no formal agreement guiding them in the treatment of prisoners, Japan's representatives had said their military would abide by the rules. And yet, as Japanese soldiers and authorities saw it, surrender was dishonourable, and on the battlefield or in the prisoner of war camps the Japanese authorities exhibited little but contempt for their prisoners. Even accounting for cultural differences, the Japanese were sadistic captors and their prisoners, over the next four years, faced starvation, malnourishment, disease, and execution.

In the first months of incarceration, the Japanese authorities refused to allow the Red Cross to inspect camps, and even withheld the names of prisoners from their families in Canada. While the Japanese did not reveal this cruel tactic to their prisoners, the silence from home left many Canadians in the camps deeply uneasy. Ray Squires confessed his private fears in his secret diary some three months after capture, writing, "I hope you know I am alive."[88] Prisoners' letters were routinely read by the Japanese and when they revealed any mistreatment they were destroyed and the author punished with isolation and starvation. At all times, rifle butts were used freely to smash bones and shatter teeth. "We took a lot of beatings," remembered Leo Berard.[89] Humiliation was also common. The Japanese guards tied naked prisoners to stakes for hours or days, even under the burning sun or, when the weather turned cold, in the harsh winter wind. The prisoners were in fragile health to begin with and many did not survive the ordeal.

Mock executions were also held, with men dragged before firing squads or forced to kneel beneath the executioner's blade. At the last moment, the sadistic guards would toss the quivering Canadians back in their cells. But the threat was always there. Sergeant John Oliver Payne of Winnipeg Grenadiers, a twenty-three-year-old from Fort Rouge, Manitoba, wrote a final letter to his mother on August 19, 1942, about his plan for an escape from North Point Camp.

> Dear Mother, I have decided, either fortunately or unfortunately as the case may be to take a chance on getting through to Chungking. I've investigated as much as possible and feel sure we stand a jolly good chance of getting there. There are numerous reasons for this step the chief being that the cholera season & fly season is starting, dysentery & Beri Beri are high in camp, and anyway I'm ruddy sick of Japanese hospitality. You share, I know, my own views on fatalism, so for that reason I know you won't condemn my judgment. So just in case I shouldn't make it you must remember that according to our beliefs I have departed for a much nicer place (I hope) although it will grieve me to exchange the guitar for a harp even though there is a higher percentage of gold in the latter. But that's enough of this drivel, I'll be able to destroy this note myself I'm sure so bye bye for now, your devoted son John.[90]

John and three Canadians who joined his escape attempt were captured after their boat capsized. Japanese military police beat them to a pulp with bats, bound their bodies with barbed wire, and later executed them.

Throughout the British and Canadians' period of incarceration, the daily nutritional intake per prisoner dropped to a starvation level of fewer than 1,000 calories. While there were periods during which a quantity of food would come into the camps, the supplies never lasted long. For the most part, prisoners subsisted on rice, rotten meat, weeds, and fish heads. In the summer months, the meagre meals had to be eaten with one hand constantly waving off the swarms of flies. But with men starving, nothing was wasted. Camp cooks threw unappetizing scraps of food into a communal stew, along with grass, buttercups, and rice, to create a frothy broth that the prisoners called the "green horror." Stray dogs and cats were consumed by the desperate men who were, in the words of Sergeant Howard Donnelly, "wasting away."[91] The prisoners, wrote Leo Berard, "appeared as if some vampire had sucked all the blood from them, with the dead blue skin and eyes with a deep distant look, staring right in front about their own height, without turning the head ... as if in a coma of hypnotism."[92] The systematic starvation affected men differently. Some prisoners could withstand the drastic weight loss—as much as a third to half of their pre-battle weight—while others saw their once-healthy bodies reduced to a bone-protruding nightmare, followed by disease and death. Rifleman D.L. Welsh of the Royal Rifles wrote his last diary entry on October 5, 1942: "never ate anything all day (could not swallow)."[93] He died shortly thereafter, at the age of twenty-one.

The prisoners played sports for a while, to stay active and keep their spirits up, but soon the malnutrition left them too tired. Disease began to claim victims. Pellagra, malaria, and diarrhea were virulent among the emaciated prisoners. "Those men with dysentery," recounted Vince Calder, "had to head for the toilet 40 to 50 times a day."[94] Bleeding body sores plagued the gaunt scarecrows, and prisoners found to their horror that they were able to pull out their own teeth from their grey, squishy gums. Parasitic worms infested almost everyone. Beriberi was another killer, brought on by a lack of vitamin B1. Starving bodies ballooned as fluid accumulated in tissue and skin became doughy. The disease caused a burning sensation in the feet,

or extremities felt as if they were being jabbed repeatedly with needles. "I would find them rocking back and forth," remembered one of the camp's doctors, "and crying with pain."[95] One horror was called "Hong Kong balls," which caused men's testicles to be enlarged to the size of baseballs. In the Anglo-Canadian camps, men died every day from starvation and disease. Donald Geraghty of the Royal Rifles recounted that they "were burying fellas six a day."[96] Some were too bloated from the beriberi to fit in the makeshift coffins and were simply put in the ground. For a while, "The Last Post"

This is the medical ID card for Winnipeg Grenadier Private Norman Pott, age twenty-two, who died of pellagra in a Japanese prisoner-of-war camp on February 11, 1944.

was played to acknowledge a death, but eventually it was stopped by the prisoners: the plaintive call was too demoralizing, as its haunting refrains sounded morning, noon, and night.

"The will to live is very strong," believed one Canadian prisoner.[97] Rumours of rescue and food sustained many men, with Lieutenant Leonard Corrigan of the Winnipeg Grenadiers writing, "they are invaluable as topics of conversation and subjects of humour."[98] Amid the beatings and starvation, prisoners cared for one another. One of the few international reports to reach Ottawa about the Canadians in the Japanese camps in July 1943 revealed that "Medical Facilities are scandalous.... The Japanese entirely neglect medical aid."[99] The report spoke the truth. Medicine and instruments were withheld by the Japanese prison guards, and men parted with their wedding bands or pulled out their own gold-capped teeth to pay for the supplies to keep their buddies alive. "There was never enough medicine to go around," said William Bell, who was hobbled during his incarceration by multiple wounds sustained during the battle. "The doctors literally had to choose who would live and who would die."[100] One of those doctors, J.N. Crawford, the medical officer for the Winnipeg Grenadiers, wrote agonizingly, "We felt that such a power over life and death should be the prerogative of the Deity, but at the moment He seemed to have forgotten us."[101] In a twist of sick irony, Japanese guards often beat the doctors or medical orderlies, blaming them for not doing enough to keep the abused prisoners alive.[102]

While any act of disobedience resulted in a savage thrashing, a former Japanese Canadian, Kanao Inouye, known as the Kamloops Kid, took special delight in tormenting prisoners. He claimed to have been subjected to racial abuse and epithets when he lived in Canada, and now he took his revenge. "He was a sadistic maniac," wrote one prisoner, "who vented his sickness in the deliberate torture, abuse and even murder of his Canadian countrymen."[103] He kicked, smashed, and battered the Canadians relentlessly during the imprisonment, and tortured other civilians. Justice was delivered in August 1947 when the Canadian government hanged him for treason.[104]

IN THESE CIRCUMSTANCES, THE BRITISH GENERAL, MALTBY, had time to stew over why the battle had been lost. He did not blame himself. When he wrote his official dispatch, he held his soldiers responsible for the defeat, singling out the Canadians as particularly weak. With most of the official records destroyed or lost during the battle, the confusion and chaos of combat left few clear narratives. Brigadier Wallis also wrote up his account of the battle during his incarceration and was exceedingly harsh in his assessment of the Canadians, and especially the Royal Rifles of Canada—his acerbity no doubt stemming from his many disagreements with the Rifles' Lieutenant-Colonel Home. Wallis's stinging indictment—in the form of an official war diary entry that was leaked throughout the prison camps—led to acrimonious relations between the Canadians and British.[105] A number of Canadian officers refused to let their men be scapegoated and wrote their own reports of the battle when they found out. As Lieutenant-Colonel George Trist remarked with anger, "We [the Canadians] are being blamed by the Imperial staff for the early fall of Hong Kong."[106] Wallis's war diary was never published, but after the war the Canadian government, upon receiving an advance copy of Maltby's official report, formally protested the contents, which were set to be released in 1948. Maltby was out of touch for much of the battle and therefore relied heavily on Wallis's war diary; his report highlighted the lack of training of the Canadian battalions, downplayed their many brave actions during the battle, and, far worse, accused them of lacklustre fighting. Because of the Canadian government's outcry, the 1948 report was heavily expurgated, but it still stirred considerable controversy in Canada and a significant backlash from veterans. Maltby's full report was not released in its entirety until 1993, when it again provoked an angry response from Canadians.

"HOW LONG! HOW LONG! WILL THIS DAMN THING LAST," wrote a starving and despondent Major Kenneth Baird after three years of incarceration, and facing an unknowable future stretch of torture and neglect.[107] Somehow Baird and his Canadian comrades held on, but the prisoners were not liberated until after the dropping of the atomic bombs on Japan in August 1945. The survivors reported that even a few more months of incarceration and starvation would have led to mass death. As it was, the effects of imprisonment were horrendous: 264 Canadian POWs died in captivity as a result of systematic abuse, malnourishment, torture, and execution. The treatment of the Canadians in Japanese hands was far worse than it was for those soldiers, sailors, and airmen who fell into the clutches of the Nazis.

Back in 1941, the defeat of the Canadians at Christmas in Hong Kong had sent the King government reeling. It reacted with little honour, with the prime minister expending a great deal of energy in shifting blame to Crerar and Ralston. King's voluminous diary is also nearly devoid of expressions of concern for the welfare of the Canadians in captivity. Instead he worried more about the potential political fallout from having sent Canadians to the indefensible and isolated colony. The opposition Conservatives hammered away at King and eventually demanded an investigation. The Royal Commission found no evidence that the government had betrayed Canadian soldiers in the unmitigated defeat in the Far East, but few would have expected a full and frank revelation of government wartime policy during the conflict.[108]

If blame was difficult to assign, Canadians nonetheless demanded retribution for the losses. Innocent Japanese Canadians became the scapegoated victims. Immediately

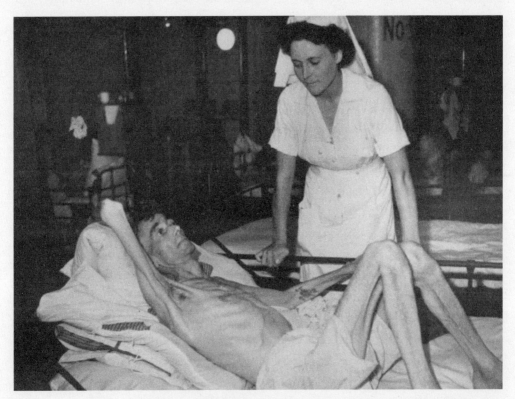

A malnourished ex-POW receiving treatment from a British nurse in September 1945.

after the Pearl Harbor attacks, some 23,000 Canadians, living for the most part on the west coast, were rounded up and evacuated to the interior. The justification for the evacuation was that members of the visible minority might have aided an enemy assault on Dominion soil, although police and military investigations had already found almost no enemy sympathizers.[109] At the same time, Japanese Canadians' civil liberties were trampled and their household and business goods sold off to despicable vultures, often their former neighbours or, in the case of fishermen, their competitors. The ill treatment of these Canadians remains a dark stain on the nation's history, although it cannot be divorced from the anger and fear felt by wartime Canadians who worried about the threat of a Japanese invasion, or from the misplaced belief that race trumped nationality.

For over seventy years, historians have since chewed over the Hong Kong operation at some length. Much of the first generation of literature, until the 1980s, condemned the Canadian and British governments for sacrificing inexperienced troops to a hopeless operation and then being all too keen to fight to the last Canadian.[110] But such accounts were delivered with a healthy dose of hindsight. At the time, the King government (if not King) and the Canadian army were anxious to see the nation's troops sent into battle somewhere, perhaps anywhere. Further, the British had their own soldiers stationed in the isolated garrison; desperate to deter the Japanese—to the point where they sent two capital ships to that theatre—they were in dire need of help from allies. Contrary to early opinion, the calamity that resulted was not an imperial conspiracy. The King government acted with naiveté and lacked the means to independently assess intelligence coming from the Far East, but Ottawa wanted to do its part in defending the far-flung British Empire. Its soldiers fought with enormous bravery and distinction, and they paid a heavy price, but they were not sacrificed in any different way than other soldiers, sailors, or airmen who are sent into desperate situations and battles.

IN EARLY 1942, the Rising Sun flag was raised over much of East Asia. In five months, the Japanese created a new empire, incorporating the natural resources of the Dutch East Indies (now Indonesia), Hong Kong, the Philippines, Malaya, and Burma, as well as much of China. These swift and shocking victories were capped off by the

British capitulation in their seemingly impregnable fortress at Singapore. There, the British army collapsed in the face of Japanese pressure, the garrison surrendering on February 15, and some 80,000 British, Australian, and Indian troops were captured.[111] The sinking of the *Prince of Wales* and *Repulse* only added to the severe blows to British prestige. Churchill nearly wept at the losses, and, in the case of Singapore, at the clear failure of command and willpower. Defeat and disgrace in the Far East doomed the Empire, and with it, Churchill's hollow hope of keeping it intact.

While the British Empire sagged under the onslaught—and with India and Australia threatened with invasion—the Americans were only temporarily dazed. The strike against the US navy at Pearl Harbor had seemed a crushing blow, but the Japanese bombers had not sunk the aircraft carriers that were safely at sea. They had missed the oil storage facilities and only lightly damaged the dockyard. Most of the sunken warships, including three battleships and three cruisers, were raised and repaired. Amid this resurgence, the Americans were united in rage against the sneak attack and responded with a formidable commitment to victory.[112]

Churchill's greatest fear was that the full might of the US forces would be thrown against the nation's new Asian enemy, causing it to ignore Nazi Germany. But Hitler saved Churchill from having to negotiate for ongoing American support by declaring war against the United States on December 11, 1941, in one of his most monumental blunders. The Führer was driven by hatred and hubris, and by his long-standing belief that a Germany that ruled Europe would eventually face off against the United States for global dominance. Hitler's declaration of war allowed Roosevelt to order a two-front war, against both the Japanese and the Nazis, and it was the final step in transforming the conflict into a global war. When Churchill and King heard the news of Germany's declaration, both men gasped at Hitler's strategic ineptitude, but also recorded their jubilation, knowing that the odds had tipped in their favour. The Western Allies were also willing to support the monster, Stalin, following the axiom that the enemy of my enemy is my friend. Whatever had happened on the Eastern Front or in the Far East, there would be much hard fighting and many horrendous casualties before the Thousand Year Reich was brought down.

CHAPTER 5

THE WAR AT SEA

While the Canadian army drew upon inspiration from the exploits of Sir Arthur Currie's Canadian Corps during the Great War, the nation's navy had a less storied history. The Royal Canadian Navy (RCN) was nearly stillborn in 1910, when a plan for a modest fleet of close to a dozen warships was cancelled, and had since been kicked around as a political football with few champions. During the Great War, the RCN had carried out good work on the open seas, ensuring safe passage for merchant ships through the all-important transatlantic shipping routes, but closer to home it had been unable to defend the east coast against U-boat attacks in the summer and fall of 1918, when German raiders had unleashed a series of high-profile, low-impact attacks on close to two dozen small vessels.[1] To redeem the RCN's undistinguished wartime experience, and forge bonds in local communities across the Dominion, senior naval brass had cleverly established reserve units in 1923, just as the militia had done since before Confederation. Nevertheless, the service had twice faced near dissolution in the interwar period, and had survived mainly by entwining itself with Britain's Royal Navy. As all Canadians knew, the Royal Navy had an illustrious history as Britain's first line of defence, and it was the mechanism through which London projected worldwide power and guarded the empire's vast trade network.

Despite the Canadian navy's lacklustre history, it was better equipped than the other two arms. The fleet, by the end of 1939, consisted of three auxiliary ships, four minesweepers, and seven modern destroyers: HMCS *Assiniboine*, *St. Laurent*, *Fraser*, *Ottawa*, *Restigouche*, and the slightly older *Saguenay* and *Skeena*. The most recent destroyers displaced 1,360 tons each, had a top speed of 31 knots (about

57 kilometres per hour), and were equipped with main armaments of four 4.7-inch guns. To man the ships and shore establishments there were 2,967 naval personnel, a mixture of professionals and reservists.[2] As each destroyer required a crew of 181 officers and men, barely enough sailors were available even to man these warships.

The RCN was on a war footing beginning on August 28, almost two weeks before Canada declared war. On September 1, as war with Germany seemed to loom, HMCS *Fraser* and *St. Laurent*, two of the four destroyers on the west coast, steamed around North America by way of the Panama Canal to arrive in Halifax at mid-month. The other two destroyers initially were left to guard the west coast in anticipation of a Japanese attack, so poisonous were that country's relations with the United States; but eventually they too were sent to the RCN's primary battleground, the Atlantic. The Allies' ability to maintain and guard the supply route between North America and Britain would in some degree determine the outcome of the war.

The Royal Navy had always protected the merchant ships that linked Britain's worldwide empire, but the Great War revealed the threat of the German U-boats to disrupt seaborne supply lines. In September 1939, the roughly 4,000 British merchant ships were immediate targets. But Hitler had underestimated the value of the U-boats and had instead put resources towards building enormous warships to rival those of the Royal Navy, even though bombers and aircraft dropping torpedoes had already demonstrated their vulnerability to airborne attack. Germany's *Bismarck*, 251 metres in length, with a crew of more than 2,000 and bristling with long-range guns, epitomized the new capital ships. The British Admiralty initially feared that the Kriegsmarine's two modern battlecruisers, three pocket battleships, eight cruisers, and twenty-two destroyers could devastate the merchant navy around the globe. The German naval high command was less optimistic. Admiral Erich Raeder noted, "It is self-evident that the navy is in no manner sufficiently equipped in the fall of 1939 to embark on a great struggle with England." His forces were vastly outnumbered by the Royal Navy and, he believed, his ships and sailors could "only show that they know how to die with honor."[3] In October, the *Admiral Graf Spee* and *Deutschland*, loose in the Atlantic shipping lanes, caused great consternation to the British admiralty, but did relatively little damage as they had difficulty finding merchant ships to sink. The German warships and surface raiders had little impact, and most were soon hunted down and destroyed in naval battles, or bottled up by mines and aircraft and forced to stay close to home.

It was the U-boats that wrought havoc, even though at the start of the war the Germans had only fifty-seven, of which twenty-seven were long-range, ocean-going submarines.[4] The U-boats in the Great War and now in this conflict were not true underwater vessels: they frequently ran on the surface, although low in the water. They were vulnerable when on the water, but also fast, at about 17 knots, and able to dive rapidly, usually in less than half a minute.[5] Underwater, they were slow but difficult to detect with the Allies' rudimentary sonar. Germany's U-boat fleet underwent a rapid expansion during the war, and it was these subs that were unleashed against the merchant ships to cut the critical logistical lifeline from North America that supplied Britain with food, material goods, and munitions. For the Allies to win the Battle of the Atlantic, the U-boats would have to be defeated.

THOUGH U-BOATS STAYED CLOSE TO THEIR BASES in the first year of the war, the merchant ships sailing to Britain faced the horrors of the most inhospitable and dangerous waters in the world. The North Atlantic was pitiless in the winter, and only slighter better in summer. The Atlantic's driving gales, wild waves, and unpredictable weather left even seasoned sailors anxious for the survival of their battered ships. But the northern route was the shortest across the Atlantic, and so this is where Canada's war at sea was fought.

The Canadian ports of Sydney and Halifax, along with Newfoundland's St. John's, offered shelter from the howling Atlantic storms, and they would become crucial bases from which merchant ships left for the frightful eastward trip. In 1939, the nation had few coastal guns. Even Halifax was grossly ill-equipped in terms of defence, with a single 4.7-inch gun, five RCAF seaplanes that lacked bombs, and two light Royal Canadian Mounted Police (RCMP) patrol boats.[6] A year earlier, in the fall of 1938, Chief of the Naval Staff Percy Nelles had described the fortifications as "near tragic," and they had been little improved since then.[7] Halifax, like the rest of Canada, was vulnerable, and although the U-boats never slipped into the harbour, the possibility kept authorities awake at night. Nor was their worry misplaced: in October 1939, a German U-boat captain achieved stunning success at

Scapa Flow, Scotland—the Home Fleet's war station and main anchorage—torpedo-ing the battleship *Royal Oak*. In a scramble to offer some protection, steel netting was soon slung up along the entry points across the Halifax harbour, but the worry never entirely disappeared.

For the first full year of the war, the main battleground was in British waters. The Admiralty was very cautious in requesting resources from King and the Canadians, as the senior Royal Navy officers were aware that the Canadians were hypersensitive about losing control of the Royal Canadian Navy. But the British navy desperately needed additional warships. While King was wary of being perceived in Quebec as kowtowing to the imperials—a concern that extended to putting the navy under Admiralty control—he would not go so far as the Irish, who had used the Statute of Westminster and the independence that came with it to demand that the Royal Navy abandon its base at Queenstown. This lack of Irish cooperation had been a major blow to the Royal Navy, and the King government had already announced publicly that British warships could use Canadian bases. The prime minister even agreed to a request by Nelles that the Canadian navy act in "closest cooperation" with the Royal Navy and ultimately serve under its operational control.[8] The Canadian government continued to throw its weight into the Empire-wide war effort, aware that Britain was on the front lines of battle and that Canada too would soon face the U-boats.

THE SINKING OF *ATHENIA* ON SEPTEMBER 3 revived memories of the Great War, and prompted the Royal Navy to study the vulnerability of the merchant marine. Accordingly, the Admiralty ordered that merchant ships be grouped in convoys and protected by warships to save them from being picked off by U-boats one at a time. The Admiralty put its considerable skill and resources towards establishing a system to coordinate the successive group sailings. The first convoy sailed from Halifax across the Atlantic on September 16, 1939. HX-1, consisting of 18 merchant ships, was escorted by two Canadian destroyers, *St. Laurent* and *Fraser*, which had arrived from the west coast only the day before. Moving out to sea with their vulnerable charges in line, the two destroyers handed the civilian ships over to two Royal Navy cruisers about 600 kilometres into the Atlantic (about forty-eight hours from shore), and returned to Halifax. The RCN did not yet have the ships or personnel to take convoys across the entire Atlantic, but it would expand rapidly. The need was desperate: soon two convoys were departing every week.

As long as the U-boats were confined to European waters, the Canadian naval authorities had time to work on their convoy system. Bringing the ships safely into harbour, unloading and loading them, and then grouping them again for the return voyage was exceedingly complicated.[9] At any given time, Halifax's Bedford Basin could have dozens of merchant ships waiting for cargo, a crew, a convoy, or the necessary warship escorts. This was the unglamorous side of war, but one essential to success. "The last two months in 1939 were frantic in the Halifax area," recounted Commander Horatio Nelson Lay, a long-service RCN officer who happened to be Prime Minister Mackenzie King's nephew. "We had hundreds of ships waiting for Convoy and our Escort Force consisted of only [seven] destroyers."[10]

Merchant ships forming up for a convoy in the safety of Nova Scotia's Bedford Basin.

Ships that could maintain speeds of 15 knots or more were generally safe from U-boats, which could reach a maximum speed of about 17 knots but needed targets far slower in order to position themselves before unleashing their torpedoes. Of the 3,500 merchant ships that sailed in convoys throughout 1939, only 5 were lost, although some 90 other vessels, displacing 421,156 tons, were sunk in all theatres as they sailed unprotected in the first four months of the war.[11] However, as the Allied war effort increased in intensity, more supplies were needed and older and slower merchant ships were pressed into service. A new Canadian navy had to be born to protect them. It was forged in the furnace of battle.

"GENTLEMAN, A BLOODY WAR AND A SICKLY SEASON!" was one of the traditional wardroom toasts in the Royal Canadian Navy, reflecting the junior officers' desire to rise through the ranks through the loss, if necessary, of more senior officers due to violence or disease. During the Battle of the Atlantic, the substantial expansion of the fleet, combined with the steady sinking of ships and destruction of men, made this toast a reality for many a subaltern.

The RCN consisted of three organizations. The professional force, the Royal Canadian Navy, was about 1,600 strong at the start of the war; these sailors had made naval warfare their profession. Most of the officers enlisted at about sixteen years of age, and had been trained at the naval college and on Royal Navy ships—experience known as "Big Ship time"—in order to learn their trade.[12] They would form the nucleus of the Canadian wartime navy. Because much of the training was done on Royal Navy ships, it is not surprising that nearly all of the Canadian officers revelled in British naval traditions and were sometimes accused by their compatriots of being "little Englishmen," with false accents and a class-inspired approach to enforcing discipline.

Second, there was the Royal Canadian Naval Reserve (RCNR), which drew upon the merchant navy or the pool of men who made their living as fishers. These men had vast experience at sea, which meant that they were also often rough and ill-disposed to submit to naval discipline. They had a reputation collectively as unorthodox captains of their ships, but they played a fundamental role in the first three years of the war, before other officers could be trained to take command.

Finally, the officers of the Royal Canadian Naval Volunteer Reserve (RCNVR) were recruited early in the war from yacht clubs and universities, or from the naval reserves. Some of these sailors had experienced no more than desultory summer training. Most had some seafaring experience, but this was a far cry from possessing modern warfighting skills. It was the ordinary sailors of the RCNVR who would form the bulk of the expanding navy, eventually making up 84 percent of the force. The majority of recruits who enlisted over the early months and years of the war would serve as part of the RCNVR. They then would be posted on all ships, but especially the smaller minesweepers and corvettes. The recruits were required to have a grade eight education and be between the ages of eighteen and thirty-two, but rarely did the lack of a birth certificate prevent enlistment, and younger boys slipped easily into the service.[13] Lieutenant William Pugsley estimated that the average age of crews was around twenty.[14] "Crews were young," remembered another officer, James Lamb. "Officers and men were mostly right out of high school, and anyone over thirty found himself nicknamed 'Pappy,' and the oldest man on the ship."[15]

The Volunteer Reserve drew from across the country. A widely held belief among Canadians was that the majority of recruits came from the Prairies. They did not: Ontario and British Columbia supplied the most sailors. Members of the RCNVR were more likely to be Canadian-born than RCN officers and personnel,

The Wavy Navy

Portrait of Royal Canadian Naval Volunteer Reserve sailors. The RCNVR took their informal name, "the Wavy Navy," from the cuffs on their uniform.

and this added to the perception that the RCNVR was more egalitarian and less disciplined, and it likely was.[16] While the flood of "prairie sailors" was a myth, thousands still enlisted from farms and communities located nowhere near open water. The lure of the seafaring life for men who, over the preceding decade, had known only dust and crop failure, was powerful. Ethnic minorities, such as blacks and Japanese, were blocked from serving, and the Volunteer Reserve was also an English-language service that offered no allowance for French Canadians. Within these significant limits, the RCNVR was, as recruiters and propagandists claimed, a "People's Navy," representing in terms of education and background a broad cross-section of the population.

The three categories of sailor in the Canadian navy were distinguished by the distinctive stripes on the cuffs of their uniforms. The RCN had broad straight stripes; the RCNR had criss-crossed stripes; and the RCNVR had wavy stripes. The most numerous group, the RCNVR, called themselves the "Wavy Navy," in reference to their stripes. There was a popular saying, remembered Lieutenant Geoffrey Hughson, who served on HMCS *Huron* and lost a brother in Normandy, about the three organizations in the RCN: "RCNVR officers were possibly gentlemen pretending to be sailors; and RCNR officers were sailors pretending to the gentlemen, [while] RCN (permanent force) officers were neither, pretending to be both."[17] As the saying implied, friction existed between regulars and volunteers, which was replicated to a lesser degree in the army, though nearly absent in the air force. None of it had much effect on morale or fighting efficiency, and the three naval organizations were frequently lumped together with little distinction under the title of Royal Canadian Navy. Canadian sailors of all stripes knew their common enemy.

THE U-BOATS STRUCK HARD against marine traffic beginning in the summer of 1940. With their occupation of France, the Germans acquired new naval bases on the Bay of Biscay that gave ready access to shipping coming and going from Britain. Soon the U-boats had extended their operational range 1,500 kilometres to the west and, with improved technology, could stay out for longer on patrol. Britain took urgent measures to improve the defences close to home in the summer and fall of 1940, but the Germans built additional U-boats so they could sustain operations farther and farther out in the Atlantic beyond the reach of British defences, especially patrolling aircraft. Having established through bitter experience that the Royal Navy could not be defeated in surface action, the Germans increasingly turned to the expanding U-boat force to take up the attack. This would be a war of interdiction, with the aim of cutting Britain off from its food supplies and fuel. Two hundred and seventeen merchant ships were lost to U-boats in the last half of 1940, about a third of them in convoys.[18] To protect against this threat, the Royal Navy needed to provide better protection for the merchant ships, and senior naval commanders called on the Canadians for a more active participation in the coming campaign.

What was needed was an easy-to-build but effective anti-submarine warship. What the British came up with was the corvette. Roughly 60 metres long, 10 metres in beam, and with a displacement of 860 to 950 tons, the corvette design was based on that of a whaling vessel. The corvettes were made to be sailed close to land and never intended for Atlantic crossings, but the warship was a good model for hunting U-boats and it carried a 4-inch Mk. IX gun that fired a 31-pound shell to a range of 12,000 metres, as well as depth charges filled with high explosives to blow submarines out of the water. The corvette was not fast: its top speed was only 16 knots, although some commanders could drive it harder for short periods, pushing the 2,750-horsepower steam engines nearly to the breaking point. While the corvette paled in comparison to the much larger and more robust destroyers and frigates, it was surprisingly tough and nimble, with a tight turning circle that gave it an advantage over U-boats above or below the water. For the King government, the most significant advantage of the corvette was that its relatively simple design meant it could be manufactured in Depression-wracked shipyards and it cost a modest $500,000 per vessel. Orders soon were placed with Canadian manufacturers to build corvettes for both the RN and RCN.

The navy also requested Bangor-class minesweepers, for which contracts were let early in 1940. By the late summer of that year, sixty-four corvettes and twenty-four minesweepers were under construction in shipyards on the Great Lakes, the upper St. Lawrence River, and the British Columbia coast. Few Canadian workers had experience building warships, and they ran into shortages of material and skills. A further frustration in the initial stages was an irksome delay on the part of the

A corvette, HMCS Galt, *under construction at the Collingwood Shipyards in October 1940.* Galt *was launched about three months after this photograph was taken.*

British in sending over designs and drawings. However, by the end of the year, the first fourteen corvettes were launched, and almost immediately thrown into battle. By January 1942, sixty-three corvettes had been built, and sixty-two more would follow.[19] The aggressive building program meant that there was a desperate need for new crews but too little time to train them. Survival in the war against the U-boats would have to be learned the hard way: on the ships, at sea, and against the enemy in battle.

"THE CORVETTE WAS THE BACKBONE of the Canadian navy," wrote Louis Audette, an RCNVR corvette and frigate commander during the war.[20] James Lamb, another Canadian corvette captain, believed that the corvette "played a greater part in the growth and character of the Canadian navy than it did in any other naval force.... More than any other ship, weapon, or aircraft, the corvette had a distinctively Canadian connotation, her limitations and capabilities reflecting to a remarkable degree those of a new and growing Canadian navy, so that she came almost to reflect the character of the men who sailed in her."[21] The humble warship battled against the odds, the enemy, and the vile weather to deliver victory.

On the first corvettes, the forecastle, or "fo'c'sle," located at the front of the ship, had a raised deck that ended some 4.5 metres in front of the bridge section. This was soon recognized as a poor design because it allowed waves to spill over the forward quarters. As one sailor remarked, "For much of her time at sea, a corvette was, for all practical purposes, semi submerged," leaving "her well-decks perpetually awash, and her superstructure bombarded by flying spray, up to and over the height of her bridge and funnel."[22] With decks under water for much of the time, went the joke, corvette crews deserved the submariner's higher rate of pay. Getting food was no joking matter, however, as the galley was on the other side of the fo'c'sle's gap and sailors had to traverse the open space with grub in hand. Many a meal ended up on the water-slick steel decks. The short fo'c'sle was by all accounts a miserable feature, but the main problem with the design was that the corvettes were never meant for the wide-open ocean.

The ship was initially configured for a complement of four officers and forty-eight ratings, but the addition of new armaments and technology eventually required a doubling of the crew to about a hundred men. This made for a crowded, as well as a wet, ship. In heavy seas, the corvettes climbed the crests of waves, only to plunge into the troughs before battling up to the crest again. "The violence of the rolling, pitching and pounding was incredible," recounted Lieutenant R.J. Pickford, captain of HMCS *Rimouski*.[23] Jim Galloway, a nineteen-year-old seaman in *Agassiz*, remembered one terrible storm in December 1943 during which every blow from the angry sea "would buckle your knees and jar your teeth as a shudder went through the whole ship."[24] Knee and hip joints soon felt like bone grating on bone. Seawater swept through hatches and flowed freely in the mess deck where the sailors ate and slept. With each climb and drop of the ship, the foul tide of water rushed back and forth, carrying clothing, paper, and anything that had fallen from hook or flat surface during the rough ride. The smell of men at close quarters, stagnant water, wet clothes, and dirty feet contributed to a nearly indescribably nauseating stench. Over

HMCS Windflower, *one of the first corvettes manufactured in Canada, was sunk when it collided with another ship on December 7, 1941.*

the five years of war, the corvette would earn Churchill's description of the vessels as the "cheap and nasties."[25]

AS NEW SHIPS WERE BUILT, the need for trained personnel became acute. Chief of the Naval Staff Percy Nelles—a career officer who was a cadet from the first graduating class of 1909–1910 and had served on Canadian and imperial warships for three decades—agonized over how to employ his small staff of professional RCN officers and men, numbering about 1,600. Those who wanted operational posts used their connections to serve with the Royal Navy or on the most modern Canadian warships—the destroyers, which, throughout much of 1940, were serving in British waters. These posts were, after all, the glamorous (and more comfortable) jobs. Very few RCN officers commanded corvettes. Into the gap stepped experienced merchant mariners or sailors of the RCN Reserves. There were not a lot of these old seamen, however, and often they were too salty or undisciplined to be given—or to keep—a King's commission. The ratings on the lower decks were almost exclusively formed from the RCNVR, and most of these former civilians had little seafaring experience. New men received only basic training that focused on marching, rope-tying, rudimentary seamanship, communications, and rifle drill—at least until February 1941, when a more formal eight-week course was established. Even then, there was much that could not be taught in a classroom. "The strain of command, particularly in those early years, was almost more than men could bear," wrote Hal Lawrence, an RCNVR officer. "Not only were the ships ill-armed and under-equipped, the crews inexperienced and undisciplined, the escort groups uncoordinated and ill-trained, the weather, particularly in the winter months, simply indescribable, but the shortage of escorts and the size of convoys—up to a hundred ships—imposed intolerable demands on the early corvette commanders. Each convoy trip was a test of endurance."[26]

Even with the new builds underway, the navy lacked sufficient escort warships, especially destroyers, to protect the freighters and tankers whose cargoes were so vital to Britain's survival. Churchill turned to Franklin Roosevelt and in September 1940, the neutral Americans completed the "destroyers for bases" deal, which saw the Americans acquire naval access to British bases in exchange for its provision of fifty Great War–era destroyers.[27] Though the American destroyers were outdated and ill-suited for crossing the Atlantic, they were better than nothing and were almost immediately pressed into service. Canada initially received six, all of which took their names from rivers near the Canada–United States border: HMCS *Niagara, St. Croix, St. Clair, St. Francis, Annapolis,* and *Columbia.*[28] The vessels were known colloquially as "four-stackers" (because of their four funnels) and their crews soon learned first-hand about their deficiencies, particularly in heavy seas. "How those things could roll!" remembered George Coles, who served on one of the American destroyers in 1941. They were built narrow for speed, but, lacking stability, were tossed about in the rough Atlantic seas.[29] The ships were also badly insulated, so that the internal pipes built up enormous condensation in cold weather and, according to Engine Room Artificer Jack Kimber, "it was almost like being in a rain storm."[30]

HMCS Niagara *was one of the American four-stack destroyers taken on strength by the Royal Canadian Navy in late 1940.*

When the destroyers joined the Canadian fleet in December 1940, the navy brass was forced to further dilute its experienced crews in order to find some 1,500 seamen to man them. For all their weaknesses, the new destroyers offered added protection to merchant ships in coastal waters and far out-gunned any U-boat they might encounter. Prime Minister King beamed with pride when he thought about them, writing in his diary about the navy's ongoing sacrifice and its rapid maturation, which was in lockstep with "Canada growing into a nation."[31]

The Germans sank 700,000 tons of shipping in the last three months of 1940, and most of the losses were in British waters.[32] The Royal Navy was desperate to shore up its convoy and coastal defences. Fourteen new Canadian corvettes were available at the end of the year, and even though Canada desperately needed them, most were sent to Britain. Yet because Canada lacked armaments, several of the corvettes were not equipped with the 4-inch gun. Fake wooden guns did little to quell the sailors' feeling of helplessness when they set sail from Halifax in late 1940, but they crossed the Atlantic unscathed. When the corvettes neared the Western Approaches, the area off the west coast of Ireland, they were greeted by a Royal Navy escort. The experienced British sailors were little impressed by the undersized warships, and the admiral aboard the battleship HMS *Rodney*, when studying HMCS *Mayflower*, remarked with horror, "My god! Since when are we clubbing the enemy to death!"[33] Such was the unpreparedness of the RCN in 1940. One of Canada's most experienced fighting captains, J.D. "Chummy" Prentice, who had retired from the Royal Navy in 1934 but had recently come out of retirement at age forty-one, summed up the limitations of the RCN with a very Canadian analogy: "It is as though we were attempting to play against a professional hockey team with a collection of individuals who had not even learned to skate."[34]

Overseas losses during operations in 1940 further reduced the number of Canadian ships. HMCS *Fraser* was accidently cut in half by the British cruiser HMS *Calcutta* in June, and another newly commissioned destroyer was lost on October 23 when HMCS *Margaree* collided with a merchant ship while running convoy duties from Londonderry, Northern Ireland, on a rainy night. *Margaree* lost 140 sailors; among the dead were many who had joined the ship from the doomed *Fraser*. For these early accidents, the CN earned from crusty Royal Naval types the unfair moniker of "the Royal Collision Navy."[35] The name did not stick, but the losses accumulated.

THE BRITISH ADMIRALTY responded to the U-boat threat by extending warship protection to convoys further into the North Atlantic. The longer trips tied up more
resources and thinned out the available protection. Some of the slack was taken up
by the RAF Coastal Command's shore-based aircraft patrols. Though the early seaplanes and light bombers had rudimentary navigational systems and ineffective aerial bombs, their mere presence forced U-boats to dive for cover. This was especially
useful if U-boats were encountered while they were shadowing convoys, because
the submerged subs then almost always lost contact with their prey. But fuel was
limited and the planes could stay in the air only for so long. In addition, the daily
roulette of bad weather often grounded the planes, and thick cloud cover sometimes
made it pointless to send them up. Worse still, no matter how long the aircraft flew,
enormous tracts of the ocean remained where U-boats could hide. One region in
particular became known as the Black Pit or the Air Gap. It extended some 600
kilometres from east to west and 1,000 kilometres from Greenland in the north to
the Azores Islands in the south. The main trade routes between Britain and North
America passed right through this area. Long-range seaplanes could be pushed about
1,000 kilometres from Ireland, Iceland, and Newfoundland, but much of the mid-
Atlantic could never be reached by supporting aircraft. And foul weather, all too
frequent on the Canadian side of the Atlantic, further curtailed missions because
planes consumed fuel faster when they battled wind and storms.

New four-engine bombers went into production beginning in late 1941. These
planes—the Halifax, Lancaster, and American-made Liberator—might have been
used to help close the Air Gap, but they were in short supply and were earmarked for
Bomber Command. Coastal Command pleaded for some of the bombers to harass
U-boats, but Churchill and most of the senior air marshals insisted that the striking
power of the four-engine "heavies" should not be wasted in circling vast, empty spaces
of ocean.[36] For his part, Karl Dönitz, the decorated U-boat commander whose goal
was to sink any ship carrying supplies to Britain, wrote that seaplanes were effective
in keeping his U-boats at bay, and he feared the day when the Black Pit would no
longer be a safe haven.[37] But until late 1942, Coastal Command remained critically
short of long-range, four-engine bombers.[38]

In Canada, the RCAF's Eastern Air Command, responsible for air operations on
the Atlantic seaboard to protect shipping and seek out U-boats, spent much of the

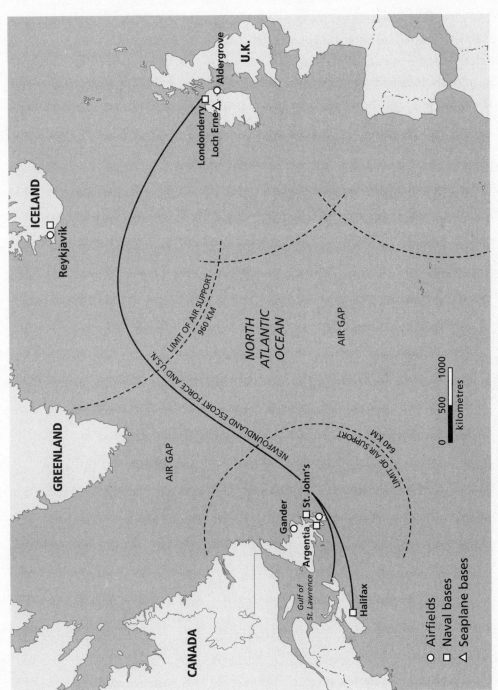

The North Atlantic Air Cover, May 1941–February 1942

early part of the war trying to purchase American aircraft with a long-range capability. In 1939, Canada had only a single maritime aviation squadron, No. 5, at Dartmouth, which flew the Supermarine Stranraer flying boats. It was soon joined by No. 11 Squadron, which operated Lockheed Hudson bombers, and No. 10 Squadron, which flew Douglas Digby bombers. The Hudsons had a range of about 500 kilometres, which allowed them to push over the ocean to look for U-boats, while the Digbys had an even greater range and could stay in the air longer—about 12 hours. By the spring of 1941, the long-range Catalina (a 105 PBY flying boat) and, in the fall, the RCAF version, the Canso, also flew protective air coverage. The twin-engine flying boats had a cruising speed of about 180 kilometres per hour, and while the U-boat

Lockheed Hudson two-engine bomber flying patrol in support of convoys. The bombers were a threat to U-boats that were far from their home bases and vulnerable to air attacks.

crews often saw the flying boats before they could close the distance and drop depth charges, their presence again forced the Germans to dive. The Catalinas and Cansos became steadily more effective over the course of the war as their range was increased by modified fuel tanks from about 700 to 1,000 kilometres, and their ability to stay aloft was extended to twenty-five hours. Gradually, they closed parts of the Air Gap, although the Atlantic continued to provide U-boats with ample hiding places.

To avoid the worst of this wreck-infested hunting ground, the convoys were routed further north, where the weather was harsher and the storms wilder, but the break in air coverage less pronounced. Iceland was occupied by Britain in early 1940, following the German occupation of Denmark. In July 1940, some 2,500 Canadians

Merchant ships sailing in a tight convoy.

were sent there as Z Force, a mixed battle group of the Royal Regiment of Canada, Les Fusiliers Mont-Royal, and the Cameron Highlanders of Ottawa, to prevent the Axis powers from gaining a foothold in the western Atlantic. Long-range seaplanes and bombers would eventually fly out of Iceland to provide cover for the convoys. It was a tough posting for flyers, soldiers, and airmen: the bleak and barren wasteland offered few amenities, and the Icelandic people, who viewed the Allies as invaders, were as cold as the winds that blasted the aircraft and ships. As one of the Cameron Highlanders observed ruefully, "The Icelanders for the most part resented our occupation ... and wanted nothing to do with the troops of any nationality."[39]

"CONVOYS ONLY WENT AS FAST AS THE SLOWEST SHIP," recounted Harry Urwin of the RCN, who served on convoy duty for thirty-two months.[40] Some of the old ships pressed into service were dangerous to the more modern vessels because of their slow speed and propensity to fall out of line when their boilers broke down, and so the authorities separated out the slow from the fast. Starting in August 1940, most of the slow convoys, ships that chugged along between 7 and 9 knots, formed up and left from Sydney, on Cape Breton, Nova Scotia. "These convoys were endurance tests for ships and crew alike," wrote one Canadian sailor, with the protective warships generally finding themselves at sea 30 percent longer than those vessels that protected fast convoys.[41] Regular convoys could make the voyage across the Atlantic in ten to twelve days, but the slower convoys packed with rusting relics could take fourteen to sixteen days, and even longer if steaming into winter storms.

Organizing the convoys was trying in the extreme. Ships arrived from all over— Boston, New York, Baltimore, the Caribbean—and then waited in the safety of the maritime ports, behind submarine nets and long-range coastal guns, for their proper pairing with the corvettes, frigates, and destroyers, and a sufficient number of other merchant ships that steamed at similar speed. The final convoy could be as few as two dozen ships or a multinational grouping of more than 100 vessels. Determining a ship's speed, and therefore if it was earmarked for a slow or fast convoy, and then trying to chivvy the beast of the convoy into sailing formation, was a hair-whitening exercise. Each convoy had an identifying code. For example, "HX" denoted Halifax to UK; "SC" denoted Sydney to UK. Westbound convoys were prefixed "ON" (the

United Kingdom to Halifax) or "ONS" (the same, but a slow convoy). A sequential number was applied to each unique convoy—"ON 42," for example, or "SC 108"— and each of these convoys had its own stories of trial and desperation.

"The convoy," recalled Charles "Pat" Nixon, commander of the destroyer HMCS *Chaudière*, "represented a vital ingredient of our relentless, unwavering determination to win this war."[42] When the orders to sail were given, the ships steamed out of harbour, taking several hours to find their place in the convoy. The merchant ships were tightly packed in rows and columns. Only about 600 metres separated the vessels in front and back, and about 1,000 metres separated the columns. Nonetheless, the slow-moving box of ships covered dozens of square kilometres of ocean. Merchant mariner Ralph Burbridge, who eventually captained steamships, remembered that they were ordered to change course "every fifteen or twenty minutes. You had the clock set to ring a bell and then you'd change course another away. The whole idea of zigzagging was that the enemy submarines never got a chance to set their angles

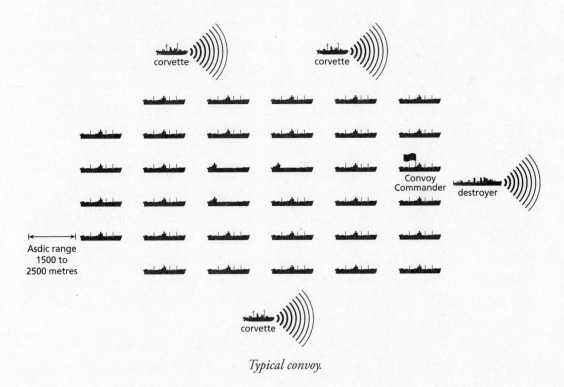

Typical convoy.

right, for firing their torpedoes, because as soon as they'd think they got it right, the convoy would suddenly go this way and then go that way."[43] While this zigzagging presented a more elusive target for the enemy, the ships found it exceedingly difficult to maintain formation in the dark, in rough waters, and with the use of haphazard communication—usually flags, shaded Aldis signal lamps, sirens, horns, or rockets. Canadian seaman Paul Brick grimaced at the memory: "There was always a near collision in every convoy, nothing ever went smooth."[44]

On December 7, 1941, in the face of heavy fog caused by the cold Labrador Current running into the warm Gulf Stream, the corvette HMCS *Windflower*, along with a destroyer and five other corvettes, was part of an escort for convoy SC 58. The pea soup haze reduced visibility to almost zero, and in its manoeuvres *Windflower* lost the convoy. *Windflower*'s captain became worried about his charges and unwisely turned into the convoy to look for the vessels. At 9:20 A.M., the fourth ship in the port column, the 10,000-ton Dutch freighter *Zyphenberg*, emerged from the fog a mere 400 metres from *Windflower*. Horns blared, but there was no time to avoid a collision. *Zyphenberg* sheared off 8 metres of the corvette's stern. The stunned Canadian sailors had little time to prepare themselves to abandon ship. The cold water rushed into the vessel through its gaping wound, hit the hot boiler, and *Windflower* blew up within a minute of the collision.

Zyphenberg could not stop to pick up survivors, for fear of being rammed by a ship steaming hard from behind, but its blaring horn alerted others. HMCS *Moose Jaw* steamed to the area. The corvette's crew could see little in the fog, although the shouts of sailors drew assistance, and ropes and scramble nets were lowered. Few of the freezing men had the strength to swim towards safety or even grasp the lifelines. Another British corvette moved aggressively to the scene of the accident, assuming *Windflower* had been torpedoed. Sonar pings rebounded from the now sinking corvette; the British warship mistook it for a German U-boat and attacked it with depth charges, killing the ship a second time. The blowback of the blast caused damage to the British ship and likely killed some of the survivors left in the water, although most of them undoubtedly had already succumbed to hypothermia.

Jim Sharpe was in *Windflower* when it exploded, and was thrown into the freezing water. He remembered seeing the ship's Christmas turkeys bobbing on the swell, as he, too, was buoyed by his life jacket. Within minutes he lost feeling in his extremities and was close to death when he was finally pulled into a lifeboat. "All that time in the water, my outstanding reason for living was thoughts of my wife, who was pregnant with our first child."[45] It would have been easy to accept the water's cold embrace, but Jim Sharpe had found his reason to live. Twenty-three others died in the explosion, from the depth charge blasts, or from the ocean's icy grasp.[46]

HOWEVER DEMORALIZING THE COLLISIONS within a convoy, the real threat was the U-boat. The convoy commodore was at the head of the formation, generally in a destroyer, while corvettes took up their posts on the flanks, and, if there were enough of them, also at the rear. While the warships were always spoiling for a fight, their role was to engage the enemy U-boats, either pushing them away from the convoy or forcing them to submerge, which would allow the surviving merchant ships to steam off at top speed. Fleeing was always the best tactic for civilian ships.

The convoy, wrote Hal Lawrence, was a moving "community of between four and five thousand souls, covering an area of nearly one hundred square miles."[47] The most vulnerable and valuable ships—those with ammunition or oil—were placed in the centre of the convoy, shielded by the merchant ships on the outer edges and the roving warships. These merchant ships on the convoy's outside columns—including those in the worst spot in the bottom right corner, where the Germans most often attacked and which was known ghoulishly as "coffin corner"—were sometimes equipped with torpedo nets that were lowered when an attack was anticipated, in the hope of catching or deflecting a torpedo. The nets were not very effective and they slowed a vessel by at least 2 or 3 knots; few sailors had much faith in their ability to protect against the fast travelling torpedoes that cut through the water, leaving, at night, a phosphorescent wake. Moreover, as German captains gained experience, the more aggressive among them penetrated to the centre of the enormous convoys in the dark, burrowing for the prizes at the core.

Heavy storms broke up the formation, scattering the rust- and salt-streaked ships. "Gale after gale shrieks down upon us, howling out of the north," wrote James Lamb, a corvette captain. "Fierce winds tear at our rigging, snatch the tops off waves and send them flying above our mastheads, stinging our faces and blinding our eyes.

Mountainous waves crash inboard, making our upper decks impassable, sweeping over our forward gun and crashing against our superstructure with an impact that jars us to the keel."[48] In fighting the weather and sea, storm-lashed ships were blown out of formation and fuel was consumed at a higher rate. The old clunkers and dilapidated coal burners often broke down, dropped out of the convoy, and were left behind as easy, immobilized targets. With only a few corvettes and a destroyer, the convoy commodore agonized over detaching one of his warships to protect the laggard. The stricken merchant ship was usually left to its fate.

THEIR LONG BLACK HULLS made the German submarines look like what they were: sleek killing machines. The Type VIIC U-boats—the workhorse of the fleet from 1941 onward—could remain at sea for up to three months. Crewed by about fifty sailors each, the U-boats could outrun a corvette on the surface, although they made only about 7 knots when submerged. Depending on their size, the U-boats carried a number of torpedoes, fourteen in the case of the Type VIIC, twenty-two in the larger Type IX. U-boats initially were armed with compressed-air-driven torpedoes, their warheads fitted with magnetic detonators that exploded on contact with a ship, but these "fish" were not reliable and were soon replaced by electrically driven torpedoes. The Type IX's torpedoes were 7 metres long and 53 centimetres in diameter, and carried 280 kilograms of explosive charge in the warhead. A single torpedo fire could deliver a fatal blow. The U-boats were also armed with an effective 88mm deck gun, which could hole the hulls of merchant ships. When facing a stronger opponent— anything at the frigate class or above, or airplanes—the U-boats would crash dive to escape, and could submerge quickly by allowing water into the main ballast tanks. While they were vulnerable to depth charges, especially during the first part of a dive when they were close to the surface, the explosive devices had to detonate fairly close to the sub—less than 6 metres away—to shatter its steel hull.

The U-boats lurked in the Atlantic, ready to strike. "You could almost smell them," recounted Bill Nelligan, who served on several Canadian vessels during the war. "You'd worry yourself sick. Where the hell are they?"[49] Then, without warning, a merchant ship would explode in the night. The blinding light was seen for kilometres and the smell of cordite and burning debris polluted the air. The shock passed rapidly through the small city of ships. Last messages sent out location, and then the battle was underway. All ships went to action stations, with desperate watches scanning the dark waters under the weird illumination cast by magnesium flares slowly descending by parachute. Light was the best defence against U-boats on the surface, although the flickering starshells and flares offered strange, fleeting shadows, which led constantly to false sightings.

While the British Admiralty had expected the U-boats to fire their torpedoes underwater, Dönitz pushed his U-boat captains to strike fast on the surface. The subs worked their way into the convoys under cover of darkness, running low on the surface of the water, where their trimmed-down profile made them nearly invisible. U-boat skippers manoeuvred for the perfect shot before their torpedoes were launched—aiming to catch a vessel broadside from about 1,000 metres. Less than

A German U-boat prowling for prey. Note the low profile in the water and the main armament, an 88mm deck gun.

a minute after firing, an explosion signified a hit. Depending on the damage done and the cargo on board, stricken ships might either limp forward on reduced speed, lie dead in the water, or slide quickly beneath the surface. Experienced U-boat captains slipped away, submerged, before warships could steam to the area. The killers moved through the wreckage, generally emerging from the wake of the convoy before surfacing and steaming ahead at full speed to catch the convoy again for another run several hours later.

But not all U-boats shot and ran. Without harassing Allied air cover, the U-boats were free to prowl within the convoy, and so warship tactics involved turning inward, hoping to encounter the enemy on the surface within the convoy's own ranks. Burning ships and flares provided some light, but convoys were spread out and a few corvettes could never patrol that entire space. Worse still, the early radar systems were rarely able to locate the U-boats as they sped away. So the subs stalked the convoy, picked off their victims, and moved out again, leaving wreck and ruin behind.

MOST CANADIAN CREWS HAD VERY LITTLE TRAINING in anti-submarine warfare, either before or during the early part of the war, as there were few officers to teach them their trade. They had only limited equipment to detect submarines underwater, and had no access to friendly submarines to practise against in mock battles, the most realistic and valuable way to prepare for combat. "The enemy, the U-boats, were unseen," remembered Anthony Griffin, a Royal Canadian Naval Volunteer Reservist who enlisted in 1939 and eventually commanded the corvette HMCS *Pictou.* "They were faster than we were on the surface, so that if they did come to the surface and you chased them, you had a very small chance of overtaking them."[50] If the U-boats could be caught at the right distance, the corvette or destroyer's guns could pound them, but the subs were a slim, low-lying target and it was not easy to depress the guns to hit them at close range. For in-close fighting, the best weapon and tactic for the inexperienced corvettes was ramming the enemy. One of the few advantages to the Allies was that U-boats were exceedingly wary of engaging in sea battles, for any significant damage thousands of kilometres from their home bases could prove to be fatal.

In the first three years of the war, the Allied tactics were ineffective and the weapons at the disposal of the corvettes were limited. RCN crews could fire their guns, ram, or drop depth charges over the side, but the challenge was first to find the enemy to attack. When a submarine was forced underwater, the Allied ships sought them out with "asdic," an underwater detection device that the Americans called "sonar." Asdic, in that unimaginative British way, was an acronym for Anti-Submarine Detection Investigation Committee. The device worked by converting an electrical impulse into a sound wave transmitted through the water; the sound beam was fixed at an angle of about 45 degrees below horizontal, and the sound wave moved outward on a narrow beam until it reached an object—hopefully a U-boat—and then rebounded with a "ping" sound. If the sound wave hit nothing, it simply lost strength at around 1,500 to 2,500 metres, depending on the current, water temperature, and salinity of the water. But then another sound wave was sent out. In watching warships track for submerged U-boats, Lieutenant-Commander Alan Easton, a corvette captain, was reminded of "dogs with their noses to the ground trying to pick up a scent."[51]

A different kind of radar was required to detect U-boats on the surface. In May 1941, Canadian corvettes began to be equipped with the Type SW1C (Surface Warning—One Canadian) device. Radar, wrote Lieutenant Dudley King, "was the eyes of the fleet and kept U-boats from approaching a convoy on the surface undetected." While the SW1C, with its lightweight rotating antenna, had been able to detect some vessels in calm water, in the mid-Atlantic the signals were scrambled by the heavy swell of the waves.[52] Experience showed that the SW1C could rarely detect a U-boat trimmed down with only its conning tower visible, which is how the German boats frequently approached convoys in the dark. Lieutenant-Commander Allan Stevens wrote of one absurd case of a convoy trying to track a U-boat that had just sunk one of its ships, and then finding that its SW1C could not even pick up an iceberg floating in the vicinity.[53] The U-boat, not surprisingly, escaped.

The British had the more advanced 271 radar set, which produced a search beam on a narrow wavelength of only four inches to detect vessels on the surface. While rough seas could still mask the U-boat signature on the 271 set, the device was better than the Canadian radar. The Royal Navy first equipped its own ships with the 271, as well as a few of the modern Canadian destroyers that served in British waters.

Without an effective scientific liaison with the British, the Canadians continued to suffer equipment shortages and to be neglected by their allies.[54]

Throughout the war, the British were invariably a full generation of radar ahead of the Canadians, and one of the great failings of Percy Nelles, as Canadian chief of the naval staff, was not to push harder for the British to share their advanced technology. Hindered by a staff that should have given him better support, Nelles nonetheless did not fully grasp the value of the radar and was timid in dealing with his Royal Navy counterparts. He simply assumed the Brits would share what they had. They did not—or they did, but not in a timely manner. Hundreds, perhaps thousands, of men died because of the Canadians' inability to find the enemy, divert ships around enemy concentrations, or attack these concentrations effectively.

CANADIAN CORVETTES LACKED not only the most advanced radar, but also a modern gyro compass that allowed for more precise navigation.[55] Having to rely on a magnetic compass, with its wandering needle, made it far more difficult to mount accurate depth charge attacks or to pass bearings quickly from ship to ship, and especially to coordinate movements and attacks. During the critical years of 1941 to 1943, the Canadians fought nearly blind because of obsolete equipment and technology. They nonetheless destroyed fourteen U-boats during this period—far fewer than their British and American counterparts, but still an important contribution to the campaign.[56]

When the warships did locate a submerged submarine, they dropped depth charges over the side. Jim Peters of Moose Jaw, Saskatchewan, was responsible for the depth charges on HMCS *Regina*. "They would call down, 'set the depth for fifty feet,'" he remembered. "So you'd turn a little knob on the depth charge and then you'd hear, 'roll one on the right rail' or the starboard rail. So we'd pull the handle and we'd go, 'roll two.' ... And that's what got the submarine."[57] The depth charge was a blunt weapon, but as Canadian signalman William Acheson, who served on the HMCS *Ottawa* in the early part of the war, wrote when his destroyer shattered the hull of a submerged Italian submarine in November 1940, "It was a bit of all right while it lasted but I'm certainly grateful that I was on top and not below."[58]

The depth charges looked like oil drums. They weighed about 420 pounds, of which about 300 pounds was TNT or amatol. The early versions were simply rolled off the ship in a concentrated grouping of five or ten, and as they sank, a hydrostatic valve triggered the firing mechanism at a preset depth. A depth charge assault, like an artillery bombardment, was directed towards saturating an area with high explosives, in the hope that one might detonate close enough to the U-boat to cause damage. There was rarely such a thing as a precision strike. Later in the war, a depth charge thrower, which resembled a giant mortar, was developed to hurl the heavy drums into the air. British ships would be equipped in 1942 with a variety of depth charge thrower, the Hedgehog, which fired a series of depth charges in front of the warship.

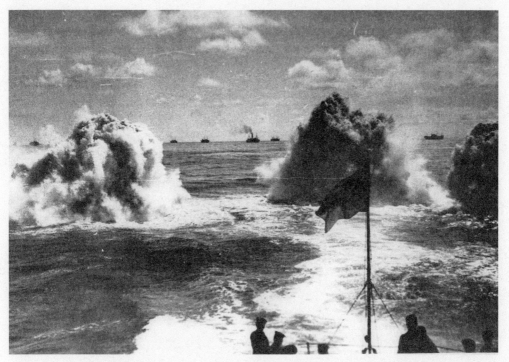

While the U-boats had all the advantages in battle, corvettes defending against the attacks could strike by ramming or by using deck guns and depth charges. The depth charges were filled with 300 pounds of TNT and were rolled off the stern of the boat to explode in the water at a predetermined depth.

The charges exploded only when they made contact with an object, so it was easier to stay in contact through asdic with a submerged U-boat because the pursuer's sonar contact was not scrambled by the noise of random explosions. Canadian ships would not receive these weapons until 1943.

Despite its imprecise nature, a depth charge was still a fearful weapon, and corvette crews soon learned that the explosion could lift the stern of the corvette right out of the water. In some instances, it even broke bottom plates in the warship's hull. Allen Hurst of the RCNVR described the explosions from depth charges as sounding "like hammers beating all around the hull of the ship," while Alastair Stewart cringed at every depth charge blast, as the blowback "blew out every light bulb in the ship."[59] The blast was far worse for the U-boat crew, who held their collective breath with every explosion, watching steel plates buckle or spring leaks and praying that the boat's structural integrity would hold.

In the early part of the war, Frank Curry remarked on the frustrations of pursuing the U-boats and, when they finally tracked one, being unable to kill it. "Time and again, we muddled through, attacking submerged U-boats, driving off a faint shadow on the surface in the pitch dark, holding asdic contact and throwing pattern after pattern of depth charges at our unseen but not unheard enemy. Inevitably we lost contact. Inevitably we were left unsure whether we had succeeded in destroying or even damaging the attacker. But we always tried to stick to the cardinal rules: protect the convoy; save the convoy from attack, never leave the convoy open to U-boats."[60] While success against the U-boats was often measured by how many vessels were destroyed, the Canadians knew that their primary goal was to see their merchant ships to safety. But it was harder to defend than attack, and almost all the advantages went to the U-boats as the warships groped to find their enemy. "In the beginning, we were outclassed and we took a beating," recollected Mike Morey, who served on several corvettes. "I used to have a saying; every time we left port I'd say, 'Kiss your backside goodbye.'"[61]

BY THE SPRING OF 1941, the British had extended the anti-submarine protection of convoys well into the central North Atlantic by basing escort groups of destroyers, corvettes, and other anti-submarine warships in Iceland. These groups came out and relieved the escorts based in Britain. The strategy did not stop the U-boats, although there were more contacts and sinkings from warships and bombers. The Germans reacted rapidly to the new threat and were soon hunting in strength as far west as Newfoundland. In May 1941, after HX 126 from Halifax was attacked before the Iceland escort ships could reach the scene, the British asked the RCN to operate from St. John's, Newfoundland. The RCN warships would join convoys passing south of Newfoundland and accompany them towards Iceland, refuel there, and then join westbound convoys heading back towards Canada. While Newfoundland remained a separate colony under London's direction, its geography, economy, and the shared British connection meant that Canada treated the defence of Newfoundland as falling within its own influence. A year earlier, in June 1940, Canada had moved No. 10 Squadron of Eastern Air Command to the northern Newfoundland airport at Gander, thereby extending the squadron's range farther into the Atlantic.

In the continuing effort to refine convoy protection, the Newfoundland Escort Force was established in May 1941, under command of Commodore Leonard W. Murray. Born in Granton, Pictou County, Nova Scotia, Murray was a member of the first class to graduate from the Royal Naval College of Canada. After that, he served on Royal Navy ships and in increasingly prominent positions in the RCN. He was seen as more bookish than salty—although widely regarded as a fine seaman—but earned a high reputation as a dependable sailor in Ottawa and London. As the senior Canadian officer in the Battle of the Atlantic, he was responsible for the convoys in much of the waters off the east coast of Canada. In the summer of 1941, after the threat of an invasion of Britain was much reduced, the surviving Canadian destroyers were recalled to Canadian waters to add hitting power to the escorts, and these warships were soon augmented by a growing number of corvettes coming out of Canadian dockyards.

The first Newfoundland Escort Force (NEF) convoys sailed from St. John's on June 2, 1941, and would continue to support HX and SC convoys to Iceland, where they handed off the merchant ships to Royal Navy groups and then shepherded the westbound convoys back to North American waters. While the northern route to Iceland added several days to the crossings, the Allies hoped to avoid the U-boat wolf packs—concentrations of U-boats that hunted and killed together—waiting along the traditional, more southerly routes. The NEF, though administered by Murray, remained under overall command of the British Admiralty, specifically Western Approaches Command in Liverpool, which was the only headquarters that had a full array of command, control, and intelligence assets to control the transatlantic convoys.

The British Empire was riding high, for once. Royal Navy warships and torpedo bombers sank the mighty German battleship *Bismarck* on May 27, 1941. A few months earlier, a more important but shrouded victory had occurred when the British broke the German Enigma naval codes between land headquarters—Befehlshaber der Unterseeboote (BdU)—and the U-boats at sea. In spite of incredibly complex encryption involving millions of permutations, the British, with the assistance of Polish mathematicians who had fled their overrun country, had hacked into the system used by the U-boat headquarters to coordinate their captains in the Atlantic. Crucial to their breakthrough was a captured Enigma machine—a typewriter-like encoder/decoder—which now allowed the British to read German messages, albeit after a delay. This information was known as Ultra, for "ultra secret"—beyond top secret—and it was limited severely in its distribution, so fearful were the Allies of alerting the Germans to the breakthrough. The Allies usually faced a lag time of several days in breaking the enemy codes, but knowing where the U-boats were and where they were going allowed the Admiralty to steer convoys away from danger zones. An incalculable number of ships were saved in this way, although Ultra had to be used sparingly for fear of alerting the Germans. Such was the fine line in the intelligence war: some units had to be sacrificed so that some secrets could be held for future use.

On June 16, 1941, forty-nine merchant ships set sail for Britain from Halifax in convoy HX 133, first picking up their RCN escorts from Newfoundland. Due to the ongoing problem of overstretch, the NEF escort force was weak, consisting only of the destroyer HMCS *Ottawa*, three corvettes, and a British armed merchant cruiser. The operation was plagued with trouble from the start. Deep fog shrouded the convoy, and it was so densely packed that a number of merchant ships collided. However, the fog was greeted positively by many of the sailors because it hid them from the U-boats that they knew were lurking in their path across the Atlantic.

For weeks, the U-boats had little success in catching convoys on the open seas, so now the subs moved more aggressively into the western regions of the Atlantic, focusing on St. John's. The Admiralty had intercepted messages indicating that this was the German plan, but the officers did not push the convoy further north, afraid that the move would arouse suspicion in BdU.[62] Submarine *U-203* spotted the convoy on June 23, about 700 kilometres south of Iceland. It reported back to BdU and, as per the established doctrine, was instructed to shadow the convoy. As one Canadian sailor noted, "A sighting by one U-boat would bring the remainder slipping silently up for the kill."[63] The Admiralty intercepted some of the messages from German U-boat headquarters, and sent a desperate warning to the convoy to drastically alter its course at night in the hope of deceiving the stalking German vessel. The convoy nearly escaped, but *U-203* observed the change in direction and attacked, firing three torpedoes. One found its mark, striking the Norwegian merchant ship *Soløy*. The battle had begun.

The RCN warships, inexperienced and lacking inter-ship communications equipment, were not effective in defending against the threat. *Ottawa* swept across the rear of the convoy, firing illuminating star shells in the hope of catching the U-boat on the surface, but the other corvettes attacked in a random, uncoordinated fashion. *U-203* dived under the convoy, leaving the corvettes to search fruitlessly with their unreliable sonar. And then *U-371*, summoned by the first sub, joined the attack and took down a merchant ship that had fallen astern of the convoy because of engine problems. With blood in the water, more U-boats converged on the vulnerable convoy, desperate for a kill after a long period of fruitless hunting.

In a bizarre turn of events, a second convoy, OB 336, almost blundered into the battle. The Admiralty had sent it a warning to stay clear of the area, but an inexperienced telegraphist had been unable to decode the message and left it unread for more than a day. The convoy commander realized to his horror that he was leading his charges into a slaughterhouse and made an abrupt turn, losing only a single merchant vessel before steaming to safety. The U-boats decided not to chase OB 336 and focused on the already overwhelmed ships in HX 133.

With no way to outrun the U-boats, the beleaguered RCN ships and merchant vessels were under continuous, intense pressure over an exhausting seven-day period. Day and night, sailors were called out to action stations, after asdic or surface radar identified U-boats in the water. Exhaustion plagued the crews. Even with Sunderland flying boats keeping the U-boats submerged during daylight hours, the Canadian warships could not keep the subs from returning, especially at night. Four more vessels were sunk. A fleet of five additional British warships was directed to the convoy, hoping to stave off a more comprehensive catastrophe. Equipped with more effective surface radar, and with better tactics and luck, the British vessels sank two of the U-boats. This success made the Canadians look even more impotent in losing six of their charges to the U-boats, and HX 133 was a stern wake-up call that the RCN needed more ships, better technology, and sufficient time to train crews to work together to hold off the U-boat onslaught.

THE U-BOATS PRESSED THEIR ADVANTAGE throughout the summer of 1941. With more boats entering the Atlantic and moving into the western regions, they spoiled for action against Allied shipping. Between April and August, shipping displacing some 1,630,000 tons had been lost.[64] The Canadian-escorted convoys, in particular, suffered grave losses over the summer, and some of the ungenerous officers in the Royal Navy sneered at the Canadians' difficulties. Few allowances were made for the enormous expansion of the Royal Canadian Navy, its shortage of destroyers, or the substandard technology on the corvettes. In fact, the corvettes, which had been pressed rapidly into service, were derided by many British naval officers, often because they were rusted. This deterioration was not a reflection of the corvette crews' ineffectiveness, but rather of Canadian shipbuilders' failure to properly weather the steel in the shipyards. But the Canadians' rust-streaked ships were perceived by some to symbolize shoddy discipline and weakness.

Convoy SC 42 departed Sydney, Nova Scotia, on August 30, 1941, under the protection of the Newfoundland Escort Force. The sixty-seven ships bound for Liverpool were designated a slow convoy, and many of the old vessels threw up black smoke—which could be seen even at night at about a dozen kilometres—as they struggled to keep up to the main body. To protect the convoy, the overstretched RCN could afford only four warships.

SC 42 was organized into twelve columns, with the destroyer HMCS *Skeena* in the lead and three corvettes, HMCS *Alberni*, *Orillia*, and *Kenogami*, guarding the flanks. The four warships were far too weak a force to protect so many merchant ships over such a large area—about 100 square kilometres of ocean.[65] The wind had an edge to it, and two skyscraper icebergs were passed in the heavy fog on the second day of sailing. The floating ice mountains gave more than a few surprised sailors the shivers, for any collision would have been fatal. By the eighth day, the seas were raging, slowing the convoy to a creeping 5 knots. Most of the new RCN seamen had spent a good part of the trip vomiting.

Skeena's captain, Commander Jimmy Hibbard, affectionately known as Jumping Jimmy on account of his enthusiasm on the bridge, had been fighting the U-boats for more than a year, and he sensed approaching trouble. On September 9, amid foul weather and gales, SC 42 was spotted by a U-boat, which soon directed additional boats to the sector. A fruitless attack that day by an overeager U-boat alerted the convoy to the danger, but there were not enough warships to defend against a sustained enemy push, even as two additional Canadian corvettes steamed at full speed to support them.

A bright moon shone that night on the southern side of the convoy, showing the freighters and ships in silhouette. Eleven U-boats attacked.[66] The U-boats steamed silently into the convoy, trimmed down so that only the conning tower remained above the water, like a shark's fin. SS *Muneric* was the first to die. Its entire crew of sixty-one, as well as two stowaways, were lost. The convoy broke into evasive manoeuvres, engaging in emergency turns and zigzags, while the warships tried to locate the U-boats.

The most inexperienced Canadian ship, the corvette *Kenogami*, spotted a U-boat on the surface after firing a starshell to illuminate the surface, but it had not been equipped with smokeless powder, so after the first shot from its 4-inch gun, the gunners were shooting blind. The U-boat slipped away. Frustration mounted. False sightings from panicking merchant ships dragged the corvettes all over the shifting battlefield as they raced dangerously up and down the disintegrating columns, trying to catch U-boats on the surface. In one twist of fate, HMCS *Skeena*, the only destroyer and therefore the best gunned and fastest war vessel, was racing down a column of ships at 18 knots, only to pass by a U-boat, *U-652*, headed in the opposite direction, low in the water. *Skeena* was too close to the U-boat to depress its guns to fire, and was too far away to ram. The Canadians watched helplessly as the U-boat slid by, almost mocking them. More merchant ships were savaged in the dark. The debacle was turning into a massacre. Machine-gun tracers lit the sky and depth charges blasted the waters, but the Canadian escorts were chasing shadows.

"Wreckage littered the water: boats, floats, rafts, some with wildly waving men clinging to them, others empty," reported one sailor.[67] Corvettes and merchant ships slowed to try to grab a few survivors, but to break rank in the convoy was to invite death in the running battle. Most of the sailors in the dark sea were left there, soon to succumb to hypothermia. Those that were pulled out often had hands and feet that were black from frostbite.

The terrible night of the 9th was not leavened by the light the next day, as the U-boats continued to challenge the convoy. Few moments of glory redeemed the hours of horror. *Skeena*, in a skilful attack against the submerged *U-85*, dropped a number of depth charges that severely damaged the hull of the German U-boat, forcing it back to base. Two corvettes, *Chambly* and *Moose Jaw*, arrived as more ships were burning during the night on September 10, and immediately swept the seas with their asdic and surface radar. For a second straight night, the Allied seamen found little rest. Lieutenant W.H. Willson of HMCS *Skeena* remembered, "I was so God damn exhausted.... A series of sinkings and continuous ringing of that bloody [alarm] bell.... People don't realize there is a point at which you cease to function with any rational approach at all. You're just going through the motions."[68]

HMCS *Chambly* detected *U-501* at around 10 P.M. on September 10 and dropped a five-depth-charge spread. It damaged the U-boat, forcing it to the surface, nearly alongside *Moose Jaw*. Commanded by Lieutenant Freddy Grubb, the only prewar officer on board and a captain at the age of twenty-six, *Moose Jaw* was on its first cruise. Most of the young crew was wretchedly ill from days of prolonged seasickness, but they manned the guns and depth chargers. *Moose Jaw* fired a single round at *U-501*, but then the 4-inch gun jammed, as the inexperienced gun crew had failed to cock the weapon. Grubb roared, "Stand by to ram." The corvette lurched forward at full steam, crashed into the already damaged U-boat, and ran over it with a grinding scream of metal tearing metal. In a bizarre incident, the German captain, Korvettenkapitän Hugo Forster, leapt from his damaged conning tower onto the corvette's forecastle. Grubb was mystified to see the enemy captain abandon his ship, especially when *U-501* limped away, leaving its captain behind.[69] The corvettes pursued the damaged, captainless U-boat, guns firing, and pounding the vessel with shells. Mortally wounded, *U-501* surrendered a little before midnight.

Canadians boarded the sub in the hope of securing its codebooks, but the vessel was doomed and, as water flooded into the various compartments, there was a frantic race to get topside before it went to its grave. Canadians and Germans went into the water, and when the two corvettes switched on their 10-inch signal lamps to find the bobbing men, the Germans screamed, "No lights! No lights!" fearing that their rescuers would fall victim to one of their own U-boats. Thirty-seven men were pulled from the water. One Canadian, Stoker W.I. Brown, failed to escape from the submarine, and eleven other Germans were killed.[70] *U-501* was the first German sub sunk entirely by the RCN, but it was meagre reward for the terrible lashing endured by the convoy, which was harassed through the night and the next morning. Finally, on September 11, supporting airplanes from Iceland forced the U-boats off their kill.

The Canadians on that day handed the mangled convoy over to a British escort group, which consisted of five destroyers, two sloops, and two corvettes. This was the kind of escort strength that the Canadians needed to defend against multiple U-boat attacks, but few Brits made note of the Canadians' scant resources. Instead, the grim tally of loss was recorded: 15 destroyed merchant ships and tankers, carrying some 70,000 tons of cargo, including 1,000 truckloads of wheat, an almost as large quantity of chemicals required for manufacturing explosives, and enough steel and ore to build several destroyers. It was a grim indication that the under-strength Canadians were too often, as one official report observed, thrust into "a hopeless situation." However, even in this "appalling tale of disaster," the report noted, the outgunned Canadians had shown "energy and initiative throughout, probably thereby averting worse disaster."[71] It was scant encouragement and the RCN sailors and merchant seamen faced an enemy growing in strength and force.

CHAPTER 6

LIFE ON A CORVETTE

"Wartime service at sea in corvettes, frigates or destroyers is guaranteed to instill a profound respect for nature's power," warned Lieutenant Geoffrey Hughson. "Sometimes it seems that the real opponent is the sea itself."[1] The winter weather in the North Atlantic was, as one sailor remarked, "a terrible awakening."[2] Massive waves—the Green Ones, in the sailor's slang—battered the ships, sweeping over them from bow to stern, tearing away lifeboats from their moorings, and knocking about 420-pound depth charges like marbles. "The waves were so high that when you would crest one, it looked like you were looking 40 or 50 feet, maybe 75 feet down into a trough," remembered Seaman Gerald Bowen. "You would crest that wave and you'd fall into the trough. Everybody just held on. Then of course the next sea would come in.... We lost all track of time."[3] The monstrous waves seemed to grab the upper deck, wrenching the corvette out of the water and then dropping it down with a thundering crash; it was known as "hitting milestones," and it was stomach-shuddering in its power. "As the ship rolled and pitched, you were thrown around continuously, not daring to move without holding fast to something," reported Signalman Howard Cousins of HMCS *Algoma*.[4] Stomachs were emptied. Men were injured. It was a mad ride.

Lieutenant L.B. "Yogi" Jenson, the second-in-command or "Jimmy the one" aboard HMCS *Niagara*, wrote of one dawn where the faint light revealed "a wilderness of large, bitterly cold waves with streaming greybeards." He was on the bridge looking down and he saw the ordnance artificer coming along the starboard side. "As I watched, a large wave came up over the deck beside him and lifted him overboard to vanish instantly. He was a young man of cheerful and gentle nature, devoted to his work."[5] They searched for two hours, but the unfortunate sailor never surfaced.

The sea and the ship are at the core of the naval experience. These expensive vessels take sailors in and out of battle, and ease them through hostile environments. Yet the ship does not function without a crew, whose individual members can be too easily forgotten in the broader narrative, or simply lumped together in the story recorded by the ship's commander. It is the crew that fights the ship and keeps it seaworthy, and without high morale and efficiency, they would have little chance of surviving the trials of the North Atlantic. "Facing the dangers of the sea and the violence of the enemy creates a very special bond between men," wrote Lieutenant Commander Allan Stevens, who served on half a dozen warships during the war.[6]

The North Atlantic was violent and dangerous.
Most sailors felt they battled both the German U-boats and the seas.

The corvette was crowded. The crew's mess deck was the space for living, sleeping, eating, and relaxing off duty. It included two triangular compartments, each a mere 7 by 10 metres, where some sixty or so sailors were crammed. The chiefs and petty officers had a separate area, and the officers, their wardroom. In the mess deck, benches—which also doubled as lockers—were positioned around the perimeter, and at the centre was a large table that was used for everything. Canvas hammocks hung from every conceivable spot of the deckhead, and men slept at all times because of the watch-keeping schedule. On the overcrowded HMCS *Sackville*, John Margison remembered that the "micks"—the hammocks—were slung three deep.[7] Even then, on most corvettes, there were rarely enough swinging beds, and so new sailors were directed to the benches. Here, men learned to sleep propped up, with at least one leg on the floor to balance against a sudden lurch in the ship. To wake up face down in a puddle of stagnant water, with cockroaches crawling over one's body, was not the glory of war that any sailor had imagined.

Dim red and blue emergency lights provided a haunting glow, and there was a constant coming and going of men as the four-hour watches ended and new ones began. All sailors slept in their clothes for fear of the torpedo blast that would send them scrambling for safety in darkness, as power was usually lost. A jacket or sweater was always kept free, with heavy seaboots ready for searching feet. The working rig was a denim shirt and cotton dungarees. Men wore layers of clothing in all but the warmest weather. Discipline was looser on corvettes than on destroyers: the sailors took pride in their weathered boats and casual dress. When they were at sea, especially in good weather, members of a corvette's crew could be seen wearing hockey sweaters or other unconventional clothing, leaving the "pusser" and by-the-books British looking down on them as mismatched pirates—pirates, that is, who supported the Montreal Canadiens or Toronto Maple Leafs.[8]

"You were always trying to dry your clothes," recounted gunner Max Reid. "Even when you went to bed you were quite wet and cold … you always seemed to be shivering."[9] Water dripped from the condensation forming on the deckhead and, during storms, the sea found its way into most parts of the ship, creating a sloshing swill of foul-smelling water. In one storm, Lieutenant-Commander Alan Easton noted how there was "Water rushing from end to end of the mess carrying everything movable on its tide and crashing abruptly against the bulkhead."[10] Wet and stinking bundles of duffle coat and oil-skin were hung from any spare hook, or left in a corner to add to the stench.

The irony was not lost on sailors that while everyone was damp, hardly any fresh water was stored on the ship, and almost all of that was earmarked for cooking. This made showering impossible, except for the occasional sponge bath. One sailor

Sailors eating dinner in the seamen's mess of the corvette
HMCS Kamsack *underneath the swaying hammocks.*

remarked, "When you are in a ship you go with about a two-litre jug to the galley every day. [The cook] fills it up with water, takes ½ for cooking and gives you the other half. That's what you live on for water. That's for drinking, cleaning your teeth, laundering, you name it. Which meant that you never laundered, hardly ever cleaned you teeth and it was really just for drinking water."[11] The shortage of water also meant that many men developed "sailor's skin," a nasty irritation resulting from the lack of water and the harsh soap needed to scrub away the oil.[12]

George Richmond, from Thunder Bay, Ontario, enlisted at seventeen and remembered how the sailors were routinely "seasick, and you can add that to the cocktail on the floor."[13] The chronically seasick, wrote James Lamb, lived "at sea in a sort of half-world, between life and death, sustained only by a handful of crackers or soup for all the days and weeks of a voyage. Seasickness—real seasickness—is endured by these few with a resolute bravery that sometimes awes their heedless and healthy shipmates."[14] Ray Culley went to sea before his nineteenth birthday and served as a visual signalman in HMCS *Summerside*. His first trip out of St. John's harbour introduced him to the bane that stalked sailors:

> Ten minutes past the gates you were hit suddenly and very forcibly with a rolling and pitching sensation, as if you were standing on a cork in a bowl of water. It never relented and was compounded by very thunderous waves of ocean water, called "green ones," which landed with a thud and when they hit you they left a very hard salty film on your face, hands, or outer garments. The pitching and rolling were relentless, and after only a few minutes you were completely void of any nourishment you had consumed within the past eight hours. You hung on to whatever was handy, be it a railing, bulkhead, fellow rating, officer, whatever. You also knew in your heart of hearts that you were going to DIE![15]

Culley survived the sickness and fourteen trips across the Atlantic, but the first few hours of every voyage left him spewing.

John Peterson, who enlisted in the navy when he came of age in 1944, recounted the many cases of seasickness on the corvettes: "You see them crawled up in a corner just moaning and groaning."[16] Such was their misery, with no relief. The violently sick gravitated to the upper deck during their off hours, finding safe haven behind the single funnel. It provided a little shelter from the howling winds. There, the huddled ill—known as "the Funnel Gang"—found some comfort from heat radiating up from the warm engine room. Seasickness did not just strike landlubbers or the inexperienced. Frank Curry wrote of his first major ocean-crossing in HMCS *Kamsack*, where most of the crew, even "hardened Newfoundland fishermen, who had years of rough seagoing behind them," all suffered "the misery of the deadliest plague of the sea, seasickness."[17] While most sailors got over the sickness, some never did. Harry Barrett always spent his first ten to twelve hours at sea after a spell on land throwing up continuously. He remembered a fellow sufferer who lost thirty pounds in a two-week crossing; reduced to a mere skeleton of a man, he had to be drafted ashore on medical leave, never to return to a ship.[18]

With vomit added to the stale water in the mess deck, and to the body odour of men living too close together, the fug from the below deck was something to behold. Moreover, the portholes had to be closed at night for fear of allowing light to escape and attract U-boats, and so the mess decks were impregnated with a dreadful stink. "The smell in the mess decks was forever a stench of wet clothing, sea spew, and dampness that would never go away until you arrived in port, opened scuttles and deadlights, and scrubbed with disinfectant," recounted Clifford Ashton, who served nearly three years at sea on several ships.[19] "Please take it from one that was there," advised Al Bonner years after the war. "The stench of the foul air in the forward mess deck was indescribable!"[20]

SAILORS HAD TO EAT. Somehow the cook made meals for 60 to 100 crew members, three times a day, in what often resembled a roller coaster. The galley was about 4 metres long and 3 metres wide, and the stove and pots were designed to be locked in place. While a railing was fastened in front of the stove for the cook to hold on to, ladling stew or keeping boiling potatoes in their pots was a skill unto itself. There were few cooks whose arms did not bear the scars of their daily kitchen affrays.

Breakfast was oatmeal porridge and, when supplies lasted, eggs and toast, sometimes known as "chicken on a raft." However, the switch from real eggs to powdered came distressingly fast, particularly on ships leaving Britain, where there were always shortages of fresh food. "Red lead and bacon" was one of the staples on the corvettes, and served at breakfast and lunch. It consisted of cans of tomatoes thrown in a pot with fatty bacon, and whatever else that could be found in the victualling store to stiffen the fare. The sight of barely cooked bacon floating like turds in a red sauce was enough to make more than a few sailors lose what was left in their stomach. And yet the dish recurs so often in sailors' memoirs that they appear to have enjoyed something of a love–hate relationship with "red lead." Bangers and mash was another staple, even as the sausage seemed, according to Lieutenant Geoffrey Hughson, to be made of "80% sawdust."[21] Because of the shortage of water, the chalky, chunky powdered milk was thick enough to be gag-worthy, and many young men turned to Coca-Cola, which they brought on board and drank morning, noon, and night. Some in the Royal Navy even took to calling the Canadian navy the "Coca-Cola navy."

Lieutenant Richard Pearce of the corvette HMCS *Arvida* wrote, "The bread loaves got smaller each day as the green mould was cut away."[22] As fresh food was eaten or rotted, sailors turned towards canned goods, and found innovative ways to prepare meals. Complaints were common, but few men gave up on the meals that came from the galley. Patrick Nelson, who commanded ships in both the RCN and RN, remarked of his generation and their expectations: "We were mostly children of the Depression in Canada and brought up pretty frugally and I don't recall actually having serious trouble about the food or the rations."[23] Many sailors were used to belt-tightening and going hungry.

CORVETTES WERE NOT EQUIPPED with a loud speaker system, and so most orders—other than the alert station's alarm bell and direct communication to the boiler room—were transmitted through the traditional bosun's call that was carried through the voice pipes that ran through the ship. While detailed commands through the voice pipes could also be attempted, they were usually garbled and difficult to decipher. So the bosun used a whistle to make his calls, modulating the sound by opening and closing his fist, and these signals were understood by all sailors. It was the whistle that communicated to the men "hands to dinner" and times for watch change.

Each crew member was assigned regular tasks as well as additional duties when

Sailors stood watch in good weather and bad in search of enemy U-boats.

ordered to action stations. A ship had many specialized branches. The seamen looked after operations on deck, including radar and guns; the torpedo hands were responsible for electrical matters and torpedoes; the communication hands oversaw visual and radio signalling; the supply hands served as cooks and stewards; the asdic section sent out the sonar pings and listened for their echoes; and then there were the men in the bowels, the engine room and stoker crews, who kept the vessel at speed. Each branch had a chief petty officer or a petty officer, and there were, of course, the officers of the ship, all of whom reported to the captain.

The seamen were also required to engage in mundane maintenance. Steel ships required constant chipping of old paint and the application of new coats, as well as attention to the spreading rust spots. A couple of weeks in the Atlantic, wrote one officer, and a ship was "covered with rust and crap."[24] Months of continuous service left corvettes with dangerous rust holes in the deck, and ships were forced periodically to go for more extensive repair, known as a refit.

The other primary duty for most seamen was watch. The crew was organized into three watches: Red, White, and Blue. Each sailor put in an eight-hour day, divided into two four-hour shifts. Those on watch stood in the crow's nest, on the bridge, and on the quarterdeck, surveying the sea. A four-hour watch was long, boring, and cold. Jeffry Brock, a Canadian who commanded a series of British warships, wrote of being reduced to the "match stick trick." While on watch he was often so "weary, sick, and exhausted" that he propped open his eyelids by inserting matchsticks, broken at both ends, between the upper and lower lids.[25] Seaman James Galloway recounted one of his first watches onboard HMCS *Agassiz* (pronounced Aga-see and named after a farming community in the Fraser Valley, British Columbia), where he was desperately afraid that he would miss a lurking U-boat in the gloom. "My eyes were aching, as were my hands from holding up the binoculars."[26] All of this was made worse by his constant vomiting. The first lieutenant scolded Galloway for the mess and gave him two buckets: one to clean up the wheelhouse and the second into which he could direct his spew.

A watch might be blessed by a cloudless, clear sky, stars abright, and the sea lapping gently at the ship. For these the crew were thankful. On dirtier nights they were blasted by gales, the frenzied wind lashing and nearly tearing oil skins from a seaman's body.

The midnight watch was a bone-chiller. To be roused from only a few hours of fitful sleep to face the roiling sea was a bitter experience. Strong men survived it through gritted teeth and set jaw. In the winter, the weather was so frigid that, according to one witness, the "life seemed to drain slowly out of the ends of the body."[27]

"When you went to action stations on the upper deck, or if you were an upper deck man and your watch was up there, you put on every bit of clothing you had," remembered Gerald Bowen, whose father survived the trenches of the Great War and whose brother was serving in the current conflict. "You had sweaters on and pants and big sea socks and sea boots and then you put a duffel coat on and if it was a stormy night, you'd put an oil skin over that, then over the top of that, you had to put your lifejacket. It was a very miserable existence."[28] Water still found its way down the backs of necks. Most men developed their own technique for avoiding this wet intrusion, usually some variation of a rolled-up towel worn as a scarf to sop up a measure of the leakage; but by the end of a watch, few men were dry.

Relief from the toil and hardship came in the form of the beloved kye, a viscous drink made from a block of coarse chocolate, scoops of sugar, and canned milk. Kye, according to Lieutenant A.G. W. Lamont, "brightened one's life…. Nothing else could have approached its magic in raising flagging spirits on watch in the small hours of the morning."[29] In a proper pot of kye, according to one veteran of the North Atlantic, a spoon would "stand vertical in the cup at boiling temperature for at least 10 seconds before touching the side."[30] Served piping hot, it provided both comfort and caffeine, and tasted damn fine despite a frothy coating of fat. Harry Barrett remembered that the steaming cocoa's "welcome warmth could be felt to your very toes."[31] But one was never warm for long, even in the summer, although the beauty of a still sea and a rising sun was something at which to marvel. Yet there was always the chance in the North Atlantic that the sea would shift from beautiful to bad in a frighteningly short time. "No corvette sailor ever talked of 'ruling the waves' or 'conquering the deep,'" wrote James Lamb, and all sailors were wary of nature's power.[32]

The winter months brought the added danger of a ship icing up, as the heaving water sprayed the vessel and froze to anything made of metal. Sailors called this "white mist." When the air temperature dropped to freezing, or below, water droplets almost instantly turned to ice. It was as if the ship had been stricken by some terrifying mottling disease, as ice seemed to grow from every structure, as if it were alive. In a short period of time, the ice could thicken dangerously to 20 or 30 centimetres, adding enormous weight to a 60-metre corvette.[33] The ship became a block of ice, but the weight was distributed unevenly, with ice coating one side more than the other and leaving it vulnerable to the crashing waves. "Every man on board had to turn to and chip ice," recounted Gerald Bowen. "You used hammers, you used axes, you used crowbars, you used anything. You used your fists trying to get rid of the ice because if it built up to a sufficient weight, you might keel over."[34] The crew carried out their work as the waves pummelled them again and again. Even if he was tied down by lifelines, a sailor could be swept overboard by a rogue wave. After a few hours of this labour, a man was nearly done in. Still the sailors worked with the fury of the

Ships iced up dangerously in the harsh North Atlantic. When they did,
the entire crew chipped and smashed the ice to relieve the weight on the ship.

condemned, desperate to break the icy grip that might soon become a death grip. No Canadian warship ever went down from ice buildup, but all faced the possibility.

Good weather or bad, sailors were instructed to wear their deflated rubber life jacket, nicknamed a Mae West, around their waists. But many found them bulky and kept them in their lockers, observing mordantly that if a man fell into the Atlantic in winter, it did not matter if he was wearing a life vest or not, because the cold would kill him in minutes. However, the life jacket allowed countless sailors to chortle that they had slept with the movie star Mae West, or lain on her ample bosoms, or engaged in all manner of less printable activities. In 1943, the Mae West was replaced by a fuller, heavier life jacket, with a collar that kept an unconscious head out of the water. It also had a battery-powered blinking red light so that the wearer could be more easily spotted in the water. Many would-be rescuers found, tragically, that the light blinked on relentlessly, long after a man had succumbed to the freezing Atlantic.

Asdic and radar were crucial in the war against the U-boats, and the operators aboard a warship had a heavy responsibility in providing early warning against enemy attacks. Underwater submarine detection had been available since the last months of the Great War, but it was an unheralded aspect of naval warfare, and the Canadian navy had few experts in the difficult art. The corvette asdic operators were situated in the wheelhouse. They wore headphones and directed the sonar beam using a simple hand wheel, while listening to the pings and echoes for signs of a sub. The work of the "ping merchants" was mentally exhausting, and on destroyers they were cut off from most human contact, as they sat in the belly of the vessel. They worked on a two-and-four routine: two hours of listening and then four hours off, followed by the same again. The monotony was debilitating. A contact brought an adrenaline rush, but most of the return "pings" did not indicate enemy vessels. "Reverberations and tiny echoes from seaweed, fish, debris, fainter and fainter as the pulse of sound energy went out from the ship," described Hal Lawrence. "Then, ping, again. Hour after hour, watch after watch. The asdic set had been going since sailing and wouldn't stop until we reached safe haven."[35] After a few months of service, Frank Curry nearly collapsed from the strain of asdic operations and the responsibility for "safeguarding the ship ... and the whole wing of the convoy."[36] Another operator remembered how the pings invaded his sleep, noting, "After two weeks at sea, we were completely drained, never getting a decent rest."[37]

"YOU GOT TO KNOW A PERSON inside and out aboard ship," observed Bill Nelligan.[38] There were no secrets in the mess deck. These were "chummy" ships, one sailor remarked.[39] Chummy they were, but not everyone was the best of friends. In the close living, the braggarts and liars were soon spotted, and arguments were not uncommon. Hal Lawrence, who served on many ships in his five and a half years of war service, wrote that while he loved most of the men he served with, he also learned "how to live and work cheek-by-jowl with men I actively disliked."[40] While a few bad seeds marred every crew, the young sailors banded together to deal with the constant adversity of life at sea. There were far more friendships than enmities, more good will than ill.

"Escorting convoys during the Second World War, was, for just a little under 100 per cent of the time, extraordinarily dull work," penned Lieutenant L.B. Jenson.[41] To pass the time and pinch some pleasure, almost everyone smoked. Most sailors stocked up on their favourite brand when they were in port. When the supply of North American cigarettes was exhausted, they turned to the British standard cigarette, the Churchman's No. 1, which was generally despised, but not enough to keep it from a man's lips. As Gerald Bowen remarked, "One of the most beautiful moments when you're at sea was when you came down off watch and you went into the mess deck and somebody would have made a pot of tea and you'd have a cup of tea and a cigarette and nothing, nothing has ever tasted as good."[42] The bluish haze below deck was enough to make new men gag, but the tobacco aroma also masked some of the stench. Smoking was prohibited above deck. "At lookout stations, at the guns or on the bridge, the glow of a cigarette could mean a torpedo, and death," wrote Lieutenant Geoffrey Hughson.[43]

"Up spirits" was piped daily at 11 A.M. All crew members over the age of twenty-one were given grog, a 2.5-ounce tot of rum mixed with two parts water, although some men preferred it with Coca-Cola. Chiefs and petty officers, and occasionally an old hand, could ask for the rum neat; however, undiluted navy rum was not for amateurs. One administering officer remarked that the rum "went straight down to your boots." It was tough on the gut, but the "rum issue was the high point of the day for most men and was a major factor in maintaining morale."[44] While most men were classified "Grog," those who chose temperance received an extra twenty-five cents a day in pay. Despite the not insubstantial bonus, the abstainers were in a minority, although all the young sailors under twenty-one were automatically "T," for temperance. Most young sailors seem to have skirted the rules, and there are few mentions in letters, diaries, or memoirs of underage sailors not getting their rum.[45]

Singing was a common pastime, and often done with well-lubricated throats after the daily grog. "Sing-songs, limericks or parodies of songs were very popular, particularly 'That was a Cute Little Rhyme, Sing us Another One, Do.' Of course, 'Roll Out the Barrel' and 'Roll Along, Wavy Navy,' were all sung with gusto," recalled Al Bonner.[46] "I served with one captain who had the greatest collection of pornographic songs that it is possible to imagine," wrote Hal Lawrence, "and he sang them with an irrepressible gusto in a powerful, sonorous baritone, slapping his palms against his belly in the more rhythmic choruses and urging us to sing louder."[47] As sailors' speech was already "salty"—with John Peterson, who served on the corvette, HMCS *Midland*, reporting that on a ship, "every other word is an F word"—songs demanded even more scandalous language, metaphors, and unadulterated vulgarity.[48]

The most famous, and dirty, song—although many vied for that plum recognition—was "The North Atlantic Squadron":

Away, away with fife and drum,
Here we come, full of rum.
Looking for women who peddle their bum
In the North Atlantic Squadron.
When we arrived in Montreal, she spread her legs from wall to wall.
She took the Captain balls and all in the North Atlantic Squadron.

We were seven days at sea, the Captain took to buggery.
His only joy was the cabin boy in the North Atlantic Squadron.

A-sailing up and down the coast, now here's the thing we love the most,
To fuck the girls and drink a toast to the North Atlantic Squadron.

Accolades and cheer were heaped on the singer who added original verses, and they never seemed to run dry, as amateur lyricists found new ways to describe improbable sexual gymnastics, loose women, and amorous farm animals. Like the popular and equally filthy "Mademoiselle from Armentières" from the previous war, few of the verses of "The North Atlantic Squadron" were written down, even as they remained legendary in the hearts of sailors and sung in closed company during the postwar years.

Commander Jeffry Brock recounted that while he was busy at sea, he still had time to consume 600 to 700 books during the war years.[49] While most sailors did not have that sort of aptitude, during less boisterous times William P. Vradenburg, who served in HMCS *Capilano*, along with many of his mates passed off-hours by reading detective stories. "Whenever I was in port, I would pick up pocket books that I could stick in the top of my boot."[50] Lying in his hammock, Vradenburg generally did not get far into his novels before nodding off. "You never felt that you had fully caught up on your sleep, never."[51] With all the noise and commotion, it is a testament to the deep fatigue that plagued all men that anyone slept at all.

A poker game was underway day and night on the main table. The sharks ate the guppies, but the fish kept coming back. These men were accustomed to living with worse odds and higher stakes in the U-boat war. Gerald Bowen recounted how he sat down for some poker and "within five minutes the old hands had cleaned me out."[52] He endured a long month without tobacco and treats, an experience that taught him early in his career not to gamble, something he stuck with throughout his life. Most of his shipmates took longer to learn that lesson, if they learned at all. Lieutenant L.B. Jenson thought he had a gambling-free ship but found out after the war from old shipmates that the poker games ran continuously.[53] The officers were excluded from most of the lower deck's secrets.

A vibrant oral culture developed in the lower decks. Sailors talked and pontificated. There were some who were inveterate liars and stretched their stories with relish. Others had lived rich, wild, and occasionally desperate lives. New men learned from their briny elders about sex, prostitutes, and the mysteries of that world. There was shameless gossip and a constant exchange of rumours, yarns, and salty dips—nearly all of which were wildly wrong or exaggerated. Legends were shared that told of drinking, seafaring, and even of monsters of the deep. Superstitions were reinforced or discussed in hushed tones. New men learned, for instance, not to whistle on board the ship: the practice was said to invite storms.

Such seafaring traditions and legends forged bonds within the crew, but most sailors also kept up their connection to Canada, chiefly through letters. The return mail was often waiting in port. The missives "assuaged a terrible longing on the part of every one of the crew, a longing that ate and ate at a man's heart," wrote one sailor. Often accompanying the letters were packages filled with treats and cigarettes. "The arrival of mail," wrote one veteran of the seas, "was a great occasion, magically restorative of morale and spirit to such an extent that the senders could hardly have imagined."[54]

Letters from loved ones were central for morale, but Frank Curry felt a compelling need to create order and sense out of the chaotic war around him, and so he kept a

Card games ran day and night in the tight confines of the mess deck. Sailors who lived by the long odds of their dangerous profession did not seem to mind losing big stakes in games of chance.

diary. This was forbidden for security reasons and, he reported, when it was "discovered by my shipmates, [it] became a source of endless jokes at my expense. I think they were both puzzled and suspicious about my desire to write about our experiences. Wasn't it bad enough to have to go through it all without re-living it again on paper?... But despite the many reasons for letting it go, I spent five long years jotting down the feelings, the events, the exhilaration, the fury of war, and the magic of the hours of respite."[55] Torpedo man John Peterson also kept a diary that he hid on his body throughout his wartime service for fear that it would be read or stolen: "It didn't give me much space to write much. But a little note here and a little note there. Because I wanted to remember when the war was over a couple little things. Because you forget about things."[56] While some sailors felt the need to record their war, others were happy to ignore all thoughts of moments past or future, and simply to survive the present.

Sailors faced death every day, but many did it with a smile. Humour, pranks, and jokes were common. Should we expect any different from adolescents and young men? Sub-Lieutenant Ray Richardson of the RCNVR, who served in several corvettes over five years, shared the story of a prank played on a hapless crew member. During one convoy crossing that took them close to the English coast, HMCS *Mimico* picked up the corpse of a pilot who had crashed his Spitfire. "We sewed the body up in canvas ... and put him under the forward gun platform.... The midnight watch wanted to pull a joke on one of our fellows in the watch called 'Happy.' He was a great lad, but perhaps a little gullible." The body of the flyer was transferred to a secure spot and one of the men was sewn up in some canvas. Happy was told to move the body. "As soon as Happy got a few feet carrying the body at the head end, the lad inside the canvas started to moan and wriggle. The poor guy was so frightened he ran the full length of the ship screaming bloody murder." While the joke was crude, Richardson shared that he and his mates would do anything to "generate a laugh" and to "take our minds off the daily miserable work at hand."[57]

Even the cockroaches could be conscripted into the fun. All ships were infested. The little monsters normally stayed out of heavily trafficked areas, but an unwary hand moving crates or baggage was more likely than not to be shocked by the discovery of a swarming mass of shiny, black uglies. Ray Culley remarked that prior to slicing the bread, "one had to remember to hit the end of the bread with the handle of the knife, until all the cockroaches scrambled out of the air holes."[58] By some accounts, sailors had to learn to sleep with their mouths closed for fear of cockroaches dropping from the deckhead. Still, it was said that cockroaches killed the bedbugs, which made them the lesser of two evils. The phlegmatic sailors found a way to make the cockroaches work for them, trapping them and entering them in races. "Each had his speedster in a matchbox and put up a shilling, a starting and finishing line was drawn on a table, money was put in a pot and the race was on," wrote George Zarn, who served aboard the armed merchant cruiser HMCS *Prince Robert*.[59]

EVEN WITH THE PRANKS AND FUN, with the endless chat and cigarettes, and all of it enlivened by kye and grog, the war at sea wore down the Canadian sailors. They were pushed too hard, lacking enough ships to cover the convoys and enough time at the end of their arduous voyage to recover before doing it again. A saying in the corvettes, recounted Bill Perry of Victoria, British Columbia, who served on a number of ships including the *Alberni*, was that the sailors were "fed up, fucked up and far from home."[60] Captain E.B.K. Stevens wrote a report in October 1941, warning of the enormous stress on the Newfoundland Escort Force ships' crews: "Recently corvettes have escorted convoys east-bound for sixteen days and then after between four and eighteen hours in harbour have returned with west-bound convoys, this voyage lasting between fourteen and sixteen days. This is quite unacceptable. There seems to be a strong tendency to estimate the endurance of these small ships principally on their fuel carrying capacity. This is not only fallacious, but positively dangerous.... Unless very urgent steps can be taken ... I must report that grave danger exists of breakdowns in health, morale and discipline."[61] The RN and the United States Navy also commented in official communication that the RCN, and particularly the NEF, was stretched too thin. The Canadian crews were at sea about twice as frequently as their counterparts in the RN.[62]

Most convoys never encountered U-boats, but the subs always lurked out in the open seas, and the threat weighed heavily on the sailors' minds. The strain was even worse when a U-boat was spotted trailing a convoy, and all the marked ships knew that it was holding back, vectoring other U-boats to the coordinates. James Lamb remembered the rising stress provoked by knowledge that a sub was on their trail: "We steam on, everyone on tenterhooks; on the bridge and in the messdecks the tension is almost palpable. Yet at sea we are all fatalists."[63] Sailors worried about the odds, but, as Ralph Burbridge revealed, "We were always hoping that if someone's going to get it, it'll be someone else, you see. Everybody has that. It doesn't matter whether you're on a naval ship or a merchant ship, or in the trenches, I guess, or in a plane."[64] If death was coming, every sailor had to believe that it would not strike at him. That was one of the mental tricks that allowed sailors to keep functioning. But of course the fear found ways to creep into a man's mind. Often it came on during the pitch dark of a midnight watch. What was out there? What was to be one's fate? Not even sleep brought escape from the tentacles of the deep. "I couldn't fall asleep when I turned in, although I was exhausted," wrote Hal Lawrence. "I would stare at the ship's side by my bunk and think, 'If a U-boat has worked herself up on the bow of the convoy, at, say, two miles, and if she is firing a spread of torpedoes, say,

The fear of a sudden U-boat attack weighed on all seamen.

now, then it will take the fish three minutes to arrive.' And then I would count up to a hundred and eighty seconds. One, two, three, four.... Then I would say, 'Well, I guess she didn't fire. But, if she were firing now. One, two, three, four, five...' And in the morning I'd tell myself that it was just another form of counting sheep."[65]

Life on board a corvette was mentally and physically exhausting. But these were tough men. They had grown up during the Depression and had known hardship all their adult lives. And, as many sailors recounted, they survived the bitter sea conditions particularly because they were young. Since they knew of no better or different life, they endured the privation and eventually shrugged it off. They might have been cynical and satirical. They groused and grew angry at their plight. But they knew what they were doing was important for the war effort. "I had a great feeling for the merchant sailors that were on those ships," remembered Frank Curry. "If we got a convoy through without losing a ship, surely we were doing our job!"[66] Despite the hardship, the weather, the rough crossings, and the terror of being hunted, morale remained high in the little corvettes. Herb Jones remarked proudly of his crew on the HMCS *Dauphin*, "my predominant memories remain of a very close comradeship, unselfish sharing, tremendous 'esprit de corps' and pride in our ship and the Navy."[67]

CHAPTER 7

BOMBER COMMAND

Fighter Command had saved Britain from Hitler's invasion, but even before that hard-won victory, Prime Minister Winston Churchill told his cabinet, "The fighters are our salvation, but the bombers alone provide the means of victory."[1] Churchill ached to strike back at Germany after its victory over Western Europe, and he wanted revenge for the Blitz. The British prime minister was a long-time proponent of air warfare, and he wrote to his friend and confidant Lord Beaverbrook in the summer of 1940, "There is one thing that will bring ... [Hitler] down, and that is an absolutely devastating, exterminating attack by very heavy bombers from this country upon the Nazi homeland."[2]

The Royal Air Force had established Bomber Command as an independent arm on July 14, 1936, when it had created three other separate commands: Fighter, Coastal, and Training. Bomber Command's motto was "Strike Hard, Strike Sure," and the new command allowed for a specialization of bombing, with the strategic aim of knocking out the nerve centres of the enemy: command and control functions, logistical pathways, and essential war-related factories. This was an offensive force, and the more enthusiastic proponents of air power believed that massed aerial bombardment would destroy civilian morale and end wars in a matter of weeks.

In September 1939, Bomber Command went to war with 23 front-line bomber squadrons, totalling 280 planes. These were all twin-engine machines—Bristol Blenheims, Armstrong Whitworth Whitleys, Handley Page Hampdens, and Vickers Wellingtons—modern for the time, but dwarfed by the immense four-engine bombers of only a few years later. The two-engine planes were slow, could not fly far into Germany, had a low service ceiling, and were poorly equipped to defend themselves against enemy fighters. They also carried a small bomb load, boasted few navigational electronic aids, and had only primitive bombsights. At first, senior Bomber Command officers believed their planes could fly daylight precision bombing runs, despite prewar tests showing that bomber crews regularly missed their targets (even those without protective anti-aircraft fire, also known as flak). But early operations during the war revealed that aircraft were vulnerable to both ground fire and enemy fighters—unable to fly above the former or defend against the latter. Dozens of bombers were shot down in the first months of the war; additional crews were trained and factories built more planes, and then the new ones were shot down too.

"Bombing up" a Vickers Wellington to carry out a sortie against an enemy target.

The hundreds of Canadians serving in the RAF at the start of the war found themselves the first of their countrymen in battle.[3] Flight Lieutenant T.C. Weir piloted a 44 Squadron Hampden on September 3 in an offensive sortie against German naval vessels—the first Canadian to engage in action during the Second World War. Two days later, Sergeant Albert Price from Vancouver was killed in a bombing run over Wilhelmshaven, Germany.[4] Another Canadian, Alfred Thompson, was shot down on September 8, two days before Canada officially entered the war. He spent every day of Canada's war as a prisoner.[5]

In September 1939, even as the Germans pounded the Polish cities from the air, the British bombing policy was tentative and restrained. Fearing reprisal attacks against British citizens and anxious to hold the moral high ground, Prime Minister Chamberlain limited the bomber attacks to useless propaganda leaflet raids and only marginally less useless strikes on enemy shipping or factories far from civilian centres.[6] No matter the target, the bomber crews rarely hit their objectives and almost always took significant casualties.

Everything changed with the German offensive of May 1940. On May 13, the Luftwaffe bombed Rotterdam in the hope of smashing critical war industry, but those bombers, like the British ones, could barely hit a city let alone pinpoint specific buildings. Nonetheless, in the blaze of bombs, about 1,000 citizens were killed and the Dutch people surrendered rapidly. Hitler and his air marshals took note of how bombing could lead to a collapse of civilian morale and avoid the need for a costly land war.

The British also took note. Churchill sought ways to hurt the surging German forces, and with a new offensively minded chief of the air staff, Sir Charles Portal, the two war leaders moved towards a more aggressive stance in the bombing war. The forty-seven-year-old Portal was quiet but shrewd, and he well understood that his bombers were unable to pick off enemy targets from 15,000 feet when opposed by enemy flak and fighters, and were even more inaccurate when flying in darkness. He pushed the government towards using its only offensive weapon to target industry and factories in cities, aware that should his aircrews miss their primary targets they would still inflict damage on the enemy.[7] The government remained wary of advocating a policy of bombing civilians, but the decision making was moving from black and white to grey, and soon the bombers were striking cities in the hope of damaging war industry. Few in the British high command, either civilian or military, believed that bombing could win the war on its own, especially after its own people withstood the sustained aerial blasting of their cities, but it was one of the few means of taking the battle to Germany.

While civilian casualties were still to be avoided, the new bombing strategy after the fall of France saw an emphasis on attacking German airfields, rail lines, and oil refineries. Damaging German industry, and thus hurting the war machine, became the bomber's goal. The Germans, upon studying the bomb dispersal patterns, found the British bombs falling all over the countryside, far from cities—seemingly providing evidence of British bombers who were dead set on killing farmers' animals and ploughing fields. These aimless strikes perplexed the Germans, sparking new fears that the British were embarking on some indecipherable strategy.[8] In reality, the RAF's bombers were targeting factories in urban areas, but they were so inaccurate that they were, quite literally, missing the cities, with their bombs off the mark by dozens and dozens of kilometres.

As evidence of the RAF bombers' ineffectiveness accumulated, and as the losses mounted, the command had absolutely no other choice but to switch to night bombing. By the late summer of 1940, almost all of the bomber missions were carried out at night. Darkness provided some cover from enemy defences, but the crews now faced even greater difficulties in reaching the blacked-out cities and then hitting specific targets within them. As one distressed senior RAF commander wrote, "The constant struggle at night is to get light on the target." He warned about "a never ending struggle to circumvent the law that we cannot see in the dark."[9] Yet even as the bombers struggled in their night battles, Churchill and the senior RAF staff insisted on their missions, viewing these operations as crucial to showing the United States that Britain was willing and able to hit back even as the government, people, and military pulled themselves up from the bloodied mat where they had been driven by relentless blows. The bombers became the vanguard of their attack.

RAF BOMBER COMMAND had little impact on the enemy's ability to wage war in 1940 or 1941. When the RAF and RCAF bombers, usually numbering between 50 and a 100, found their targets, the bombing did surprisingly little damage. And each night, the bombers ran the gauntlet of fire, with aircrews watching their comrades getting hit by flak and disintegrating into fiery fragments both on their outward flight and on their return. The German night fighters were just as deadly as the British fighters had been, and often the bombers flew in small groups, with stragglers drifting off into the darkness. This lack of cohesion allowed individual bombers to become easier targets for the fighters, and also meant that the planes arrived over the target at different times. Those arriving late found the city's defences prepared. Senior RAF officers naively believed that the bombers would be able to defend themselves against enemy fighters if they flew in tight formations with their gunners sending out a hail of bullets. But maintaining close formations was difficult, and the small calibre guns on the bombers—.303, the same as a rifle shell—lacked stopping power. Unless they were fired in concentration, with several gunners training on a single enemy craft, the machine guns were no match for the cannon fire from Luftwaffe fighters. Flight Sergeant Arthur Wahlroth of the RCAF's No. 405 Squadron, who flew in the summer of 1941, wrote that "if the whole sky was not erupting around you," then the fighters were coming. "Sometimes you could smell it, hear it, feel it" coming from above— and experienced pilots corkscrewed downward, seeking cover in clouds.[10] The cost of attacking was cripplingly high. Mike Lewis, from Welcome, Ontario, enlisted in the RAF in 1938 and flew Hampden medium bombers with No. 44 Squadron. He survived sixty-one operations before his bomber was raked with fire, forcing the crew to ditch. Lewis was made a prisoner for the last three years and eight months of the war. When patriated home, he was informed that of the thirty-eight comrades with whom he went through training, only six had survived the war. Lewis, who went on to serve in the postwar RCAF, recounted that unlike later in the war, when there were limited operational tours, the airmen of the early war flew until they were shot down. "These determined men went unrewarded for their magnificent efforts."[11]

The gradual switch from the ineffective bombing of specific targets to area-bombing entire cities meant an acceptance of civilian deaths. In July 1941, a series of British government and air force documents advocated for the bombers to strike at German workers in the hope of wearing down morale and slowing work in support of the state.[12] The British did not set out to kill women and children, but a rationale gradually emerged as it was understood that the bomber was more of a hammer than a scalpel. Was it right to target the enemy soldier or airman, but not the civilian who built his weapons or supported him through war work? The answer seemed clear to those fighting the Nazi regime, and, in any case, the enemy had already crossed that line by deliberately targeting British civilians. Looking back, RCAF Flight Lieutenant Joseph Deutscher declared, "The evil of Nazism had to be crushed and I'm glad I did my share in destroying it." Deutscher became a priest after the war, but not because of his guilt over his actions in Bomber Command; in fact, this man of God assumed that in a total war the entire civilian sector of the war economy was a legitimate target. "If we killed German factory workers who worked in a shoe factory rather than a munitions plant, then we prevented shoes from reaching the German fighting forces."[13]

British Prime Minister Sir Winston Churchill watches a Stirling four-engine bomber taking off.

Churchill and his fellow civilian and military leaders had their reasons for striking back with the bombers, and they were supported by a large proportion of the British people. While early public opinion polls indicated that the British people were not overwhelmingly anxious to kill German women and children, over time, as the British witnessed European and British cities targeted by German bombers, they demanded retribution.[14] The bombing of enemy cities was gradually accepted, first as an appropriate response to the Blitz, and then as an accepted strategy for taking the war to the German economy.

RCAF Navigator Ron Peel, who served with RAF No. 9 Squadron and flew in the twin-engine Wellingtons, wrote that he had no misgivings in taking part in bombing Germany by night. Daylight operations were suicide, particularly by late 1941 when Peel had begun to fly. "On all my earlier operational sorties I was given a very specific military target to attack. This I did even though fully aware that to do so would surely result in civilian casualties." With limited targeting systems and the need to fly at night, the only solution was to blanket the cities in bombs, "using much the same brutal tactics as the Luftwaffe had initiated in their destruction of much of London, Coventry, Liverpool, Hull and numerous other cities in England and the rest of Europe." Peel acknowledged, "We killed a lot of civilians."[15]

THERE WAS NO SHORTAGE OF CANADIAN VOLUNTEERS for the air force, both to serve in the established RAF and the steadily expanding RCAF. The grim memories of fathers and uncles who had survived the rat-infested trenches of the Great War, and who were traumatized by such experiences, kept many from enlisting in the infantry. John Weir of Toronto remembered being offered a commission in the Governor General's Horse Guards. He turned it down, saying, "I'm not fighting in some mud ditch."[16] He enlisted in the RCAF and flew Spitfires before being shot down in late 1941 and becoming a prisoner of war. The navy had few Great War heroics to which it could point in order to draw recruits, and for many Canadians the air force was a more attractive option. Arthur Wahlroth was born in Truro, Nova Scotia, and enlisted in the RCAF in 1940 at the ancient age of twenty-five. Most of his fellow flyers were eighteen or nineteen. He did not want to enlist in the army: "When I was a young kid, we had neighbours who had been in World War One, who had legs off and arms off and burnt faces, who had respiratory problems." He was afraid of sharks and so that ruled out the navy, in his mind. "I had been brought up on Chums books, which were full of stories, fiction mostly, about airplanes and daring stunts that were done in-between the war period and that sided me towards the air force.... When the air force gave me the opportunity to join, I jumped right in as soon as I could."[17] Donald Cheney enlisted on his eighteenth birthday in 1940, for reasons that paralleled those of Wahlroth and numerous others: "I had always wanted to fly. I dreamed about flying since I was a youngster."[18] He was bombing Germany by age twenty. Douglas Humphreys had turned nineteen only a few months before the declaration of war in September 1939. The Scottish-born Humphreys wrote, "I found the prospect of war exciting and given what had been happening in Europe over the past few years, neither I nor my friends were taken by surprise."[19] Humphreys gave up a good job and enlisted in the RCAF because, like so many others, he was "entranced by flying and like my friends I knew all about Sopwith Camels, Spads, Fokkers and other First World War aircraft. Billy Bishop was one of our heroes."[20] Tens of thousands of young Canadians were enamoured with the romance of flight. They had all been enraptured, too, by the Battle of Britain, and how the fighters saved the British people. How could square-bashing and sea-sickness compare to that?

There was no shortage of volunteers for the Royal Canadian Air Force. Inspired by the heroics of the last war and of the Battle of Britain, Canadians enlisted in large numbers in the RCAF. This poster reads: "Well done, Son! Fly and Fight with the R.C.A.F."

RCAF posters highlighted the glory of flying, and the exclusivity of being one of the "few." Colourful images labelled flyers as "men with a purpose." The tagline on some posters was "Join the team," while others offered the chance to "Fly and fight with the RCAF." There was even a poster of a proud mother cheering her dapper boy, in his RCAF slate-blue uniform, as he set off to war: "Well done, Son!" In theatres, the film *Target for Tonight* came out in the summer of 1941, which documented real airmen engaged in the bombing campaign. A camera team followed the crew of a Wellington, and the hero was the unperturbed and pipe-smoking pilot Charles Pickard. Authentic flying scenes "filmed under fire," as one theatre poster exclaimed, were interspersed with studio-shot drama segments. A critical and commercial success, the film spread the message of plucky Britain and its Bomber Command striking back.[21] Like so many young men who served in the bombers, Pickard was killed later in the war, suffering from battle stress but refusing to quit flying. Early the next year, in 1942, *Captains of the Clouds*, starring James Cagney and featuring a cameo by Air Vice-Marshal Billy Bishop, thrilled viewers and potential recruits.[22]

The advertising, posters, and movies suggested that flyers were a unique breed of warrior. In a sense they were. The air war required intense training, and the RCAF prided itself on maintaining the highest educational standards of the three services. By mid-1940, the new recruits were funnelled into the British Commonwealth Air Training Plan (BCATP), one of the marvels of the war. The plan saw training stations, schools, and airfields across Canada organized to turn out a steady stream of pilots and aircrews. The senior dominion was close enough to Britain to train airmen from throughout the British Empire and the United States, and its skies were not threatened by the Luftwaffe.

Negotiations to set up the BCATP were conducted between October and December 1939. They were sticky: Britain tried to bully the Canadians and other dominions into accepting the lion's share of the expenses. Prime Minister King was having none of that, and he pushed back forcefully, refusing to commit to the plan— which the British were desperate to get started. While King liked the idea of becoming a trainer of the Empire's airmen, he also hoped that it might be Canada's major contribution to the war, along with the supply of munitions and war materiel, all of which was in line with his policy of limited liability. The British refused to accept that notion, as they desperately needed Canada's fighting forces in the line, but the two sides edged closer to a deal that had more in common with a canny business transaction than the coming together of allies at war against a superior military foe.[23] After Canada's share of the costs was reduced (although, ironically, later in the war Canada would agree to pay almost all of the plan's $2.2 billion), King and his cabinet demanded that the Canadian airmen serve on identifiable RCAF squadrons.[24] The British balked at this but eventually gave ground. Still, for much of the war, the RAF senior brass ran interference against the agreement, and more Canadians served in the RAF than in Canadian squadrons.

While similar training plans were developed in Australia, New Zealand, and Britain, the Canadian one was the largest. The first BCATP graduates went overseas in November 1940, with legions following them. Ultimately 131,500 airmen graduated from the BCATP. More than half of them were Canadian, including 26,000 pilots, 13,000 navigators, 6,000 bomb aimers, 26,000 wireless operators and air gunners, and 2,000 flight engineers.[25] The majority of these airmen would eventually serve in the bombers, and Canadians contributed the second highest numbers to Bomber Command, forming about a quarter of the command in 1944 and a third of the force by the end of the war. Roosevelt was right to characterize Canada as the "aerodrome of democracy."[26]

"WE CAME FROM ALL OVER CANADA, from cities, small towns and farms," recounted W.H. Clever.[27] The new recruits, anxious to fly and take the war to Germany, were a little frustrated that they were first sent to one of the Manning Depots to begin basic training. The vast majority of new flyers also wanted to pilot Spitfires like the heroes overseas; instead, almost all went into Bomber Command. The disappointment was soon shed, although there would be other harsh realities to face during the long period of flying instruction. Bill McRae had roughed it before the war, but he was in "shock" when he viewed the temporary quarters at Manning Depot No. 2 in Brandon, Manitoba: "It was a former equestrian exhibition hall about the size of a hockey rink, the floor of which was now covered by at least 500 double-bunk beds.... The ablutions consisted of a long trough of galvanized metal which was the communal wash basin."[28] McRae, a future Spitfire pilot, was unimpressed by the line of toilet cubicles that had no doors. Robert Collins, 125 pounds and with a face of acne that betrayed his youth—he was twenty—was more taken with the experience, and wrote of being surrounded by hundreds of men: fat and thin, brooders to be avoided and friendly men who attracted crowds. They told crass jokes, broke wind playfully, and shouted insults. "Milling around in the buff in a room packed with other naked men, you wondered what to do with your hands.... Whatever was left of my native modesty went down the drain."[29] Collins learned, as did every recruit to the army, navy, or air force, that privacy disappeared after enlistment.

But the young men adapted well and learned to live with one another, despite coming from different regions and social classes, and having varying expectations. Among the "Acey-Deuceys," or Aircraftmen 2nd Class, much masculine jostling took place, and never-ending pranks. Nat Levitin, a future RCAF squadron leader, was waiting to go overseas at the Y Depot at Halifax when he and his mates were instructed to undergo a final medical exam. In an open room, they were told to drop their drawers for a genital examination. As they waited awkwardly for a doctor, an unknown assistant came by and swabbed each of the man's genitals with dark, brown iodine. They were then instructed to remain where they were. When the doctor arrived later, he looked rather surprised, "'What the hell's going on here?' he exclaimed, 'what are you guys doin'?' 'Well, Sir,' one of the men explained, 'your assistant has prepared us for your inspection.' After a pause, the doctor smiled, 'There's only one problem here—I don't have an assistant.'"[30]

As part of the laddish culture, nearly everyone had a nickname. Longer Christian names were abbreviated: Hal, Pete, Al. For some, surnames replaced Christian names: Woodman became Woody, Smitherson was soon Smithy, and Miller was automatically Dusty. Any Scottish name reverted to "Mac" or "Scotty." Physical features might be reflected in a name, such as Shorty or Lefty, and the linguistic innovations went on and on. New recruits were being remade into warriors, but first they had to be renamed by one another.

The Acey-Deuceys moved through a series of schools across the country, with most located in towns like Virden, Manitoba; Goderich, Ontario; and dozens of other spots that provided basic training and then more advanced skills. Alan Avant, who came from Hughton, Saskatchewan, where his family farmed, would be bombing Berlin at age twenty, but before that, he remembered, "We managed to make the transition from farm lads to fledgling pilots in a few short weeks....We were anxious

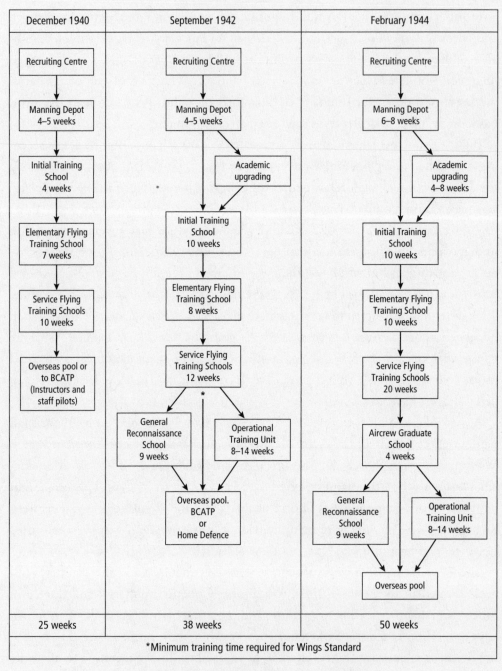

Usual sequence of pilot training in the BCATP.

to learn."[31] Indeed they were, but they were also weeded out ruthlessly. "I feel tough about washing out but I have lots of company," wrote a disappointed Miller Brittain after failing as a pilot.[32] He later served overseas as a bomb aimer, and then as an official war artist.

The 94 training schools at 231 sites across Canada required new airfields and thousands of military instructors and ground crews.[33] There were specialist schools for pilots, air observers, bombers, gunners, wireless operators, and navigators, although all instruction was in English, forcing French Canadians to adapt. Some of the trainers were prewar civilian pilots, while others had fully embraced the flying profession's daring myths. Thomas Reid observed that some of his instructors at Portage la Prairie, Manitoba, "are awful daredevils ... flying under telegraph wires, landing on top of trains, chasing cars down the highway, scaring horses to death in the fields ... one did the impossible [and] flew under a bridge ... no stunts for me, you can bet. I have too much to live for."[34] He survived his training and received the Distinguished Flying Cross for operations over Germany, but was shot down and went missing on August 10, 1943.

Across the Prairies, yellow-painted Harvards, Tiger Moths, Fleet Finches, and Avro Ansons flew over towns, and occasionally came down near them. These undersized planes—about the size and appearance of the fighters from the previous war—were a far cry from the two- and four-engine bombers overseas, but they were a sufficient introduction to the basics of flight. Nonetheless, the Canadian weather played havoc with inexperienced pilots, and many crashed when a storm blew in suddenly or when they tried to land on shimmering snow-covered terrain, where distance was hard to judge. In winter, machines froze up. In spring, everything around the base was reduced to a bog, and Kiwis, Brits, Aussies, and all the other airmen soon learned the horror of black fly season. Airmen and trainers died in accidents of all kinds. "One of our chaps had walked into a propeller and was decapitated right before our eyes," wrote one dismayed flyer.[35] Approximately 3,000 training deaths occurred in the BCATP schools.[36] They were quickly forgotten in the hurly burly of training, although mourned by their families.

Towns throughout the Dominion were soon overrun by airmen stationed at the newly built bases. Great gobs of money were to be made by supplying the bases. At the same time, the competition between the locals and the dashing young airmen could reach dangerous heights. Alcohol-fuelled, testosterone-driven bar fights were not uncommon. Howard Hewer, a nineteen-year-old BCATP recruit from Toronto, remembered how he and his mates overran Calgary. They found the locals friendly but the regional militia unit was not keen to see airmen encroaching on their territory, especially at the Saturday night dances. Hewer remembered, "By now we were wearing a white flash in our wedge caps, a piece of flannel inserted into the front fold of the cap to show that we were under training for aircrew."[37] The fledging airmen proudly wore their uniforms and wedge caps to dances, and then wondered why the women recoiled from them in horror. Only later did they discover that the local militia soldiers had spread a story that the white flash was a signal that the wearer had contracted a venereal disease.

The Canadian-run British Commonwealth Air Training Plan was a major contribution to winning the Second World War. But numerous accidents occurred and some 3,000 aircrew died during the course of the war.

At the end of their training, the BCATP airmen received their "wings." They were pinned on by senior RCAF officials and, sometimes, by Great War aces, among them Billy Bishop, now an air vice-marshal. The wings were worn with pride and Martin Cybulski-Ross spoke for many when he enthused, "We god damned well earned them!"[38]

THE BCATP FLYERS CROSSED THE U-BOAT-INFESTED ATLANTIC to Britain and were sent to Bournemouth on the south coast. Before the war, Bournemouth was a resort town that catered to the middle-aged and elderly who sought to escape to picturesque beaches and lush parks. Now, the beaches were mined and barbed-wired kill zones cordoned off in anticipation of an amphibious invasion. Bournemouth was also occasionally raided by German fighters that slipped across the Channel, flying low and fast, to shoot up the town before returning home. Known as "tip and run" raids, these encounters reminded airmen that there was a war on.

The once elegant hotels were increasingly run down, but were still occupied cheerfully by Canadians attached to the RCAF Personnel Receiving Centre, which would send flyers off to Advanced Flying Units for further training. The airmen received new battle dress, clothing, food coupons, and pay. Canadians overran the town, moving freely and in groups, visiting the pubs, cinemas, and dance halls. The training was not arduous, and Harlo Jones, a future RCAF bomber pilot, noted, "Most of our days in Bournemouth were spent killing time." However, Jones wrote of one memorable occasion: "Once we were paraded to a movie theatre where we were shown some real horror movies, about VD. That did leave an impression!" But some of the effect was lost when the last VD film included a beautiful young starlet who was supposedly the carrier of VD. The young men in the audience began to whistle and cheer, with shouts and catcalls, including "I'd take a chance on her any day."[39] The air force, like the other services, attempted to limit the ravages of VD, but its approach was clumsy. Young men who sought to live in the moment and contemplated the prospect of sudden death daily would have been a tough audience in any event.

After Bournemouth, finally the airmen would be introduced to two- and four-engine bombers. At the Advanced Flying Unit (AFU), the airmen met instructors who were tour-expired veterans of active combat operations. Most carried themselves with a quiet air of authority and many wore gallantry awards. Some of the new recruits were brassy and anxious to fly, but the smart ones also realized that the instructors had much to share with them, having beaten the long odds in the air war.

But there were also long-service RAF NCOs and officers who delighted in belittling the Canadians, and many of the Dominion's airmen felt that they were singled out for prejudice. The new flyers, who were soon to pole-vault in rank over the hardscrabble NCOs, did not readily accept the harsh words and general degradation. Flight Sergeant Joseph Harrison wrote of the friction in No. 1 AFU, where the RAF "personnel who greeted us obviously resented our presence if not our very existence. They appeared to consist entirely of bitter disgruntled permanent force NCOs who weren't about to take any insubordination from these young 'instant NCO' colonials."[40] Pilot Officer George Brown, who had enlisted in November 1941 from Brandon, Manitoba, wrote of his advanced flying training at No. 3 AFU at Bobbington, Worcestershire, "The Commanding officer was very anti-colonial and did not hesitate to vent his feelings on us Canadians. No wonder so many of the Canadians took a violent dislike to the English military."[41]

So many complaints were made that the RCAF conducted a study in 1942 to determine the effects of this conflict on morale. The report concluded that while tension existed at the training bases, few accounts of disunity were found in the operational units, where airmen of all nationalities flew together and relied on each other for survival. Moreover, the report concluded that the Canadians were not blameless and liked to play up their supposed unique national characteristics: "There seems to be a certain degree of truth in allegations made both by RAF and RCAF officers that Canadian airmen are harder to discipline than other airmen of the RAF. This surprised us." The report's authors felt that there were some Canadians who saw themselves as "tough guys" and got into trouble: "Canadians have no veneration for spit-and-polish" discipline, such as saluting crisply and keeping uniforms along uniform regulations.[42] At the same time, many imperials betrayed their own prejudices, believing, "The New World—the Americans and Canadians alike—is impetuous, enthusiastic, sometimes childish, often self-assured and usually not a little boastful. It likes to seem 'tough,' and it likes to show off."[43]

Instructors tried to put crews into the air for eighty hours of flying, with much of this being, in airmen's parlance, "circuits and bumps" (takeoff and landing) and "stooging" around England. The "heavies"—Lancasters, Halifaxes, and Stirlings— were needed for front-line action, so the training schools used the outdated and battle-scarred two-engine bombers from the early years of the war. Mechanical failures were frequent and hundreds of crews were killed as the old beasts crapped out in mid-air and plummeted to earth. But more deaths occurred through pilot error. Sergeant pilot Arthur Wahlroth recounted his experience of training on Whitley bombers in early 1941:

> These things were big, bigger than any aircraft ever seen before. They were definitely prewar. They were heavy to fly, although they did fly very nicely. It took two of us to fly the things. They gave us circuits and bumps at first, of course. And then they took us to places where we had to drop bombs and eventually we got into the turret and shoot out drogues [aerial targets] for the other craft there. So we had a rounded out education. The Whitley had one idiosyncrasy that we didn't like very well. Because the tail was so far up behind you, you trimmed the machine tail heavy so you didn't have to carry the weight on the control column. And if you were in a hurry when you took off and you just ducked down to trim and you didn't take it a turn and a quarter all the way to neutral, but only took it a quarter of a turn, when you took off, you sped down the runway. When you gained flying speed, the aircraft would rear up in the air and fall up on one wing and drop to a conclusion. I lost several friends this way.[44]

RCAF navigator Robert Kensett wrote that the Whitley was known as the "flying coffin" at his training unit. There were "twenty-nine crews, each with seven men, in our course," he reported, "and by the time the course ended nine aircraft had crashed, killing sixty-three airmen."[45]

AS HEAVIER BOMBERS WERE MANUFACTURED and rushed into service, the number of crew members per plane changed, as did their responsibilities. At the start of the war, most of the bombers carried two pilots. The other crew members were tasked with a number of roles: the navigator was also the bomb aimer, and the wireless operator was also the mid-upper gunner (who studied the skies for enemy aircraft and fired from the top of the bomber). In 1941, the second pilot was removed and a flight engineer was added to the crew. Most of these engineers had been ground crew members who understood the technical challenges of the machine. They were responsible for the plane in flight and for assisting the pilot. As one Canadian remarked, "it was almost a given that on every operation something would malfunction."[46] The wireless operator monitored the Allied and enemy air waves. And then a second air gunner was added, and because the navigator's job was found to be full-time, a bomb aimer now became a part of the crew. With the tail-gunner isolated in the rear, that made a crew of seven in the big, four-engine planes.

The new flyers were formed into flying crews at the RAF Operational Training Units. The approach of action brought with it an initiation into the culture and mores of their unique trade. The airmen's uniforms, insignia, and rank structure all served to distinguish them from the other services. "Almost every air force officer removed the stiffener from his hat, whereupon the hat soon lost its shape and looked like it might belong to a veteran of the Battle of London," wrote Flying Officer Charlie Hancock. "The floppy hat remained the mark of experience."[47] The slate-blue uniform was much prized, the flying badge worn above the right upper jacket pocket and the wings above the left. The fighter pilots embraced a culture of bravado and dash, and one of these signs was the seemingly nonchalant leaving of the top button of their tunics undone in "fighter boy style"; in contrast, the bomber boys left the bottom one undone. But both pilots and bombers took great pride in their uniforms and, as one British flyer remarked, "Air Force Blue, at that time the most famous colour in the world."[48]

The airmen developed their own idiosyncratic language for their specialized work. RCAF Flight Lieutenant Ron Peel wrote of his slow adoption of flyers' slang: "I learned that aircraft were 'kites' and that if somebody got killed they 'Got the chop,' 'Came a cropper,' or 'went for a Burton,' a popular dark ale. A hazardous event was a 'Shaky do' and a crash was a 'prang.' Violent evasive action was 'jinking.' ... Sound information was 'Gen' and its opposite 'Duff Gen.'"[49] Anything that was good was "wizard." A "wizard prang" was slightly different—an exciting or risky operation, either in the air or in the bars pursuing drink or women. Planes were also known as "crates" or "birds," but each type had an affectionate name: Halifaxes were "Hally Bag," Typhoons were "Tiffies," the Wellington was a "Wimpey."

Once they looked and sounded the part, the airmen finally were forged into a flying team. "Crewing up" was brilliant in its simplicity and worked against everything in the hierarchical military forces, where a superior was always giving orders or barking at a junior. Herded into a hangar, loosened up with a bit of beer, the men were left to decide their own crews, and their own fate. The navigators, wireless operators, gunners, bomb aimers, flight engineers, and pilots all milled around. "Nobody told us anything about how to form a crew," remembered Stan Coldridge, who would pilot Halifaxes. "You just sorted it out yourself."[50] Canadian pilot Harlo Jones wrote of the bewildering affair. "I was at somewhat of a loss how to proceed but upon looking around the room I spotted a man wearing a navigator's wing sitting quietly amid the turmoil.... I approached him and asked if he would like to crew up with me." The man agreed and they exchanged names. "We chatted for a moment before being approached by a bomb-aimer, a rather nice looking man who appeared to be twenty-one or twenty-two years old, and we accepted his offer to join us. Within a few minutes we had acquired a wireless operator, Don Howard, from Renfrew, Ontario, and as we stood chatting two rather diminutive but sturdy men approached us.... They were to become our two air gunners, Harold Sharpe from Calgary, and Ralph Syer of Hamilton.... Meanwhile, the other fifty or so types in the room had similarly sorted themselves out. It was a strange experience but it seemed to work out well for most of us."[51]

New families were born and old ones were lost. Walter Irwin came through the BCATP system as a pilot who would later be commissioned as a navigator, and he made good friends throughout the various training schools. But after crewing up, he lost touch with the other flyers, who were sent off to their new squadrons. He regretted that he never "found out who survived the war and who did not."[52] Flight Sergeant George King wrote in a letter to his loved ones in Canada that his fellow bomber crew members "are sure a fine bunch of fellows." The five Canadians and two British airmen were, King felt, "just like brothers."[53] Crews formed a close-knit family, and were further welded together over time by their sharing of danger and reliance upon one another for survival. Like all families, they were not without strife or conflict, but generally their bond allowed for an airman to cope with the relentless stress of combat. Parents, family, girls, community, and national identity were all important—critically so at times—but it was the relationship among the crew that mattered most.

After crewing up, the finishing school was the Heavy Conversion Unit. It was here where the crews were allowed to fly the precious four-engine bombers, Lancasters and Halifaxes. As one awed new Canadian remarked of the Lancaster, "this was an aircraft worthy of one's respect."[54] Pilot Officer Andy Carswell joined the RCAF at eighteen and was overseas the next year. His final training session, which lasted for a month or so, was on the big bombers at a conversion unit. In his words, the other members of the aircrew "sat in the airplane, scared to death while I learned to fly the Lancaster."[55] They survived, although Carswell and his crew were shot down on their fourth operation. There was no easy way to learn how to fly the bombers. Even after months of theoretical lessons and dozens of hours in the air, the training crews suffered a litany of disasters, crashes, and deaths. By the end of the war, Bomber Command lost 47,268 who were flying on operations, while another 8,305 were killed in training or by accident.[56]

Most Canadians who trained in the BCATP and later in England put in at least a year, and some as many as two, before reaching a front-line operation squadron. Sergeant Erle "Dusty" Miller, who had enlisted from the Ottawa Valley in May 1940, wrote after nearly twelve months of instruction with no end in sight, "this place is more like college life than war life."[57] It was estimated that each airman cost about 10,000 British pounds to train, or about two million Canadian dollars today—which made it all the more depressing that many aircrews were killed during their first operation.[58] While one could scarcely imagine better prepared warriors, there was a quantum difference between training and combat. Nothing could prepare the Canadian airmen for the deadly skies over Europe.

CHAPTER 8

THE STRUGGLE TO SURVIVE

"The reputation of the RCN in this war depends on the success or failure of the NEF," wrote Commodore L.W. Murray of the Newfoundland Escort Force (NEF) and its role in protecting the North Atlantic convoys.[1] The mauling of SC 42 in September 1941 was a wake-up call for the RCN. But the endless stream of convoys across the Atlantic, and the need to protect them over the course of that year, meant that the RCN had little time to train its crews. Indeed, officers were hard pressed even to manage regular repairs and maintenance, such as cleaning boilers and repairing rust holes. In October 1941, Captain E.B.K. Stevens warned Murray that "unless very urgent steps can be taken ... I must report that grave danger exists of breakdowns in health, morale and discipline."[2] A month later, Murray received another insistent memorandum from one of his captains that claimed starkly, "RCN corvettes have been given so little chance of becoming efficient that they are almost more of a liability than an asset."[3] The NEF had initially planned for each ship and its crew to have ten to twelve days to recover at the end of a run, but this interval had been chiselled away to only two or three days. Even though the number of Canadian corvettes had risen from thirteen at the beginning of 1941 to sixty-six by the end of the year, Canadian crews were overworked and wearing out from lack of rest and recuperation.[4] Ottawa and London knew the Canadians were being pushed to the limit, but the coming year would afford few opportunities to pull warships from convoy duty and to train crews in the new anti-submarine tactics that had emerged from battle. The Canadians would have to push on as best they could.

The formal entry of the United States into the war after Pearl Harbor compelled Churchill and his senior military staff to go to Washington to draw up a combined strategy for the war against the Axis. Code-named Arcadia, the conference lasted from December 22 to January 14, 1942, and it was where the Anglo-American alliance was forged. To coordinate the multi-front war, the Combined Chiefs of Staff was created to harmonize the western Allies' strategy—with the Russians continuing to fight their own war, almost entirely alone, albeit heavily supplied by the United States, Britain, and Canada. One of the most pressing Allied issues was the coordination of the navies to protect merchant shipping.

In early 1942, more American warships were ordered to the Pacific theatre in the campaign against Japan, leaving the Canadian navy to pick up the slack on the Atlantic seaboard. Convoy protection remained the RCN's primary goal: about three quarters of all Canadian ships were under the NEF's command and serving on the North Atlantic. Yet despite Murray's protests to Ottawa that his ship crews and officers were wearing out, he received little assistance from Naval Service Headquarters. No new destroyers were made available.[5] Notwithstanding the shortages of ships and the overwork of crews, the Canadians tried to follow the Royal Navy's lead by forming semi-permanent escort groups of six warships that would fight and train together with the objective of coordinating effective attacks against U-boats. Creating stable fighting escort groups made sense, and like bomber crews or infantry platoons that forged links of camaraderie through close service and combat, escort groups of half a dozen warships honed their skills in unison. But the constant pressure to support the convoys—which always outnumbered the groups—meant that Canadian ships were repeatedly detached from their own group to serve in another. The ship's crews found themselves at the foot of a steep learning curve, having to adjust to new ships on every convoy—with all the ships' individual strengths and weaknesses, and their different methods of attacking U-boats and defending against them. The lack of a stable working relationship among ships was a major reason the RCN fell behind the Royal Navy in destroying U-boats.

While the Canadian warships struggled to meet the conflicting demands being made of them, they got some help in the form of land-based patrolling aircraft. The RCAF's Lockheed Hudson, which had a patrol range of about 500 kilometres, and the Consolidated Catalina flying boats (and the Canadian version, the Consolidated Canso flying boat), with a longer range of about 700 kilometres (later extended several hundred additional kilometres), provided support in keeping the snapping wolf packs at bay.

Flight Lieutenant Clare Annis, who served in Eastern Air Command and retired as vice-chief of the air staff, remembered, "The RCN was generally most anxious to work with us and although there was a keen rivalry between the Services cooperation was good."[6] The Canadians and Americans also coordinated their patrols, with the experienced Canucks sharing lessons with their American counterparts. In turn, the United States contributed its essential airpower assets, although these dwindled as

The Royal Canadian Navy played a crucial role in protecting the convoys sailing from North America to Britain throughout 1942. Shortages of warships meant that the Canadian sailors were overtaxed in their long voyage across the Atlantic.

the Pacific theatre sucked in all resources, to the point where the American coastal air forces were reduced by the end of the year to just three squadrons. The Canadians had eight.[7]

Patrol aircraft such as the Canso undoubtedly offered a measure of security to the ships below, even though their crews often flew for hours on end without seeing a trace of the enemy. The aircraft initially were equipped with nearly useless radar, leaving many observers joking that the "Mark I eyeball" was the best available method of spotting U-boats. The German subs had a lot of ocean to hide in. Just the same, the vessels were more cautious when weather permitted aircraft to fly. Their captains preferred the easier pickings found outside the aircrafts' range, and they retreated

Maritime airpower kept U-boats from patrolling too close to land. While U-boats tended to dive rapidly when the seaplanes or bombers appeared overhead, a handful of U-boats were sunk or damaged in 1942 from such attacks.

from the coastal waters where any attack that damaged their boat would leave them vulnerable and thousands of kilometres from their bases.

For the Canso or Hudson crews, the aerial patrols meant endless of hours of eye-straining boredom. Whales and schools of fish broke the monotony and quickened the pulse momentarily, but only rarely was the sleek, black hull of a U-boat encountered. Sentries on board the subs were on the lookout too. When they saw the Allied flying boats, they shouted out a warning and scuttled into the boat as the captain ordered a crash dive. U-boats could disappear in thirty seconds—not much time for their pursuers to react. Aboard the Canso, the crew also jumped to action, manning machine guns and preparing the depth charges. The U-boats usually got away, but they fled for their lives, knowing that over the next few hours, Allied planes and, depending on their location, other Allied warships, would criss-cross the area dropping depth charges in what might turn out to be a lengthy and terrifying time for the U-boat caught in the dragnet.

One of Eastern Air Command's No. 10 Squadron crews, piloted by Squadron Leader Norville Small, engaged a U-boat on April 28, 1942, dropping two depth charges about fifteen seconds after the sub dived. Oil and debris floated to the surface, but it was not a lethal blow. Small admitted as much in his report: "The captain of the aircraft feels that though the possibility of a clean kill is not very strong, he is certain that he definitely made their back teeth rattle."[8] Three months later, Small—now commander of the new No. 113 Bomber Reconnaissance Squadron—led his Lockheed Hudson (its bottom painted white to make it difficult for the U-boat spotters to locate)—back to the ocean for Eastern Air Command's first kill. On July 31, his Canso caught *U-754* on the surface and bracketed it with depth charges as it attempted to dive.[9] A few seconds later the U-boat broke the surface of the water, and Small's Hudson machine-gunned the vessel. The U-boat sank beneath the waves again, and Small witnessed an underwater explosion and oil swirl up to the surface.

No. 113 Squadron had twelve additional depth charge attacks on U-boats from June to November 1942. No other U-boats were confirmed as kills, but all were wary of the aerial threat. Small was an inspired and resourceful leader, and in the late fall of 1942 he moved back to No. 10 Squadron at Gander, Newfoundland, which was re-equipping with Cansos. U-boat packs were known to be hovering beyond aircraft range in the Black Pit east of Newfoundland. Small encouraged his crews to strip the Cansos of excess weight by removing everything that might be considered extraneous from the planes, even welded-down equipment. Thus lightened, the Cansos extended their range from about 700 to 1,000 kilometres, which enabled them to launch several attacks against U-boats caught on the surface as they recharged batteries and ventilated the interior.[10] Small led by example and took the same risks as his men; he and his crew were killed in a January 1943 accident when, in the interest of providing convoy protection, he pushed his Canso's range and endurance too far, and his plane did not return from a patrol.

A steady increase in the number of Cansos and other aircraft throughout 1942 allowed the air force to provide more frequent patrols. Allied intelligence—using Ultra and other sources—also became increasingly adept at directing convoys away from U-boat-infested areas, and aircraft towards them. The system was enhanced over time, and bombers could be put into the air in fifteen minutes when intelligence relayed the U-boat's coordinates. There remained an enormous ocean to cover, but it helped to know where to look.

The aerial defenders would have been more effective had they been equipped with long-range bombers like the type used to hammer German cities. However, these were jealously guarded by Bomber Command and the politicians, all the way up to Churchill, who wished to reserve them as an offensive weapon to strike Germany and also appease the growing demands of Stalin for assistance in drawing off enemy strength.[11] This prime example of inter-service rivalry was damning for the Admiralty in its desperate battle throughout 1942 and much of 1943 to close the Black Pit, which remained, as RCN officer Thomas Pullen observed, "where the fighting and the killing was the heaviest."[12] It could have been closed with the assignment to Coastal Command of forty or fifty four-engine long-range bombers outfitted with extra fuel tanks. While Churchill wrote in his postwar memoirs, "The only thing that ever really frightened me was the U-boat peril," at the time he declined to allocate the resources needed to fight that battle.[13] This was one of Churchill's great strategic errors in the war, although also an indication of the enormous pressure on the prime minister to show the British people and his ally, Stalin, that Britain could still hit back. Nonetheless, thousands of lives were lost as the U-boats ravaged the convoys.

THE OVERSTRETCHED NEWFOUNDLAND ESCORT FORCE was renamed the Mid-Ocean Escort Force (MOEF) in February 1942. To increase efficiency, the Atlantic convoys were directed along a more southward crossing, right through the German U-boat concentrations, because the northern route near Iceland added extra days to the journey and left too many ships damaged by the harsh weather. The MOEF was also ordered to protect the convoys along the entire Atlantic route, from Newfoundland's Grand Banks to Ireland, thereby eliminating the need to hand off in the mid-Atlantic, which had proven to be challenging as convoys missed their rendezvous and stragglers caused delays. The final destination was Londonderry, Northern Ireland, a 2,800-kilometre run from Newfoundland. Canadian sailor James Lamb recounted that the layovers, short as they were, were not purely rest stops. The worn-out crews had to use the time to "refuel, load food and ammunition for the return voyage, and attempt to repair and maintain their battered ship and armament." The reorganization of the convoy system meant that the Canadian crews had to quicken their turnaround in port in order to get on to the next convoy. "It was like a continuing bad dream," wrote Lamb, "an endless round of misery and hardship and strain which tested officers and men, but above all, captains, to the limits of human endurance, and sometimes beyond."[14]

The strain on the RCN only increased in early 1942. New U-boats were being manufactured at the rate of twenty a month, and Dönitz shifted additional U-boats from the Mediterranean to North American waters in order to catch inexperienced American crews in their vulnerable vessels. Fourteen U-boats were also sent to Canadian waters in early January 1942 and, over the next two months, they sank about two dozen merchant ships. The numbers would have been higher if the RCN had not reacted so aggressively to the threat. By mid-January the navy had established inshore convoys for ships travelling between east coast ports, especially Halifax, Sydney, and St. John's. Air patrols also were increased, which made enemy daylight operations dangerous. While no U-boats were sunk in Canadian waters, the German captains were shaken by both the terrible weather and the stepped-up defensive measures, and soon opted to take their boats further south for easier pickings and warmer climates. The Americans made things easy because they had not yet introduced coastal convoys or city blackouts. In March and April, 125 ships were

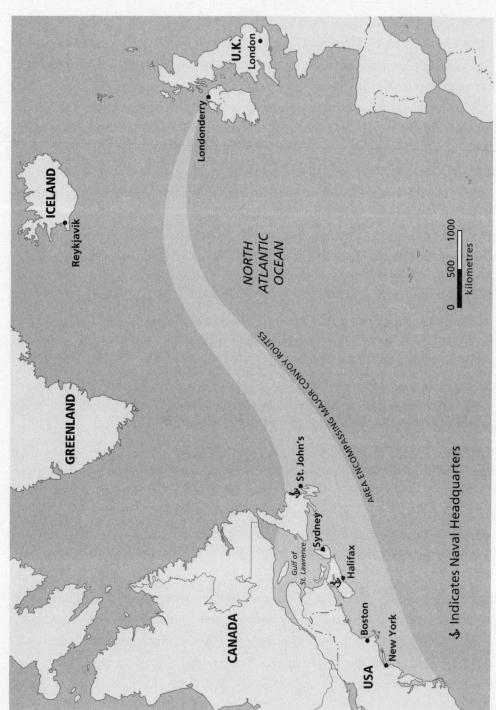

THE NORTH ATLANTIC, 1939–1945

sunk in American waters in what the U-boat captains described as "the American turkey shoot."[15]

Despite the steady loss of merchant ships in its home waters, the United States refused to redirect its forces away from the Pacific. The Canadians shuddered at the southern slaughter, and in March 1942 they acted to assist the hard-pressed Americans. And so began the Triangle Run, in which Canadian corvettes, supplemented by smaller Bangor-class minesweepers pressed into ocean service because nothing else was available, escorted vessels from Boston, and later New York, to Halifax. From there, an inshore convoy took the vessels to east of Newfoundland where they were handed over to the Mid-Ocean Escort Force, which then took the convoy across the Atlantic. At St. John's, Newfoundland, the corvettes picked up newly arrived merchant ships coming from Britain and guided them back to one of the US ports. Even though the Canadian escorts groups were relatively weak, the U-boats tended to avoid armed vessels, and they drifted even further south in April and May, where large oil tankers emerged unguarded from Caribbean waters. The RCN's experience and expertise saved dozens, perhaps hundreds, of merchant ships in North American waters. However, the introduction of the Triangle Run further diluted the strength of the Canadian navy, which remained hard pressed to meet its multiple commitments.

IN THE MIDST OF THESE GRIM DEVELOPMENTS, in the summer of 1942, the RCN pulled one of its new corvettes, *Montcalm*, from active duty in a venture to raise the profile of the Canadian navy, its ships, and its sailors. The National Film Board had produced several short films related to the navy early in the war in its popular *Canada Carries On* series, and now, with *Montcalm* providing the backdrop, the service received star treatment. Hollywood's Universal Pictures produced the film *Corvette K-225*, in which a Canadian captain—played by Randolph Scott, an American actor known chiefly for westerns—and his crew struggled against the odds in the harsh North Atlantic. The credits concluded with an expression of fine fighting sentiments: "She will carry on, and those who come after her, for her name is legion, and the legend of her and of those who fight in her is an inspiration for all men who believe in courage and hope."[16] The RCN received a much-needed boost in its public profile.

Many of the imperial naval officers looked down on the Canadian civilian-sailors as rowdy, uncontrollable, and ill-disciplined frontiersmen who were out of place in the "Senior Service."[17] Commander Frank Layard, a Canadian regular force officer serving in the RN, was occasionally embarrassed by the behaviour of Canadian sailors and officers who refused to follow strict naval traditions, but he was equally discomfited by the anti-Canadian attitude so often adopted by British officers. After watching *Corvette K-225*, Layard wrote in his diary that it was "very good," but it "depicted something so entirely different from the RN as to be almost completely unrecognizable. But of course the RCN is very different."[18]

Some Royal Navy officers and NCOs delighted in calling the Canadians "colonials," implying they were inferior in bearing and performance. Such snubs and sneers were also experienced by Canadian flyers and soldiers, and had been as far back as the Great War and before, when Canadians served in South Africa. Imperial condescension was especially prevalent in the Royal Navy, however, with its iron-clad traditions and hidebound unwillingness to accommodate national differences. Some Canadian officers, and especially the professionals, contributed to the problem, as they sought to emulate all things British, even the RN's class-based discipline, which made for such a wide gap between officers and enlisted men.[19] While the RCN was hardly democratic, insofar as officers gave orders that were to be followed without question by lower ranks, it was widely acknowledged that the atmosphere was more relaxed on Canadian warships—and especially corvettes—than on their British counterparts. "Most of us, officers and men, spoke with about the same accent and, for the most part, came from similar social backgrounds and basic schooling," wrote L.B. Jenson. "Our war went on for years in small, crowded and uncomfortable ships on one of the roughest, coldest and most soul-destroying stretches of ocean in the world, the North Atlantic. I have often wondered if some of us should have been a bit more 'Canadian' instead of trying to be so 'pusser' and British."[20] The RCN automatically turned to the RN for its traditions and guidance, but over the course of the war a distinctly Canadian identity emerged.

Each Canadian warship had its own personality. The naming of ships was important, and unlike the United States and Britain, Canada avoided naming ships after military, national, or political figures, except in the case of the interwar destroyers *Champlain* and *Vancouver*.[21] The British took a different tack when they named their

Flower Class corvettes (logically enough) after flowers, a practice that saw U-boats chased by the likes of HMS *Buttercup*. Canadian corvettes, in contrast, were linked to cities, which reinforced the notion that this was a citizen navy. Cities such as Moose Jaw and Verdun adopted their namesake ships (in the case of Verdun, the rejigged name of HMCS *Dunver*), and patriotic groups sent the sailors presents and care packages. Strong links developed between the fighting ships and the communities that supported them.[22] Quesnel, British Columbia, was honoured to have a corvette named after the village, and the municipal clerk advised the minister of national defence in April 1943 that "the citizens of this town have made numerous gifts to the officers and crew of this Corvette." These gifts included knitted socks, sweaters, and a "large quantity of smokes."[23] The destroyer HMCS *Ottawa* was adopted by its namesake city, and the mayor donated a piano to the ship, which, according to sailor Cliff Ashton, led to many nights of "bawdy songs or chanties."[24]

The gun shields of Canadian warships were decorated with creative imagery. This one, from HMCS Calgary, *featured a sailor mounted on a shark and blazing away with his pistol.*

A unique Canadian identity was also revealed in the ships' gun-shield art. Comical, aggressive, or lewd, these unofficial insignia, which never would have been allowed in the RN, reflected the distinctive character of the ships and their Canadian crews, which invariably included an amateur or even professional artist. Disney characters were popular, as were scantily clad women, but many ships' crews embraced even more creative imagery. HMCS *Calgary* featured a sailor riding a shark, firing off his six-shooter, while HMCS *Moose Jaw*'s crest showed a fire-breathing moose chasing a fleeing Hitler. HMCS *Wetaskiwin*'s insignia was a classic: it portrayed a queen, her legs outstretched, sitting in a pool of water, a visual play on the ship's name: the "Wet Ass Queen." These crests, wrote one corvette captain, "would have been the despair of the Royal College of Heralds, [but] were nonetheless lively, if not down-right lurid."[25] A green Maple Leaf funnel badge, displayed in the last two years of the war, was perhaps the most emblematic symbol of this emerging sense of identity.

AS AMERICAN AND CANADIAN DEFENCES tightened up along the eastern seaboard, Dönitz ordered his U-boats to push southward into the Caribbean to attack tankers carrying crude oil from Venezuela and Colombia. The oil was the lifeblood of the war industries of the United States and Canada, and by early April 1942 the U-boats were wreaking havoc on the vulnerable tankers. Later that month, the United States panicked when seventy-nine ships were lost in the Gulf of Mexico and off Florida, all but cutting off the supply of fuel and oil to Canada.[26] The Americans announced a retreat, declaring a temporary moratorium on allowing tankers to head north. Vice-Admiral Percy Nelles, after being urged on by the King government, decided to intervene. "To hell with that," he said, "we'll get our own."[27] And they did. A number of corvettes were peeled off from northern convoy runs to head south and guard the tankers. They ran through fiercely contested waters, but took their charges past the lurking U-boats and back to Canada. While the convoys were weak—only a hand-ful of corvettes and limited air cover—they were better than nothing. The Halifax to Trinidad run was one of the most successful of the entire war: the RCN guided vessels from May to July without losing a single one of their thirty-seven charges.[28]

The escorts continued after that, although at a less desperate pace. One notable surface engagement took place on August 28, when the corvette HMCS *Oakville* engaged *U-94* after it had been brought to the surface by depth charge attacks from an American PBY flying boat. Closing the distance rapidly, *Oakville's* 4-inch guns raked the submarine on the surface, eventually blowing away the enemy's main deck gun, and then ramming and shattering its hull with depth charges. As the Germans prepared to abandon their boat, Lieutenant Hal Lawrence and a single comrade, Petty Officer A.J. Powell, leapt to the enemy deck and scrambled down into its bowels. They shot a few of the enemy sailors who were slow to surrender, and led the rest topside off the listing vessel. Though he was unable to recover the logbook, Lawrence was awarded the Distinguished Service Cross and later immortalized in one of the "Men of Valor" Canadian propaganda posters. The sinking marked another Canadian victory in foreign waters.[29]

Canadian warships escorted oil-carrying tankers out of the Caribbean over the summer of 1942 and ensured that the lifeblood of industry was not cut off by enemy U-boats.

By that point, however, the war had come to Canada. U-boats slipped into the St. Lawrence River in May. The river was the key Canadian inland waterway: more than a quarter of Canadian shipping carried goods to and from the cities, towns, villages, and shipyards that dotted the edges of the artery. For some time the navy had anticipated U-boat incursions into the target-rich water, and had planned an elaborate defence, but most of the warships the plan required had been siphoned off in previous months for more pressing duties.

During the early hours of May 12, *U-553* slid into the St. Lawrence and sank two steamers that were sailing unescorted to Halifax, where they were to join up in a convoy to cross the Atlantic. Government censors tried to cover up the losses, but as survivors were picked up by local fishermen and bodies washed up along shore, soon the red-pen brigade could do little to kill the story.[30] Wild rumours fed fear and speculation. Canadian warships rushed into the waters, hoping to catch the enemy sub, but warm freshwater from the St. Lawrence and cold saltwater from the Gulf met and created layers that interfered with asdic. U-boats could rest easily in the stratified waters, nearly undetectable until they rose at night to recharge their batteries. Eastern Air Command scrambled most of its fifty available aircraft, but they had the nearly impossible task of patrolling some 140,000 square kilometres of water. Over the following five months, from May to September, Eastern Air Command aircraft made seven attacks on U-boats, and several more on unfortunate whales, but no U-boats were destroyed in the St. Lawrence.[31]

In early July, *U-132* went for the Canadian jugular. A number of ships were sunk while travelling in convoy. The thin veneer of protection had been pierced, both in reality and perception. Ships exploding at night in the heart of Canada led to another round of screaming editorials to the effect that the nation was under Nazi attack. It was, but the hysterical reaction was disproportionate to the operational loss. Corvettes and aircraft renewed the search for the enemy boats, but their task remained exceedingly difficult. The Canadians were fighting blind. The Germans, on the other hand, had acquired a new technological advantage. The U-boats were now equipped with the Funkmessbeobachtung 1 radar detector, which allowed them to intercept Allied radar transmissions and steer away from danger.[32] The radar detector worked only on certain wavelengths, but these, unfortunately, were the ones employed by most Canadian warships. This was an advantage enjoyed by the U-boats over the RCN, but not over the Royal Navy, which operated on different wavelengths.

The losses mounted throughout July and August, as more emboldened U-boats gathered at the mouth of the St. Lawrence for their prey to come to them. On August 27, *U-517* sank the American troopship *Chatham*, although only 13 of the 562 passengers were lost because the vessel sank slowly. Even warships were not safe. The efficient killer, *U-517*, ambushed HMCS *Charlottetown*, sending two torpedoes into its hull on September 11, a year and a day after it was launched. The corvette was mortally wounded, but most of the sixty-four crew got off the ship before the sea

Flower Class corvette HMCS Charlottetown *was sunk by* U-517 *on September 11, 1942, in the St. Lawrence River.*

closed around it. As *Charlottetown* went down to its grave, the ship's depth charges exploded. The shock waves killed several sailors in the water.

The attacks created anxiety in Quebec. Rumours and accusations proliferated to the effect that the federal government was deliberately denuding defences to punish the province for its perceived lacklustre support of the war effort. A divisive plebiscite held in April 1942 by the King government had asked all Canadians to release the government from its promise never to impose overseas conscription. English Canada voted decisively in favour of the resolution, while Quebec was adamantly opposed. The wily and fearful King privately hoped that the U-boat attacks would spur Quebeckers to accept the plebiscite's outcome. However, there was little give in Quebec, and even limited conscription remained deeply unpopular. King had a mandate to bring in conscription, and was being urged aggressively to do so by his obstinate defence minister, J.L. Ralston, but the prime minister refused to enact conscription until he absolutely had to. From his lips sprang one of the most famous political utterances in Canadian history: "Not necessarily conscription, but conscription if necessary." Now, as so often, King played for time.

But something had to give. On September 9, the RCN was further weakened when the King government agreed to the Admiralty's request for Canada to send sixteen of its corvettes (and one British corvette) to assist in the protection of troops for Operation Torch, the amphibious invasion of North Africa, set for early November 1942.[33] While no Canadian army formations would be involved in the forced landing, the Dominion again sacrificed its own naval forces for the greater Allied good. U-boats still were hunting in Canadian waters, and the RCN would have even fewer resources with which to meet the threat. It was the final straw. On the same day, the King government made the painful decision to close commercial traffic on the St. Lawrence. The action, which seemed drastic when it was taken, hurt trade, but not as much as was expected, as the decision was made late in the shipping season and other ports handled much of the diverted traffic.[34] Nevertheless, Canadians viewed the RCN as having suffered a serious defeat.

That perception was compounded on October 13 when the Newfoundland railway ferry SS *Caribou* sailed from Sydney harbour in a 180-kilometre night passage to Port aux Basques, Newfoundland. On the moonless night, *U-69* stalked the ferry, manoeuvring itself for hours until it had the perfect shot. It fired at a distance of 650 metres at 3:21 A.M., while most of the crew and passengers were slumbering. The torpedo ripped through the hull and, minutes later, the ferry's boilers blew up. The broken ship plunged into the freezing water, and of the 237 passengers and crew, which included civilians and military personnel, only 101 survived.[35] Among the dead were 10 children and 18 women. The terrible loss of *Caribou* was the grim capstone to the RCN's failure to protect the river and the surrounding water ways.

The Battle of the St. Lawrence had witnessed a frustrating and fearful season of losses: 21 ships were sunk and many others damaged. Close to 300 sailors perished. And not a single U-boat was sunk. For Canadians, it appeared to be an unmitigated disaster. The great irony of the battle is that, without access to German records, the RCN and Eastern Air Command had no way of knowing how successfully they had harassed and intimidated the Germans, who were eventually driven out of the Gulf, having exacted a relatively light toll. Air patrols by the Canso flying boats were particularly effective in forcing the subs to submerge in sudden terror.[36] The RCN's strength was, as always, in prevention rather than profile-raising sub-killing.[37] The latter was more glamorous, but the former was what would eventually win the Battle of the Atlantic.

REAR ADMIRAL LEONARD MURRAY offered generous praise late in the war for the merchant navy: "The very outcome of the war depended on those embattled, rust-streaked ships sailing through the long, bitter years. The real

This poster celebrates the heroics of the Merchant Navy, described here as the "Fourth Arm of the Service." It reads, in part, "Men of Valor, They fight for you."

heroes were the merchant seamen who sailed them. They hung on and stuck it out during the dark days when they were subjected to fierce attacks against which there was only the lightest defence."[38] Echoing Murray's generous sentiment, Canadian newspapers, politicians, and sailors took to calling the merchant mariners the "fourth arm" of the military in the war against Hitler.

Before the war, Canada was a seafaring nation, but it was not a mercantile power. In 1939, it had only thirty-seven ocean-going merchant ships. The two largest companies were Canadian National Steamships Company and Imperial Oil Steamships, although new ships built in the rejuvenated Canadian shipyards and captured vessels were soon added to the registry. Canadian shipyards produced two types of cargo ships: the first, named for forts, at 4,700 tons, and the second, named after parks, displaced 10,000 tons. The Park ships—flat-bottomed, slab-sided, enormous vessels—began to sail in 1942 and were the more numerous of the two. Canadian mariners also served in all manner of vessels from other nations, which was the source of one of the challenges officials had in tracking their number during and after the war. By war's end, about 12,000 deep-sea Canadian merchant seamen served on ships, and Canada launched 354 10,000-ton and 43 4,700-ton vessels. The new Crown corporation, the Park Steamship Company, incorporated in April 1942, coordinated the movement of 183 of the merchant vessels produced in Canada during the course of the war.[39]

With these new ships came the need for new sailors. Most of the professional mariners came from coastal steamers, tugboats, and the established fishing fleets, and these experienced seamen were augmented by those with minor physical debilities, especially poor eyesight, who had been turned down by the military and still sought to do their bit for the war effort. Earl Wagner was one who had been denied entry into the RCN for being underage at fifteen: "There were those people like myself who were rejected, too young.... I was called up later on, but I was in the merchant navy so they didn't take me anyway."[40] An analysis of a large number of mariners found that most came from small towns and villages in rural Canada, especially Nova Scotia and Quebec.[41] There was also the usual assortment of ne'er-do-wells, alcoholics, and men running away from their lives, mixed up with those seeking adventure and a steady paycheque, as well as underage boys and men aching to serve the Allied war effort.

Even though the merchant navy and its supplies were one of the essential keys to victory, the mariners rarely received the same respect as the sailors of the RCN. Captain Earl Wagner survived the Battle of the Atlantic as a merchant seaman, first sailing at age eighteen. Sixty years later, he bristled at how he and his comrades were mistreated because of "damned myths!" The merchant mariners were, it was believed by many, "over-paid, over-sexed, undisciplined, mercenaries."[42] "I got paid $45 a month and they put a 35 percent war bonus on top of that," recounted Wagner.[43] This was far from a king's ransom, although the issue of pay was complicated, and often mariners aboard ships carrying explosives received added danger pay.[44] Rumours circulated that the merchant mariners received enormous sums for their dangerous work, but comparisons suggest that while the mariners made a little more than the ordinary seamen in the service, senior RCN officers received more generous compensation than their equivalents on the merchant ships. Moreover, the mariners had to pay income tax, unlike servicemen, which increasingly ate into their paycheques.[45] But the perception of rich rewards for high danger was widely held at the time and in the war's aftermath. An undercurrent of angry rumour was directed against the merchant seamen who were accused of dodging their responsibility in serving the nation. After the conscription crises of 1942 and 1944, the mariners were sometimes denigrated as freeloading and unpatriotic for their "limited" service.[46] The merchant seamen's lack of a uniform—in all but a few cases—seemed to confirm that they were not another of the service arms, but instead civilians looking to profit in the war zone. For decades after the war, Canadian merchant seamen were denied veteran status and most forms of government compensation.

BRITAIN'S MAIN LIFELINE was from North America, but convoys sailed from around the world, and in all theatres of war. Outward-bound, the ships sat deep in the water as their elephantine hulls were crammed with food, munitions, and all the supplies that were required to keep the island kingdom in the war. The 9,140-ton American Liberty ships, of which some 2,751 were produced during the war, had a cargo-carrying capacity slightly less than that of the Canadian-made Parks, but they could still transport an astonishing 2,840 jeeps, 440 light tanks, or 3,440,000 daily rations.[47] Each ship that was sunk by the U-boats stopped this critical materiel from reaching British citizens or Allied fighting forces. Each ship that made it through the torpedo gauntlet allowed the Allies to fight for another day. Imports to Britain in 1940 had been 38.1 million tons. They fell in 1941 to 27.7 million and in 1942 to 20.8 million.[48] Had the figure fallen much lower, the Nazis would have achieved their aim of strangling the British war effort.

The merchant navy relied on the warships for their protection. Angus McDonald left high school to enlist in the merchant marine, and he remembered the vulnerability of the civilian vessels in the convoy, and their need to rely on the protective warships: "We were just like sheep, surrounded by these little sheepdogs.... They had pretty sharp teeth! So we in the merchant navy had a lot of respect for both the Royal Canadian Navy and the Royal Navy."[49] In turn, the crews of the warships were impressed by the quiet courage of the mariners. "The merchant seamen," recounted Roy Ernest Eddy of HMCS *Outremont*, "were the heroes of the war. They'd get sunk so many times, they'd go back and have a recuperation period and, first thing you know, they'd be on another ship."[50] Corvette commander Alan Easton spoke of the ships he guarded in U-boat-infested waters: "It was the merchant seamen who took the real onslaught of the enemy at sea. Their ships could hardly fight back against the elusive submarine and, due to their ponderous bulk, could not manoeuvre quickly to avoid the attacker.... The men who lived in these ships could not have been unaware of their vulnerability. They pushed their ships along, never knowing when they would be singled out for extinction."[51]

Joseph Dempsey, an RCN seaman attached as a DEMS (Defensively Equipped Merchant Ship) gunner to a civilian ship, recounted that he and his fellow trained gunners "got along great with the merchant seamen."[52] There were nearly 1,600 DEMS gunners on merchant ships in the war, with one of them, Douglas Baird, writing, "The gunners manned literally anything that could float and carry a gun, whether in convoy or sailing independently."[53] Small ships might have a single combatant at watch with an old Lewis machine gun, while more modern vessels, like the Park steamships, often had numerous armed sailors operating multiple gun platforms, including a 12-pounder, a 4-inch gun, and seven Oerlikon heavy machine guns to protect against dive-bombers. They offered at least some protection against the U-boats, and the larger ships could throw down significant firepower, even though it was an uneven fight at the best of times. DEMS gunner Max Reid believed that he and his fellow armed seamen were there primarily to provide "psychological comfort to the merchant seamen on board, particularly when sailing independently."[54]

"We are asking a lot of the morale of an inexperienced crew, to expect them to be happy, and remain fighting fit and aggressive," wrote one concerned RCN officer of the merchant mariners. "It should also be remembered that this fortitude is being expected from men who have seen gasoline tankers disintegrate in five seconds, less than half a mile away from them, and who have been through the harrowing experience of seeing men with lights on their shoulders bobbing up and down in the water and shouting for help."[55] Week after week, stricken vessels limped into harbour in the United Kingdom and along the North American seaboard, great jagged holes in them from torpedo blasts, or lashed from the cruel North Atlantic. Or they never arrived at all, lost to the depths. However, most did survive the deadly struggle with the enemy. From 1940 to 1945, 7,357 merchant ships left Canadian ports, carrying 41,480,161 tons of cargo.[56] And while the vast majority of merchant ships—some 99 out of 100 that sailed—made it to their destination, the odds of surviving were far more grim in the first three and a half years of the war, when several thousand merchant ships were torpedoed and defeat seemed the likely destination on the horizon.[57]

EACH SAILOR KNEW that his ship might fall victim at any moment during the long journey across the Atlantic. "We went to bed with one eye open and a life jacket," remembered Jack Smith.[58] Mariners ran through their ship's evacuation plan over and over again in their minds. "Every night you went out you never knew if you were comin' back," recounted Jack Matthews. "I was lucky if I did get an hour or two sleep at night."[59] "Your whole thinking changed with the cargo," wrote another experienced merchant mariner. "If you were carrying foodstuffs you had a little better feeling. Wheat or general cargo, you had a pretty good chance of getting away [if the ship was hit by a torpedo]. If you were carrying ore, once you were hit you just went plop, straight down. Those guys that were carrying this casing oil and hydrochloric acid and sulphuric acid—10,000 tons of that—how do you think they felt? A lot of them as a result of that became heavy drinkers."[60]

It was estimated that fewer than 50 percent of the merchant crews ever survived a torpedo attack. They were either killed in their bunks or at their stations from the initial explosion, blown apart when their cargo ignited, or unable to scramble out of the dead ship as it sank quickly into the deep.[61] Imagine the terror of those final minutes: racing minds pushing back against panic, as searching hands tried to negotiate the pitch-black corridors of the ship, praying for an exit from the steel coffin. These were pathways that had been travelled thousands of times, but never in inky darkness, with adrenaline surging and, as water rushed into the ship, in a frantic race against time.

Those who made it to the deck had little time to take stock of their chances. In those desperate last moments, men who kept their heads threw on extra layers of clothes and a life jacket. Another jacket or a heavy sweater kept warmth in the body but would weigh a man down, and so a life jacket was essential to keep him buoyant. But none of this mattered in the dead of winter, when going into the water was a death sentence. Even in the summer, the North Atlantic water was bone-chilling. Bill Nelligan, who served five and a half years on the North Atlantic and had one of his ships torpedoed, recounted that within seconds of immersion, "Your limbs would start to go numb and your heart would be jumping."[62] To survive even initially, a man had to swim like mad away from the ship, because the suction from its sinking could pull a sailor to his doom. If he survived all of the trials, he had to find his way, usually in the dark, into a small boat or Carley float. Time permitting, these crafts and floats were launched from the ship before it was claimed by the ocean, and this gave the sailors a fighting chance of being rescued.

"Be harsh," Admiral Dönitz said to his U-boat captains when he learned that some collected survivors against his orders. "Remember that the enemy takes no regard of women and children in his bombing attacks on German cities."[63] Allied ships similarly were ordered to steam ahead rather than break convoy ranks. "We could never stop to pick up the survivors," recollected merchant mariner Elwyn Elliot.[64] A ship that was immobile was an easy target for U-boats. William P. Vradenburg, who enlisted in May 1944 in the RCNVR and saw action later in the year, described the first time he witnessed the death of a torpedoed merchant ship. From the mess deck he heard two muffled explosions. He raced up on deck, unsure of what to do. The skipper saw the milling crowd of scared sailors and told them, "No sweat! Nobody's got a[n] [asdic] trace. We're not going to action stations right now." They steamed on. "This was, I think, one of the first times I ever realized that, when a ship got torpedoed, the escorts do not go over and pick up anybody.... We did not talk about it.... If you went over the side, mister, you were for the fish."[65]

While the convoy could not stop, generally a rescue boat would be dropped out of line and, after the warships chased off the U-boats, begin the search for survivors. Seventeen-year-old Paul Bender of the merchant navy sailed on *Nailsea Moor*, a rescue ship in several convoys, and he was shaken by the state of the survivors, many of whom "were injured, some quite horribly. After picking up the living, or near living, we then picked up body parts which might be identified so that next-of-kin could be informed."[66] Despite the nature of their task, the rescue ships were also targets for

Canadian sailors being rescued on the North Atlantic. Many sailors were not so lucky and died from exposure or dehydration.

the U-boats when they slowed to gather the scattered survivors. During the course of the war, 29 dedicated rescue ships saved more than 4,000 sailors on the high seas.[67]

In the long wait for the arrival of the rescue boat or other vessels, heavy seas might carry a Carley float or life craft out of the path of friendly ships, and hours at the mercy of the sea could see survivors alive but with little hope of rescue as they drifted kilometres from the initial sinking. In their boats or rafts, they huddled together for warmth and human contact. As the injured slowly succumbed to their wounds, the dead were sometimes stripped of their clothes so that others might add layers to their own. If the rafts or lifeboats were properly stocked with food and water, the survivors could survive for weeks, but that simply prolonged the agony of an end through dehydration or exposure. Many lifeboats were found months later carrying sun-shrivelled corpses. It was a long, lonely, and agonizing death.

For those in the water or in lifeboats, there was indescribable relief when a ship was sighted on the horizon, and men yelled themselves hoarse to draw its attention. As the rescue ships or returning warships drew near, scramble nets were lowered down the side for survivors to come aboard, although this ascent also was fraught with danger. The wet nets were not easy to navigate at the best of times, and for those suffering from wounds, hypothermia, or simply caked in bunker fuel, the climb of 7 to 10 metres to the top was nearly impossible. It was heartbreaking for those on the ship to watch as exhausted men slipped back into the water, sometimes to be crushed by the lifeboat against the ship's hull or, even more ghastly, to be dragged into the ship's screws and torn apart. It was not unknown for sympathetic sailors on board to shimmy down the ropes to carry up the helpless, but there was always a rush against time. Most sailors had witnessed incidents in which the water was just too rough to make a safe transfer, and had seen survivors marooned in the lifeboats, unable to take the final steps to safety. Keith Shufelt, who enlisted when he was nineteen in January 1941 and served on HMCS *Lachine*, remembered when his captain, anxious because U-boats were thought to be lurking in the vicinity, left some of the sailors in lifeboats to their fate: "It was quite horrifying, and I had many nightmares."[68]

Making it aboard ship did not mark the end of the ordeal. The wretchedly tired and cold men plucked from the sea frequently suffered from exposure and hypothermia. The worst cases had blackened, frost-bitten limbs that usually became infected with gangrene and had to be amputated. Almost all who had spent time in the water were covered in thick bunker oil that clung to hair and clothes like tar. "I saw men die as a result of heavy fuel oil clogging their beards and choking them," wrote Allan Stevens.[69] Harry Boyd, who served on two corvettes and rescued many seamen during the course of the war, remembered that in some cases, "Mouth, nose and everything else were sealed up with oil. Sometimes the lips came off when they cut through."[70] Jeffry Brock, another long-service veteran of the Atlantic, recalled that "many survivors pulled from the sea were so filled up and choked with bunker fuel oil that they did not last long.... These memories come back to haunt."[71] Help often came too late or was not enough, even though crews provided those they picked up with blankets, clothes, rum, and medical attention.

A photograph of the survivors of *Lady Hawkins*, the Canadian National Steamships Ltd passenger ship torpedoed on January 19, 1942, provides stark testimony to the resilience required of the mariners during the Battle of the Atlantic.[72] Carrying 2,908 tons of general cargo and 322 passengers and crew members, the unescorted ship was hit by *U-66* with two torpedoes, and it sank in 30 minutes about 240 kilometres from Cape Hatteras, off the American eastern seaboard. There were 71 survivors. The photograph captures 15 of the mariners staring into the camera, their faces filled with relief. The gaunt seamen look weather-blasted. The survivors—mainly merchant mariners, but also a family with a three-year-old girl—had lived for five days in an open 20-metre lifeboat before they were picked up by SS *Coamo*. They had faced the sea and won. Many of them had been torpedoed before, but five days in an open boat on the ocean was enough to break men. Yet

Thick bunker oil from a sunk vessel coats this sailor.

one of the merchant mariners stares defiantly at the camera. He holds up his fingers in a victory sign. It is also the cockney gesture for "up yours." Both sentiments were in ample evidence among the crew of *Lady Hawkins*, and the thousands of others of the merchant navy, who, despite being targets for the U-boats, remained unbowed.

Defiant survivors of Lady Hawkins.

CHAPTER 9

STRIKING BACK

Flying Officer Charlie Hancock and his bomber crew discovered that no accommodations had been made for them when they arrived at the Royal Canadian Air Force base at Linton-on-Ouse, Yorkshire, to serve with No. 408 Squadron. "On the first night I slept in a bed used the night before by a member of the Jones crew, which had not returned from operations," he recounted. "It felt a bit creepy, but it would happen again and one had to get used to it."[1] The dead were a heavy presence as bomber crews took off each night and disappeared into the darkness. New flyers like Hancock were there to replace the vanished.

RCAF Wireless Operator Howard Hewer also wrote of finally arriving at RAF Station Marham in August 1941 to serve with No. 218 Squadron. He had spent months training and he felt ready for battle. He and his crew were greeted by a cheerful squadron commanding officer, who told them, "The glamour period is over. You got in for a penny, but now you're in for the pound." The officer concluded his talk with a stark prediction: "I think it is only fair to tell you that casualties in this command have been high, and that they are on the rise as we make more and more flights further into Germany. I must tell you then that many of you will not be with us a few weeks or a month from now." Hewer left the talk feeling sick. The next day, he was even more disturbed when the squadron medical officer lectured the crew on the terrible nature of burns that were so common to airmen. He offered some useful observations to the new flyers, but concluded fatalistically: "I hope it doesn't happen to any of you, but in the event that you find yourself trapped in a burning aircraft, with no chance of escape, best to get things over with in a hurry.

What I suggest you might do is lean directly over the flames, open your mouth, and inhale strongly. The fire should scorch the lungs and cause almost instant death, much preferable to burning slowly. Well, good luck chaps."[2] These types of warnings to new airmen were not meant to unnecessarily scare, but were simply part of the harsh reality of flying in a bomber: the life expectancy of new crews could be measured in weeks.

WHILE THE BOMBERS COST tens of thousands of dollars each, the high command had little inclination to spend lavishly on the bases that were being built across eastern Britain. Some were prewar RAF stations, featuring winterized multi-storey facilities and established messes, but many were wartime throw-ups, which meant corrugated iron huts for the crews' living quarters and for rest and relaxation. The huts were poorly insulated and were heated by a central coke stove that threw off little warmth. The iron beds and rough blankets were no great comfort, although airmen always lived better than the ground-pounders in the field or the sailors on the sea-swept corvettes.

The first overseas RCAF bomber unit, No. 405 Squadron, was activated on April 23, 1941, in 4 Group, and it flew Wellingtons out of Driffield in Yorkshire. It was formed initially from experienced Canadian and Commonwealth crews already flying in the RAF, but it would only be 50 percent Canadian by the fall of 1941. A wing commander led the bomber squadron, which consisted of two flights of eight aircraft plus a few spares, each led by a squadron leader. The squadron contained about 200 airmen, supported by several hundred ground crew and service staff. No. 405's first operation was on June 12, when the twin-engine Vickers Wellingtons bombed a railway marshalling yard at Schwerte, near Dortmund. Later that month, No. 405 Squadron was joined by No. 408 Squadron; Nos. 419 and 420 then stood up at the end of the year. While Canadian in name, most of the aircrew in the new squadrons were drawn from across the Empire, although the number of Canadians increased throughout the year and into the next as casualties whittled away at the original number, and BCATP-trained flyers arrived from across the Atlantic. Throughout 1941, Canada began to build a massive bomber force that would culminate in fifteen squadrons within an all-Canadian bomber group.

IN THE SUMMER OF 1941, wishful thinking augmented by poor follow-up to assess the damage left the Bomber Command air marshals and senior officers believing they were hurting the German war machine more than was really the case. For months, the air force brass were convinced that German industries were being destroyed and civilians being driven to the edge of panic. Just one more operation, they believed, might push Germany towards capitulation. Some of the air crews flying at the time had their doubts. Bomber pilot John Gee remarked that the two-engine bombers had virtually no navigational equipment. "Here we were flying 500 to 600 miles over enemy territory, trying to locate a target in total blackout, often with cloud below us and a lot of industrial haze. It's not surprising that our bombers were [off target by] 5, 10 miles."[3] The bombsights were not accurate and a miscalculation of wind speed by a mere 5 kilometres an hour caused a bombing error of more than 100 metres.[4] Eventually, in August 1941, D.M. Butt, a member of the cabinet secretariat, was instructed to study photographs and operational reports to more accurately gauge Bomber Command's achievement. His report revealed that only one-third of the missions in the previous two months had struck within 7 kilometres of their targets; the remaining two-thirds were even more wildly inaccurate. Moreover, the farther away a target was from Britain—such as those in the industrial Ruhr valley—the less likely they were to be hit with any accuracy.[5]

The Butt report's conclusions challenged the power of the bombers. Churchill fumed and considered reallocating resources, but he needed the bombers to hit back against Germany, or at least to show that the British bulldog had some bite.[6] The chiefs of staff concluded that a renewed offensive should be made against Germany's major industrial centres, with the bombers taking to area bombing. If pinpoint accuracy was not possible, then entire cities would be smothered in high explosives. The chiefs also persuaded themselves that area bombing would crack German civilians' morale. To make all of this happen, a new front-line force would have to be constructed, and it would have to be equipped with larger four-engine bombers. Even with the acknowledged failure of bombing up to that point, the Allies had few other ways to take the war to the Germans.

The smashing arm of Bomber Command became the four-engine bombers, with their ability to fly farther, carry a heavier payload, and survive more devastating punishment from flak or cannon fire than their smaller predecessors. The four-engine Short Stirling began to fly in February 1941, while the Handley Page Halifax entered battle a month later, and the iconic Avro Lancaster started flying operationally by year's end. The Lancaster was initially the more robust machine. Statistics recorded between August 1941 and October 1942 revealed that Halifax crews were lost at nearly twice the rate of counterparts on Lancasters. Early versions of the Halifax had difficulty gaining height with heavy bomb loads, were sluggish in flight, and were hampered by faulty exhaust shrouds that were so ineffective that enemy fighters could see the exhaust flames from over 500 metres. But officials studied these defects, funded new research, and gradually rectified the problems—eventually reaching the point where the Halifax was on par with the Lancaster and both were usually loved

A Handley Page Halifax flying over a smoke-obscured target in the Ruhr.

by their crews.[7] The Stirling was significantly slower, with a top speed of 420 kilometres per hour, and could attain an altitude of just 17,000 feet when fully bombed-up, which made it vulnerable to flak fire. While the poor performance of the Stirling was recognized early in 1942 due to the crippling loss rates, the planes, even with the defects, continued to fly. Any and all bombers were required in the war against Germany.[8] It would take almost two more years to phase out the Stirling.

ON FEBRUARY 24, 1942, Bomber Command received a new commander-in-chief. Air Marshal Sir Arthur Harris, a Great War veteran who had risen steadily through the RAF, while seeing action in India and Mesopotamia in the 1920s, was to become Bomber Command's greatest champion. Often bad-tempered and bristling for a fight, Harris held strong and unswerving opinions about how to wield the bombers

Sir Arthur Harris was air officer commanding-in-chief, Bomber Command, from February 1942 to the end of the war. Canadians served under Harris's command and he was a vigilant proponent of attacking German cities to drive the enemy from the war.

effectively. While Harris was a dominating personality, he was also a forward-thinking commander, and in his previous position as the AOC (air officer commanding-in-chief) of 5 Group he had urged his airmen and staff officers, and later operational scientists, to constantly improve the destructive power of the bombers and to find ways to aid the air crews in their battles over Europe.[9]

Harris is regularly portrayed in history books as the architect of Bomber Command's aerial campaign to destroy Germany. Indeed, he pursued that policy with zeal, writing, for example, in April 1942, "We have got to kill a lot of Boche before we win this war." It needs to be remembered, however, that Policy Directive Number 22 was issued on Valentine's Day, 1942, ten days before Harris took over.[10] This directive stipulated that the primary objective of Bomber Command was to crush the "morale of the enemy civil population and, in particular, of the industrial workers."[11] Harris was not a lone wolf. The strategy of laying waste to entire cities that he implemented was not only supported firmly but also set in place by Sir Charles Portal, the chief of the air staff, and Prime Minister Winston Churchill. The two men knew now that individual factories were nearly impossible to hit, but they also believed that entire cities could be carpeted in fire and high explosives to disrupt water and electricity, destroy housing, and kill and maim civilians. In the process, war industries would be damaged and the workers who kept them going would be killed. Relentless blows from the bombers would ultimately disable the German war machine. Harris merely applied previously established policy, albeit with a fierce conviction that bordered on the evangelical.[12]

Canadians flying in Bomber Command were not dismayed by their mission any more than were their British and Commonwealth comrades. Flight Lieutenant Warren Duffy, an RCAF pilot in No. 57 Squadron, RAF, wrote in July 1942, "The RAF are sure doing a big job now, as you read in the newspapers.... They asked for it, and now they're really getting it, and I don't mean maybe. That's the way it should be, eh.... That may sound funny but the more operations I do the keener I get about doing them. 'Jerry' has a lot coming to him, and I sure want to be in on it."[13] Many others echoed his sentiments. Hugh Bartley, for example, from Heddingly, Manitoba, a pilot with No. 128 Squadron, RAF, said this of his fellow airmen: "We took the view, in many cases, and certainly the British population did, that as you sow, so shall you reap. And we had all been to London and places like that where the East End was all smashed to smithereens. So we didn't have too damn much sympathy."[14]

THE ALLIED BOMBING STRATEGY forced the Germans to protect their homeland. The Kammhuber Line consisted of belts of interconnected aerial defensive zones, where long-range Freya radar stations tracked the incoming Allied bombers and alerted a second, short-range radar system known as Würzburg that directed night fighters to engage the incoming enemy bombers. After the bombers passed through this fire-and-fighter screen, they encountered the defences of each German city, which were protected by additional fighters, anti-aircraft guns, and searchlights to guide them. Even though the guns were operated mainly by adolescents and old men—young, able-bodied men having been conscripted for service abroad—combat veterans usually filled leadership roles. As the bomber war intensified, however, increasing numbers of soldiers were ordered back from other theatres to defend German cities.

In the early part of the war, the first-line German night fighters were the Messerschmitt Bf 110, a twin-engine fighter, and the Junkers Ju 88, a converted twin-engine bomber. Neither had fared well in the dogfights over Britain, but on the defence, with their ability to hunt relatively slow-moving Allied bombers with no fighter protection, they were extremely effective. The Bf 110 was fast, at 525 kilometres per hour, and was typically armed with five 7.9mm machine guns and two 20mm cannons. The latter fired a shell that was as long as two index fingers, and it could open up a bomber like a tin can. The single-seater Messerschmitt Bf 109, which had been in service since the Spanish Civil War and was flown by many of the Luftwaffe's highest scoring aces, was an even deadlier opponent, but most of the 109s were posted to the Eastern Front, the Mediterranean, or the Middle East. By late 1941, the Focke-Wulf Fw 190 had come on strength in greater numbers; armed to the teeth with four 20mm cannons, it also proved to be an agile fighter. The German night fighters took their toll. One Canadian pilot wrote of the enemy fighters, "They were killers in our book, killers who had every advantage over us, the prey they stalked."[15]

The need for the Germans to defend their cities forced them to divert resources away from the fighting fronts. This especially assisted Soviet forces on the Eastern Front, as the dual-purpose anti-aircraft and anti-tank gun, the 88mm flak gun, was devastating on the battlefield. Because thousands of these guns were situated through-out the Reich to protect the cities against bombers, the Wehrmacht's anti-tank defences were significantly weakened from 1942 onward. Moreover, it was estimated that the 88mm guns expended some 16,000 shells to bring down a single aircraft, so an enormous amount of ammunition was wasted that might otherwise have been used on the forward lines.[16] These home defences became a considerable drain on German resources, and would eventually by manned by over 900,000 troops.

THE BOMBER AIRCREWS went "over the top" two or three times a week in a relent-less battle of attrition. Flying Officer Ron Peel completed his first tour of operations in May 1942 and would eventually wear the Distinguished Flying Cross, but in the

Thousands of German 88mm flak guns defended Western Europe and Germany against Allied bombers. While the guns could throw up a deadly rain of shells, it was the bomber threat that forced Hitler to pull back these defences to guard the cities.

process he witnessed many comrades lose their lives. When another mate was killed in early July 1942, he confided despairingly to his diary, "It seems that all whom I befriend 'get the chop.'"[17] Yet even as the casualties mounted, more aircrews were trained and more squadrons stood up for battle. Seven new RCAF bomber squadrons were formed in 1942, including No. 425 (Alouette), the only French-Canadian squadron. The Alouettes became a proud symbol of French Canada's contribution to the war effort, although like most Canadian squadrons it contained Canadians from across the country, representing several nationalities.

Each squadron had its own separate identity. Besides being numbered between 400 and 450 (save for a few oddities), each was also given a title or nickname, with many linked to Canadian animals, birds, or cities. The third overseas bomber squadron, No. 419, was formed in December 1941 and soon gained its identity from its commanding officer, Wing Commander John "The Moose" Fulton, of Kamloops, British Columbia. He was an inspiring leader who flew regularly with his aircrews. The Moose, with his carrot-coloured hair and engaging smile, was a mere twenty-six years old, but soon the squadron took to calling themselves the "Moosemen." A great outpouring of grief took place when Fulton was killed on July 28, 1942, in an operation against Hamburg. A badge incorporating the image of a moose was later commissioned for the Squadron. No. 408 Squadron took on a goose as its emblem, while 420 Squadron adopted a snowy owl. Thunderbirds were embraced by 426 Squadron, bison by 429, and a porcupine by 433. No. 415 Squadron took the name Swordfish when it was in Coastal Command, and kept it after moving to Bomber Command. Other squadrons were linked back to Canadian cities, such as 405 (Vancouver) Squadron and 432 (Leaside) Squadron, while 434 (Bluenose) Squadron was not a town but reflected the maritime heritage of many of its members. Perhaps the most interesting name was acquired by 427 (Lion) Squadron, which was linked to a Hollywood studio, MGM. Hollywood actors from the studio—including Lionel Barrymore, Van Heflin, and Spencer Tracy—offered their names to individual bombers in the squadron. The crews fought among themselves for the honour of representing MGM's cinematic bombshell, Lana Turner.[18]

IN MARCH 1942, morale among the aircrews was at a grievous low as a direct result of the withering casualties that Bomber Command had taken. After having lost more than a thousand crews in the previous twelve months, the bomber armada had grown little in the attritional battles.[19] Harris needed a high-profile victory. To achieve it, he coordinated Bomber Command's resources to attack the port of Lübeck. The city along the northern coast of Europe, on the shore of the Baltic Sea, was the major centre for Red Cross shipments in and out of Germany, which were crucial for the comfort of prisoners of war. It also happened to be an easy target for the Allied aircrews to locate and it was lightly defended. In the early hours of March 29, 80 hectares of the city core, in which most of the buildings were made of wood, were burned to the ground when 234 bombers struck. Some 520 civilians were killed and another 785 injured.[20]

Harris now had evidence that a German city could be virtually destroyed, and he was anxious to follow the Lübeck operation up with a more spectacular one. With the support of Portal and Churchill, he planned a thousand-bomber raid on May 31, 1942, against Cologne. Almost every available bomber was thrown into the mix, including obsolete or run-down machines pulled from Training Command, to achieve what was planned—as much as a publicity coup as an operational victory. Studies had demonstrated that German fighters patrolled sectors of space, and when the bombers flew independently, they could be picked off with relative ease. On this raid, the bombers were channelled into a stream—a bit like a naval convoy. By using this system, a concentration of bombers would punch through the enemy defensive grid with minimal losses, and would be over the target and its defences in less time than if bombers flew on their own.

On the night of May 31, the 1,047 bombers—including 78 from RCAF squadrons—crashed through the German defences and converged on Cologne, Germany's third largest city. In 90 punishing minutes, the bombers dropped 500 tons of high explosives and more than 1,000 tons of incendiaries on the city. The high explosives blew up buildings, cracked water mains, and shattered glass, all of which contributed to the spread of the fires ignited by the incendiaries. The death toll was 469, but some 13,000 homes were destroyed, along with 36 factories. Within days, thousands of citizens fled the city.[21] RCAF navigator Ray Silver, who was shot down returning from Cologne, remembered the fiery cloud that arose 7 kilometres from the city below into the illuminated sky: it "was at once a torch of hope for enslaved millions and a preface to Armageddon."[22]

THE BOMBER CAMPAIGN OVER EUROPE was not the only aspect of the Allied air war. Thousands of Canadians served in RCAF and RAF formations in other capacities around the globe. RCAF bomber squadrons also took the war to the Axis in the Mediterranean and the Far East. One such RCAF squadron, No. 413, was formed at Stranraer on the southwest coast of Scotland in June 1941, but its Catalinas and crew were transferred to Coastal Command and flew out of Ceylon (modern-day Sri Lanka) in early 1942. The airmen swept the Indian Ocean in long, monotonous flights, staring endlessly at the open water as they patrolled for U-boats or any sign of the enemy. On April 4, Squadron Leader Leonard Birchall of St. Catharines, Ontario, piloting a Catalina flying boat, sighted a Japanese fleet about 500 kilometres south of Ceylon and sent off a warning message just before he and his crew were shot down by a dozen enemy fighters. Birchall and five of his crew survived the crash, but two were machine-gunned while they floated helplessly in the water.[23] Churchill labelled Birchall "the saviour of Ceylon" after the British defenders, alerted to the impending attack, repelled the Japanese raid. The Canadian airman was awarded the Distinguished Flying Cross for his actions on this day, though he would exhibit even more impressive feats of bravery in the brutal Japanese prisoner of war camps, where his calm leadership saved lives. Birchall stuck up for his men against the cruel oppressors and, on one occasion, when a Japanese guard was pummelling a defenceless man, Birchall entered the fray and struck the Japanese guard. He was sentenced to death and forced to undergo a mock execution that was stayed at the last moment.[24] Birchall, shaken but undeterred, continued to defend the rights of British prisoners of war, perhaps a far greater deed than that for which he is better known.

In the same Pacific theatre of war, RCAF Flying Officer R.W. Eves remembered that "Burma, during the war, was something you didn't want to miss, but you wouldn't want to do it again, either."[25] The RCAF had two Transport Command squadrons in Burma providing airlift to the British Fourteenth Army, which was fighting the Japanese. Perpetually short of ammunition and food, the Fourteenth fought an aggressive action against the enemy, holding down significant resources. The supplies carried in by the RCAF's Douglas C-47 Dakotas were vital in the inhospitable campaign, and, as RCAF pilot Bob Farquharson of No. 435 Squadron remembered, "We dropped absolutely everything. If somebody at the front had lost his eyeglasses or his false teeth, we flew in eyeglasses and false teeth. We flew in ammunition, clothing, rations."[26] In just two weeks in January, for example, No. 436 Squadron reported that it had lifted 2,500 tons of cargo and 735 passengers during 2,087 hours of flying.[27] Atholl Sutherland Brown, an RCAF pilot in the Burma theatre, spoke for many of his comrades, both in the air and on the ground, when he wrote that "their efforts and sacrifices were unrecognized and largely forgotten in the panorama of the war."[28] As many as 7,500 Canadian airmen served in the Far East and Pacific theatre of war, most with RAF squadrons, and according to one source, 431 of them were killed.[29]

WITH BOMBER COMMAND expanding into its role as an offensive strike force, Fighter Command also sought influence in the battle over Europe. The Spitfires and Hurricanes of 1940 had saved Britain, but Fighter Command had lost its raison d'être when the Germans had pulled back their bomber assaults the next year. By summer 1941, RAF and RCAF fighters were patrolling across the Channel, hoping to engage the Luftwaffe in battle and wear down its strength. As part of these engagements, twelve RCAF fighter squadrons were deployed: eight were day fighters, three were night fighters, and one—No. 418 Squadron—was an intruder unit whose fighters sought to harass enemy planes as they left or returned from their bases.

Aggressive fighter sweeps varied in scale from "rhubarbs," in which a few pilots "stooged" across the Channel to shoot up targets of opportunity, to more organized mayhem, known as "rodeos," in which larger numbers of fighters sought out the Luftwaffe, their actions usually based on intelligence relating to the location of enemy squadrons. A third type of operation, "circuses," saw several squadrons and light bombers attacking predetermined sites. The bombers were used as bait to draw out the Luftwaffe, which was then fought off by the escort wing and, if the trap was fully sprung, jumped by a high-cover squadron. But the Luftwaffe refused to fight according to the RAF's plans. Flight Commander Wilf Burnett of No. 408 Squadron, RCAF, recalled that the circuses had little effect on the enemy: "They were not prepared to sacrifice their fighters against a massive number of fighters, so they stayed on the ground and left us to the anti-aircraft gunners. We got quite a hammering from the anti-aircraft fire."[30]

While the RAF and RCAF concentrated their forces in the hope of wearing down the German defences as they "leaned into France," they faced a skilled enemy who were directed onto targets by ground radar, and who, should they be driven down by enemy fire or mechanical failure, had the same advantages as the RAF during the Battle of Britain, in that they could be flying again within days, or even hours, if they survived the drop unscathed. In any battle, the Allied pilots always had to keep one eye on the steadily dropping fuel gauge. Nonetheless, the premier fighters for the two sides, the Bf 109 and the Spitfire, engaged in wild dogfights in the skies over Europe. The Spitfire—all metal and with seemingly razor-thin wings—was more nimble and could turn more sharply, which was critical in a dogfight; but the Bf 109, which

Spitfire Vs of No. 403 (Wolf) Squadron, RCAF, in an operation against German forces in Europe.

could climb to 30,000 feet, often roared out of sun or clouds for the decisive first strike. The arrival of the Focke-Wulf Fw 190 by late 1941 provided a new advantage to the Luftwaffe, and it took some time for improved Spitfires—the Mark V and Mark IX—to hold their own in single combat. But the upgraded Spitfires and Fw 190s were close enough in technological effectiveness to ensure that pilot skill rather than engineering determined the outcome of their battles.

The RCAF pilots honed their tactics over time, learning to fly in the "finger four" position, so named because it resembled the fingers on an outstretched hand. In combat, the four fingers broke off to the basic two-plane fighting unit, a leader and his wingman, one the "shooter" and the other the "eyeball." The wingman defended the more experienced leader, and stuck close to him through twists and turns, watching for enemy fighters coming from behind, above, or below. With the Spitfire V's two 20mm cannons protruding from the leading edge of the wings, as well as four additional machine guns also in the wings, the aircraft had enough ammunition for six seconds of fire. But even a short burst sent hundreds of shells in a lethal cone of fire between 200 and 400 metres ahead of the gunsight.

Flying Officer Hugh Godefroy, who flew Spitfire VBs with No. 401 Squadron, described one chaotic battle on October 17, 1941, when he and his RCAF comrades were jumped by fifteen Bf 109s: "I fired at every 109 that came in front of me. Two peeled off from above and attacked head on. I flew straight at them, firing back, and they went by on the other side firing. Then I ran out of ammunition and I held the Spitfire in tight shuddering turns to avoid being shot down from 25,000 feet. At 15,000 feet I recovered from the spin and at 10,000 feet, I started to pull out and headed for the White Cliffs of Dover." He landed to find that of the twelve pilots who had begun the patrol, five had gone down in flames, including his wingman. Over the following months, Godefroy observed that the Spitfires were as good as or better than the 109s, but the Fw 190s were a very tough opponent. In many battles, he said, the Allied fighters, who had more total planes than the Germans, were outnumbered in the fierce battles over European soil, as the Luftwaffe vectored fighters to the battles when it suited their forces or simply avoided combat when it did not. The Spitfires and Hurricanes were often reduced to "dogfighting to survive and running out of ammunition; sometimes hit in several places and [where it was always a] struggle to get back to base."[31] Godefroy survived 77 sorties in 1941 and the early part of 1942 and returned for a second tour later in the war, for a total of 144 sorties. He was awarded the Distinguished Service Order and the Distinguished Flying Cross and Bar, and he made it back to Canada.

Between mid-June and December 1941, the RAF lost 395 pilots (killed, missing, or taken prisoner), against 154 Luftwaffe losses, of whom about half survived to fight for Germany another day.[32] However, at the time, RAF and RCAF pilots reported shooting down some 731 enemy aircraft, revealing a wide margin of error and again demonstrating the difficulty of determining kills in air combat. It was a common tactic, for example, for the fighters of both sides to mimic a dying spiral, and then to pull out below cloud cover and race back to safety. While the RCAF Spitfire squadrons gave a good account of themselves (having converted from Hurricanes in the fall of 1941), the battle went against the side that fought on enemy terrain and far from their base. Douglas Lindsay, a decorated RCAF pilot who served on Nos. 403 and 516 Squadrons, said he survived the war likely because he knew "how to get out of trouble when trouble presented itself. You have to have some thought about your own survival. I can think of some individuals who went headlong into everything, and they didn't last more than three or four trips."[33] Even with the losses, Allied output of fighter aircraft and trained pilots was soon dwarfing that of the Germans. And their activities all had the effect of reducing the pressure on the bombers that continued to raid German cities, while also allowing photo reconnaissance units to build up photographic evidence of German defences for the day when the Allies would storm France's shores. Flying Officer Frederick Wilson of Thunder Bay, Ontario, survived two operational tours and observed, "One thing about a Spitfire, you were master of your own destiny, and you could either fly the damn thing and be as good as the next guy, or you couldn't; and if you couldn't, you paid the consequences. You bailed out, cracked up, or died."[34]

THE TINY ISLAND OF MALTA became another key battleground in the Mediterranean. Both the Royal Navy and Royal Air Force used it as a base of operations from which to attack German and Italian convoys supplying Rommel's desert army in North Africa. The Axis powers saw Malta as a thorn in their side that caused them much misery, and they bombed it relentlessly from Sicily. The besieged Allied fighter squadrons on that bomb-pocked island fought some of the most intense aerial battles of the war. The Malta garrison somehow survived the continuous attacks of 1941 and, in April of the next year, its starving civilian population, most of them living underground in vast rat-infested caves, was awarded collectively the George Cross for bravery. More than 100 Canadians and Americans served on the island, often engaging in pitched battles against German and Italian fighters. Malta became a story of resistance for the Empire, a miniature Battle of Britain, where the RAF struggled against overwhelming odds while striking back at the enemy. Eighty Axis ships were sunk in the first seven months of 1942, and another 150 were sent to the bottom in the final five months. It was estimated that 60 percent of the Axis supplies

Seen here writing a report, George Beurling, from Verdun, Quebec, was Canada's highest-scoring ace of the war, with twenty-nine kills.

coming from the sea in the autumn of 1942 were destroyed by the Royal Navy and the fighters from Malta, and this interdiction had a profound impact on Rommel's ability to wage war in the desert.[35]

Pilot Officer R.W. "Buck" McNair had scored a kill against a Bf 109 in England with No. 401 Squadron, RCAF, before he arrived in Malta in March 1942. During a three-month tour of frenzied and nearly continuous combat, he shot down nine enemy aircraft and, by the end of the war, after commanding No. 126 (Canadian) Wing of the RAF's Second Tactical Air Force, was Canada's sixth-highest scoring ace, with sixteen victories. John McElroy finished the siege with ten victories, while Rod Smith recorded six. Five of the top twenty Allied aces in the blistering battles over Malta were Canadian—but all were eclipsed by Canada's highest-scoring ace of the war, George Beurling.[36]

A lanky, good-looking lad from Verdun, Quebec, Beurling learned to fly at fourteen and was in combat with the RAF at age twenty. Posted to Malta in June, he immediately showed his prowess in the air and also developed a reputation for being a lone wolf. In a period of formation flying, Beurling's tactics harkened back to those of Billy Bishop of the Great War—another Canadian ace who enjoyed flying alone and killing swiftly. Beurling was seen by many fellow airmen and administrators as reckless and undisciplined; on the ground, he was insubordinate, moody, and even a little strange. He did not drink in the mess, which set him apart, and for a fighter ace with an international reputation, he was shy. One Canadian ground crewman remembered that after shooting down an enemy plane, Beurling flew across the aerodrome and executed a "victory roll" before he landed. According to the crewman, "Victory rolls had been outlawed because too many very enthusiastic, second-class pilots couldn't do the roll and would kill themselves." Beurling was reprimanded. After shooting down another plane, he again buzzed the base, flying upside down. "So, they pulled him up on the carpet and said, 'We told you if you ever did that again we'll have to ground you.' Buzz snapped back, 'I didn't do it the same way this time. I did it upside down! That's Buzz Beurling."[37]

Like most aces, Beurling had incredible vision, quick reflexes, and was a master of the art of deflection shooting: leading his target with fire, which required split-second calculations involving angles, speed, and almost knowing what your enemy was about to do before he did, to ensure that he flew into the stream of shells. But Beurling also killed within an intimate range. Beurling described one of his victories: "I closed up to about thirty yards ... I was on his portside coming in at about a fifteen-degree angle ... it look[ed] pretty close. I could see all the details in his face because he turned and looked at me just as I had a bead on him.... One of my can[non] shells caught him right in the face and blew his head right off."[38] Beurling was relentless in hunting the Axis fighters and bombers that blasted the Malta defences. At the same time, he continued to rouse the ire of many of his British colleagues, who well understood the eccentricities of pilots but for some reason found Beurling's beyond the pale. He acquired the nickname "Screwball," although within six weeks of being posted to the island, he had claimed seven kills. Beurling remained an unstoppable force over Malta and was awarded four gallantry medals in four months. By the time he was wounded and shot down in the sea on October 14, he had twenty-nine kills. In the vicious air war over Malta, where the Allied fighters were always outnumbered and suffering from overwork, where they slowly succumbed to malnourishment and were plagued by the "Malta Dog" (dysentery), Beurling and his mates bested the enemy time and time again. The RAF needed more screwballs.

Like Major Billy Bishop in the previous war, Beurling became a national hero. He was pulled back to Canada, much against his will, to sell war bonds and put a human face on the war. The media dubbed him "Buzz" Beurling, which was probably better than "Screwball" and certainly a name more befitting one of Canada's first heroes of the war. He was also known as the Knight of Malta. By all accounts, he was generous and friendly on the cross-Canada tours, even though the introverted, blue-eyed hero found the adulation painful and he was jittery from the long-term effects of the Malta ordeal.

Upon his return to the front, Beurling was transferred to the RCAF and flew with No. 403 Squadron, but he scored only two more victories before he was pulled from operations in January 1944 for what his superiors believed was reckless behaviour in the air. It would be a blow to Canadian morale if the nation's hero was killed in combat. But the fighter ace was lost without the thrill of flight and fight, and he was released from the RCAF in August 1944. He was killed four years later in a crash near Rome while ferrying an aircraft to Israel in the 1948 Arab–Israeli War.

Whether fighting over Britain, "leaning into France," or battling over Malta, fighter pilots earned a reputation as dashing, heroic figures. These "knights of the sky" built upon the image of the gallant fighters of the Great War, who were also feted for their aerial combat skills. The fighter pilots were portrayed as lone heroes engaging the enemy in the battlefields of both the air and the imagination. The exhilarating prospect of soaring into the endless blue skies captivated civilians of all nations, but the cruel, dark reality of vicious air battles, the stark certainty of confrontations in which opponents either killed or were killed—or scurried like mad for cover—exacted an emotional toll on all who participated in the aerial battles.

"DO YOU REALIZE that we're winning this war, that the tide is definitely on the turn, that light is beginning to break?" wrote RCAF Flying Officer Thomas Reid to his fiancée on June 12, 1942. "The cost of winning is fearful—we feel sick every time a new casualty-list comes out, because some of our pals are named in every one—but we're winning."[39] It may have felt to Reid that the Allies were now winning the air war, but to date, in fact, Bomber Command had made little impact on the enemy's ability to wage war. The cost to Bomber Command was heavy, and Reid, like so many other flyers, would eventually have his name added to the casualty lists when his bomber was shot down a year later.

As German defences were strengthened by the addition of fighters and flak guns, the bombers needed new ways to overcome the enemy, and preferably to get to the targets and out of enemy air space as rapidly as possible. Allied scientists and researchers pored over reports and aerial photographs, seeking methods to equip the navigators and pilots with technology that would enable them to better locate their targets. In early 1942, the RAF introduced the navigational aid Gee. The original system, and the evolutions that followed, vectored the bombers to their targets. The navigator watched his Gee box, a cathode-ray receiver that sat on one side of the navigator's worktable, as it received signals from fixed bases in England and allowed constant triangulation to place the location of the aircraft. Navigators studied the receiver and factored in speed and wind—which could push the bomber off its intended path—to stay on target and within the relative protection of the bomber stream. "Through the use of Gee," remarked RCAF Flight Lieutenant John Patterson, "the navigator could quickly and accurately determine his aircraft's position," which aided bombers in finding their targets.[40]

Oboe, introduced in 1943, was similar to Gee in that it allowed aircraft to pick up pulses from two ground stations. It improved upon the accuracy of Gee, but most crews did not like it because the bomber had to fly a straight course to get a proper reading, and this left the aircraft vulnerable to enemy fire. The best device was H2S, downward-looking terrain-mapping radar used operationally for the first time in January 1943, which provided a picture of the ground features over which the bombers flew by bouncing pulses from the plane to the earth and back again, much like a warship's asdic. Water, irregular surfaces, and built-up areas were all reflected on the navigator's screen. "Things such as buildings gave a stronger reflection than trees or water," recounted one RCAF navigator, and "cities were normally easy to pick up."[41] While these early computer-like screens assisted the navigators, they could be jammed and would often malfunction, and so more often conventional maps, astronavigation, and dead reckoning were the most trusted methods employed to get to and from the objective, although they did nothing to ensure that bombs landed accurately on their targets.

The most important innovation was not technological but doctrinal. To assist in leading the bomber stream to targets, pathfinders were introduced in August 1942. While Harris had initially opposed the creation of a target-finding force for fear of drawing off the best crews into an elite formation, he was overruled by Portal. These aerial rangers became the spearhead of the bomber stream.[42] Typically flying de Havilland Mosquito light bombers—a fast, wooden machine—the pathfinders arrived first over the target and dropped coloured flares to pinpoint and highlight the area to be bombed by the follow-on force. The timing was critical: the pathfinders had to be close enough to the stream that German ground defences had no time to light decoy flares outside the city or to mask the dropped flares. After they dropped their first round of flares, the pathfinders continued to fly over the city to ensure that the bombers' high explosives and incendiary bombs landed in the intended area, as a common tendency of those bombers arriving at the end of the stream and encountering a sea of fire below them was to drop their loads short, a phenomenon known as "creep-back." And so there were generally two waves of pathfinders: those that marked the target area with flares, and then a second group that dropped another round of sky markers that renewed aiming points or corrected previously obscured targets. As one Canadian pilot—later a pathfinder in No. 614 Squadron—wrote, "Quite often the falling bombs would scatter the target indicators on the ground and the pathfinder aircraft would have to keep circling the area and replenish the markers."[43] These elite bombers flew circuits for twenty or thirty minutes over their targets and were subject to ground fire the whole time. Casualties were high. The pathfinders were experienced, second-tour aircrews and wore their badge with pride. They accepted the danger.

While technological advances, the introduction of pathfinders, and the sheer number of heavy bombers all helped to raise the level of intensity and violence in the battles over Europe, dropping bombs from 18,000 feet or higher when visibility was impaired by plumes of smoke, smog, and flames was never an exact science. But it did not have to be. Any strike against an enemy city was a blow against the

A collection of RAF and RCAF bombs, including incendiaries and high explosives,
with the most common armament in the foreground, the 4,000-pound high explosive.

enemy's infrastructure and morale. And the strikes got harder. From January 1942 on, Lancaster and Halifax bombers usually carried a "cookie," a 4,000-pound bomb that contained about 3,000 pounds of amatol, a high explosive material made from TNT and ammonium nitrate. The cookie occupied the centre of the bomb bay, and there were usually additional 500-pound high explosive bombs placed fore and aft of it, plus dozens of 4-pound incendiary bombs. The bomb load was about five and a half tons. Later, this was increased yet again, until the Lancaster was capable of carrying loads as great as 12,000 pounds, albeit at the cost of reducing speed to a lumbering crawl.

The cookie, an ugly green-painted cylinder, blasted buildings, blew off roofs, collapsed walls, and killed in a wide radius, while the 500-pounders buried themselves in structures before exploding from the inside. Timed fuses could delay the explosion by a few seconds or a few hours. All of these bombs burst water pipes and cut gas mains, the latter leading to secondary fires that were often ignited by the bombers' incendiaries. Because the bombs were made in different shapes and sizes and possessed different aerodynamic qualities, they never landed in the same spot. However, this lack of a consistent and tight bomb pattern was inconsequential when the target was an entire city.

Carpet bombing kilometres of urban centres created scenes of genuine horror on the ground and resulted in vast physical damage, and yet German industry was barely slowed by the bombings in 1942. While the damage wrought by the bombers grew in intensity, the war industries were made more efficient as the duplication in the industrial sector was eliminated and procedures were streamlined. Albert Speer, Hitler's minister of armaments and war production, was responsible for much of this increased output.[44] Speer was also able to draw upon the vast occupied territory in the east for additional raw material and slave labour. Statistics would later show that between February and August 1942, German production increased by 27 percent for guns, 25 percent for tanks, and 97 percent for ammunition. And this was a period when Bomber Command dropped 28,000 tons of bombs and lost 852 aircraft.[45] What the stark numbers cannot reveal is the degree to which the destruction of infrastructure, the killing of workers, and the disruption of German society actually slowed the rate at which Speer was able to increase production. Might the increases above have doubled or tripled without the bomber's hammer blows? The bombing campaign of 1942 had few measurable successes, but with more bombers carrying heavier payloads, the next year would see German cities gutted, civilians killed in shocking numbers, and industrial production severely curtailed.

In 1942, German civilian morale, much like that of the British during the Blitz, was not crushed. But as the aerial assault thickened, there was little escape for those who lived in the cities. Hundreds and then thousands, and then tens of thousands, were killed. When the high explosive reverberations stopped and the fires burned down, the survivors crept from their blackened concrete bunkers and underground silos to return to their neighbourhoods and houses, to salvage their losses, to gather their precious items, and to bury the dead. The workers went back to manufacturing guns and war supplies, and continued until the next air raid drove them underground again. Yet while buildings and factories might be rebuilt, there was no restoring the charred bodies of loved ones and friends. And such attacks were also debilitating for the German troops at the front, anxious for their families who faced the bombs alone.

Churchill continued to press for the full-fledged bomber offensive, even though he knew by now that it would not, by itself, win the war, as some of the more enthusiastic bomber barons claimed. The bomber war was also popular with British civilians, who had faced the Blitz and now watched the same weapon used against the aggressor. A *Daily Express* headline captured the angry sentiment of millions of Britons on the day after the first thousand-bomber raid against Cologne: "The Vengeance Begins!"[46]

CHAPTER 10

A SORTIE AGAINST A CITY

"There's a war on tonight." The call from air force group headquarters to the squadron usually came in the early morning. An operational board was updated with the list of crews scheduled to fly that night, but no target was announced. "Prior to briefing," however, "we'd try and find out how much petrol was being loaded on the aircraft, and by that we could tell how far the trip was going to be," remarked Flight Lieutenant W.E. Vaughan.[1] Rumours were rife, and some cheeky men even placed wagers on the target. Other flyers, more philosophical, wondered if this sortie, whether it was a hop across the Channel or a drive deep into Germany, might be their last. New men were particularly likely to be nervous, but so too were those who were inching their way towards the end of their thirty-operation tour. When the tour ended, they would be given a rest as a trainer in Britain or Canada, before being required to return six months later for a second tour. Flying Officer Murray Peden described the cumulative strain after nearly two dozen operations: "Each time I found myself on the battle order, the ordeal of waiting—an ordeal punctuated by the ritual of air test, briefing, and flying meal—seemed intensified, the muscles of the abdomen hardening until they felt like the extended ribs of a miniature umbrella."[2]

The aircrews moved into the briefing room—usually in the early afternoon if it was a night operation, which was almost always the case—and sat together as a crew. Over a hundred men might be packed into the space. RCAF Flight Sergeant B.G. McDonald observed that the green crews were seated in the front rows, while the more experienced hands grabbed the seats behind them. But, "as casualties occurred, [the new crews] moved back, row by row. It wasn't unusual for a new crew to be in the front row one night, and two weeks later, to be occupying the fifth or sixth."[3]

When the men were settled and the door closed, the squadron's commanding officer called the room to attention and said some introductory words before handing the podium over to his lead briefers to describe the target and its importance. A curtain would be pulled aside to reveal a large map on which pins and coloured strings were arranged to indicate the path leading to the target. The flight into enemy air space was rarely a straight line: its turns were intended to deceive the German defenders about the squadron's true destination. The revelation of the target brought murmurs, sighs, and even catcalls. Objectives in France required less time in the air

Briefing of the aircrews of Nos. 431 and 434 Squadrons, RCAF,
before an operation against Nazi-occupied Europe.

and were generally safer. Cities in the Ruhr Valley, one of the major German industrial centres and known satirically to most airmen as "Happy Valley," were obscured by smog and protected by thousands of anti-aircraft guns and searchlights, and were always more costly in terms of crews lost. The most fearful target was Berlin—the "Big City"—as it was far inside enemy territory and surrounded by legions of guns, fighters, and searchlights.

The navigators and bomb aimers took special note of the bomber stream's approach, highlighting the turns in mid-air to avoid German cities protected by flak, as well as known enemy air defences, especially the expected patrol grids occupied by night fighters. It was also crucial to remember the colour of the flares that would be used to illuminate ground targets, because the defenders set all manner of decoys. The intelligence officer ("Spy" in flyer slang) detailed what was known about the city's defences. "If 'Spy' was foolish enough to predict light enemy flak over an area we considered to be hot," recounted one indignant Canadian flyer, "someone invariably would pipe up with, 'Yeah, that's what you told us the night we lost thirty aircraft.'"[4] The flyers did not want to be sold a bill of goods—their lives were on the line.

The weather briefing was given by "Cloudy Joe," as the meteorological officer was called, although he also went by a number of unprintable nicknames. Types of clouds and when they were expected to break, potential icing situations, and wind speed were all provided, although experienced airmen were skeptical about the quality of the "gen" (information) for a target that was five to seven hours away. The cloud cover was rated out of ten; full cover, "10/10," meant that a target was entirely concealed and almost always led to the scrubbing of the operation. The denser the cloud cover, the less likely the bombers would hit specific targets on the ground. However, aircrews generally wished for some cloud cover to facilitate their escape after they dropped their payload. A full moon made the German countryside visible to the bombers but also made their planes easy targets for the night fighters and the ground defences. Despite the increased vulnerability it brought with it, a "bomber's moon" was not a sufficient obstacle to force the cancellation of a mission. Flight Lieutenant Douglas Baird of No. 408 Squadron, RCAF, remembered that his anxiety rose as the briefing progressed until he found himself, by the end of it, "shaking like a leaf."[5] Flight Lieutenant John Zinkhan recollected that his mind often drifted during the briefing and "without exception, I was on edge, wondering if it would be our turn next to go 'for the chop.'"[6] Many others weighed the same odds.

WHEN THE BRIEFING WAS OVER, the aircrews had several hours to kill. Most talked over the operation or mused about the quality of the gen. "Every aircrew hated and feared the endless hours between briefing and actually taking off," recounted Douglas Harvey, a No. 408 Squadron pilot.[7] Flight Lieutenant Ross Baroni witnessed the growing strain as thoughts turned to the long night ahead, noting, "we kept pushing it behind ... trying to put it aside. You had a job to do. To stay true."[8] Flyers tried to catch a few hours of sleep, but nerves were frayed and rest was elusive.

A Halifax at rest and soon to be "bombed up." A four-engine heavy bomber needed about 8,000 litres of aviation gasoline and carried about five and a half tons of bombs.

All phone lines were cut at the base after the briefing, leaving airmen no opportunity to reveal the target by accident, or to say goodbye. RCAF Warrant Officer Al Bridgwater recalled, "After briefing, most chaps would write letters," and these were normally left with a chum.[9] Putting pen to paper for mothers, fathers, and children was no easy task for these anxious men. Some of their brave veneer crumbled as flyers sought the phrases and sentiments that would convey comfort should they fall.

Later in the day, most of the aircrews were driven out to check their "birds," which had been readied by the dedicated ground crews who were "bombing up" the machines. Filling the Lancasters with a full load of about 8,000 litres of aviation gasoline took the better part of half a day. The bombs were transported on trolleys to the hard standings from the protected bomb dumps. Like most airmen, Flight Lieutenant Leslie McCaig had a close relationship with the ground crew. "These poor devils work hard and I have the utmost respect for them," he wrote in his diary. "Those assigned to a kite treat it like a baby if they like the crew—they work all hours and never get any credit for it. We know how valuable they are but unfortunately the public does not."[10]

Crews that survived a few operations on a specific bomber routinely stayed with the same plane. Bombers were tracked alphabetically, A-Able, S-Sugar, or V-Victor. Each machine was also commonly distinguished by its nose art, a more informal name, and marks indicating the tally of successful sorties. The nose art was an emblem of service and survival: the aircrews who "owned" the bombers after completing a number of operations chose the design. The metal canvas invited all manner of representations, but the young bomber crews (like their naval counterparts) were attracted mostly to cartoon characters or women in risqué poses. A number of Canadian symbols were also used, such as the Maple Leaf, or icons connecting the flyers to their hometowns. The nose art was a part of bomber culture, and as Jack McIntosh of No. 419 Squadron, RCAF, claimed, "The name and nose art made it feel she was 'our' aircraft and would always bring us home."[11]

IN THEIR TOPSY-TURVY WORLD, the bomber crews slept by day and flew by night; consequently, they were given a solid breakfast at dinner time, usually real eggs and bacon. This was a luxury in wartime Britain, but appropriate for a "last meal," as

Flight Lieutenant Ross Baroni of No. 434 Squadron, RCAF, called it.[12] It was reserved for those crews flying on a particular night; the flyers who were not on duty suffered through the usual gamey mutton, mountain of potatoes, and waterlogged Brussels sprouts. Few of them complained too loudly, however, as their evening was free. They could go to a movie or a pub while their mates kitted up for the operation.

Crew members handed over their wallets and personal effects to the intelligence section for safekeeping. This was to ensure that personal information was kept from the enemy in case the bomber was shot down and its crew captured. They kept their identification tags so that they would be known in death and, equally important for many, given a burial according to their faith. Having stowed away their kit and created next-of-kin bags, which separated out potentially embarrassing items such as letters to girlfriends and salacious material, the crews went to pick up their flying kit.

The aircrews were issued warm flying boots, a white turtleneck sweater, and white silk gloves. A Mae West life jacket was required and worn around the waist. Escape kits were handed out and kept in the inside pocket of the battle dress tunic. These contained French, Belgian, German, and Dutch currency, as well as maps, matches, razors, food, gum, and a compass. All flyers wore a leather helmet with an oxygen mask. Earphones for the intercom system were built into the flying helmet and the speaker was in the oxygen mask, all of which went active when the flyer plugged into the bomber's electrical system. Finally, the crews were issued with parachutes. Members of Britain's Women's Auxiliary Air Force or the RCAF's Women's Division, which had been established in the summer of 1941, handed out the parachutes with a cheerful smile, a quip, and light flirtation. Theirs was not an easy task: they handed out parachutes to young flyers, many of whom would never return. Day and night, these women packed the life-saving parachutes, making sure the silk was carefully stuffed into the tight packages, but aware that their actions were the difference between life and death for innumerable airmen. A few wags attempted well-worn jokes, along the lines of, "Shall I bring it back if it doesn't work?" but most airmen simply inspected their bags in silence. "When our crew went to draw parachute packs," recounted one Canadian pilot, "we would not take one that had 13 in the number. Number 27013, for example, was out on that account; and so was Number 28021, because the digits there added up to 13."[13]

"Am convinced that fatigue is an indirect cause of many losses," wrote Flight Lieutenant Leslie McCaig in his diary. "Two nights in a row are too many for any crew."[14] The relentless demands of the bomber war were hard to bear, and all of the crews that had flown for any length of time were tired and worn out. Small comforts were offered to alleviate the strain. A thermos of coffee or tea and a chocolate bar or a sandwich were available from the kitchen. These could be taken on the mission to keep hunger at bay and supply energy on a long flight. Many flyers relied on barbiturates to offset the lack of sleep. "We called them 'wakey wakey pills,'" wrote pilot Douglas Harvey.[15] The medical officers prescribing the pills warned that they should not be taken until the plane was in flight, but more than a few men wolfed them down on the ground, eager for the rush to keep them alert. The medical officer's

Canadian airmen kitting up with cold-weather flying suits.

warning was a sensible one, however, because operations were often scrubbed at the last moment because of poor weather or mechanical failure. The unfortunate airman who swallowed the pills prematurely, only to find himself grounded for the night, would be climbing the walls of his Nissen hut while his mates slept. Inevitably, some airmen became addicted to the "bennies" (Benzedrine), but Harvey never felt the need to use them. "How could anyone fall asleep over enemy territory," he mused, "with every gun on the Continent trying to shoot you down?"[16]

THE AIRCREWS FACED DEATH TOGETHER. Crews drew upon one another for strength and they demanded that their tight-knit group not be broken up. Having a member of the crew drop out, even for a single sortie, often meant that the senior squadron officers allowed the whole crew to sit out the mission, unless a "maximum effort" was demanded that night. Flying Officer Mike Harrington remembered when one of his crew got married, and they were ordered to fly while their mate was on his brief honeymoon. Harrington was aghast, believing that "when a crew changed, it broke up the harmony and teamwork and you might end up getting the 'chop.'"[17] He pleaded successfully for his crew to be left out of the operation. And indeed there were many examples of new men not working out. Arthur Bishop, who saw the end of thirty-five operations in 1942, observed that "few men survived a full tour." He remembered that a new gunner, just added to their crew, broke down on his first sortie as the bomber approached the heavily defended Ruhr Valley.[18] He started to scream hysterically into the intercom and kept on screaming, his voice rising and falling in naked terror, until one of the crew members eventually cut his intercom cord. The crew worried about the loss of the rearward eyes that the gunner was meant to supply, but no one went back to check on him, even as they imagined him still screaming through the roar of the engines on the long flight home.

As the sun sank on the horizon, the aircrews convened at their aircraft. "You would walk around them and kick the tires," recounted RCAF flyer Arthur Wahlroth. "You would get inside and you would do your walk around inside to find out that all your oxygen connections and your inter-plugs were working."[19] Then the crews exited the bird and waited for a sign that the operation was either a go or cancelled due to bad weather. Clouds over the base meant a difficult landing later, but it did not necessarily mean clouds were over a target. Most men chain-smoked while they waited, since most crews had the sensible policy of forbidding smoking when in the air because of the oxygen and other flammables on board. Other men threw up.

Airmen fingered their talismans as the tension rose. Most crews, according to one Lancaster pilot, were "totally superstitious."[20] Flyers carried lucky charms, pieces of clothing like a girlfriend's scarf, or other personal items infused with magical qualities, and almost all airmen dressed in the same set of clothes on every operation. Flight Lieutenant W.E. Vaughan spoke of his crew's many superstitions: "We had one mid-upper gunner who chalked his wife's name on the bomb-bay. Tom, our skipper, always wore a pair of long green socks that went right up his legs, and before take-off he always had to urinate on the left front tire."[21] Robert Kensett, a twenty-one-year-old RCAF navigator serving in No. 158 Squadron, RAF, wrote of a gift

Bomber Command aircrew with good luck charm.

from his girlfriend—a little leprechaun made of pipe cleaners, covered in green felt and wearing a little cap: "He was my good luck charm, and I carried him everywhere with me tucked into the breast pocket of my battledress."[22] The little leprechaun was so central to Kensett's crew's well-being that when he forgot one time to bring it along on an operation, the rest of the crew became frantic: they found him a bike and insisted on sending him back to his room to fetch it. The superstitions bordered on the absurd. Michael Kutyn, an RCAF navigator who flew with No. 10 Squadron, RAF, professed not to be superstitious, but then observed, "Some letters of the alphabet assigned to aircraft seemed to be luckier than others. The letter 'O' seemed to be a lucky letter with this squadron. During the years No. 10 Squadron was in bomber command, no aircraft bearing the letter 'O' had been shot down over enemy territory."[23] All such magical thinking helped to ward off fear of the unknown. With so little control over their destiny, airmen hoped that items imbued with a sort of otherworldly power—which they had discovered or cultivated—would protect them.

THE CONTROL TOWER FIRED A FLARE to indicate that the operation was on. A last cigarette was stubbed out, and bladders were emptied in a ritual dampening of the rear tire. The mind raced in anticipation of what lay ahead. Flight Lieutenant Jack Singer wrote about his fears, acknowledging that "sometimes it took all my courage to climb back into the aircraft for start-up."[24] As the crew hauled themselves aboard, they were greeted by the smell of raw gas, oil, and hydraulic fluid. Airmen found the odour calming, as was the act of linking into the crew intercom, which drew together all seven members. They were isolated in their bird and relied implicitly on one another to survive the night. The repetitive pattern of checking equipment was, according to one Canadian navigator, "a small piece of insurance in an uninsurable world."[25] Pre-flight tension was always palpable, but as Flight Lieutenant Leslie McCaig of No. 426 Squadron, RCAF, confided in his diary, "there is something decidedly comfortable about bomber work—others willing to share your fate."[26]

Engines coughed, rumbled, and then roared as the bombers taxied out of their dispersal area. Pilots acknowledged the thumbs-up signal from their ground crews. Flying Officer George Williams described the difficulty in getting bombers off the ground without hydraulic controls. As the bomber built up speed, "you had to lift off the ground by brute force, and by the time you were airborne you had worked up a real sweat." When a bomber was at its maximum bomb load and fuel, the flight engineer usually had to assist the pilot at the controls. "The Lancaster engines produced 4,800 horsepower and that was a heck of a lot of torque. You had to shove the column forward to lift the tail off the ground as fast as you could or you wouldn't be able to pick up any speed. Once the air speed was up, then you pulled back on the controls, but by then you were flying and your flying surfaces were supported by air pressure."[27]

The first bombers circled the airfield waiting for the rest of the squadron. When all the planes were airborne, they flew together along the coast to the crossing point, before turning east to the Continent. The rumble of a bomber's engines was tremendously loud and drowned out all talk that was not on the communication link. And the interior of the plane was cold. The bombers were not pressurized and only poorly heated. In winter, at 18,000 feet, the temperature was often minus 50 degrees Celsius outside, and almost as cold inside. It was usually a miserable and frigid flight as the crew members sat for hours on end, with little chance to stretch or move.

THE HEAVY BOMBERS—the Halifaxes and Lancasters—had a crew of seven. While the Lancaster overshadows the Halifax in popular memory, the two aircraft were very similar. If crews survived a tour of operations, they inevitably credited the type of aircraft in which they flew, and defended its reputation fiercely in a friendly—or not so friendly—rivalry. On any bomber, the pilot was the captain and his word was the final authority on all issues. The cockpit was on a raised platform and next to the pilot, although slightly lower, was the flight engineer. He had an uncomfortable seat that he gave up to a "second dickey" if the crew was taking on an inexperienced pilot to give him a taste of battle. Otherwise, the flight engineer assisted the pilot, watched fuel consumption, changed over gas tanks, and, when necessary, dealt with mechanical failure or the damage from flak. Almost all engineers were former ground crew and British because the BCATP did not train engineers in Canada until late in the war.

The bomb aimer was situated beneath the pilot, in the nose of the Lanc, looking down into the darkness through a transparent Perspex cupola. He manned twin .303 machine guns, although he rarely had anything to fire at since few fighters attacked head on. As the bomber closed on its target, the bomb aimer moved away from his turret and lay flat, looking through the bombsight to find some recognizable geographical feature on the ground. He was assisted by the navigator, who was situated behind a curtain that shrouded his work and kept light from spilling out into the cockpit. In the Lancaster, the rudimentary heating duct was located near the wireless operator and navigator, so they sweated uncomfortably while their mates worried about frostbite. The navigator had a table for his maps and charts, and consulted an instrument panel showing airspeed and other details that he required to plot the machine's course and location. An H2S screen was also usually at his elbow. Most bomb aimers and navigators tried to get some time in at flying, for if the pilot was killed or wounded, someone would have to take the bomber home.

"Tail-End Charlie" was the loneliest and coldest position in a bomber,
but it was critical in providing early warning of enemy nightfighter attacks.

The wireless operator manned the radios. He spent most of the time listening to broadcasts from home base and watching the Fishpond radar, which was a rudimentary screen that tracked the bombers in the stream, all moving at roughly the same speed. "If a spot of light suddenly began to drift across the screen or change position radically," wrote RCAF navigator Robert Kensett, "there was a good chance it was a fighter plane trying to infiltrate the stream."[28] This gave the crew early warning of a possible attack, but no protection. That role fell to the gunners. In the bomber's fuselage was the mid-upper gunner in a bubble turret armed with two .303 Browning machine guns. He was ensconced uncomfortably in a seat slung below the turret, an arse-freezer that he occupied for hours. Even worse was the situation of the tail gunner, known affectionately as "Tail-End Charlie." He was crammed into a rotatable turret as he scanned the darkness for the waspish night fighters. "We were the eyes of the crew," said Fraser Muir of Westville, Nova Scotia. "We couldn't for a second stop searching the skies for enemy aircraft but also our own aircraft."[29] If an enemy fighter began its attack run—and this was usually done from a pilot's blind spot—the rear gunner shouted out warnings to the skipper for evasive action and fired his four .303 Brownings. The Brownings had limited stopping power against enemy fighters unless they were unleashed at close range, and many bombers later were provided with two more powerful .50-inch machine guns. Tail-End Charlie was a lonely position, and it took a special man to sit in the frigid cold, watching the skies for lurking killers.

SQUADRONS OF BOMBERS from bases across Britain formed up into the bomber stream, a dense formation of planes flying through the night. On the large raids, the stream was packed several kilometres high and wide, with a tail that stretched back dozens of kilometres. Flying in pitch darkness, without lights, often meant that it was only the navigator who kept the bomber on its path, while the gunners watched anxiously for friendly planes drifting into their air space. With a stopwatch in hand, the navigator had his turning points and time over targets scribbled down to ensure that the bomber stayed in the stream. Bomber Pilot David Chance praised his crew: "My navigator was good. We were always in the middle of the stream."[30] To drift out of the stream made one vulnerable to being picked off by night fighters, who preferred to attack stragglers.

The bombers climbed steadily to their required height—the higher the better to avoid flak. Oxygen was need at altitudes above 10,000 feet. Most bombers could fly at 16,000 to 18,000 feet, and later in the war to 20,000 feet, although full bomb and fuel loads dragged them down. To see the Halifaxes and Lancasters pushing through the clouds, like giant whales through the surf, was awe-inspiring, especially when hundreds of them broke together through the cushion of white. It was a view reserved for air warriors. But above the clouds, the moon illuminated the strange battlefield. Soaring in the bright moonlight was a "beautiful but sinister sight," recounted RCAF Flight Lieutenant Alex Campbell.[31]

"Flying consists of hour upon hour of utter boredom punctuated by moments of sheer terror," wrote Les Morrison, RCAF Lancaster pilot.[32] Despite the minutes of fright, it was difficult for the airmen to remain alert for hours on end. "Imagine what it was like to be confined in a cramped position for all that time, particularly at night," ruminated John Patterson. "Think of the gunners and bomb-aimers like me sitting in a turret for hours with no room to stretch, with no food except perhaps a chocolate bar, with conversation over the intercom restricted, subjected to the constant noise from the engines and expected to be alert at all times."[33] The intense cold, engine roar, and unyielding monotony dulled the senses.

The bombers faced fire from anti-aircraft batteries along the occupied French coast, and from major urban centres; the latter were avoided when possible. Experienced pilots also weaved their planes slightly, alternately climbing and descending a few hundred metres, always presenting a shifting target for the enemy. "The only place we couldn't see was just where we needed it most—underneath," wrote Lancaster pilot Walter Thompson. "I tried to remedy this by flying a constant and pronounced corkscrew path, asking the crew to look below as I alternately banked one way then the other."[34] Both pilot and crew knew that these manoeuvres brought with them the danger of colliding with another bomber, and so the team kept watch.

As the stream penetrated deeper into German air space, some bomber forces split away towards different targets to throw off the enemy's defences. For the same reason, the bomber stream followed a zigzag path. German radar regularly picked up the mass of bombers and sent warnings to the cities that seemed to be in their path. These early warnings gave civilians time to reach their air raid shelters, but the zigzagging also meant that half a dozen cities or smaller centres might face disruption, rather than the single target. Each feint brought terror to hundreds of thousands of civilians.

"Once we were over enemy territory, we were silent," remembered Halifax bomber pilot Stan Coldridge. The wireless operator listened "to the radio all the time going back and forth across the range in order to pick up recalls from Britain or tune in to German broadcasts to see if German fighters were being scrambled."[35] Any distraction might draw away eyes from sentry duty or mask, even for a second, the telltale sounds of a crew member who spotted an enemy fighter. The crew was wired into the intercom system, and when a flyer wanted to speak he switched on his microphone, and then, when he was done, he switched it off. Leaving it on stopped others from using it, and most pilots wanted to hear only from the navigator as he offered minor flight corrections, or from the gunners, who might scream out an alarm calling for immediate evasive action. When the bombers approached the target, fatigue gave way as adrenaline kicked in.

"WHEN WE GOT OVER THE TARGET," said Lancaster pilot Donald Cheney, "all hell broke loose."[36] Experienced crews learned that it was best to be at the front of the bomber stream and at a higher altitude than the others. The bombers nearer the ground were often victims of medium flak that could be thrown up from the flak guns in almost solid shot. Meanwhile, those at the end of the stream were obvious targets because, by the time they were over their destination, the guns were alerted and often had the range of the incoming planes. It was always a challenge to run the German defences, but it was far more costly to do so when the defences were prepared. After hours of sitting and staring into darkness, the final run over the target was a pyrotechnical marvel. The ground defences operated high-powered searchlights that cut the night sky in the hope of illuminating the bombers for the flak guns. The long white beams weaved back and forth, directed by a bluish radar-guided master light. "One of the terrors was, of course, to be coned by search lights," recalled Cheney. "One searchlight would pick you up and be able to hold onto you. If he could hold onto you for up to 30 or 40 seconds, then five or six or a dozen other search lights [would join it], then you would be coned. When you were coned, you couldn't see a thing inside of your cockpit. You were totally and absolutely blinded. And then, of course, you were a dead duck target for either fighters or for flak."[37]

When a bomber was caught in the steadily expanding cone of light, the pilot had few options. Within seconds, high explosives and shrapnel would be detonating or whirling through the air around the plane. Flight Lieutenant Walter Irwin, who served as both navigator and pilot in heavy bombers, wrote, "It was estimated that once a battery of search lights locked onto a plane, your chance of surviving was about 50%."[38] Twisting or turning was pointless: the searchlight operators were too canny to be thrown off and the beam too broad. Only an immediate corkscrew dive gave one a chance to evade the blinding lights. Lancaster pilot Les Morrison was coned over Kiel in the final months of the war. It was his first time, and as the spotlight grabbed the plane, he knew the Lanc had only seconds before other searchlights joined the first. He cut off the four throttles, pulled up the nose sharply, lowered the flaps, and dropped the wheels—this was the equivalent of braking abruptly in a car. The Lanc convulsed as if suffering an epileptic seizure. He pulled the plane over in a near-stall turn, and then rammed it forward straight down the beam of the searchlight. For those flak teams on the ground, it must have looked like the bomber was diving straight at them. As he plummeted thousands of feet, the bomber and the wind screaming in different tones, Morrison broke off his suicide plunge, shot out of the illuminating ray, and escaped into darkness.[39]

While Morrison survived, other crews did not. A desperate dive was dangerous at the best of times, as the chance of crashing into other planes was high, and the manoeuvre was performed in blinding light, with the control panels obscured. The g-force pushed the human body to the limit when the aircraft dropped thousands of feet in a matter of seconds, and many pilots were afflicted with temporary blindness as the blood pressure in the brain dropped and blood to the eyes was cut off. A longer and more rapid descent often could lead to a loss of consciousness.[40] If the pilot did elude the two-million-candlepower searchlights, he could choose to flee the battlefield for the long trip home, or, depending on his sense of duty, return to the bedlam to drop his load.

Once they closed in on their targets, those members of the crew looking down could see the winking flak and streams of coloured tracers rising up to meet them.

Flight Sergeant Miller Brittain described the elusive patterns of fire: "Jerry sends up something to scare us that is the most beautiful of all. A great red flare burst and out of it come long silver streamers like some sort of enchanted tree."[41] Bombers in the stream that were hit by the shellfire caught fire, flared, and exploded. Their surviving comrades in other bombers searched the skies, frequently in vain, hoping to see parachutes. The pilot could not afford to be distracted, even by the loss of comrades: he had to hold his aircraft steady for the final run. Air Gunner Flight Sergeant B.G. McDonald sought to capture in words the sights during a raid over Germany, but observed solemnly, "No mere mortal can possibly do justice to the violent scene that unfolded before our eyes."[42] Sergeant Edison DeMone, who was shot down on his second operation, described the flaming inferno below as "one that I shall never forget."[43] Another airman, a pilot, noted, "Looking down from the bomb run was

A bomber over its target.

often like looking into a blast furnace. Usually a mass of flames, bursting bombs, flak puffs, tracer bullets, shells, flares, and clouds obscured ground features. I can remember seeing only one target clearly during my thirty ops."[44]

The bomb aimer, by this point, was lying face-down in the Perspex nose. He stared through the bombsight looking for geographical features and targets. The bombsights were rudimentary at the start of the war, but they went through a series of improvements, culminating in the very good Mk XIV, which was introduced in May 1942. The Mk XIV system was an automated course-setting sight that corrected for wind through a mechanical computer to update the sights in real time as the aircraft weaved in the air. It required less time—around ten seconds—of flying level to pick up targets on the ground. The improved sights allowed the bomb aimer to be more accurate, but the system was not perfect. Bombs of different configuration and weight—high explosives and incendiaries—fell in widely dispersed patterns from a height of 18,000 feet.

The crew was silent on the intercom as the bomb aimer called out corrections to the pilot. It was difficult for pilots not to flinch as they flew through the black puffs of flak exploding above, below, and in front of them, buffeting the bomber, even sending pieces of jagged steel through the wings or fuselage, but the final run had to be straight. It was a time to tighten the hold on the control column stick, suck in one's gut, and clench one's buttocks. All around the bombers, comrades' planes were on fire or exploding in mid-air, sending pieces of aircraft and body parts tumbling through the night sky. Meanwhile, the bomb aimer uttered his simple instructions: "Left, left, left, right, left, left, left, right, right ... get on the target," as recounted by Sergeant Pilot Arthur B. Wahlroth of No. 405 Squadron.[45]

On the right-hand side of the bomb aimer's compartment were the switches for bomb selection and the bomb release button, known as the "bomb tit." The switch was on the end of a wire and the bomb aimer gripped the tit, holding it firmly as he prepared to jettison his deadly cargo. When satisfied that he had visually acquired the target or the pathfinder's flares marking the aiming points, he called for the bomb bay doors to be opened, which sent freezing air roaring through the fuselage. The pungent smell of cordite from exploding flak was a stark reminder to the cocooned airmen of the danger outside. And then it was "bombs gone."

THE BOMBS DROPPED into the scorched city below, sending shock waves rippling across the plumes of fire, dust, and smoke that obscured entire city blocks. Lancaster pilot Donald Cheney, who survived thirty missions, described the mayhem: "The fires from the altitude we were flying, which would be about 18 to 19 thousand feet, looked like glowing white metal. They seemed to expand and contract and expand and contract. They looked almost like white amoeba that you would see in a microscope. It was the most incredible sight."[46] RCAF Flight Lieutenant W.E. Vaughan, who flew twenty operations during the war, remembered that "Always in the back of my mind was the bombing of civilians.... Sometimes we hit strategic targets and other times there were near misses. But civilians were always killed.... More than once I wondered, 'How many people will those bombs kill?' However, you couldn't dwell on it. That's the way war is." Pilot Les Morrison recalled, "We received no quarter and yielded none." As such, he felt no compunction in dropping the bombs on cities. "At the same time," he continued, "aerial bombardment was a remote and impersonal form of warfare. Intense preoccupation with technical complexity, against a background of personal danger, insulated bomber crews from contemplation of the human factors involved.... I never met the enemy in person, nor did he meet me.... I never saw at close quarters the death and destruction delivered by a bombing attack." Guilt welled up in some airmen, but the very remoteness of the environment they worked in provided some comfort. Morrison believed—as did many other airmen—that in the total war, everything on the ground was a target, and success for him was to "see the raging fires and plumes of smoke rising to 20,000 feet behind us, as we beat our way back to the security of Yorkshire."[47]

The plane bucked when the bombs were released, as it was lightened by several tons. The pilot fought the upward jump and waited for the camera attached to the release wire of the bombs to take the picture of the falling ordnance. The thousands of pounds of high explosives and the incendiaries were followed by a flash flare dropped by the same plane and capable of generating a level of 170 million candlepower to illuminate the sky at about 4,000 feet. The flare allowed the camera to get a picture of the bomb pattern as it fell. In order to acquire the necessary photograph, however, the pilots had to keep level for a dozen or so seconds after bombs away. This was, according to mid-upper gunner Fraser Muir, "the longest and scariest time."[48]

A German woman flees a bomb blast.

Staff officers and specialized interpreters later pored over the pictures to determine the accuracy of the attack and discover whether a crew was a "fringe merchant" that dropped its bombs off-target on purpose to avoid the most intense defensive fire.

When the bomb aimer finally signalled that the photographs were taken, the pilot could begin to gain altitude and fly clear of the worst of the battle zone. Now the greatest danger was that the bombers would drift into one another or be struck by another plane's bombs. Halifax pilot Larry Keelan was always anxious about flying near another attacker's string of bombs. He relied on his "mid-upper gunner to keep a close eye on other planes and scream like hell if he thought I should take evasive action."[49] Flying Officer Mike Harrington, a Lancaster rear gunner, recalled an operation against a refinery at Bochum. His bomber dropped its load, but then the mid-upper gunner shouted, "'Dive to starboard, skip. There's a kite above us with the bomb doors open.' Before the ship could even move, a cookie from the plane above went right through our fuselage, only twelve inches behind the pilot."[50] After plummeting several thousand feet, the pilot regained control. The crew breathed a sigh of relief to find they were still alive—the bomb that struck them was not set to explode at that height or on contact. Their troubles weren't over, however: the damaged bomber was later a target for a night fighter that raked the plane with cannon fire, forcing the crew to bail out over Germany. Most aircrews escaped the friendly fire, but there were other dangers on the way home.

Flight Lieutenant Leslie McCaig wrote in his diary of his crew's sortie over Hanover in October 1943, when a Bf 110 crossed in front of his Lancaster's nose while chasing another bomber—likening it to a "sleek shark on his predatory mission."[51] The Allied attackers now became defenders, with all available crews scanning the skies and manning their guns. "After leaving the target area, I always feel sort of relieved," said bomb aimer John Patterson in his diary. "I guess everyone does. There is a strong temptation to relax, which is a very dangerous practice, as fighters may be waiting for us to leave the target area."[52]

"Some of the fellows went as fast as they could get home," recounted Flying Officer David Chance, who survived thirty-three missions. "Others stooged along, in the normal way. It was best to stay with the stream because if you got ahead of it or away from it, you were a target for night fighters."[53] There was safety in numbers: the night fighters picked off planes on the outside, below or above the stream. Wounded planes, trailing smoke or limping back on three engines, were a prime target, and the crews knew it. Theirs was a terror-filled journey.

The most important set of eyes belonged to the rear gunner. "Gunners were a different breed from other aircrew; but rear gunners were different again, even from the mid-upper gunner in the same crew," observed one pilot.[54] Nearly folded into a ball, legs cramping and stiff with cold, they scanned the skies for hours on end,

A Halifax III of No. 429 Squadron, RCAF, over Mondeville, France. In this rare photograph, a friendly bomb dropped from a bomber above the plane has blown away its starboard tailplane. The wounded plane crashed minutes later.

looking for a darting shadow that might signify an enemy fighter. If the Tail-End Charlie spotted a fighter or saw tracer shells dancing out of the darkness, he shouted into the intercom, and the pilot went into immediate evasive manoeuvres, typically a corkscrew dive. As bomber pilot Harlo Jones commented, "This manoeuvre involved a sharp diving turn toward the direction from which the fighter was attacking, then rolling out and climbing in the opposite direction. The object was to increase as much as possible the angle of deflection a fighter would have to allow when attacking, making a miss more likely and, at night, hopefully eluding the fighter in the process."[55] Sergeant Jim Finnie, an RCAF rear gunner, remarked, "When you're under attack, your gunners are really in control of the aircraft."[56] The gunners also had their machine guns, and although these were underpowered in comparison to the cannons on the night fighters, they could still send a hurricane of lead at an enemy plane, driving it down or away in search of easier prey.

In addition to the enemy fighters, the bombers had to deal with other perils, such as harsh weather, ice forming on the wings, and mechanical failure. Flight Lieutenant John Zinkham remembered returning from an operation and having to pass through a storm cloud. "No sooner did we get into it than we felt its fury. That old 'Hallybag' bounced and lurched around like a sheet of paper in a tornado.... Anything that happened to be loose just bounced off the ceiling, walls and floor.... Heavy bolts of lightning flashed all around us. The thunder was so loud it literally shook the big machine.... The pummelling that old Halifax took would have torn a weaker airplane apart."[57] Somehow their plane survived.

Most experienced airmen were exposed to the terror of flying through clouds and feeling the bird become more sluggish as it iced up and lost altitude. There seemed to be otherworldly problems too. In a raid over Hamburg in August 1943, Douglas Harvey described the ice building up on his aircraft as it passed through a storm. Lightning lit up the clouds around them, stunning in its ferocity and beauty. And then "sparkling blue flames leaped and snaked" within his cockpit, playing over his instrument panel.[58] He knew this was St. Elmo's fire—an uncanny weather phenomenon that manifests itself within electric fields—but nonetheless was shocked by its spectral quality, the flames seeming almost alive. Another pilot, Les Morrison of No. 424 Squadron, described being bathed in St. Elmo's fire, his Lancaster "outlined as though by bright blue neon tubes. The propellers formed four dazzling rings of blue fire. The windows were framed in dancing blue flame. It was an awesome sight.... It also played havoc with my radio, setting up a blaze of static in my headphones which was quite intolerable."[59]

It wasn't just strange weather phenomena that reinforced the flyers' superstitious tendencies. Mechanical failures often were attributed to tricksters from some other dimension. Gremlins, according to RCAF Flying Officer John Clark, were the "mythical creatures that were supposed to be the cause of unexplained accidents generally and, in Air Force terms, the cause of accidental operations of aircraft in flight."[60] Bomb aimer John Patterson wrote to his mother about the gremlins that plagued the planes: "I am of the opinion that there are both Allied and enemy gremlins. Different crews have reported gremlins in the engines that caused them to stutter and backfire until they finally stopped. One crew had two engines fail by enemy gremlins but our Allied gremlins put up a grim fight and were able to keep the two other engines going.... An aircraft detailed to bomb a German city turned around in circles and no one yet seems to know the reason. They are blaming the magnetic gremlins who seem to take great enjoyment in playing with aircraft compasses.... They play queer tricks on aircrews."[61] The magical, and at times malicious, gremlins added to the danger of a sortie, and in the unpredictable world of the flyer—where mechanical failure was always a possibility—it was less disquieting to ascribe a breakdown to mischievous entities than to bad luck.

During the long flight home, crew members faced their own internal issues. The seven- or eight-hour flights, when combined with bursts of adrenaline-fuelled stress, often precipitated a need to urinate or defecate. Neither was easily achieved in the unpressurized and freezing bombers. Many pilots were unwilling either to turn the plane over to the primitive automatic pilot or to make the long trek to the rear of the plane where the portable toilet, known as an Elsan, was located, so they simply peed in a can. As one pilot observed, "It took a very urgent need to crawl to it [the Elsan] through the guts of the bomber, especially if flying over enemy territory."[62] Sergeant Don McCann recalled that Tail-End Charlies were stuck in their tiny rear gun bubbles for the entire flight. They had no choice but to "take a leak right there in the turret."[63]

RCAF navigator Robert Kensett described the challenges posed by an upset stomach, which often were in evidence after the stress and excitement of passing over enemy terrain and targets. After establishing plotting tracks for the pilot, Kensett made his way to the rear of the Halifax, not pleased with having to use the toilet, but certain that he would not make it back to the aerodrome without an accident. He disconnected his oxygen and the intercom wire, and headed through the narrow fuselage, his bulky uniform catching on things, his head giddy from lack of oxygen. He arrived at the throne, a square, box-like structure out in the open, with a lid that lifted up to reveal the seat and bowl. Light-headed, he plugged the oxygen back in and began to rid himself of his clothes. First the parachute came off, then the straps over his shoulders, and his one-piece flying suit, and the layers beneath it. "Sitting on the toilet with your posterior bare, you felt most vulnerable. It was stupid to think that your trousers and flying suit offered any protection whatsoever against bullets, shells and anti-aircraft fire, but in your mind, they did."[64] After flushing out his deposit over France, the exposed and shivering navigator eventually returned to his seat.

In the long hours that passed as they flew back to safe territory, the night fighters trailed the bomber stream, looking for targets. Sometimes the rear gunners spotted them, and urged the pilot to drift away into the enveloping night. Flight Lieutenant Bruce Betcher of No. 419 Squadron described what it was like to be pursued by a Ju 88 night fighter: "He was gently weaving on a parallel course about a hundred feet down and two hundred yards to starboard.... The thought occurred to me that if we dived by we might give him a blast," but Betcher decided against it. When later he was asked by the base's intelligence officer why he had not engaged the enemy, he replied, "Have you ever heard of the sheep attacking the wolves?"[65]

Enemy fighters sought to climb above the stream, and then fired off flares to illuminate the skies. Once a bomber was located, the German pilot might choose to attack it, but some experienced stalkers held off for hours, trailing the bomber stream, working their fighter into its interior, hoping that the bomber crews would let down their guard as they moved out of Germany into France, and ultimately back to the safety of British air space. Allied aircraft had an IFF (Identification Friend or Foe) signal that pulsated out from their birds. If it was turned on and working, it signalled their own anti-aircraft defences not to open fire. But a Luftwaffe fighter in the middle of the stream could sneak past these defences unnoticed. At some point, the fighter would strike. A particularly effective ploy was to follow the bombers back to their bases and attack them as they circled the airfield waiting for their turn to land, or, even riskier, to shoot up the planes once they were on the ground. Of course, such a raid left the night fighter deep in enemy air space after having stirred up a hornet's nest. Daring becomes recklessness at some point. Fighter pilots also yearned for home.

THE MAJORITY OF BOMBERS returned to base unscathed, but some were ripped open by flak or a fighter attack, their engines knocked out, while smoke-blackened turrets hinted at disasters inside the plane. Most bombers had also exhausted all but the last vapours of fuel. Instruments might be malfunctioning or damaged.

*A tired Halifax pilot of No. 405 Squadron, RCAF, sipping his coffee
(likely laced with rum) after a July 1942 air raid against Germany.*

Crippled aircraft had priority to land, while the rest circled and tried not to collide in the clouds before the control tower called them down. Shot-up bombers often landed hard, on one wheel or their belly, skidding along, veering off the runway, crashing through bushes, buildings, or trees, and suffering any of the other disasters that could befall mammoth planes landing in distress. Others burst into flames on impact. Many of the planes carried corpses.

"Always on arriving back at base, after a successful mission, one had the most wonderful feeling of euphoria," wrote bomber pilot Walter Irwin. "I guess it stemmed partly from the satisfaction of a job well done, but mostly from a profound feeling of relief at still being alive."[66] Mosquito pilot George Stewart, who completed fifty operations before the age of twenty-one, found satisfaction in "the tired and almost drunken feeling we had after landing and getting out of the kite."[67] The ground crews waited for them. No matter the hour, there were trucks on hand to pick up the flyers with their rubbery legs and aching shoulder muscles, and to drive them to the official debriefing. Most of the crews had gone eighteen to twenty hours without sleep and were dehydrated from heavy sweating, lack of water, and reliance on oxygen. At the debriefing room, airmen received a stiff tot of rum, which could be taken straight or mixed into coffee, with refills for those flyers who had endured particularly difficult sorties. Murray Peden, a Canadian pilot in the RAF's No. 214 Squadron, wrote that coffee laced with Lamb's rum "tasted terrible but worked therapeutic miracles."[68]

Coming from darkness into the light of the debriefing room, combined with the belly warmth of rum, soon got tongues wagging. The debriefing officer, who was occasionally a member of the Women's Division of the RCAF, queried the men about weather conditions, aircraft problems, and enemy defences. As one Canadian airman remembered, "They were especially interested in the raid itself and the damage inflicted to the target and the exact time that any of our own aircraft were shot down."[69] Some of the aircrews were skeptical of the value of this information, and gave pat or flippant answers. However, most flyers tried to convey accurately what they saw from their bird's-eye view over the conflagration. The bomber's own aerial photographs—a six photo sequence—formed the final picture of the raid.

When debriefing was concluded, the airmen returned their equipment and parachutes, went to the mess for a meal, and then to bed. Most were wrung out like dishrags, chain-smoking, with bleary eyes and shaking hands. The airmen noted the empty beds and wondered if their chums had landed at another base, bailed out over Europe, or been killed in a fiery crash. The bone-deep exhaustion pushed some immediately into a slumber, but others lay restlessly awake, with the wakey-wakey pills still coursing through their system, or simply unable to calm the mind as it replayed the night's events. And for those who drifted off, most knew that they would soon do it all again, in the seemingly never-ending battles of the bomber war.

CHAPTER 11

DAY OF DESTRUCTION

The Canadian soldiers in Britain were restless. The lead elements of the 1st Canadian Infantry Division had arrived in late 1939 and had been joined by tens of thousands of comrades during the subsequent three years. Relentless training had lost its appeal, and in some places—especially in small town pubs—the Canadians were wearing out their welcome. The number of crimes committed by Canadians was on the rise, as was the incidence of out-of-wedlock pregnancy.[1] Senior commanders worried that the Dominion's army-in-waiting was degenerating into an army in stagnation while the navy and air force were fighting on multiple fronts. Defending the coast against a phantom invasion was a far cry from the glory of Currie's Canadian Corps on the Western Front during the last war. The Canadian Army needed action.

The British were also under pressure. Stalin's forces on the Eastern Front had absorbed the German onslaught of 1941. In the process, they had lost millions (killed, wounded, and captured), together with thousands of tanks, guns, and aircraft. They had been badly mauled, but they had turned back the Wehrmacht at the gates of Moscow. The Soviets subsequently lost even more men in battle in 1942 in a series of shambolic defeats, but German soldiers had suffered too, as they faced the brutal winter, chronically hungry and often seeking shelter rather than victory. The Soviet soldiers fared worse, but remained unbroken—forced to fight by political officers willing to use mass execution as a motivator, and by the knowledge that the Germans, should they catch them, would either murder them outright or starve them to death. In the Far East, the Japanese had overrun Hong Kong, Malaya, Singapore, and much of Burma with incredible speed. In the course of 90 days, the British lost 2 capital ships, 200 aircraft, and 166,000 men, of whom 130,000 were taken prisoner.[2] British and Commonwealth forces were driven to defeat by a Japanese army inferior to their own in number. Only in North Africa had the British shown any signs of resilience. The fighting there took place in seesaw battles, both sides alternately attacking and defending, tethered to long and unstable supply lines, until Rommel's Afrika Korps humiliated the British Eighth Army at Tobruk in June 1942.

But the primary battlefield lay on the Eastern Front, where the Soviets bore the brunt of the Nazi war machine—more than two-thirds of the German army. Stalin pleaded with the West for some kind of relief. By this, he meant the opening of a new front, which came to be known as the Second Front, to siphon off German forces.[3] While Churchill sympathized with the Soviet position—or, more accurately, was wary of how a Soviet collapse would allow his enemy to divert military resources to the Western Front—he blanched at the thought of invading Europe before the necessary resources were in place. The brash and reckless Americans, who were mistrustful of the seemingly gun-shy British, demanded an early invasion of Europe, preferably in 1943. There was even insane talk of going in 1942. The British, staggered by this exuberance, pointed to reams of studies that showed the Allies lacked enough bombers, fighters, warships, landing craft, or trained soldiers to successfully launch an amphibious attack, let alone supply it against the inevitable German counterattack. Passion over reason almost prevailed, and Churchill's counter-claims made him seem timid as the impatient Yanks gnashed their teeth over the delay. Churchill, seeking to hold off his allies, proposed that a series of small-scale attacks might draw off some of the enemy's resources. This failed to satisfy Stalin, who believed the Allies were all too happy to see the Communists and Nazis bleed each other white, just as he had once hoped the democracies would do in the West, but some form of attack was better than nothing. Meanwhile, Churchill and Roosevelt sent mountains of war supplies through the sea lanes to Stalin's forces—a staggering $9.3 billion in aid from the United States between 1943 and 1945—and kept up the important bombing campaign against German cities and infrastructure.[4]

CHURCHILL TURNED FOR ADVICE to Lord Louis Mountbatten, the handsome second cousin to the future Queen Elizabeth, known to friends as "Dickie." The ambitious naval captain had lost three ships during the early years of the war, but he retained his cavalier cheerfulness. Promoted far beyond his competence, Mountbatten was given command of the Combined Operations Headquarters in March 1942, at the rank of vice-admiral. He came with an aggressive mandate: to take the war to the Germans in a series of escalating raids.

The first raids had been launched in June 1940, and many had followed since then, usually conducted by British commandos. They enjoyed modest success: more often than not, the commando units limped back to Britain after taking grim casualties. At best, these "butcher and bolt" operations were mere pinpricks against the German-controlled Continent, but still they appealed to Churchill as a means of keeping the Germans on their toes.[5] Aware that Churchill wanted larger and more aggressive raids, Mountbatten, now elevated to a position on the Chiefs of Staff Committee, set out to plan a newsworthy operation that would boost morale and placate Stalin. But Mountbatten had a peculiar headquarters, which was staffed by misfits and castoffs from other services. Among its failures was its inability to process intelligence, and so it relied on the other services for information.[6] This failure would eventually result in a misreading and gross underestimation of the strength of enemy forces in Dieppe.

IN APRIL 1942, First Canadian Army was established in England, eventually consisting of two corps of three infantry divisions, two armoured divisions, and two armoured brigades. This was the first and last time in Canada's history that the nation fielded an army in battle. In the absence of General Andrew McNaughton, who was on leave due to illness, Lieutenant-General Harry Crerar was now in temporary command of the army. Crerar had arrived in England in late 1941, having given up his appointment as chief of the general staff in Canada to take over I Canadian Corps. The fifty-three-year-old career soldier was aware of his lack of command experience, having never commanded at the brigade or divisional level, and he was anxious for an operation in which to prove himself. He had shown that he was willing to send Canadian infantry battalions to Hong Kong to see Canada pull its weight in the Empire's war effort, and when he heard that a major raid was to be directed at the French coast, he again pushed aggressively for his forces to be involved. The Canadian government of Mackenzie King had no say in the matter, having generally abdicated operational control over the deployment of its overseas forces. As the plan took form, the target turned out to be the French resort town of Dieppe, long a popular destination for vacationing British tourists because of its casino and picturesque coastline. Close to 5,000 of the 6,000 troops assaulting the town and surrounding area would be Canadian.

The British agreed to the Canadian request to take the lead in the raid, even though Mountbatten's headquarters would continue to plan the operation. The 2nd Canadian Infantry Division, under the command of Major-General J. Hamilton Roberts, was selected for the assault by General Bernard Montgomery, then commander of South Eastern Command, in which the Canadians served. "Ham" Roberts, a fifty-year-old professional soldier with a jowly, bulldog face, had risen to prominence after saving the guns in the embarrassing June 1940 sojourn to the Continent, and had subsequently proven himself to be a good trainer of men. His division was considered to be the best in the Canadian Army. He was optimistic about the raid's chance of success, even though much of the planning was out of his hands. In one pep talk to his men, he told them that the forthcoming operation would be a "piece of cake." The statement would come back to haunt him.

The 2nd Division underwent intense training, including moving to and from landing craft and assaulting beaches. At the same time, Mountbatten's headquarters refined the plan, which was increasingly heralded as a dress rehearsal for the eventual invasion of Europe. It would be a test of combined arms and inter-service cooperation, as well as a chance to challenge German defences. As these expectations were raised, the raid took on the scale and substance of a major operation. Everyone involved in the planning knew casualties would be sustained: they were inevitable in an attack from the sea against a fortified port. Speed and surprise would, it was hoped, carry the day.

There was a second, secret component to the Dieppe operation. The British were desperate to acquire German intelligence documents, code books, and possibly one of the new four-rotor Enigma encryption machines. Since early 1942, the German wireless communications from the U-boats in the Atlantic to their shore-based headquarters had gone dark, leaving British cryptologists unable to read the chatter that had been so essential in guiding the Allied high command and saving merchant shipping. A number of "pinch" raids had been pulled off by British commandos to gather secondary bits of intelligence, but more information was needed to break the codes. Now, at Dieppe, a larger raid by Royal Marine commandos would go in behind the Canadian main assault with the goal of ransacking a local German naval headquarters. Though this part of the raid was cloaked in secrecy to avoid letting the Germans know what the British cryptologists were up to, it could succeed only if the main Canadian assault made headway into Dieppe, blasting and breaking everything in its path. But while the operation was expected to provide valuable information to assist in breaking the U-boat codes and gaining an upper hand in the Battle of the Atlantic, the failure of the Royal Navy to devote any of its large ships to the Dieppe operation would suggest that this stealth raid did not matter as much to the navy as some historians have sensationally claimed—going so far as to argue that the entire Dieppe raid was but a cover for the commando pinch.[7] It was not. The navy saw an opportunity to add the pinch operation to the already ballooning Dieppe raid in the hope of gaining advantage should the operation be a success.

After months of training and marshalling of resources, Operation Rutter was set for early July. But a German air raid on the concentrated troop ships that had gathered for the assault left the planners worried that the German pilots would report what they had seen and so destroy the chance for surprise. While this did not happen, poor weather on July 8, with rough, choppy waters, would have disrupted the embarkation of soldiers into the landing craft (a procedure that had been identified as a problem during training over the previous month), and that would have led to an uncoordinated assault on the targets.[8] Surprise and shock were vital to the success of the raid; uncoordinated landings would lead to disaster. Rutter was cancelled. Many of the Canadians were disappointed to hear the operation had been scrubbed—Canadian journalist Ross Munro reported that some cried openly.[9] Even though everyone involved in the raid was sworn to secrecy, soon the Canadian soldiers and British sailors talked about the botched raid that the bloody "red tabs"— the staff officers and commanders—had failed to pull off.

MOUNTBATTEN'S HEADQUARTERS conducted a post mortem in the days that followed the scuttling of the plan. With unpredictable weather having ultimately led to the cancellation, Mountbatten wondered if the operation could be remounted.

Perhaps the element of surprise had not been blown? Even if it had been, the Germans would never believe that the same operation would be directed against the same target. Mountbatten chewed over this tasty morsel and decided to tee up the operation again. It was to be top secret. No record has ever been found of the order to remount the raid, which has led some historians to believe it was done without Churchill's knowledge.[10] This seems unlikely, however, because Mountbatten and Churchill worked closely together, Mountbatten had Churchill's full support for mounting raids in general, and Churchill still needed an operation to pacify Stalin. This last factor became even more pressing in July after convoy PQ 17, taking supplies through the Arctic Ocean to the Soviet Union, was savaged, losing twenty-four of thirty-five merchant ships. Ship-borne aid was temporarily curtailed, and Churchill quaked a little at having to explain this to Stalin. When he had his first face-to-face meeting with the Russian dictator in Moscow in early August, Churchill spoke of an upcoming major raid—thus leaving little doubt that he was in the know about the Dieppe raid, despite the absence of a paper trail.[11] That is not to say that Mountbatten's plan was not foolhardy: he ordered the new raid to be directed against the same target, using the same troops, apparently in the belief that the Germans—should they have got word of the previously cancelled operation—would assume that no one in their right mind would order such an attack.

The Canadians began to feel uneasy. The optimistic Crerar commented on August 11 that "given an even break in luck and good navigation, the demonstration should prove successful."[12] This was scarcely an expression of unbridled enthusiasm. But the Canadians had asked to be involved in the operation, and now Crerar and McNaughton, who had returned to command the army, felt that their hands were tied.[13] It would have taken enormous courage to turn down the operation after asking to be a part of it, and after the Canadian Army's years of relative inactivity.

There were other problems. Mountbatten's command was to coordinate the three major services, but the operation had lost its lustre and it was difficult for the service heads to see how success, as it related to their particular arm, would be achieved and measured. The navy wanted little part in this operation. Its forces already were spread thinly in several theatres of war and desperately trying to keep from losing the Battle of the Atlantic. When Mountbatten asked Admiral Sir Dudley Pound for a battleship to supply crushing firepower with its 15-inch guns, the admiral, still sore about the loss of his two capital ships to land-based aircraft in the Far East, replied, "Battleships by daylight off the French coast? You must be mad, Dickie!"[14] The Royal Navy was willing to commit only eight small "Hunt" class destroyers equipped with relatively weak 4-inch guns. This disastrous shortcoming in firepower might have been made good if Sir Charles Portal, chief of the air staff, had been willing to devote his formidable bombing force to smashing the Germans, but he too refused to risk his assets. The withdrawal of the air element represented another major change from the original Rutter plan, but Portal was concerned about German anti-aircraft defences, and he also knew that the bombers would have grave difficulty in targeting the rather narrow enemy fortifications along the landing sites. The likelihood of significant French civilian casualties was another consideration: any bomber strike would almost certainly hit the residential areas near the beach. Moreover, with the concentrations of German Luftwaffe warplanes in the area, Portal and the air officer commanding-in-chief of Bomber Command, Arthur Harris, believed that the bombers would be savaged by flak and fighters. Events would prove that their misgivings were unwarranted: the Luftwaffe was surprised by the heavy raids that commenced the operation, and a bombing run would likely have achieved its objective and returned home by the time the enemy mounted any sort of defence. Bomber Command bowed out of the operation, allowing only eight squadrons of Hurricane fighter bombers and five squadrons of medium bombers to soften up the defences. The one positive contribution to the planning was made by RAF Fighter Command, whose senior officers were always spoiling for a fight. Forty-eight squadrons of Spitfires—six of which were RCAF—were committed in the hope of bringing the Luftwaffe to battle, which was in accordance with the air arm's aggressive policy of "leaning into" Europe. However, the ineptitude demonstrated by Mountbatten's headquarters in corralling the proper assets revealed scandalous deficiencies in planning for the operation that was set for August 19, 1942.

WHILE MOST OFFICERS would readily acknowledge that no plan survives contact with the enemy, few battles begin without some semblance of a plan. For the raid on the 19th, the primary landing beach in front of the town of Dieppe would be

assaulted by the Royal Hamilton Light Infantry and the Essex Scottish, both drawing their recruits from southwestern Ontario. The infantry was to be supported by
Churchill tanks of the Calgary Regiment, as well as artillery, engineer, and medical
units. In the aftermath of the wide-ranging tank battles of France, the Middle East,
and the Russian steppes, the Allied planners put enormous faith in the power of the
tank to suppress and overcome enemy defences. On the far flanks, about three kilometres from each of the outside beaches, British commandos were to knock out a
series of coastal battery positions that could rake incoming Allied ships. Closer to the
main Dieppe beach, the village of Puys to the north was the objective of Toronto's
Royal Regiment of Canada and the Black Watch (Royal Highland Regiment), while
Pourville to the south of Dieppe was to fall to the South Saskatchewan Regiment
and the Queen's Own Cameron Highlanders of Canada. The objective on these
two flanking beaches was to destroy guns on the headlands that overlooked the
main beach. A floating reserve consisting of the Fusiliers Mont-Royal (FMR) from
Montreal was to be ordered forward onto the main beach to exploit the initial push
into the town. Additionally, a secret reserve of 250 British Royal Marines was to
land behind the FMRs to punch through the centre to the German headquarters at
the Hotel Moderne. Here, it was hoped, the marines would capture key intelligence
documents or codes to the German Enigma machine. The flanking beaches and
operations were to be assaulted concurrently at 4:50 A.M., a time of day known as
nautical twilight, just as the horizon was becoming discernible. The primary assault
on Dieppe would follow half an hour later to allow time for the guns along the cliffs
and headways to be captured. Nowhere in the planning documents does this discrep-
ancy of thirty minutes square with the operation being based on surprise and shock.
Once ashore, the Canadians were to hold the town for one tidal period, about six
hours, before landing craft returned to take them off the beaches.

Mountbatten's staff put much stock on landing in the dark to ensure that enemy
defenders, should they be alerted, would have few identifiable targets. The planners
placed far less emphasis, and disastrously so, on suppressing the mortar, machine
gun, and sniper positions that honeycombed the cliffs overlooking Dieppe and the
landing beaches. Even though these positions were camouflaged and almost invisible on the aerial photographs, common sense dictated that the Germans would

hold the high ground that allowed them to sweep the beaches with enfilade fire. Mountbatten's planning officers hoped that the light bombers and Spitfires might stun, or even demolish, these positions, but this wishful thinking was unsupported by experience. Airpower, to that point in the war, had been unable to take out camouflaged ground forces in hardened positions. For these strongpoints to be neutralized, the beach landings at Puys and Pourville had to be a complete success, or the landing on the main beach had to be so rapid as to overrun the enemy and pass through the kill zone. This was just one of the many examples of Mountbatten's deficient planning. Another equally egregious oversight was the failure to plan the withdrawal: how were the troops, at the end of the six hours, going to retreat to their landing crafts and pull back to the waiting ships if they simultaneously were engaged in a firefight with the enemy? The FMRs, supported by a new wave of Churchill tanks, were to hold open the perimeter, but the planning documents do not explain in any detail how this last wave was to be pulled off the beach while being pressed back by German defenders-turned-attackers, who would be surging in strength even as the Canadians were drawing down their forces in retreat. Too much of the plan was left to chance and hope, all of which was contingent on a coordinated surprise landing on several fronts.

The raiders were to demolish fortifications, wreck harbour facilities, kill Germans, and then withdraw. A radar station in the Pourville sector was a target of opportunity and it was hoped that actionable intelligence would be gathered there, while the marines' raid on the German headquarters, if successful, would serve up a grab bag of intelligence goodies for the cryptologists at Bletchley Park, the British intelligence-cracking unit. It is unclear how these new codes would have assisted the wizards at Bletchley Park, as the Germans would have known that their codes had been snatched, and therefore compromised, and so it is highly unlikely that they would have resulted in any long-term reading of the enemy's signals. But the cryptologists had proved effective in the past in breaking enemy transmissions by using only scraps of information gleaned from obscure sources. While the strategic goal of pressuring the Germans to guard against a second front and, hopefully, pull back military resources from the east, was worthy—as was the dress rehearsal aspect of the raid for a future invasion—the tactical goals of the raid were almost trivial.

Dieppe would be a hard nut to crack. The 90-kilometre front of the Dieppe sector was held by the 302nd Infantry Division. It consisted of three regiments of infantry augmented by artillery and anti-aircraft units, including sixteen 10cm field howitzers, eight French 75mm guns, and two batteries of 37mm and 20mm anti-aircraft guns.[15] While the entirety of the French coastline was indefensible, the Germans had focused on the port of Dieppe, which they had spent months fortifying with wire entanglements and concrete barriers. They demolished anything along the beaches that could be used for cover. In fact, turning Dieppe into a designated "Defended Area" had been the Germans' only goal in that sector, and though some of the best and most aggressive German units and formations had been transferred to the Eastern Front, the garrison had trained intensely to repel an amphibious landing. The Germans were ready for battle, with multiple machine guns, light mortars, and medium artillery all situated to saturate the beaches with intense fire.[16] At the same time, throughout August the German high command had issued warnings to the various garrisons along the coast, reminding them to be vigilant—not because of leaked information, but simply as a precaution on days when the tides were low and advantageous for an amphibious landing. August 19 was singled out as a possible invasion day, and the entire German garrison was at the alert.

IN THE DAYS LEADING UP TO THE OPERATION, the Canadians were first put in isolation and then transferred to the waiting warships. Many infantrymen assumed it was another training operation, but the tension was more palpable, and soon rumours and information leaked by officers revealed the nature of the raid. Most of the confident Canadians were aching for battle and prepared themselves for the coming fight as the sun set on August 18.

The Allied operation got off to a poor start in the early morning of the 19th, when British warships and other Allied vessels steaming to the beaches ran into a German inshore convoy at 3:47 A.M. off Berneval, on the left flank. The sharp firefight was heard by the German coastal defence troops, but they interpreted it as another regular Royal Navy assault against their convoys, and no additional alarm was raised. However, the brief sea battle had a deleterious effect on the commando units that were directed to the northern flank against Berneval, as the battle scattered their small boats and many never landed at their assigned targets. The commando raid against

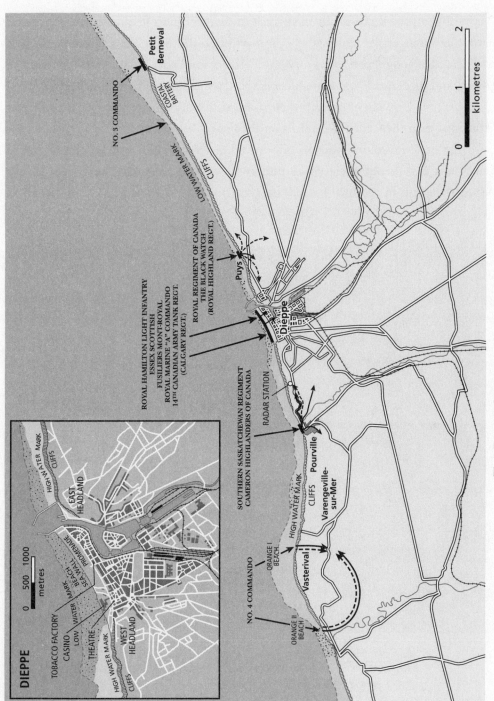

The Dieppe Operation, August 19, 1942

Berneval had little success, but the assault on the southern flank, against the coastal battery at Varengeville, achieved its objectives as Lord Lovat's No. 4 Commando unit of 252 raiders fought their way forward.[17] The commandos bore up well against the enemy, and their attack was a model operation, knocking out the battery in sustained and fierce fighting. They achieved their mission, although this success ultimately had little impact on the Canadian attacks on the Pourville beaches.

By the time the commandos had destroyed or screened the guns to the south, the Canadians' assault was already well underway, with the attacking battalions having begun their run-in around 3 A.M., after having moved from large troop ships to

Landing craft carrying Canadian troops ashore to Dieppe, August 19, 1942.
Because of the long run-in to the beaches, many of the landing craft
were late in dropping the infantry on their objectives.

smaller landing craft. They faced about a 15-kilometre voyage to the beach, which took some two hours, and despite the gentle breeze and the full moon, the distance was too great to allow for the coordination of multiple vessels. It all but guaranteed that some of the dozens of landing crafts would arrive late.

AT PUYS, THE GERMANS had established concrete machine-gun positions along the chalk cliffs that rose 60 metres from the narrow cove. The beach was a mere 200 metres long and 15 metres deep at high tide. The two machine-gun positions in bunkers on the flanks of the beach, along with three machine guns situated along the cliffs, could rake the entire area. Quite apart from the barrier imposed by the terrain and the careful placement of the machine guns, the beach was blocked by a 3.5-metre concrete seawall and dense coils of barbed wire. It was lunacy to expect any force to land under these conditions.

The Royal Regiment of Canada sent all four companies, some 554 strong, into the beach area, backed by another 111 officers and men from the Black Watch (Royal Highland Regiment). The landing flotilla would come ashore in three separate waves, but the five first-wave landing craft drifted off course during their lengthy voyage, leaving them to close on the beach about twenty minutes late, around 5:10 A.M. Dawn was breaking, and the Canadians were visible for hundreds of metres before they reached land.[18] The German defenders, roused by the fighter-bomber attack against various fortifications along the main Dieppe beach to the south, watched the unreal spectacle of the Canadians chugging stolidly towards their gun emplacements. Ammunition was checked and rifle triggers fingered nervously. Even though the defenders numbered a mere two platoons, a total of around 100 soldiers, every single one of them had time to line up their Mauser rifles or heavy machine guns under the glow of aerial flares, and simply wait for the steel doors of the landing craft to drop.

Private Alfred Moody was on one of the lead landing craft. When the ramp dropped, a number of men were bowled over by machine-gun fire. "How anybody could get through it and still live, I still don't know," Moody wrote. "I looked out there and saw all these little white things going by. Every one of these was their tracer bullets. For every one you saw, there was four or five you didn't see. I saw guys falling, and said to myself, 'This is sheer madness.'"[19] He hesitated for a second, but then he and his surviving platoon mates pushed forward into the cold water, waded awkwardly to the beach, and then ran to the seawall, which seemed to offer some cover. When Moody glanced behind him, he saw dead and dying Canadians all over the beach and dozens more lying in bloodied piles inside the yawning landing craft.

Many of the Germans were shooting through the narrow slits in concrete pill-boxes, leaving little opportunity for Canadians to take them out. A few officers and men ran through the firestorm to throw grenades at their enemy, but most of these Royals paid for their bravery with their lives. The terrible crossfire on the beach was thickened up by machine gunners raking the ground from the cliffs, while mortar teams lobbed their bombs into the confined beach area to devastating effect. The only protection was afforded by the seawall, and even this was partially enfiladed by machine-gun fire from the eastern cliff. Lance-Corporal L.G. Ellis of A Company made the run from his landing craft to the wall with his platoon around him. When he arrived, he was alone. Every single one of his platoon mates had been cut down by bullets or mortar fragments.[20] Private Peter Macleod had a very short battle. As he left the landing craft, a bullet slammed into his face. The slug tore out his eye, sending him flopping back into the crimson-stained water. Stunned by the trauma, he nonetheless dragged himself forward out of the water, already choked with bodies, and was shot in the leg before he reached the seawall. Then, in his words, "all hell had let loose."[21] He got a bandage on his leg, but agonized over finding a way to stop the bleeding from his shredded face. As he was trying to wrap a bandage around his eyes, he was shot again in the head. He slipped into unconsciousness, but somehow survived his wounds.

The wall protected the men if they hugged it tightly, but it was also a trap. Once there, it was very difficult for the attackers to get up and keep moving. The Royals' platoons were scattered along the barrier, and many of the junior officers and NCOs had been shot down. The top of the wall was fringed and blocked by three layers of barbed wire, and more rows of wire lay beyond it that were, according to one rifleman, "virtually impassable."[22] Fire from the Germans intensified as they found their range, and the Canadians could do little in reply. Both of the regiment's 3-inch mortar teams had been wiped out, the first without launching a single bomb, while the second managed to get off just three bombs before the entire team was killed. From the wall, riflemen snapped off a few rounds from their Lee Enfields, and the Bren gunners laid down some fire, but with the Germans camouflaged and protected, not much could be seen, let alone hit.[23] And anyone who exposed themselves for long was a target for riflemen from above. "The Royals were shot down in heaps on the beach without knowing where the firing was coming from," remarked one eyewitness.[24]

The second wave of landing craft landed at about 5:35 A.M., but dozens of infantrymen never even passed out of the steel confines. The sailors took in living Canadians, dropped the ramp, saw most of their infantry comrades torn apart by machine-gun fire, and then pulled back off the beach with their bleeding cargo. The wounded riflemen writhed in agony, their screams echoing inside the confines of the steel craft, while mortar fire crashed down in the water and bullets pinged off the sides. When the third wave, consisting of the Black Watch, arrived and surveyed the beach, its officers looked for an opportunity to reinforce success. None could be seen. But no news had been received from the Royals because all the wireless sets were broken, and the Black Watch made the fateful decision to continue with the landing. Perhaps more experienced officers would have aborted the mission. As it stood, 111 Black Watch troops came ashore in a slightly secluded part of the beach, but were funnelled back to the seawall, where they had little impact on the battle. Only a single Highlander from the Black Watch got off the beach and returned to Britain.

The seawall soon resembled a charnel house. Blood flowed from bodies, forming puddles or soaking into the sand. The journalist Ross Munro was on one of the landing craft and miraculously survived the dropping of the ramp and the staggeringly heavy fire that ripped men apart around him. As he looked out over the open bow, he saw dozens of slain Canadians floating in the water, crumpled on the beaches, or lying motionless along the seawall. "It was brutal and terrible and shocked you almost to insensibility."[25]

Even amid the horror, some of the junior officers and NCOs struggled on, ordering forward Bangalore torpedoes—long, thin tubes filled with explosives—to blow a ragged hole through the barbed wire. About half a dozen riflemen passed through the gap before German fire found it. The storm party encountered additional barbed wire obstructions beyond the first barrier and found themselves without Bangalores.

They were reduced to snipping the metal strands by hand, using wire cutters. But soon several Germans had turned their attention to this threat, and at least one Canadian was riddled with machine-gun fire here, his body left tangled in the wire. All of the riflemen would have been annihilated if one of their comrades from the seawall had not thrown a smoke grenade. The Canadians ran back to the uncertain safety of the beach.

In another section of the fire-swept front, on the eastern headlands, the Royals' commanding officer, Lieutenant-Colonel Douglas Catto, a Great War artilleryman and Toronto architect, was able to rally about two dozen men who were partially protected from the enemy fire by a shallow curvature that jutted into the seawall. They tried to move forward up a narrow staircase, but it was blocked by barbed wire. With no Bangalore torpedo, they spent thirty excruciating minutes cutting the wire by hand. Each man took his turn in the dangerously exposed position, including the colonel, while the others laid down fire. Their determination paid off and they were eventually able, around 7 A.M., to race up the stairs to the top of the cliff, where they cleared a number of positions. Unfortunately, their exit from the beach was soon thereafter blocked by enemy riflemen and machine gunners who swept it with continuous small-arms fire. Catto's battle group swept along the cliff, and eventually turned in an attempt to complete their objective in connecting with the Essex Scottish on the main beach. It would have been wiser to try to engage the Puys beach defenders who were shooting vulnerable Canadians below. Their decision to turn towards Dieppe ensured that no other Canadians made it to the top.

Nothing prepared the Canadians trapped on the beach for the cacophony of noise in the battle zone. Or for the mauling. Heaps of bodies lay along the seawall. One observer described the beach as pure "carnage ... the whole slope was just littered with khaki bodies of the wounded and killed Royals."[26] This unfettered butchering went on for some three hours before most of the Royals surrendered around 8:30 A.M. Catto's group at the top of the cliff held out until the afternoon, but it too was in a futile position and eventually downed arms. Only 67 of the 554 Royals got off the beach, and many of them were wounded in the second-wave landings, having never stepped off their landing craft. Riflemen killed many Canadians who sought to swim away, while others drowned from their exertions. A number of the landing craft braved the fire in an attempt to pick up survivors, but several were blown apart by mortar bombs or, in one tragic case, were so heavily laden with the wounded that the craft capsized, leading to a mass drowning. In the end, some 227 Royals were killed, including 20 men who died of their wounds in captivity or after returning to England. The Royal Regiment of Canada lay in ruins, one full company of the Black Watch was killed or captured, and the German guns on the eastern headland overlooking Dieppe were intact.

AT THE POURVILLE BEACHES to the south of Dieppe, the navy put the twelve landing craft carrying about 500 infantrymen of the South Saskatchewan Regiment ashore on time at 4:50 A.M., while the Queen's Own Cameron Highlanders of Canada were to come in half an hour later in a second wave, although they were delayed another thirty minutes after that. The Pourville beach was much longer than that at Puys, but like the other, it was dominated by cliffs on both sides. The enemy strongpoints here would have to be knocked out early in the battle. However, more than half of the South Sasks—A (Able) and D (Dog) Company—landed in the wrong place, on the west side of the Scie River (furthest from the main Dieppe beaches), which divided the front.

On the eastern side of the river, C (Charlie) Company of the South Sasks advanced on the village of Pourville, which consisted of a few blocks of red-brick buildings and houses with white picket fences. Terrified French civilians sought cover in cellars or attics, praying for the storm to pass over them. When the Canadians encountered German resistance, they pinned the enemy down with Bren gun- and rifle fire, allowing other units to advance on the flanks and bomb them into submission. Their Sten guns—a submachine gun with forty-seven parts—were much less effective than the Brens or the Germans' machinengewehr 34, and most jammed at some point in the battle. Still, the Germans were either killed or driven out of Pourville by around 5:30 A.M., and the Sasks on the eastern side of the Scie fought their way forward, some 3 kilometres, occupying hills southwest of the village.

Private W.A. Haggard, who took over his platoon when his NCO was gunned down, later claimed, "The Canadian troops showed themselves far better soldiers than the Germans whom they encountered. Their morale was excellent, and they were ready to fight, whereas the enemy infantry gave in easily when it came to close quarter fighting."[27] However, Haggard's optimistic assessment was contradicted in an official report by the Cameron Highlanders, which observed that the German defenders were well trained, resilient, and flexible: "Machine guns were situated to cover all beaches, about 800 yards to the rear. They were well prepared sites and camouflaged. The snipers were numerous and very accurate, well-spread out, pre-determined positions, very hard to locate.... They changed positions frequently, kept away, moved back when our troops advanced and followed our troops as they withdrew."[28] Further to the rear, a few German 81mm mortars harassed the village and beaches with bomb fire that exploded and sent hundreds of slivers of metal in all directions.

In response to the Canadian inroads, the Germans rushed forward reinforcements. Some of these made for the heights of Pourville (closest to Dieppe), which

A Hunt Class destroyer firing in support of Canadians on the beaches.
The destroyers had little impact on the battle.

overlooked the landing sites. The South Saskatchewan attack party that sought to clear that position and reach the radar station (about halfway between Pourville and Dieppe) was turned back with heavy casualties, and thereafter the Germans could fire down and into the Canadians advancing off the beach. Royal Canadian Artillery forward observers sent coordinates back to the Royal Navy destroyers by wireless to drench the positions with shellfire, but either the observers or the gunners were unable to spot the camouflaged German strongpoints.[29] A few salvos of 4-inch shells slammed into the cliff face, but did little to slow the rate of enemy fire.

The advance was harder on the western side of the river, where the Sasks were soon pinned down at the only bridge across the Scie. It was covered by enemy mortar and machine-gun fire. Bodies piled up. Watching the Germans gain the initiative as the Canadians were cut down crossing the 24-metre bridge, Lieutenant-Colonel Cecil Merritt, the youthful commander of the South Sasks, whose moustache lent only slight gravity to his baby face, moved up from his forward headquarters on the beach and rallied his men. Merritt raced back and forth as bullets and shrapnel whirled through the air and, at around 5:50 A.M., led his men across the bridge, shouting encouragement and somehow escaping unscathed. Many of his men were not so fortunate, and soon the bridge was heaped with bodies. Merritt survived and continued to throw himself into battle, later racing forward into heavy fire before tossing a grenade and blowing up a machine-gun position. Their colonel's inspiring leadership notwithstanding, the South Sasks who crossed the bridge made little progress.

Back at the beach, the Queen's Own Cameron Highlanders of Canada landed late, at around 5:50 A.M. They took fire from about 1,000 metres out, bullets ringing off the steel hulls of the landing craft. As men cringed inside the fragile vessels, a brave piper stood up on the fo'c'sle to inspire his comrades. Much of the skirling wail from his instrument was lost in the unremitting noise of battle, but the Highlanders charged into the fight. Their commanding officer, Lieutenant-Colonel Alfred Gostling, was shot down by machine-gun fire almost as soon as he hit the beach.

The Highlanders pushed forward, platoons and sections fanning out from the landing sites, driving through Pourville and engaging a number of enemy defenders who had been bypassed by the South Sasks. About 1.5 kilometres inland, a series of houses hid enemy riflemen. Company Sergeant Major George Gouk remembered that an ad hoc Highlander battle group "got busy ... and were doing a fairly good job cleaning them out with rifles and grenades when all of a sudden they opened up on us with their mortars." Casualties mounted, but "there was no stopping the boys then, they were seeing their pals for the first time being killed and wounded at their side and the only thought that seemed to be in everyone's mind was to have revenge."[30] The houses were cleared with bombs and bullets.

Around 9:30 A.M., with the Germans now holding much of the high ground along the headways and cliffs that separated the main beach from the Pourville landing site, the Canadians began their methodical retreat. It was now that the most conspicuous flaw in Mountbatten's plan was revealed. Once engaged with the enemy in close-quarters combat, the two Canadian battalions had no way to withdraw to the landing craft unless a sizable force was left behind to cover the retreat. Moreover, as long as the Germans held one of the cliffs, they could pour fire into the beach area and engage the in-bound landing craft. "The boats started coming into the teeth of it all," wrote Private Clarence Bourassa of the South Saskatchewan Regiment. "They came through a wall of lead and fire, not a one turned back."[31] Bourassa survived the mad scramble to the boats, but was killed two years later in Normandy. The navy bravely took the remaining Camerons and Sasks out, but Major A.T. Law, now leading the Queen's Own Cameron Highlanders of Canada, remembered bitterly that his men "suffered more heavily during the last phase of the withdrawal than during all the previous stages of the operation."[32]

The vice was tightening on the Canadians, and the only way to hold off the enemy and forestall even greater carnage was to leave behind a sacrificial force. Lieutenant-Colonel Merritt chose to stay back and orchestrate the desperate defence. He was wounded several times, but still had the strength and courage to race out under fire, grab a wounded Canadian, and drag him back to the seawall where the Canadians made their desperate stand. As one of the Camerons observed of the South Sasks' commander's actions, "It wasn't human, what he did."[33] Merritt, who survived the battle to face three years of imprisonment, was awarded the Victoria Cross for his "matchless gallantry and inspiring leadership." The rearguard of about 250 men, nearly evenly split between the two regiments, continued to fight against impossible odds until about 1:30 P.M. Their brave actions had bought enough time for about 600 of the 1,200 men who landed to get away.

WITH THE FLANKS UNSECURED, the centre could never hold. The Royal Hamilton Light Infantry and Essex Scottish motored towards the main beach at 5:20 A.M., between ten and thirty minutes later than the assaults on the Puys and Pourville. Their staggered run-in was meant to give time for the forces north and south of Dieppe to immobilize the guns along the white cliffs that towered over the main beach, but now it was evident—and this should have been anticipated by the planners—that the fighting on those two beaches had alerted the German defenders in the town of Dieppe and along the high cliffs that overlooked it.

The 4-inch guns of destroyers pounded the fortifications on the Dieppe beach to no avail: the defenders were holed up in the hotels, a tobacco factory, churches, and the long esplanade. The gun positions closer to the beach or camouflaged on the cliffs, as well as the pillboxes, concrete bunkers, hidden snipers' posts, and artillery, were not easy to either locate or silence. Before the Canadians landed on the main beach, fifty-eight Hurricane fighter bombers shot up the town, directing 20mm cannon fire into known enemy positions, but the Germans were not suppressed for long by this drive-by shooting. Denis Whitaker, a former professional Canadian Football League player and a captain in the Royal Hamilton Light Infantry, wrote later of the sinking feeling in his stomach as his landing craft closed in on the beach: the fortifications looked "terribly wrong. Everything was intact!"[34]

Off the 1.6-kilometre stretch of beach, the Germans had installed underwater mines that blew a number of landing craft out of the water, the blast ripping through metal and flesh. The craft that negotiated the mines were hit with withering fire from machine-gunners and riflemen who tracked their movement from hundreds of metres out. To add to the carnage, several of the landing craft were hit with mortar fire and opened up like tin cans.

"The instant we jumped from our boats," recounted Private Joseph Johnston of the Rileys, as the Hamilton boys were known, "we were ... swept with a murderous crossfire."[35] Scores of men died instantly, but their comrades plunged forward, down the landing craft ramps and into a firestorm. A concrete seawall halfway to the town, similar to the seawalls on other beaches, became the focus for many of the soldiers caught in the kill zone. However, unlike the others, this wall was uneven in height, ranging from about 1 to 2 metres high, and beyond it was a broad esplanade, which offered little cover.

Mortar fire crashed down along the beach, and proved the most deadly German weapon. The bombs exploded on the egg-sized chert, sending steel fragments and stone splinters in all directions. The soldiers either crouched behind the seawall or retreated and took shelter among the landing craft that were now riddled with holes and taking on water. All the while, snipers in the town picked off NCOs and officers, and anyone who seemed to be coordinating the advance.

The battle broke down into a series of isolated engagements as the front-line formations lost all coherence. It was nearly impossible to advance past the thick rows of barbed wire, which was coiled 1 metre high and 5 metres deep beyond the seawall. Many of the Bangalore torpedoes had been lost and their carriers killed. Furthermore, the relative safety of the wall made it very hard for the infantry, once they stopped there and lost momentum, to start again. Matters were made worse as many officers and NCOs were already down and voice commands were all but lost in the whirlwind of destruction.

Lieutenant-Colonel Fred Jasperson, commander of the Essex Scottish, wrote shortly after the battle about the stunning brutality of combat on the beach that

Official war artist Charles Comfort tried to capture the chaos of the Canadian attack on the main beach.

day. "The scene of it," he wrote, would be "imprinted on my mind forever."[36] Men's arms and legs had been amputated by shells; long ropes of entrails lay in gruesome clumps next to bodies. Three times, ad hoc Essex battle groups tried to breach the barbed wire beyond the seawall, and each time they were forced back with casualties. In the end, only a small group of Essex, led by Company Sergeant Major Cornelius Stapleton, made it off the beach. They charged for cover in the hotel and killed a number of riflemen. Stapleton would be awarded the Distinguished Conduct Medal for this action, but such small victories were the exception. The vast majority of the battalion simply endured the crippling fire on the beach.[37] More experienced soldiers might have found a way forward, but this seems unlikely in the face of the hopeless position and the defenders' strength.

THE 14TH CANADIAN ARMY TANK BATTALION, better known as the Calgary Regiment, was the first unit of the Canadian Armoured Corps to go into action during the Second World War. But because of a navigational error, they were about fifteen minutes late touching down on the main beach, arriving a little after 5:30 A.M. At that point, the battle there was already shaping up as a bloodbath. Could the tanks reverse the infantry's grim fortunes?

More than half of the Churchill tanks were equipped with the powerful 6-pounder gun (the others had the wimpy 2-pounder), which would have been useful in the first critical minutes of the battle, and in trading return fire with the Germans. In fact, the Canadians had high expectations with respect to their armour, hoping it would shock the enemy, even though the infantry had had only a few opportunities to train with tanks in mock battles.[38] As it was, the Germans, far from being surprised, could see the landing craft ferrying in the 45-ton Churchills, and directed their fire in an attempt to stop them before they had a chance to play their part. A weak smoke-screen did little to obscure the landing, although the lumbering beasts, which had been fitted with waterproof material, drew considerable fire that allowed some of the exposed Canadian riflemen on the beaches to pull themselves to cover. A number of tanks were damaged or sunk before they made it to the beach, but twenty-seven tanks eventually made it ashore and brought their guns to bear on the enemy.[39]

The Churchill tanks ground up and down the beach, their coaxial Besa machine guns cooking off 7.92mm small-arms ammunition, and the 6-pounder throwing armour-piercing, solid-shot shells at enemy fortifications. While the firepower had an immediate impact on the enemy, the solid shot was not as effective as high explosive shells that might have done more damage. At the same time, the tanks had difficulty in finding purchase on the shingle. Incredibly, Mountbatten's planners had not warned the Canadians that they would encounter the chert, even though tens of thousands of British vacationers had visited Dieppe before the war. Between six and nine of the tanks were disabled because stones were caught between their treads and bogey wheels, eventually breaking the track.

Far more damning to the operation's success was the inability of the tanks to get off the 200-metre-wide promenade between the beach and town, because the exits were blocked by concrete metre-and-a-half-high barriers. The Royal Canadian Engineers were to have removed these obstacles earlier with explosives, but the engineers had almost all been killed or wounded.[40] And so the tanks rumbled back and forth on the beach and the promenade, attempting to avoid the wounded and dead Canadians that littered the ground, hurling shells into enemy positions, but always suffering from constricted vision and suffocating heat that, according to Trooper Dennis Scott, began to melt the paint on the interior of the tank.[41]

The German anti-tank guns, the impotent 37mm, had little effect against the Churchill's armour, but the pounding against the steel hull created splash—little bits of metal that flew around the interior—injuring the troopers. The German fire was more effective in dislodging the tank tracks. When that happened, the resolute tankers kept firing from their immobile, yet still hardened, positions. The Churchills blasted away at the enemy until they ran out of ammunition, and even then the tanks remained deadly. Lieutenant Edwin Bennett, a twenty-year-old tank commander who was blinded in one eye by a sliver of metal during the battle, remembered seeing a German soldier advance on the tank with a stick grenade in his hand. He was ground to death under the tank's tracks when Bennett ordered his driver to run him over.[42]

The tanks added firepower to the Canadian attack. But they did not turn the tide of battle.

ABOVE THE TERRESTRIAL BATTLEFIELD, the RAF and RCAF fought in the largest air battle that had been seen to that point in Western Europe, committing 863 pilots to drawing out and destroying the Luftwaffe. Throughout the long day, Spitfires, Hurricanes, and P-51 Mustangs engaged Focke-Wulf Fw 190s and Messerschmitt 109s, with some of the RAF and RCAF pilots flying up to five sorties.[43] The Germans had the advantage of fighting on the defensive, but throughout the battle flaming aircraft on both sides crashed down to earth.

RCAF pilot John Maffre would serve in a number of squadrons during the war, but he flew his first operation over Dieppe, in a Spitfire V with No. 416 Squadron. Just twenty years of age at the time, he described the scene as a "tapestry of aircraft, wheeling all over the place—just nothing but aircraft."[44] In the whirling confusion of combat, Maffre temporarily lost his leader. "I was number two, and my number one and I got separated for a moment." That was when he noticed "tracer bullets going past your wingtip, and you realize that some SOB is trying to kill you…."[45] Maffre survived the battle and the war, as did his twenty-four-year-old brother, Jim, who served in Coastal Command, although two of their other brothers were killed while flying with the RCAF.

Don Morrison flew a Spitfire with No. 401 Squadron, RCAF, in the air battle. The twenty-one-year-old already had four kills to his credit and would get his fifth on the 19th, when he tangled with an Fw 190. "As I closed to about 25 yards, I opened up with a two-second burst of cannon fire," Morrison recalled. "As both the enemy aircraft and I went into thin cloud he exploded. Suddenly my windshield and hood were covered with oil and there was the clatter of debris striking my aircraft. I imagine it punctured my radiators. The engine started to cough and the aircraft shuddered violently."[46] Morrison ditched his plane and parachuted into the water. Parachuting into water was often a death sentence, but he was able to climb into a small inflatable dinghy (attached to the parachute) and was eventually rescued. It was his seventh Spitfire, and he would lose another when he was shot down over Calais a few months later, leaving his left leg in the plane as he was wrenched out. That ended his war as a fighter ace, and he was a prisoner until liberation.

Bruce and Douglas Warren were twins who served together in Fighter Command and flew together in No. 165 Squadron, RAF. The twins had been briefed the night before to prepare for a massive battle, and been warned that, in the course of it, the Royal Navy would fire on anything below 7,000 feet. Douglas Warren revealed,

"My twin brother and I were ... especially interested in the Dieppe operation as we were the only Canadians in the squadron. We were in the air at first light, and could see the battle area alight with tracers, with many fires on the esplanade of Dieppe. Several landing craft were grounded offshore." They spent the morning chasing enemy fighters that raked the infantry pinned on the beach. The first sortie was at dawn, followed by a second one at lunch. At noon, "there were many dogfights, and Dornier 217s [bombers] were dive-bombing our ships. Our section of four attacked a Dornier from astern and rear quarter. It appeared that the pilot bailed out while the rear gunner was still firing at us!" Even at thousands of feet above the battlefield, the Warrens could see that the battle was going against the Canadians, and he and his brother fought with added desperation to relieve the strain on the ground forces. "We had no trouble appreciating what our boys were going through down below."[47]

When the fighting on the beaches hit a fever pitch, at around 8:30 A.M., the first German bombers targeted the ships and beaches. The Ju 88s were very effective in swooping down from a high altitude and dropping their bombs close to the ground, and at least two Churchill tanks were knocked out this way. The Germans were out-numbered for most of the battle, but they could stay in the air longer, and the Allied fighters coming from across the Channel had only a limited time—sometimes as little as ten minutes—in which to do some damage. The Canadian and British pilots had to worry both about the enemy and their own fuel tanks. Consequently, there were periods when few Allied fighters were positioned over the beaches and the skies swarmed with the Luftwaffe, as well as the opposite situation—a seeming armada of Allied fighters and no enemy planes. By the end of day, the RAF and RCAF had lost ninety-nine aircraft. The Allied flyers claimed that even more Germans were shot down, but later figures revealed the number was forty-eight.[48]

ON THE MAIN DIEPPE BEACH, the Essex Scottish remained pinned down, but on the right flank a few aggressive battle groups from the Royal Hamilton Light Infantry pressed into the casino overlooking the Promenade. The Rileys fought through the inside of the large building and were largely protected by its walls from the fire directed at the beach. Sergeant George Hickson of the 7th Field Company, Royal Canadian Engineers, was attached to a group of Rileys as they moved through the labyrinthine interior. They overran a German concrete casement, chiefly by throwing hand grenades at the enemy, and then set about blowing up machine-gun posts and a gun battery, the latter unmanned because the Germans were already either dead or captured. At one point, the group heard a sniper firing at the Canadians on the beach from the other side of a concrete barrier. Sergeant Hickson set a high explosive, 3-pound plastic charge and blew him and the position to rubble.[49] Another group of Rileys, led by Captain A.C. Hill, fought its way through a number of buildings in Dieppe. French civilians were, peculiarly, still on the streets; some of them greeted the Canadians, while others pointed to where enemy soldiers lay in ambush. After a series of firefights, there was nowhere for the Highlanders to go, and because they were running low on ammunition, they retreated back to the beaches.

"The beach was a deathtrap," recounted Lieutenant-Colonel Robert Labatt, commander of the Royal Hamilton Light Infantry.[50] It was also a mass of confusion, with almost all communication cut between the survivors on the beaches and the headquarters on HMS *Calpe* several kilometres out at sea. Signalmen were dead or their radios destroyed, leaving only crackling dead air for General Hamilton Roberts to interpret as he waited anxiously for news. But then, at 6:10 A.M., a garbled message from shore seemed to indicate that the Essex Scottish had pushed into town. Roberts clung to the hope implied by the message, even though the ominous radio silence and the obvious signs of fierce fighting on the beach, and, much closer, the return of landing craft shot up and filled with bloodied and broken bodies of his troops, indicated that it was likely untrue. Roberts could have sent liaison or intelligence officers forward. Instead, wishing to exploit success and turn the tide, he ordered into battle Lieutenant-Colonel Dollard Menard's Fusiliers Mont-Royal. The 584 French-Canadian soldiers never faltered, even as enemy fire raked their small unarmoured boats during the run-in. They hit the beaches around 7 A.M. and ran headfirst into the storm.

A few made it through the firezone, but most of the FMRs took cover along the western end of the beach, under the cliffs or behind burning landing craft and immobilized tanks. Lieutenant-Colonel Dollard Menard was struck by shrapnel in the shoulder (the first of a number of wounds he endured that day). "You say a bullet or a piece of shrapnel hits you but the word isn't right. They slam you the way a sledgehammer slams you. There's no sharp pain at first. It jars you so much you're not sure exactly where you've been hit or what with."[51] Stunned and driven to the ground, Menard came to as bullets potted the stones around him. He stumbled for cover, past the bodies of men who would never rise again.

Sergeant-Major Lucien Dumais was one of the lucky ones. He and a few mates made it off the landing craft before it reversed violently and pulled away from the beach. Firing and advancing towards the casino, they found it already cleared by the Rileys. After an hour of fighting, Dumais and a Bren gunner knocked out two German machine-gun positions, and eventually met up with elements of the retreating Rileys. They carried wounded men back to the beach and loaded up a landing craft under smoke cover. Dumais nearly made it onto the landing craft too, but it pulled away and he sank about 3 metres under water, his hobnailed boots taking him down.[52] He swallowed a lot of the sea before he swam back to the beach, where he was eventually taken prisoner. He later escaped and made his way back to England.

THROUGHOUT THE LATE MORNING, one tank after another had been put out of action or had run out of shells. The fusillade from the pinned-down Canadians gradually dropped off as they succumbed to wounds, burned through their ammunition, or simply gave up fighting. Still the German counterattack was stymied by pockets of resolute attackers-turned-defenders. One German observed that the Canadians took "effective cover behind their dead comrades" and "shot uninterruptedly at our positions. Thus with their bodies these dead soldiers provided their comrades with the last service of friendship."[53] The plan to send the Royal Marines to penetrate to the German headquarters was partially cancelled after the FMRs were cut to ribbons, although dozens of commandos were carried right into the battle on fast boats, where they suffered the same fate as the Canadians. With the main beach a ruin of blood, tangled metal and bodies, the challenge now was to see how many men could be saved.

The landing craft arrived on the beaches a little after 11 A.M. in staggered and scattered individual runs. Despite covering fire from the destroyers' guns, many were holed and sunk by the Germans who fired from the cliff tops. Observant Canadians would have seen the stakes driven at intervals into the shingle: these were distance markers for the mortar men who methodically blasted every sector of the shallow beach where the Canadians were hanging on by their fingertips.[54] As one German artillery officer recalled of the target-rich scene, "Two whole regiments ... clinging tightly against the concrete wall.... Everywhere along the whole strand our shells were exploding, their effect multiplied ten times by the exploding of the stone splinters."[55] Nonetheless, many Canadians continued to hold off the enemy, and to buy time for the landing craft to begin the evacuation.

The unwieldy landing craft were easy targets for the German gunners, snipers, and mortar teams, who often held their fire until men ran from their protected positions at the seawall into the open, yawning mouths of the waiting boats. Enemy fighter pilots also took low-flying runs to rake the beaches and water with cannon fire. A desultory smokescreen provided some concealment for the trapped Canadians, but much of it

A view of the carnage inside a landing craft.

dissipated just as the landing craft hit the beach. Nonetheless, the officers and men of the Royal Navy, according to one Canadian infantryman, "showed a complete disregard for death and carried on as if this action was an every-day occurrence."[56]

On the beach, brave Canadians rushed back and forth between the seawall to the beaches to pull injured comrades to safety. Honorary Captain J.W. Foote, the burly chaplain of the Royal Hamilton Light Infantry, was a non-combatant who worked relentlessly on the wounded, bandaging, giving morphine, and offering last rites. During the withdrawal, Foote carried several Canadians to the landing craft, risking his own life to save others. On one of the landing craft, wounded men called out for Foote to stay, but he was heard to say, as he returned to the beach, "the men ashore would need me far more in captivity than any of those going home."[57] For his self-sacrifice and devotion he was later awarded the Victoria Cross.

The surviving Canadians could see that the landing craft would never be able to take them all off. Too many landing craft had been destroyed, including six of the eight meant for the Essex Scottish. In desperation, some of the Canadians stripped down to their shorts, intending to swim back to the waiting ships. German snipers showed no mercy, picking them off, driving bullets through bobbing heads and exposed backs. Even more devastating were the German bombers that swooped down and dropped high explosive bombs into the water. Private Geoffrey Ellwood, a signaller attached to the Essex Scottish, recounted seeing "parts of bodies flying up—heads, arms, legs. This brought everybody [the swimmers] back to shore. And afterwards, the bodies and debris were washed ashore. A good six or eight feet along the water's edge was just bodies and parts of bodies just floating there."[58]

Some 33 landing craft were destroyed by enemy action, mortars, and mines during the frantic battle. But amid the carnage about 400 Canadians were brought back to the ships. It is surprising that anyone at all got off the beach.

THE SHOOTING ON THE MAIN BEACH finally ended at around 2 P.M. For the shell-blasted soldiers, the quieting of the guns brought some relief. Hands up and heads bowed, the Canadians were led from the corpse-strewn beaches and through Dieppe. Despite the ferocity of the battle, the captors treated the Canadian prisoners fairly gently, considering their propensity for murdering those who fell into their hands. While cases of physical abuse were recorded, and some of the more grievously wounded Canadians were executed on the beach, most were simply herded towards prison cages. In town, injured men were cared for, although almost all the surgery—from amputations to deep-tissue cutting—was conducted without anaesthetic, due to the chronic shortage of medical supplies experienced by the Germans on all fronts.[59]

On the beaches, the Germans combed through the wreckage, looking for souvenirs and for documents that might shed light on why the raid had been launched. Propaganda photographs were taken to highlight the achievement of the gloating supermen who had defended Europe from "invasion." The ugly task of stacking the Canadian dead, like seeping cordwood, and of collecting body parts, was conducted without picture-taking.[60]

Over the coming days, the Canadian survivors—those who made it back to England and those made prisoners—tried to reconstruct their traumatic experiences.

The aftermath of the raid. The Germans used photographs of the victorious battle as effective propaganda.

The death of comrades tore at the mind, and the battle was reduced to a vague memory of fading faces, dying screams, and the pain of irreparable loss. Men looked for their friends, counted heads, and compared notes, wondering who had got back to safety and who had been left behind. Grief turned to anger as most of the Canadians concluded that the Germans had known about the raid in advance. This wasn't the case, but the defenders knew that an attack was most likely to be launched in the period when the moon and tide were favourable, as they were on August 19, and long-standing orders had put the coastal garrisons on alert. The Germans did not need forewarning: their defences were in place. They simply responded efficiently when the attack came.

While the lopsided battle favoured the Germans, they nonetheless suffered 591 casualties in all three services. The final toll on the Canadians was far worse. Of the 4,963 Canadians who embarked in England, only 2,211 returned. Of those, 589 were wounded but survived, while in 28 cases the wounds proved to be mortal. Another 1,946 Canadians were captured, and at least 568 of them were wounded. Seventy-one would die in captivity. In nine hours of battle, the Canadians had 836 killed, and six of the seven Canadian battalions sent into battle lost their commanding officers.[61] Dieppe was the single most costly day for the Canadian Army during the Second World War.

Notwithstanding the resounding failure, prepared communiqués went out throughout the British Empire and the United States claiming success and lauding the Canadians prowess in battle. The eye-popping fabrications that the assault was "decisive," or, as the *Toronto Star* reported, that it helped "Smash Nazi Opposition," might have made even inveterate deceivers like Stalin blush.[62] But over the coming weeks, the whitewash was slowly revealed for what it was, and some brave newspapers questioned the government's account, especially when, in mid-September, the Department of National Defence released a staggering 134-page list of the Canadian casualties.

Major-General Roberts wrote a ludicrous appreciation of the battle in its aftermath: "All the men who returned are in wonderful spirits," he concluded, "and have expressed their desire to go back at the enemy again as soon as possible."[63] Roberts must have known better. The Canadian general was scapegoated by his superiors after the battle; he never complained or spoke publicly of his role in the raid, but his career was all but finished. Removed from command after a polite delay of a few months, he was cast aside to oversee reinforcement units. Some of the Dieppe survivors never forgave him. Every year until his death in 1962, on the anniversary of the battle, unknown Canadian veterans of the raid sent him a stale piece of cake, a harsh reminder of his earlier cheery prediction that the operation would be a "piece of cake." Admiral Mountbatten sought to forget the mess, shifting blame and emphasizing the claim that Dieppe taught valuable lessons for future operations, even going so far as to later claim that the D-Day landings of June 1944 would have failed without Dieppe. It was a hard sell because it was untrue. At least, no scholar examining the record has been able to draw a direct line connecting the two operations. Mountbatten's royal blood protected him, however, and he went off to an even higher-profile position as Supreme Allied Commander in Southeast Asia.

THE DIEPPE RAID comprised but a single day in the six-year war, but it remains hotly contested by generations of soldiers, historians, and commentators.[64] Success has a thousand fathers, goes the saying, while defeat is an orphan. But the defeat at Dieppe was multi-sired. Mountbatten and his staff were guilty of poorly coordinating the various arms involved in the operation, of failing to pick the right target, and of orchestrating a misguided multi-timed beach landing. None of the friction of war was taken into account. The plan's success was predicated on surprise, speed, and darkness. Instead, what the Canadians got was an alert enemy that used its tactical advantages of terrain and firepower to shock and then shatter the raiders. Dieppe was launched to appease both the Americans and the Soviets, both of whom demanded action. If the raid was mounted with too little careful thought, the Canadian high command of Crerar and McNaughton has to wear some of the blame. These generals accepted the flawed plan with little protest. Braver commanders would have questioned the operation, rather than roll the dice and look skyward. One British admiral, Sir Bertram Ramsay, observed, "Dieppe was a tragedy, and the cause may be attributed to the fact that it was planned by inexperienced enthusiasts."[65]

At a strategic level, the raid confirmed in Churchill's mind the difficulty of opening a second front. Amphibious attackers had to bring everything into battle—from ammunition to reliable communication systems to medical facilities—and an assault from the sea introduced new factors to disrupt plans, from the challenges of combined-arms warfare to different service cultures, and more opportunities for the fog of war to obscure and confuse. If Dieppe served any purpose, it was that of stiffening Churchill's resolve to postpone the invasion of Europe until the Anglo-American military commanders could gather the necessary forces, and until the Battle of the Atlantic was won. While additional lessons were processed from the difficult American experiences in the Pacific campaign, as well as landings in the Mediterranean, Dieppe always remained a sepulchre to remind senior officers of the folly of shoddy planning and misplaced hope. The preparations for D-Day would be far more thorough. The application of overwhelming firepower in June 1944 was a lesson learned from Dieppe. Or the lesson learned was not to allow inter-service rivalry to dictate operations: on D-Day a central headquarters exercised control over both bombers and warships. None of this is to suggest, as Mountbatten claimed, that Normandy was won on the beaches of Dieppe, only that Dieppe caused Allied planners to be more careful than they might otherwise have been. They had seen what failure looked like.[66]

The Russians were unmoved by the failure of Dieppe. They had the equivalent of scores of Dieppe-like slaughters weekly, at times daily, but the Americans sheepishly dialled back their pressure on Churchill for the invasion of Europe, at least for the short term. In the Canadian Army, the raid provoked a seemingly paradoxical pride: censors who read the troops' letters home observed that morale was "enhanced" by the raid. In fact, the message implicit in the letters was that of a "great feat which was accomplished [that] has completely vindicated the Canadians as first-class fighting men."[67] It may seem odd that the Canadians took a somewhat perverse satisfaction in their battered glory, but such is sometimes the way of soldiers. Canadians also celebrated the costly stand made by the 18,000-strong Canadian Division at the Battle of Second Ypres in April 1915, where 6,000 soldiers were killed, wounded, and made prisoner in a few days of intense fighting.

The Germans also took away lessons from their resounding victory. They concluded that an amphibious landing could be defeated on the beaches, especially if an Atlantic Wall of some 15,000 fortifications was built before the next invasion.[68]

They therefore clung to a thin defence that covered much of the French coast rather than constructing a defence-in-depth from which to launch rapid counterattacks. The Germans were also led to believe that the Allies would have to capture a port to meet the logistical needs of ground forces after they landed, and so they went about fortifying the ports along the coast. These issues would be critical two years later, when the Germans confronted the five-division landing on D-Day.

Critics of Dieppe have argued that the Allied operational and tactical appreciations could have been learned without the destruction of the Canadian force. That is certainly true, but lessons learned in blood are those that are remembered longest. None of this smoothes away the jagged scar of Dieppe that runs through the Canadian psyche to this day.

CHAPTER 12

BACKS TO THE WALL

The number of U-boats rose to nearly 200 in the summer of 1942, about half of them in the Atlantic. The pickings along the eastern seaboard were no longer so easy, now that the Americans had introduced convoys, blacked out cities, and increased aircraft patrols. Consequently, Dönitz shifted many of his U-boats to the mid-Atlantic, where they renewed the assault on convoys sailing to the United Kingdom. Canadian maritime defences had improved significantly since the start of the war, but even the modified Canso flying boats could fly no farther than about 1,000 kilometres off Newfoundland. Beyond that, the U-boats could operate free from the prying eyes and exploding bombs of Allied seaplanes. Intercepted enemy communications sometimes made it possible to route the convoys around the areas of U-boat concentration, but when the surface vessels encountered the wolf packs, the odds were always against the prey. The RCN escorts tried to hold off the U-boats, as they sought to save the merchant ships. Killing the enemy was not the RCN's first priority, although all captains looked for the opportunity.

In fact, Canadian warships had sunk only one Italian and one German U-boat in the first three years of the war. That changed in the summer of 1942, when they destroyed five U-boats in three months. The kills were largely due to finding U-boats on the surface and pursuing them doggedly, with surface radar and then asdic and depth charges when they dived. The most spectacular engagement occurred in early August, when convoy SC 94, which consisted of thirty-three merchant ships steaming in an easterly direction, came under attack.[1] It was a slow convoy, at 7 knots, pursued by a wolf pack of sixteen boats. The first victim was a merchant ship that was torpedoed on August 5. This was only the prelude to a fierce battle as U-boats shadowed the convoy, waiting for the protection of nightfall before unleashing hell.

The convoy's best weapon was HMCS *Assiniboine*, a River-class destroyer armed with four 4.7-inch guns, which was accompanied by six corvettes. Together the ships sought to hold the U-boats on the perimeter through the night of August 5 and the next day. The crews were at their battle stations constantly, all eyes straining to catch a glimpse of an enemy conning tower or torpedo's wake. Asdic and surface radar revealed several U-boats and sent the corvettes racing across the water, but they were always gone when the Canadians arrived. The *Assiniboine*, faster than the smaller escorts, was in constant pursuit as well. It chased off and damaged a U-boat on the 6th. Later that day, the warship gave chase to *U-454*, which was spotted in the fog, and forced it to submerge and lose contact with the convoy. At 6:36 P.M., as *Assiniboine* returned to its position in the vanguard, its radar—the newer and advanced Type 286—detected a submarine on the surface. The destroyer revved up to 22 knots and raced towards *U-210*, aiming to ram it. The warship shook as it churned through the water. Commander John Stubbs ordered the crew to prepare for battle.

Lieutenant Rudolph Lemcke on *U-210*, an experienced naval officer who had recently been transferred to the U-boat arm, was horrified to see the Canadian destroyer loom out of the fog, a mere 50 metres away. *U-210* lurched to action, managing to avoid the lethal ram, and its crew began to fire on the larger warship. *Assiniboine* manoeuvred for a shot with its 4.7-inch guns, seeking to open the distance, but the U-boat was too close. Nonetheless, its 50mm-calibre machine guns raked the German vessel, which responded with its 20mm flak gun. Allan Riley, a sparker (radio operator) experiencing his first battle, recounted the shock of feeling the U-boat shells tearing through the ship.[2] The depth charge men were at their stations, anxious to release their deadly packages, but the manoeuvring went on, both ships firing and neither able to gain advantage.

For half an hour, the two snarling beasts circled each other, hammering away with their guns, slipping in and out of the fog. The U-boat sought to evade the destroyer on the surface and find safety in a fog bank, for if it had dived it would have been blown out of the water by depth chargers. The *Assiniboine* was bigger and had larger

HMCS Assiniboine *trading blows with* U-210. *This remarkable photograph shows the U-boat barely escaping one of* Assiniboine's *attempts to ram.*

guns, but the U-boat was adept at staying inside the turning circle of the much larger ship. The submarine's 20mm flak gun's shells raked the destroyer, causing significant damage. "There was so much smoke and the smell and the taste of cordite was awful," remembered Aimé Dorion, who was passing shells to the forward gun. "I was scared.... I never prayed so much in my life but I kept on handing up the shells."[3]

One of the stranger non-combatants on board *Assiniboine* was Dr. Gilbert Tucker, a mild-mannered official naval historian. Anxious for some experience at sea, he had begged for passage on the destroyer. Throughout the convoy crossing, Tucker had sought Nelsonian action and had been grumbling that he got only a lot of empty water and sea-sickness. Now he was on the deck, watching one of the RCN's most thrilling naval engagements of the war. Shells ripped through the air and steel plating around him; he responded by cheering on his crew and shouting epithets at the enemy. An experienced medical officer saw the dangerously exposed historian and shouted, "Get your head down, you silly old bastard!" but Tucker refused to miss what was unfolding before him.[4]

German shells riddled the *Assiniboine*'s bridge, and soon started a fire. A number of the crew were hit by shrapnel and pieces of metal coming off the ship. Ordinary Seaman Kenneth Watson of Revelstoke, British Columbia, a member of "A" gun crew on the forecastle, was clipped in the arm and knocked down. When the eighteen-year-old scrambled up to pass another shell, he was hit directly be enemy fire and torn to pieces, his body thrown across the deck.

Another fire broke out near the flag deck. As smoke poured from the bridge structure, First Lieutenant R.L. Hennessy organized a fire control team using hoses that snaked along the starboard waist. In the wheelhouse—where the ship's direction was controlled—Chief Petty Officer Max Bernays, an experienced sailor who had put in more than thirteen years on the oceans, and two junior mates, responded to Commander Stubbs's commands from the bridge. As the smoke filled the wheelhouse, Bernays ordered his two companions out and remained at the helm, even as shell fragments whirled around him and fires encroached. Commander Stubbs continued to communicate from the bridge to Bernays, who, in the course of the engagement, carried out 130 telegraph orders, performing the job of three men— and doing so even after shell splinters gouged his face.

Assiniboine, pounded relentlessly by the U-boat's gun, was on fire and smoking badly. The crew on the U-boat must have thought that they might escape. Yet the submarine too had been struck repeatedly by shells, and had barely missed destruction three times when it avoided ramming attempts. The dogged *Assiniboine* would not be deterred, however, and it finally silenced the U-boat's main gun with machine-gun fire, in addition to smashing one of the port trimming tanks. More devastatingly, the bridge had been peppered with gunfire, leaving most of the senior German officers dead, including Lemcke. When the electric motors caught fire, the U-boat slowed. Unable to escape another ramming, the desperate crew finally dived, knowing that they would likely fall victim to depth charges, but aware that staying on the surface meant death. Stubbs ordered the destroyer full speed ahead. All hands prepared for impact. The destroyer ran over the U-boat, crushing it in a clash of grinding metal.

After smashing U-210 *with shellfire, this photograph captures the death blow delivered by HMCS* Assiniboine *as it rams the stricken submarine.*

The mortally wounded U-boat dived to about 20 metres, but foundered as water poured in through the crushed tower. The engineer officer, now in command, ordered the tanks blown, and the sub floated back to the surface—only to be run over by *Assiniboine* one more time. As the desperate Germans sought to escape the dead vessel, they found to their collective horror that the conning tower hatch was jammed, trapping them inside. As the sea rushed in, the desperate sailors worked feverishly and eventually pried it loose. Some thirty-eight men were picked up from the water, shortly after the sea closed permanently over *U-210* at 7:14 P.M.[5] "The Bones," as *Assiniboine* was affectionately known, limped back to St. John's, battered but victorious after its classic duel.

Commander Stubbs was awarded the Distinguished Service Order, but would not live to see the end of the war. He was killed when *Athabaskan* was sunk in April 1944. Bernays's actions, believed the senior naval brass, were worthy of a Victoria Cross, and the RCN put forward the recommendation through the governor general. The Admiralty refused to support it, however, arguing that Bernays's bravery, while incredibly important during the battle, did not warrant the Empire's top honour. Canada's high commissioner in London, Vincent Massey, was at a loss as to what to do, and he seems not to have pressed the case as effectively as he could. Bernays was instead awarded the Conspicuous Gallantry Medal, making him one of only two members of the RCN to receive this prestigious award. During the course of the war, no Canadian was awarded a Victoria Cross while serving on a Canadian warship. Only Lieutenant Robert Hampton Gray of the Royal Canadian Naval Volunteer Reserve, a Fleet Air Arm pilot on a British aircraft carrier, was awarded the VC posthumously for his uncommon valour in continuing an attack, while mortally wounded, against a Japanese warship in the last days of the Pacific war. The Royal Navy high command appeared to have an anti-Canadian bias when it came to recognizing gallantry.[6] The Royal Navy had a maximum strength of 863,000 men and women; 22 of its members were awarded the Victoria Crosses, and 60 were given Conspicuous Gallantry medals. The RCN, on the other hand, with a maximum strength of approximately 96,000 men and women, received just one Victoria Cross and two Conspicuous Gallantry Medals. The statistics are damning. The bias may not have been entirely against dominion sailors. Historically, the Royal Navy tended to award the Victoria Cross for big-ship actions rather than U-boat skirmishes. The senior RN officers were never quick to change their collective mindset.

The RCN sank two U-boats in the defence of SC 95, and was proud of the achievement, even though the convoy still lost eleven ships to the wolf pack. As one experienced Canadian officer noted, "The number of escorts that we had were so few it was impossible to give the Halifax convoys really adequate protection."[7] They did the best with what they had.

THE APPROACH TO ST. JOHN'S, NEWFOUNDLAND, was staggeringly beautiful. Alan Riley, then a signaller on board HMCS *Galt*, remembered that the entrance to the harbour looked like it had been "carved by a giant axe, allowing the sea to pour through a thousand-yard channel."[8] In St. John's—known affectionately as "Newfy John" or the "Hole in the Rock"—ships' crews became familiar with one another, and with the locals. Sailors got their land legs quickly as they strolled along the narrow, cobblestone streets. They were flush with cash—at least those who had not had to pay off gambling debts—and so the movie theatres were always full and the bars saw men packed inside shoulder to shoulder. "Beer was often in short supply," wrote Frank Curry of HMCS *Kamsack*, "but it didn't take long for us to discover the joys of Newfoundland's famous Screech." Curry was not the last visitor to Newfoundland to find that the overproof rum looked "innocent," but that it was "powerful enough to knock out even the hardiest of drinkers."[9]

Hal Lawrence remembered the raucous times in the St. John's bars, filled to the gills with sailors, airmen, army grunts, uniformed women, and even the occasional civilian. Songs of service, humour, and vulgarity could bring the entire bar thumping to a new beat, and the "The Three Bastards" was a popular one. Lawrence described a night of revelry when a Wren—a member of the Women's Royal Canadian Naval Service—sat at the bar singing,

If I were a marrying girl,
Which thank the Lord I'm not, sir,
The sort of man that I would wed
Would be a rugby scrum-half.

And then the bar shouted out the chorus,

> Oh, he'd push hard
> And I'd push hard
> And we'd push hard together;
> We'd be all right in the middle of the night
> Pushing hard together.[10]

And of course, there were other verses in which different rugby players sought to try different "positions" with the ladies.

Officers had a private club known as the Crowsnest, which was open day and night but was located perilously at the top of a steep fifty-nine-step outside staircase. Comfortable leather chairs awaited those who made the death-defying climb. Paintings of the crests of Canadian ships were hung on the walls. In a corner, a spike had been driven into the floor, put there by the commanding officer of HMCS *Spikenard* the night before it sailed and was sunk, leaving only eight survivors.[11] "It was a home to all of us in the escort ships," said one officer fondly.[12]

Harry Barrett grew up loving the sea. He enlisted in the RCNVR in February 1942 and was drafted for a short period to HMCS *Saguenay*. In early December, he was transferred to *Assiniboine* and waited for the ship's return to join the crew, staying at the Knights of Columbus Hall in St. John's. On December 12, 1942, a fire broke out in the attic and spread throughout the building. The power went out, and a packed crowd stampeded, trampling men under foot. Barrett was driven to the ground in the panic, but managed to find his feet and was more or less carried out the door by the crowd. He escaped just as a ball of flame blew out the doors and windows. "The sudden stench of burning hair and flesh, some of it mine, was sickening," he remembered.[13] The building was soon engulfed in flames and dozens were trapped inside, burned alive or taken down by smoke inhalation. Barrett went back to the ruins the next day to search through the charred remains for his friend. He found him, one of the ninety-nine dead.[14]

Despite the overcrowding of every known bar, theatre, or eatery, the Canadian and British naval personnel tended to get along well in ports, and while some tension existed among the senior brass, most Canadian sailors liked their British counterparts. The Royal Navy sailors were known informally as "juicers" or "limeys," after the long tradition of issuing lime juice to sailors to prevent scurvy. Canadian Army personnel and RCAF flyers were also stationed in St. John's, and generally eyed one another warily from across the bar or street, but "our greatest rivals," recounted Frank Curry, were the Americans from Fort Pepperall and the US warships.[15] Even if an occasion skirmish or pitched battle took place between the various national forces, much affection was felt towards the Newfoundlanders who found their city overrun by soldiers, sailors, and airmen. "Kind, friendly, generous and decent, rich and poor alike, they could not have been more supportive of all these strangers who had descended upon them" wrote Lieutenant L.B. Jenson of the RCN.[16]

In contrast to St. John's, Halifax was an emotionally cold town, and Haligonians did not welcome the tens of thousands of service personnel who passed through, or who arrived on temporary leave. B.G. Macdonald, an RCAF air gunner who was shipping out for England, remembered the dreary streets and the inhospitable people. In one unhappy interaction, he was stung when he and a group of airmen passed two civilians and one of them shouted out, "So long, suckers!"[17] Macdonald shrugged it off, but he worried that perhaps his hasty enlistment, while so many stayed behind, might indeed have made him a sucker. Paul Brick sailed for four years in the merchant navy during the war and he remembered that almost everyone called Halifax "Slackers," and that anyone from there was a "slacker." George Zarn declared that "all sailors hated" the city.[18] This was certainly not the case, as many sailors remembered fondly their time there, but tension was indeed present between the RCN and civilians, the latter feeling their city was under occupation, and the former bristling at the ungrateful behaviour of the civilians.

Equally unpopular with sailors was Iceland. The Icelandic people made few attempts to make the harbour friendly for sailors or airmen. "I don't know of any [sailor]," wrote Hal Lawrence, "who ever had a hospitable word said to him by an Icelandic man or woman."[19] The inhabitants kept to themselves, and their chill was little surpassed by the dreadfully strong winds that blew down the fjord in Reykjavik and Hval Fjord. Nonetheless, the otherworldliness of the country made an impression on many Canadians. In November, when only a few hours of sunlight graced the skies, Lieutenant Dudley King of HMCS *Arvida* recalled, "Iceland appeared to be a bleak, windswept country devoid of trees. During the dark hours there were some spectacular displays of the aurora borealis."[20]

Sailors on the inshore convoy run to New York or Boston had generally happier experiences. Not much was rationed in the United States, and the harbour-front economy catered cheerfully to the seamen. Much love was also heaped across the Atlantic, on the inhabitants at the end of the "Newfie-Derry run." Londonderry, Northern Ireland, was the rest spot for most Canadian sailors, and much like St. John's, war transformed Londonderry into a thriving naval base. "Never did anything look so softly green and lovely as those Irish hills towering on the starboard side of that beautiful spring day," recounted a mesmerized Doug Murch of Cambridge, Ontario, a coder on HMCS *Agassiz*.[21] "A Guinness is good for you," went the advertisements, and many seamen agreed. However, wherever a sailor found his port, the turnaround was always too swift. Another convoy always was waiting to be shepherded to safety.

NOTWITHSTANDING ITS VICTORIES, the RCN continued to be plagued by an insufficiency of destroyers and corvettes, which left convoys vulnerable. The shortage was felt even more acutely after Canadian escort operations were moved from Iceland to Ireland in February 1942. Most of the old American-built destroyers could not safely make the Atlantic crossing, and so the Canadian corvettes and remaining destroyers were pressed into service over the longer route. At the same time, the technology gap continued to widen between the RN and the RCN.

In early 1942, the most modern British destroyers were equipped with HF/DF sets, known as "Huff-Duff"—a high-frequency direction finder that provided another method of intercepting German U-boat wireless signals as they were broadcast back to their home base. The German naval command, under the firm direction of Admiral Dönitz, demanded constant updates from the ocean-going U-boat captains. Their messages were coded and made unreadable by the four-rotor Enigma machine throughout much of the year, but the signal alone could be tracked, thereby locating concentrations of U-boats.[22] Even if the convoy lacked enough time to move hundreds of kilometres north or south of a wolf pack, if the escort group warships had two Huff-Duff sets (and this was the goal of the British Admiralty), then the operators could vector onto the U-boat chatter, locate it, and find a path around the U-boat concentration. Or the destroyers could steam at full speed towards the U-boats and compel them to dive, thereby giving the merchant ships time to pass over them.[23] Either way, HF/DF gave the destroyers a sword-and-shield capability and, more importantly, usually purchased time for the convoys to escape. But no Canadian ship was equipped with HF/DF until late in the year, and then only after much pleading by senior RCN officers. The failure to equip Canadian warships with the most modern technology played out with deadly results during the battle of convoy ON 127 in early September 1942.

The senior officer of the convoy was Lieutenant-Commander Andrew "Dobby" Dobson of HMCS *St. Croix*. He had at his disposal HMCS *Ottawa* as a second destroyer, and four additional corvettes. The escort group left Londonderry on September 5, 1942, to rendezvous with the thirty-four ships in convoy ON 127. Seven German U-boats had also caught wind of the convoy and waited for it to steam into their lair. The U-boats struck on September 10, at about a third of the distance between Londonderry and Newfoundland, when two merchant ships were hit by torpedoes. The convoy was spread out over a dozen kilometres in nine columns, however, and the warships had little idea where the U-boats were skulking, so they arrived too late at the scene of the ship's destruction. Desperate to catch the enemy, Dobson ordered *Ottawa* and HMS *Celandine* to sweep with *St. Croix* down through the convoy, hoping to catch one of the U-boats in the convoy's wake. It was a dangerous manoeuvre, and could have led to a head-on collision, but the hope was that it might surprise the enemy. They found nothing. Late in the day, another tanker was "fished." Lieutenant L.B. Jenson of *Ottawa* wrote in anguish, "It seems too strange when it is a beautiful day and one sees dreadful things happening. It is like a nightmare. Ships should only be sunk and people killed on dark, gloomy days."[24]

With three ships sunk and another damaged, the water was filled with debris, flotsam, dead bodies, and lifeboats. Standing orders were to abandon the survivors for fear the U-boats would move in on any stationary vessel, but that struck the Canadian and British officers as inhumane. And so, as the merchant ships continued to steam ahead, the warships picked up the half-drowned seamen, leaving themselves vulnerable as they lay stopped in the water. It was a time of high stress: all day, the anxious crews had seen torpedoes racing through the water, narrowly missing the zigzagging ships.

Darkness brought no relief. The U-boats continued to attack throughout the nights of September 11 and 12. The attackers had worked out an efficient tactic: they built up speed during the day, sailed around the convoy beyond visual range, and then positioned themselves in front of the convoy to line up new targets. Aware that the U-boats would begin their attack runs as the sun set, the RCN warships illuminated the sky with starshells and spotlights, and searched the water in methodical patterns. Again, no U-boats were caught on the surface. It was frustrating and terrifying to watch the merchant ships picked off, one after another. More tankers were hit. Some sank while others attempted to keep up with the convoy, their hulls ripped open and smoking. By the next day, September 13, the convoy appeared to have outrun the U-boats, but another straggling vessel was torpedoed and sunk. "Every day we were losing ships," remembered a desperate Steve Logos, who served on *Ottawa*.[25]

With all the crews tense and sleep deprived, after living for days with the threat of death, there was no relief until long-range aircraft from Newfoundland—about

HMCS Ottawa *sank an Italian sub in November 1941 but was sunk in turn by German U-boat U-91 on September 14, 1942, as part of convoy ON 127.*

725 kilometres away—found the ravaged convoy. Most of the warships were short on fuel, having expended reserves by chasing phantom U-boats; they would be hamstrung if the subs attacked again. But then they got word that two additional destroyers were coming to support them: it seemed the danger was past. They let down their guard. The weary found sleep.

But that night, at 12:05 A.M. on the 14th, *U-91*, a Type VII boat on its first patrol, fired a spread of two torpedoes at *Ottawa*. One torpedo went racing by the ship. The second hit. There was a tremendous blast and the entire ship was briefly shrouded in an orange glow. And then the power went out. Thomas Pullen, the second-in-command, raced from his cabin, feeling along the walls in the blackness. When he went topside, he was greeted by the smell of sulphur and found to his shock that the forward section of the ship had been blown off. Twisted and torn steel created an apocalyptic scene. Far worse was the stoker's living quarters, which had taken the full force of the explosion. The dead and wounded lay under debris. Pullen looked up to see a number of bloodied bodies impaled on the overhead fittings.[26] The detonation had hurled these men upwards and left their corpses skewered on the jagged deckhead ceiling, bodily fluids raining down on the wounded below. Lieutenant J.B. Jenson also survived the attack, and described a group of the wounded: "Men with grotesquely twisted limbs were lying there; it was like a scene from hell."[27]

Sid Dobing enlisted in the Royal Navy as a Boy Seaman in May 1939, and served on several British destroyers until his parents wrote to the naval authorities in 1942, demanding that he be returned to Canada. He was sent home but re-enlisted as a nineteen-year-old and was training as a torpedo man on HMCS *Ottawa* when it was hit. After the strike, Dobing recounted his horror at assisting comrades in the bowels of the dead ship. The torpedo blast had compressed the steel frames of the doors, so that the men in the sonar compartment, deep below deck, could not be released. "Every effort was made to get them out ... and we could hear them shouting, crying."[28] The trapped men called up the voice pipes with shrieking, desperate pleas for help and—when they realized they would never be released from their pitch-dark coffin—cries for their mothers.

Despite the gaping hole, the ship was afloat, although dead in the water. The sailors knew it would not last for long, as it was vulnerable to a second attack. About ten minutes after the first hit, *Ottawa* was struck by another torpedo, this time striking below the Number Two boiler room, breaking the ship's back. The captain called out to abandon ship. The vessel had lost power, and few of the 180 men in the destroyer's company heard the order, but all knew that the second torpedo blast had sealed the destroyer's fate.

A few men were hurled overboard by the second explosion, but climbed back aboard the ship to stay out of the numbing cold. The desperate crew, finding temporary safety on the deck, but operating in the dark and aware the ship could go down at any time, scrambled to release the ship's Carley floats. A number of them had been blown up, damaged, or were already in the water, but those that remained were lowered over the side. Overcrowded and in rough seas, a few of the boats flipped, drowning several exhausted and wounded men, some of whom, surprisingly, given their profession, did not know how to swim.[29] Within a few minutes, *Ottawa* listed and began to go down. Survivors still on deck dived into the water and swam for their lives to escape the suction created by the sinking vessel.

Before going in the drink, Lieutenant Jenson had inflated his Mae West to keep him buoyant. He was warmly dressed in a heavy sweater, shirt, battledress trousers, and wool socks, but he had kicked off his shoes because they would have filled with water and dragged him down. "Clothes keep one warm in water just as in the open air," Jenson noted, "and men with less died more rapidly."[30] Thomas Pullen also went into the water, dressed in layers, but almost drowned as his seaboots filled up and dragged him down like weights on his feet. He was able to kick them off, and he resurfaced into a slurry of bunker oil and broken wood.

The survivors swam or rowed away from the destroyer, but turned to watch sadly as it gave an inhuman groan. The ship's stern rose above the surface, its rudder and propellers briefly visible, before it slipped under. Jenson worried that the depth charges on board might go off and kill them all, but they had been disarmed by their attentive crews. More oil rose from the ship, like blood from a mighty beast, and soon, as the polluted waves broke over them, all the men in the water were slathered in the viscous black muck.

The few Carley floats were packed with survivors—both from *Ottawa* and merchant ships' crews who had been picked up from the sea in the previous days—and so a number of men, like Pullen, had to stay in the water, holding on to ropes with hands that soon lost feeling from exposure. Few of the dry men offered to change places with those in the water, knowing that it was a virtual death sentence. They averted their eyes. Those in the water knew their fate, and throughout the night, many fell away, too exhausted to hold on to life.

Jenson was luckier than Pullen, as he had been pulled into a float. He sat shivering in his wet clothes, and soon turned to prayer. In the distance, he could hear depth charges exploding and he knew the battle with the U-boats continued. It meant that danger still lurked beneath the surface, and no warship could break off combat to look for the survivors. Much to the horror of all, the floats were slowly drifting away from one another and becoming lost in the night. Merchant ships continued to steam past. Men cried out, shouting pleas and curses. They went unanswered.

After several hours, when all the ships were gone and the depth charge attacks faded, darkness and desolation settled in. But then one of the groups of men huddled in a Carley float started to sing songs from the Great War, such as "Pack up Your Troubles" and "It's a Long Way to Tipperary"—cheerful tunes that had sustained a previous generation in the sometimes cold, muddy, and hopeless trenches. Jenson tried a few bars, but found his jaw paralyzed by the cold. Still, he took comfort in the familiar music. As the night wore on, he lost feeling in his extremities, except for his hands, which felt like they were on fire from a brush he'd had with a jellyfish. The pain reminded him that he was still alive.

And then, out of the darkness loomed the corvette HMS *Celandine*. It sounded no horns and flipped on no searchlights, for fear of attracting the U-boats. In the dark, the crew desperately gathered all those they could find. It was a race against time. How long would the ship stay vulnerable in the water? Would its crew find all of the Carley floats that had drifted far from one another? The warship's steel hull could be seen occasionally in the gloom, and the sound of the rescue of the survivors carried in the stillness. At the last moment, *Celandine* turned towards Jenson's boat, skilfully coming alongside, with the scramble net let down the hull. Jenson began to climb, but he was so weary that he fell back into the water. Someone hauled him out, a spluttering, exhausted mess, barely alive.

Another corvette, *Arvida*, picked up twenty-two men from *Ottawa*. Lieutenant Dudley King, the second-in-command, was overseeing the rescue operation when he saw two men in the water, flailing and sinking under the surface only to rise again.

Judging that they could not swim to the net, he jumped into the water. "By the time I reached them, one man had gone, but I managed to grasp the other who was covered with oil, only to lose my grip.... The man sank out of sight." Years later he wrote, "It always has haunted me that I did not save him."[31] Life was but a grasp away, but often that was too far in the cold Atlantic.

Thomas Pullen, too, was saved, along with 75 other men; 137 went down with *Ottawa* or perished in the sea. In the end, ON 127 lost seven merchant ships and a destroyer, and four additional ships were damaged. It was a clear-cut victory for Dönitz and his U-boat captains. Yet in the kill-and-be-killed Battle of the Atlantic, *U-91*, which delivered the death blow to HMCS *Ottawa*, was itself sunk in February 1944 on its sixth patrol. Few of *Ottawa*'s survivors would have shed a tear for the ship, but maybe a shudder was in order for the German crew who went down into the dark depths, forever.

IN THE BATTLE'S AFTERMATH, the British were scathing in their condemnation of the Canadians for the drastic losses and the ineffectiveness of their sweeps.[32] The usual explanations came from Ottawa about why their warships had failed, but the refrain seemed less convincing as the trail of sunken ships and bloated corpses grew ever longer. The Canadian failure was all the more apparent because the British warships were beginning to incorporate their effective surface radar, especially the Type 271 sets, into new tactics that allowed them to hunt U-boats and take control of the sea lanes. Captain H.C. Fitz, an American naval officer, reported on meetings with his Royal Naval counterparts around this time, observing, "There is no doubt that the British naval officers as a class think the Canadians very ineffective. In all the time I was there I did not hear one single word in their favour."[33]

The merchant ships took a battering in 1942, with some 7.8 million tons sunk.[34] Allied shipping capacity had been reduced sharply by the losses, and was further stretched by the North Africa and Pacific campaigns. In light of this dilution of capacity, the British became acutely concerned about the continued security of merchant shipping in the Atlantic. There was open speculation in the Allied halls of power and in the fourth estate that Britain might be starved out of the war. It seemed unlikely, but no one wanted to test whether it might turn out to be true. When the Admiralty examined its reams of statistics, one depressing series of numbers, gathered between July and December 1942, revealed that Canadian escorts in the MOEF, which numbered about 35 percent of the total Allied fleet in the North Atlantic, had been responsible for safeguarding about 80 percent of the shipping lost to U-boats.[35] Merchant ships fared far worse when escorted by Canadian warships. The numbers did not lie, although they offered no clue as to the real reasons for the losses: the failure to equip the RCN ships with the proper technology, the shortage of destroyers and corvettes, and the too-eager desire of the Canadians to meet the Admiralty's demands for escort work that could not be achieved with their worn-out crews. A rest was needed.

In mid-December 1942, Churchill wired a birthday message to William Lyon Mackenzie King. The two had an uneasy relationship, but they had grown closer during the war. King remained wary of the British exerting pressure on his government,

Survivors of a torpedoed merchant ship in a small boat awaiting rescue.

demanding more and more forces to the point where the strain would lead to conscription. Churchill was content to accept the Canadians' substantial commitments on the land, in the air, and at sea, but he excluded King and his cabinet from any influence over the strategic direction of the war. This was fine with King, who was firmly committed to skilfully guiding Canada's domestic war effort, but perhaps this arrangement was not fully befitting Canada's massive contribution of munitions, supplies, and fighting forces. Yet now, given the desperate situation in the Battle of the Atlantic, Churchill observed that analysis of transatlantic convoys revealed the RCN was suffering from overstretch and needed time to regroup and train for the brutal year that was to come.[36] If King agreed, much of the RCN would be pulled off the critical North Atlantic run and redirected to the less intense United Kingdom-to-Gibraltar route. In his more than fifteen years as prime minister, King had delivered his share of harsh messages wrapped in soft padding; now he was on the receiving end. King and the cabinet agreed the RCN should take a break from its arduous assignment. The Canadian admirals were less sanguine and refused to accept the snub gracefully. Time and time again, the government had denuded the fleet to assist the Allied war effort—and now this vote of non-confidence. But the die had been cast. The British not-so-veiled declaration of incompetence was a blow to the navy's prestige and pride, even though its senior officers had long demanded a slowing of the frantic operational pace in order to upgrade equipment and training. Christmas 1942 was the low point of the war for the Royal Canadian Navy.

THE BATTLE OF THE ATLANTIC was, according to one senior Canadian officer, the "trench warfare of the seas."[37] And in this war of attrition, by the end of 1942 it appeared that the Allies were losing. The Royal Canadian Navy entered the fifth year of the war battered and badly bruised. The citizen navy had seemingly failed in the defence of the St. Lawrence River, and it had been pulled temporarily from convoy duties by the British. Despite these embarrassments, the navy had shepherded thousands of war-winning merchant ships across the Atlantic. One Royal Navy official report noted candidly in January 1943, "The Canadians have had to bear the brunt of the U-boat attack in the north Atlantic for the last six months."[38] In the Atlantic battlefield, by the end of 1942, the Canadian navy supplied warships for 48 percent of the convoys as opposed to 2 percent for the US navy, while the other half was picked up by the Royal Navy.[39] It was the RCN who had guided the merchant ships to safety and kept Britain in the war. And despite the terrible losses, the lifeline Canada provided was never cut. The steady attack against the merchant navy was an ongoing threat, but Britain's wartime production never slowed down, and all the hardships caused by shortages of food were borne. While the Battle of the Atlantic was a test of endurance, not a single month of the war passed when 95 percent of the shipping did not arrive in British ports, and throughout the war 99 percent of shipping leaving from North America arrived at its destination.[40] By any account, this was a monumental victory for the Allies, and especially the hard-pressed RCN. Despite tactical stalemate, and occasional defeat, the Canadians could claim strategic victory.

By January 1943, the RCN had about 200 warships, and about as many ships again being built, including modern frigates and destroyers. That same month, three of Canada's four escort groups were transferred to British command, and the Canadian role in the North Atlantic was much reduced for several months. But by February, when the U-boats began yet another campaign in the North Atlantic, the desperate Admiralty again needed Canadian warships. By March, most of the Canadian escort groups were returned to North American waters, where they began the Atlantic crossings anew. It was not much of a rest.

A casualty of the RCN's failure in destroying U-boats was Vice-Admiral Percy Nelles, the naval chief of staff, who was brought down by a palace revolt led by his own reserve officers. He had never been an inspiring commander, and he had failed signally to convince the British to share their resources, but he had overseen the largest expansion of the Canadian navy in its history. The whispering campaign against him that led to his removal was internecine infighting at its worst. Nonetheless, the ongoing and debilitating equipment crisis that plagued Canadian warships on the Atlantic apparently bypassed Ottawa, as few of the senior politicians seemed even aware of the issue. This did not reflect well on naval defence minister Angus Macdonald, or on Nelles. As one desperate sailor wrote, "In retrospect, it appears to have been an almost nightmarish example of how a military Headquarters can become so remote from the realities as actually to stultify its own *raison d'être*. They were living in cloud cuckooland, while sailors were dying."[41] The King government dropped its senior naval officer in January

1944, replacing him with the vice-chief, Rear-Admiral G.C. Jones, who had no operational service during the war, but was adept at political manoeuvres. Jones's appointment was not the solution to the equipment problem. It did, however, shake up the naval service. While viewed by many as the viper that had brought down Nelles, Jones proved to be an effective chief, and was more willing than his predecessor to show his displeasure with the Admiralty.[42] Under Jones's command, the Canadians embraced the new *King's Regulations for the Canadian Navy*, another small yet important step in distancing the Dominion's navy from that of Britain, as the document provided Canadian rules and regulations to guide the actions of its sailors and forces.

Before Nelles was driven out, the Canadians gained a significant new command. With British, Canadians, and Americans in the western Atlantic, the nations controlled multiple and overlapping jurisdictions. Canada's two commands at Halifax and Newfoundland had learned to work together, but they were responsible only for waters inside the twelve-mile territorial limit, beyond which command devolved to the British (even though Canadian warships continued to take convoys through those waters). Nothing about this arrangement adequately reflected the exertions of a nation that had been at war since 1939 and had contributed significantly to the struggle. The Canadians demanded more control. After a series of meetings, the Americans and British eventually agreed, on April 30, 1943, to the appointment of Rear-Admiral Leonard W. Murray as Commander-in-Chief Canadian North West Atlantic. Murray, who had command experience in the RN and RCN, was the only Canadian theatre commander. He was responsible for Allied forces—air, land, and naval assets—in a large zone, stretching from 47 degrees west and south to 29 degrees north.

THE GERMANS WERE WINNING the Battle of the Atlantic in early 1943. In March, Dönitz deployed more than 160 U-boats in the Atlantic, and they tore into the convoys, sinking 108 merchant ships weighing in at 627,377 tons.[43] The lifeline was being gnawed through. Desperate discussions were held at the Admiralty on the merits of abandoning the convoy system and letting the merchant ships sail by themselves, making every vessel responsible for its own survival. Perhaps, if the enemy's prey was scattered, the fleet would suffer fewer wolf pack slaughters?[44] The Royal Navy was saved from this gut-wrenching decision later in the month when its cryptologists broke the German naval cipher codes, Triton, and the convoy controllers were able to divert some of the vessels away from the massacre that awaited them. As always, running from the wolves made more sense than trying to fight through them.

And then a nearly miraculous turnaround occurred, especially as improved Allied tactics and technology were finally providing the warships with tactical and technological advantages over the enemy. Convoy support groups, including four increasingly experienced RCN U-boat-hunting formations, known as C groups, were taking the battle to the German U-boats when they converged on the convoys. The convoys retained their close protective escorts, but the support groups also accompanied them and could be detached to go on the attack. The support groups were

B-24 Liberator bomber flying protective cover over a convoy.

now, in the words of Rear-Admiral Louis-Philippe Brodeur, able to "destroy the present submarine menace."[45]

The convoys were also assisted by long-range aircraft that caught more U-boats on the surface or forced them to be submerged for longer periods. After the brutal losses of shipping in late 1942, Churchill and his staff had finally agreed to divert some VLR (Very Long Range) bombers from the offensive against German cities and assign them to U-boat patrols. The American-built, four-engine VLR Liberators, with their range of 1,600 kilometres, were devastating against U-boats in British waters. The RAF also agreed to send fifteen of their Liberators to the RCAF for the summer of 1943, and these bombers flew from Newfoundland to drive German U-boats back deep into the Atlantic.[46] Eastern Air Command's Canso flying boats and other aircraft were also aggressive and effective, leading to the sinking of three U-boats in 1942 and another three in 1943.[47] The unspectacular, lumbering Canso patrolled deep into the Atlantic, and several of No. 5 Squadron's crews dropped depth charges on surprised U-boats, damaging a number of them in February 1943. Despite these victories, in Ottawa there was grave disappointment that no RCN ships could claim to have destroyed a U-boat during the reversal of German fortunes in April and May 1943, although HMCS *Drumheller*, fighting as part of the C2 support group, was credited with a shared kill after a May 13 depth charge attack on *U-753*.[48]

The high-water mark of the U-boat campaign in the Atlantic was May 1943. Up to that point, 2,190 Allied ships had been sunk.[49] Even with a mass of new constructions, particularly the American Liberty ships, more vessels were lost than built until late summer 1943. But with the hunting groups, long-range bombers, and new-build escort aircraft carriers, the U-boats were being hounded. From April 10 to May 23, in twelve convoy battles, the U-boats sank only twenty ships, and at the cost of twenty-two U-boats. In all of May, Dönitz lost thirty-five U-boats, a crippling blow to his force in the North Atlantic.[50] With the Air Gap almost closed by long-range bombers, the hunters became the hunted. Dönitz, whose own son was killed during this striking reversal, pulled back the U-boats to safer waters on May 24.[51] During these remarkable two months, and those that followed, the sea channels were not free of the U-boats, but the steel gauntlet that had been squeezing Britain's throat was finally pried loose.

CHAPTER 13

MAKING AN IMPACT

While the Allied small-boat and amphibious raids against the French coast were at best pinpricks, and at worst an amateurish debacle (as in the case of Dieppe), the bombers were striking painful blows against the Nazi regime and the German people. And the order to attack cities and civilians came from the very top. When Roosevelt and Churchill met in Casablanca in January 1943, they set the strategic direction for the bombing campaign in the last two years of the war.

This meeting, which saw the American and British administrations working together to prosecute the war against Germany, took place as the German Sixth Army was facing annihilation at Stalingrad on the Eastern Front. Stalin demanded that the Allies do their part in the war against Germany and, with the invasion of Europe put off for at least a year, the Allied leaders ordered that the aim of the bombing campaign would be "the progressive destruction and dislocation of the German military, industrial and economic system. And the undermining of the morale of the German people to a point where their capacity for armed resistance is fatally weakened."[1] There was no grey area here; it was a stark order to attack the cities, smash societies, and kill civilians. The American and British bombers in the Combined Bomber Offensive would strike the Germans "around the clock."

Air Officer Commanding-in-Chief Arthur Harris, of RAF's Bomber Command, took to his orders with enthusiasm and continued to stand up new bomber squadrons. The British Commonwealth Air Training Plan continued to prepare thousands of airmen of all nationalities for service, and the location of the system in Canada meant that the majority of airmen were Canadian. By war's end, the senior

Dominion's flyers formed nearly a third of the total Bomber Command force.[2] Prime Minister King was well aware of the scale of this effort and demanded that the imperials follow a policy of Canadianization, meaning that the nation's airmen would serve together in identifiable RCAF squadrons. Together with his minister of national defence for air, Charles "Chubby" Power, King pressured the British throughout the war to ensure that Canadians flew together. The RAF senior command stonewalled Ottawa's requests, however, and diverted recruits to British squadrons. Significantly more Canadian RCAF flyers—some 93,844—flew in RAF units than in RCAF ones. But the RCAF was expanded throughout the war, eventually consisting of thirty-eight overseas squadrons.[3]

Halifax bomber attacking sites in France.

Les Morrison, who enlisted in the RCAF in 1942, when he was eighteen, took enormous pride in his uniform, the coveted wings, and the shoulder patches "emblazoned with one word, Canada." He believed, "they became a reflection of our intense pride."[4] "I am sure proud of our democracy," wrote another Canadian, having in mind the differences in class-consciousness in Canadian and British society.[5] Canadians serving overseas in either RCAF or RAF squadrons often saw themselves as deeply and intimately linked to Britain, but also as separate. Unlike in the Great War, when about half of Canadian soldiers were British-born, in this conflict, the proportion was far smaller: the vast majority of Canadian service personnel now were Canadian-born. With their own uniforms, units, and symbols, most Canadians took pride in their distinctive status.

The flip side of the men's pride in Canada was often a yearning for home. Soldiers and airmen wrote of missing Canadian food, gum, and leisure activities, as well as their families and community. Arthur Wilkinson penned a letter to his mother on April 14, 1940: "I listened to the hockey game on the radio last night, between New York Rangers and Toronto. Rangers won the Stanley Cup. It was grand to hear Foster Hewitt's voice and hear the crowd yell. It made me sort of homesick."[6] RCAF Sergeant Earle Miller from Renfrew, Ontario, saw a film titled *Untamed*, and wrote home about it in December of that same year: "It was all about Canada in the wilds.... This doc in the States was told to take a trip for change so he took a geography book and opened it up to a map of Canada. There was seven Sergeant Air Gunners sitting with me and we all stood up and clapped. It was hunting and fishing. Good Old Canada."[7]

Whether or not they missed "Good Old Canada," most Canadians fit in easily within the RAF squadrons. They found camaraderie and kindred spirits among young men from many nations in the shared struggle. When inter-nation tension occurred, it stemmed chiefly from class prejudices in British society or hidebound adherence to RAF customs. The civilian airmen sometimes chafed at military discipline and taunts reflecting on Canada's colonial past. Many Canadians in uniform held a perception that they were a unique breed of tough, northern warriors who came from an egalitarian society that prized independence and initiative. Not all British officers treated Canadians with disdain, but "some of the English boys looked upon the Canadians as uncouth Colonials," remembered Flight Lieutenant Arthur Wahlroth of No. 405

Squadron. "A few of us used to foster this impression by going into the kitchen before dinner and getting a strip of raw meat, then walk through the mess chewing on it. It tasted like hell, but they thought we were real backwoodsmen!"[8]

THE CANADIAN GOVERNMENT and RCAF headquarters overseas kept pressing for the creation of an all-Canadian bomber group—the air force equivalent of an army. Each of the RAF bomber groups, of which there were initially five, had around a dozen squadrons, all taking their orders from Harris's headquarters. An all-Canadian group would allow the RCAF to distinguish itself within the larger Allied war effort and, equally importantly to senior airmen, would provide much-needed opportunities for Canadians to fill critical command and staff positions. The King government greased the deal by agreeing to pay to equip and maintain it. Commander Harris was not pleased with the idea, feeling the Canadians were too inexperienced to carry off the administrative and planning work, but the decision was out of his hands: 6 Group was activated on January 1, 1943.

The creation of the group was met with little enthusiasm on the part of Canadian aircrews. As one Canadian report in late 1941 observed, Canadianization was tolerated, but most Canadians already fighting were more interested in "getting on with the war" and were "unlikely to be in a mood to seriously contemplate 'official policy on 'Canadianization.'"[9] Little had changed two years later. Canadians in established aircrews did not want to be torn from their mates and parachuted into a sprog squadron of neophytes. They knew that their chances of survival were better when they worked with experienced crews. In the end, the policy was haphazardly applied to the waves of airmen coming out of the BCATP. "Although proud to be a Canadian in the RAF," recounted RCAF Flight Sergeant B.G. McDonald, "it didn't make any difference to me which squadron I was on as long as it was an RAF Lancaster one."[10] For McDonald and many of his comrades, the issue was less about nationalism or identity, and more about having access to the best machines. For those who flew night after night, simply surviving mattered more than flag waving.

Under the command of Air Vice-Marshal George Brookes, 6 Group consisted initially of six obsolete twin-engine Wellington squadrons and three four-engine Halifax squadrons. Over time, the number of squadrons would rise to fifteen.

Brookes had served in the Great War as an aviator, had enjoyed a distinguished career as a Permanent Force RCAF officer, and had served competently in various commands since the start of the war. He faced more than a few challenges in establishing the new unit. Many Canadian flyers felt that they had not received their fair share of medals, which rankled. More serious was the failure to get the most up-to-date bombers. The Wellingtons were slowly taken out of front-line service and replaced by more modern Halifaxes and Lancasters, but as long as they were in use, the outdated Wellingtons were a problem. Flying at a lower altitude made them more susceptible to flak, and the two-engine bombers were also more vulnerable and less robust than their four-engine cousins.

The Canadians requested the more powerful Lancaster bombers, but the RAF was reluctant to supply them. The RAF suffered from a shortage of bombers in 1943, and Harris believed in rewarding experienced squadrons with newer aircraft. He equipped the long-service RAF squadrons with the best bombers, and sent Halifax bombers to the Canadians to replace the Wellingtons. The Halifax was a good plane, and on par with the Lancaster, although less sturdy in absorbing flak or fighter fire, but the Canadians found themselves with the fault-prone Mark II and V variants, which added to the fledgling group's problems. There was grumbling in the RCAF overseas command and from Minister of Air Chubby Power that the Canadians were being shorted, just as the RCN suffered while the RN favoured its own with the newest equipment. Harris's policy of rewarding experienced squadrons with better bombers was not unreasonable, but the Canadians were finding out that it was difficult to be the junior partner in a military alliance.

All of the best aerodromes were also already taken by British air groups. The 6 Group squadrons were spread out over a number of airfields among the rolling Yorkshire hills in the north of England. Consequently, the Canadians had to fly at least half an hour longer than squadrons stationed further to the south in order to reach their objectives. The extra distance put considerable strain on crews who already were in the air for six or seven hours, a strain made worse if their plane was shot up and returning after sustaining damage. Many of the northern airfields were so close together that circling aircraft preparing to land were held in dangerously overlapping flight patterns. It was also a notoriously cloudy area of England, often blanketed by industrial smog from Leeds and Middlesbrough, which, again, led to a higher occurrence of aircraft accidents. In a final most unhelpful move, three of the group's most experienced RCAF squadrons were ordered to North Africa in early 1943, to take part in the bombing of Sicily and Italy. With inferior aircraft, far-flung northern bases, and a lack of experienced squadrons, it is not surprising that 6 Group performed less effectively than most RAF groups in its first year of operations.

In the early months of 1943, only 17 percent of Bomber Command crews could be expected to complete their tours: the majority were shot down before their sixth mission.[11] The odds were even worse for the Canadians. Flying outdated Wellingtons, 6 Group posted losses of a crippling 9 percent per mission in June 1943, when anything above 5 percent was viewed as unsustainable, in terms of both aircraft lost and the crushing effect on morale.[12] Writing at this time, RCAF navigator George Brown, who sortied against Duisberg, Bochum, Dortmund, and Dusseldorf, and who saw his bomber twice caught in searchlight cones and riddled with flak fire, observed, "I think that these raids toughened us. Either that or we accepted the fate that it was inevitable that our turn would come and it was only a matter of time."[13]

THE BOMBERS LEANED HEAVILY against the German cities throughout 1943. The policy that had been decided at Casablanca was reaffirmed at the May 1943 Washington conference. It authorized around-the-clock bombing, with the Americans flying by day and the British and Commonwealth forces at night. While the Canadian government had no control over this policy, neither did it raise any objection to it. And none of this was a secret. The British government occasionally downplayed the effects of the bombing or evaded direct questions about whether civilians were targeted, but the hammering of German cities was widely reported in British and Canadian newspapers—and rarely condemned by politicians, the media, or civilians.[14] In fact, the newspapers offered graphic accounts of the bombing and even provided justifications for them.[15] On July 30, 1943, for example, *The Vancouver Sun* labelled the raid on Hamburg a "heavy terror attack" that caused "extensive fires in several areas of the town and high casualties among the civilian population."[16] Moreover, the RCAF historical section produced several wartime best-selling histories that made no secret of how the bombers were striking back against the Germans.[17] As further evidence that the Allied bombing policy reflected the convictions of most Canadians, the Canadian Institute of Public Opinion took two polls in January and June of 1944. These revealed that between 76 and 80 percent of the Anglo-Canadian public supported the bombing of Germany.[18] Targeting civilians was central to the bombing strategy, and most Canadians, like their British cousins, understood that the workers in German urban centres supported an odious Nazi regime that had put millions to the sword. Though almost no one in Canada knew of Hitler's horrifying Final Solution, which would eventually entail the murder of six million Jews and other unlucky innocents, these crimes were known to Churchill, Roosevelt, and select senior military officers by the midpoint of the war. These leaders were therefore further steeled in unleashing the full range of weapons at their disposal.[19] There would be no let-up against the barbarous Nazi regime.

This cartoon, published in The Halifax Herald *on July 31, 1943, makes stark reference to the "Allied Air Offensive" against the city of Hamburg. The city is being put through a meat-grinder.*

"Bombing of Cities is a crime," wails Hitler, while standing on a mountain of victims from "Warsaw, Rotterdam, Coventry, Belgrade, etc."

The US Eighth Army Air Force—the "Mighty Eighth"—had begun European operations in August 1942, sending its bombers into enemy air space during the day. Soon the USAAF squadrons learned the hard way—just as the RAF had done—how skilled the German defenders were, and American aircrews suffered horrendous losses from blanketing anti-aircraft fire. Their B-17 Flying Fortresses carried around 4,000 to 5,000 pounds of bombs (about half that of a Lancaster) and were armed to the teeth (each aircraft had at least ten .50-calibre machine guns), but they were no match for the swift German fighters.[20] Even with these visible setbacks, the Americans made far-fetched claims for their bombers, saying that they were better at targeting factories and munitions plants and avoiding homes and schools. This was nonsense: there was no such thing as precision bombing from 20,000 feet. One postwar study of fifty-seven American "precision" strikes on three separate synthetic oil plants revealed that only 2.2 percent of the bombs hit buildings and equipment, while no less than 87.1 percent were spread uselessly over the countryside.[21] Even the American official history observed that in January 1945, when the Luftwaffe was all but destroyed and after enormous progress had been made in tactics and technology, the 8th Air Force "had an average circular probable error of two miles on its blind missions which meant that many of its attacks depended on effectiveness on drenching the area with bombs."[22] The RAF, RCAF, and USAAF all bombed German urban centres, killing widely and indiscriminately: nothing else was possible with the available technology and the fierce German defences.[23]

THE FLYERS PAID A HEAVY PRICE for Bomber Command's gains. RCAF navigator James Baker, writing to his mother in January 1943 during the final stages of training, did not sugar-coat the nature of the task that lay ahead: "We are going to have a terrific fight on our hands. We're going to lose a lot of men and a heavy price is going to be paid amongst the Air Crews. We all realize that and there is no use tying to dodge the fact. We are all going into this with our eyes open. God knows after 3 years of war, we ought to know what to expect. We must go forward and if we fall, it is God's Will. Each of us hopes that he won't be the one that is unlucky."[24] By mid-1943, the corpse counters at Bomber Command headquarters concluded that an airman had a 17 percent chance of completing a thirty-operation tour, while only a dismal 2.5 percent saw a second tour to the end.[25] "If you live on the brink of death," wrote Halifax pilot Flight Lieutenant Denis Hornsey, "it is as if those who have gone have merely caught an earlier train to the same destination, and whatever that destination is, you will be sharing it soon, since you will almost certainly be catching the next one."[26]

But not all aircrews accepted their likely end with such fatalism. Throughout 1943, 6 Group squadrons had a high "turn back rate," meaning that bombers returned to base without completing the sortie. These crews were often accused of lacking a sufficiently aggressive spirit to "push home the attack."[27] The charge seems unfair as the bombers frequently experienced mechanical failure, and any delay from a blown engine left the bomber straggling behind the stream and therefore a prime

RCAF flyers buried at an air base. Their planes made it home, but they did not survive.

target for enemy fighters. Nevertheless, the commanding officer, Air Vice-Marshal George Brookes, had little sympathy for "boomerang crews" who turned back before completing their mission.

Flying Officer Alex Nethery, a bomb aimer with No. 427 Squadron, RCAF, recounted the tale of his first operation with a nervous crew and, at the last moment, a new navigator. The navigator got confused and took the bomber off course, eventually leading it to London, where it was nearly shot down by friendly anti-aircraft fire. The bewildered sprog crew was terrified by the searchlights and flak, and the skipper banked the bomber sharply to escape. Somehow the navigator got confused again and took them back to London, where they were fired at again. By now, there was no way to catch up to the bomber stream. There was the added risk in this particular mission of running into the returning bombers, because the operation followed a nearly straight flight path both to and from England. The pilot made the hard call: the crew jettisoned their bombs over the sea and sheepishly returned to the squadron. "When we arrived back at the base, we did not get a very good reception," Nethery remembered. "We were then told there was going to be a raid the next night and we were going—regardless! The powers that be seemed to imply there was a little lack of moral fibre on our part."[28] Nethery was clearly no coward and would survive fifteen operations with No. 427 Squadron and another fourteen as a navigator with No. 405 Pathfinder Squadron, RCAF. Pilot Douglas Harvey had experiences similar to Nethery's, writing that by 1943, "the climate of trust that had marked our earlier operations vanished, and the interrogations after a raid turned bitter as accusations were flung at the crews."[29] Canadian flyers reacted badly to being treated as delinquents by senior officers who urged them to "press on" but rarely experienced the same dangers as the crews.

The photographs, showing the bomb pattern when the planes' payload was released, allowed the scientists, boffins, and staff officers to develop tools to improve the bomb aimers' accuracy, but photographs also revealed when a crew dropped their bombs short or avoided a target altogether. The crews tended to resent this monitoring, and some figured out how to deactivate the cameras. Official reports drew attention to the issue in guarded language, saying, for example, that the failure of numerous cameras "could not definitely be explained," especially considering that the cameras worked fine before take-off and upon landing.[30] It is impossible to estimate how many crews found ways to avoid completing their missions, but it does not appear to have been widespread or epidemic. The vast majority of bomber crews pushed on.

GENERAL SIR ALAN BROOKE, the chief of the imperial general staff and Churchill's primary military advisor, did not believe that bombing could win the war. He did think, however, that the attacks were worthwhile, and that they would "bring the horrors of war home to the German people."[31] He also argued that the bombing campaign had, in effect, opened a second front against the Nazis. Stalin had demanded that the Allies somehow relieve the pressure on the Eastern Front, and a cross-Channel invasion was out of the question in 1943. The bombing campaign helped to placate the Soviet tyrant by drawing off significant German hitting power.[32] It forced the Germans to pull back from the east thousands of fighters and anti-aircraft guns in order to defend the Reich. Many of these weapons, such as the 88mm anti-aircraft gun, could also be employed in an anti-tank role.[33] The hard-pressed German army needed every gun at its disposal as it was now outnumbered by the Red Army, and the removal of thousands of these guns from the Russian steppes had a significant impact on their campaign. Late in the war, the Germans had 22,000 light and medium anti-aircraft guns, as well as 11,000 heavy 88mm guns guarding their cities within range of the bombers. In contrast, they had only 12,000 other anti-aircraft guns in all theatres of war, from Italy to the Balkans to the Eastern Front.[34] The bombing campaign also siphoned off fighters from the Eastern Front and the Mediterranean, and by April 1944, the Luftwaffe was reduced to 500 aircraft of all types against more than 13,000 Soviet planes.[35] By mid-1943 more than 40 percent of German weapons production was devoted to aircraft that were largely employed in the defence of Germany, while tanks and self-propelled guns had fallen to just 6.27 percent.[36] There were other ways to measure the effectiveness of the bombers.

The bombing campaign was weighted heavily on the industrial heartland of Germany, the Ruhr. Between March and June 1943, the cities of Duisburg, Bochum, Krefeld, Dusseldorf, Dortmund, Wuppertal, Mulheim, Gelsenkirchen, and Cologne were hit; more than 15,000 civilians were killed and thousands of buildings destroyed. The nation's propaganda minister, Joseph Goebbels, confided his shock and fury in his diary after the spring aerial attacks: "We find ourselves in a situation of helpless inferiority."[37] While the Ruhr presented many targets, it was far from Britain and protected by dense pockets of anti-aircraft batteries, as were the approaches to it over northern France, Belgium, and the Netherlands. The Allied fly-ers took terrible casualties as a result, but their sacrifice was not wasted. The German war industry had continued to increase output, year after year, as armament minister Albert Speer tightened slack in the system, increased productivity through the use of slave labour, and pressured the heads of industry to carry on despite the terror from the skies. From February 1942 to May 1943, wartime production, particularly arma-ments (as other industries were scaled back), almost tripled.[38] This was an impres-sive achievement, and yet barely enough to stave off the Red Army on the Eastern Front. In the summer of 1943, Hitler and Speer needed more, and were planning to increase steel production for weapons by 2.8 million tons per month. The massed bombing attacks against the Ruhr severely disrupted the plan. Instead of an increase, production of steel fell by 400,000 tons per month.[39] Bomber Command was hav-ing a direct impact on the Nazi war machine.

THE CITY OF HAMBURG was subjected to four major attacks in late July. This was Germany's second largest city, with a population of 1.8 million, and the site of fac-tories that manufactured aircraft and submarine parts. In the late hours of the 24th, 792 British and Canadian bombers took off with Hamburg as their destination. The bomber crews were aided in their attacks by a new low-tech defence system: the bombers approached the target and airmen shovelled aluminum foil strips—code-named "Window"—from their bomb bays and flare chutes. The tens of thousands of strips of foil, each ten inches long and three-quarters of an inch wide, effectively blinded the German radar-controlled anti-aircraft guns. And then they dropped their bomb loads. Just twelve planes were lost in the raid, and large parts of the city were burned to the ground. Two additional American attacks over the next two days were followed by another RAF and RCAF operation on the morning of July 28, when 787 bombers returned to the still-smouldering ruins of the city.

The heat of summer, high humidity, and collision of two weather fronts, combined with 2,313 tons of high explosives and incendiaries—the most bombs dropped up to that point in history in a single operation—created a massive firestorm. The man-made tempest, fed by cooler air on the ground and super-heated air above it, generated a peak temperature of 700 degrees Celsius and produced upward-flowing winds that rose to the sky like a monumental fountain. The conflagration sucked in oxygen to fan the flames to create a gale force vortex that uprooted trees and pulled houses into pieces. The flames burned higher and hotter. Fleeing citizens, some with their hair on fire, were lifted off their feet by winds that reached speeds of 110 kilometres per hour and dragged them into the incinerating heart of the storm. One civil defence report noted, "The scenes of terror are indescribable. Children were torn from their parents' hands and whirled into the fire."[40] Entire blocks were consumed in the blaze, terrified civilians were cooked alive in the streets, cowering mothers and children suffocated from lack of oxygen in shelters, and even those who dived into the canals for safety were later found boiled alive. In the scorched streets, corpses were reduced to charred bones, mummified remains, and coagulated human body fat.[41]

This was the brutal, horrifying potential of the raids. Almost all of the bombers involved in the operation survived the mission, but more than a few airmen who looked back must have shuddered at the devastation in their wake. The appalling butcher's bill for the four aerial attacks was 42,600 killed and 37,000 wounded.[42] Much of Hamburg was reduced to ashes.

Some 900,000 stunned survivors fled the dead city, spreading disorder and panic throughout the surrounding countryside. Shocked Nazi officials feared that the bomber campaign would be unstoppable now that the Allies had reached this new level of ferocity. The attacks on Hamburg had killed almost as many people than were massacred during the six-month Blitz against Britain. In the horrendous aftermath, trains filled with quicklime were sent to the city to dissolve the charred bodies that were too numerous to bury. Some 40,000 houses, 275,000 apartments, 277 schools, and 58 churches were destroyed. Another 260 factories were burned out.[43] Hitler raged about the ineffectiveness of the city's defences, and ordered more fighters and anti-tank/anti-aircraft guns pulled back from the fighting fronts to further fortify the cities, thus undermining his generals on the Eastern Front and in the Mediterranean.[44]

Speer observed, darkly, that six more such raids in quick succession would cost Germany the war. In fact, it was impossible to replicate the conditions that had produced the firestorm: the precise concentration of aircraft in time and space, the weather and wind, the topography, and the mass of buildings on the ground. But that did not stop the wild rumours that circulated throughout Germany after the raid—the whispered speculation that the Allies had developed some new, terrifying weapon. The summer of bombing put a terrible strain on Germany's home front, and the raids continued to kill by the thousand, culminating in another smaller firestorm on October 22 in Kassel, where 6,000 civilians were killed. While German civilians had been able to shrug off all but the worst effects of the bombing campaign from 1939 to 1942, now, in the summer of 1943 and until the end of the war, the intolerable tension caused by the nightly sirens, the blasted houses, the killing of neighbours, and the terror-filled nights spent in bunkers and dugouts led to growing disillusionment with the war and the Nazi regime. The citizens of Essen, a steel production centre, endured 635 warnings of enemy aircraft approaching from 1939 to 1943, plus another 198 warnings over the last two years of the war.[45] Each potential threat drove citizens to the shelters. As often as not, the Allied bombers veered off for other targets, but each false warning reminded the entire city that no safe refuge was to be had. A postwar survey of German civilians revealed that the disruption and fear precipitated by the bombers was the most trying aspect of the war, and far more damaging to morale in 1943 than the defeats at the fighting fronts, including the disaster of Stalingrad.[46] The war was being brought home and no one in the burned out, moonscape cities could pretend that Germany was not paying a steep price for its warmongering and unfettered aggression.

"WAR TO US IS SPASMODIC," wrote Flight Lieutenant Leslie McCaig in his diary.[47] The flyers fought a stop-and-start war, flying into danger for a few hours then returning to the relative luxury of a bed, a warm meal, and stiff drinks. The airmen served on both a martial and a domestic front. They did not endure the extended misery experienced by soldiers in the field. Nor did they suffer through the long, monotonous periods of waiting, broken by brief bouts of terror, as sailors did. Instead they were jolted fitfully, almost daily, between danger and safety. There were also many nights when they prepared themselves for battle only to find their mission scrubbed because of poor weather or mechanical failure. "The effect of these cancellations was traumatic," remarked wireless operator Howard Hewer. "Each man had psyched himself up for the raid in his own private way. To have the raid cancelled at the last minute ... imposed more stress on the aircrews than an actual operation."[48] Stopped in their tracks, with adrenaline pumping through their systems, the airmen had nowhere to go but back to the mess.

The mess was the flyers' retreat from the outside world. Men read quietly, wrote letters home, and smoked until their fingers were stained yellow. Most officers' messes had comfortable chairs, libraries, and games. They created a shared space where airmen could talk about their operations, their near misses, and those who never returned. None other than Air Vice-Marshal Donald Bennett, the first commander of Pathfinder Force, suggested that the lessons of battle were "taught mainly through gossip," or informal learning, "and not through classroom stuff."[49] Mess chat saved lives.

"Parties were frequent and frequently riotous," recalled RCAF navigator Douglas Humphreys.[50] Alcohol played an important role. Twenty-year-old J.K. Chapman remembered, "Many of our drinking parties were wakes for crews who had been lost the night before. In part they followed the old dictum: 'Eat, drink and be merry, for tomorrow we may die.'"[51] The men had so many opportunities to drink, and so much peer pressure to join in, that it was hard to resist. Twenty-eight-year-old Flight Lieutenant Leslie McCaig's diary is an endless recitation of nights out and mornings hung over. "We drink more as time goes on," he wrote. This resort to self-medication was not without purpose, however. Martin Schellin, a mid-upper gunner in No. 407 Squadron, RCAF, remembered years after the war that the booze, songs,

The strain of sustained operations is etched into the face of this Canadian airman. He has earned his rest.

pranks, and adolescent camaraderie "seem silly as hell now but were a real part of life then." With alcohol used as a means to relax, socialize, and forget, as one Canadian wrote, "Tomorrow was a hundred years away."[52]

Music was important too. Almost all the messes had a piano and all had a gramophone on which to play the latest hits. Young men were used to singing at church, during school, or at home, and found it easy to sing in the company of their friends. In this new war, First World War songs were recycled, as were more modern, bawdy music-hall pieces. Multiple versions of each song were developed, and what they had in common, said pilot Douglas Harvey, "was the foul language of the work-a-day air force, language born out of loneliness, frustration and fear.... Helpless to control our lives, we turned to song to express the insanities of the moment."[53] Anodyne songs such as "The Quarter Master's Stores" were absorbed and reworked with new lyrics to better suit the moment:

> There was flak, flak, bags of bloody flak,
> In the Ruhr, in the Ruhr.
> There was flak, flak, bags of bloody flak,
> In the Valley of the Ruhr.
>
> My eyes are dim I cannot see,
> The searchlights they have blinded me.
> The searchlights they have blinded me.

Flight Lieutenant Harlo Jones, an RCAF No. 408 Squadron bomber pilot, recalled a ditty they sang to the tune of "Bless Them All":

> They say there's a Lancaster leaving the Ruhr,
> Bound for old Blighty shore,
> Heavily laden with terrified men,
> Shit scared and prone on the floor.
> There's many a Junkers that's hot on their tail,
> Many a Messerschmitt too.
> They've shot off our bollocks and fucked our hydraulics
> So cheer up my lads, bless them all.[54]

Flight Sergeant B.G. McDonald enjoyed a rousing untitled, anti-authoritarian song that was sung to the tune of the popular "Lili Marlene":

> Coming out of briefing,
> Getting into the kites,
> Down the effing runway,
> And off into the night,
> We've left the flare-path far behind,
> It's effing dark, but never mind,
> We're pressing on regardless,
> For the CO's DSO.[55]

Irreverent, hyper-masculine, and super-sexualized songs were the flavour of the day: they made fun of the airmen's grim fate, took the piss out of their officers, and, of course, poked fun at the Führer. One of the favourites was sung to the tune of "Colonel Bogey":

> Hitler has only got one ball.
> Goering has two but they are small,
> Himmler, is somewhat sim'lar
> But Goe-bals has no balls at all.[56]

This one remained popular well after the war. Vulgar and cheery, the songs reflected the desperate mindset of young men who faced death almost nightly. And why not sing out your fears? In a saying popular among flyers at the time, "There's fuck all else to do."[57]

"Most of us had a sort of perverted sense of humour," said RCAF Flight Lieutenant John Zinkhan. "We were always playing pranks on each other. I guess this was a sort of safety-valve for inner tensions."[58] In addition to cards and darts, new games were devised, fuelled partly by alcohol and the high pain tolerance of youth. The mess game "Chesterfields" involved two teams cheered on by the bibulous crowd. Bets were placed. After an appropriate wind-up of taunts and boasts, each team picked up a chesterfield and charged at the other, ramming the couches together in a wood-splintering crash. If the chesterfields survived the first impact, they did it again until one of them lay broken on the floor. A variation played at No. 109 Squadron, RAF, was "High Cockalorum," in which teams of men climbed onto their partner's shoulders to wrestle or ram others to the ground. "The game could get quite violent," remembered Ron Peel, a Canadian navigator in the squadron, "as all roared around the room with a full head of steam often generated by the consumption of more than a little alcohol."[59]

"There are absolutely no women around our mess which makes it much easier," wrote Canadian pilot Jack Small, who did not survive the war.[60] One Canadian airman recounted how a fellow dominion flyer, an Australian pilot, amazed new and old hands by drinking his beer in the mess and then eating the glass. "He snapped off pieces of the glass with his front teeth and carefully manoeuvred the pieces with his tongue between his molars. Then he would grind the glass, with a horrible sound, before washing it down with beer."[61] Drunk newcomers, urged on by mates or puffing their own chest, tried to emulate the freak show, and almost always ended up with bleeding gums and lacerated tongues, to the howls of delight from their comrades. Other playful and painful tricks involved sneaking up behind a man, spraying him with lighter fuel, and lighting his jacket on fire. A less dangerous gag was to "pants" a man by grabbing his trousers and pulling them down. All of this, no doubt, was more amusing in the boozy mess environment than in the retelling.

D.J. Matthews, an RCAF navigator in No. 547 Squadron, RAF, described yet another diversion in a letter to his wife: "Late in the evening F/O Hemiston organized a work party to pile up furniture as a makeshift scaffold across the floor of the ante room. He was then passed shoes that had been ground thoroughly into the soot of the fireplace. Putting these on his hands he produced a realistic path of excellent footprints up one wall, across the ceiling, then down another. It was our parting shot after a couple of months' [of] open warfare with two unpopular 'wingless wonders' commonly spoken of as 'V.D.' and 'Joe Syph.'"[62] Again, through drinking, songs, pranks, and their own closed culture, this unique community banded together against the hazards of their duties, and against those who did not share the danger, especially the "wingless wonder" staff officers.

Airmen lived for the moment, wringing all they could from simple pleasures. "Morale was important in the air, as well as on the ground, to survive and keep your sanity," said Flying Officer Alex Nethery, who completed twenty-eight operations with his band of brothers. "Our crew did things together.... In a strange country the crew took the place of the family and friends left behind in Canada."[63]

NEARLY ALL THE AIR BASES were close to villages or cities to which the flyers would more or less regularly escape. These excursions were one of the defining experiences of bomber crews and RCAF personnel in their non-flying hours. Much as they valued the seclusion of the mess, they also needed sometimes to put a distance between themselves and their base. While the sailors were at sea and the infantry fighting in other theatres of war, the aircrews were a part of the home front, and were daily in contact with the British people. Those civilians, in turn, saw the bombers rumbling through the skies and had frequent encounters with the young men who had enlisted to defend them.

Few airmen had cars, but most could secure a bicycle, which, according to twenty-one-year-old Flight Lieutenant George Joseph Chequer, was "worth its weight in gold."[64] Many of the bikes were known as "stand up and begs," because the rider holding the high handlebars looked like a dog on its hind legs, but they got the airmen around. Some of the more adventurous Canadians purchased motorcycles, but petrol was expensive and driving on the English roads in the blackout was not for the faint of heart. Flying Officer Bob Wallace wrote to his girlfriend, Norma Etta Lee, an air traffic control operator in Canada, that his mate had bought a motorbike and wanted Wallace "to buy one but there is lots of ways to get killed over here without going looking for it on a motor-cycle."[65] As the Germans were reputed to have said, "Give the Canadians enough motor-cycles, and we don't need to worry about them."[66]

Canadians in those years came from a puritanical country where drinking establishments were dreary, dingy, and reputedly frequented only by degenerates. In Britain, in contrast, the pub was the community meeting place, filled with good cheer and boisterous folk. The airmen had money to burn and many came straight from battle after less than a day's rest. "There is no doubt that we took them over and in the course of doing so we drank too much," said Bon Cassels, a wartime navigator with No. 428 "Ghost" Squadron.[67] Pubs also offered the opportunity to meet local women, as did the dances arranged by various benevolent organizations. Flying Officer Ron Peel, who enlisted as an eighteen-year-old in September 1940, wrote of his experiences at the dance halls as "innocent fun and relaxation." Many of his older or more experienced fellow airmen—and all service personnel—used them as a place to meet new friends and lovers.[68] The music was lively and the atmosphere genial. The quickstep, slow foxtrot, waltz, and tango were all popular, as well as novelty dances such as "Doing the Lambeth Walk." More than a few hardened combat veterans studied dance guides to rectify the problem of two left feet.

Whether in the pubs, the dance halls, or the shops and streets, the British people rarely complained about the Canadian interlopers. They knew that the high-spirited young warriors who sang too loudly and drank too much risked everything for them.

CHAPTER 14

TEST OF BATTLE

The tide was turning. After four years of catastrophe, defeat, and desperate defence, the Allies had clawed their way back on land, in the air, and at sea. In the Pacific, the Americans won a stunning naval victory at Midway in June 1942, in which they crippled Japan's ability to project power by sinking four aircraft carriers. In the North Atlantic, in May 1943, German U-boat losses forced a retreat to safer battlegrounds closer to European waters. Throughout 1942 and growing in intensity in the first half of 1943, German cities were pounded by the British, Canadian, and American bombing campaign.

In another morale-raising victory for the Allies, the Germans were finally cleared from North Africa after a see-saw campaign in which the British overpowered the Italians in late 1940, failed against General Rommel's Afrika Korps in 1941, and then regrouped the following year. The enormous logistical challenges resulting from fighting in the desert led to the irony of an initial victory resulting in lengthening supply lines and then dangerous overstretch, as both sides lunged at one another repeatedly until approaching the point of exhaustion. In the end, Eighth Army commander General Bernard Montgomery's cautious tactics, materiel advantage, and determined troops were too much for the Germans, who were beaten at El Alamein in late October and early November, 1942.[1] This victory boosted the flagging spirits of the British people and vastly enhanced Montgomery's reputation as a battlefield commander, although he was much assisted by the Malta defenders, the Desert Air Force, and the Royal Navy, which combined to weaken Rommel's forces that were slowly strangled along overextended supply lines.[2]

After El Alamein, the Germans retreated westward, fighting and sometimes winning a series of skilful rearguard actions. The Germans were doomed, but Hitler made the fateful decision to order additional divisions to the front in what was already a hopeless cause. The influx of American troops with the November 1942 Operation Torch landings in northwest Africa tipped the balance of forces decisively in the Allies' favour. The Axis powers in Tunisia were finally done for in early May of 1943, when 250,000 troops (including 100,000 Germans) surrendered. This defeat compounded Hitler's humiliation as the German Sixth Army was annihilated at Stalingrad in January 1943. A quarter of a million Germans were killed or led into captivity at Stalingrad, adding to the 80,000 lost since the commencement of the battle a few months earlier.[3]

The Nazi forces went on the defensive in their global war. The question was, where should the Allies strike next? The enormous logistical challenge of moving several hundred thousand Allied troops from North Africa to another theatre of war weighed heavily on Allied commanders. Transport vessels that ventured into the Atlantic or the Mediterranean would be vulnerable to U-boats. It made sense to avoid the risk and, as Churchill suggested, employ those troops to attack German- and Italian-held Sicily. This would open up the Mediterranean to merchant shipping, and then, if all went well, would clear the way for an attack up the "soft underbelly" of Europe and knock Hitler's ally Mussolini from the war. Anyone who had ever seen Italy's hills, valleys, and rocky terrain knew the absurdity of describing Italy as a soft underbelly, but Churchill was more interested in rhetoric than reality. The Americans argued that it made more sense to focus on Germany than on its weak ally, Italy, and that meant the long-awaited cross-Channel invasion of Europe. They remained impatient with the British; some even sneered that Britain's Mediterranean strategy was primarily intended to shore up its crumbling Empire. That was always a concern for Churchill, but what really disturbed him was the prospect of sacrificing tens of thousands of Allied soldiers in a failed invasion. At Casablanca, and five months later in

Washington, Churchill convinced Roosevelt to accept the Mediterranean theatre as the next target and to continue building up forces and materiel in Britain for the European invasion. Churchill and Roosevelt were further bound together when, in January 1943, they publicly pledged that the Allies would accept nothing less than the "unconditional surrender" of the Axis powers. This commitment was made to the Allied peoples, to Stalin (who they feared would make a separate peace with Germany), and to those citizens of European nations who had endured Nazi occupation and oppression.[4] The Axis and Allied forces now had no other option but to fight to the bitter end.

ALTHOUGH PRIME MINISTER William Lyon Mackenzie King had avoided involvement in setting Allied strategy for fear of being entrapped in an ever-expanding war effort, his war cabinet, led by Minister of National Defence J.L. Ralston, pushed hard for inclusion in the Sicily campaign. Canadian newspapers taunted the government, charging that the Dominion's overseas soldiers were sitting out the war and letting others do the fighting. Meanwhile, reports of brawls, drunkenness, and debauchery on the part of Canadian troops were played up in the British press, and invariably found their way back to Canada though letters, rumours, or direct reports. The overseas military authorities pleaded that the number of incidents was low considering the size of the force, but a perception was growing on the home front that the Canadians, some of whom had been in England since late 1939, were bored and anxious for battle.[5] Ralston finally prevailed upon the cabinet, and the British found room in the Sicily invasion force for the well-trained 1st Canadian Infantry Division and an armoured brigade.[6]

"The acid test of sovereignty," wrote First Canadian Army commander General A.G.L. McNaughton, "is the control of the armed forces." McNaughton wanted to avoid splitting his large army (three infantry and two armoured divisions, and two tank brigades), for fear that it would be used piecemeal by the British without regard for Canadian sensitivities.[7] McNaughton, a fierce nationalist, argued that the army should be a semi-permanent, autonomous fighting formation. In this regard, he took his lead from the commander of the four-division-strong Canadian Corps in the previous war, Sir Arthur Currie, who had insisted that the four divisions fight together. The Corps had become a symbol of Canadian national aspirations because it remained an identifiable fighting unit.[8] While McNaughton did not demand that he, as army commander, set strategy, he had a responsibility as head of a national army both to his Allied commanding officers and to Canadian political leaders. The army, in his mind, had to remain a coherent formation to provide the necessary clout for his voice to be heard.

But McNaughton also understood the importance of seeing some of his Canadian officers and units gain battlefield experience, and realized the importance of washing away with a victory the bad taste of the Dieppe raid. He had allowed 348 Canadian officers and NCOs to serve with British First Army in Tunisia, and the men who survived gained valuable experience. Yet under pressure both from London and Ottawa, McNaughton eventually agreed to his army's temporary dismemberment, although his obstinate protest angered the British high command, some of whom, including Chief of the Imperial General Staff General Alan Brooke, undermined him with Ralston and actively sought his removal.[9] King was shielded from McNaughton's warnings by Ralston, who was anxious to see the army in action, but it appears fruitless to look for any sort of Canadian strategy relating to the war effort other than a desire to be involved in the fighting. King's primary aim at the outset had been to keep his ground forces out of combat to avoid both casualties and conscription; now he lost that battle with his own ministers, who were desperate to see Canadians serve somewhere—anywhere. This achievement was probably enough for most Canadians, but Ralston, King, and the cabinet should have forged a more coherent policy for Canada's involvement in the overseas campaigns that spanned the globe.

SICILY IS A MOUNTAINOUS ISLAND, extending about 250 kilometres from east to west, which sits astride the Mediterranean shipping routes some 90 kilometres north of Malta. For much of the first half of the war, Axis air forces and navies used it as a forward base from which to harass Allied shipping. Indeed, they were so successful in this pursuit that they all but drove Allied merchant vessels out of the Mediterranean, forcing them make a detour thousands of kilometres long around the Cape of Good Hope. The capture of Sicily would assist the Allied global marine strategy and, with the island's 1,115 kilometres of coastline and numerous landing areas, the Italians and Germans would face a monumental challenge in defending against an invasion. However, the interior of the island was a defensive planner's dream. It featured steep cliffs, the 3,000-metre-high snow-capped Mount Etna in the northeast, poor interior roads, and countless sharp grades leading to hilltop towns and villages. While this was a minor theatre of war for Hitler and his generals, as almost all of their energies were focused on the collapsing Eastern Front, the Axis strategy was to hold off the Allies before retreating back to Italy, where precious industrial resources could be exploited in the North. But Sicily was not held lightly: defending it were some 200,000 Italian troops and two effective German divisions totalling 31,000 men. And over the course of the campaign, another 40,000 Germans were sent to shore up the island's defence, including two regiments from the 29th Panzer Grenadier Division and two regiments from the 1st Parachute Division, plus additional fortress battalions and anti-aircraft units.[10] The Italians were a doubtful quantity in military terms, but the Germans were expected to fight resolutely.

British intelligence used its spies and turned enemy agents to sow disinformation regarding the timing and location of the attack. The Germans were fooled, and moved a panzer division and more than 200 aircraft to repel a fake invasion aimed at the Peloponnese region in Greece. They also shifted troops to the Balkans and Sardinia.[11] Their subterfuges were successful, but the Allies still had the enormous challenge of transporting their forces from North Africa and Tunisia, and of coordinating that armada with the Canadian and British convoys sailing from Britain and then launching synchronized amphibious landings. A single U-boat torpedo could kill thousands of vulnerable soldiers in transit. The entire operation was fraught with peril.

AFTER THREE FULL YEARS OF WAITING FOR ACTION, a diarist for the Royal Canadian Regiment summed up the Canadian soldiers' reaction to the news that the 1st Division was being sent into battle: "'No more Home Guard' is our feeling! At last our training and our courage is going to be put to the test."[12] The Canadians were ready to leave, and some, at least among the British civilians, were ready to see them go. "A Canadian soldier on leave has visited my home," one British woman informed military authorities. "As a result, both my daughter and I are pregnant.

Not that we hold it against your soldier, but the last time he was here he took my daughter's bicycle which she needs to go to work. Can you get him to return it?"[13]

By late April 1943, the staffs of the 1st Canadian Division and the 1st Canadian Army Tank Brigade were engaged in the complex task of arranging transport for 25,000 men, their kit, equipment, and everything else needed to sustain a distant campaign. Senior commanders also ordered a process of toughening up, which included long-distance marches, small-unit tactics, and training in scrambling up and down nets to get into landing craft. "We had become hardened," wrote Gunner Ben Malkin, a Jewish-born Canadian who would later serve as a war correspondent.[14] Most regiments were ordered to weed out their over-age NCOs and privates; they had provided fatherly stability during the time in England but were not fit for harsh campaigning.[15] That was a young man's game.

Regulations stipulated that the infantry were to be between the ages of eighteen and forty-five, but, on average, they were in their early twenties, and thousands were teenagers. Like their fathers, more than half had not made it out of middle school; the average education level was about grade seven. One in ten was illiterate. Officers were better educated, but all Canadians in the Depression years were confronted with difficult decisions about schooling, and many were forced to abandon formal instruction to put food on the family table. The Canadians had inherited the Great War soldiers' reputation as wild men from the northern icescapes of the Empire, sturdy in temperament and tough in outlook. But their average height was five foot seven. They weighed about 135 pounds at enlistment, and despite bulking up with the intense training and starchy food in England, this was no army of Spartans bred for battle.[16] Nonetheless, they were ready to fight.

Everyone tied up loose ends. Letters were written to family members informing them that mail would be forwarded to an unknown destination. Some English girlfriends were abandoned, while other lovers promised to wait for one another. It would be a long wait. John MacQueen was desperate to marry his girl, Margaret, whom he had met two years earlier. He managed to find a barrel of beer, and his mates hoarded their Spam to feed the forty guests in a snap wedding. His mother, in Sydney, Nova Scotia, sent along silk for Margaret's dress. Rationing still made it difficult for the bridesmaids to be outfitted in matching dresses, but they cobbled together some material. It was a glorious wedding, but as MacQueen noted, he shipped out a few days later and "Peggy and I did not see each other again for two years."[17]

New weapons were issued. The trusted Bren gun remained the primary light machine gun: one was issued for each section of ten men. Able to lay down bursts of fire, and deadly to a range of about 500 metres, the Bren gunner provided heavy firepower to a section, with three of them grouped at the platoon. The thirty-round curved magazine emerged from the top of the gun like a menacing fin, and it could be pulled out and a new one jammed in with only a few seconds of break in fire. The number two on the gun was laden down with ammunition and ready to take over if the trigger man was killed or wounded. The Canadians were also surprised to find themselves issued with the Thompson submachine gun, which reminded them of Al Capone and his American gangsters. It was a better weapon than the British-made Sten gun, but the soldiers had little time to train with it. Most infantrymen remained riflemen, equipped with the .303 Lee-Enfield rifle and its skewer-type bayonet. The rifle was similar to what their fathers used in the Great War, although the bayonet was severely shortened from the 17-inch sword bayonet of the trenches. Most generals assumed there would be few bayonet fights, but official and eye-witness accounts over the coming months would reveal a surprisingly high incidence of hand-to-hand combat. Hand grenades were essential for clearing enemy strongpoints, and most soldiers stuffed their pockets with them when they went into battle.

An infantry battalion had a full strength of 850 (38 officers and 812 other ranks). A commanding officer and his headquarters company of around 100 consisted of a signals and administrative platoon to communicate with the four rifle companies and support company. The rifle companies were the core of a battalion's fighting strength and were expected to take the highest casualties. Each company was led by a major and his four lieutenants, and had a strength of 120 other ranks, divided into three rifle platoons of three sections each, and a headquarters. At the lowest level, a section was a mere eight riflemen and two junior non-commissioned officers (a corporal and a lance-corporal), and they knew each other as intimately as brothers.

To augment a battalion's firepower, a fifth company, the support company, consisting of 7 officers and 184 other ranks, had four platoons: the mortar platoon of six 3-inch mortars could provide plunging fire; eight Universal Carriers—an all-purpose lightly armoured tracked vehicle with Bren guns—that were useful for moving men and ammunition, and for providing added firepower; an anti-tank platoon of about sixty other ranks that manned six 6-pounder guns (named because of the weight of the projectile), and were meant to backstop the rifle companies against armoured attacks or soften up structures during battle; and, finally, a pioneer platoon employed to clear mines, maintain positions, and do anything and everything ordered by the commanding officer. The support company represented a significant change from the Great War battalions, which were heavier at about 1,000 men and much more reliant on riflemen. The Second World War battalions had more firepower and greater mobility, with about 120 vehicles ranging from the Universal Carriers, to jeeps, to several types of supply truck.

Over the preceding three and a half years, the Canadians had undergone intense preparation for battle. Long marches were used to get the men in shape, and longer ones to punish them. Battle drill had been introduced in 1941, and it toughened soldiers through gruelling physical activity, while also exposing them to the hardship of combat conditions, including live fire drills that saw men wounded and killed. One excited Canadian wrote home, "We have just come back from Battle Camp in the mountains of Wales. No kidding, Mom, your son is almost a Commando now. I think I've had everything fired at me including the kitchen sink. It really is quite a thrill to be under fire. It certainly gives you lots of confidence and that's what an officer needs in this man's war."[18] Infantrymen in sections and platoons learned to support one another and advance upon a dug-in enemy position by laying down fire and rushing forward.[19] A section of riflemen, backed by Bren gunners, were trained to infiltrate forward under a cover of bullets and mortar bombs, build up their own volume of fire—applied continuously rather than in isolated sniper battles—and then, while the enemy was seeking cover, to move around points of resistance, finding the gaps in the defence and attacking from multiple directions.[20] The key to success, as in the Great War, was to cross the enemy's firezone as rapidly as possible. However, on the battlefield, with voice control lost in the cacophony of shelling and small-arms fire, and men spread out on the broken terrain, they had to be their own leaders. It took time for soldiers in combat to distinguish between the sounds of enemy and friendly shells and bombs. Those who had not yet learned the difference flopped at every crash and snap and slowed the advance. Experience was always bought with blood, but training reduced the amount to be paid.

Units practised fighting as a platoon of thirty-five or so members. Then they worked with other platoons to manoeuvre on the battlefield, and after that with companies, and finally in battalions. From there, the Canadians engaged in combined arms exercises over large tracts of the English countryside, where divisions and corps learned how to advance in unison and to overcome the friction of moving tens of thousands of men and mountains of supplies along constricted road systems. As the infantry mastered fighting together in a series of large-scale training exercises from 1940 to 1943, commanders wielded together infantry, artillery, armour, combat engineers, and other formations, to coordinate attacks and augment combat power.[21]

Throughout training, soldiers were taught to kill. It was an unnatural act for nearly all men, but relentlessly driving bayonets into human-sized bags, shooting at

Canadian infantrymen engaging in battle drill training in England.

life-sized targets, and listening to lectures about enemy atrocities combined to wear away at the individual's instinctive reluctance to take life. Some men later found that they rarely fired their weapons on the battlefield, never saw the enemy, and never overcame their abhorrence of killing. For most, however, the psychological rewiring for combat occurred the moment they entered the No Man's Land, where others were trying to kill them.

THE 1ST CANADIAN INFANTRY DIVISION—known as the Red Patch, for the battle patch first issued during the Great War—was commanded by Major-General H.L. Salmon, a respected professional soldier. He had trained his three infantry brigades intensely—each of them made up of three infantry regiments. In the 1st Brigade was the prewar regular unit, the Royal Canadian Regiment, known for its attention to "spit and polish" discipline. The brigade was also home to the Hastings & Prince Edward Regiment, a rural militia regiment that had recruited through Ontario's central counties. They called themselves the Plough Jockeys, and were also known informally as the "Hasty Ps." "Farmers know a lot about life, and a lot about death," wrote one of their officers. "They have what is so important for infantrymen—an eye for movement, for weather and for ground. And they grow up knowing how to use a rifle."[22] The Hasty Ps wore their rural roots as a badge of honour, and their origins especially set the unit apart from the third regiment in the brigade, the 48th Highlanders of Canada, one of the oldest and wealthiest of militia regiments, which drew from Toronto. The brigade was commanded by Brigadier Howard Graham, long-time militia officer and former mayor of Trenton.

The 2nd Brigade consisted of Princess Patricia's Canadian Light Infantry, a professional regular battalion from Western Canada, first raised for overseas service in 1914. The Seaforth Highlanders of Canada, a long-standing militia regiment from Vancouver, and the Edmonton Regiment, which recruited in northern Alberta, rounded out the brigade. The three Western battalions were commanded by Christopher Vokes, a hard-drinking and rough-hewn regular soldier. Each regiment had its own identity, culture, and reputation to forge or protect. Richard Malone, brigade major for the 2nd Brigade, remarked on the regimental rivalries, noting how each regiment looked "down its nose slightly at its sister formation."[23] It was not uncommon to see fists fly in regiment-defending pub brawls. At the same time, the Patricias, Seaforths, and Eddies would not stand for their brigade mates being battered by others, and often rushed in to save a flailing 2nd Brigade man in a fight with soldiers from regiments outside the brigade or division. Notwithstanding black eyes and broken noses, these rivalries promoted loyalty and pride.

The 3rd Brigade was also commanded by a professional officer, M.H.S. Penhale, and it consisted of a Quebec battalion and two Maritime units. The Royal 22e Régiment, referred to as the "Van Doos," was the only French-Canadian prewar permanent infantry regiment. The Carleton and York Regiment recruited from the Saint John River Valley in New Brunswick, and the West Nova Scotia Regiment was formed from Nova Scotians and Prince Edward Islanders. The 1st Division also included the Saskatoon Light Infantry, which operated 4.2-inch mortars and Vickers machine guns, and the 4th Princess Louise Dragoon Guards, a reconnaissance regiment known as the Plugs, which moved in armoured cars and Universal Carriers.

The division also controlled its own sizeable force of gunners, with three field artillery regiments, each consisting of three eight-gun batteries. The workhorse of the artillery was the 25-pounder, of which each division had seventy-two (increased to ninety-two by the end of the war). The gun, with its stabilizing trail, fired a 25-pound shell, an upgrade from the Great War's 18-pounder artillery piece. Despite the killing power of a 25-pounder shell exploding above ground and spraying an area with shell splinters and a killing blast, the shell had to land within about a metre of a target in a slit trench to kill the occupant from the shock wave blast.[24] A well-dug-in defender would be protected from all but a nearly direct hit. The anti-tank regiment used a mixture of the 6-pounders and the new 17-pounders, which surprised gunners with their spectacular muzzle-flash; the blast had a tendency to sizzle off the hair, eyebrows, and moustaches of gunners who leaned in too close. The 17-pounder fired an armour-piercing capped ballistic cap (APCBC) at 885 metres per second. It was less effective than the best German anti-tank gun, the 88mm Pak 43, but a year later, in Normandy, the Canadian anti-tank guns would be equipped with a tungsten-carbide armour-piercing discarding sabot (APDS) shell, which did in fact make the 17-pounder more effective than the much-feared German 88.[25] The medium artillery consisted of the 5.5-inch howitzer, which fired an 82-pound high explosive shell to a range of 18,200 metres. Rounding out the division were anti-aircraft gun teams, engineer companies, a signals squadron, and service and medical units.

Tanks were not part of an infantry division, and were grouped in independent brigades generally controlled at the corps or army level. This isolation made infantry and tank training more difficult, and the Canadians had engaged in only the most limited tank and infantry interaction over the preceding four years. The 1st Canadian Army Tank Brigade (soon renamed 1st Canadian Armoured Brigade) consisted of about 3,500 men. The brigade's 200 or so Sherman tanks were divided into three regiments: the Ontario, the Three Rivers, and the Calgary. The new M4A4 Sherman had replaced the Churchill that had gone into battle at Dieppe, although many British tank regiments would use it throughout the war. Sand-coloured paint and red, white, and blue aircraft-identification markings, in the form of a bull's eye, were added to the Sherman's hull. The Shermans had a better design than the Churchills, with a lower profile and a bigger main gun in the 75mm, and were about on par with the German Panzer IVs, although inferior to anything larger, such as Panthers and, later, the feared Tiger tanks. Wearing their iconic black berets, the tank men would spearhead the armoured formations going into their first sustained campaign of the war.

Disaster almost immediately struck the Canadian division, as a result of accident rather than enemy fire. General Salmon and several staff officers set off for Cairo in late April to be a part of the planning operation, but their airplane crashed in England, killing all on board. The Canadian division was decapitated. General McNaughton acted quickly to appoint Major-General Guy Simonds, a forty-year-old Royal Military College graduate, to take Salmon's place. Forceful, aloof, and ruthless, Guy Simonds, nicknamed the "The Count" for his cold manner, had little time for fools or failure. While he had been too young to serve in the Great War, he had been a leading military intellectual in the lean 1930s, when he wrote in *Canadian Defence Quarterly*, the military's service journal, on the use of armour on the battlefield. Even though Simonds had limited command experience—and rose to take over a division without ever having fought in battle—he would play a critical role in Canada's army over the next two years.

THE CANADIANS DEPARTED from a number of ports in the United Kingdom in mid-June, to arrive off Algiers on July 5. As the ninety-two ships that bore them steamed southward, the soldiers lined the rails admiring the beautiful seas. They learned that the wan Scotland sun was far different from that of the Mediterranean sky, which soon left the fish-white Canadians looking like burn victims. Those young soldiers who mastered their roiling stomachs were jocular and loose, playing cards day and night, singing lusty songs, and writing touching letters home. Men abandoned the crowded, humid, and stinky mess decks, known as the "slave quarters," when they

Major-General Guy Simonds, on the right, commanded the 1st Canadian Infantry Division in Sicily and would rise to become Canada's best general of the war.

could, to find spots on the upper deck in which to hide and sleep, even as they were hounded by military police and chivvied back to the depths of the ship.[26] German subs were a worry for all. Over a two-day period, on July 4 and 5, U-boats sank three of the convoy's transport ships. The two subs were chased off, and both would be sunk within the year; luckily, none of the destroyed ships were troop carriers. Nonetheless, 58 Canadians were killed, and more than 500 vehicles—along with signals equipment and about half of the division's anti-tank guns—sank out of sight.[27]

While supposed clairvoyants fed rumours early in the voyage on the force's final destination, it was identified by degrees through lectures and loose talk among the officers.[28] The soldiers' woollen battledress was replaced with khaki shorts and shirts. They were briefed on the dangers of tropical diseases. *A Soldier's Guide to Italy* was a useful little pamphlet for an introduction to the climate, culture, and people of Sicily and Italy, although it seemed more useful for planning a vacation than for fighting a war. Everyone knew they were bound for Sicily long before it was officially announced.

On July 9, as 3,000 ships closed on Malta, they were united in a single massive armada some 100 kilometres long. That night, the fleet was pounded by a heavy gale. The storm passed, but many hoped it was not an omen for the battle that was soon to be joined. "Hour by hour the tension mounted," wrote Lieutenant Farley Mowat of the Hastings & Prince Edward Regiment, who was known as Squib to his mates because of his small stature. "All around us the sea and air were pulsing with gathering power as more and more convoys hove into view; new packs of grey destroyers foamed up to guard our flanks; and the planes patrolling overhead multiplied like shrilling locusts."[29] Officer and men alike worried about their own inexperience and what it might be like to face the battle-hardened German soldiers. Captain B.G. Parker penned in his personal diary, "Hard to believe that we shall be in action in a few hours."[30]

GENERAL DWIGHT D. EISENHOWER was destined for greatness. The fifty-two-year-old American had been a prewar staff officer and stuck in the stagnant US military at the rank of major for sixteen years. Yet he was jovial, hard working, and a favourite of General George Marshall, who would rise to chief of staff to the army during the

Second World War. Eisenhower was given a number of critical staff appointments early in the war, performed them well, and rose rapidly, bypassing many other officers above him in rank. The general had the ability to make those working for him strive to tremendous heights while at the same time earning their deep respect. In his first wartime command, overseeing the Torch landings in North Africa half a year earlier, and then the fighting in Tunisia, Eisenhower had led the raw American troops effectively, even though there had been numerous challenges and problems. Now he had the enormous responsibility and burden of commanding the multinational invasion of Sicily, known as Operation Husky. The balding Eisenhower was cheerful and optimistic as he chain-smoked through the day, weighing the hundreds of options in front of him, delegating authority, and soothing bruised egos. Unlike most other great fighting Allied generals of the coalition, he took into account a number of different points of view before issuing his orders, and he was sensitive to the cultural differences between his American colleagues and their British counterparts. These differences sometimes kept him awake at night, but he rarely unleashed his frustration and anger on his subordinates, and he tended to work well with the senior naval and air force commanders. His relationship with his multinational army was more difficult. The commander of the ground forces was General Harold Alexander, an experienced and brave British career soldier who was well respected by almost everyone until he received overall command. In that role, he was too gentle in coordinating the actions, or corralling the egos, of his difficult army generals, General Bernard Montgomery, commander of the British Eighth Army, and General George Patton, commander of the United States Seventh Army.[31]

From the start, the Americans and British had a different vision for attacking the island. The Americans wanted an aggressive plan that saw their army land divisions at different points around the island in order to confuse the enemy and cut off retreating forces that would seek safety on the Italian mainland. But Montgomery was adamant that a more cautious plan was required, one that did not divide the Allied ground forces and leave them susceptible to counterattack. The Germans, despite being outnumbered, were masters at exploiting weakness. The ferret-faced Montgomery—who in his baggy uniform might have been mistaken for a shopkeeper rather than a general—had supreme confidence in himself as a soldier. His success in North Africa confirmed in his mind that a "tidy battlefield" was the approach that would beat the Germans, and by "tidy" he meant a methodical application of heavy firepower and careful preparation of his forces for a decisive battle. He was no proponent of blitzkrieg, even though he understood the power of an armoured thrust. With his brassy confidence and insufferable self-regard—even if he was typically correct—he was not an easy man for his peers and superiors to like. He was, however, much beloved by his Eighth Army troops, who had followed him in and out of the hell of North Africa. Montgomery ultimately prevailed in modifying the Sicily plan, and then he gloated about his victory.[32] Patton was furious—not least because the Americans were left without a port through which to unload supplies, which would hamper their advance. The American general raged that it was nothing short of a "British plot."[33] Since Alexander was playing favourites by supporting Montgomery over Patton, and barely concealed his lack of faith in the newly arrived American soldiers, who had been uneven—and at times inept—in the final battles in Tunisia, the Americans were right to be livid. Eisenhower watched all of this warily, concerned that his coalition forces would savage one another before they confronted the enemy.

In the short time between the Axis surrender in Tunisia in May and the Allied landings at Sicily in mid-July, enormous energy and planning went into the assault landing. Rather less thought was put into how to drive the Axis formations back and, equally important, how to ensure that when the enemy was defeated on Sicily, they did not cross the Straits of Messina to regroup on the Italian mainland. But the most pressing and immediate challenge was the amphibious landing on the beaches; it was there that Eisenhower expected a lot of his soldiers to die.

The key to the invasion was to pulverize the enemy's beach defences, overwhelm its air force, and land in strength before the inevitable counterattack threw the Allies back into the sea. Montgomery assumed that "resistance will be fierce and a prolonged dog-fight will follow the initial assault."[34] The Royal Canadian Army Medical Corps—which had almost 1,800 officers and orderlies to support the invasion—planned for 3,200 casualties to come through the Canadian sector alone in the first six days of battle.[35] The casualties were expected to be at least as heavy on the American and British beaches.

Seven divisions would come ashore on twenty-six beaches, along a 70-kilometre stretch of the southern coast. The Americans were to land in the southwest, the Canadians in the south on the Pachino Peninsula, and the British to the southeast.

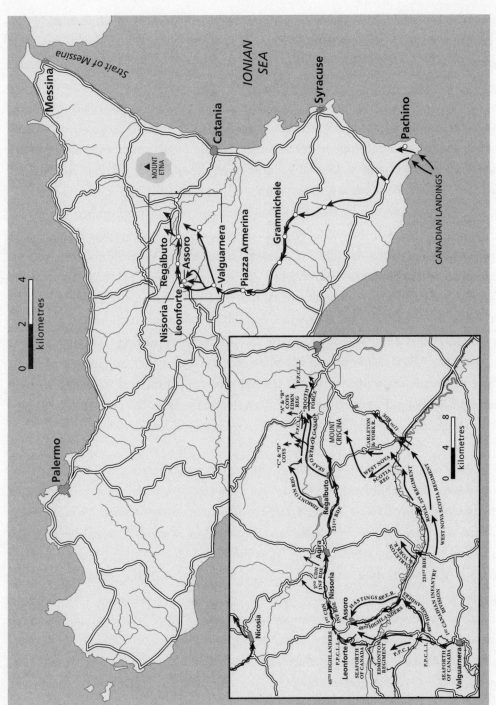

Messina

Strait of Messina

Palermo

MOUNT
ETNA

Nissoria
Leonforte
Regalbuto
Assoro
Valguarnera
Piazza Armerina

Catania

IONIAN
SEA

Grammichele

Syracuse

Pachino

CANADIAN LANDINGS

0   2   4
kilometres

Nicosia

1ST CDN
INF BDE

2ND CDN
INF BDE

Agira

Nissoria

48TH HIGHLANDERS
P.P.C.L.I.

Leonforte

SEAFORTH
OF CANADA

EDMONTON
REGIMENT

P.P.C.L.I.

SEAFORTH
OF CANADA

Valguarnera

Assoro

HASTINGS & P.E.R.

48TH HIGHLANDERS

48TH HIGHLANDERS

CARLETON
& YORK R.

1ST CANADIAN
INFANTRY DIVISION

EDMONTON REG

"C" & "D"
COYS

"A" & "B"
COYS
EDMN

P.P.C.L.I.

"BOOTH"
FORCE

P.P.C.L.I.

Regalbuto

231ST BDE

SEAFORTH OF CANADA

MOUNT
CRISCINA

WEST NOVA
SCOTIA
REG

CARLETON
& YORK R.

3RD BDE

ROYAL 22ND REGIMENT

WEST NOVA SCOTIA REGIMENT

CARLETON
& YORK R.

231ST BDE

0   4   8
kilometres

SICILY, 1943

The lessons learned from Dieppe ruled out an assault on a fortified port, so it was crucial for the Allies to capture a number of airfields to allow for the movement of materiel, as army divisions consumed about 500 tons of supplies daily. Because the beaches were spread out, and the landing forces were vulnerable to counterattack, the warships, with their enormous guns, were expected to support the shallow landing by hurling shells over the troops heads, targeting the few built-up positions within range, and, when it developed, meeting any enemy attack in strength. Allied fighters would provide an aerial umbrella, holding back the far fewer German and Italian fighters and bombers, while also harassing ground forces.[36]

The Axis defenders had more than 230,000 troops on Sicily (a number that would grow to 270,000 with the addition of German defenders). Allied intelligence estimates suggested, however, that the southern beaches would be lightly defended by unmotivated Italian garrison units. Most Allied soldiers sneered at the Italians, but it was not difficult to sweep a beach with a machine gun, and regardless of their unit's less than impressive martial reputation, some Italians would certainly fight for their lives. Still, the real fear was of the Germans. The two hard-hitting German divisions terrified the Allied planners, and Eisenhower warned that they might be enough to drive his forces, unsteady from their landings, back into the sea. Churchill winced at such defeatist talk, and raged that Stalin's armies faced 185 divisions.[37] The attack went ahead, but apprehension was rife within the Allied high command.

THE ARMADA HAD 6 BATTLESHIPS, 2 aircraft carriers, 15 cruisers, 119 destroyers, and more than 2,000 landing craft to ferry the invaders from their troop ships to the beaches. Four RCN Landing Craft Flotillas, consisting of some 400 Canadian sailors, were involved in the operation. Amphibious operations were always risky, but they were all the more challenging in difficult weather. Although the storm on the 9th had blown itself out, the seas remained rough, and they broke relentlessly against the ships' sides.

Above the ships, wave after wave of bombers flew from North Africa, smashing enemy fortifications, as they had been doing for six weeks prior to the landing on July 10.[38] As part of the bomber armada, three RCAF squadrons—Nos. 420, 424, and 425 of 331 Wing, commanded by Group Captain Larry Dunlap—contributed to the mayhem. On the 102 nights 331 Wing spent in theatre, its two-engine Wellington MK Xs launched a total of 2,182 sorties in 82 separate operations against Sicily and Italy.[39]

Under a cloud-covered moon, the heavily laden infantry were ordered into the landing craft late on July 9. In some instances, the troops embarked on the LCAs (Landing Craft Assaults) that were on board and were lowered into the water from winches and davits. In others, soldiers scrambled down nets that hung along the ships' sides, holding on for dear life, aware that a misstep in the dark would result in drowning or being crushed between the hulls of the two vessels. No cases of infantrymen losing their lives were reported, but the descent into the landing craft, heaving wildly from the rough water and packed with troops, took longer than expected.

"Our LCAs really took a beating," reported eighteen-year-old Canadian bowman Fred Turnbull, who operated the ramp on one of the assault vessels. "At 1:00 AM, the Flotilla formed up in line ahead and we started on the first seven-mile run-in."[40] Private George Ableson, who turned thirty years old that fateful night and wondered if he would see one more day, wrote to his parents describing the rough voyage: "I was seasick, and there was nowhere to be seasick except right in front of you because we were jammed in there like sardines. There were 39 of us I think it was, in a space that seemed no longer and only a little wider than the corridor from your living room down to the boys' back bedroom."[41] A chunky broth of mutton-stew-vomit sloshed over the Canadians' boots as their landing crafts pitched and yawed.

HMS *Roberts*'s 15-inch guns reverberated through the night, and soldiers could feel the blast through their bodies and aching teeth. Other warships sent their shells landward in a display of pyrotechnics and fury. The infantry came ashore at around 2:45 A.M., expecting a hostile reception. "I couldn't get over the feeling of being there, right in the middle of an invasion," remarked Private George Reid of the Seaforth Highlanders. "I feared this is going to be another dammed fiasco like Dieppe."[42]

It wasn't like Dieppe at all.

Most of the Italian troops surrendered at first sight. Others had been blown to bits by the advance bombardment. Major T.M. Powers, the second-in-command of the Royal Canadian Regiment, wrote that Able Company had only two killed and three wounded in stray bullet fire "but captured 250 Italian prisoners who, it is estimated, could have held out for least two days if they had the heart to fight."[43] Few of the Canadian assault groups encountered much opposition, although several platoons of the spearhead regiments had been dropped on the wrong beaches, and a few were stuck on hidden shoals. The infantry groused that it was nothing but snafus and sandbars, but nothing was lost except a bit of pride as landing craft foundered far from shore. It was much worse in the air, as British and American paratroopers were fired on by Allied anti-aircraft guns because of miscommunication and apprehension that somehow the Germans were attacking. More than 250 men were dropped short and drowned.

As dawn broke, the Canadians were driving hard on their objective, an airfield at Pachino. Marching rapidly through vineyards and dusty open fields, they secured the airfield after a brief fight and a few dozen casualties. The blazing sun rose to reveal as successful an amphibious invasion as any of the planners could have hoped for. The defenders either melted away before the onslaught or surrendered. Canadian officers soon found that few Germans were among the 720 prisoners, and no one expected the Germans to give up so easily in the battle to come.[44]

BEHIND THE LEAD ASSAULT WAVES came 160,000 Allied soldiers, 600 tanks, and 14,000 vehicles. The challenge for the staff officers and beach masters was in sorting out traffic jams and ensuring no friendly fire incidents occurred as trigger-happy soldiers stumbled upon their mates ahead of them, shooting before asking questions. The Canadians, as a lead formation, were ordered to march. Pushing deeper into the interior was made difficult for Simonds's men because so many of the division's jeeps had been sunk on the voyage, and it became necessary to shift vehicles to forward units and to starve others. Canadian officers were reduced to begging, borrowing, and stealing from their British and American comrades.[45] As vehicles were slowly gathered, the ground-pounders pounded the roads. Army boots soon reduced feet to a welter of oozing and bleeding blisters. Some Canadian units requisitioned mules. The bad-tempered animals could carry a heavy load and withstand the heat, but sitting atop an ass was a far cry from blitzkrieg.

While the Americans on the Canadians' left flank met and defeated a fierce German counterattack on July 10 and 11 with the aid of naval fire and overwhelming air

support, Simonds's troops marched northward into the interior. Their most immediate enemy was the hammering heat. The infantry were kitted out in tropical gear,
with shorts and short-sleeved battle dress, but soon, through trade with the Sicilians,
the Canucks acquired sun hats, top hats, and even parasols, with the result that the
mismatched force, according to one lieutenant-colonel, "began to look more like an
army of pirates than soldiers."[46]

Canadians in a Universal Carrier. They have acquired an umbrella to ward off the sun.

In temperatures above 40 degrees Celsius, backpacks bit deep into reddening skin and every man suffered in the blast furnace. The Shermans were equipped with virtually no ventilation, and the tankers endured nearly intolerable heat and dangerous dehydration. All soldiers emptied their canteens rapidly before they learned to conserve their water in a practice known to the military hierarchy as "water discipline"—which really meant suffering from intense thirst. Wells were few and far between in the parched terrain, and potable water had to be boiled or chlorinated to avoid parasites. All the while, the Canadians stumbled forward, kilometre after kilometre, through flour-like dust so pervasive that it found its way into every orifice of the body. One Canadian officer, upon seeing British troops of the 7th Black Watch—of Monty's famed Eighth Army—observed that they "looked lean and hard ... compared to them we look raw indeed."[47]

As the Canadians lurched into the interior, they were dismayed by what they saw of the conditions in which most Sicilians lived. Major Alex Campbell of the Hastings & Prince Edward Regiment wrote to his mother that the pathetic civilians "are practically starved and their homes are just hovels."[48] The Sicilians at first stared back at the Canadians with suspicious and sullen glances. They had known only hardship from other occupiers and supposed liberators. But soon they were, as an officer in the Seaforth Highlanders of Canada wrote, standing "in the streets waving and clapping their hands at us. Wine and fruit were passed out to the troops, the hatred of Mussolini and the Germans always being expressed time and time again."[49] The Allied soldiers were warned not to loot Sicilian homes and businesses, but almost nothing was left to take, and most Canadians found themselves passing out gum or sun-melted chocolate bars to the barefoot, grubby children that clamoured around them.

WITHIN A FEW DAYS OF THE ALLIED LANDING, the Germans realized that Sicily was lost. The Italian forces were fleeing or surrendering en masse, to the point where the frustrated German commander, Field Marshal Albert Kesselring, wrote angrily, "The Italian coastal divisions were an utter failure, not one of their counterattack divisions reaching the enemy in time or even at all.... Cowardice or treachery?"[50] The Allies had put too many men and armour onto the southern beaches, and after the thrust against the American beachhead failed, the Germans planned a measured retreat to the northeast corner of the island. From there, they could cross the straits to the Italian mainland. It would be a fighting retreat, with rearguard units holding ground in a series of concentric lines to slow the attackers marching north. The poor road system all but channelled the Allies into chokepoints and ambushes. Sicily became an enormous traffic jam. If the Allies had not commanded the air, the Luftwaffe would have transformed the lines of stalled and idling trucks carrying supplies and munitions into a wasteland of burning wrecks.

The Allied plan was to split Sicily in half, but the British and American generals continued to fight over access to the few available roads.[51] The British forces had landed on the east coast, and had a direct road system northwards to Messina. It made sense for them to drive hard along the paved roads and cut off the German escape route to the Italian mainland. But this plan left the Americans on the left flank with no suitable role to play. The rapid advance of the Eighth Army from July 10 to 12 emboldened Montgomery, and on the 12th his enthusiasm turned to bravado when he convinced Alexander to give him three paved roads previously designated for Patton's army, further driving the Americans to the periphery. The Americans were furious, and not without justification: it was a terrible error on Alexander's part to allow Monty to bully the Yanks.[52] Montgomery—described aptly by one of his contemporaries as "small, alert, tense, rather like an intelligent terrier who might bite at any moment"—had little interest in the niceties of coalition warfighting.[53]

All went well at first, as Italian resistance continued to collapse, but as Montgomery drove his exhausted troops forward through blinding heat and clouds of dust, they hit a wall. Hitler, indicating his desire to hold Sicily, had begun to release elite German formations from Italy. One of these formations, the German 1st Parachute Division, made a stand outside of Catania, about halfway up the eastern coastline, early on July 14. The three battalions of German paratroops, along with some Italian units that now had their backbones stiffened, dug in to block the British advance.[54] The potted and hilly countryside was a far cry from the terrain of North Africa, and Montgomery's experienced desert rats were stopped cold at several bridges that the Germans held in a death grip. After days of intense fighting and heavy casualties, a frustrated Monty saw his dream of galloping to Messina collapse.

Patton, unhappy in the role of bystander, consulted Alexander and flung his forces westward on July 17, in a deep advance towards Palermo, Sicily's capital. He masked the drive as a reconnaissance, but he intended to gain some glory for his army, and for himself, by becoming Sicily's liberator. The Germans, already in retreat from the western portion of the island, wondered why Patton was hell-bent on capturing empty ground. They did not yet understand Patton's fierce need for fame.

GENERAL MONTGOMERY WROTE to one of his generals on July 15 that operations were "slow and sticky" around his primary front at Catania.[55] That was, for Montgomery, a typical understatement: the British advance was in fact blocked. To solve the problem, Monty planned a left hook, using the Canadians to circle around the enemy positions towards the scorched interior and, from there, to burrow their way into the midst of the retreating German and Italian forces, which would be fighting for their collective lives to reach Messina.

The Canadians, serving as part of 30 Corps in Montgomery's Eighth Army, charged into the Sicilian badlands early on July 15. General Guy Simonds's inexperienced division was to have been a reserve formation for the campaign, to give the men time to acclimatize to combat; now it was the vanguard of the Eighth Army. On the first day of the advance, around 9 A.M. on July 15, the Canadians ran into a significant enemy force at Grammichele, a town built in 1683 and home to some 13,000 Sicilians. Reconnaissance units of armoured carriers rolled into an ambush where the main road crossed a wide hollow that was visible from at least a kilometre away. It left the Canadians in a natural kill zone. "From the crest and forward slopes of the mile-long escarpment the Germans were firing down upon our column with everything they had—and they seemed to have just about everything," wrote one Canadian trapped in the open ground.[56] But the lead units of the Hastings & Prince Edward Regiment did not panic; they scrambled for safety, regrouped and, supported by Sherman tanks of the Three Rivers Regiment, surged into and around the town in a textbook advance from three directions. Even with a supporting artillery barrage snarling overhead, the Canadians had their work cut out for them, as they faced a dug-in enemy, a concentration of 20mm guns and tanks, and further off, the terrifying 88mm German anti-tank guns. These deadly guns, the same type

*Canadian Sherman tank in Sicily. The Sherman's main gun
was a 75mm cannon, but the .50-calibre machine gun in the
flexible mount on the turret top could also lay down devastating fire.*

used to shoot down bombers over European air space, fired armour-piercing shells that tore through tank armour. The first Shermans burst into flames. It looked like a slaughter in the making, but one of the Bren-gun carriers, with no room to retreat, burst forward in a frontal assault. Somehow the carrier survived the charge over open ground and its machine gun cut down the enemy gunners. Other German defenders of the Hermann Göring Division, along with elements of an elite Italian division, were defeated by the Hasty Ps, who converged on the enemy in the wake of the Bren-gun carrier. These tactics, honed in battle drill over years, destroyed the enemy or drove them back. Within a couple of hours, Grammichele fell to the Canadians, at the cost of twenty-five casualties. Two 20mm anti-aircraft guns, an Mk III tank, and two Mk IV tanks were also destroyed, although the 88s escaped.[57] The Canadians had been bloodied, but had shown surprising tactical expertise in defeating the dug-in Germans.

FIELD MARSHAL KESSELRING had thrown the better part of two divisions into the Catania sector, and his forces were holding up the British advance. Meanwhile, his formations on their right flank were slowly pulling back to the northeast of the island. But they had to hold vital roads in the centre of Sicily to carry out the withdrawal, and it was the Canadian division that was now driving forward along these lines. British intelligence reported that Italian battalions and brigades were everywhere collapsing, but the still-strong 15th Panzer Grenadier Division was tasked to defend along the critical roads in the centre of the island, especially around the mountain-top towns of Valguarnera and Leonforte. Simonds's division was ordered to drive the enemy from these fortresses.

The way forward was not easy. The task of the Canadians was to march to contact. Ambushes were frequent. German mortars were sighted to land in predetermined positions, such as road junctions or areas that had to be crossed by advancing troops. Short bursts of machine-gun fire, the crump of mortar shells, and the sharp crack of sniper fire regularly drove the Canadians to ground. One Canadian infantry officer observed, "The use of the mortar by the Hun is so accurate that it is an art."[58]

"One cannot see the enemy," complained Lieutenant Robert Thexton of the West Nova Scotia Regiment, speaking for most infantrymen who were caught in these crossfires.[59] Nonetheless, lead Canadian units struck back, firing wildly until they caught sight of the Germans' camouflaged position or a muzzle flash. Even to glimpse the enemy was difficult, and made even harder by the glare of the sun, leading some clever infantrymen to fashion a form of sunglasses by tearing off the goggles from captured Italian gas masks. Trading fire with the Germans pinned down the defenders, whereupon the Canadian gunners—several kilometres to the rear—were called on to saturate the front with high explosives and shrapnel. Hitler's forces anticipated

Gunners from the 7th Battery, 2nd Field Regiment,
Royal Canadian Artillery, fire their 25-pounder field gun.

this tactic and usually bugged out before the bombardment, but an inspection of enemy ambush sites sometimes revealed blood and body parts. The Canadians continued to move forward again, leading with their chins.

The Germans, according to one Canadian officer, "fight a stout delaying action against the first attacks, and when we stop to catch our breath he pulls out hell-bent-for-leather."[60] Every road was mined and strewn with rubble. It all had to be rebuilt or cleared by the engineers and pioneers before the infantry and armour could resume the drive northward. All the while, the Canadian riflemen humped forward under their heavy loads, acting as the bait. Private Rudy Cormier of the Carleton and York Regiment, twenty years old and recently married in England, wrote of his rapidly dawning understanding of the battlefield, noting that when the firing started, "we knew that two or three inches could make the difference between life or death."[61] With the newly acquired battlefield awareness—including a suddenly developed capacity to find cover almost instinctively—came the growing realization that death could claim any man. Lives were snuffed out by stray shells and random sniper fire. Men prepared for the losses as best they could, but it was always a shock. Death in battle was ugly. "I never realized before that a dead man's bowels move," wrote Strome Galloway, an RCR officer. "Surely this is the final humiliation in life."[62]

Piazza Armerina fell to the 2nd Canadian Infantry Brigade on July 16, pushing the Germans who had retreated from Grammichele back again. Another two days of advancing against sniper fire left the 1st Canadian Infantry Brigade closing in on Valguarnera on July 18, where a pitched battle was fought against a strong force from the 104th Panzer Grenadier Regiment. The Canadians attacked and manoeuvred around it, eventually cutting off several roads as they encircled the enemy. Farley Mowat, a young man with an interest in poetry and birds, and later one of Canada's best-known storytellers and writers, described one of the brief, butchering affrays in which his company took part: dozens of Germans packed into six trucks drove straight into his company's ambush. The battle did not last long, and soon white flags ended the carnage. The number of German wounded was appalling. "We could do almost nothing for them," recalled Mowat. "We had no medical supplies to spare, or even any water." Having rounded up the Germans, one of the Canadians suggested that it would be more humane to put them out of their misery.

Their company commander, Major Alex Campbell, who earlier had gunned down about two dozen of the enemy with his Bren gun in a frontal assault, put an end to that talk. "There'll be no killing prisoners! Try anything like that and I'll see you court-martialled on a murder charge!'" It seemed an odd statement to Mowat, but he reflected that "the line between brutal murder and heroic slaughter flickers and wavers ... and becomes invisible."[63]

LATE ON JULY 18, Valguarnera fell to the Canadians at the cost of 145 casualties. Some 250 Germans were made prisoners and at least another 180 were killed or wounded, but the main prizes were further down the road, at Leonforte and Assoro.[64] Through burning heat and across a scarred landscape of dried watercourses, Simonds's division advanced towards the two dusty towns that perched on a high ridge overlooking the road. Here all three battalions of the 104th Panzer Grenadier Regiment, together with supporting Italian troops, intended to make a stand. They were hundreds of metres above the Dittanio valley and shielded by cliffs, with a clear field of fire between them and the road below.

Simonds had little room to manoeuvre his brigades, although the regimental commanders sent companies and platoons forward in a series of fire and flanking movements. But with the Germans dug into a nearly invulnerable position, attacks from any and all directions could be tracked and adjustments made; within a few minutes, a Canadian feint was reduced to a frontal assault into rapid-firing MG-42s, concealed rifle fire, and a storm of mortar bombs. The Canadians inched their way forward in search of an opening in the enemy defences.

On July 20, Simonds's forces were variously arrayed around the German defences. The 2nd Brigade stood at the foot of Leonforte; the 1st Brigade prepared to overrun Assoro; and the 3rd Brigade and the attached 231st Malta Brigade stood ready to act as a flanking force and to guard against counterattack. Deliberately cratered and blocked roads slowed the final advance towards Assoro. The enemy poured fire into the lead Canadian units and harassed the engineers who were filling in holes and removing obstructions. Mines further constrained movement as nine tanks from the Three Rivers Regiment were disabled. That same day, during a reconnaissance of the ground over which the Hastings Regiment would attack Assoro, the unit's commanding officer, Lieutenant-Colonel Bruce Sutcliffe, was killed by shellfire. His intelligence officer, Lieutenant Battle Cockin, was also fatally wounded. But he lived long enough, while coughing up blood, to warn the second-in-command, Lord Tweedsmuir, son of Governor General John Buchan, "For God's sake, don't go up that road."[65]

"Tweedie," as some of the soldiers called him mockingly behind his back, was a soft-spoken, fair-haired, kindly young man with a tendency to stutter. He was out of place in a battalion of farmers, even though he was an uncommonly good soldier. Aware that a frontal assault on Assoro would only end in a massacre, Lord Tweedsmuir and Major Alex Campbell led about eighty men (twenty of the fittest men from each company) up a nearly impossible path on the 300-metre Assoro cliff face. Their objective was the ancient Norman castle, on the highest peak, which dominated the German-held village.[66] Even while travelling in the dark, some men worried that their dank body odour might betray them: after less than a fortnight in the field, the soldiers had begun to trust their heightened olfactory sense as a guide to danger. With every slip possibly alerting the enemy, the Canadians moved over treacherous rocks, felt their way across ravines, and clawed up the vertical heights with finger-tearing speed. The Germans had left no guards because they thought the climb was impossible.

At about 7 A.M. on July 21, the Hasty Ps finally pulled themselves to the top, muscles screaming in agony, but having made it undetected. They had a commanding view of the Germans below them. The enemy had no way of knowing that the attackers had few heavy weapons and little ammunition, and the fierce firefight that erupted that morning spooked the panzer grenadiers, who were dismayed to find Canadians looking down on them when they had spent days preparing for an attack from every other direction. They fought back with desperate intensity, sending artillery shells into the rocky Canadian defences. Farley Mowat was there, and noted that the "fury of that barrage was paralyzing. I lay flat on my belly behind a section of stone fence, scrabbling at the rock-hard ground with my tin hat in a frenzied attempt to burrow into the heart of the mountain."[67] Somehow the Canadians withstood the bombardment. The situation became more perilous as the exposed Hastings' ammunition ran low, but using a wireless set, the officers were able to contact the gunners of the 7th Medium Regiment, Royal Canadian Artillery, whose 5.5-inch howitzers laid down punishing fire while an officer called in the coordinates. The Germans took cover, and eventually the Hasty Ps were joined by reinforcements from the RCR.[68] One of the minor tragedies of the war was that, with most of the Hasty Ps' officers either killed or wounded in the coming weeks, no one was left to write up the recommendations for gallantry awards until much later in the campaign. Consequently, not a single member of the Hastings & Prince Edward Regiment received a medal for what remains one of the most audacious small-unit Canadian actions of the war.

The Germans did not retreat immediately. Assoro fell to the 48th Highlanders on July 22, after they completed their own epic scaling of steep terrace walls to the west of the town and drove the grenadiers back at the cost of thirty-seven killed and wounded.[69] The commander of the 15th Panzer Grenadier Division, smarting after having his carefully set defensive line unhinged, reported candidly that the Canadians exhibited "fieldcraft superior to our own troops."[70]

ON THE SAME MOUNTAIN RIDGE, to the west of Assoro, Leonforte was a significant town of 22,000, perched atop a 600-metre rise that was approachable only from a few twisting roads. Most of the Canadian guns could not register on the position, generally firing short or beyond, and so Simonds's staff planners were forced to turn to plunging mortar fire that was much less effective than artillery in softening up the enemy positions. The Seaforths prepared for a daylight advance on the afternoon of July 21, but were cut up badly by enemy and friendly fire. "They knocked the hell out of us," wrote Private George Reid of the fire from his own guns: "Several shells landed in the headquarters area, killing and wounding a lot of men."[71] Reid dove for cover in a slit trench, trying to fit his six-foot frame into the tiny hole. He made it, but was later blown clear out of the trench when a shell landed about two metres away. Reid survived, but about thirty of his comrades were killed or wounded.

Under the cover of twilight, at 9 P.M. the Edmonton Regiment took over from the shaken Seaforths and advanced into the heavily armed town behind an artillery barrage that rocked the ground and sent up a thick cloud of dust. To thicken up the firepower, the two companies of the Eddies were supported by the mortars and Vickers machine guns of the Saskatoon Light Infantry (SLI). Lieutenant Howard Mitchell, who commanded an SLI mortar battery, observed, "No one can properly describe a barrage. There were flashes and explosions of guns behind. There are the hissing and swishing of shells passing overhead. There were the flashes and explosions ahead. All mixed up in one continuous din."[72]

Within the ruined village, the Western Canadians met a roughly equal number of Germans in hand-to-hand combat. In the chaos, communication was severed. The fighting units at the front eventually were entirely cut off from Vokes's brigade headquarters. The Germans surged forward and the Eddies were threatened with destruction. Lieutenant-Colonel Jim Jefferson eventually found a cowering boy in the rubble of a building and convinced him to carry a message back to Brigadier Vokes asking for tank reinforcements. The grimy lad ran through the hail of mortar and shrapnel fire and delivered the message.[73] Throughout the city, the Eddies battled the Germans during the night, holding on by their fingertips.

The engineers of the 3rd Field Company, Royal Canadian Engineers, worked under harassing mortar and small-arms fire to rebuild a blown bridge leading into town and finished in the early hours of July 22. Around 9 A.M., a flying column of the Princess Patricia's Canadian Light Infantry, riding on tanks and self-propelled guns, crashed through the outskirts of the city and into the ruined core. Their charge was eventually halted by enemy fire, and the infantry scrambled from their steel steeds, firing and advancing on the enemy. One of the Patricias' officers described the scene: "It soon deteriorated down to house to house fighting and there was much confusion. Whole companies seemed to be missing and each small group thought itself the sole survivor of the larger body—everybody seemed to think that all was lost.... Little by little, however, small groups began to come back and it was found that picture was not as black as it seemed."[74]

The fog of war blanketed the smash-up fighting. The words of the French general Ferdinand Foch, written during a battle in 1914, help to explain what happened next: "Hard pressed on my right. My centre is yielding. Impossible to manoeuvre. Situation excellent. I attack." The Canadians drove forward. Lieutenant-Colonel Jim Jefferson of the Edmontons recounted how the timely arrival of the leading Three Rivers Regiment's Sherman tanks caught the enemy as they were manoeuvring towards his headquarters: "The Canadian gunner was lightning fast on the trigger and the enemy tank exploded almost in our faces."[75] It was one of three enemy Mark

IV tanks knocked out in the battle in exchange for one Sherman. Sergeant W.R. Campbell of the Three Rivers Regiment offered a glimpse into the cat-and-mouse tank battles that developed in the narrow streets: "We flushed out a German tank on a side street, and, followed by Sergeant Gallagher in 2B, we chased it through a maze of narrow back streets until the German tank commander set a trap at a major intersection. In a close range exchange of gunfire, the German Mark IV tank damaged my Sherman, starting a fire in the ammunition bin. Trooper Lund, the driver, smartly reversed and backed the tank around the corner. The German tank was also hit, but managed to escape along the main street and get out of town."[76] While the Shermans were often outgunned by the German tanks, they did have an advantage in the tank's hydraulic turret traverse, which allowed them to bring their guns to bear more rapidly. Their twin .30-calibre machine guns and the .50-calibre machine gun on the turret also provided significant firepower when engaging enemy infantry.

Much of the fighting came down to the relentlessly brave infantrymen pushing forward. One of the Patricias, Private S.J. Cousins, upon finding his platoon pinned down by enemy fire, advanced with an NCO and another private. The two other men were cut down, but Cousins rose from his cover and leapt forward alone into a hail of bullets. Firing his Bren gun from the hip, he closed on a machine-gun position, killing the five defenders. After catching his breath—and no doubt patting down his torso in search of bullet holes—he charged another machine-gun position, clearing it with accurate fire. Cousins saved numerous lives, but lost his own later that day. His grateful mates believed he should have been awarded the Victoria Cross, but the award was downgraded to a Mentioned in Despatches.

Leonforte had fallen by the afternoon of July 22. After a few more hours of fighting, the Patricias were able to drive east and west of the town to create a buffer zone against counterattack. Fifty-six Canadians were killed during the battle, and another 105 were wounded.[77] "I've seen a lot since I wrote you last," Private George Ableson told his parents after the battle, "by which I mean a lot of bloodletting and the kind of butchery that goes with war." In the ruins of Leonforte, the dead lay near the sleeping, and the two were hard to distinguish from each other, as all were covered in a fine layer of dust. In spite of the campaign's terrible carnage, Abelson noted, "I think more about the things of life than about the things of death."[78]

THE AMERICANS SEIZED PALERMO on the same day that Leonforte fell. Patton strode into the Sicilian capital trailing an army of reporters and cameramen. A chastised Montgomery, aware that his "stolen road" incident had angered the Americans and thinned out his own advance, and with his main force stalemated on the eastern corridor, ordered an aggressive drive from the now bloodied Canadians, who continued to defy the odds by breaking the German centre. With the 1st US Infantry Division pushing hard on the left flank, a Canadian thrust would collapse the German front and bag thousands of prisoners, while funnelling the Germans into a more narrow retreat route that would leave them vulnerable to Allied fighters and bombers.

*Lieutenant-Colonel Bert Hoffmeister leads the Seaforth
Highlanders of Canada in a long climb through the Sicilian hills.*

The Canadian victories at Leonforte and Assoro had completely upset the German line of defence. They had captured at least 435 prisoners and had inflicted hundreds of additional casualties on the enemy. Although these two victories were soon overshadowed by subsequent events, it is worth remembering these remarkable feats of battle by the raw Canadian division, which had driven back a strong force from nearly impregnable positions. Now Simonds's division was ordered to march again, towards Agira, about 12 kilometres to the east, along the main highway.[79]

Montgomery deemed the Canadian advance critical for opening up the clogged roadways. Intercepted intelligence revealed that the Germans, too, regarded these arteries as vital and that they planned to make a stand at Agira to hold their escape routes open. The 1st Canadian Infantry Division would be supported by significant airpower and long-range artillery.[80] The aerial support had its effect, and the Germans retreating from Leonforte and Assoro were torn apart by Allied Kittyhawk fighter-bombers of the Desert Air Force. Some sixty-five German vehicles and guns were destroyed as they moved along the open roads. The dug-in defenders further to the east, however, were little affected by the bombing and strafing.[81] The Allies had absolute command of the air, but German official reports noted, "In spite of ceaseless employment of the air force the campaign has proven that the air force alone cannot force decisions in battle. After initial losses the troops did adapt themselves to a degree that could never be reached in training."[82] The best way to kill Germans from the air was to upset their dug-in positions and drive them back over open ground.

The Germans held Agira in strength—this was another village atop a mountain overlooking a series of valleys—but they had also prepared a forward defence. Throughout the hilly and broken terrain to the west of Agira, a large composite force made up of all three battalions of the 104th Panzer Grenadier Regiment, and additional elements of the 15th Panzer Grenadier Division, held three ridges around the village of Nissoria, a huddle of stone hovels and non-descript buildings. Nissoria could barely be found on maps, but the German forces were entrenched in the surrounding hills. Sacrifice troops were dug in to the frontal slope, allowing them to fire directly on advancing Canadians. When shelled or driven back, they would retreat to the reverse slope of the ridge and, with additional troops, wait for the Canadians to come over the top of the ridge and then fight another battle on the other side.

The march to Nissoria in temperatures above 40 degrees Celsius was a brutal one. As the Canadians closed on their objective, several skirmishes involving the 1st Brigade's regiments west of Nissoria revealed that the Germans were dug in. Simonds wisely pulled back, regrouped, and planned a set-piece battle, sticking close to the main road to ensure that his tanks could support the infantry. The operation was also heavily supported by division and corps artillery, consisting of five field and two medium regiments of guns, as well as air power in the form of ninety medium bombers and more than a hundred Kittyhawk fighter-bombers.[83]

The bombers had little impact in dislodging the defenders. They were good for morale, however, and one Canadian report noted, "the sight of our bombs falling on the enemy immediately opposite him does give the Infantryman considerable satisfaction."[84] Artillery was also effective in saturating the enemy positions. But one German official report by the 15th Panzer Grenadier Division scorned the Canadian and British reliance on gunfire "to save blood by use of considerable material," dismissing it as a "rigid tactical doctrine." The Allies saw it as a prudent use of resources and a husbanding of manpower that they could not afford to lose.[85] Whichever view of this firepower-reliant doctrine was more accurate—as an approach that saved lives or as one that limited the initiative of troops at the front by tying them to artillery bombardments—the battles in the latter half of the Sicily campaign relied heavily on artillery. Elaborate preparations were required to coordinate the coming battle; the artillery ammunition alone had to be transported in forty-three trucks driving continuously for twenty-two hours.[86] Situating guns in the uneven and rough terrain was also difficult, and Canadian gunners—especially those on the 25-pounder—carved out unorthodox positions, blowing holes in the rock with demolition charges and hanging off the ridges like mountain goats. As the Saskatoon Light Infantry war diary recorded before the battle, "the first flush of attack is over and now the division is settling in to a hard grind."[87]

At 3 P.M. on July 24, the guns opened up and the hard grind began. Despite intelligence suggesting heavy concentrations of Germans in the area, Simonds unwisely ordered only a single Canadian infantry battalion forward. It was not enough. The Royal Canadian Regiment supported by Sherman tanks from the Three Rivers Regiment advanced across the ground west of Nissoria and then into the town, moving behind a creeping barrage, which leapt forward at a quick pace of 200 metres every two minutes. The barrage tore up the ground in front of the Royals and there was little resistance from the enemy. But much of the battlefield was soon obscured by dust and artillery explosions, making it difficult for the RCRs and the Shermans to keep direction and to support one another. The debris and explosions also made it almost impossible for the forward artillery observers to correct the fall of artillery shells for the gunners kilometres to the rear.

Even as the artillery fire swept over the front, the entrenched troops from the 2nd Battalion of the 15th Panzer Grenadier Division remained in their fortified positions. Some were killed or buried alive—their bodies later found horribly twisted, faces contorted in grimaces that betrayed how agonizing their last minutes of life had been—but when the barrage passed over them, the survivors were ready for the Canadians moving forward in the open.[88] German mortar bombs fell amid the Royals' lead platoons, which were advancing in sectional rushes. Soon enemy machine-gun

Canadian mortar crew firing at German targets near Nissoria, late July 1943.

fire was added to the destruction. A Canadian artillery smokescreen offered some cover, but it blew away too quickly.[89] Ten of the Shermans were knocked out by rapid-firing German 88s—four of them totally smashed and six later recovered and repaired to run again. The Canadian armour was not helpless, however, and one battered Sherman—hit an astonishing seven times—continued its gritty advance, eventually destroying three German Mk II tanks and killing dozens of enemy soldiers.[90]

Caught in a crossfire of small-arms and mortar fire, the Royals searched desperately for an exit from the kill zone. Two of the companies, Able and Baker, found a sheltered gully running east. They took it, eventually finding themselves behind the enemy lines, halfway to Agira. It was a lucky move, but fate works in many ways, and while the RCRs held a commanding position behind the enemy, they were cut off from their own artillery, as none of their short-wave radios—the temperamental No. 18 sets—worked in the hilly terrain. As in other battles that had been fought over the previous two weeks, communication was proving to be an Allied weakness, making it difficult to coordinate units in combat. The Royals now were ripe for a killing blow. They found cover, prepared themselves to hold off counterattacks, and waited for reinforcements.

Back at brigade and division headquarters, the fog and friction of war left the commanders with little knowledge of what was happening at the front. One RCR company had been mauled badly, and two had disappeared. Had they been annihilated? Reports later filtered in that the regiment's colonel had been killed in the fighting when he advanced too far in search of his missing companies. The situation did not look good. Simonds, urged on by his British corps commander, Sir Oliver Leese—who, along with Montgomery, was desperate to dislodge the German defence and continue the push to Messina—unwisely ordered another frontal assault, throwing the Hastings & Prince Edward Regiment into the battle against a ridge to the east of Nissoria. The Hastings officers, including Lord Tweedsmuir, had no chance to reconnoitre the ground, and their plan was simply to infiltrate forward in the darkness. They set off during the early hours of July 25, eventually running into machine-gun nests, but the single-file lines of infantry shook out from their formation and rushed forward, overcoming the enemy positions by complex outflanking manoeuvres. As one strongpoint after another was destroyed, the Germans laid down punishing artillery fire and the Canadian losses mounted. Lord Tweedsmuir, severely wounded in the leg, was among the casualties. By the end of the day, the Hasty Ps suffered eighty killed and wounded, the heaviest single-day loss of any Canadian regiment during the Sicily campaign.

Even as the Hastings soldiers continued to engage the enemy, and felt they were getting the upper hand, they were ordered to withdraw, since in the judgment of their commanders the depleted companies were strung out and ripe for a counter-attack.[91] One of the RCR officers, Strome Galloway, observed proudly but sadly, "Our men have plenty of guts. They walked through hell yesterday, but all in vain."[92] The Canadians gave up most of the ground they had captured as they regrouped for a new assault. Two more days of battle over the hills east of Nissoria followed. Canadian companies and platoons ghosted forward at night, slipping past geographical bottlenecks to silence German machine-gun nests. It was a slow and methodical approach designed to avoid a frontal assault where the enemy held the high ground. Meanwhile, the two "lost" RCR companies continued to huddle behind the front lines, using their deep lodgement to shoot up enemy trucks and troops that blundered into their camouflaged positions.

All along the front, the Canadians bit into the enemy lines, nibbling forward, wiping out the enemy positions with grenade, rifle, and machine-gun fire. Finally, as the light faded on July 26, two companies of the PPCLI, aided by an eighty-gun artillery barrage, spearheaded a 2nd Brigade attack and cracked the German outer defences east of Nissoria.[93] "The results of the artillery barrage," said Lieutenant Jack Wallace, a tank commander with the Three Rivers Regiment, left "the badly pock-marked ridge littered with German dead."[94] Sixty bodies were found and another 150 Germans, many of them wounded, were taken prisoner. The Seaforths and Edmontons leapfrogged through the corpses at dawn the next day, capturing key ridges, and then moved towards Agira. Another fierce day of fighting took place around the western and northern hills of Agira, in an operation codenamed Grizzly, and "It was not until the enemy were engaged with the bayonet," observed one Eddies officer, "that the situation began to clarify itself."[95] With the back of their defensive line broken, the Germans pulled out of Agira on July 28, and retreated towards Messina.

"English and Canadians harder in the attack than Americans," noted one German report on the recent fighting, adding that the Canadians were "very mobile at night, [making] surprise break-ins, clever infiltrations at night with small groups between our strong points."[96] While much credit for the victory goes to the skill of the Canadian infantryman, the opening set-piece battle was poorly planned. Simonds's 1st Division headquarters underestimated German strength, and the general and his

Infantrymen of the Princess Patricia's Canadian Light Infantry in action near Nissoria.

staff were slow to reinforce the RCRs. However, when these rigidly planned assaults broke down, the Canadians had success in allowing the company and platoon commanders to infiltrate forward, using their battlecraft, snaking through the rough terrain to winkle out the enemy and take down larger positions. At one point in the battle, an under-strength Eddies company of 40 men drove 150 Germans from a dug-in position.[97] All over and across the hills, gullies, and ridgelines, the Canadians engaged the enemy in a series of brutal hand-to-hand assaults that they consistently won. As one Canadian officer observed, "I suggest you give the infantryman his head" in future battles.[98] By that he meant that the infantry should be allowed to fight their way forward, using the terrain and their own initiative to dislodge the enemy rather than relying on firepower. However, that would not be the case in most of the future battles, and Canadian commanders remained deeply tied to the set-piece attack that relied heavily on artillery to pave the way for armour and infantry. With these tactics, they were adhering to an attack doctrine in which Montgomery also believed, and one that had achieved historic success in the Great War. It was a ponderous approach to battle that often sacrificed some of the initiative accrued by allowing the infantry to penetrate forward, but there were few junior officers at the sharp end who wanted to attack without suitable artillery support. As it stood, the battle for Nissoria and Agira had cost the Canadians 438 casualties, although the division's staff estimated that at least 325 Germans were killed and an equal number were wounded, and some 430 Germans taken prisoner.[99] The Canadians had decisively beaten the Germans, who were again forced into retreat.

THE CANADIANS CAMPAIGNED FOR ANOTHER WEEK, into early August, capturing one last major town, Regalbuto, which the Hermann Göring Division had been ordered to hold "at all costs."[100] From July 30 to August 2, three Canadian battalions—the 48th Highlanders, RCRs, and Hastings—manoeuvred around the dug-in and camouflaged German defenders, and eventually closed a complex pincer on the enemy. On August 2, the surviving Germans, pounded by artillery and bomber attacks, and defeated by the Canadian infantrymen, set off on another headlong retreat where, again, they were subjected to heavy bombardment and raking cannon fire by the Desert Air Force. Simonds's division was now fought-out and, after another couple of days of desultory fighting, it was finally pulled from the line for a much-needed rest. In the final week of battle, from July 31 to August 6, the Canadians lost 106 killed and 345 wounded.[101]

Removed from combat, the men were given lectures by officers and sermons by the padres. Trophies were shown off, especially the prized Luger pistols, German forage caps, and Iron Crosses. Survivors processed their grief and attempted to come to terms with the loss of friends who were closer than brothers. They then put pencil to paper as they wrote letters to grieving families. Most of the combatants recharged their personal batteries after weeks of sleep deprivation, but no one slept too long, what with the flea bites and unrelenting heat. The company or platoon scroungers made the camps liveable, working their magic to find chairs, tables, and other amenities to augment the homeless men's lives. Battle-hardened veterans cracked a smile as they sat under stitched-together gas capes and drank brackish water in "borrowed" china. Some entrepreneurial Sicilians circulated through the various regiments selling what they could, while a series of enterprising barbers made their way through the ranks, scissors-first, clipping shaggy manes. The mail finally caught up, as did food parcels of treats, cigarettes, and clothing.

Yellow grapes grew in profusion, and trees could be found bearing pears, peaches, and pomegranates, although throughout the campaign the Canadians were warned to stay away from fruits and vegetables because Sicilian farmers fertilized the soil with animal and human waste. While the Allied troops were issued vitamin C pills, more than a few Canucks could not avoid plucking ripe fruit; many later found their insides running with gippy tummy or something worse, such as jaundice or diphtheria.

The millions of black flies found their way on to every bite of food and into open mouths. They were annoying, but the mosquitoes carried death. "We take malarial pills four days a week, yellow and bitter they are, and have given up our shorts for long trousers to keep the mosquitoes from our knees and legs," wrote Major J.D. Forin in early August.[102] Not all men were diligent in accepting their awful-tasting mepacrine pills, which sometimes caused cramping and diarrhea and gave a jaundice-like hue to the skin. Others, driven by fear or wagging tongues, gave credence to the rumours that whispered the medicine induced sterility.[103] Even though the men had undergone intense pre-campaign preparation and discussion about how to treat malaria, it was a difficult disease to combat. The soldiers were ordered to wear long pants to reduce the number of mosquito bites, but few emulated Major Forin by following the order. It was just too hot.

Dozens and then hundreds of Canadians succumbed to malaria. Shivering and shaking, the feverish victims lay limp with sweat and their internal demons. More than 1,200 Canadians were afflicted by the disease during the campaign, although most of the losses came at the end of the fighting.[104] The outbreak in Sicily—later labelled by the official historian of the medical corps as a "medical disaster"—persuaded the Canadians to embrace more diligent anti-malarial discipline, and they were much more effective in warding off the disease during the Italian campaign.[105]

TO THE NORTH OF THE CANADIANS, the final drive to Messina was made by American forces, with the crazed Patton urging on his formations, slapping shell-shocked soldiers in hospitals, threatening to shoot his own men when he saw them at rest, breaking into tears, and remaining entirely unrepentant about his wild outbursts. Messina was seized on August 17 after another race between the British and Americans that went to the Yanks. American GIs chided the first British soldiers to arrive at Messina, "Where've you tourists been?"[106] Montgomery was indeed embarrassed at how his vaunted Eighth Army had been held up, and how Patton had overshadowed him. The campaign ended in victory—and in tragic farce. Before Messina fell, the Germans, in a dangerous but daring manoeuvre, ordered the withdrawal of 55,000 of their own battle-trained troops and 70,000 Italians from the northeastern tip of the island to the Italian mainland. With them would go almost all their heavy weapons, including forty-seven tanks, ninety-four guns, and several thousand vehicles.[107] The Allies' inability to close the Strait of Messina was a monumental failure for Eisenhower, who had played a minimal role in coordinating the fighting on the ground but should have been gathering military assets to block the retreat.[108]

The German ships that crossed the 3 kilometres of open water were ripe targets for bombers and fighters flying out of North Africa and from the newly acquired airfields in Sicily. But in another example of inter-service clashing, the Allied bombers directed only about one quarter of their operations against the bottled-up Axis forces at Messina and against the tip of the Italian mainland. The mystified Germans, who had expected to lose thousands of men in a ghastly turkey-shoot, saw their chance and began to move their troops by daylight.[109] The Allied naval command was equally inept. Fearful of losing their capital ships, they refused to let them engage at close quarters, even though they would have encountered little resistance among the German ferries.[110] This series of Allied blunders revealed the failure of the high command that had put all its energy into planning the amphibious landing—as hideously complicated as it was—and then given little thought to what to do afterwards. No doubt the entrenched Germans and Italians would have made the Allied naval armada and bombers pay for their attacks—Messina and the Italian mainland bristled with about 500 anti-aircraft guns—but much damage would have been wrought against the enemy, who could have been killed in the open rather than fought again in the coming months in the mountainous Italian terrain. What should have been a death blow against the German garrison was stayed at the last moment.

The Sicily campaign was nonetheless a victory. It gave the Allies another much-needed morale boost and revealed a vast improvement in American fighting skills. The seizure of the island opened the Mediterranean sea lanes and a more direct supply route for war materiel and aid to be sent to the Soviet Union. New airfields were created in a few days, and bombers were able to strike deeper into Italy, bringing the war to the already wavering Italian people whose cities were protected by relatively few anti-aircraft defences.[111] News of the Hamburg firestorm on July 28 soon spread, and the bomber threat caused something like panic among Italian civilians. More significantly, Mussolini, sick and lost, wasted in body and mind, was forced out of power on July 25 by the Italian royal family and parliament. Sicily drove a spike through the Axis alliance, and all but knocked Italy out of the war.

The Sicily campaign saw the Italians lose 147,000 killed, wounded, and captured—the majority in the last category—while the Germans absorbed 29,000 casualties, of which about 22,000 were killed and wounded. Almost all of the front-line German fighting units had been devastated, losing more than half their strength. Another 78 tanks and armoured cars, 287 guns, and 3,500 vehicles were destroyed or left on the island following the German retreat. The Allies, in turn, took nearly 20,000 casualties: 12,000 sustained by the British and Canadians, and 7,402 by the Americans.[112] Axis material losses alone, when combined with the sizeable casualties (even if one excludes the surrender-prone Italians), told the story of an overwhelming Allied victory.

The Canadians had done well in the thirty-eight-day campaign, better than they or anyone had expected. Montgomery had never planned for the Canadians

General Bernard Montgomery addressing Canadian troops
from his favourite position, atop a Universal Carrier.

to play such a prominent role, but his failure to bypass Catania thrust Simonds's division into the spearhead against a well-entrenched enemy. The Canadians had responded magnificently, even as they were bloodied by 2,310 casualties, including 562 killed.[113] One in eight Canadians was killed or wounded, and the casualty rate was much higher among the infantry. More than 100 gallantry medals were awarded to Canadians for bravery in battle, but, as one early campaign chronicler wrote, "for each brave deed recognized by an award there were doubtless several more that passed unnoticed."[114] The Canadians' collective mettle had been tested, and they had not been found wanting.

While the Canadians at the sharp end had fought tenaciously, their senior generals struggled to master their commands. Simonds encountered significant challenges in controlling and communicating with his forces, but he had been supported by his superior, Montgomery, who had given him time to learn in battle conditions. Montgomery continued to believe that Simonds possessed the right skills for divisional command. Unfortunately, their close relationship led to an unseemly row with McNaughton, who had travelled to the Mediterranean to see his Canadians in battle at the end of the campaign. McNaughton remained the Canadian Army commander and was well within his rights to visit his soldiers in the field, but Simonds, who dreaded the thought of entertaining the charismatic general, asked Montgomery for support. The abrasive British general showed no hesitation in blocking McNaughton's visit to Sicily, and an embittered McNaughton left without

The Canadians emerged from their trial-by-fire campaign in Sicily hardened for further battles.

seeing his boys. McNaughton was insulted, but Simonds may have needed the gesture to continue to develop as a divisional commander. McNaughton took a long and silent flight back to England.

Montgomery visited the Canadians several times in the field, typically standing on the roofs of cars or in the backs of jeeps to be seen by his troops. Now, in dusty fields in the country that the Canadians had helped to free from Nazi oppression, Monty congratulated them and, at one gathering, said, "I regard you now as one of the veteran divisions of the Army.... I knew the Canadians on the Western Front in the last war and there were no finer soldiers anywhere."[115] In private, he had written no less effusively earlier in the campaign, "They are a grand Division and when we get them tough and hard and some of the fat off them, they will be absolutely first class."[116] After a month of combat, the Canadians had shed the fat from four years of service in England. In the surviving photographs, many of the dust-covered, bare-kneed soldiers look very young, almost like Boy Scouts, albeit armed to the teeth. Youth and endurance helped these tough men to deal with the strain of combat, but the short campaign had aged and hardened them, and even the most optimistic knew that there would be many more difficult battles before the Germans were broken and they could go home.

CHAPTER 15

THE ITALIAN CAMPAIGN

General Bernard Montgomery's Eighth Army landed on the Italian boot at Calabria on September 3, two days after the fourth anniversary of Hitler's invasion of Poland. The veterans of North Africa and Sicily, with the now battle-hardened 1st Canadian Infantry Division in the vanguard, came as an invading force, but the Italians had been wavering since Mussolini's removal from power by the Italian king on July 25. Anxious to avoid pitched battles on their soil, frantic Italian emissaries met with the Allied high command to discuss terms. September 8 was the date set in secret for their surrender, but like so much else the Italians did during the war, they bungled the peace, with disastrous consequences. The Germans caught wind of the overture and moved first. Despite being outnumbered by their former allies, Hitler's forces disarmed more than a million Italian combatants, murdered some 12,000 officers, and eventually imprisoned 650,000 soldiers. They made the transition easily from ally to occupier. Hitler had to shift numerous divisions to the Italian theatre, but he compensated for some of this manpower drain by plundering Italy for fuel, food, supplies, and armaments—including 5,568 guns, 8,736 mortars, 977 tanks, and 1,173 anti-tank guns.[1] In early September, the German high command issued this laconic order: "Italian armistice does not apply to us. The fight continues."[2]

Before the Italian surrender, the Canadian run-in to Reggio di Calabria on the Italian mainland was made behind an ear-shattering barrage from 800 naval guns, rockets, and long-range howitzers. Starting at around 2:30 A.M. on September 3, the box-like landing crafts carrying thousands of infantry cut through the cordite and smoke, lurching and jolting their way over the swells, trying to avoid other vessels in the darkness. There was little enemy resistance. The Germans, anticipating a punishing naval bombardment, had pulled back from the beaches, while the Italians surrendered several forts with high-calibre guns that could have made the Eighth Army pay heavily for its landing.

Lieutenant Robert Thexton of the West Nova Scotia Regiment wrote of the strange feeling of touching down on Italian soil and finding no one shooting at them. That changed quickly. Thexton noticed a group of soldiers running towards them from the 5th British Division's sector. He steadied his men, noting they were British troops, but no sooner had he said this than one of the British soldiers threw himself down, aimed his Bren gun and fired. "He must have been a rotten shot because, although he fired a whole magazine at us and bullets were whizzing past our ears, not one touched us. We were very fortunate to escape being killed." Thexton responded to the assault with a litany of swear words, and finally one of the British soldiers blurted out, "Cor, it's the bloody Canadians!"[3] Thexton later realized that perhaps the conical armoured corps steel helmets that he and his carrier platoon soldiers wore gave the Tommies the impression that they were Italian. Thexton led his troops inland until he was shot in the chest a few weeks later. He returned to battle the next year.

The spearhead of the Canadian division—the Carleton and York, West Nova Scotia, and Royal 22e Regiments—pushed through the darkness, making room on the beachhead for the rest of the division to follow. After Montgomery's almost unopposed landings, the American Fifth Army landed at Salerno, south of Naples, about 450 kilometres north of the British Eighth Army on September 9. Patton had been moved to Britain to command a follow-on army intended for employment in the invasion of Europe, the hero of Sicily leaving in disgrace after reporters filed stories that he had slapped and belittled American GIs who were battle-shocked. He was too good a general to be fired, but it would be some time before he returned to Eisenhower's good books. Patton's place was taken by Lieutenant-General Mark Clark, who planned for only a British and an American corps to put ashore along a 50-kilometre front, landing a day after the Italians formally surrendered. The Americans expected a cakewalk. The Germans were having none of that.

At the front, from the mountainous high ground that ringed Salerno, the Germans launched relentless assaults against the Allies' two corps in the shallow beachhead. The situation was desperate, as fierce battles threatened to annihilate the Anglo-American force. Theatre commander General Harold Alexander intervened, propping up a flagging and stunned Clark, and refusing to initiate any plan for an evacuation. As Clark's forces buckled under the German onslaught, Alexander ordered into battle the Allied capital warships, which rained down their enormous shells on the German lines. From above, bomber attacks added to the storm, eventually making the German lines untenable. Canadian airmen did their bit as three RCAF bomber squadrons carried out 571 sorties to assist the hard-pressed troops on the ground.[4] A week of fighting eventually drove the Germans out of the blistering firezone, but the 8,659 casualties to the Allies were a reminder that while the Italians had packed it in, the Germans remained a combat-effective force.[5]

THE INVASION OF ITALY WAS CONDUCTED, as in Sicily, without much thought given to strategy, beyond pushing northward and defeating the enemy as it was encountered. With little imagination and less flair, the campaign had all the makings of a Great War battle of attrition. While General Alexander continued to oversee the ground forces, he let his army commanders take the lead. Montgomery's Eighth Army was ordered to fight up the eastern side of Italy, while General Clark's Fifth Army would take the west, punching through the Liri Valley to Rome, which hopefully would fall by Christmas. Unfortunately, Clark had almost the same arrogance, ego, and distrust of the British that Patton exhibited.[6] Even more unfortunately, while Patton was a thrusting, aggressive general who got battlefield results, Clark lacked experience and picked fights with everyone over real and imagined slights. He was overwhelmed for much of the time and yet he was vain—demanding, for example, that he be photographed only on his "good" (left) side.[7] One of his staff officers considered him "a goddamned study in arrogance."[8] Monty remained unrepentant for his snubbing of the Americans during the Sicilian campaign, and Alexander did little to force him into greater cooperation. The relationship between Clark and Montgomery deteriorated immediately, as the Americans fought for their lives at Salerno while Montgomery's army faced little opposition and marched at a leisurely pace—according to the Americans. In fairness to Montgomery, the 450 or so kilometres of poor roads over which the British army travelled required daily feats of engineering.[9]

If the Allied strategy appeared slapdash at best, the Germans were also unsure about how to best defend Italy. Field Marshal Albert Kesselring, commander of the German forces in the south and a former Luftwaffe operational commander, had recovered from his defeat in Sicily, partially because he had been allowed to save much of his army by ferrying it over to the Italian mainland. At fifty-seven, Smiling Albert, as he was known informally, had a keen mind and great determination, and understood implicitly the advantages enjoyed by defenders holding ground of their choosing.[10] He demanded a forward defence and a slow, measured fighting retreat, even as other senior generals in theatre and in Berlin—including the much-respected Field Marshal Erwin Rommel, commander of Army Group B in northern Italy— argued for a longer pull-back to a more stable northern line, fearful that a rapid Allied advance would cut off and destroy the German divisions in the south. Hitler eventually sided with Kesselring because the Führer had begun to refuse any and all retreats, even strategic ones, for fear that they would be construed as defeats.[11] In this case, though, the Nazi regime remained desperately short of all raw materials, and the Romanian oil fields now were crucial to the war effort.[12] Every Allied step northward through Italy brought British and American long-range bombers closer to targeting the oil as well as the northern industrial centres of Turin and Milan. But in order to protect these vital industries and resources, the German high command had to pour infantry divisions and aircraft into Italy, both to bolster defence and to pacify the Italians.[13] This commitment—which eventually rose from sixteen to twenty-three divisions in mid-October—bled off important reinforcements that were needed elsewhere.[14] Hitler's determination to defend Italy turned the country into a violent battleground, which ultimately played into the Allies' plan of holding the enemy while building the forces necessary for the invasion of Europe.

IN THEIR LONG MARCH NORTHWARD, the Canadian khaki-coloured columns snaked along winding roads leading up and over hills, moving from gravel and dirt roads to narrow animal paths. While the weather was blessedly cooler than in Sicily by day, the nights were cold and the Canadians were still wearing their summer kit. A stiff shot of rum got the chilled and cramped men moving in the morning, but laden down with rations, picks, bandoliers of ammunition, and their weapons, they found the march through the mountains tough. It was no surprise that the infantry attached themselves like leeches to trucks when they could.

At every step, the Canadians encountered evidence of the Germans' scorched earth policy. Enemy combat engineers revealed again their skill at demolition work by blowing bridges and fouling wells across the Allied advance.[15] The narrow roads were particularly dangerous, and even without German obstructions the Royal Canadian Army Service Corps was required to work wonders in moving up supplies, often leapfrogging dumps forward in complicated convoys, and even using jeeps when the trucks could not make it across the crumbling roads.[16] "Mines were an ever present danger," wrote Lieutenant Howard Mitchell of the Saskatoon Light Infantry, a mortar and machine gun support unit. "Usually they were simple mines with explosives in a metal container. The detonator was set off by contact." The Canadian engineers had mine detectors that alerted users to the metal parts of the mines, but the Germans used about thirty types of mines and many explosives were encased only in wood, making them difficult to locate.[17] Mitchell testified to seeing on one stretch of road "three vehicles blown up on the same day" and noted, "The effect of such uncertainty on morale was very great."[18] The mine's upward blast frequently broke the driver's legs and caused internal organ damage. The infantry on foot had to worry about anti-personnel schu-mines. One of the variations, the Bouncing Betty, jumped out of ground when stepped on, exploding at waist height, where it scattered lethal fragments into bellies and genitals. "There was nothing more terrifying to men than mines," wrote one Canadian. "You just never knew when your next step would be your last. Just the thought of being blown all to ratshit was too horrible to think about."[19]

In the division's advance wave were the Princess Louise Dragoon Guards, a reconnaissance regiment that roamed forward on Universal Carriers. These lightly armoured tracked vehicles were open on the top, and designed to carry light machine guns or mortars as well as the infantry's PIAT (Projector, Infantry, Anti-Tank weapon, similar to the American Bazooka). "Those patrols into unknown territory were a time of fear and danger," remembered one corporal engaged in recce work. Most carriers advanced until they drew fire.[20] The riders were protected by thin metal plating to the height of their upper chest, but were totally vulnerable to sniper fire and mortar air bursts. The terrible roads led to the death and wounding of others. So many accidents occurred with the Universal Carriers that some Canadians labelled them "Hitler's secret weapon."[21] The carriers were, nonetheless, more agreeable than the many mules employed by the Canadians to haul gear and supplies. Whether by motor, mule, or foot-slogging, travel was always slow.

The Canadians had many encounters with peasants during their long trek north, including pockets of Fascist supporters who did little more than offer disagreeable glances. But most Italians sought to curry favour by trading information about German strongpoints or booby-traps. Desperation forced many Italians to seek Allied goods, and Canadians swapped canned meat and vegetables for grapes and

Canadian soldiers in their long march northward.

wine. Pius Girouard, a twenty-six-year-old bilingual New Brunswicker serving with the Royal 22e Régiment, remembered with satisfaction how he bartered soap to the Italians in return for wonderful spaghetti meals.[22] After passing by farms or villages, soldiers marched on with their helmets full of eggs and bread speared on bayonets. A few men who spoke Italian could be found in most battalions, which eased the burden on officers as they tried to soothe angry farmers who had just lost a pig to some sticky-fingered Canadian or seen their fence posts disappear as firewood. Ample supplies of chocolate bars and cigarettes lowered tempers, but exasperated Canadians, fed up with wailing farmers, were also not reluctant to utter threats or simply march away.

On September 17, Alexander ordered Montgomery to seize Potenza, a town 80 kilometres inland from the Salerno beaches, through which key roads intersected. Montgomery called on a mechanized Canadian battle group—named Boforce after its charismatic leader, Lieutenant-Colonel M.P. "Pat" Bogert of the West Nova Scotia Regiment—to drive north and seize the junction. Besides the West Novas, Boforce consisted of tanks from the Calgary regiment backed up by artillery support. Though the Allied air forces had bombed the city for more than a week, wounding or killing some 2,000 civilians, Potenza did not fall until September 20, when the Canadians bashed their way into town at the cost of a mere twenty-seven casualties.[23] The Germans had underestimated the ability of the Canadians to leap forward over the 70 kilometres of rough roads and were forced to scuttle away, their planned retreat disrupted. Alas, few other innovative armoured thrusts like that of Boforce would succeed during the Italian campaign, as the German defences tightened up.

IN EARLY OCTOBER, Ultra intelligence cracked messages sent at the beginning of the month from Hitler to Kesselring, ordering the field marshal to hold several main lines of defence, with a strategic goal of stopping the Allies south of Rome. The German retreat halted and their lines congealed. The enemy occupied the best ground, mostly overlooking the Allied advance across open spaces, and always registered with pre-determined artillery and mortar fire. Every step would now be contested.

The Canadians remained on the leading edge of the Eighth Army in September and early October. Their orders were always to push ahead, with the lead units having little time to reconnoitre their advance. Private George Reid, a Seaforth veteran of the Sicily campaign, wrote of his time in a scout patrol, "Every pillbox we came to and passed, I would thank God. I was really a believer in the Lord. And the laws of average. I kept telling myself they haven't made a shell or built it yet [with his name on it]. The trouble was, I was not as sure as I was at first in Sicily. And my nerves were getting worse."[24] Twenty-year-old "Speed Reid," as his mates called him, would later catch shrapnel through his calf and spend two years as a prisoner, during which he was forced to work in a salt mine. His weight dropped from 170 to 105 pounds and he barely survived his incarceration.

Despite a slew of ambushes and shellings, there were few major stand-up battles. It remained the weather and terrain that tormented the soldiers. Hill after hill greeted the Canadians in a mind-numbing series of exhausting climbs. Henri Mazerolle of the Carleton and York Regiment remembered with disgust that one advance towards the village of Caprica saw the regiment "drive their trucks through clouds to reach it."[25] Roll-overs were common. "They seem to like sticking us right up in the hills," wrote one gunner, "so we have nicknamed ourselves, 'Monty's mountain goats.'"[26]

The weather turned foul in early October. Foot-sore soldiers had trekked some 700 kilometres since the initial invasion. Now rain and cold temperatures kept the Canadians huddled under their gas capes and shivering over fires. They had been given winter kit by now, but it had done little to relieve their wretchedness. Drizzle seemed to greet them every morning when they emerged soggily from their slit trenches in the ground. Sergeant Kenneth MacNeil of the West Nova Scotia Regiment wrote to his wife about the importance of the "slittie": "A slit trench is the only shelter a fellow has, he must dig his own and to his own taste. If he doesn't dig deep enough, it's his own funeral and very often is."[27] Most soldiers got, as a Canadian observed, "slit trench religion," even if their conversion led to raw and bleeding hands.[28] Despite the misery of living in the ground like animals, it was hard to kill a man below ground. But he could easily get sick. Malaria and jaundice soon took down hundreds of Canadians. Shell- and sniper fire, along with traps and mines, also made permanent claims on the ranks: from October 1 to 15, 147 Canadians were killed and 401 wounded, almost five times as many deaths as in the previous month.[29] After six weeks of this hard campaigning, noted Lieutenant Farley Mowat, most of the men were "fatalistic with fatigue."[30]

Small comforts provided some solace. Tea was important in keeping up morale. Most platoons had a dented bucket that they used daily to brew it. A few handfuls of tea leaves and water taken from any source, including the radiators of vehicles, were boiled up, typically by digging a shallow hole, filling it with gasoline, and setting it aflame. Precious sugar was pulled from a dry sock. Anything else that looked appetizing might be added to the "char," and then it was served around, a wee bit of pleasure in a harsh environment.

A private in the Edmonton Regiment digs a slit trench for safety.

For the leading units, compo rations came up in wooden cases filled with canned goods, tinned meat, beans, cheese, and a few of life's essentials, such as toilet paper.[31] Even battle-hardened men marvelled at the margarine—or what was labelled as such—as the bricks that arrived at the front did not melt and were nearly impossible to cut. Private Bruce Walker, a twenty-two-year-old in the 48th Highlanders of Canada, remembered that the wooden cases were filled with all manner of canned

Canadians in Italy were desperate for news from home.
These two Canucks study their Maclean's *magazines.*

meats and treats, but often you'd open them up and "find out that somebody had been in it and taken the cigarettes, or taken the chocolate bars, or taken the candies, or whatever." Everyone had their favourite compo meal, but most agreed on the worst: "They had one real dandy called Haricot and Ox-tail Stew, and it had great ox-tail bones in it. It got so you couldn't even trade it to the Italians, because they got wise to it and wouldn't take it."[32] The meat and vegetable stew was charmingly renamed by the men as "muck and vomit." Fruit was almost always lacking, and Captain M. Pariseault of the Royal 22e Régiment complained in an official document that the men hated the British food and "they never got canned fruits or other delicacies made in Canada."[33] Nonetheless, most of the soldiers had iron stomachs and had learned during the Depression to never pass up a meal.

Nearly all the soldiers smoked. The officially rationed cigarettes came up in tins of fifty, with seven cigarettes doled out per man, per day. Multiple brands were received, but one of the more common—and despised—were the Indian-made V for Victory cigarettes. The smokes, according to Walker, consisted of "half camel manure, [with] the other half straw."[34] When the Vs were smoked, remembered one Canadian, they gave off the aroma of someone who "had just shit his pants."[35] Nonetheless, as Private Jack Shepherd of the Hasty Ps noted, "if they cut off our smokes the whole system [and war effort] would collapse."[36]

No one below the rank of major knew much about what was happening outside the regiment, although battle surveys conducted among officers observed time and time again that morale was raised when soldiers were informed of plans that affected them and were taken into the commanding officers' confidence.[37] Too often that didn't happen, and the vacuum was filled by rumour. Good and bad information was shared freely, some men eating it up and trying to piece together the war, while others shrugged it off, caring only what happened to their section or platoon. One officer called the rumours—and especially the far-fetched ones about the division being sent back to Canada—"latrine-ograms," on the theory that they originated in the toilets and their value was worth about as much as what was deposited there.[38]

One of the rumours came true in late October when the 1st Canadian Division was pulled out of the line. Campobasso, a town in the interior with a population of some 17,000, had become an Allied rest centre that provided food, shelter, drink, and entertainment for the troops. The Canadians overran the place and soon it became known as Canada Town, its streets renamed after Canadian landmarks. The Italians catered to the soldiers, who with their accumulated pay were anxious to drink the sour red wine, to watch a film, to get some rest and a meal. The Salvation Army and YMCA offered huts in which to read a book or write a letter home. Life flowed back into worn bodies. Music played a key role in rousing the weary. There were "heated arguments," wrote one Canadian, over who was better, Frank Sinatra or Bing Crosby.[39] Almost all could agree on the appeal of the haunting German song "Lili Marlene," whose popularity crossed national boundaries. As one Canadian observed, "many a lonely soldier is swept away on the currents of emotion which well up in his lonely heart, as this devastating war song reflects the frustrations of his own love-life."[40]

Italian prostitutes converged on the area, and padres and officers who preached abstinence found themselves in a losing battle. Venereal disease rates skyrocketed. According to a contemporary medical report, "Investigations of prostitutes, who are numerous, reveal that they are universally infected, and that over 50 percent of the so called amateurs are likewise suffering from these diseases."[41] Prophylactics were issued but seem to have been used haphazardly. The army grudgingly set up treatment centres where soldiers could have their genitals disinfected after intercourse. Posters throughout the town warned of the dangers of VD, but, as C.E. Corrigan of the Royal Canadian Army Medical Corps remarked, the drawings of a curvaceous young woman "in a most seductive pose" that illustrated the signs tended to entice, rather than discourage, the young, sex-starved Canadians. More effective, believed Corrigan, was a crude sign that warned, "VINO + VENUS = VEEDEE."[42]

THE COLD WEATHER OF OCTOBER worsened in November. The already abominable roads were reduced to glutinous bogs. This climate, wrote Farley Mowat, "must be the worst in the whole bloody world. It either burns the balls off you in the summer, or freezes them off in the winter. In between, it *rots* them off."[43] Everyone was soggy. Their socks were perpetually wet and their unwashed bodies reeked like mouldy cheese. The burning heat of Sicily looked profoundly attractive in retrospect.

The rain and mud aided the German defenders. Hitler now had twenty-three divisions spread throughout the country, although many in the north were tasked to put down with much violence any Italian resistance to the occupation. It would not be easy for Alexander's eleven divisions to punch through these German forces, even though they had faced about the same number in the south.[44] "If we can keep him on his heels until early spring," wrote Eisenhower of the Germans, "then the more divisions he uses in counter-offensives against us, the better it will be for Overlord [the planned invasion of Europe] and it then makes little difference what happens to us if Overlord succeeds."[45] So now the strategy was reduced to this: to tie up the enemy until the invasion and ensure that the twenty-three divisions in Italy were not sent to France to shore up the defences there. There would be no let-up in the campaign. The American Fifth Army was ordered to march on Rome, although it first had to crash through several defensive positions, including the vaunted Gustav Line anchored by the mountain-top Benedictine monastery at Cassino. Monty—of course—hoped to beat the Americans to the Eternal City, and starting on November 28, he drove his Eighth Army, with its British, Canadian, Indian, and New Zealand divisions, to attack the Germans blocking their advance along the eastern coastal plain north of the Sangro River, then past the small port of Ortona, where it would pivot westward along the main highway through the Apennines to Rome.

While the Eighth Army made some initial progress in its late-November offensive and the drive to reach the lateral road leading to Rome, the advance fell far short of Montgomery's bombastic reference to a mighty "crack that will be heard all over Italy."[46] The Bernhardt Line was broken as the Eighth Army crossed the Sangro, but Kesselring rushed reinforcements forward to re-establish a new line north of the Moro River. In fact, because the Allies were able to deploy only eleven divisions in the entire theatre, and the Germans had ten south of Rome, the enemy had many advantages. They were fighting on the defensive and employing the natural barriers formed by the terrain, including rolling hills, rivers, and broken ground—advantages augmented by the vile weather conditions as winter set in and slowed the advance of large formations. Traditional military thinking suggests that the attacker as a rule needs a three-to-one ratio in its favour if it is to dislodge a dug-in defender. Granted, the Allied divisions were larger and could be grouped against areas of weakness, and they had nearly complete command of the air; but with the force ratios involved, there would likely be few rapid victories.

AFTER MONTGOMERY'S CRACK was absorbed by the enemy, the Canadians were put back into the line on the night of December 1–2, to replace the 78th British Division, known as the Battleaxe division, and now badly blunted after sustaining almost 5,000 casualties. The Canadian objective was to cross the Moro River and capture the Adriatic port of Ortona, in what would become one of the defining Canadian battles of the war. The Germans were determined to make a stand both in the town and south of it along several defensive positions. The 90th Panzer Grenadier Division—one of the elite formations from Rommel's Afrika Korps (although destroyed and rebuilt since then)—was ordered to keep the Canadians from advancing into Ortona. "The Krauts would run no more," wrote one Canadian. "We were now going to find out how either side would fare in a toe-to-toe battle."[47]

The Germans' Winter Line—where they planned to dig in and hold off the Allies—was hinged on the Ortona front and protected by the Moro River, which flowed into the Adriatic about 6 kilometres south of the town. It was more a stream than a river, but its soft bottom and high banks made it a serious obstacle to armoured vehicles. The Moro passed two main roads that led from the south: the relatively new Route 16 snaked along the coast, while an older road passed through the village of San Leonardo, north of the Moro, and then to the Ortona–Orsogna road that ran from northeast to southwest. With the December rain turning the clay soil into gluey mud, the roads took on considerable importance in the Canadian advance towards the town.

The Canadian divisional commander, Major-General Guy Simonds, was invalided out for medical care when he came down with jaundice at the end of September. He was replaced by Major-General Chris Vokes, a professional soldier, blunt in speech and with a reputation for pressing his own troops hard in battle. Vokes ordered two Canadian brigades into the line for an attack in the early hours of December 6, positioning the 1st Canadian Infantry Brigade along the Adriatic coast and the 2nd Brigade inland. The new divisional commander had proven his aggressive nature in Sicily, but he was a conventional commander, with no great flair. Montgomery believed that he would "never be anything more than 'a plain good cook.'"[48] Vokes was more bloody-minded than battle-smart.

As orders were passed down to the battalions, the senior officers met in O (Orders) Group to go over the operation. From there, company commanders went back to

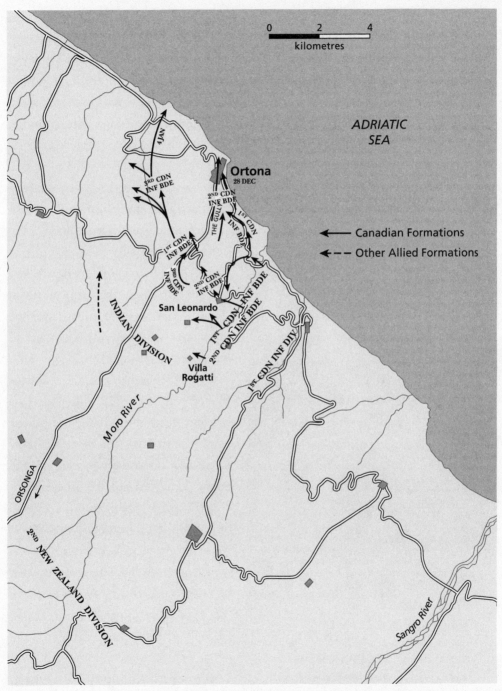

ADRIATIC
SEA

0   2   4
kilometres

Ortona
28 DEC

3RD CDN
INF BDE

2ND CDN
INF BDE

1ST CDN
INF BDE

THE GULLY

1ST CDN
INF BDE

4 JAN

← Canadian Formations

←-- Other Allied Formations

3RD CDN
INF BDE

2ND CDN
INF BDE

San Leonardo

1ST CDN INF BDE

2ND CDN INF BDE

1ST CDN INF DIV

Villa
Rogatti

INDIAN DIVISION

Moro River

ORSONGA

2ND NEW ZEALAND DIVISION

Sangro River

THE ADRIATIC SECTOR: NOVEMBER 28, 1943–JANUARY 4, 1944

explain the plan to their junior officers, who in turn briefed the platoon and section NCOs. The Seaforth Highlanders were to cross the Moro in the early hours of December 6 and capture the village of San Leonardo astride the centre road, while the PPCLI were to push to the west and overrun Villa Rogatti, a rump of high ground isolated by several deep ravines and held in strength by the Germans. On the far right, along the coast, the Hastings & Prince Edward Regiment were to establish another foothold across the Moro. While the plan was straightforward in concept, regimental officers worried about the lack of information that was provided, especially related to enemy strength, and though the warning had come down from division headquarters to expect a dug-in enemy with heavy weapons support, the operation felt like a rush job with little time for the intelligence sections to gather tactical information.[49] Vokes

Chris Vokes commanded the 1st Canadian Infantry Division at the Battle of Ortona. He was a hard-thrusting general, but he lacked an intuitive control over battle.

hoped to surprise the Germans, and so there would be no supporting artillery barrage, although the guns were on standby. Few of the combat-hardened Canadians expected the Germans to leave their front door open.

Using their battlecraft, the Seaforths filtered into the night, following gullies and dead ground to close on the enemy positions. On the left, Baker Company discovered a seam in the enemy defences, but the other advancing companies ran into an alert enemy only 100 metres beyond the river, and were forced to go to ground as fifteen to twenty machine guns opened up across the front, sweeping all of the approach routes.[50] The German MG-42, known as the Spandau, fired at an alarming rate, some 1,200 to 1,500 bullets a minute. To the west, under the cover of darkness, the PPCLI routed German outposts, as they closed on their objective. At Villa Rogatti, the scouting Patricias found multiple machine-gun nests, but Lieutenant-Colonel Cameron Ware believed they could be taken in a daring attack. Surprise rather than firepower was the key, and three companies converged on the Germans and cut through them. The panzer grenadiers were killed or captured in wild fighting, and when their comrades counterattacked at first light, the PPCLI, with the support of British tanks from the 44th Royal Tank Regiment that had been rushed forward, blasted the enemy relentlessly. In the words of one Canadian gunner, it "felt like a minor earthquake."[51] The German attack disintegrated under fire, but the day was not yet won.

Later on December 6, starting around 1:30 P.M., the Germans attacked with a formidable force of nine Mk IV tanks and supporting panzer grenadiers, but the Canadians were in an effective position along a ragged grove of olive trees and vineyards, and backed by tanks and anti-tank guns behind the Moro.[52] British Sherman tanks were hull-down, with only their long-barrelled guns and turrets visible. As the Germans surged forward, mounds of brass cartridges from the forward Shermans marked the defensive lines. One official report exclaimed, "Tanks to hard-pressed infantryman are blessings from the God of War."[53] By the end of the day, the PPCLI had defeated five counterattacks, and they counted about 100 dead Germans on the battlefield amid 5 burning Mk IV tanks. "It was a fair massacre," remembered Lieutenant-Colonel Ware. "We allowed them to come ... within fifty metres before anti-tank fire was opened."[54] The cost to the Patricias was sixteen killed and missing and about fifty-two wounded, as well as two destroyed British Shermans.[55] The Seaforths were less successful in their attack about 3 kilometres downstream. They had no tank support because the Shermans on that front had been unable to cross the Moro and climb its muddy banks. The PPCLI eventually handed over Rogatti to British troops, and they and the Seaforths then pulled back across the Moro to shorten the Canadian lines.

On the right flank, across the river mouth, the Hastings & Prince Edward Regiment had clawed their way across the Moro, but it was under heavy fire throughout the morning. The lead companies suffered severe casualties. They could not call down artillery fire because of faulty No. 18 wireless sets (which had also failed repeatedly in

Sicily), but they held on. When Dog Company was thrown into the line a few hours later, the Germans faltered, and, with communication restored to the rear, a crushing Canadian artillery bombardment kept the enemy from counterattacking the Hasty Ps' 600-metre-wide and 500-metre-deep bridgehead. After licking their wounds, the Germans returned that night, and were beaten back again. One report observed, "By morning a large number of enemy dead were in and around our positions."[56] On December 7, with the Germans massing for an armoured thrust, desperation drove the Hastings soldiers to manhandle two 6-pounder anti-tank guns across the river and up the steep banks. It was a difficult manoeuvre, but fear fuelled the straining muscles. The guns opened fire in time to fling the Germans back; they left 170 dead over the two days of fighting.[57]

The battles to the south of Ortona saw both sides rely heavily on massed mortar and shellfire, and the bombardments were the most intense faced by Canadians to that point in the war. The 1st Canadian Division's gunners fired, according to one report, "until the paint curled back from the red-hot steel and the men reeled in the pits from exhaustion and were sick from the blast."[58] The endless cannonade from both sides was a sonic bombardment of the senses. Hardened men broke under the strain. Lieutenant Farley Mowat fought desperately against the dread that lay like a worm in his belly. Writing in retrospect with grim honesty, he remembered that after hearing that one good chum had been incinerated when a phosphorous grenade exploded in his face, he gulped down a few swallows of rum: "It did not restore my failing courage but at least it helped a little to deaden the throbbing fear."[59] There was no shame in fear: few were immune in this wasteland of battle. Mowat, having steadied himself, once again led his dwindling platoon back into combat.

Dark smoke drifted across the battlefield, lit by muzzle flashes and geysers of mud erupting from large-calibre shells. Dead men and eviscerated mules fouled every road, ditch, and crater, while burned and smouldering vehicles littered the landscape. On December 8, the RCRs and 48th Highlanders renewed the push north of the Moro behind an artillery barrage that was thickened up by 180 Kittyhawk bombers from the Desert Air Force (DAF).[60] The DAF was grounded for much of the month by the poor weather and thick cloud cover, but when they could unleash their bombs, they were a welcome sight for the Canadian infantry. However, it was mainly the artillery that paved the way forward, laying down a wall of steel and high explosives. Bruce Medd, a thirty-nine-year-old forward artillery observer attached to the 48th Highlanders, reported that when the guns started firing, "It was just like a machine gun." He remembered seeing some of the infantry crying openly: "They were afraid but they carried on just the same."[61]

Behind a scorching artillery barrage from 350 guns, the RCRs attacked laterally at 4:30 P.M. along the river, heading towards San Leonardo. But the enemy front-soldaten—who had been exhorted by their commanders, "the watchword for one and all! 'Into the Ground!'"—were ready for the assault.[62] Advancing with all four companies, the Royals ran into an enemy counterattack. Both sides were shooting and lunging across the contested ground. Dozens of minor battles broke out in a melee. The Royals were forced to dig in about halfway to their objective, strung out in a vulnerable position. With German armour massing to deliver the coup de grâce, and the RCRs without tanks or their anti-tank guns, the Canadian regiment's only recourse was to call down the division's artillery fire on the forward companies. Orders were given to burrow deep. The Germans coming overland were caught in the open by withering shellfire, although some of the Royals were killed too. The stunned grenadiers retreated. On the left flank, the Highlanders, with tanks assisting the advance, inched forward against fierce opposition but failed to reach their object-ives at the Ortona–Orsogna road junction. As one of the 48th Highlander infantry-men put it, "They threw hate at us across the gully from several directions."[63]

On the Canadians' left flank, further inland, the New Zealanders and Indian troops were grinding their way forward, attacking and defending against German assaults as the enemy sought to keep them driving around Ortona, with the ultim-ate goal of pushing north to Pescara, a coastal town like Ortona but on a direct road to Rome. As early as December 7, the German army commander had recognized that despite the wide army front, "the centre of gravity remains on the coast."[64] Reinforcements and artillery batteries were rushed to the Canadian, New Zealand, and Indian sector. Throughout the battle zone, the enemy-held ground favoured the defenders, who had a nearly uninterrupted view of any assault. This meant that their artillery could hammer the attackers: even the New Zealand and Canadian sup-port units to the rear were targeted—a new and unwanted experience. At the front, devastated farmhouses were fought over in see-saw battles. Vineyards became the site of mass killing. Irrigation ditches were held with brutal tenacity. The battlefield soon resembled the shell-blasted, muddy wasteland of the Great War's No Man's Land. Each advance swallowed up more gummy landscape, but at a growing cost in lives. And still they fought.

Amid the chaos, a team of embedded historical officers recorded the conflict. Since Sicily, a small group of combat historians and war artists had been instructed

A private in the Edmonton Regiment uses a blasted wall for cover.

to gather historical evidence of the Canadians in battle and to paint their actions. In Italy the chroniclers grew in number, with Captain Eric Harrison, a prewar professor of history at Queen's University, and Captain Sam Hughes, grandson of the erratic minister of militia from the Great War, documenting the war for future generations.[65] Official war artists, such as Charles Comfort, Alex Colville, and Lawren P. Harris (son of the Group of Seven painter), also travelled along the front, sketching and creating water colour paintings of the battlefield, engagements, and Canadian soldiers, before returning to London to work up larger oils.[66] The historians and war artists also acted as eyewitnesses to battle. At Ortona, war artist Charles Comfort wrote of the fighting that "raged with demonic fury. Day after hellish day men clubbed and smashed one another at close quarters for desperate short-range objectives.... The bomb, the Brens, the PIATs, the grenades; rallying around the tanks as they roared out of harbour at last light; flanking the position under covering fire, rushing in the half-light, through sheets of blinding flame, hurling the grenades and closing in through lacerating, pounding, light-stabbed darkness."[67]

IN CONJUNCTION WITH THE RCR ATTACK on December 8, Canadian combat engineers on the left flank had begun to bridge the Moro, eventually manhandling a bulldozer to the front to reduce the height of the far bank, even though, according to one eyewitness, it made "as much noise as an entire tank brigade" and attracted mortar bombs.[68] Working under fire and suffering twenty-two casualties in the process, the engineers were able to establish bridges for the tanks to cross on the morning of December 9, allowing Canadian Shermans to crash through the German defences on the north side of the river. A number of tank battles took place on the 9th, with the Shermans manoeuvring in the mud for advantage and hammering shells at Panzer Mk IIIs and Mk IVs. The German Mk IIIs were inferior to the Shermans, but the Mk IVs were about on par with the Allied tanks, although with better armour and a more powerful gun.

The Seaforths crossed the new bridge clinging to the Shermans of the 14th (Calgary) Canadian Armoured Regiment. A few of the tanks rolled over, sliding down the 10-metre embankments at either end of the fragile bridge, and another was knocked out by a mine, but four crashed forward to San Leonardo, with thirty-nine Seaforths, led by Lieutenant John McLean, catching a ride. The tip of the spear now had pierced as far as the village, and the rest of the Seaforths, along with fifty-one tanks, slipped across the Moro to hold San Leonardo against enemy counterattack. Forward observation officers corrected the blind gunners to the rear, and the 25-pounders and 5.5-inch medium howitzers laid down thousands of shells to join the 65,000 they would fire over the four-day battle.[69] Hull-down, the Shermans blasted away at the enemy, securing a few kills of enemy tanks at a face-to-face range of just 150 metres. Major Ned Amy, a twenty-five-year-old Maritimer commanding A Squadron of the Calgary tanks—who would be awarded the Military Cross for his gallant leadership—remembered a weary Seaforth Highlander rifleman rushing over to his tank after the Germans had been turned back. The rifleman whooped and yelled out, "You big cast-iron, son-of-a-bitch, I could kiss you!"[70] By the end of the day, San Leonardo was in Canadian hands for good, but only twenty-four tanks remained.[71]

The Seaforths now were dug-in on the crossroads at San Leonardo, and the Hastings & Prince Edward Regiment linked up with the RCRs. The latter unit's soldiers were spread out over the muddy hills and fields, including one mound of smoking ruins known as Slaughterhouse Hill. Together, they blunted several German thrusts on December 9, which one report described as "furious and almost suicidal" in their intensity.[72] The German grenadiers were eventually driven back, leaving some 200 corpses and writhing injured on the battlefield.[73] After four fierce days of fighting, the Canadians held a ragged line beyond the Moro, consisting of slit trenches and a few strongpoints that were linked by nightly patrols. The road to Ortona appeared to be open. But between the Canadians and their goal lay the formidable position that came to be known as the Gully, a deep trench 5 kilometres long that ran across the front, ranging from 200 metres wide at the Adriatic to about 80 metres further inland, and measuring about 60 metres deep. It was filled with thorny acacias, olive trees lined its slopes, and the Germans were dug-in all around it. Crossing the Moro had been the hardest battle of the Italian campaign, but the fighting to follow would be every bit as tough.

THE PATRICIAS, THE "LOYAL EDDIES" (the Edmonton Regiment had received the designation of "Loyal" the previous month), and the Seaforth Highlanders now confronted this unexpected obstacle, a cut in the terrain that was barely noticeable

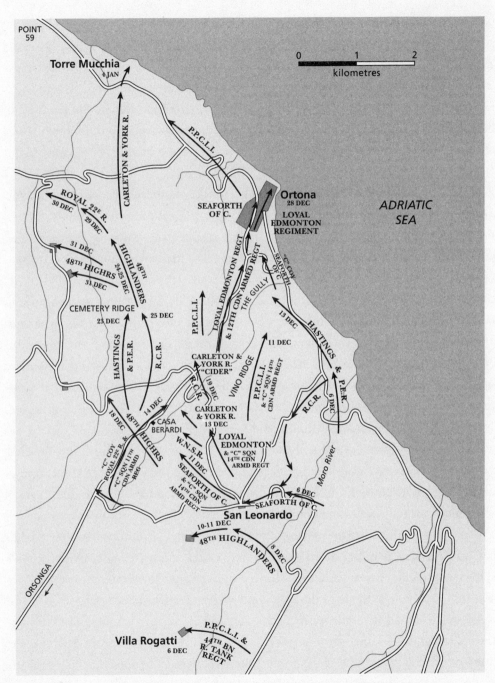

POINT
59

Torre Mucchia
4 JAN

CARLETON & YORK R.

P.P.C.L.I.

0   1   2
kilometres

ROYAL 22E R.
30 DEC

29 DEC

SEAFORTH
OF C.

Ortona
28 DEC

LOYAL
EDMONTON
REGIMENT

ADRIATIC
SEA

31 DEC

48TH HIGHRS
31 DEC

48TH
HIGHLANDERS
24-25 DEC

"C" CDN
SEAFORTH
OF C.

CEMETERY RIDGE
23 DEC

25 DEC

13 DEC

HASTINGS &
P.E.R.

HASTINGS
& P.E.R.

R.C.R.

P.P.C.L.I.

LOYAL EDMONTON REGT
& 12TH CDN ARMED REGT

THE GULLY

VINO RIDGE

11 DEC

CARLETON &
YORK R.
"CIDER"

19 DEC

R.C.R.

CARLETON &
YORK R.
13 DEC

P.P.C.L.I.
& "C" SQN 14TH
CDN ARMD REGT

R.C.R.

6 DEC

14 DEC

CASA
BERARDI

W.N.S.R.
11 DEC

LOYAL
EDMONTON
& "C" SQN
14TH CDN
ARMD REGT

Moro River

18 DEC

48TH
HIGHRS

"C" COY
ROYAL 22E R. &
"C" SQN 11TH
CDN ARMD
REG

SEAFORTH OF C.
& "C" SQN
14TH CDN
ARMD REGT

SEAFORTH OF C.

6 DEC

San Leonardo

10-11 DEC

48TH HIGHLANDERS

8 DEC

ORSONGA

Villa Rogatti
6 DEC

P.P.C.L.I. &
44TH BN
R. TANK
REGT

THE CROSSING OF THE MORO AND THE BATTLE OF ORTONA:
DECEMBER 6, 1943–JANUARY 4, 1944

on maps but was now revealed as a significant enemy position that was held in strength. Vokes's division used December 10 to close the distance between the Moro and the south bank of the Gully, though not before discovering that the Germans still had some fight in them. A group of Loyal Eddies encountered a section of Germans advancing with arms raised seeking to surrender. When the Canadians revealed themselves, a hidden machine gun raked them, cutting several down.[74] An enraged Vokes warned all his formations to accept the surrender of enemy troops with extreme caution.

On the opposite bank of the Gully, the northern side closest to Ortona, the Germans were dug-in and ready for battle. The high banks of the Gully were a thick wall of soil that acted as a reverse-slope position that was nearly impossible to strike with artillery fire because the shells arced over the enemy hugging the banks. Only a limited number of howitzers and mortars—the 4.2- and 3-inch—could provide the necessary plunging fire, and the effects of these bombardments went largely unseen. The infantry took matters into their own hands. Patrols by scouts and snipers collected information by crawling through the muck and spying on the enemy. Lieutenant-Colonel Jim Jefferson, commanding officer of the Loyal Eddies, noted after the battle the "absolute necessity of aggressive patrolling." At the same time as they gathered information, the scout platoons engaged in heavy sniping and "were out almost continuously picking off Germans."[75]

One by one, the enemy positions on the south side of the Gully were snuffed out. But the Germans also had established camouflaged machine-gun positions on the forward slope of the Gully—in and up the opposite bank—that could sweep the ground across which the Canadians had to cross. These positions were difficult to strike with Allied artillery shellfire, and even a single German MG-42, a belt-fed machine gun that laid down scything fire, could annihilate a company. As one soldier remarked, "every time the MG 42 opened up, you'd swear someone was tearing a long strip off a tarpaulin or a window-blind, they were that fast."[76] All the roads were infested with anti-tank mines, and any attempt to outflank the Gully to the west would have seen the Canadians subjected to intense fire from an increased number of artillery guns, as the German batteries there had tripled in number from twenty-six to seventy-six—becoming one of the heaviest concentrations of enemy firepower on the Italian front.[77] With limited tactical options and almost no room to manoeuvre, the Gully required another frontal assault by the Canadians against a deeply fortified position.

A series of probing attacks on the 10th, marred by confusion stemming from sporadic communication, ended in failure when the Canadians were stopped short of Vino Ridge (a tangle of vineyards and olive groves protected by mines and machine guns on the south side of the Gully). The West Nova Scotia Regiment and tanks from the Ontario Regiment continued to test the enemy defences along the Gully at 6 P.M. on the 11th. Infantryman John O'Brien of the West Novas, who operated the No. 18 wireless set, wrote that he never saw a German during the engagement, although his position was pounded by enemy mortar fire. "In a very short time there were casualties everywhere," he recalled. [78] By the end of the bombardment, every man in the vicinity was hit except O'Brien: two dead and ten wounded. It was nearly as bad throughout the battalion, which sustained sixty casualties, including the inspiring commander, Lieutenant-Colonel Pat Bogert. After a week of heavy fighting, the effective strength of the battalion had been reduced to a meagre 150 men.[79]

General Vokes was stymied. Having failed on the right, he now sought to drive on the left, sending forward the fresh Carleton and York Regiment at 6 A.M. on December 13, along with some support on the flanks from the fought-out PPCLI and West Novas. The New Brunswickers of the Carleton and Yorks advanced in rainy weather that reduced visibility, while the heavy cloud cover also made air support largely ineffective. A creeping barrage chewed up the earth in front of them, crashing through the enemy lines around the Gully, but the German defenders—the 3rd Parachute Regiment—remained well protected on the reverse slope. The defenders re-emerged from their protective dugouts and positions to engage the Canadians when the barrage swept over them.[80] The guns might have had greater effect if the Canadian maps had been more accurate, but these atrocities—Italian sheets with British grid numbers superimposed on them—were out by as much as 500 metres.[81] The German guns had no such deficits. Stupefied by the bombardment and paralyzed by the scything machine-gun fire, the Canadian survivors dug into the slop for cover.

Vokes had shot his bolt. Eight of the nine Canadian infantry regiments at his disposal had been committed and chewed up in the meat-grinder. The Germans were suffering too. Intercepted intelligence reports indicated on December 13 that the 90th Division was all but destroyed as a fighting force and could no longer be relied upon for a robust defence.[82] To hold the Gully, the German high command cycled in battle-hardened paratroopers from 1st Parachute Division, which Canadian intelligence later lauded, saying there were "no better German tps [troops] in this theatre."[83]

Both sides were being ground down. The Canadians continued to press forward, still sending battle patrols ahead to look for gaps in the enemy line. But there was never enough time to gather intelligence. Finally, one of the patrols found a way through the Gully, at its head, during the dark hours of December 13, and returned to guide a West Nova platoon through it, aided by three Ontario tanks. In the ensuing battle, the Shermans and West Novas smashed two German Mk IV tanks.[84] These burned-out tanks became grim markers for soldiers navigating forward and back across the battlefield. Even though the Canadians had knifed through the position, few forces were left to exploit the break in the enemy line. As the paratroopers massed for a counterattack, the West Novas, despite being supported by the Seaforths, were forced to withdraw. Hunched over, slathered in mud, the hollowed-eyed Canadians retreated back through shell craters that reeked of corpses and cordite.

Meanwhile, the pressure to get on with the battle—coming from corps headquarters, and ultimately from Montgomery—was never-ending. In his last hope, Vokes—whom some of his men now called "The Butcher"—sent his final undamaged battalion, the Royal 22e Regiment, through the southwestern end of the Gully at 7 A.M. on December 14.[85] The Van Doos were accompanied by the last seven tanks of the Ontario Regiment, and a bombardment that included the division's artillery pieces and that of the British 5th Corps. The rolling barrage tore up the ground as the two lead companies crossed No Man's Land. But again, enough German defenders survived to emerge from the smouldering wasteland and fire into the advancing forces. A camouflaged enemy tank held up the drive until lead elements were able to manoeuvre close to it, at which point Sergeant J.P. Rousseau fired his hand-held anti-tank launcher, the PIAT, in an attempt to disable the beast. The under-powered PIAT often failed to penetrate German armour, but in this case the 2.5-pound hollow-shaped bomb bore through the Mk IV's armour beneath the turret and detonated the tank's ammunition, blowing it up from within. One Canadian reported seeing more than thirty pieces of the tank spread over the battlefield.[86] But the stiff German defence had cost the Van Doos dearly: half of the officers and men were killed or wounded, and the survivors seemed destined for failure. The French-Canadians would not be stopped, and aggressive platoons found ways to move forward, raking the enemy positions with Bren gun- and Lee-Enfield fire. When the Germans struck

Private Edmund Arsenault of the West Nova Scotia Regiment
aiming a PIAT anti-tank weapon from a slit trench near Ortona, Italy.

back, Sherman tanks from the Ontario Regiment, led by Major H.C. "Snuffy" Smith, knocked out two German Mk IVs before the enemy armour withdrew in confusion.

Captain Paul Triquet, a thirty-three-year-old professional soldier from Cabano, Quebec, slight in build but aggressive in nature, gathered the shot-up soldiers and told them the only way to survive was to punch forward. Pius Girouard of the Van Doos, who had traded soap for spaghetti earlier in the campaign, found himself in a field of mud. Triquet crawled past him and told him to advance, but on his knees, as the Germans were sweeping the area with fire. Next to Girouard, one of his mates wiggled forward on his elbows until he took a bullet in the face. A little while later, Girouard was shot in the throat and left for dead. When his position was overrun, Germans captured him and carried him to a barn. He did not expect to live, and remembered, "I only wanted to see my father and my mother before I died."[87] He was rescued by his regiment later in the day, and spent years undergoing painful operations and rehabilitation to repair his throat. Even then, he never regained full command of his voice.

At around 8:30 A.M., Triquet's company, now reduced to two dozen men—down from the eighty-one that had started only a few hours earlier—continued to fight their way forward. At around noon, mud-encased and stiff with cold, they were still 200 metres from their target: Casa Beradi, a three-storey farmhouse situated on the critical road to Orsogna and now fortified by the Germans, which had blown-out windows giving it a death's head aspect. The French-Canadian captain rallied his men, now down to fourteen in number, exposed himself to fire, coordinated the tank movements, and finally captured the farmhouse by 3 P.M.

Possession of Casa Berardi allowed the Canadians to turn the enemy's flank and, as Vokes's noted in his official report, it "gave us domination."[88] Through the rest of the day and into the 15th, the enemy counterattacked but were beaten back from the road junction. Four burning German tanks were left on the chewed-up battlefield. Triquet received the Victoria Cross for his inspired leadership, and other survivors, including tank commander Smith, received gallantry awards. The French-Canadian hero would later be pulled back to Canada to recover from the ordeal and to sell the war in Quebec.[89]

Despite the heroism of the Royal 22e Regiment, the Canadian division had been battered severely. Several battalions, notably the West Novas and the Carleton and York Regiment, now were almost ineffective because of the casualties they had taken.[90] As they had done during the Sicily campaign, the Canadian divisional command, this time with Vokes at the helm, had thrown Canadian battalions into the line one after another. As Vokes wrote after the battle, "Once battle is joined, the fog of war descends, as communications invariably become difficult, and the development of the operation must be based on the scantiest of information or a mass of conflicting reports. One often had to depend on instinct and chance one's aim.... No training exercise in which I have taken part has adequately demonstrated the 'fog of war'. It is complete and utter."[91] Indeed it was, and only experience and an innate feel for the unfolding battle guided good commanders. Vokes, unfortunately, had shown little intuitive understanding of what his Canadians faced in crossing the Moro and attacking the Gully, and British corps and army commanders, unhappy with the rate of advance, questioned his tactical sense in not massing the attack. However, it is not evident that a larger, concentrated Canadian attack would have overpowered the German advantages of terrain and firepower. It might only have created a target-rich environment for the mortars and shellfire to snuff out more Canadian lives. What is clear, though, is that by the end of the battle, too few reinforcements were left to support success and too often operations were initiated without adequate coordination. This was smash-mouth warfare, in which firepower chewed up bodies relentlessly.

"WHERE IS THE LINE between aggressive action and unnecessary risk?" wondered Lieutenant Howard Mitchell, after burying a friend who had the top of his head blown off in the fighting to cross the Moro.[92] Did the Canadian division have the strength for an assault on Ortona? Vokes consulted senior Canadian officers and decided that so much had been sacrificed already that Ortona had to be captured by his men. A defeat or withdrawal—even handing over the untidy front to a British unit—would have grim consequences for his soldiers' morale and would deliver a devastating blow to the division's reputation. The Canadians would fight on.

Ortona, an ancient town reportedly founded by the Trojans after the fall of Troy, was a mere 450 metres across. But they would be a tough 450 metres. Many of the town's stone buildings were more than 500 years old, with deep cellars and underground passages that linked them to other structures. Above ground, the town was

cut through with narrow streets commanded by four-storey houses that stood shoul-
der-to-shoulder, often with shared walls. Churches abounded, and there were three
large, open squares. These were vacant now, thousands of the inhabitants having
fled. The German defenders, members of the elite 1st Parachute Division—many
of whom were veterans of the Sicily and Crete campaigns—would fight among the

Exhausted and wounded Canadians emerging from battle.

remaining Ortonese. The parachutists, masters of demolition, had prepared their defences carefully. Most of the narrow streets were choked with rubble; only a few were left open to draw the Canadians into kill zones.

Ortona could not be approached from the sea, as its shoreline was protected by cliffs and steep banks. The Canadians would have to go through the town, while also pushing around it to the west. It was here, outside Ortona, that the Germans stacked at least four battalions, aware that the Canadians and, further to the west, Indian soldiers, would attempt to slip past. There would be no rapid flanking movement in the mud and against fierce opposition, and snow and rain still grounded most of the Desert Air Force aircraft, which might otherwise have been useful in bombarding the German supply lines to the north.[93]

On the morning of December 21, after several days of pauses and probing, often under cover of smoke bombs, Brigadier Bert Hoffmeister ordered the Loyal Edmonton Regiment and the Seaforth Highlanders of Canada into Ortona. The handsome, boyish-looking Hoffmeister had proven himself to be an aggressive regimental commander in Sicily, and had been promoted to command the 2nd Brigade early in the Italian campaign. A militiaman who inspired almost everyone he met, he had studied the lessons of the battlefield, and he spent much of the next week infiltrating forward, providing encouragement to his men, and leading from the front.[94] But now the hard part was up to the Loyal Eddies, who entered Ortona with a forward company marching on either side of the main road. Many of the sombre soldiers calculated worriedly who among them, far from the open spaces of Alberta, would soon be buried in this ancient town. The Loyal Eddies stalked through the labyrinth of streets, as the tanks of the Three Rivers Regiment ground forward, their machine guns raking doorways and entrances. To the west of the Eddies, the Seaforths infiltrated forward through the outskirts of Ortona, hoping to locate the hidden Germans in order to bring down artillery fire. The Germans would not be drawn out, preferring to see the Canadians commit themselves deeper into the town.

Urban warfare was different from anything the Canadians had encountered so far. Two fresh battalions from the 1st Parachute Division were well established in the town, and soon they began to spring traps on the advancing Canadians. German machine guns swept the streets: frequently two or more provided an overlapping scythe of fire, and sometimes a third operated from an upper-floor window.[95] Snipers took down their human prey from ingeniously camouflaged positions. German parachute combat engineer Carl Bayerlein later remembered, "Using our engineers' explosives, we blew up entire lines of houses to hold up the advance of enemy tanks. In the mountains of rubble thus created, booby traps were emplaced."[96] The Canadians' tanks moved forward cautiously, wary of mines and enemy paratroopers employing the anti-tank rocket-launcher panzerfaust for the first time in the campaign. Enemy tanks half buried in the rubble, hull down, with only their guns protruding, were also difficult to spot until they started firing.[97]

Ortona's buildings, so crammed together, restricted movement and effective observation. When Canadian platoons advanced, officers had difficulty corralling their men and giving voice orders. Half-sections of soldiers skulked forward, slowly inching their way into danger, clearing one position after another. An intelligence log (a track of radio communications) for the Loyal Eddies provides a glimpse into the nature of combat on the 21st: "Enemy have dug in and blown houses to make strong p[oin]ts. Streets have been barricaded and heavily mined. Fighting heavy. Progress slow due to having to clear houses.... 2 enemy A/Tk [Anti-tank] guns knocked out patrols will be active tonight." And the next morning, at 6:32, the log reported, "enemy heavily dug in along south bank ... posn at church ... believed to be HQ ... won heavily held. Hv [Heavy] enemy shelling and mortaring during the night."[98]

"They set up some first class booby traps," remembered Sergeant A.J. Rudd of the Loyal Eddies. "You might see a nice Bible or piece of stained glass laying about a house. Items like these were usually connected to at least a pound of explosives."[99] Toilet flush chains were an easy way to set off the igniter to a well-placed bomb.[100] The Germans also laced entire houses with explosives. One platoon of Edmontons was caught in such a trap: the building collapsed and buried them alive. Lance-Corporal Roy Boyd was the only survivor, dug out from the rubble three days later. The enraged Eddies pushed on, through the dust and smoke, seeking out the enemy in close-quarters combat. By the third day of the operation, the three forward companies of the Eddies were down to sixty men each. The Seaforths were not much stronger. But the Canadians continued to divide up the town and drive the enemy back systematically, house by house.

The Canadians soon developed methods of fighting in this built-up environment. Initiative passed to junior officers and senior NCOs. Because so many snipers were hidden in and on the buildings, the Canadians avoided the deadly open plazas and streets. The Three Rivers Regiment took to blasting every building. The Seaforths and Eddies infantry, grateful for the firepower, watched for enemy infantry or panzerfaust teams that tried to creep up and destroy the tanks. The commanding officer of the Loyal Eddies, Lieutenant-Colonel Jim Jefferson, wrote that the PIAT was useful for "shooting up houses and proved an ideal weapon for street fighting," but that it took enormous courage to engage a tank with what appeared to be a pea-shooter, and it was nearly suicide if the tanks were protected by infantry.[101] More important in taking the fight to enemy tanks were the infantry support guns: the 6-pounder and

Canadian soldiers frantically dig out one of their comrades who was buried alive when a German explosive brought down a house on him and his platoon. He survived. Everyone else in his platoon was killed.

the deadlier 17-pounders wielded by the 90th Anti-Tank Battery. Both guns were used to blow holes in the walls of houses to allow the infantry through to avoid the German kill zones. They were even more deadly when shells were fired through an open window to bounce around the granite walls and make a mess of the defenders inside. Even in the face of such horror, the resilient German paratroopers frequently fought to the last gasp. The battle-hardened Seaforths were a little shocked when they found one paratrooper, his eyes torn out by shrapnel, yelling hoarsely while still clutching his weapon: "I wish I could see you—I'd kill every one of you."[102]

Three Rivers Sherman tank battling through the streets of Ortona.

The Canadians adapted quickly to their new fighting environment. When they came to understand that almost all the ground-level doors of buildings were booby-trapped or covered by fire, the Canadians jumped from balcony to balcony. When this was not possible, they began to "mouse-hole" or "house-hole" from building to building. Beginning at the top, they used an explosive charge, and occasionally German anti-tank Teller mines, to blast holes through adjoining walls. Any Germans on the other side were killed or stunned, and the Canadians then quickly tossed in No. 36 fragmentation grenades, which detonated into some eighty fragments that cut into anything, and anyone, within an 18-metre radius. Before the dust settled, the Canadians scrambled through the hole and crept from room to room. As one officer reported, "'No risks were taken and [No.] 36 grenades were thrown into any room which gave reason for suspicion before we actually entered."[103] Each room was methodically cleared: first with grenades and then with Thompson and Bren machine guns. Afterwards, the Canadians worked their way down, spraying stair-wells with small-arms fire and tossing more grenades ahead of them. The Germans were at a grave disadvantage in trying to throw their "potato mashers" up the stairs. Through bitter experience, the Canadians became masters of urban warfare, and were acknowledged as such throughout the Eighth Army.[104]

"In very hard house to house fighting and at the cost of heavy casualties to his own troops, the enemy advanced to the market square in the southwestern part of the town," observed one German report of the Canadian steady advance. "The battle there is especially violent."[105] The losses were significant on both sides, but the German paratroopers were steadily driven back, even as they tenaciously infiltrated back at night into cleared houses, sniping at the Canadians the next day. To silence the enemy threat, Canadian engineers soon took to demolishing key structures, even though they were painfully aware of the damage they were wreaking on the town. Stunned Italian families who took shelter under the rubble and in cellars struggled to pass through the Canadian and German lines, calling out piteously at night to be allowed safe passage. Others simply stayed hidden and hoped the storm would blow over them. Lieutenant Howard Mitchell of the Saskatoon Light Infantry recounted the story told by his batman, who stumbled upon an Italian family holed up in a house: "There he had found two children, killed in their high chairs. The wailing mother was with them. The father and some other men were huddled around doing nothing. The children had been dead for some time."[106] Throughout the town were pathetic graves—often unmarked, under piles of rocks and rubble—for the 1,300 Ortonese who were killed in the fighting.[107]

As the battle raged on, a glimpse of combat was captured by the Canadian Army Film and Photo Unit. These combat cameramen, wielding cameras instead of rifles, rode on tanks or crept through the maze of streets, documenting what they saw

Canadian infantry clearing out German troops with hand grenades in the battle for Ortona.

on film.[108] At one point, Sergeant Jack Stollery, a member of the unit, was moving through the rubble-strewn streets with the Three Rivers Regiment. After a short battle, with both Germans and Canadians advancing and retreating, he found himself ahead of the Sherman tanks and facing the enemy with only his camera. He beat an escape to safer ground, but the gritty battle footage was soon being shown in theatres across Britain and Canada. War correspondents such as Matthew Halton and Ralph Allen also broadcast from the town, providing hour-by-hour progress to Canadians at home. Ross Munro, a twenty-nine-year-old Canadian Press journalist had scored a monumental scoop in reporting the Canadian landings at Sicily. By drafting his story on the beaches and getting a naval contact to send it back on the wires to London, he had avoided the formal censors and told the world of the Canadian part in the invasion. Now, at Ortona, the Canadian war correspondents, or "warcos" as they were commonly known, were again bringing news of the overseas battle to Canadians. No tape recorders existed at the time, and to record the sound of combat a technician accompanied the reporter into battle with the bulky equipment needed to cut a phonograph record. Some of this high-quality front-line Canadian reporting was picked up by the BBC and American radio networks, which further publicized the battle on the Adriatic coast and the men who were winning it. In one report, the CBC's Matthew Halton, creeping past Canadian and German corpses and fearful of snipers, provided an eyewitness account of the fierce fighting: "The Germans were superb—admit it freely—and when that is said, our Canadians were better. The Boche had all the cards—the prepared positions, the hundreds of booby traps and mines; we had to seek him out and kill him man by man."[109] Halton became the most famous Canadian overseas voice of the war, reaching millions across the Dominion.[110]

Major Jim Stone, a company commander for the Loyal Eddies, remembered, "Street-fighting is won by the men, not by the weapons—the men actually in contact with the enemy, mostly commanded by junior NCOs."[111] Battles raged back and forth in the ruins, with little respite for Christmas. Some of the soldiers in the forward units munched on cold pork chops brought forward in Universal Carriers, and both the Eddies and Seaforths cycled units from the front line to ensure that most of the infantry had a chance to partake of a festive dinner. The drawn and dirty Seaforths had their meal on white table cloths in the bombed-out church of

Santa Maria di Constantinopoli, in the southern outskirts of the town. The cooks had scrounged apples and oranges, nuts and mixed vegetables. A few pigs provided the main course. Against a backdrop of distant machine-gun fire and exploding shells, carols were played on an organ and a few men took to singing before the Highlanders went back into the line, and to the killing. Maurice White, an infantryman of the Loyal Edmonton Regiment, shot and killed a German on Christmas Day; he lost

A member of the Canadian Army Film Unit captures the experience of battle.

no sleep over his actions at the time, believing, "You either shoot somebody or they shoot you." But after the war, and particularly every Christmas for more than sixty years, he reflected on the strange juxtaposition of the 1943 Christmas celebration and the ongoing organized murder.[112] The paratroopers were no less resolute or cold-hearted, but the German high command concluded on December 25 that holding Ortona "costs so much blood that it cannot be justified."[113]

While the Seaforths and Eddies clawed their way forward in Ortona, the 1st Brigade was advancing through the muddy terrain 3 kilometres west of the town, hoping to outflank the German defenders in that sector.[114] Beginning on December 23, the Hastings fought their way forward through fierce German resistance, with the 48th Highlanders eventually leapfrogging them to take Cemetery Ridge, a key position that overlooked Ortona and would make the German position there untenable. But the Germans refused to retreat, and instead launched counterattacks against the Highlanders. Battles were fought day and night.[115] The Canadians held their ground.

Bone-chilling wind and snow slowed operations. The soldiers subsisted on cigarettes, cold rations, and rum. The Van Doos and the Carleton and Yorks continued the drive, but it was slow, grim fighting, not dissimilar to the bog battles of Passchendaele a generation earlier. There were brutal see-saw engagements over non-descript, blasted hilltops and knolls of blackened trees, where the veterans of Sicily died alongside new recruits. On January 4, the Carleton and Yorks, exhausted and roughly handled in several battles, finally captured Point 59, near Torre Mucchia, on the Adriatic coast overlooking Ortona. The evicted surviving defenders of Point 59 joined the paratroopers from Ortona who had filtered away from the town in the early hours of December 28, leaving it in Canadian hands. As one German paratrooper remarked, "Our main desire: to sleep for once without being shelled."[116] The Battle for Ortona was over.

"EVERYTHING BEFORE ORTONA WAS A NURSERY TALE," remarked Major-General Vokes.[117] The Canadian division suffered 2,339 casualties and 1,617 sick in the month of December, with all of the infantry battalion's rifle companies reduced by more than 50 percent.[118] Veteran soldiers were not easy to replace. The Canadians dug in for the winter and licked their wounds.

Padre Eldon Davis, a keen observer of the Canadian soldier, wrote, "Everyone was scared at the front.... Training and discipline will help most soldiers to carry out their duties in spite of their fears, but it doesn't alter the fact that everyone in their right mind is scared when bullets and shell fragments are flying and bombs and mines are exploding."[119] All soldiers were worn down by combat, of course, but also by lack of sleep, poor food, and exposure to harsh weather. Over time, these cumulative pressures eroded the will, eventually leading to physical and mental breakdowns. During and after the long Ortona battle, some 587 Canadians were diagnosed with battle exhaustion.[120] Captain R.R. Johnston, a twenty-three-year-old who served with the Canadian Field Artillery, noted, "Men must be watched for signs of strain, bad cases

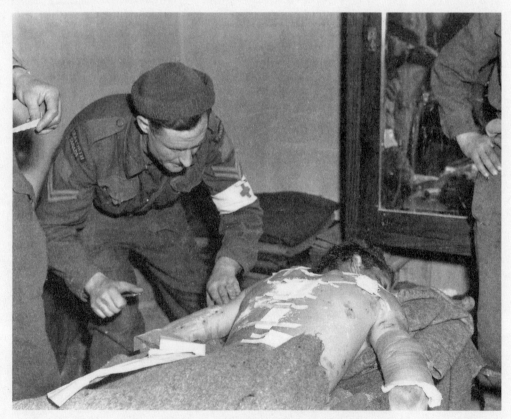

*Medical staff at a regimental aid post care for a wounded
Canadian whose back has been shredded by shrapnel.*

should be sent to the MO [medical officer] at once or sent to echelon," as the effect of their presence was detrimental to group morale.[121] The impending breakdown was often visible: broken bodies, bloodshot eyes, and lined faces; nightmares that left men moaning and screaming; chronic trembling and uncontrollable tics. The advanced cases mumbled gibberish, exposed themselves dangerously to enemy fire, developed paralyzed limbs, or slipped into a catatonic state. Similar mental wounds had been witnessed during the Great War, when the stress injury had been labelled "shell shock." A generation later, the military and medical profession had a better sense of how to treat most of the wounded. Much of the damage was caused by sleep deprivation. Rest stations were established close to the lines, where men were sedated and allowed to sleep for two or three days straight.[122] Many recovered sufficiently to return to the front. Others did not, the strain of battle having ravaged their minds.

Captain Strome Galloway of the RCRs wrote of the intense fighting from Sicily to Ortona. His regiment, like the others in the 1st Canadian Infantry Division, had been decimated. The battalion had landed 756 strong in Sicily, and less than half a year later, more than 550 originals had been killed, were wounded or missing, had been taken prisoner, or had fallen victim to malaria and jaundice. New men flooded the ranks and changed the culture of the regiment. The veterans tried to inculcate the spirit of the battalion into the new men but found they were a dying breed. "The Old Regiment had completely passed away," lamented Galloway. In fact, it would be destroyed several times more over the coming year and a half of fighting. But for the first veterans, Galloway noted, "Ortona was the watershed of the war."[123] Ortona had capped off the campaigning year—a brutal and mad battle for a town that no one in Canada had heard of. They knew of it now.

THE END OF
THE BEGINNING

The Battle of Ortona, wrote a Canadian corporal of the 48th Highlanders of Canada, "was like a raving madhouse."[1] The same could be said of the multiple night battles fought by the bomber crews who took their war birds over the burning German cities, evading the flak curling upward from the guns below; or of the Hurricane and Spitfire fighter pilots who held off the screaming Fw 190s; or of the weather-blasted sailors and merchant mariners who sailed through the U-boat gauntlet of the North Atlantic. Canadians in combat bore the pressure and paid the price in the worldwide war against Hitler and his forces.

The Western Allied strategy involved several interrelated but cascading campaigns that needed to be won before an Anglo-American invasion of Europe would be possible. The U-boats had to be defeated along the sea lanes to allow the uninterrupted movement of war supplies, food, and reinforcements to reach Britain and then, eventually, to support the Second Front in Europe. All other campaigns flowed from the victory at sea, and the Allies could not, for example, invade German-occupied France if the U-boats were mauling their ships in the Atlantic. Churchill and Roosevelt seemed to grasp this reality, but resources remained scarce for the naval and coastal air forces, due to competing demands for other strategic objectives, and this was never as apparent as it was when the warlords failed to allocate four-engine VLR bombers to close the Air Gap in the Atlantic. And so it fell to the navies to fight their desperate battles against the submarines from the first day of the war, until they finally turned the tide in May 1943, and then beyond, as they drove the U-boats back into European waters. The Canadian navy, which expanded more than thirty-three-fold during the course of the war to counter the threat posed by its enemies and meet the needs of its friends, played a heroic and at times desperate role in winning the Battle of the Atlantic. The U-boats did extraordinary damage and scored high-profile sinkings against them, but the Canadian navy never faltered in its unglamorous work. The litany of destruction obscured the reality that, even when the U-boat wolf packs were at their most pernicious, the vast majority of merchant navy vessels arrived safely at their destination. This steady infusion of goods kept Britain in the war and would allow, in 1944, for the cross-Channel invasion.

The second major strategic objective of the Western allies was to relieve the pressure on Stalin's beleaguered armies in the east. The battle on the Russian steppes was fought with unparalleled ferocity and savagery, as Hitler's forces carried out the Führer's genocidal policy of annihilation. Behind the deep Nazi military advances of 1941 came the Einsatzgruppen, death squads that targeted and murdered hundreds of thousands of Jews, Communists, and others they looked upon as undesirable or merely expendable. Stalin's forces barely survived the onslaught, yet counterattacked at Moscow in late 1941. A year later, at Stalingrad, they stopped the Germans for good. The tragic raid against Dieppe was a direct result of the need to relieve pressure on the east, although the operation was incompetently planned and revealed a disheartening degree of inter-service rivalry. The Canadians on the beaches, like their comrades in Hong Kong, were committed to battle to fulfill higher strategic objectives in the global war.

A critical component of the Second Front strategy was the bomber offensive against German cities. The survival of Britain had hinged on the fighters, the integrated radar system, and the dedicated expertise of ground crews during the Battle of Britain, but it was the bombers that allowed the Allies to take the war to the Nazi heartland. While the German economy was ill-prepared for an intensive war of attrition in 1941, productivity was steadily improved, industry was enlarged and made more effective, and slave labour was incorporated to feed the war machine. German production rose steadily in 1942 and the first half of 1943, but then all but flat-lined in the second half of the year. It was the full weight of the bomber offensive in 1943 that slowed production and undermined the German war effort. The modest high explosive payloads of the two-engine bombers in 1941 and 1942 were superseded in 1943 by hundreds of howling, death-dealing Lancasters and Halifaxes. For the civilians, war workers, and armed combatants on the ground, the terror was inescapable, and morale in the totalitarian state plummeted. The bomber crews paid for their nightly operations with crippling casualties, but they stood the course and the German cities and civilians that fed the Nazi armed forces suffered an appalling blitz that was unique in the history of human warfare.

But Germany was too strong to be defeated by anything less than continuous attacks across continents. The war in the air was one way to wear down the Nazi war effort, but it could not succeed on its own. Direct engagement with the German land forces was required. Although the war in the Soviet Union made the difference between victory and defeat, in the Middle East, the Eighth Army won and lost in see-saw battles until, by late 1942, the Germans were on their back heel and, with the assistance of American forces, were driven to capitulation in early 1943. While the Americans ached to begin their assault on Europe, even as they continued their victorious and relentless campaign in the Pacific to close in on Japan, Churchill held off his brash allies and succeeded in convincing them of the importance of first invading Sicily, and then undermining Germany's Fascist ally, Italy. It was on the inhospitable island of Sicily that the Canadian army fought in its first sustained operations of the war, save for the two battalions lost at Hong Kong. Brutal heat, clouds of dust, and malaria-carrying mosquitoes made for a cruel battlefield, and casualties were run up against a fierce and dedicated enemy. In every engagement the Germans held the best ground, but time and time again the Canadians bested them, killing, capturing, and driving them back. General Simonds's division made a name for itself in Sicily, and the Canadians continued to carry the battle to the enemy in Italy, their efforts culminating in the mud and misery of the Moro and the bloodstained streets of Ortona.

At home, by 1941 the Canadian economy was geared for the war effort. Full employment had been achieved as the nation supported its allies by turning out thousands of trucks, tanks, bombers, and weapons of war. Tens of thousands of Commonwealth flyers were trained across the Dominion, preparing them for the air battles over Europe. At the helm of the state was the unwarlike William Lyon

Mackenzie King, guiding his nation to greater exertions to support those on the battle front.

WAR IS ABOUT COMBAT AND DEATH. The warriors' first encounter with dead bodies led to a morbid fascination with the things that were once men and then a grim understanding that combat left the living broken, traumatized, and motionless forever. Death came in many ways. High explosive shells and bullets eviscerated bodies and tore off limbs. The frigid waters of the Atlantic killed men silently and left almost no trace. Death came in the dark sky, when fighters and bombers disappeared without warning. However it struck Canadians from 1939 to 1943, death came too often, decimating the young and shattering the hopes of the old. Despite the gathering losses, which numbered in the thousands—killed at sea, on land, and in the air—Canadians refused to be cowed. They fought on. And their fighting forces steadily improved. In war, amateurism kills soldiers, sailors, and airmen. Dieppe was a bungled mess. On the Atlantic, the merchant ships were hopeless victims if they did not sail in the complicated convoys, and even then it took years of training before the protective screen of warships could fight in a coordinated matter to hold off the U-boats. In the air war, sprog crews died on the first sortie—cannon fodder for the night fighters and flak. The Germans had a head start in established doctrine, tactics, and technology, and they proved to be extraordinarily good at fighting, whether on the offensive or in orderly retreat. They too had learned through failure, although earlier in the war. But the Canadians honed their combat skills and, by 1943, consistently drove the Axis formations back in battle.

The Canadians made their mark as an identifiable force, just as Prime Minister King had demanded at the beginning of the war. The corvettes, the cheap and nasties of the Atlantic, had been thrown against the U-boats in a lopsided battle. The destroyers were better suited for sub-hunting, but it was the corvettes that guided the merchant ships to safety, and the battered little corvettes best epitomized Canada's naval effort. Above the convoys were the Canso flying boats. Bloated, impossibly slow, but with enormous endurance, they helped the hard-pressed sailors hold off the wolf packs. Overseas, RCAF fighters and bombers defended Britain and took the war to Germany. In all services, the maple leaf and other Canadian badges were worn with pride. Ships' names and bombers' nose art reflected the connection of Canadians to their home cities and symbols. The culmination of Canada's growing status in the Allied air war was the creation of RCAF's 6 Group in January 1943. It is no small achievement that eventually a third of all of Bomber Command personnel were Canadians.[2] On land, the Canadians fought as identifiable units at Hong Kong, Dieppe, Sicily, and Italy, and by 1942 the First Canadian Army was the largest land formation ever raised in the Dominion's history. While Canadian service personnel were less interested in waving the flag than they were in simply surviving, over time an identity was hammered out, pride was forged, and a nation showed its mettle under duress.

How Canadians fought in battle has been the focus of much of this book. Picking through the entrails of combat is a bloody business. The Canadians faltered at times, but they were learning their grim art and finding ways to meet and defeat their opponents. "The Tommies will have to chew their way through us inch by inch and we will surely make hard chewing for them"—such was the determined sentiment of a German paratrooper killed at Salerno, his resilience captured in a letter found on his corpse.[3] His tough outlook epitomized the attitude of many German troops during the war. The Tommies, GIs, and Canucks, as well as all the other Allied fighting forces and men, were indeed chewing through the Germans on multiple fronts, and were no less determined in battle. There were few easy victories. While the full industrial might of the United States, Britain, and Canada was out-producing Germany by 1943, these material advantages still required the proper application of force on the battlefield and the intangible human spirit in combat. The tide had turned at sea and on some battlefields in the Mediterranean and the Soviet Union, but only the foolhardy or the naive were predicting an early victory. Many long and costly battles would be fought before Hitler's forces were driven back from the lands they had overrun. Sacrifices were demanded of all Canadians, but few doubted the justice of their cause as they sought to free millions of oppressed peoples and to end the horrific slaughter in a war of utter necessity.

ENDNOTES

INTRODUCTION: THE WAR AGAINST HITLER (PP. 1–11)

1. Mark Harrison, "The Economics of World War II: An Overview," in Mark Harrison (ed.) *The Economics of World War II: Six Great Powers in International Comparison* (Cambridge, 1998) 7, 8, 13. John Ellis, *Brute Force: Allied Strategy and Tactics in the Second World War* (New York: Viking, 1990). For a more complex analysis of victory, see Richard Overy, *Why the Allies Won* (London: Pimlico, 1995) and Paul Kennedy, *Engineers of Victory: The Problem Solvers Who Turned the Tide in the Second World War* (Toronto: HarperCollins, 2013).

2. For casualties by service, see C.P. Stacey, *Arms, Men and Governments: The War Policies of Canada, 1939–1945* (Ottawa: Queen's Printer, 1970) 66. Stacey calculates 42,042 deaths. Added to this are another 1,629 Canadian and Newfoundland merchant mariners who lost their lives. See W.A.B. Douglas, Roger Sarty, and Michael Whitby, *No Higher Purpose: The Official Operational History of the Royal Canadian Navy in the Second World War, 1939–1943* (St. Catharines: Vanwell, 2002) 634.

3. Barney Danson, *Not Bad for a Sergeant: The Memoirs of Barney Danson* (Toronto: Dundurn, 2002) 10.

4. Roger Sarty, "Uncle Bill's Service in Bomber Command, 1942–1944, Family Memory and the Written Record," *Canadian Military History* 15.3&4 (Summer–Autumn, 2006) 94–5.

5. Thomas G. Lynch (ed.), *Fading Memories: Canadian Sailors and the Battle of the Atlantic* (Halifax: Atlantic Chief and Petty Officers Association, 1993) 178.

6. Barbara Dundas, *A History of Women in the Canadian Military* (Montreal: Art Global, 2000) 52.

7. J.L. Granatstein, *Canada's Army: Waging War and Keeping the Peace* (Toronto: University of Toronto Press, 1993) 191.

8. Dominion Institute, The Memory Project, interview, Yvonne Jukes.

9. Carolyn Gossage, *Greatcoats and Glamour Boots: Canadian Women at War (1939–1945)* (Toronto: Dundurn, 1991) 127.

10. See Jeffrey A. Keshen, *Saints, Sinners and Soldiers: Canada's Second World War* (Vancouver: UBC Press, 2004) 178–9; Ruth Russell, *Proudly She Marched: Training Canada's World War II*

Women in Waterloo, Volume I: Canadian Women's Army Corps (Kitchener: Canadian Federation of University Women, 2006) 45–6, 50; Quote from Gossage, *Greatcoats and Glamour Boots,* 47.

11. Canadian War Museum [hereafter CWM] oral history interview, 31D 5 FLEMING, page 7.

12. Bill McNeil, *Voices of a War Remembered: An Oral History of Canadians in World War Two* (Toronto: Doubleday Canada, 1991) 31–2.

13. McNeil, *Voices of a War Remembered,* 37.

14. See Cynthia Toman, *An Officer and a Lady: Canadian Military Nursing and the Second World War* (Vancouver: UBC Press, 2007).

15. See Ruth Roach Pierson, *They're Still Women after All: Canadian Women and the Second World War* (Toronto: McClelland & Stewart, 1986).

16. Stanley Scislowski, *Not All of Us Were Brave* (Toronto: Dundurn, 1997) 11.

CHAPTER 1: RELUCTANTLY TO WAR (PP. 13–30)

1. See Margaret MacMillan, *The War That Ended Peace: The Road to 1914* (London: Penguin, 2013); Christopher Clark, *The Sleepwalkers: How Europe Went to War in 1914* (London: Harper, 2013).

2. On inflation, see Richard J. Evans, *The Third Reich in Power* (London: Penguin, 2005) 5.

3. On veterans, see Deborah Cohen, *The War Come Home: Disabled Veterans in Britain and Germany, 1914–1939* (Berkeley: University of California Press, 2001).

4. Ian Kershaw, *Hitler, 1936–1945: Nemesis* (New York: W.W. Norton, 2000) xliii.

5. See Richard Bessel, *Political Violence and the Rise of Nazism: The Storm Troopers in Eastern Germany, 1925–1934* (Yale: Yale University Press, 1984); Ian Kershaw, *The "Hitler Myth": Image and Reality in the Third Reich* (Oxford: Oxford University Press, 1987).

6. On Great War tactics and fighting, see Bill Rawling, *Surviving Trench Warfare: Technology and the Canadian Corps, 1914–1918* (Toronto: University of Toronto Press, 1992) and Tim Cook, *Shock Troops: Canadians Fighting the Great War, 1917–1918, volume II* (Toronto: Viking, 2008).

7. Timothy Snyder, *Bloodlands: Europe between Hitler and Stalin* (New York: Basic Books, 2010) 53, 81.

8. Robert Bothwell and John English, "'Dirty Work at the Crossroads': New Perspectives on the Riddell Incident," *Historical Papers* 7.1 (1972); Brock Millman, "Canada, Sanctions and the Abyssinian Crisis of 1935," *The Historical Journal* 40.1 (March 1997).

9. See James S. Corum, *The Roots of Blitzkrieg: Hans von Seeckt and German Military Reform* (Lawrence: University Press of Kansas, 1992).

10. Robert H. Whealey, *Hitler and Spain: The Nazi Role in the Spanish Civil War, 1936–1939* (Lexington: University of Kentucky Press, 1989).

11. Jurgen Forster, "From 'Blitzkrieg' to 'Total War': Germany's War in Europe," in Roger Chickering, Stig Förster, and Bernd Greiner (eds.) *A World at Total War: Global Conflict and the Politics of Destruction, 1937–1945* (Cambridge: Cambridge University Press, 2005) 96.

12. Williamson Murray and Allan R. Millett, *A War to Be Won: Fighting the Second World War* (Cambridge: Harvard University Press, 2000) 13.

13. Max Hastings, *All Hell Let Loose: The World at War (1939–45)* (London: HarperCollins, 2012) 14.

14. *Democracy at War: Canadian Newspapers and the Second World War:* The Hamilton Spectator *and Its Archive*, 4 September 1939, www.warmuseum.ca/cwm/exhibitions/newspapers/hamilton_e.shtml.

15. Tim Cook, *Shock Troops: Canadians Fighting the Great War, 1917–1918, volume II* (Toronto: Viking, 2008) 611–20.

16. J.L. Granatstein and J.M. Hitsman, *Broken Promises: A History of Conscription in Canada* (Toronto: Oxford University Press, 1977).

17. J.L. Granatstein and Robert Bothwell, "'A Self-Evident National Duty': Canadian Foreign Policy, 1935–1939," *Journal of Imperial and Commonwealth History* 3 (1975), 222.

18. S.W. Dziuban, *The Military Relations between the United States and Canada, 1939–1945* (Washington: United States Army in the World War II, Special Studies, 1959) 4.

19. Desmond Morton, *A Military History of Canada*: *From Champlain to Kosovo*, Fourth Edition (Toronto: McClelland & Stewart, 1999) 178.

20. Roger Sarty, "Mr. King and the Armed Forces," in Norman Hillmer, et al. (eds.), *A Country of Limitations: Canada and the World in 1939* (Ottawa: Canadian Committee for the History of the Second World War, 1996) 217–46.

21. J.L. Granatstein, *The Last Good War: An Illustrated History of Canada in the Second World War, 1939–1945* (Vancouver: Douglas & McIntyre, 2005) 6; Library and Archives Canada [hereafter LAC], digitized diary, William Lyon Mackenzie King personal diary, 14 November 1938 [hereafter "King diary"].

22. John Marteinson and Michael R. McNorgan, *The Royal Canadian Armoured Corps* (Toronto: Robin Brass, 2000) 77–8.

23. House of Commons debates [hereafter Hansard], 30 March 1939.

24. See Terry Copp, "Ontario 1939: The Decision for War," *Ontario History* 86.3 (1994) 269–78.

25. On guiding Canada into the war, see Lita-Rose Betcherman, *Ernest Lapointe: Mackenzie King's Great Quebec Lieutenant* (Toronto: University of Toronto Press, 2002); King diary, 1–10 September 1939; Tim Cook, *Warlords: Borden, Mackenzie King, and Canada's World Wars* (Toronto: Allen Lane, 2012) 208–13.

26. See Irving Abella and Harold Troper, *None Is Too Many: Canada and the Jews of Europe, 1933–1948* (Toronto: Lester & Orpen Dennys, 1982).

27. J.K. Chapman, *River Boy at War* (Fredericton: Goose Lane, 1985) 11–13.

28. Robert Crozier, *Looking Backward: A Memoir* (self-published, 1998) viii.

29. Gordon Brown and Terry Copp, *Look to Your Front ... Regina Rifles: A Regiment at War, 1944–1945* (Waterloo: Laurier Centre for Military Strategic and Disarmament Studies, 2001) 4.

30. Terry Copp, *Fields of Fire: The Canadians in Normandy* (Toronto: University of Toronto Press, 2003) 15–16.

31. See Jonathan F. Vance, "Understanding the Motive to Enlist," in Sherrill Grace, et al. (eds.), *Bearing Witness: Perspectives on War and Peace from the Arts and Humanities* (Montreal and Kingston: McGill-Queen's University Press, 2012) 28–40.

32. Mathias Joost, "Racism and Enlistment: The Second World War Policies of the Royal Canadian Air Force," *Canadian Military History* 21.1 (Winter 2012) 17–19, 22.

33. Scott Sheffield, "Fighting a White Man's War?": First Nations Participation in the Canadian War Effort, 1939–1945," Geoffrey Hayes, et al. (eds.), *Canada and the Second World War: Essays in Honour of Terry Copp* (Waterloo: Wilfrid Laurier Press, 2012) 71.

34. Whitney Lackenbauer, "'A Hell of a Warrior': Remembering Sergeant Thomas George Prince," *Journal of Historical Biography* 1 (Spring 2007) 31.

35. Cynthia Commacchio, "'To Hold on High the Torch of Liberty': Canadian Youth and the Second World War," in Geoffrey Hayes, et al. (eds.), *Canada and the Second World War: Essays in Honour of Terry Copp* (Waterloo: Wilfrid Laurier Press, 2012) 35–6.

36. George S. MacDonell, *One Soldier's Story (1939–1945) From the Fall of Hong Kong to the Defeat of Japan* (Toronto: Dundurn, 2002) 3, 6.

37. Ian Miller, "Toronto's Response to the Outbreak of War, 1939," *Canadian Military History* 11.1 (Winter 2002) 10–11.

38. David J. Bercuson, *The Patricias: The Proud History of a Fighting Regiment* (Toronto: Stoddart, 2001) 152.

39. Terry Copp, *No Price Too High: Canadians and the Second World War* (Toronto: McGraw-Hill Ryerson, 1996) 39.

40. C.P. Stacey, *Six Years of War: The Army in Canada, Britain and the Pacific* (Ottawa: Queen's Printer, 1955) 34.

41. Stephen J. Harris, *Canadian Brass: The Making of a Professional Army, 1860–1939* (Toronto: University of Toronto Press, 1998).

42. Stacey, *Six Years of War*, 50; Jonathan Vance, *Maple Leaf Empire: Britain, Canada, and the Two World Wars* (Don Mills: Oxford University Press, 2011) 149.

43. Robert Bryce, *Canada and the Cost of World War II: The International Operations of Canada's Department of Finance, 1939–1947* (Montreal and Kingston: McGill-Queen's University Press, 2005) 22–3; King diary, 18 September 1939.

CHAPTER 2: THE FALL OF FRANCE (PP. 31–44)

1. Halik Kochanski, *The Eagle Unbowed: Poland and the Poles in the Second World War* (London: Allen Lane, 2012) 84. Also see Alex B. Rossino, *Hitler Strikes Poland: Blitzkrieg, Ideology, and Atrocity* (Lawrence: University Press of Kansas, 2003).

2. Kochanski, *The Eagle Unbowed*, 105.

3. On King's cabinet, see J.L. Granatstein, *Canada's War: The Politics of the Mackenzie King Government, 1939–1945* (Toronto: Oxford University Press, 1975).

4. *Toronto Daily Star*, 18 January 1940.

5. For the campaign, see J. Murray Beck, *Pendulum of Power: Canada's Federal Elections* (Scarborough: Prentice-Hall of Canada, 1968) 223–40.

6. Brown and Copp, *Look to Your Front*, 3, 7.

7. John Marteinson (ed.), *We Stand on Guard: An Illustrated History of the Canadian Army* (Montreal: Ovale Publications, 1992) 227.

8. Bercuson, *The Patricias*, 157.

9. LAC, RG24, National Defence, v. 13721, "Report on a Press Clipping," December 1939.

10. LAC, RG24, National Defence, v. 6917, CMHQ Report No. 51, "Censorship of Mail, Canadian Army Overseas. Field Censors' Notes as Material for History," 31 October 1941.

11. Melynda Jarratt, *War Brides: The Stories of the Women Who Left Everything Behind to Follow the Men They Loved* (Toronto: Dundurn, 2009) 15.

12. Michael Pearson Cessford, *Hard in the Attack: The Canadian Army in Sicily and Italy, July 1943–June 1944* (Ph.D. dissertation, Carleton University, 1996) 29.

13. R.H. Roy, *The Seaforth Highlanders of Canada, 1919–1965* (Vancouver: The Seaforth Highlanders of Canada, 1969) 78.

14. Adam Tooze, *The Wages of Destruction: The Making and Breaking of the Nazi Economy* (London: Allen Lane, 2006) 371.

15. For the failure of the French army, see Robert Doughty, *The Seeds of Disaster: The Development of French Army Doctrine, 1919–1939* (Hamden: Archon Books, 1985); and Eugenia C. Kiesling, *Arming Against Hitler: France and Limits of Military Planning* (Lawrence: University Press of Kansas, 1996).

16. Karl-Heinz Frieser (with J.T. Greenwood), *The Blitzkrieg Legend: The 1940 Campaign in the West* (Annapolis, MD: Naval Institute Press, 2005) 90.

17. For the campaign, see Julian Jackson, *The Fall of France: The Nazi Invasion of 1940* (Oxford: Oxford University Press, 2003).

18. CWM oral history interview, 31D 1 NIXON, page 6.

19. King diary, 23 and 24 May 1940.

20. Norman Gelb, *Dunkirk* (New York: William Morrow and Company, 1989) 309; and W.J.R. Gardner (ed.), *The Evacuation from Dunkirk: Operation Dynamo, 26 May–4 June 1940* (London: Frank Cass, 2000).

21. See Martin S. Alexander, "After Dunkirk: The French Army's Performance against 'Case Red', 25 May to 25 June 1940," *War In History* 14.2 (April 2007) 219–264; Hastings, *All Hell Let Loose*, 67.

22. J.L. Granatstein, *Canada's Army: Waging War and Keeping the Peace* (Toronto: University of Toronto Press, 2002) 262.

23. CWM, 1982624-001, Composition of Advance Party, no date.

24. Alta R. Wilkinson (ed.), *Ottawa to Caen: Letters from Arthur Campbell Wilkinson* (Ottawa: Tower Books, 1947) 24.

25. See various reports in LAC, RG 24, v. 10854, 232.C1 (D8).

26. G.W.L. Nicholson, *The Gunners of Canada: The History of the Royal Regiment of Canadian Artillery*, volume II (Toronto: McClelland & Stewart, 1967) 72.

27. Ashley Jackson, *The British Empire and the Second World War* (New York: Hambledon Continuum, 2006) 1.

28. Daniel Byers, "Mobilising Canada: The National Resources Mobilization Act, the Department of National Defence, and Compulsory Military Service in Canada, 1940–1945," *Journal of the Canadian Historical Association* 7.1 (1996); C.P. Stacey, *Arms, Men and Governments: The War Policies of Canada, 1939–1945* (Ottawa: Queen's Printer, 1970) 33–4.

CHAPTER 3: THE BATTLE OF BRITAIN (PP. 45–58)

1. Hugh Halliday, *No. 242 Squadron: The Canadian Years* (Stittsville: Canada's Wings, 1981) 17–18.

2. Wayne Ralph, *Aces, Warriors & Wingmen: Firsthand Accounts of Canada's Fighter Pilots in the Second World War* (Mississauga: John Wiley & Sons, 2005) 69.

3. Halliday, *No. 242 Squadron*, 37–8.

4. See David Ian Hall, *Strategy for Victory: The Development of British Tactical Air Power, 1919–1943* (Westport, CT: Praeger Security International, 2008); Ian Gooderson, *Air Power at the Battlefront: Allied Close Air Support in Europe 1943–45* (Routledge, 1998) 23–4.

5. *The Canadians at War 1939/45* (Montreal: Reader's Digest, 1969) 40.

6. Hastings, *All Hell Let Loose*, 72.

7. See Fred Pollock, "Roosevelt, the Ogdensburg Agreement, and the British Fleet: All Done with Mirrors," *Diplomatic History* 5 (1981) 203–19.

8. See David Reynolds, "Churchill and the British 'Decision' to Fight on in 1940: Right Policy, Wrong Reasons," in R. Langhorne (ed.), *Diplomacy and Intelligence during the Second World War* (Cambridge: Cambridge University Press, 1985) 147–67.

9. See Anthony J. Cumming, *The Royal Navy and the Battle of Britain* (Annapolis, MD: Naval Institute Press, 2010).

10. Robert Jackson, *Before the Storm: The Story of Bomber Command, 1939–1942* (London: Cassell & Co., 2001 [original 1972]) 117.

11. P.M.H. Bell, *Twelve Turning Points of the Second World War* (New Haven: Yale University Press, 2011) 21; Copp, *No Price Too High*, 48.

12. John Terraine, *The Right of the Line: The Royal Air Force in the European War, 1939–1945* (London: Hodder and Stoughton, 1985) 194.

13. Air Ministry, Air Historical Branch, *The Rise and Fall of the German Air Force* (London: HMSO, 1983) 80.

14. Robert Bracken, *Spitfire: The Canadians* (Erin: The Boston Mills Press, 1995) 11.

15. Brereton Greenhous and Hugh A. Halliday, *Canada's Air Forces, 1914–1999* (Montreal: Art Global, 1999) 59–60.

16. Richard Collier, *Eagle Day: The Battle of Britain* (London: Sphere, 1981) 128.

17. Arthur Bishop, *The Splendid Hundred: The True Story of Canadians Who Flew in the Greatest Air Battle of World War II* (Toronto: McGraw-Hill Ryerson, 1994) 40.

18. Jean Portugal, *We Were There: A Record for Canada*, volume 7 (Shelburne: The Royal Canadian Military Institute Heritage Society, 1998) 3239.

19. David Bashow, *All the Fine Young Eagles: In the Cockpit with Canada's Second World War Fighter Pilots* (Toronto: Stoddart, 1997) 25.

20. Granatstein, *The Last Good War*, 42.

21. Horst Boog, "The Luftwaffe's Assault," in Paul Addison and Jeremy A. Crang (eds.), *The Burning Blue: A New History of the Battle of Britain* (London: Pimlico, 2000) 48.

22. Brian Bond, "Introduction," in Paul Addison and Jeremy A. Crang (eds.), *The Burning Blue: A New History of the Battle of Britain* (London: Pimlico, 2000) 11.

23. On heroes, see Garry Campion in *The Good Fight: Battle of Britain Propaganda and the Few* (Basingstoke: Palgrave, 2009).

24. Steven Casey, *Cautious Crusade: Franklin D. Roosevelt, American Public Opinion, and the War Against Nazi Germany* (Oxford: Oxford University Press, 2001) 26.

25. Hastings, *All Hell Let Loose*, 187.

26. Tami Davis Biddle, *Rhetoric and Reality in Air Warfare: The Evolution of British and American Ideas about Strategic Bombing, 1914–1945* (Princeton: Princeton University Press, 2002); Phillip S. Meilinger, "Trenchard and 'Morale Bombing': The Evolution of Royal Air Force Doctrine Before World War II" *The Journal of Military History* 60.2 (1996); Tim Cook, "Against God-Inspired Conscience: Perceptions of Gas Warfare as a Weapon of Mass Destruction, 1915–1939," *War & Society* 18.1 (May 2000) 47–69.

27. Keith Lowe, *Inferno: The Fiery Destruction of Hamburg, 1943* (New York: Scribner, 2007) 52; Patrick Bishop, *Bomber Boys: Fighting Back, 1940–1945* (London: Harper, 2007) 74. Also see Juliet Gardner, *The Blitz: The British Under Attack* (London: Harper, 2012).

CHAPTER 4: THE WAR IN THE FAR EAST (PP. 59–94)

1. On trucks, see Graham Broad, "Not Competent to Produce Tanks: The Ram and Tank Production in Canada, 1939–1945," *Canadian Military History* 11.1 (Winter 2002) 26.

2. Paul Marsden, "The Costs of No Commitments: Canadian Economic Planning for War," in Norman Hillmer, et al. (eds.), *A Country of Limitations: Canada and the World in 1939* (Canadian Committee for the History of the Second World War, 1996) 199–216; Robert Bothwell, "'Who's Paying for Anything These Days?' War Production in Canada, 1939–1945," in N.F. Dreisziger (ed.), *Mobilization for Total War* (Waterloo: Wilfrid Laurier University Press, 1981); Robert Bothwell and William Kilbourn, *C.D. Howe: A Biography* (Toronto: McClelland & Stewart, 1979).

3. See Graham Broad, *A Small Price to Pay: Consumer Culture on the Canadian Home Front, 1939–45* (Vancouver: UBC Press, 2013).

4. Galen Perras, *Franklin Roosevelt and the Origins of the Canadian-American Security Alliance, 1933–1945* (Westport: Greenwood Press, 1998) 1–23.

5. For the ramifications, see Colonel C.P. Stacey, "The Canadian-American Permanent Joint Board on Defence, 1940–1945," *International Journal* 9.2 (Spring 1954) 107–24; Stacey, *Arms, Men and Governments*, 489–90.

6. Geoffrey P. Megargee, *Inside Hitler's High Command* (Lawrence: University of Kansas Press, 2000) 87.

7. Gerhard L. Weinberg, *Germany, Hitler, and World War II* (Cambridge: Cambridge University Press, 1995) 160.

8. Tooze, *The Wages of Destruction*, 424.

9. John Erickson, *The Soviet High Command: A Military-Political History, 1918–1941* (London: Macmillan, 1962) 506; Snyder, *Bloodlands*, 117.

10. Megargee, *Inside Hitler's High Command*, 112–4.

11. For Stalin's plans, see Viktor Suvorov, *The Chief Culprit: Stalin's Grand Design to Start World War II* (Annapolis: Naval Institute Press, 2008).

12. See William R. Trotter, *A Frozen Hell: The Russo-Finnish Winter War of 1939–1940* (Chapel Hill: Algonquin Books of Chapel Hill, 1991).

13. MacGregor Knox, *Hitler's Italian Allies: Royal Armed Forces, Fascist Regime, and the War of 1940–1943* (Cambridge: Cambridge University Press, 2000) 18–20.

14. Charles Burdick and Hans-Adolf Jacobsen (eds.), *The Halder War Diary, 1939–1942* (Novato: Presidio, 1988) 244.

15. Evans, *The Third Reich*, 175.

16. R.L. DiNardo, *Mechanized Juggernaut or Military Anachronism? Horses and the German Army of World War II* (New York: Greenwood Press, 1991) 35–54.

17. For the failure of the German army in planning Barbarossa, see David Stahel, *Operation Typhoon: Hitler's March on Moscow, October 1941* (Cambridge: Cambridge University Press, 2013).

18. For the German army, see Omer Bartov, *The Eastern Front 1941–1945: German Troops and the Barbarisation of Warfare* (Basingstoke: Palgrave Macmillan, 2001) and Stephen G. Fritz, *Ostkrieg: Hitler's War of Extermination in the East* (Lexington: University Press of Kentucky, 2011).

19. Hans-Neinrich Nolte, "Partisan War in Belorussa, 1941–1944," in Chickering, et al., *A World at Total War: Global Conflict and the Politics of Destruction, 1937–1945* (Cambridge: Cambridge University Press, 2005) 275.

20. Tooze, *The Wages of Destruction*, 481; and see C.R. Browning, *The Origins of the Final Solution: The Evolution of Nazi Jewish Policy, September 1939–March 1942* (Lincoln: University of Nebraska Press, 2004).

21. Stig Forster and Myriam Gessler, "The Ultimate Horror: Reflections on Total War and Genocide," in Chickering, et al., *A World at Total War: Global Conflict and the Politics of Destruction, 1937–1945* (Cambridge: Cambridge University Press, 2005) 66.

22. See Gotz Aly, et al., *Cleansing the Fatherland: Nazi Medicine and Racial Hygiene* (Baltimore: Hopkins Fulfillment Service, 1994).

23. Richard J. Overy, *Russia's War: A History of the Soviet War Effort, 1941–1945* (London: Penguin, 1997) 117; Omer Bartov, *Hitler's Army: Soldiers, Nazis, and War in the Third Reich* (New York: Oxford University Press, 1991) 87; Snyder, *Bloodlands*, 175–7; Evans, *The Third Reich at War*, 184–5.

24. See Klaus Reinhardt, *Moscow—The Turning Point: The Failure of Hitler's Strategy in the Winter of 1941–42* (Oxford: Berg, 1992).

25. Evans, *The Third Reich at War*, 214.

26. Mark R. Peattie, Edward J. Drea, and Hans J. van de Ven (eds.), *The Battle for China: Essays on the Military History of the Sino-Japanese War of 1937–1945* (Stanford: Stanford University Press, 2010) 115.

27. Sheldon H. Harris, *Factories of Death: Japanese Biological Warfare 1932–45 and the American Cover-Up* (Northridge: California State University, 1994).

28. For the importance of Hong Kong as a primary port for the Chinese army, see Franco David Macri, *Clash of Empires in South China: The Allied Nations' Proxy War with Japan, 1935–1941* (Lawrence: University Press of Kansas, 2012) 124.

29. Kent Fedorowich, "'Cocked Hats and Swords and Small, Little Garrisons': Britain, Canada and the Fall of Hong Kong, 1941," *Modern Asian Studies* 37 (February 2003) 133.

30. Galen Roger Perras, "'Our position in the Far East would be stronger without this unsatisfactory commitment': Britain and the Reinforcement of Hong Kong, 1941," *Canadian Journal of History* 30.2 (1995) 232–59; Christopher M. Bell, "'Our most exposed outpost': Hong Kong and British Far Eastern Strategy, 1921–1941," *Journal of Military History* 60.1 (1996) 61–88.

31. For Canadian strategy in the Pacific, see Timothy Wilford, *Canada's Road to the Pacific War: Intelligence, Strategy, and the Far East Crisis* (Vancouver: UBC Press, 2011); Stacey, *Six Years of War*, 442; Macri, *Clash of Empires in South China: The Allied Nations' Proxy War with Japan, 1935–1941*, 273–85.

32. Paul Dickson, "Crerar and the Decision to Reinforce Hong Kong," *Canadian Military History* 2.1 (Spring 1994) 102.

33. Richard J. Aldrich, *Intelligence and the War against Japan: Britain, America and the Politics of Secret Service* (Cambridge: Cambridge University Press, 2000) 19–67.

34. See Terry Copp, "The Decision to Reinforce Hong Kong, September 1941," *Canadian Military History* 20.2 (Spring 2011) 9–12.

35. Hong Kong Veterans Commemorative Association, "Vince Calder's Story," 1, www.hkvca.ca.

36. George S. MacDonell, *One Soldier's Story, 1939–1945* (Toronto: Dundurn, 2002) 16.

37. Reader's Digest, *The Canadians at War, 1939/45* (Montreal: Reader's Digest Association, 1986) 124. On deficiencies in defence, see David Macri (ed.), "The Fall of Hong Kong: The Condon Report," *Canadian Military History* 20.2 (Spring 2011) 65.

38. Terry Copp, "The Defence of Hong Kong, December 1941," *Canadian Military History* 10.4 (Autumn 2001) 10.

39. Oliver Lindsay, *The Lasting Honour: The Fall of Hong Kong, 1941* (London: Hamilton, 1978) 13.

40. Tony Banham, *Not the Slightest Chance: The Defence of Hong Kong, 1941* (Vancouver: UBC Press, 2003) 337, note 13.

41. John Dover, *War without Mercy: Race and Power in the Pacific War* (New York: Pantheon Books, 1986); S.W. Kirby, *The War Against Japan, Volume 1: The Loss of Singapore* (London: HMSO, 1957) 116; Directorate of History and Heritage, Ottawa [hereafter DHH], 503/D33, Lieutenant-Colonel George Trist, Report on the Part Played by the Winnipeg Grenadiers in the Defence of Hong Kong, North Point Camp, April 1942.

42. British Broadcasting Corporation [hereafter BBC], *WW2 People's War*, Maurice Parker Memoir, A4642887, no page.

43. See Alan D. Zimm, *Attack on Pearl Harbor: Strategy, Combat, Myths, Deceptions* (Philadelphia: Casement, 2011) for recent scholarship into the multiple debates and myths surrounding the battle.

44. Hong Kong Veterans Commemorative Association, "Alfred Babin's Story," no pagination, www.hkvca.ca.

45. Kirby, *The War against Japan, Volume 1*, 468.

46. Leo Paul Berard, *17 Days until Christmas* (self-published, 1997) 67.

47. Hong Kong Veterans Commemorative Association, *Bob Clayton's Story*, no pagination, www.hkvca.ca.

48. BBC, *WW2 People's War*, Maurice Parker Memoir, A4643255, no page.

49. Berard, *17 Days until Christmas*, 75.

50. DHH, 593.013 (D10), Colonel Doi's Battle Progress Report, 9–10.

51. DHH, 593 (D26), Notes on Interview, Major Nicholson with Lieutenant-Colonel H.B. Rose, 8 & 9 June 1946, page 2.

52. Major Kenneth G. Baird, *Letters to Harvelyn: From Japanese POW Camps: A Father's Letters to His Young Daughter during World War II* (Toronto: HarperCollins, 2002) 21.

53. DHH, Hong Kong Honours and Awards file, E.I. Bennett.

54. Carl Vincent, *No Reason Why: The Canadian Hong Kong Tragedy—An Examination* (Stittsville: Canada's Wings, 1981) 153.

55. Hong Kong Veterans Commemorative Association, "Tom Marsh" [memoir], Chapter 4, "War in Earnest," no pagination, www.hkvca.ca.

56. Brereton Greenhous, *"C" Force to Hong Kong: A Canadian Catastrophe, 1941–1945* (Toronto: Dundurn, 1997) 82–3.

57. Daniel Dancocks, *In Enemy Hands: Canadian Prisoners of War, 1939–45* (Edmonton: Hurtig, 1983) 223–4.

58. Hong Kong Veterans Commemorative Association, "William Bell's Story—Battle and Capture," no pagination, www.hkvca.ca.

59. Cameron Pulsifer, "John Robert Osborn: Canada's Hong Kong VC," *Canadian Military History* 6.2 (Autumn 1997) 79–89.

60. MacDonell, *This Soldier's Story* (1939–1945), 33.

61. Banham, *Not the Slightest Chance*, 121.

62. Nathan Greenfield, *The Damned: The Canadians at the Battle of Hong Kong and the POW Experience, 1941–45* (Toronto: HarperCollins, 2010) 56; Copp, *No Price Too High*, 75.

63. See Tyler Wentzell, "Brigadier J.K. Lawson and Command of 'C' Force at Hong Kong," *Canadian Military History* 20.2 (Spring 2011) 15.

64. Banham, *Not the Slightest Chance*, 318.

65. Vincent, *No Reason Why*, 203–4.

66. Stacey, *Six Years of War*, 482.

67. Oliver Lindsay, *At the Going Down of the Sun: Hong Kong and South-East Asia*, 1941–1945 (London: Hamish Hamilton Ltd, 1981) 236.

68. Reader's Digest, *The Canadians at War, 1939/45* (1986) 112.

69. BBC, *WW2 People's War*, Maurice Parker Memoir, A4643255, no page.

70. Nathan Greenfield, *The Damned: Canadians at the Battle of Hong Kong and the POW Experience, 1941–45*, (Toronto: HarperCollins, 2010) 163–4; Copp, "The Defence of Hong Kong, December 1941," 17.

71. Fedorowich, "'Cocked Hats and Swords and Small, Little Garrisons,'" 153.

72. Extract from the Report of the Historical Section, Cabinet Office, London, cited in *Canadian Military History* 2.2. (Autumn 1993) 113.

73. Winston Churchill, *The Grand Alliance* (Boston: Houghton Mifflin Company, 1950) 635.

74. Greenfield, *The Damned*, 218.

75. CWM, 20080086-001, Raymond Elliot, diary, 25 December 1941.

76. Hong Kong Veterans Commemorative Association, "Vince Calder's Account," no pagination, www.hkvca.ca.

77. Stacey, *Six Years of War*, 479.

78. CWM, 20050094-002, War Diary and Letters of A. Ray Squire, letter 22 February 1942.

79. Copp, *No Price Too High*, 76.

80. "Report by Miss Kathleen G Christie, Nurse with the Canadian Forces at Hong Kong, as given on board SS Gripsholm, November 1943," *Canadian Military History* 10.4 (Autumn 2001) 30; Patricia Roy, et al., *Mutual Hostages: Canadians and Japanese during the Second World War* (Toronto: University of Toronto Press, 1990) 68.

81. Hong Kong Veterans Commemorative Association, "Alfred Babin's Story," no pagination; and Ibid., "Bob Clayton's Story," no pagination, www.hkvca.ca.

82. Bill McNeil, *Voices of a War Remembered: An Oral History of Canadians in World War Two* (Toronto: Doubleday Canada, 1991) 101.

83. Dancocks, *In Enemy Hands*, 227.

84. Stacey, *Six Years of War*, 488.

85. Lawrence Lai Wai-Chung, "The Battle of Hong Kong: A Note on the Literature and the Effectiveness of Defence," *Journal of the Royal Asiatic Society Hong Kong Branch*, 39 (1999) 123–7.

86. Greenhous, *"C" Force*, 98.

87. Hong Kong Veterans Commemorative Association, "William Bell's Story—Prisoner of War," no pagination, www.hkvca.ca.

88. CWM, 20050094-002, War Diary of A. Ray Squire, 29 March 1942.

89. Berard, *17 Days until Christmas*, 121.

90. CWM, 19950077-001, John Oliver Payne, letter to mother, 19 August 1942.

91. Dancocks, *In Enemy Hands*, 234.

92. Berard, *17 Days until Christmas*, 141.

93. CWM, D.L. Welsh, 19810684-004, diary, last entry.

94. Hong Kong Veterans Commemorative Association, "Vince Calder's Story," no pagination, www.hkvca.ca.

95. CWM, MHRC, J.N. Crawford, "A Medical Officer in Hong Kong" (1946), 7.

96. Dancocks, *In Enemy Hands*, 238.

97. MacDonell, *One Soldier's Story*, 52.

98. Leonard Corrigan, *A Hong Kong Diary Revisited: The Family Remembers* (Baltimore, Ontario: Frei Press, 2008) 191.

99. LAC, A.G.L. McNaughton papers, MG 30 E133, v. 141, file 3-3-1, Conditions in Hong Kong P/W Camps, 4 July 1943.

100. Hong Kong Veterans Commemorative Association, "William Bell's Story—Japan and Camp 3D," no pagination, www.hkvca.ca.

101. CWM, MHRC, J.N. Crawford, "A Medical Officer in Hong Kong," (1946) 6.

102. CWM, 19830038-001, Donald Geraghty, diary, page 14 [October 1942].

103. MacDonell, *One Soldier's Story*, 51.

104. Patrick Brode, *Casual Slaughter and Accidental Judgements: Canadian War Crime Prosecutions, 1944–1948* (Toronto: Osgoode Hall, 1997) 173.

105. For Wallis's account, see Greenfield, *The Damned*, Appendix II, 385–92. For one of the Canadian responses, see DHH, 503 (D33), Lieutenant-Colonel George Trist, Report on the Part Played by the Winnipeg Grenadiers in the Defence of Hong Kong, North Point Camp, April 1942.

106. Carl Vincent, *No Reason Why: The Canadian Hong Kong Tragedy* (Stittsville: Canada's Wings, 1981) 228.

107. Baird, *Letters to Harvelyn*, 180.

108. Mark Bourrie, *The Fog of War: Censorship of Canada's Media in World War Two* (Vancouver: Douglas and McIntyre, 2011) 142–55.

109. Ken Adachi, *The Enemy That Never Was: A History of the Japanese Canadians*, 2nd edition (Toronto: McClelland & Stewart, 1991); Stephanie Bangarth, *Voices Raised in Protest: Defending North American Citizens of Japanese Ancestry, 1942–49* (Vancouver: UBC Press, 2008).

110. For the Hong Kong historiography, see Galen Perras, "Defeat Still Cries Aloud for Explanation: Explaining C Force's Dispatch to Hong Kong," *Canadian Military Journal* 11.4 (Autumn 2011) 37–47.

111. Colin Smith, *Singapore Burning: Heroism and Surrender in World War II* (London: Penguin Group, 2006); Brian Farrell and Sandy Hunter (ed.), *Singapore, Sixty Years On* (Singapore: Eastern Universities Press, 2002).

112. Gerald F. Linderman, *The World within War: American's Combat Experience in World War II* (New York, 1994) chapter 4.

CHAPTER 5: THE WAR AT SEA (PP. 95–131)

1. Michael Hadley and Roger, *Tin-Pots and Pirate Ships: Canadian Naval Forces and German Sea Raiders, 1880–1918* (Montreal: McGill-Queen's University Press, 1991).

2. W.A.B. Douglas, et al, *No Higher Purpose*, 28.

3. Murray and Millett, *A War to Be Won*, 236.

4. John Keegan, *The Second World War* (London: Penguin, 1989) 105.

5. David Mason, *U-Boat: The Secret Menace* (Ballantine's Illustrated History of World War II) (New York: Ballantine, 1986) 14.

6. W.A.B. Douglas, Roger Sarty, and Michael Whitby, *No Higher Purpose: The Official Operational History of the Royal Canadian Navy in the Second World War, 1939–1943, volume II, part 1* (St. Catharines: Vanwell, 2002) 55.

7. LAC, Ian Mackenzie papers, MG 27 III-B-5, v. 32, file X-51, Nelles to deputy minister, 30 September 1938.

8. Douglas, *No Higher Purpose*, 56.

9. See Arnold Hague, *The Allied Convoy System, 1939–1945: Its Organization, Defence, and Operation* (St. Catharines: Vanwell, 2000).

10. H. Nelson Lay, *Memoirs of a Mariner* (Stittsville: Canada's Wings, 1982) 100.

11. Eric J. Grove, *Defeat of the Enemy Attack on Shipping, 1939–1945* (Hull: Ashgate, 1997) 302; Holger H. Herwig, "Germany and the Battle of the Atlantic," in Chickering, et al. (eds.), *A World at Total War: Global Conflict and the Politics of Destruction, 1937–1945* (Cambridge: Cambridge University Press, 2005) 75.

12. Richard H. Leir, "'Big Ship Time': The Formative Years of RCN Officers Serving in RN Capital Ships," in James A. Boutilier (ed.), *RCN in Retrospect, 1910–1968* (Vancouver: UBC Press, 1982) 74.

13. David Zimmerman, "The Social Background of the Wartime Navy: Some Statistical Data," in Michael Hadley (eds.), *A Nation's Navy: In Quest of Canadian Naval Identity* (Montreal and Kingston: McGill-Queen's University Press, 1996) 256–79.

14. William Howard Pugsley, *Saints, Devils and Ordinary Seamen: Life on the Royal Canadian Navy's Lower Deck* (Toronto: Collins, 1945) 19.

15. James Lamb, *The Corvette Navy: True Stories from Canada's Atlantic War* (Toronto: Macmillan of Canada, 1977) 11.

16. Richard Mayne, "The People's Navy: Myth, Reality, and Life in Canada's Naval Reserves 1939–1945," in Richard Gimblett and Michael Hadley (eds.), *Citizen Sailors: Chronicles of Canada's Naval Reserves* (Toronto: Dundurn, 2010) 58–9.

17. Canadian War Museum, Military History Research Centre, 20110062-014, Geoffrey Hughson, "I was going to write a book," 10.

18. Murray and Millett, *A War to Be Won*, 239.

19. J.H.W. Knox, "An Engineer's Outline of RCN History," in James A. Boutilier, *RCN in Retrospect, 1910–1968* (Vancouver: UBC Press, 1982) 105.

20. Ken Macpherson and Marc Milner, *Corvettes of the Royal Canadian Navy, 1939–1945* (St. Catharines: Vanwell, 1993) 6.

21. James B. Lamb, *The Corvette Navy: True Stories from Canada's Atlantic War* (Toronto: Macmillan of Canada, 1977) 1–2.

22. Lamb, *The Corvette Navy*, 113.

23. Mark Lynch, *Salty Dips*, volume II (Ottawa: Naval Officers' Associations of Canada, 1983) 102.

24. Edward O'Connor, *The Corvette Years: The Lower Deck Story* (Vancouver: Cordillera Publishing, 1995) 17.

25. Lawrence Paterson, *The First U-boat Flotilla* (Barnsley: Leo Cooper, 2002) 37.

26. Hal Lawrence, *A Bloody War: One Man's Memories of the Canadian Navy, 1939–45* (Toronto: Macmillan of Canada, 1979) 46.

27. See Philip Goodhart, *Fifty Ships That Saved the World* (London: Heinemann, 1966) 144–66.

28. Roger Sarty, "Rear-Admiral L.W. Murray and the Battle of the Atlantic," in Lieutenant-Colonel Bernd Horn and Stephen Harris (eds.), *Warrior Chiefs: Perspectives on Canadian Military Leaders* (Toronto: Dundurn, 2001) 170.

29. Thomas J. Lynch (ed.), *Fading Memories: Canadian Sailors and the Battle of the Atlantic* (Halifax: The Atlantic Chief and Petty Officers Association, 1993) 78.

30. Lynch (ed.), *Fading Memories*, 91.

31. King diary, 4 November 1940.

32. Murray and Millett, *A War to Be Won*, 239.

33. Thomas Lynch, *Canadian Flowers: History of the Corvettes, 1939–1945* (Halifax: Nimbus Publishing, 1983) 10.

34. LAC, RG 24, v.11929, file 00-220-3-6, Prentice to Captain (D), Newfoundland, 4 November 1941.

35. Mac Johnston, *Corvettes Canada: Convoy Veterans of WWII Tell Their True Stories* (Toronto: McGraw-Hill Ryerson, 1994) 36.

36. John Buckley, *The RAF and Trade Defence, 1919–1945* (Keele: Ryburn Publishing, 1995) 123–4.

37. DHH, 79/446, BdU War Diary, 3 September 1942.

38. See Richard Goette, "Britain and the Delay in Closing the Mid-Atlantic 'Air Gap' during the Battle of the Atlantic," *The Northern Mariner* 15.4 (October 2005) 19–41.

39. Lieutenant-Colonel Richard M. Ross, *The History of the 1st Battalion Cameron Highlanders of Ottawa (MG)* (Ottawa: Published by the regiment, 1948) 15.

40. Dominion Institute, The Memory Project, oral history, Harry Urwin, www.thememoryproject.com.

41. Frank Curry, *War at Sea: A Canadian Seaman on the North Atlantic* (Toronto: Lugus, 1990) 60; Roger Sarty, *War in the St. Lawrence: The Forgotten U-boat Battles on Canada's Shores* (Toronto: Allen Lane, 2012) 47.

42. Charles Patrick Nixon, *A River in September: HMCS Chaudière, 1943–1945* (Montreal: John Mappin, 1995) 5.

43. CWM oral history interview, 31D 3 BURBRIDGE, page 18.

44. Mike Parker, *Running the Gauntlet: An Oral History of Canadian Merchant Seamen in World War II* (Halifax: Nimbus, 1994) 28.

45. Johnston, *Corvettes Canada*, 65.

46. Marc Milner, "The Accidental Enemy: Navy, Part 41," *The Legion* online, October 2010.

47. Lawrence, *A Bloody War*, 92.

48. Lamb, *The Corvette Navy*, 32.

49. William Horrocks (ed.), *In Their Own Words* (Ottawa: Rideau Veterans Home Residents Council, 1993) 168.

50. Dominion Institute, The Memory Project, oral history, Anthony Griffin, www.thememoryproject.com.

51. Alan Easton, *50 North: An Atlantic Battleground* (Toronto: The Ryerson Press, 1963) 65.

52. Captain Dudley King, *Reminiscences* (self-published, 1999) 90–1.

53. Allan W. Stevens, *Glory of Youth: A Narrative of My Experiences as an Officer in the Royal Canadian Navy from 1939 to 1945* (self-published, 1995) 68.

54. David Zimmerman, *The Great Naval Battle of Ottawa* (Toronto: University of Toronto Press, 1988); F.A. Kingsley (ed.), *The Development of Radar Equipment for the Royal Navy, 1935–1945* (London: Macmillan Press for the Naval Radar Trust, 1995).

55. Marc Milner, "The Implications of Technological Backwardness: The Royal Canadian Navy, 1939–1945," *Canadian Defence Quarterly* 19.3 (Winter 1989) 48.

56. W.A.B. Douglas, Roger Sarty, and Michael Whitby, *Blue Water Navy: The Official Operational History of the Royal Canadian Navy in the Second World War, 1943–1945, volume II, part 2* (St. Catharines: Vanwell, 2007) 568–9.

57. Historica-Dominion Institute, *We Were Freedom: Canadian Stories of the Second World War* (Toronto: Key Porter, 2010) 33.

58. DHH, Bio File, William Acheson, diary, 6 November 1940.

59. Jean Portugal (ed.), *We Were There: The Navy, the Army and the RCAF: A Record for Canada*, volume I (Shelburne: Battered Silicon Dispatch Box, 1998) 176; CWM oral history interview, 31D 3 STEWART, 5–6.

60. Curry, *War at Sea*, 59.

61. Horrocks (ed.), *In Their Own Words*, 162.

62. On the interception, see David Syrett, "The Battle for Convoy HX 133, 23–29 June 1941," *The Northern Mariner* 12.3 (July 2002) 44.

63. Lawrence, *A Bloody War*, 95.

64. Christopher Bell, *Churchill & Sea Power* (New York: Oxford University Press, 2012) 224.

65. Roger Sarty, *Canada and the Battle of the Atlantic* (Montreal: Art Global, 1998) 68.

66. For the battle, see W.A.B. Douglas and Jurgen Rohwer, "'The Most Thankless Task' Revisited: Convoys, Escorts, and Radio Intelligence in the Western Atlantic, 1941–1943," in James A. Boutilier (ed.) *RCN in Retrospect, 1910–1968* (Vancouver: UBC Press, 1982) 187–234; and Bernard Edwards, *Attack and Sink!: The Battle for Convoy SC 42* (Wimborne Minster: New Guild, 1995).

67. Lawrence, *A Bloody War*, 51.

68. Donald Graves, *In Peril on the Sea: The Royal Canadian Navy and the Battle of the Atlantic* (Toronto: Published for the Canadian Naval Memorial Trust by Robin Brass Studio, 2003) 96.

69. RG 24, v. 11334, file 8280-SC 42, Report of Proceedings, *Moose Jaw*, 6 November 1941.

70. RG 24, v. 6901, NSS 8910-339/21, Report of the Boarding Party; Marc Milner, "The Fate of Slow Convoy 42: Navy, part 33," *Legion Magazine* (18 June 2009) online, no page.

71. Douglas, *No Higher Purpose*, 255.

CHAPTER 6: LIFE ON A CORVETTE (PP. 133–152)

1. CWM oral history interview, 20110062-014, Geoffrey Hughson, "I was going to write a book," 12.

2. Frank Curry, *War at Sea: A Canadian Seaman on the North Atlantic* (Toronto: Lugus, 1990) 42.

3. CWM oral history interview, 31D 1 BOWEN, G, page 11.

4. Mac Johnston, *Corvettes Canada: Convoy Veterans of WWII Tell Their True Stories* (Toronto: McGraw-Hill Ryerson, 1994) 113–14.

5. Latham B. Jenson, *Tin Hats, Oilskins & Seaboots: A Naval Journey, 1938–1945* (Toronto: Robin Brass Studio, 2000) 184.

6. Allan W. Stevens, *Glory of Youth* (self-published, 1995) 49.

7. John Margison, *H.M.C.S. Sackville, 1942–1943: Memoirs of a Gunnery Officer* (Cobalt: Highway Book Shop, 1998) 20.

8. Jenson, *Tin Hats, Oilskins & Seaboots*, 201.

9. CWM oral history interview, 31D 1 REID, 14.

10. Easton, *50 North*, 192.

11. CWM oral history interview, 31D 1 REID, 14.

12. Bill Rawling, *Death Their Enemy: Canadian Medical Practitioners and War* (self-published, 2001) 167.

13. Dominion Institute, The Memory Project, oral history, George Richmond.

14. Lamb, *The Corvette Navy*, 25.

15. Ray Culley, *His Memories Can Survive* (self-published, 2003) 20.

16. CWM oral history interview, 31D 1 PETERSON, page 9.

17. Curry, *War at Sea*, 27.

18. Harry B. Barrett, *The Navy & Me* (self-published, 2003) 126.

19. DHH, Bio file, Clifford Ashton, interview (April 1993) 6.

20. Lynch (ed.) *Fading Memories*, 74.

21. CWM, 20110062-014, Geoffrey Hughson, "I was going to write a book," 3.

22. CWM, MHRC, Richard C. Pearce, "Recollections," 9.

23. CWM oral history interview, 31D 1 Patrick Nixon, page 14.

24. Jenson, *Tin Hats, Oilskins & Seaboots*, 200.

25. Jeffry Brock, *The Dark Broad Seas: Memoirs of a Sailor, Volume I* (Toronto: McClelland & Stewart, 1981) 38.

26. Johnston, *Corvettes Canada*, 104.

27. William H. Pugsley, *Saints, Devils and Ordinary Seamen: Life on the Royal Canadian Navy's Lower Deck* (Toronto: Collins, 1945) 4.

28. CWM oral history interview, 31D 1 BOWEN, G, page 11.

29. A.G.W. Lamont, *Guns Above, Steam Below in Canada's Navy of WW II* (Ely: Melrose Books, 2006) 47.

30. Margison, *H.M.C.S. Sackville, 1942–1943: Memoirs of a Gunnery Officer*, 16.

31. Barrett, *The Navy & Me*, 124.

32. Lamb, *The Corvette Navy*, 115–16.

33. Pugsley, *Saints, Devils and Ordinary Seamen*, 83.

34. CWM oral history interview, 31D 1 BOWEN, G, page 12.

35. Lawrence, *A Bloody War*, 59.

36. Curry, *War at Sea*, 67.

37. Johnson, *Corvettes Canada*, 30.

38. Horrocks (ed.), *In Their Own Words*, 169.

39. Lamb, *The Corvette Navy*, 11.

40. Lawrence, *A Bloody War*, 12.

41. Jenson, *Tin Hats, Oilskins & Seaboots*, 116.

42. CWM oral history interview, 31D 1 BOWEN, G, page 12

43. CWM, 20110062-014, Geoffrey Hughson, "I was going to write a book," 4.

44. Jenson, *Tin Hats, Oilskins & Seaboots*, 175.

45. Curry, *War at Sea*, 71.

46. Lynch (ed.), *Fading Memories*, 72.

47. Lawrence, *A Bloody War*, 11.

48. CWM oral history interview, 31D 1 PETERSON, page 22.

49. Brock, *The Dark Broad Seas*, 159.

50. CWM oral history interview, 31D 1 VRADENBURG, page 18.

51. CWM oral history interview, 31D 1 VRADENBURG, page 18. Also see CWM oral history interview, 31D 3 STEWART, page 6.

52. CWM oral history interview, 31D 1 BOWEN, G, page 12.

53. Jenson, *Tin Hats, Oilskins & Seaboots*, 176.

54. Lamont, *Guns Above, Steam Below*, 74.

55. Curry, *War at Sea*, 70.

56. CWM oral history interview, 31D 1 PETERSON, page 18.

57. Portugal, *We Were There*, volume 1, 150–1.

58. Culley, *His Memories Can Survive*, 30.

59. Zarn, *Prairie Boys Afloat*, 86.

60. Johnston, *Corvettes Canada*, 16.

61. RG 24, v. 11929, file 00-220-3-6, Stevens to Commanding Officer, Newfoundland, 16 October 1941.

62. Milner, *North Atlantic Run*, 80.

63. Lamb, *The Corvette Navy*, 36.

64. CWM oral history interview, 31D 3 BURBRIDGE, page 17.

65. Lawrence, *A Bloody War*, 82.

66. Lynch (ed.), *Fading Memories*, 78.

67. O'Connor, *The Corvette Years*, 53.

CHAPTER 7: BOMBER COMMAND (PP. 153–172)

1. Bishop, *Bomber Boys*, 48; also see Sir Martin Gilbert, *Finest Hour—Winston Churchill, 1939–1941* (London: Heinemann, 1983) 655–6.

2. Richard Overy, "Allied Bombing and the Destruction of German Cities," in Chickering, et al., *A World at Total War: Global Conflict and the Politics of Destruction, 1937–1945* (Cambridge: Cambridge University Press, 2005) 288. On Churchill and bombing, see Christopher Harmon, *"Are We Beasts?" Churchill and the Moral Question of World War II "Area Bombing"* (Newport: Naval War College, 1991) 8–10.

3. See Les Allison, *Canadians in the Royal Air Force* (Roland: L. Allison, 1978).

4. Norman Shannon, "The Cattle Boat Brigade," *Airforce* (October 1996) 9.

5. Jonathan Vance, "Their Duty Twice Over: Canadians in the Great Escape," *Canadian Military History* 3.1 (1994) 111.

6. Peter Gray, "The Gloves Will Have to Come Off: A Reappraisal of the Legitimacy of the RAF Bomber Offensive Against Germany," *Air Power Review* 13.3 (Autumn/Winter 2010) 24–5.

7. Denis Richards, *Portal of Hungerford* (London: Heinemann, 1977) 160.

8. Richard Overy, *The Bombing War: Europe, 1939–1945* (Penguin: Allan Lane, 2013) 84.

9. Randall Wakelam, "Strike Hard, Strike Sure: Bomber Harris, Precision Bombing, and Decision Making in RAF Bomber Command," in Geoffrey Hayes, et al. (eds.), *Canada and the Second World War: Essays in Honour of Terry Copp* (Waterloo: Wilfrid Laurier Press, 2012), 161.

10. Arthur B. Wahlroth, "Wellington Pilot," *Canadian Aviation Historical Society (CAHS)* 19.2 (1981) 55.

11. William J. Wheeler, *Flying Under Fire: Canadian Fliers Recall the Second World War* (Calgary: Fifth House, 2001) 12, 28.

12. Overy, *The Bomber War*, 257–9.

13. Bernie Wyatt, *Maximum Effort: The Big Bombing Raids* (Erin: Boston Mills Press, 1986) 153.

14. Overy, *The Bomber War*, 180–1.

15. Ron Peel, *My Time at War ... and a Little Bit More* (self-published, 2004) 57–8.

16. Blake Heathcote, *Testaments of Honour: Personal Histories from Canada's War Veterans* (Toronto: Doubleday, 2002) 119.

17. CWM oral history interview, 31D 1 WAHLROTH, page 1.

18. CWM oral history interview, 31D 1 CHENEY, page 1.

19. CWM, 20020026-003, D.J.R. Humphreys, A Personal Memoir, 1939–1945 (self-published, 2000) 1.

20. CWM, 20020026-003, D.J.R. Humphreys, A Personal Memoir, 1939–1945 (self-published, 2000) 3.

21. Michael Paris, *From the Wright Brothers to Top Gun: Aviation, Nationalism and Popular Cinema* (Manchester: Manchester University Press, 1995) 142–3.

22. For air mindedness, see Jonathan Vance, *High Flight: Aviation and the Canadian Imagination* (Toronto: Penguin, 2002).

23. For other challenges, see Andrew Stewart, "The 1939 British and Canadian 'Empire Air Training Scheme' Negotiations," *Round Table* 93 (2004) 739–54.

24. J.L. Granatstein and Dean F. Oliver, *The Oxford Companion to Canadian Military History* (Toronto: Oxford University Press, 2011) 64.

25. Brereton Greenhous and Hugh A. Halliday, *Canada's Air Forces, 1914–1999* (Montreal: Art Global, 1999) 55.

26. F.J. Hatch, *Aerodrome of Democracy: Canada and the British Commonwealth Air Training Plan* (Ottawa: Directorate of History, 1983) foreword.

27. Les Perkins, *Flight into Yesterday: A Memory or Two from Members of the Wartime Aircrew Club of Kelowna* (Victoria: Trafford, 2002) 25.

28. Bill McRae, "Bed and Breakfast: A Canadian Airman Reflects on Food and Quarters during the Second World War," *Canadian Military History* 9.1 (2000) 61.

29. Robert Collins, *The Long and the Short and the Tall: An Ordinary Airman's War* (Saskatoon: Western Producer Prairie Books, 1986) 18.

30. Cy Torontow (ed.), *There I Was: A Collection of Reminiscences by Members of the Ottawa Jewish Community Who Served in World War II* (Ottawa: Jewish War Veterans and the Ottawa Jewish Historical Society, 1999) 54.

31. DHH, Bio file, Alan Frederick Avant, citation of award, n.d; and Avant to W.A.B. Douglas, 2 June 1981.

32. CWM, 19770102-006, Miller Gore Brittain, letters, May 15th, 1943.

33. Granatstein and Oliver, *The Oxford Companion to Canadian Military History*, 64.

34. CWM, 20010200-002, Thomas Reid, letter, 26 February 1941.

35. Glen Hancock, *Charley Goes to War: A Memoir* (Kentville: Gaspereau Press, 2004) 70.

36. Granatstein and Oliver, *The Oxford Companion to Canadian Military History*, 64.

37. Howard Hewer, *In for a Penny, in for a Pound: The Adventures and Misadventures of a Wireless Operator in Bomber Command* (Toronto: Anchor Canada, 2004) 14.

38. Martin Cybulski-Ross, "Wanderers by Night," *CAHS Journal* 25.2 (1987) 46.

39. Harlo Jones, *Bomber Pilot: A Canadian Youth's War* (St. Catharines: Vanwell, 2001) 88–9.

40. CWM, 20080118-007, Joseph Harrison, *An unexpected enemy*, 3.

41. CWM, 20030316-001, G. Stuart Brown, *My Life in the R.C.A.F.*, 7.

42. Queen's University, Charles Power papers, box 64, file D1086, Morale Survey, by Parks and Vlastos, [1942].

43. Queen's University, Charles Power papers, box 64, file D1086, Morale Survey, by Parks and Vlastos, [1942].

44. CWM oral history interview, 31D 1 WAHLROTH, page 7.

45. Robert C. Kensett, *A Walk in the Valley* (Burnstown: General Store Pub. House, 2002) 35.

46. David Bashow, *None but the Brave: The Essential Contributions of RAF Bomber Command to Allied Victory during the Second World War* (Kingston: Canadian Forces Defence Academy, 2009) 66.

47. Hancock, *Charley Goes to War*, 163.

48. Martin Francis, *The Flyer: British Culture and the Royal Air Force, 1939–1945* (Oxford: Oxford University Press, 2008) 24–5.

49. Peel, *My Time at War*, 35.

50. Stan Coldridge, *Recollections of Stan Coldridge (Halifax Pilot)* (self-published, 2008) 1.

51. Jones, *Bomber Pilot*, 115–16.

52. Walter Irwin, *World War II Memoirs* (self-published, 1998) 3.

53. Stephen L.V. King (ed.), *Your Loving Son: Letters of an RCAF Navigator* (Regina: Canadian Plains Research Centre, 2002) 74.

54. Walter R. Thompson, *Lancaster to Berlin* (London: Goodall, 1985) 54.

55. Dominion Institute, The Memory Project, interview, Andy Carswell.

56. Terraine, *Right of the Line*, 681–2.

57. Emily Gann, "Correspondence, Camaraderie, and Community: The Second World War for a Mother and Son," Carleton University: MA thesis, 2013, Erle Miller to Gladys Miller, 25 April 1941.

58. Sir Arthur Harris, *Bomber Offensive* (London: Greenhill Books, 1990, first published 1947) 263–5.

CHAPTER 8: THE STRUGGLE TO SURVIVE (PP. 173–198)

1. Marc Milner, "Fighting the U-boats, 1939–45," in Richard H. Gimblett (ed.), *The Naval Service of Canada: 1910–2010* (Toronto: Dundurn, 2010) 87.

2. LAC, RG 24, v.11929, file 00-220-3-6, Strain on personnel ... , 16 October 1941.

3. LAC, RG 24, v.3892, NSS 1033-6-1, Commanding Officer, HMCS *Chambly*, to captain D, Newfoundland, 4 November 1941.

4. Robert C. Fisher, "The Impact of German Technology on the Royal Canadian Navy in the Battle of the Atlantic, 1942–1943," *The Northern Mariner* 7.4 (October 1997) 2.

5. Sarty, "Rear-Admiral L.W. Murray and the Battle of the Atlantic," 177.

6. DHH, Bio file, Clare L. Annis, interview, [1979], 7.

7. Brereton Greenhous and W.A.B. Douglas, *Out of the Shadows*, 78.

8. Larry Millberry and Hugh Halliday, *The Royal Canadian Air Force at War, 1939–1945* (Toronto: Canav Books, 1990) 106.

9. See Richard Goette, "Squadron Leader N.E. Small: A Study of Leadership in the RCAF's Eastern Air Command, 1942," *Canadian Military Journal* (Spring 2004) 44–5; W.A.B. Douglas, *The Creation of a National Air Force: The Official History of the Royal Canadian Air Force,* volume II (Toronto: University of Toronto Press and the Department of National Defence, 1986) 519–21.

10. Douglas, *The Creation of a National Air Force*, 541.

11. Duncan Redford, "Inter and Intra-Service Rivalries in the Battle of the Atlantic," *Journal of Strategic Studies* 32.6 (2009) 899–928.

12. T.C. Pullen, "Convoy O.N. 127 & the Loss of HMCS *Ottawa*, 13 September 1942: A Personal Reminiscence," *The Northern Mariner* 2.2 (April 1992) 6.

13. Bell, *Churchill and Sea Power*, 254–82; Winston Churchill, *Their Finest Hour* (London: Cassell, 1949) 598.

14. Lamb, *The Corvette Navy*, 47.

15. Sarty, *Battle of the Atlantic*, 98; David M. Kennedy, *The American People in World War II: Freedom from Fear, Part Two: Freedom*, 141.

16. Michael L. Hadley, "The Popular Image of the Canadian Navy," in Michael Hadley, et al. (eds.) *A Nation's Navy: In Quest of Canadian Naval Identity* (Montreal: McGill-Queen's University Press, 1996) 44–6.

17. Milner, "RCN Participation in the Battle of the Atlantic," 163.

18. Michael Whitby, "The Strain of the Bridge: The Second World War Diaries of Commander A.F.C. Layard, RN," in Colonel Bernd Horn (ed.) *Intrepid Warriors: Perspectives on Canadian Military Leaders* (Toronto: The Dundurn Group, 2007) 84.

19. William Glover, "The RCN: Royal Colonial or Royal Canadian Navy," in Michael Hadley, et al. (eds.), *A Nation's Navy: In Quest of Canadian Naval Identity* (Montreal: McGill-Queen's University Press, 1996) 71–90.

20. Jenson, *Tin Hats*, 172.

21. Michael Whitby (ed.), *The Admirals: Canada's Senior Naval Leadership in the Twentieth Century* (Toronto: Dundurn, 2006) 22.

22. Serge Durflinger, "'Nothing Would Be Too Much Trouble': Hometown Support for H.M.C.S. Dunver, 1943–1945," *The Northern Mariner*, Vol. XII, No. 4, October 2002, 1–12.

23. RG 24, v. 3990, file 1057-1-5, Municipal Clerk to Minister of National Defence, 6 April 1943.

24. Lynch (ed.), *Fading Memories*, 103.

25. Lamb, *The Corvette Navy*, 5. Also see Thomas G. Lynch and James B. Lamb, *Gunshield Graffiti: Unofficial Badges of Canada's Wartime Navy* (Halifax: Nimbus, 1984).

26. Jürgen Rohwer, *Axis Submarine Successes of World War Two: German, Italian, and Japanese Submarine Successes, 1939–1945* (Annapolis, MD: Naval Institute Press, 1999) 92–9; Robert Goralski and Russell Freeburg, *Oil and Water* (New York, 1987) 112.

27. Robert Fisher, "'We'll Get Our Own': Canada and the Oil Shipping Crisis of 1942," *The Northern Mariner* 3.2 (1993) 33–39.

28. Douglas, et al., *No Higher Purpose*, 412.

29. Hal Lawrence, *A Bloody War* (Toronto: Macmillan of Canada, 1979) 98–103.

30. On censorship, see Mark Bourrie, *The Fog of War: Censorship of Canada's Media in World War Two* (Vancouver: Douglas & McIntyre, 2011).

31. Hugh Halliday and Brereton Greenhous, *Canada's Air Forces, 1914–1999* (Montreal: Art Global, 1999) 87.

32. Fisher, "The Impact of German Technology," 5.

33. Shawn Cafferky, "A Useful Lot, These Canadian Ships: The Royal Canadian Navy and Operation Torch, 1942–1943," *The Northern Mariner* 3.4 (October 1993) 1–17.

34. Milner, "Fighting the U-boats, 1939–45," 94.

35. Douglas How, *Night of the Caribou* (Hantsport: Lancelot Press, 1988) 276–9.

36. Douglas, *Creation of a National Air Force*, 501–2; Douglas, *No Higher Purpose*, 449–451 and 461–2.

37. See Roger Sarty, *War in the St. Lawrence: The Forgotten U-boat Battles* (Toronto: Allen Lane, 2012); and Roger Sarty, "Ultra, Air Power, and the Second Battle of the St. Lawrence, 1944," in Timothy J. Runyan and Jan M. Copes (eds.), *To Die Gallantly: The Battle of the Atlantic* (Boulder: Westview, 1994) 186–209; and House of Commons, Debates, 17 March 1943, 1344.

38. Tony German, *The Sea Is at our Gates: The History of the Canadian Navy* (Toronto: McClelland & Stewart, 1990) 192.

39. J. de N. Kennedy, *History of the Department of Munitions and Supply: Canada in the Second World War,* volume I (Ottawa: King's Printer, 1950) 505.

40. Parker, *Running the Gauntlet*, 65.

41. Jay White, "Hardly Heroes: Canadian Merchant Seamen and the International Convoy System," *The Northern Mariner* 5.4 (1995) 27–8.

42. Lynch (ed.), *Fading Memories*, 127.

43. Parker, *Running the Gauntlet*, 64.

44. White, "Hardly Heroes," 27–8.

45. Halford, *The Unknown Navy*, 71–76.

46. Doug Fraser, *Postwar Casualty: Canada's Merchant Navy* (Lawrencetown Beach, NS: Pottersfield Press, 1997) 32, 116.

47. Graves, *In Peril on the Sea*, 130; David Edgerton, *Britain's War Machine: Weapons, Resources, and Experts in the Second World War* (London: Allan Lane, 2011) 161.

48. Granatstein, *The Last Good War*, 41.

49. Lynch (ed.), *Fading Memories*, 143.

50. Dominion Institute, The Memory Project, oral history, Roy Ernest Eddy.

51. Easton, *50 North*, 94.

52. Dominion Institute, The Memory Project, oral history, Joseph Dempsey.

53. CWM, 20030169-013, "DEMS, Wrens, R.C.N.S and Little Green Apples," 1.

54. Max Reid, *DEMS at War! Defensively Equipped Merchants Ships and the Battle of the Atlantic, 1939–1945* (Ottawa: Commoners' Publishing Society, 1990) 1.

55. Douglas, et al., *No Higher Purpose*, 297.

56. Graves, *In Peril on the Sea*, 59.

57. Halford, *The Unknown Navy*, 27.

58. CWM oral history interview, 31D 3 SMITH, 26.

59. Parker, *Running the Gauntlet*, 71.

60. Parker, *Running the Gauntlet*, 30.

61. Watt, *In All Respects Ready*, viii.

62. Horrocks (ed.), *In Their Own Words*, 171.

63. Clay Blair, *Hitler's U-boat War: The Hunted, 1942–1944* (New York: Random House, 1996) 552–4.

64. Dominion Institute, The Memory Project, oral history, Elwyn Elliot

65. CWM oral history interview, 31D 1 VRADENBURG, page 16.

66. Torontow (ed.), *There I Was*, 17.

67. B.B. Schofield and L.F. Martin, *The Rescue Ships* (Edinburgh and London: William Blackwood and Sons) 1968.

68. Lynch (ed.), *Fading Memories*, 31–2.

69. Stevens, *Glory of Youth*, 76.

70. Horrocks (ed.), *In Their Own Words*, 166.

71. Brock, *The Dark Broad Seas*, 127.

72. For a list of merchant ships sunk, see Robert Fisher, "Canadian Merchant Ship Losses, 1939–1945," *The Northern Mariner* 5.3 (1995) 57–73.

CHAPTER 9: STRIKING BACK (PP. 199–221)

1. Hancock, *Charley Goes to War*, 201.

2. Hewer, *In for a Penny, in for a Pound*, 55–6.

3. Richard Overy, *Bomber Command, 1939–1945* (London: HarperCollins, 1997) 76.

4. Greenhous, et al., *The Crucible of War*, 531.

5. On bombing, see W. Hays Parks, "'Precision' and 'Area' Bombing: Who Did Which and When?," *Journal of Strategic Studies* 18.1 (1995) 145–74.

6. Martin Gilbert, *Winston S. Churchill, Vol. 6: Finest Hour, 1939–1941*, 1205.

7. Stephen J. Harris, "The Halifax and Lancaster in Canadian Service," *Canadian Military History* 15.3 & 15.4 (Summer–Autumn, 2006) 10–12.

8. See Peter Lewis, *The British Bomber since 1914: Fifty Years of Design and Development* (London: Putnam, 1967).

9. For the constant search for improvement by Harris and Bomber Command, see Randall T. Wakelam, *The Science of Bombing: Operational Research in RAF Bomber Command* (Toronto: University of Toronto Press, 2009) and Henry Probert, *Bomber Harris: His Life and Times* (London: Greenhill Books, 2003) 104.

10. Richard Overy, "Allied Bombing and the Destruction of German Cities," in Chickering, et al., *A World at Total War: Global Conflict and the Politics of Destruction, 1937–1945* (Cambridge: Cambridge University Press, 2005) 277.

11. Webster and Frankland, *The Strategic Air Offensive against Germany*, volume IV, Appendix 8.

12. Peter Lee, "Return from the Wilderness: An Assessment of Arthur Harris' Moral Responsibility for the German City Bombings," *Air Power Review* 16.1 (2013) 70–90.

13. CWM, 20070044-008, Warren Alvin Duffy, letters, July 25 1942.

14. Historica-Dominion Institute, *We Were Freedom*, 77.

15. Murray Peden, *A Thousand Shall Fall* (Stittsville: Canada's Wings, 1979) 250–1.

16. Williamson Murray, *Strategy for Defeat: The Luftwaffe, 1933–1945* (Maxwell Air Force Base, Alabama: Air University Press, 1983) 190.

17. Peel, *My Time at War*, 127.

18. For squadron names, see John G. Armstrong, "RCAF Identity in Bomber Command: Squadron Names and Sponsors," *Canadian Military History* 8.2 (Spring 1999) 43–52.

19. Greenhous, et al., *The Crucible of War*, 575.

20. Jackson, *Before the Storm*, 188.

21. Lowe, *Inferno*, 57.

22. Silver, *Last of the Gladiators*, 14.

23. Rob Stuart, "Leonard Birchall and the Japanese Raid on Colombo," *Canadian Military Journal* (Winter 2006–2007) 69.

24. Lynch, *Salty Dips*, volume II, 51.

25. Bernie Wyatt, *Two Wings and a Prayer* (Erin: The Boston Mills Press, 1984) 50.

26. Historica-Dominion Institute, *We Were Freedom*, 110.

27. Douglas, et al., *The Crucible of War*, 899.

28. Atholl Sutherland Brown, "Forgotten Squadron: Canadian Aircrew in Southeast Asia, 1942–1945," *Canadian Military History* 8.2 (Spring 1999) 59.

29. T.W. Melnyk, *Canadian Flying Operations in South East Asia, 1941–1945* (Ottawa: Department of National Defence, 1976) 166; Les Allison and Harry Hayward, *They Shall Not Grow Old, a Book of Remembrance* (Brandon: The Commonwealth Air Training Plan Museum, 1991); and Atholl Sutherland Brown, *Silently into the Midst of Things* (Lewis, UK: The Book Guild, 1997).

30. Overy, *Bomber Command, 1939–1945*, 65.

31. Portugal, *We Were There*, volume 7, 3306.

32. Greenhous, et al., *The Crucible of War*, 212.

33. Ralph, *Aces, Warriors & Wingmen*, 174.

34. Portugal, *We Were There*, volume 7, 3280.

35. Jackson, *The British Empire and the Second World War*, 129.

36. Dan McCaffery, *Hell Island: Canadian Pilots and the 1942 Air Battle for Malta* (Toronto: James Lorimer, 1998) 184–5.

37. Wyatt, *Two Wings and a Prayer*, 59.

38. Brian Nolan, *Hero: The Buzz Beurling Story* (Toronto: Lester & Orpen, 1981) 84.

39. CWM, 20010200-002, Thomas Reid, letter, 12 June 1942.

40. John Patterson, *World War II: An Airman Remembers* (Burnstown: General Store, 2000) 75.

41. Wyatt, *Two Wings and a Prayer*, 69.

42. See Air Vice-Marshal D.C.T. Bennett, *Pathfinder: A War Autobiography* (Manchester: Crecy, 1983).

43. Irwin, *World War II Memoirs*, 15.

44. Evans, *The Third Reich at War*, 327.

45. Douglas and Greenhous, *Out of the Shadows*, 180–1.

46. Bishop, *Bomber Boys*, xxxiv.

CHAPTER 10: A SORTIE AGAINST A CITY (PP. 223–250)

1. Wyatt, *Maximum Effort*, 35.

2. Peden, *A Thousand Shall Fall*, 425.

3. B. Graham McDonald, *Have No Fear: "B.G." Is Here* (self-published, 2007) 124.

4. McDonald, *Have No Fear*, 153.

5. DHH, Bio file, Douglas Baird, Interview, 28 January 1983, page 23.

6. Wyatt, *Maximum Effort*, 38.

7. J. Douglas Harvey, *Boys, Bombs, and Brussels Sprouts: A Knees-up, Wheels-up Chronicle of World War II* (Toronto: McClelland & Stewart, 1981) 51.

8. CWM oral history interview, 31D 4 BARONI, page 18.

9. Wyatt, *Maximum Effort*, 35.

10. CWM, 20060191-003, Leslie McCaig diaries, 28 August 1943; Arthur B. Wahlroth, "Wellington Pilot," *CAHS* 19.2 (1981) 57–8. On the groundcrews, see Mary C. Pletsch, "The Guardian Angels of this Flying Business: RCAF Ground Crew in 6 Group," (MA thesis, Royal Military College of Canada, 2002).

11. Caitlin McWilliams, "Camaraderie, Morale and Material Culture: Reflections on the Nose Art of No. 6 Group Royal Canadian Air Force," *Canadian Military History* 19.4 (Autumn 2010) 30. Also see Steven Fochuk, *Metal Canvas: Canadians and World War II Aircraft Nose Art* (St. Catharines: Vanwell, 2000).

12. CWM oral history interview, 31D 4 BARONI, page 7.

13. Peden, *A Thousand Shall Fall*, 427–8.

14. CWM, 20060191-003, Leslie McCaig diaries, 1 September 1943.

15. Harvey, *Boys, Bombs, and Brussels Sprouts*, 17.

16. Harvey, *Boys, Bombs, and Brussels Sprouts*, 18.

17. Wyatt, *Maximum Effort*, 57.

18. Murray Winston Bishop and Arthur Adelbert Bishop, *The Bishop Brothers of New Minas in World War Two* (self-published, 2003) 33, 29.

19. CWM oral history interview, 31D 1 WAHLROTH, page 12.

20. Harvey, *Boys, Bombs, and Brussels Sprouts*, 48.

21. Wyatt, *Maximum Effort*, 47.

22. Kensett, *A Walk in the Valley*, 53.

23. George Kutyn, *Diary of R.C.A.F. Serviceman Michael Kutyn* (self-published, second edition, 2010) 22.

24. Jack W. Singer, *Grandpa's War in Bomber Command* (Ottawa: The War Amps, 2012) 63.

25. Dave McIntosh, *Terror in the Starboard Seat* (Don Mills: General Publishing, 1980) 50.

26. CWM, 20060191-003, Leslie McCaig diaries, 23 May 1943.

27. Wyatt, *Maximum Effort*, 48.

28. Kensett, *A Walk in the Valley*, 51.

29. HDI, Memory Project, Interview, Fraser Muir.

30. CWM oral history interview, 31D 4 CHANCE, page 13.

31. Wyatt, *Maximum Effort*, 67.

32. Les Morrison, *Of Luck and War: From Squeegee Kid to Bomber Pilot in World War II* (Burnstown: General Store, 1999) 116.

33. Patterson, *World War II: An Airman Remembers*, 56.

34. Thompson, *Lancaster to Berlin*, 86.

35. Coldridge, *Recollections*, 1.

36. CWM oral history interview, 31D 1 CHENEY, page 14.

37. CWM oral history interview, 31D 1 CHENEY, page 13.

38. Irwin, *World War II Memoirs*, 17.

39. Morrison, *Of Luck and War*, 130.

40. Bill Rawling, *Death their Enemy: Canadian Medical Practitioners and War* (self-published, 2001) 136–7.

41. CWM, 19770102-006, Miller Gore Brittain, letters, November 8th, 1944.

42. McDonald, *Have No Fear*, 124.

43. CWM, 20040074-004, Memoirs of Sergeant Harold Edison DeMone, 2.

44. Harvey, *Boys, Bombs, and Brussels Sprouts*, 133.

45. CWM oral history interview, 31D 1 WAHLROTH, pages 14–15.

46. CWM oral history interview, 31D 1 CHENEY, page 13.

47. Morrison, *Of Luck and War*, 107.

48. Historica-Dominion Institute, *We Were Freedom*, 31.

49. Perkins, *Flight into Yesterday*, 311.

50. Wyatt, *Maximum Effort*, 57.

51. CWM, 20060191-003, Leslie McCaig diaries, 18 October 1943.

52. Patterson, *World War II: An Airman Remembers*, 64.

53. CWM oral history interview, 31D 4 CHANCE, page 25.

54. Harvey, *Boys, Bombs, and Brussels Sprouts*, 97.

55. Jones, *Bomber Pilot*, 121.

56. CWM oral history interview, 31D 1 FINNIE, page 9.

57. Wyatt, *Maximum Effort*, 83.

58. Harvey, *Boys, Bombs, and Brussels Sprouts*, 44.

59. Morrison, *Of Luck and War*, 89.

60. John Irwin Clark, *My Memoirs of the War Years* (self-published, 2005) 58.

61. Patterson, *World War II: An Airman Remembers*, 82–3.

62. Harvey, *Boys, Bombs, and Brussels Sprouts*, 136.

63. Wyatt, *Maximum Effort*, 131.

64. Kensett, *A Walk in the Valley*, 99.

65. [no author], *Memories on Parade* (Winnipeg: Wartime Pilots' and Observers' Association, 1995) 7.

66. Irwin, *World War II Memoirs*, 25.

67. George Stewart, "I'll Never Forget … ," *CAHS Journal* 12.4 (1974) 117.

68. Peden, *A Thousand Shall Fall*, 247.

69. Wyatt, *Maximum Effort*, 89.

CHAPTER 11: DAY OF DESTRUCTION (PP. 251–285)

1. For the Canadians in England, see DHH, CMHQ, Report No. 119, Canadian Relations with the People of the United Kingdom and the General Problem of Morale, 1939–1944; John Maker, "Home Away from Home: Citizenship and National Identity in the Canadian Army Overseas, 1939–1943" (Ph.D. University of Ottawa, 2010); and C.P. Stacey and Barbara Wilson, *The Half Million: the Canadians in Britain, 1939–1946* (Toronto: University of Toronto Press, 1987).

2. Copp, "The Defence of Hong Kong, December 1941," 5.

3. William Hardy McNeill, *American, Britain and Russia: Their Cooperation and Conflict, 1941–1946* (London: Oxford University Press, 1952) 189–90.

4. For supplies, see D.M. Glantz and J.M. House, *When Titans Clashed: How the Red Army Stopped Hitler* (Lawrence: University of Kansas Press, 1995); Hubert Van Tuyll, *Feeding the Beer: American Aid to the Soviet Union, 1941–1944* (New York, 1989); Wieviorka, *Normandy*, 132.

5. Bell, *Churchill and Sea Power*, 207. And see Bernard Ferguson, *The Watery Maze: The Story of Combined Operations* (London: Collins, 1961).

6. Brereton Greenhous, *Dieppe, Dieppe* (Montreal: Art Global, 1992) 48.

7. For the primary importance of the Marine raid, see David O'Keefe, *One Day in August: The Untold Story Behind Canada's Tragedy at Dieppe* (Toronto: Knopf Canada, 2013).

8. John Hughes-Hallet, "The Mounting of Raids," *Royal United Services Institute Journal 95* (November 1950) 585.

9. Ross Munro, *Gauntlet to Overlord* (Toronto: Macmillan, 1945) 305–6.

10. See Brian Villa, *Unauthorized Action: Mountbatten and the Dieppe Raid* (Toronto: Oxford University Press, 1989 (1994)).

11. For Churchill and the raid, see Winston Churchill, *The Second World War: The Hinge of Fate*, volume IV (London: Houghton Mifflin, 1950) 444; and Denis Whitaker and Shelagh Whitaker, *Dieppe: Tragedy to Triumph: A Firsthand and Revealing Critical Account of the Most Controversial Battle of World War II* (Whitby: McGraw-Hill Ryerson, 1992) 227.

12. LAC, RG 24, v. 10,765, D126, Crerar to McNaughton, 11 August 1942.

13. Paul Dickson, *A Thoroughly Canadian General: A Biography of General H.D.G. Crerar* (Toronto: University of Toronto Press, 2007) 206.

14. S.W. Roskill, *The War At Sea, 1939–1945*, volume II (London: HMSO, 1956), 129–30.

15. T. Murray Hunter, *Canada at Dieppe* (Ottawa: Canadian War Museum Historical Publication No. 17, 1982) 16.

16. LAC, RG24, Vol.10870, File 232C2 (D2), "Report by the Military Force Commander—Operation *Jubilee*, 27 August 1942."

17. See Will Fowler, *The Commandos at Dieppe: Rehearsal for D-Day* (London: Collins, 2002).

18. DHH, CMHQ Report 83, 4.

19. Dancocks, *In Enemy Hands*, 27.

20. DHH, CMHQ Report 89, Appendix D, 1.

21. Dancocks, *In Enemy Hands*, 27.

22. DHH, CMHQ Report 89, Appendix D, 1.

23. LAC, RG 24, v.10870, 232c2 (D4), Report of Weapons, Jubilee.

24. DHH, CMHQ Report 89, 4.

25. Munro, *Gauntlet to Overlord*, 325–8.

26. Dickson, *A Thoroughly Canadian General*, 205–6.

27. DHH, CMHQ Report 89, Appendix E, 3.

28. LAC, RG 24, v.10870, 232c2 (D4), Dieppe Raid, 19 Aug 1942, Report on Weapons and Tactics Pourville and Green Beach Area, 1 Sep 1942.

29. Mark Zuehlke, *Tragedy at Dieppe: Operation Jubilee, August 19, 1942* (Vancouver: Douglas & McIntyre, 2012) 250.

30. RG 24, v. 10873, 232.C2 (D65), Cameron Highlanders of Canada, personal accounts, 125.

31. Rollie Bourassa (ed.), *One Family's War: The Wartime Letters of Clarence Bourassa, 1940–1944* (Regina: Canadian Plains Research Centre, 2010) 410.

32. DHH, CMHQ Report 89, Appendix G, 4.

33. DHH, CMHQ Report 89, Appendix H, 3.

34. Whitaker and Whitaker, *Dieppe*, 242.

35. WD, Royal Hamilton Light Infantry, August 1942, Appendix 18, 24.

36. RG 24, v. 10873, (D53) 232.C2 (D57), Extract of letter from Lt. Col. F.K. Jasperson, commander of Essex Scottish, 23 Aug 1942.

37. See Sandy Antal and Kevin Shackleton, *Duty Nobly Done: The Official History of the Essex and Kent Scottish Regiment* (Windsor: Walkerville, 2006) 408–9.

38. RG24, vol.10, 872, file 232.C2(D36), Lieutenant-Colonel C.C. Mann, "Observations Upon the Outline Plan," 3–4.

39. Hugh Henry, "The Calgary Tanks at Dieppe," *Canadian Military History* 4.1 (Spring 1995) 69.

40. A.J. Kerry and WA. McDill, *The History of the Corps of the Royal Canadian Engineers, Volume 2: 1936–1946* (Ottawa: Military Engineers Association of Canada, 1966) 108–9.

41. John Marteinson and Michael McNorgan, *The Royal Canadian Armoured Corps: An Illustrated History* (Toronto: Robin Brass Studio, 2000) 138.

42. DHH Bio file, Edwin Bennett, Interview 30 September 1973, page 3.

43. Trafford Leigh-Mallory, "Air Operations at Dieppe: An After-Action Report," *Canadian Military History* 12.4 (2003) 57.

44. CWM oral history interview, 31D 5 MAFFRE, page 22.

45. CWM oral history interview, 31D 5 MAFFRE, page 24.

46. Silver, *Last of the Gladiators*, 143–5.

47. Milberry and Halliday, *The Royal Canadian Air Force at War, 1939–1945*, 216.

48. For the air battle, see Norman Franks, *The Greatest Air Battle: Dieppe, 19 August, 1942* (London: W. Kimber, 1979); Ross Mahoney, "The support afforded by the air force was faultless': The Royal Air Force and the Raid on Dieppe, 19 August 1942," *Canadian Military History* 21.4 (Autumn 2012) 17–32; Casualties in Greenhous, et al., *Crucible of War*, 242. For the official report, see RG 24, v.10870, 232c2 (D5), Report by the Air Force Commander on the Combined Operation Against Dieppe, August 19, 1942.

49. DHH, CMHQ Report 89, Appendix F, 2.

50. Greenhous, *Dieppe, Dieppe*, 108.

51. Dollard Menard and C.B. Wall, "The Meaning of Bravery," *The Canadians at War, 1939/45,* volume I (Montreal: Reader's Digest Assoc. (Canada), 1969) 196-7.

52. For Dumais's story, see DHH, CMHQ Report 89, Appendix C, 1–3.

53. Whitaker and Whitaker, *Dieppe: Tragedy to Triumph*, 247.

54. RG24, v.10873, File 232C2(D62), Lieutenant-Colonel R.R. Labatt, "Narrative of Experiences at Dieppe," 10.

55. Granatstein, *The Last Good War*, 74.

56. DHH, CMHQ Report 98, 12; LAC, RG 24, v. 10873, (D53) 232c2 (D56), Medical Observations during Combined Operations.

57. *The Canadians at War 1939/45* (Montreal: Reader's Digest, 1969) 192.

58. Dancocks, *In Enemy Hands*, 33.

59. Charles G. Roland, "On the Beach and in the Bag: The Fate of Dieppe Casualties Left Behind," *Canadian Military History* 9.4 (Autumn 2000) 12.

60. Hugh Henry, *Dieppe through the Lens of the German War Photographer* (London: After the Battle, 1993); and David Ian Hall, "The German View of the Dieppe Raid," *Canadian Military History* 21.4 (Autumn 2012) 3–16.

61. For casualties, see Stacey, *The Canadian Army, 1939–1945*, 80.

62. On selling the mission, see Timothy Balzer, "'In Case the Raid Is Unsuccessful ...' Selling Dieppe to Canadians," *The Canadian Historical Review* 87.3 (2006) 409–30.

63. RG 24, v.10870, 232c2 (D2), Report of Operation Jubillee, from GOC 2nd Cdn Div to 1 Cdn Corps, 20 Aug 1942.

64. For Dieppe in memory, see Béatrice Richard, *La Mémoire de Dieppe: Radioscopie d'un mythe* (Montreal: VLB Éditeur, 2002); Peter Henshaw, "The Dieppe Raid: A Product of Misplaced Canadian Nationalism?" *Canadian Historical Review* 77.2 (1996) 250–66; Brian Villa and Peter Henshaw, "The Dieppe Raid Debate," *Canadian Historical Review* 79.2 (1998) 304–15.

65. Nathan Miller, *War at Sea: A Naval History of World War II* (Oxford: Oxford University Press, 1995) 314.

66. Robin Neillands, *The Dieppe Raid: The Story of the Disastrous 1942 Expedition* (London: Aurum Press, 2005) 267.

67. LAC, RG24, v.12319, file 4/Censor/4/8, Field Censor (Home) Report, 20 August–3 September 1942.

68. Stacey, *Six Years of War*, 405.

CHAPTER 12: BACKS TO THE WALL (PP. 287–308)

1. See Robert C. Fisher, "Tactics, Training, Technology: The RCN's Summer of Success, July–September 1942," *Canadian Military History* 6.2 (Autumn 1997) 7–20.

2. Alan Riley, *A Sparker's War* (self-published, 2005) 31.

3. Horrocks (ed.), *In Their Own Words*, 166.

4. Riley, *A Sparker's War*, 32.

5. LAC, RG 24, v.11020, COAC 7-2-1, pt. 4, HMCS *Assiniboine*, Report of Proceedings, 10 August 1942.

6. Robert C. Fisher, "Heroism: On the North Atlantic," *The Legion* online (May 2002).

7. Lay, *Memoirs of a Mariner*, 142–3.

8. Riley, *A Sparker's War*, 22.

9. Curry, *War at Sea*, 53.

10. Lawrence, *A Bloody War*, 72.

11. Tony German, *The Sea Is at Our Gates: The History of the Canadian Navy* (Toronto: McClelland & Stewart, 1990) 112.

12. Lamb, *The Corvette Navy*, 90.

13. Barrett, *The Navy & Me*, 79.

14. Steven High (ed.), *Occupied St. John's: A Social History of a City at War, 1939–1945* (Montreal: McGill-Queen's University Press, 2010) 106.

15. Curry, *War at Sea*, 53.

16. Jenson, *Tin-Hats*, 125.

17. McDonald, *Have No Fear*, 54.

18. Zarn, *Prairie Boys Afloat*, 124.

19. Lawrence, *A Bloody War*, 75.

20. Captain Dudley King, *Reminiscences* (self-published, 1999) 79.

21. Johnston, *Corvettes Canada*, 85.

22. David Kahn, *Seizing the Enigma: The Race to Break the German U-boat Codes, 1939–1943* (Boston, 1991); and W.J.R. Gardner, *Decoding History: The Battle of the Atlantic and Ultra* (London: Macmillan Press, 1999).

23. Guy Hartcup, *The Effect of Science on the Second World War* (Basingstoke: St. Martin's, 2000) 47–9.

24. Jenson, *Tin-Hats*, 134.

25. Lynch (ed.), *Fading Memories*, 115.

26. T.C. Pullen, "Convoy O.N. 127 & the Loss of HMCS *Ottawa*, 13 September 1942: A Personal Reminiscence," *The Northern Mariner* 2.2 (April 1992) 14.

27. Jenson, *Tin-Hats*, 136.

28. Dominion Institute, The Memory Project, oral history, Sid Dobing.

29. James Goodwin, *"Our Gallant Doctor": Enigma and Tragedy: Surgeon Lieutenant George Hendry and HMCS* Ottawa, *1942* (Toronto: Dundurn, 2007) 171.

30. Jenson, *Tin-Hats*, 138.

31. King, *Reminiscences*, 85.

32. Milner, *North Atlantic Run*, 164.

33. Sarty, *Canada and the Battle of the Atlantic*, 126.

34. Paul Kennedy, *Engineers of Victory: The Problem Solvers Who Turned the Tide in the Second World War* (Toronto: HarperCollins, 2013) 7.

35. Milner, "The Implications of Technological Backwardness," 51.

36. John F. Hilliker (ed.), *Documents on Canadian External Relations XI: 1942–1943* (Ottawa: Government of Canada, 1980) 355.

37. Michael L. Hadley, "The Popular Image of the Canadian Navy," in Michael Hadley, et al. (eds.), *A Nation's Navy: In Quest of Canadian Naval Identity* (Montreal: McGill-Queen's University Press, 1996) 40.

38. Milner, "Fighting the U-boats, 1939–45," 100.

39. W.G.D. Lund, "The Royal Canadian Navy's Quest for Autonomy in the North West Atlantic, 1941–1943," in James A. Boutilier, *RCN in Retrospect, 1910–1968* (Vancouver: UBC Press, 1982) 148.

40. See Edgerton, *Britain's War Machine*, 165; Hastings, *All Hell Let Loose*, 274.

41. Richard Oliver Mayne, "Bypassing the Chain of Command: The Political Origins of the RCN's Equipment Crisis of 1943," *Canadian Military History* 9.3 (Summer 2000) 19.

42. Marc Milner, "More Royal than Canadian? The Royal Canadian Navy's Search for Identity, 1910–68," in Philip Buckner (ed.) *Canada and the End of Empire* (Vancouver: UBC Press, 2005) 275.

43. David Syrett, *The Defeat of the German U-boats: The Battle of the Atlantic* (Columbia: University of South Carolina Press, 1994) 25.

44. Marc Milner, "Royal Canadian Navy Participation in the Battle of the Atlantic Crisis of 1943," in James A. Boutilier, *RCN in Retrospect, 1910–1968* (Vancouver: UBC Press, 1982) 159.

45. Milner, *Canada's Navy*, 124.

46. W.A.B. Douglas, *The Creation of a National Air Force. The Official History of the Royal Canadian Air Force, Volume 2* (Toronto: University of Toronto Press, 1986) 537–9, 545–51.

47. Millberry and Halliday, *The Royal Canadian Air Force at War, 1939–1945*, 104.

48. Eayrs, *In Defence of Canada*, volume III, 57; Milner, *Canada's Navy*, 126; Sarty, *Canada and the Battle of the Atlantic*, 132. Also see Robert Fisher, "Axis Submarines Lost to Canadian Forces, 1939–45: Revised List," *Argonauta* 14.1 (January 1997).

49. Greenhous and Douglas, *Out of the Shadows*, 61.

50. Holger H. Herwig, "Germany and the Battle of the Atlantic," in Chickering, et al. (eds.), *A World at Total War: Global Conflict and the Politics of Destruction, 1937–1945* (Cambridge: Cambridge University Press, 2005) 82.

51. Correlli Barnett, *Engage the Enemy More Closely: The Royal Navy in the Second World War* (New York: Norton, 1991) 613; Karl Dönitz, *Memoirs: Ten Years and Twenty Days* (London: Weidenfeld and Nicolson, 1959) 338–41.

CHAPTER 13: MAKING AN IMPACT (PP. 309–328)

1. Webster and Frankland, *The Strategic Air Offensive Against Germany, 1939–1945*, volume II (London: Her Majesty's Stationary Office, 1961) 14.

2. Bashow, *No Prouder Place*, 456–7.

3. Greenhous, *Crucible of War*, Introduction, 14.

4. Morrison, *Of Luck and War*, 28.

5. Field Censor (Home) Report, 2–15 February 1942, LAC, RG24, National Defence, Volume 12319, File 4/Censor/4/5.

6. Alta R. Wilkinson (ed.), *Ottawa to Caen: Letters from Arthur Campbell Wilkinson* (Ottawa: Tower Books, 1947) 17.

7. Emily Gann, "Correspondence, Camaraderie, and Community: The Second World War for a Mother and Son," (Masters: Carleton University, 2012) 33–4.

8. Arthur B. Wahlroth, "Wellington Pilot," *CAHS Journal* 19.2 (1981) 54.

9. John A. Blythe, "The Bomber Offensive, Youth, and Canadian Nationalism," *Canadian Defence Quarterly* 7.3 (Winter 1977) 46.

10. McDonald, *Have No Fear*, 123.

11. Biddle, *Rhetoric and Reality in Air Warfare*, 214.

12. Greenhous, *Crucible of War*, 680, 757.

13. CWM, 20030316-001, G. Stuart Brown, *My Life in the R.C.A.F.*, 12.

14. See Gray, "A Culture of Official Squeamishness?," 1367–71; David Hall, "Black, White and Grey: Wartime Arguments for and against the Strategic Bombing Offensive," *Canadian Military History* 7.1 (Winter 1998) 7–19.

15. Laurie Peloquin, "A Conspiracy of Silence? The Popular Press and the Strategic Bombing Campaign in Europe," *Canadian Military History* 3.2 (1994) 23.

16. Vincenzo Field, "Explaining Armageddon: Popular Perceptions of Air Power in Canada and Britain and the Destruction of Germany, 1939–45," (MA thesis, University of New Brunswick, 2003) 68.

17. Tim Cook, *Clio's Warriors: Canadian Historians and the Writing of the World Wars* (Vancouver: UBC Press, 2006) 115–19.

18. "Britons Back Raids on Reich Yet Want to Share Post-War Food," *Canadian Institute of Public Opinion* (January 10, 1944); "Canadians and Americans See Eye to Eye on Allied Bombing of Nazi-Held Shrines," *Canadian Institute of Public Opinion* (June 3, 1944).

19. Murray and Millett, *A War to Be Won*, 374–5.

20. Laurie Peloquin, "Area Bombing by Day: Bombing Command and the Daylight Offensive, 1944–1945," *Canadian Military History* 15.3 & 15.4 (Summer–Autumn, 2006) 31–2; Bruce Robertston, *Lancaster—The Story of a Famous Bomber* (Hertfordshire: Harleyford, 1964) 126.

21. Biddle, *Rhetoric and Reality in Air Warfare*, 243.

22. W.F. Craven and James Lea Cate, *The Army Air Forces in World War II*, volume 3 (Chicago: University of Chicago Press, 1958) 723.

23. For a recent claim to American superiority, see Randall Hansen's *Fire and Fury: The Allied Bombing of Germany 1942–1945* (Toronto: Doubleday Canada, 2008).

24. CLIP, James Baker, letter, 12 January 1943.

25. Overy, *Bomber Command, 1939–1945*, 152; Greenhous, *Crucible of War*, 681.

26. Perkins, *Flight into Yesterday*, 326.

27. Greenhous, *Crucible of War*, 680.

28. Wyatt, *Maximum Effort*, 16–17.

29. Harvey, *Boys, Bombs, and Brussels Sprouts*, 157.

30. Douglas and Greenhous, *Out of the Shadows*, 188.

31. Copp, *No Higher Price*, 113.

32. Peter Gray, "A Culture of Official Squeamishness? Britain's Air Ministry and the Strategic Air Offensive against Germany," *Journal of Military History* 77.4 (October 2013) 1366.

33. Christopher M. Rein, *The North African Air Campaign: U.S. Army Air Forces from El Alamein to Salerno* (Lawrence: University Press of Kansas, 2012) 143.

34. Greenhous, *The Crucible of War*, 292.

35. Kennedy, *Engineers of Victory*, 202.

36. Phillips O'Brien, "East versus West in the Defeat of Nazi Germany," *Journal of Strategic Studies* 23.2 (2000), 89–113.

37. Evans, *The Third Reich at War*, 442.

38. Alfred C. Mierzejewski, *The Collapse of the German War Economy, 1944–1945* (Chapel Hill: The University of North Carolina Press, 1988) 17–18.

39. Wieviorka, *Normandy*, 153–4; Tooze, *The Wages of Destruction*, 597–8 and 600.

40. Reader's Digest, *The Canadians at War, 1939/45*, 278.

41. Martin Middlebrook, *The Battle of Hamburg: Allied Bomber Forces against a German City in 1943* (London: Allen Lane, 1980) 266–7.

42. Lowe, *Inferno: The Fiery Destruction of Hamburg*, 1943, 209–10.

43. Hastings, *Bomber Command*, 246.

44. Murray, *The Luftwaffe, 1933–1945*, 177–80.

45. Hastings, *All Hell Let Loose*, 487–8.

46. Evans, *The Third Reich at War*, 465.

47. CWM, 20060191-003, Leslie McCaig diaries, 2 June 1943.

48. Hewer, *In for a Penny, in for a Pound*, 92.

49. DHH, Bio file, D.C.T. Bennett, interview, 17 June 1976, page 13.

50. CWM, 20020026-003, D.J.R. Humphreys, A Personal Memoir, 1939–1945 (self-published, 2000) 52.

51. Chapman, *River Boy at War*, 57.

52. Hibbert (ed.), *Fragments of War*, 218.

53. Harvey, *Boys, Bombs, and Brussels Sprouts*, 148.

54. Jones, *Bomber Pilot*, 141.

55. McDonald, *Have No Fear*, 137.

56. Jones, *Bomber Pilot*, 155.

57. Harvey, *Boys, Bombs, and Brussels Sprouts*, 148.

58. Wyatt, *Maximum Effort*, 62.

59. Peel, *My Time at War*, 63.

60. Milberry and Halliday, *The Royal Canadian Air Force at War, 1939–1945*, 192.

61. Harvey, *Boys, Bombs, and Brussels Sprouts*, 141–2.

62. Georgina Matthews (ed.), *Wartime Letters of Flt. Lieut. D.J. Matthews to His Wife 1943–1945* (Guelph: Georgina H. Matthews, 2003) 30.

63. Wyatt, *Maximum Effort*, 23.

64. CWM,19910181-043, George Joseph Chequer, letters, March 19, 1943.

65. CWM, 20060058-001, Second World War Letter Collection of Norma Lee, June 27, 1944.

66. G.W.L. Nicholson, *Canada's Nursing Sisters* (Toronto: A.M. Hakkert, 1975) 121.

67. Bashow, *None but the Brave*, 93.

68. Peel, *My Time at War*, 36.

CHAPTER 14: TEST OF BATTLE (PP. 329–375)

1. Niall Barr, *Pendulum of War: Three Battles at El Alamein* (Woodstock: Overlook, 2005).

2. Alan J. Levine, *The War against Rommel's Supply Lines, 1942–1943* (Westport: Praeger, 1999) 30.

3. David Rolf, *The Bloody Road to Tunis: Destruction of the Axis Forces in North Africa. November 1942–May 1943* (London: Greenhill, 2001); Douglas Porch, *The Path to Victory: The Mediterranean Theatre in World War II* (New York: 2004) 412–14.

4. H.W. Koch, "The Spectre of a Separate Peace in the East: Russo-German 'Peace Feelers,' 1942–1944," *Journal of Contemporary History* 10 (1975) 531–49; Mark Perry, *Partners in*

Command: George Marshall and Dwight Eisenhower in War and Peace (New York: Penguin, 2007) 146–51.

5. DHist, CMHQ Report, No. 123, page 6; DHH, CMHQ, Report No. 119, "Canadian Relations with the People of the United Kingdom and the General Problem of Morale, 1939–1944."

6. For an account of these debates, see Brandey Barton, "Public Opinion and National Prestige: The Politics of Canadian Army Participation to the Invasion of Sicily, 1942–1943," *Canadian Military History* 15.2 (Spring 2006) 22–34.

7. C.P. Stacey, *Canada and the Age of Conflict, Vol. II* (Toronto: University of Toronto Press, 1984), 349.

8. John Rickard, *The Politics of Command: Lieutenant-General A.G.L. McNaughton and the Canadian Army 1939–1943* (Toronto: University of Toronto Press, 2010) 20. Also see Paul Dickson, "Harry Crerar and an Army for Strategic Effect," *Canadian Military History* 17.1 (Winter 2008) 46.

9. Wilfred I. Smith, *Code Word: Canloan* (Toronto: Dundurn, 1992).

10. DHH, AHQ Report No. 14, The Sicilian Campaign, Information from German Sources, 8–9.

11. Ralph Bennett, *Behind the Battle: Intelligence in the War with Germany, 1939–1945* (London: Sinclair-Stevenson, 1994) 202–5; Michael Howard, *British Intelligence in the Second World War, Volume V, Strategic Deception* (London: HMSO, 1990) 86–92.

12. G.R. Stevens, *The Royal Canadian Regiment*, volume II (London: London Print & Lithographing Co., 1967) 66.

13. Vance, *Maple Leaf Empire*, 186.

14. CWM, 19910163-014, Ben Malkin, "Sicily Invasion 20 years after."

15. DHH, 159.91013(D1) The Voyage to Sicily, [by A.T. Sesia].

16. Granatstein, *Canada's Army*, 181.

17. Horrocks, *In Their Own Words*, 157.

18. DHist, CMHQ Report, No. 123, page 10.

19. See DHH, CMHQ Report No. 123, Battle Drill Training. Also see Timothy Harrison Place, *Military Training in the British Army, 1940–1944: From Dunkirk to D-Day* (London: Frank Cass, 2000) and John A. English, *Failure in High Command: The Canadian Army and the Normandy Campaign* (Ottawa: Golden Dog, 1995).

20. Ian Gooderson, *A Hard Way to Make War: The Italian Campaign in the Second World War* (London: Conway, 2008) 133.

21. See, for example, DHH, CMHQ Report, No. 11, Canadian Corps Exercise Fox; DHH, CMHQ Report, No. 34, South-Eastern Command Exercise Waterloo.

22. Kenneth B. Smith, *Duffy's Regiment* (Don Mills: T.H. Best, 1983) introduction.

23. Dick Malone, *Missing from the Record* (Toronto: William Collins Ltd, 1946) 33.

24. John Buckley, *Monty's Men: The British Army and the Liberation of Europe* (New Haven: Yale University Press, 2013) 117.

25. G.W.L. Nicholson, *The Gunners of Canada: The History of the Royal Regiment of Canadian Artillery*, volume II (Toronto: McClelland & Stewart, 1967) 127.

26. CWM, MHRC, 19910163-014, Ben Malkin, "Sicily Invasion 20 years after."

27. CMHQ Report 126, 79.

28. Some of these rumours were captured in an amusing ship paper published by a number of war correspondents known as the *Zig Zag*. For a surviving copy, see CWM, 19820624-001.

29. Farley Mowat, *And No Birds Sang* (Toronto: McClelland & Stewart, 1979) 58.

30. Bill McAndrew, *Canadians and the Italian Campaign, 1943-1945* (Montreal: Art Global, 1996) 38.

31. W.G.F. Jackson, *Alexander of Tunis as Military Commander* (London: Batsford, 1971) 212.

32. Nigel Hamilton, *Monty: Master of the Battlefield* (London: Hodder & Stoughton, 1985) 245–84.

33. Carlo D'Este, *Patton: A Genius for War* (New York: Harper, 1995) 494.

34. Copp, *No Price Too High*, 123.

35. W.R. Feasby, *Official History of the Canadian Medical Services, 1939–1945*, volume I (Ottawa: E. Cloutier, Queen's Printer, 1953), 129.

36. Gooderson, *A Hard Way to Make War*, 40.

37. D'Este, *Bitter Victory*, 86.

38. See DHH, 181.003 (D3004), General Summary of Military and Air Situation in Mediterranean, July 1943.

39. David Bashow, *No Prouder Place: Canadians and the Bomber Command Experience, 1939 to 1945* (St. Catharines: Vanwell, 2005) 143.

40. Fred Turnbull, *The Invasion Diaries* (Kemptville: Veterans Publications, 2007) 30. Also see, LAC, A.G.L. McNaughton papers, MG 30 E133, v. 135, ME Instructional Circular No. 17, Notes from Sicily, 1.

41. Robert L. McDougall, *A Narrative of War: From the Beaches of Sicily to the Hitler Line with the Seaforth Highlanders of Canada, 10 July, 1943– 8 June 1944* (Kemptville: Golden Dog Press, 1996) 12.

42. George A. Reid, *Speed's War: A Canadian Soldier's Memoir of World War II* (Royston: Madrona Books and Publishing, 2007) 8.

43. "The RCRs in Sicily," *Canadian Military History* 12.3 (Summer 2003) 74.

44. DHH, CMHQ report 127, 12.

45. DHH, 145.2L4051 (D1), Planning and Op Husky, by Major C.F. Richardson, 4.

46. DHH, 321.009(D60), Visits—Reports, 1943, Continuation of Lt. Col Gilbride's account, 13.

47. Strome Galloway, *Some Died at Ortona: The Royal Canadian Regiment in Action in Italy* (London, ON: Royal Canadian Regiment, 1983) 34.

48. CWM, MHRC, 20100088-030, Campbell to mother, 25 July 1943.

49. War Diary, Seaforth Highlanders of Canada, 11 July 1943.

50. Albert Kesselring, *Kesselring: A Soldier's Record* (New York: William Morrow, 1954) 196; also see Harry Yeide, *Fighting Patton: George S. Patton Jr. Through the Eyes of His Enemies* (Minneapolis: Zenith Press, 2011) 204.

51. Major General David Belchem, *All in the Day's March* (London, ON: The Royal Regiment of Canada, 1978) 167.

52. Omar N. Bradley, *A Soldier's Story* (New York: Modern Library, 1999) 135.

53. Rick Atkinson, *The Day of Battle: The War in Sicily and Italy, 1943–1944* (New York: Henry Holt, 2007) 125.

54. Lee Windsor, "'The Eyes of All Fixed on Sicily: Canada's Unexpected Victory, 1943," *Canadian Military History* 22.3 (Summer 2013) 13.

55. DHH, CMHQ Report No. 135, 6.

56. Mowat, *And No Birds Sang*, 98.

57. LAC, A.G.L. McNaughton papers, MG 30 E133, v. 135, Canadian Operations in Sicily, Series 4, 7.

58. LAC, RG 24, v. 10,450, file 212C1.011 (D1), Battle Experience Questionnaire, no. 18, Captain M. Pariseault. Also see LAC, A.G.L. McNaughton papers, MG 30 E133, v. 135, ME Instructional Circular No. 17, Notes from Sicily, 7.

59. MHRC, Robert Thexton, *Times to Remember: Some Recollections of Four and a Half Years Service with the West Nova Scotia Regiment during 1940–1944* (self-published, 2008) 26.

60. Galloway, *Some Died at Ortona*, 75.

61. Ronald Cormier (ed.), *The Forgotten Soldiers: Stories from Acadian Veterans of the Second World War* (Fredericton, NB: New Ireland Press, 1992) 22.

62. Galloway, *Some Died at Ortona*, 78.

63. Mowat, *And No Birds Sang*, 112–13.

64. Windsor, "The Eyes of All Fixed on Sicily," 22; Nicholson, *The Canadians in Italy*, 99.

65. Eric McGeer, Terry Copp, with Matt Symes: *The Canadian Battlefields in Italy: Sicily and Southern Italy* (Waterloo: Canadian Battlefields Foundation, 2008) 24.

66. "The Hasty Pees in Sicily," *Canadian Military History* 12.3 (Summer 2003) 68–9.

67. Mowat, *And No Birds Sang*, 133.

68. LAC, A.G.L. McNaughton papers, MG 30 E133, v. 135, ME Instructional Circular No. 17, Notes from Sicily, Extract from the Royal Canadian Regiment diary, 5.

69. Kim Beattie, *Dileas: History of the 48th Highlanders of Canada, 1929–1956* (Toronto: published by the regiment, 1957) 271.

70. DHH, AHQ Report No. 14, The Sicilian Campaign, Information from German Sources, Appendix, Panzerdivision Hermann Goering, Brief Experience Report on the Fighting, 3.

71. Reid, *Speed's War*, 13.

72. Howard Mitchell, *My War* (self-published, n.d.) 81.

73. LAC, RG 24, Vol. 15,156, WD Princess Patricia's Canadian Light Infantry, "Princess Patricia's Canadian Light Infantry, Italian Campaign—Leonforte," July 1943.

74. DHH, CMHQ Report No. 135, 26.

75. Terry Copp, "From Leonforte to Agira: Army, Part 61," *The Legion* online, no page.

76. Marteinson and McNorgan, *The Royal Canadian Armoured Corps*, 151.

77. G.W.L. Nicholson, *The Canadians in Italy,1943–1945* (Ottawa: Queen's Printer, 1955) 110.

78. McDougall, *A Narrative of War*, 29-30.

79. DHH, CMHQ Report No. 135, 35.

80. F.H. Hinsley, *British Intelligence in the Second World War*, volume III, part 1 (New York: Cambridge University Press, 1979) 92–4.

81. Nicholson, *The Canadians in Italy*, 110.

82. DHH, AHQ Report No. 14, The Sicilian Campaign, Information from German Sources, 23; and Ibid., Appendix, Panzerdivision Hermann Goering, Brief Experience Report on the Fighting, 3.

83. WD, Royal Canadian Regiment, 24 July 1943.

84. DHH, 142.5M1009 (D9), Artillery Lessons Learned from Sicilian and Italian Campaigns, "Artillery Lessons, First Year of the Italian Campaign."

85. DHH, AHQ Report No. 14, The Sicilian Campaign, Information from German Sources, Report of the 15th German Panzer Grenadier Division on the Sicilian Campaign, 1–2.

86. Grant N. Barry, "Beyond the Consensus: 1st Canadian Infantry Division at Agira, Sicily, 24-28 July 1943," *Canadian Military History* 19.2 (Spring 2010) 43.

87. WD, Saskatoon Light Infantry, 23 July 1943.

88. William McAndrew, "Fire or Movement? Canadian Tactical Doctrine, Sicily—1943," *Military Affairs* 51.3 (July 1987) 142–5.

89. G.R. Stevens, *The Royal Canadian Regiment, volume II (1933–1966)* (London: London Printing, 1967) 79.

90. WD, 12th Canadian Armoured Regiment, Appendix, Captain W.T. Hunter's Report, 25 July 1943.

91. WD, Hastings and Prince Edward Regiment, 25 July 1943.

92. Galloway, *Some Died at Ortona*, 68.

93. LAC, RG 24, v. 10,775, Statement by Lt. Col. R.A. Lindsay, 30 July 1943; Nicholson, *The Gunners of Canada*, volume II, 150.

94. Jack Wallace, "Shermans in Sicily: The Diary of a Young Soldier, Summer 1943," *Canadian Military History* 7.4 (Autumn 1998) 66.

95. WD, Loyal Edmonton Regiment, 28 July 1943.

96. DHH, AHQ Report No. 14, The Sicilian Campaign, Information from German Sources, Appendix, Panzerdivision Hermann Goering, Brief Experience Report on the Fighting, 3.

97. Mark Zuehlke, *Operation Husky: The Canadian Invasion of Sicily, July 10–August 7, 1943* (Vancouver: Douglas & McIntyre, 2008) 345.

98. Geoffrey Hayes, "The Canadians in Sicily: Sixty Years On," *Canadian Military History* 12.3 (Summer 2003) 16.

99. Nicholson, *The Canadians in Italy 1943–1945*, 134; CMHQ Report No. 135, 64; Cessford, "Hard in the Attack," 181.

100. Nicholson, *The Canadians in Italy*, 147.

101. Feasby, *Official History of the Canadian Medical Services, 1939–1945, volume I*, 143.

102. McDougall, *A Narrative of War*, 58.

103. "Pooch" [C.E. Corrigan] *Tales of a Forgotten Theatre* (Winnipeg: D Day Publishers, 1969) 11.

104. Feasby, *Official History of the Canadian Medical Services, 1939–1945*, 139–42.

105. Denis Dubord, "Unseen Enemies: An Examination of Infectious Diseases and Their Influence upon the Canadian Army in Two Major Campaigns during the First and Second World Wars," (Ph.D. Thesis: University of Victoria, 2009) 262; G.W.L. Nicholson, *Seventy Years of Service* (Ottawa: Borealis Press, 1977) 165.

106. Sir Basil Liddel Hart, *History of the Second World War* (London: Pan, 1977) 465.

107. Robert Citino, *The Wehrmacht Retreats: Fighting a Lost War, 1943* (Lawrence: University Press of Kansas, 2012) 195; Gooderson, *A Hard Way to Make War*, 100.

108. Carlo D'Este, *Eisenhower: A Soldier's Life* (New York: Henry Holt and Company, 2002) 438.

109. Rein, *The North African Air Campaign*, 158–66.

110. Atkinson, *The Day of Battle*, 165–7; D'Este, *Bitter Victory*, 505–35.

111. DHH, 181.003 (D3004), General Summary of Military and Air Situation in Mediterranean, July 1943.

112. Porch, *The Path to Victory*, 445; Nicholson, *The Canadians in Italy*, 174.

113. Nicholson, *The Canadians in Italy*, 174–5.

114. DHH, CMHQ Report No. 135, 1.

115. Galloway, *Some Died at Ortona*, 108.

116. Hamilton, *Monty: Master of the Battlefield*, 309.

CHAPTER 15: THE ITALIAN CAMPAIGN (PP. 377–417)

1. Citino, *The Wehrmacht Retreats*, 246–8; Evans, *The Third Reich at War*, 471.

2. Martin Blumenson, *Salerno to Cassino* (Washington: US Army Centre of Military History, 1993) 69.

3. MHRC, Robert Thexton, *Times to Remember: Some Recollections of Four and a Half Years Service with the West Nova Scotia Regiment during 1940–1944* (2008) 36–7.

4. RG 24, v. 10787, 224C1.093 (D3), RCAF Participation in the Italian Campaign, September 3rd to December 31st, 1943.

5. Brigadier C.J.C. Molony, *The Mediterranean and the Middle East*, volume V (London: HMSO, 1973) 325.

6. Martin Blumenson, *Patton: The Man behind the Legend, 1885–1945* (New York: William Morrow, 1985) 210.

7. D'Este, *Eisenhower*, 455.

8. Atkinson, *The Day of Battle*, 184.

9. Trumbull Higgins, *Soft Underbelly: The Anglo-American Controversy Over the Italian Campaign, 1939–1945* (New York: The Macmillan Company, 1968) 122.

10. For an introduction to Kesselring, see Shelford Bidwell, "Kesselring," in Correlli Barnett (ed.), *Hitler's Generals* (London: Phoenix, 1995) 265–92.

11. Bruce Lee, *Marching Orders* (New York: Crown Publishers, 1995) 190. Also see Ralph S. Mavrogordato, "Hitler's Decision on the Defense of Italy," in Kent Roberts Greenfield (ed.), *Command Decisions* (New York: Harcourt, Brace & Company, 1959).

12. Tooze, *The Wages of Destruction*, 412–13.

13. Lee Windsor, "Anatomy of Victory: Allied Containment Strategy and the Battle for the Gothic Line," (Ph.D. dissertation, University of New Brunswick, 2006) 46–7; Heinz Magenheimer, *Hitler's War: Germany's Key Strategic Decisions, 1940–1945* (New York: Barnes and Noble, 1997) 237.

14. Atkinson, *The Day of Battle*, 185, 255.

15. For German orders, see DHH, Historical Report No. 18, "The Campaign in Southern Italy, Sep–Dec 1943, Information from German Military Documents," 17–18.

16. LAC, RG 24, v. 10788, 224C1.2.6013 (D1), History of RCASC—1 Canadian Corps, 1943–1944, 7–8.

17. DHH, 321.009(D60), Visits—Reports, 1943, Extracts on mines.

18. Howard Mitchell, *My War* (self published, n.d.) 83.

19. Stanley Scislowski, *Not All of Us Were Brave* (Toronto: Dundurn Press, 1997) 143.

20. Portugal, *We Were There*, volume II, 772–3.

21. Mitchell, *RCHA: Right of the Line*, 108.

22. Cormier, *The Forgotten Soldiers*, 35.

23. Lee Windsor, "Boforce': 1st Canadian Infantry Division Operations in Support of the Salerno Bridgehead, Italy, 1943," *Canadian Military History* 4.2 (1995) 51–60.

24. Reid, *Speed's War*, 22.

25. Cormier, *The Forgotten Soldiers*, 14.

26. Mitchell, *RCHA—Right of the Line*, 107.

27. CWM, 20050097-001, Kenneth MacNeil collection, letter to wife, 14 January 1945, 4.

28. Harold Russell, "24th Canadian Field Ambulance: Royal Canadian Army Medical Corps," *Canadian Military History* 8.1 (Winter 1999) 71.

29. Feasby, *The Canadian Medical Services*, 160.

30. Mowat, *And No Birds Sang*, 185.

31. DHH, 78/361, *Operational Feeding: The Use of Field Rations, 1942* (Canada: HMSO, 1942).

32. CWM oral history interview, 31D 4 WALKER, pages 10–11.

33. LAC, RG 24, v. 10,450, file 212C1.011 (D1), Battle Experience Questionnaire, no. 18, Captain M. Pariseault.

34. CWM oral history interview, 31D 4 WALKER, pages 10–11.

35. Scislowski, *Not All of Us Were Brave*, 147.

36. MHRC, Jack Shepherd, *March to Fear* (self-published, 2003) 32.

37. LAC, RG 24, v. 10,450, file 212C1.011 (D1), Battle Experience Questionnaire, no. 10, no. 16, no. 18.

38. Galloway, *Some Died at Ortona*, 83.

39. MHRC, Herbert Hoskin, *Sometimes with Laughter: Recollections 1929–1964* (self-published, 1982) 24.

40. Charles Comfort, *Artist at War* (Toronto: Ryerson Press, 1956) 50.

41. LAC, RG 24, v. 10,779, file 224.C1.013 (D8) Medical History of the War, [ca. 1 July 1944], 6.

42. "Pooch" [C.E. Corrigan] *Tales of a Forgotten Theatre*, 13.

43. Mowat, *And No Birds Sang*, 204.

44. Lee Windsor, "Overlord's Long Right Flank: The Battles for Cassino and Anzio, January–June 1944," in Hayes, et al. (eds.), *Canada and the Second World War: Essays in Honour of Terry Copp* (Waterloo: Wilfrid Laurier Press, 2012) 224.

45. Terry Copp, "The Advance to the Moro: Army, Part 66," *The Legion* (1 September 2006), unpaginated [online].

46. Hamilton, *Master of the Battlefield*, 446.

47. John O'Brien, *Through the Gates of Hell and Back: The Private War of a Footslogger from "The Avenue"* (Halifax: New World Publishing, 2010) 102.

48. Daniel Dancocks, *The D-Day Dodgers: The Canadians in Italy, 1943-1945* (Toronto: McClelland & Stewart, 1991) 125.

49. CMHQ Report No. 165, 22.

50. WD, RG 24, v. 15256, Seaforth Highlanders, December 1943, Appendix 7, report by Lt. Col. J.D. Forin.

51. Mitchell, *RCHA—Right of the Line*, 98.

52. DHH, Historical Report No. 18, "The Campaign in Southern Italy, Sep–Dec 1943, Information from German Military Documents," 51.

53. CMHQ Report No. 165, 28.

54. Bercuson, *The Patricias*, 208.

55. G.R. Stevens, *Princess Patricia's Canadian Light Infantry, 1919-1957* (Montreal: Southam Printing, 1957) 128.

56. DHH, 145.2H1013(D1), Battle of Moro River, report of the Hastings and Prince Edward Regiment, 1–2.

57. DHH, 145.2H1013(D1), Battle of Moro River, report of the Hastings and Prince Edward Regiment, 2.

58. Nicholson, *The Gunners of Canada*, volume II, 166.

59. Mowat, *And No Birds Sang*, 225.

60. CMHQ Report No. 165, 39.

61. CWM, oral history, 31D 1 MEDD, page 9.

62. DHH, Historical Report No. 18, "The Campaign in Southern Italy, Sep–Dec 1943, Information from German Military Documents," 50.

63. Beattie, *Dileas: History of the 48th Highlanders of Canada,* 423.

64. DHH, Historical Report No. 18, "The Campaign in Southern Italy, Sep–Dec 1943, Information from German Military Documents," 53.

65. See C.P. Stacey, *A Date with History: Memoirs of a Canadian Historian* (Ottawa: Deneau, 1983).

66. See Dean F. Oliver and Laura Brandon, *Canvas of War: Painting the Canadian Experience, 1914 to 1945* (Vancouver: Douglas & McIntyre, 2000).

67. Comfort, *Artist at War*, 81.

68. CMHQ Report No. 165, 42.

69. WD, Royal Canadian Artillery, 10 December 1943.

70. Daniel Dancocks, *The D-Day Dodgers: The Canadians in Italy, 1943-1945* (Toronto: McClelland & Stewart, 1991) 162.

71. CMHQ Report No. 165, 47.

72. CMHQ Report No. 165, 47.

73. Bill McAndrew, *Canadians and the Italian Campaign, 1943–1945* (Montreal: Art Global, 1996) 72.

74. WD, 1st Division, A and Q headquarters, December 1943, Appendix 10.

75. DHH, 145.2E2011 (D1), account by Lt. Col. J.C. Jefferson, 12. 1. 1944, 1.

76. Scislowski, *Not All of Us Were Brave*, 110.

77. Cessford, "Hard in the Attack," 227.

78. O'Brien *Through the Gates of Hell and Back*, 107.

79. War Diary, West Nova Scotia Regiment, 13 December 1943.

80. War Diary, Carlton and Yorks Regiment, 13 December 1943.

81. Nicholson, *The Gunners of Canada*, volume II, 170.

82. DHH, Historical Report No. 18, "The Campaign in Southern Italy, Sep–Dec 1943, Information from German Military Documents," 57.

83. G.C. Case, "Trial by Fire: Major-General Christopher Vokes at the Battles of the Moro River and Ortona, 1943," *Canadian Military History* 16.3 (Summer 2007) 21.

84. Thomas Raddall, *West Novas: A History of the West Nova Scotia Regiment* (Liverpool, NS: no publisher listed, 1947) 161–2.

85. Case, "Trial by Fire," 25.

86. DHH, 142. 4F3 (D28), Battle Drill and the PIAT, 1–2.

87. Cormier, *The Forgotten Soldiers*, 38.

88. RG 24, v. 10,881, 234C1.013 (D1), Crossing of the Moro and Capture of Ortona, HQ 1 Cdn Inf Div, 16 March 1944, 4.

89. John MacFarlane, *Triquet's Cross: A Study of Military Heroism* (Montreal: McGill-Queen's University Press, 2009).

90. LAC, RG 24, v. 10,982, Account by Captain R.D. Price, 26 January 1944.

91. DHH, 321.009(D60), Visits—Reports, 1943, Canadian Operations in the Mediterranean Area, July–October 1943 [interview of Vokes by Historical Officer Sam Hughes], 5 January 1944, 1.

92. Mitchell, *My War*, 94.

93. See Brereton Greenhous, "Would It Not Have Been Better to Bypass Ortona Completely?," *Canadian Defence Quarterly* 19 (April 1989) 51–5.

94. See Doug Delaney, *The Soldiers' General: Bert Hoffmeister at War* (Vancouver: UBC Press, 2005).

95. Ian Gooderson, "Assimilating Urban Battle Experience—The Canadians at Ortona," *Canadian Military Journal* (2007–2008) 66.

96. Carl Bayerlein, Alex MacQuarrie (trans.), "Parachute Engineers in Combat, Ortona 1943: A German Perspective," *Canadian Military History* 8.4 (Autumn 1999) 47.

97. DHH, 780.023 (D1), German Anti-Tank Weapons, Ortona, 16 April 1951.

98. RG 24, v. 10841, 230.c1 (D15) Extract from Intelligence Log, The Edmonton Regiment, 21 Dec 1943.

99. Shaun R.G. Brown, "'The Rock of Accomplishment': The Loyal Edmonton Regiment at Ortona," *Canadian Military History* 2.2 (1993) 16.

100. Bayerlein, "Parachute Engineers in Combat, Ortona 1943," 49.

101. DHH, 145.2E2011 (D1), account by Lt. Col. J.C. Jefferson, 12. 1. 1944, 4.

102. Roy, *The Seaforth Highlanders of Canada*, 272.

103. RG 24, v. 10841, 230.c1 (D15) Report of the Historical Section, General Staff Branch, Ortona, 16 Feb 1944, Appendix B, Company commander's Story Illustrating the Use of Beehives.

104. Robert Wallace, *The Italian Campaign* (Alexandria: Time-Life, 1981) 107.

105. Brown, "'The Rock of Accomplishment,'" 20.

106. Mitchell, *My* War, 95.

107. Mark Zuehlke, *Ortona Street Fight* (Victoria: Raven Books, 2011) 137.

108. Sarah Klotz, "Shooting the War: The Canadian Army Film Unit in the Second World War," *Canadian Military History* 14.3 (2005) 28.

109. RG 24, v. 15,114, Mathew Halton, Ortona transcript broadcast, 4 January 1944. On the technical nature of broadcasting from the front, see A.E. Powley, *Broadcast from the Front: Canadian Radio Overseas in the Second World War* (Toronto: Hakkert, 1975) 55–6, 61–9.

110. I would like to thank David Halton for letting me read a manuscript that he has prepared on his father, Matthew Halton.

111. Douglas Delaney, "When Leadership Really Mattered: Bert Hoffmeister and Morale During the Battle of Ortona, December 1943," in Horn (ed.) *Intrepid Warriors*, 143.

112. *We Were Freedom*, 58.

113. DHH, Historical Report No. 18, "The Campaign in Southern Italy, Sep–Dec 1943, Information from German Military Documents," 65.

114. DHH, Historical Report No. 18, "The Campaign in Southern Italy, Sep–Dec 1943, Information from German Military Documents," 64.

115. DHH, 145.2H1013(D1), Battle of the Bulge, report of the Hastings and Prince Edward Regiment, 1.

116. Bayerlein, "Parachute Engineers in Combat, Ortona 1943," 50.

117. LAC, RG 24, v. 17505, War Diary, 1 Cdn Fd Hist Section, 28 December 1943.

118. Nicholson, *The Canadians in Italy*, 338; RG 24, v. 10,881, 234C1.013 (D1), Crossing of the Moro and Capture of Ortona, HQ 1 Cdn Inf Div, 16 March 1944, 9.

119. Eldon S. Davis, *An Awesome Silence: A Gunner Padre's Journey through the Valley of the Shadow* (Carp, ON: Creative Bound, 1991) 64.

120. Terry Copp and Bill McAndrew, *Battle Exhaustion: Soldiers and Psychiatrists in the Canadian Army, 1939–1945* (Montreal: McGill-Queen's University Press, 1990) 56.

121. LAC, RG 24, v. 10,450, file 212C1.011 (D1), Battle Experience Questionnaire, No. 23, Acting Captain R.R. Johnston.

122. See Copp and McAndrew, *Battle Exhaustion*, 56–62.

123. Galloway, *Some Died at Ortona*, 217–18.

CONCLUSION: THE END OF THE BEGINNING (PP. 419–423)

1. Kim Beattie, *Dileas: History of the 48th Highlanders of Canada, 1929–1956* (Toronto: published by the regiment, 1957) 420.

2. Bashow, *No Prouder Place*, 456–7.

3. Hastings, *All Hell Let Loose*, 454.

ACKNOWLEDGMENTS

The Necessary War is my seventh book, with the second volume to follow in 2015. While each book is special and brings its own challenges and complexities, these two books are different. I wrote them while fighting cancer. I had been thinking of how to approach the books for some time and had been gathering evidence for years, but I wrote them while facing my own personal health challenge that involved several regimes of chemo and radiation therapy. I was told by many concerned friends to down tools and focus on my health, which I did, but I also clung to these books as anchors in the storm. Every two weeks I was bedridden for days on end; when I was feeling marginally better, I often worked curled up on the floor; all the while, I worried that my chemo brain fog would never lift. Throughout the process, I drew considerable strength from reading the letters, diaries, and memoirs of Canadians and from how they coped with and endured their own struggles. They had their battles, which I sought to chronicle, and I had mine. I remain awed by those young Canadians more than seventy years ago who faced death and destruction at almost every turn and, most often, found ways to keep going forward. They are an inspiration to me.

So are the friends and colleagues who agreed to read all or parts of the manuscript—many of whom are leaders in the study of the Second World War—and whose work I have used as the foundation for my own books. My colleague, Dr. Peter Macleod, read this manuscript, as he has done for all the previous ones, and he offered excellent comments. Dr. William Stewart shared his expertise freely and suggested several interesting links between the First and Second World Wars. My friend Eric Brown, a volunteer at the Canadian War Museum and a co-author of several articles with me, thoroughly edited the text and provided his own thoughts on many sections, especially those about the naval and air war. Military historian Nathan Greenfield commented expertly on the Hong Kong chapter. Dr. Alec Douglas, one of the doyens of Canadian military history, read the manuscript and pointed out sections, especially on the naval war, that might be augmented or modified. Dr. Roger Sarty, a former boss of mine from the Canadian War Museum, and a mentor, unleashed his formidable knowledge on several key chapters and saved me embarrassment by rectifying minor details. Dr. Jack Granatstein, author of over seventy books, has always been very generous towards me and he read the entire manuscript, pointing out errors of omission and commission. Professor Terry Copp provided important comments in several key areas, especially the sections on Dieppe and Italy. Dr. Steve Harris of the Directorate of History, my Ph.D. supervisor and an expert on all aspects of the war, read the manuscript and pushed me to enlarge my scope of inquiry in a number of sections. And finally, my friend and former colleague from the CWM and now professor at the University of Ottawa, Dr. Serge Duflinger, offered wide-ranging commentary on every aspect of the war. He shared his deep knowledge of the Canadian and international war effort and saved me time and time again. To the many readers who improved the manuscript, I thank you all.

I would like to thank Matthew Walthert and Sarah Cook for researching into the Canadian Images and Letters Project and the Dominion Institute Memory Project. In reading through hundreds of letters and interview transcripts, they found some gems. My agent and friend Rick Broadhead always had time to ring me and raise my spirits. Jonathan Webb, an editor and author, provided an exceptional edit and helped me shape the book, clarify the arguments, and sharpen the writing. Editorial director Diane Turbide has stood behind me from the beginning, and I'm grateful for her energy and backing. Tara Tovell provided her usual skill and patience in her line and copy editing, with this being our fifth book together. Our ongoing collaboration is a delight. It was a pleasure to work with the thorough and conscientious Mary Ann Blair in the production stages of the book. I am grateful to all, and to the many others at Penguin Canada who have worked hard on my behalf.

I am blessed with a wide circle of friends. Throughout my illness, I received encouraging words of strength from colleagues and friends at the CWM, at Carleton University, throughout Ottawa, across the country, and around the world. At the

CWM, Director General James Whitham offered unflinching support. Two friends, Serge Durflinger and Norman Hillmer, provided steadfast cheer and sensible ways to think about my illness. Our neighbours in Manor Park took our girls on play-dates and tried to keep life as normal as possible. At every turn, there was kindness and generosity.

During this time of worry, my parents, Sharon and Terry, and my brother, Graham, bore a heavy burden. They never wavered. I drew strength from them. My own family stood beside me daily in the battle for my health. Sarah, my partner and love, has been a rock for our three girls, Paige, Emma, and Chloe; together and individually they brought joy and instilled courage to keep me in the fight. I could not have done it without them. I share this book with my girls.

BIBLIOGRAPHY

CANADIAN WAR MUSEUM, OTTAWA

20030316-001, G. Stuart Brown collection

19770102-006, Miller Gore Brittain collection

20100088-030, Alexander Campbell collection

19910181-043, George Joseph Chequer collection

19820624-001, "Composition of Advance Party," no date

20040074-004, Harold Edison DeMone collection

20030169-013, "DEMS, Wrens, R.C.N.S and Little Green Apples"

20070044-008, Warren Alvin Duffy collection

20080086-001, Raymond Elliot collection

19830038-001, Donald Geraghty collection

20080118-007, Joseph Harrison collection

20110062-014, Geoffrey Hughson, "I was going to write a book"

20020026-003, D.J.R. Humphreys collection

20060058-001, Second World War Letter Collection of Norma Lee

20050097-001, Kenneth MacNeil collection

19910163-014, Ben Malkin collection

20060191-003, Leslie McCaig collection

19950077-001, John Oliver Payne collection

20010200-002, Thomas Reid collection

20050094-002, War Diary and letters of A. Ray Squire

19810684-004, D.L. Welsh collection

Military History Research Centre [hereafter MHRC], Herbert Hoskin, *Sometimes with Laughter: Recollections 1929–1964* (self-published, 1982)

MHRC, Richard C. Pearce, "Recollections"

MHRC, Jack Shepherd, *March to Fear* (self-published, 2003)

MHRC, Roy Spackman, *A Hell of a Crew*
MHRC, Robert Thexton, *Times to Remember: Some Recollections of Four and a Half Years Service with the West Nova Scotia Regiment during 1940–1944* (2008)

CANADIAN WAR MUSEUM ORAL HISTORY INTERVIEW PROGRAM

31D 4 BARONI
31D 1 BOWEN
31D 3 BURBRIDGE
31D 4 CHANCE
31D 1 CHENEY
31D 1 FINNIE
31D 5 FLEMING
31D 1 LESSARD
31D 5 MAFFRE
31D 1 MEDD
31D 1 NIXON
31D 1 PETERSON
31D 1 REID
31D 3 SMITH
31D 3 STEWART
31D 1 VRADENBURG
31D 1 WAHLROTH
31D 4 WALKER

LIBRARY AND ARCHIVES CANADA, OTTAWA

H.D.G. Crerar
Ian Mackenzie papers
William Lyon Mackenzie King
William Lyon Mackenzie King personal diary, digitized and online
A.G.L. McNaughton

DIRECTORATE OF HISTORY AND HERITAGE

DHH, Bio File, William Acheson, diary
DHH, Bio file, Clifford Ashton, interview
DHH, Bio file, Clare L. Annis, interview

DHH, Bio file, Alan Frederick Avant

DHH, Bio file, Douglas Baird, interview

DHH, Bio file, D.C.T. Bennett, interview

DHH, Bio file, Edwin Bennett, interview

DHH, 593.013 (D10), Colonel Doi's Battle Progress Report, 9–10

DHH, 593 (D26) "Notes on Interview, Major Nicholson with Lieutenant-Colonel H.B. Rose, 8 & 9 June 1946"

DHH, 503/D33, Lieutenant-Colonel George Trist, Report on the Part Played by the Winnipeg Grenadiers in the Defence of Hong Kong, North Point Camp, April 1942

CANADIAN IMAGES AND LETTERS PROJECT

James Baker

DOMINION INSTITUTE ORAL HISTORY PROGRAM

Elmer Cairns, Andy Carswell, Joseph Dempsey, Sid Dobing, Roy Ernest Eddy, Elwyn Leslie Garayt, Elliot Anthony Griffin, Yvonne Jukes, Fraser Muir, George Richmond, Harry Urwin

QUEEN'S UNIVERSITY

Charles Power papers

HONG KONG VETERANS COMMEMORATIVE ASSOCIATION

Alfred Babin's story; William Bell's story; Vince Calder's story; Bob Clayton's story; Tom Marsh's account

ARTICLES

Alexander, Martin S. "After Dunkirk: The French Army's Performance against 'Case Red,' 25 May to 25 June 1940," *War in History* 14.2 (April 2007) 219–64.

Armstrong, John G. "RCAF Identity in Bomber Command: Squadron Names and Sponsors," *Canadian Military History* 8.2 (Spring 1999) 43–52.

Bell, Christopher M. "'Our Most Exposed Outpost': Hong Kong and British Far Eastern Strategy, 1921–1941," *Journal of Military History* 60.1 (1996) 61–88.

Ballingall, Alex. "The Real Story of Canada's Worst Disaster," *Maclean's Magazine* (20 August, 2012) 20.

Balzer, Timothy. "'In Case the Raid Is Unsuccessful ...' Selling Dieppe to Canadians," *The Canadian Historical Review* 87.3 (2006) 409–30.

Barry, Grant N. "Beyond the Consensus: 1st Canadian Infantry Division at Agira, Sicily, 24–28 July 1943," *Canadian Military History* 19.2 (Spring 2010) 41–54.

Bayerlein, Carl, Alex MacQuarrie (trans.). "Parachute Engineers in Combat, Ortona 1943: A German Perspective," *Canadian Military History* 8.4 (Autumn 1999) 47–50.

Bothwell, Robert and John English, "'Dirty Work at the Crossroads': New Perspectives on the Riddell Incident," *Historical Papers* 7.1 (1972) 263–85.

Bothwell, Robert. "The Canadian Isolationist Tradition," *International Journal* 54.1 (Winter 1998–1999) 76–87.

Broad, Graham. "Not Competent to Produce Tanks: The Ram and Tank Production in Canada, 1939–1945," *Canadian Military History* 11.1 (Winter 2002) 24–36.

Brown, Atholl Sutherland. "Forgotten Squared: Canadian Aircrew in Southeast Asia, 1942–1945," *Canadian Military History* 8.2 (Spring 1999) 59–68.

Brown, Shaun. "'The Rock of Accomplishment': The Loyal Edmonton Regiment at Ortona," *Canadian Military History* 2.2 (1993) 10–23.

Byers, Daniel. "Mobilising Canada: The National Resources Mobilization Act, the Department of National Defence, and Compulsory Military Service in Canada, 1940–1945," *Journal of the Canadian Historical Association* 7.1 (1996).

Cafferky, Shawn. "'A Useful Lot, These Canadian Ships': The Royal Canadian Navy and Operation Torch, 1942–1943," *The Northern Mariner* 3.4 (October 1993) 1–17.

Case, G.C. "Trial by Fire: Major-General Christopher Vokes at the Battles of the Moro River and Ortona, 1943," *Canadian Military History* 16.3 (Summer 2007) 13–28.

Commacchio, Cynthia. "'To Hold on High the Torch of Liberty': Canadian Youth and the Second World War," in Geoffrey Hayes, et al. (eds.), *Canada and the Second World War: Essays in Honour of Terry Copp* (Waterloo: Wilfrid Laurier University Press, 2012) 33–66.

Cook, Tim. "Against God-Inspired Conscience: Perceptions of Gas Warfare as a Weapon of Mass Destruction, 1915–1939," *War & Society* 18.1 (May 2000) 47–69.

Copp, Terry. "Ontario 1939: The Decision for War," *Ontario History* 86.3 (1994) 269–78.

Copp, Terry. "The Decision to Reinforce Hong Kong, September 1941," *Canadian Military History* 20.2 (Spring 2011) 3–13.

Copp, Terry. "The Defence of Hong Kong, December 1941," *Canadian Military History* 10.4 (Autumn 2001) 5–20.

Copp, Terry. "From Leonforte to Agira: Army, Part 61," *The Legion* online, n.p.

Delaney, Douglas. "When Leadership Really Mattered: Bert Hoffmeister and Morale During the Battle of Ortona, December 1943," in Horn (ed.), *Intrepid Warriors* (Kingston: Defence Academy Press) 139–54.

Dickson, Paul. "Crerar and the Decision to Reinforce Hong Kong," *Canadian Military History* 2.1 (Spring 1994) 97–110.

Dickson, Paul. "Harry Crerar and an Army for Strategic Effect," *Canadian Military History* 17.1 (Winter 2008) 37–48.

Douglas, W.A.B. and Jurgen Rohwer. "'The Most Thankless Task' Revisited: Convoys, Escorts, and Radio Intelligence in the Western Atlantic, 1941–1943," in James A. Boutilier (ed.), *RCN in Retrospect, 1910–1968* (Vancouver: UBC Press, 1982) 187–234.

Durflinger, Serge. "'Nothing Would Be Too Much Trouble': Hometown Support for H.M.C.S. Dunver, 1943–1945," *The Northern Mariner* 12.4 (October 2002) 1–12.

Fedorowich, Kent. "'Cocked Hats and Swords and Small, Little Garrisons': Britain, Canada and the Fall of Hong Kong, 1941," *Modern Asian Studies* 37 (February 2003) 111–57.

Fisher, Robert C. "The Impact of German Technology on the Royal Canadian Navy in the Battle of the Atlantic, 1942–1943," *The Northern Mariner* 7.4 (October 1997) 1–13.

Fisher, Robert. "'We'll Get Our Own': Canada and the Oil Shipping Crisis of 1942," *The Northern Mariner* 3.2 (1993) 33–9.

Fisher, Robert. "Canadian Merchant Ship Losses, 1939–1945," *The Northern Mariner* 5.3 (1995) 57–73.

Fisher, Robert C. "Tactics, Training, Technology: The RCN's Summer of Success, July–September 1942," *Canadian Military History* 6.2 (Autumn 1997) 7–20.

Fisher, Robert C. "Heroism: On the North Atlantic," *The Legion* online (May 2002), n.p.

Glover, William. "The RCN: Royal Colonial or Royal Canadian Navy," in Michael Hadley, et al. (eds.), *A Nation's Navy: In Quest of Canadian Naval Identity* (Montreal: McGill-Queen's University Press, 1996) 71–90.

Gooderson, Ian. "Assimilating Urban Battle Experience—The Canadians at Ortona," *Canadian Military Journal* (2007–2008) 64–73.

Goette, Richard. "Britain and the Delay in Closing the Mid-Atlantic 'Air Gap' during the Battle of the Atlantic," *The Northern Mariner* 15.4 (October 2005) 19–41.

Goette, Richard. "Squadron Leader N.E. Small: A Study of Leadership in the RCAF's Eastern Air Command, 1942," *Canadian Military Journal* (Spring 2004) 43–50.

Granatstein, J.L., and Robert Bothwell. "'A Self-Evident National Duty': Canadian Foreign Policy, 1935–1939," *Journal of Imperial and Commonwealth History* 3 (1975) 212–33.

Gray, Peter. "The Gloves Will Have to Come Off: A Reappraisal of the Legitimacy of the RAF Bomber Offensive Against Germany," *Air Power Review* 13.3 (Autumn/Winter 2010) 9–40.

Gray, Peter. "A Culture of Official Squeamishness? Britain's Air Ministry and the Strategic Air Offensive against Germany," *Journal of Military History* 77.4 (October 2013) 1349–77.

Hadley, Michael L. "The Popular Image of the Canadian Navy," in Michael Hadley, et al.

(eds.), *A Nation's Navy: In Quest of Canadian Naval Identity* (Montreal: McGill-Queen's University Press, 1996) 35–56.

Harris, Stephen J. "The Halifax and Lancaster in Canadian Service," *Canadian Military History* 15.3 & 15.4 (Summer–Autumn, 2006) 5–26.

Hall, David. "Black, White and Grey: Wartime Arguments for and against the Strategic Bombing Offensive," *Canadian Military History* 7.1 (Winter 1998) 7–19.

Hall, David Ian. "The German View of the Dieppe Raid," *Canadian Military History* 21.4 (Autumn 2012) 3–16.

Harrison, Mark. "Medicine and the Culture of Command: The Case of Malaria Control in the British Army during the Two World Wars," *Medical History* 40 (1996) 437–52.

Hayes, Geoffrey. "The Canadians in Sicily: Sixty Years On," *Canadian Military History* 12.3 (Summer 2003) 5–18.

Hauner, Milan. "Did Hitler Want a World Dominion?" *Journal of Contemporary History* 13 (1978) 15–32.

Henshaw, Peter. "The Dieppe Raid: A Product of Misplaced Canadian Nationalism?" *Canadian Historical Review* 77.2 (1996) 250–66.

Henry, Hugh. "The Calgary Tanks at Dieppe," *Canadian Military History* 4.1 (Spring 1995) 61–74.

Joost, Mathias. "Racism and Enlistment: The Second World War Policies of the Royal Canadian Air Force," *Canadian Military History* 21.1 (Winter 2012) 17–34.

Knox, J.H.W. "An Engineer's Outline of RCN History," in James A. Boutilier (ed.), *RCN in Retrospect, 1910–1968* (Vancouver: UBC Press, 1982) 96–115.

Koch, H.W. "The Spectre of a Separate Peace in the East: Russo–German 'Peace Feelers,' 1942–1944," *Journal of Contemporary History* 10 (1975) 531–49.

Klotz, Sarah. "Shooting the War: The Canadian Army Film Unit in the Second World War," *Canadian Military History* 14.3 (2005) 21–38.

Lackenbauer, Whitney. "'A Hell of a Warrior': Remembering Sergeant Thomas George Prince," *Journal of Historical Biography* 1 (Spring 2007) 26–79.

Leir, Richard H. "'Big Ship Time': The Formative Years of RCN Officers serving in RN Capital Ships," in James A. Boutilier (ed.), *RCN in Retrospect, 1910–1968* (Vancouver: UBC Press, 1982) 74–95.

Lee, Peter. "Return from the Wilderness: An Assessment of Arthur Harris' Moral Responsibility for the German City Bombings," *Air Power Review* 16.1 (2013) 70–90.

Lund, W.G.D. "The Royal Canadian Navy's Quest for Autonomy in the North West Atlantic, 1941–1943," in James A. Boutilier (ed.), *RCN in Retrospect, 1910–1968* (Vancouver: UBC Press, 1982) 138–157.

Mahoney, Ross. "'The Support Afforded by the Air Force Was Faultless': The Royal Air Force and the Raid on Dieppe, 19 August 1942," *Canadian Military History* 21.4 (Autumn 2012) 17–32.

Marsden, Paul. "The Costs of No Commitments: Canadian Economic Planning for War," in Norman Hillmer, et al. (eds.), *A Country of Limitations: Canada and the World in 1939* (Ottawa: Canadian Committee for the History of the Second World War, 1996) 199–216.

Mayne, Richard. "The People's Navy: Myth, Reality, and Life in Canada's Naval Reserves 1939–1945," in Richard Gimblett and Michael Hadley (eds.), *Citizen Sailors: Chronicles of Canada's Naval Reserves* (Toronto: Dundurn, 2010) 53–74.

Mayne, Richard Oliver. "Bypassing the Chain of Command: The Political Origins of the RCN's Equipment Crisis of 1943," *Canadian Military History* 9.3 (Summer 2000) 7–22.

McAndrew, William. "Fire or Movement? Canadian Tactical Doctrine, Sicily—1943," *Military Affairs* 51.3 (July 1987) 140–5.

McRae, Bill. "Bed and Breakfast: A Canadian Airman Reflects on Food and Quarters during the Second World War," *Canadian Military History* 9.1 (2000) 60–70.

McWilliams, Caitlin. "Camaraderie, Morale and Material Culture: Reflections on the Nose Art of No. 6 Group Royal Canadian Air Force," *Canadian Military History* 19.4 (Autumn 2010) 21–30.

Meilinger, Phillip S. "Trenchard and 'Morale Bombing': The Evolution of Royal Air Force Doctrine before World War II," *The Journal of Military History* 60.2 (1996) 243–70.

Millman, Brock. "Canada, Sanctions and the Abyssinian Crisis of 1935," *The Historical Journal* 40.1 (March 1997) 143–68.

Miller, Ian. "Toronto's Response to the Outbreak of War, 1939," *Canadian Military History* 11.1 (Winter 2002) 5–23.

Milner, Marc. "The Accidental Enemy: Navy, Part 41," *The Legion* online (October 2010) n.p.

Milner, Marc. "The Fate of Slow Convoy 42: Navy, Part 33," *The Legion* online (18 June 2009).

Milner, Marc. "The Implications of Technological Backwardness: The Royal Canadian Navy, 1939–1945," *Canadian Defence Quarterly* 19.3 (Winter 1989) 46–52.

Milner, Marc. "Fighting the U-boats, 1939–45," Richard H. Gimblett (ed.), *The Naval Service of Canada: 1910–2010* (Toronto: Dundurn, 2010) 87–104.

Milner, Marc. "More Royal Than Canadian? The Royal Canadian Navy's Search for Identity, 1910–68," in Philip Buckner (ed.) *Canada and the End of Empire* (Vancouver: UBC Press, 2005) 272–84.

Milner, Marc. "Royal Canadian Navy Participation in the Battle of the Atlantic Crisis of 1943," in James A. Boutilier, *RCN in Retrospect, 1910–1968* (Vancouver: UBC Press, 1982) 158–74.

O'Brien, Phillips. "East versus West in the Defeat of Nazi Germany," *Journal of Strategic Studies* 23.2 (2000) 89–113.

Parks, W. Hays. "'Precision' and 'Area' Bombing: Who Did Which and When?," *Journal of Strategic Studies* 18.1 (1995) 145–74.

Peloquin, Laurie. "Area Bombing by Day: Bombing Command and the Daylight Offensive, 1944–1945," *Canadian Military History* 15.3 & 15.4 (Summer–Autumn, 2006) 27–42.

Peloquin, Laurie. "A Conspiracy of Silence? The Popular Press and the Strategic Bombing Campaign in Europe," *Canadian Military History* 3.2 (1994) 23–30.

Perras, Galen Roger. "'Our Position in the Far East Would be Stronger without This Unsatisfactory Commitment': Britain and the Reinforcement of Hong Kong, 1941," *Canadian Journal of History* 30.2 (1995) 232–59.

Perras, Galen. "Defeat Still Cries Aloud for Explanation: Explaining C Force's Dispatch to Hong Kong," *Canadian Military Journal* 11.4 (Autumn 2011) 37–47.

Pollock, Fred. "Roosevelt, the Ogdensburg Agreement, and the British Fleet: All Done with Mirrors," *Diplomatic History* 5 (1981) 203–19.

Pullen, T.C. "Convoy O.N. 127 & the Loss of HMCS *Ottawa*, 13 September 1942: A Personal Reminiscence," *The Northern Mariner* 2.2 (April 1992) 1–27.

Pulsifer, Cameron. "John Robert Osborn: Canada's Hong Kong VC." *Canadian Military History* 6.2 (Autumn 1997) 79–89.

Redford, Duncan. "Inter and Intra-Service Rivalries in the Battle of the Atlantic," *Journal of Strategic Studies* 32.6 (2009) 899–928.

"Report by Miss Kathleen G Christie, Nurse with the Canadian Forces at Hong Kong, as Given on Board SS Gripsholm, November 1943," *Canadian Military History* 10.4 (Autumn 2001) 27–34.

"Report of the Historical Section, Cabinet Office, London," cited in *Canadian Military History* 2.2. (Autumn 1993) 111–16.

Roland, Charles G. "On the Beach and in the Bag: The Fate of Dieppe Casualties Left Behind," *Canadian Military History* 9.4 (Autumn 2000) 6–25.

Russell, Harold. "24th Canadian Field Ambulance: Royal Canadian Army Medical Corps," *Canadian Military History* 8.1 (Winter 1999) 65–74.

Sarty, Roger. "Mr. King and the Armed Forces," in Norman Hillmer, et al. (eds.), *A Country of Limitations: Canada and the World in 1939* (Ottawa: Canadian Committee for the History of the Second World War, 1996) 217–46.

Sarty, Roger. "Ultra, Air Power, and the Second Battle of the St. Lawrence, 1944," in Timothy J. Runyan and Jan M. Copes (eds.), *To Die Gallantly: The Battle of the Atlantic* (Boulder: Westview, 1994) 186–209.

Shelley, C.R. "HMCS Prince Robert: The Career of an Armed Merchant Cruiser," *Canadian Military History* 4.1 (1995) 47–60.

Sheffield, Scott. "Fighting a White Man's War?: First Nations Participation in the Canadian War Effort, 1939–1945," Geoffrey Hayes, et al. (eds.), *Canada and the Second World War: Essays in Honour of Terry Copp* (Waterloo: Wilfrid Laurier University Press, 2012) 67–91.

Stacey, Colonel C.P. "The Canadian–American Permanent Joint Board on Defence, 1940–1945," *International Journal* 9.2 (Spring 1954) 107–24.

Stewart, Andrew. "The 1939 British and Canadian 'Empire Air Training Scheme' Negotiations," *Round Table* 93 (2004) 739–54.

Stuart, Rob. "Leonard Birchall and the Japanese Raid on Colombo," *Canadian Military Journal* (Winter 2006–2007) 65–74.

Syrett, David. "The Battle for Convoy HX 133, 23–29 June 1941," *The Northern Mariner* 12.3 (July 2002) 43–50.

Vance, Jonathan F. "Understanding the Motive to Enlist," in Sherrill Grace, et al. (eds.), *Bearing Witness: Perspectives on War and Peace from the Arts and Humanities* (McGill-Queen's University Press, 2012) 28–40.

Villa, Brian and Peter Henshaw. "The Dieppe Raid Debate," *Canadian Historical Review* 79.2 (1998) 304–15.

White, Jay. "Hardly Heroes: Canadian Merchant Seamen and the International Convoy System," *The Northern Mariner* 5.4 (1995) 19–36.

Windsor, Lee. "'Boforce': 1st Canadian Infantry Division Operations in Support of the Salerno Bridgehead, Italy, 1943," *Canadian Military History* 4.2 (1995) 51–60.

Windsor, Lee. "'The Eyes of All Fixed on Sicily': Canada's Unexpected Victory, 1943," *Canadian Military History* 22.3 (Summer 2013) 4–34.

Wentzell, Tyler. "Brigadier J.K. Lawson and Command of 'C' Force at Hong Kong," *Canadian Military History* 20.2 (Spring 2011) 14–26.

Zimmerman, David. "The Social Background of the Wartime Navy: Some Statistical Data," in Michael Hadley, et al. (eds.) *A Nation's Navy: In Quest of Canadian Naval Identity* (McGill-Queen's University Press, 1996) 256–79.

BOOKS

Abella, Irving and Harold Troper. *None Is Too Many: Canada and the Jews of Europe, 1933–1948*. Toronto: Lester & Orpen Dennys, 1982.

Adachi, Ken. *The Enemy That Never Was: A History of the Japanese Canadians*, 2nd edition. Toronto: McClelland & Stewart, 1991.

Addison, Paul and Jeremy A. Crang (eds.). *The Burning Blue: A New History of the Battle of Britain*. London: Pimlico, 2000.

Air Ministry, Air Historical Branch, *The Rise and Fall of the German Air Force*. London: HMSO, 1983.

Aldrich, Richard J. *Intelligence and the War against Japan: Britain, America and the Politics of Secret Service*. Cambridge: Cambridge University Press, 2000.

Allison, Les. *Canadians in the Royal Air Force*. Roland: L. Allison, 1978.

Allison, Les and Harry Hayward. *They Shall Not Grow Old, a Book of Remembrance*. Brandon: The Commonwealth Air Training Plan Museum, 1991.

Aly, Gotz, et al. *Cleansing the Fatherland: Nazi Medicine and Racial Hygiene*. Baltimore: Hopkins Fulfillment Service, 1994.

Antal, Sandy and Kevin Shackleton. *Duty Nobly Done: The Official History of the Essex and Kent Scottish Regiment*. Windsor: Walkerville, 2006.

Atkinson, Rick. *The Day of Battle: The War in Sicily and Italy, 1943–1944*. New York: Henry Holt, 2007.

Bangarth, Stephanie. *Voices Raised in Protest: Defending North American Citizens of Japanese Ancestry, 1942–49*. Vancouver: UBC Press, 2008.

Banham, Tony. *Not the Slightest Chance: The Defence of Hong Kong, 1941*. Vancouver: UBC Press, 2003.

Barnett, Correlli. *Engage the Enemy More Closely: The Royal Navy in the Second World War*. New York: Norton, 1991.

Barnett, Correlli (ed.). *Hitler's Generals*. London: Phoenix, 1995.

Barr, Niall. *Pendulum of War: Three Battles at El Alamein*. Woodstock: Overlook, 2005.

Bartov, Omar. *The Eastern Front 1941–1945: German Troops and the Barbarisation of Warfare*. Basingstoke: Palgrave Macmillan, 2001.

Bartov, Omar. *Hitler's Army: Soldiers, Nazis, and War in the Third Reich*. New York: Oxford University Press, 1991.

Bashow, David. *All the Fine Young Eagles: In the Cockpit with Canada's Second World War Fighter Pilots*. Toronto: Stoddart, 1997.

Bashow, David. *None but the Brave: The Essential Contributions of RAF Bomber Command to Allied Victory during the Second World War*. Kingston: Canadian Forces Defence Academy, 2009.

Bashow, David. *No Prouder Place: Canadians and the Bomber Command Experience, 1939 to 1945*. St. Catharines: Vanwell, 2005.

Beattie, Kim. *Dileas: History of the 48th Highlanders of Canada, 1929–1956*. Toronto: published by the regiment, 1957.

Beck, J. Murray. *Pendulum of Power: Canada's Federal Elections*. Scarborough: Prentice-Hall of Canada, 1968.

Belchem, Major General David. *All in the Day's March*. London: Collins, 1978.

Bell, Christopher. *Churchill & Sea Power*. Oxford: Oxford University Press, 2012.

Bell, P.M.H. *Twelve Turning Points of the Second World War*. New Haven: Yale University Press, 2011.

Bennett, Ralph. *Behind the Battle: Intelligence in the War with Germany, 1939–1945*. London: Sinclair-Stevenson, 1994.

Bercuson, David J. *The Patricias: The Proud History of a Fighting Regiment*. Toronto: Stoddart, 2001.

Bessel, Richard. *Political Violence and the Rise of Nazism: The Storm Troopers in Eastern Germany, 1925–1934*. New Haven: Yale University Press, 1984.

Betcherman, Lita-Rose. *Ernest Lapointe: Mackenzie King's Great Quebec Lieutenant*. Toronto: University of Toronto Press, 2002.

Biddle, Tami Davis. *Rhetoric and Reality in Air Warfare: The Evolution of British and American Ideas about Strategic Bombing, 1914–1945*. Princeton: Princeton University Press, 2002.

Bishop, Arthur. *The Splendid Hundred: The True Story of Canadians Who Flew in the Greatest Air Battle of World War II*. Toronto: McGraw–Hill Ryerson, 1994.

Bishop, Patrick. *Bomber Boys: Fighting Back, 1940–1945*. London: Harper, 2007.

Blair, Clay. *Hitler's U-boat War: The Hunted, 1942–1944*. New York: Random House, 1996.

Blumenson, Martin. *Patton: The Man behind the Legend, 1885–1945*. New York: William Morrow, 1985.

Blumenson, Martin. *Salerno to Cassino*. Washington: US Army Centre of Military History, 1993.

Bothwell, Robert and William Kilbourn. *C.D. Howe: A Biography*. Toronto: McClelland & Stewart, 1979.

Bourrie, Mark. *The Fog of War: Censorship of Canada's Media in World War Two*. Vancouver: Douglas & McIntyre, 2011.

Boutilier, James A. (ed.). *The RCN in Retrospect, 1910–1968*. Vancouver: UBC Press, 1982.

Bracken, Robert. *Spitfire: The Canadians*. Erin: Boston Mills, 1995.

Bradley, Omar N. *A Soldiers' Story*. New York: Modern Library, 1999.

Broad, Graham. *A Small Price to Pay: Consumer Culture on the Canadian Home Front, 1939–45*. Vancouver: UBC Press, 2013.

Brock, Jeffry. *The Dark Broad Seas: Memoirs of a Sailor, Volume I*. Toronto: McClelland & Stewart, 1981.

Brode, Patrick. *Casual Slaughter and Accidental Judgements: Canadian War Crime Prosecutions, 1944–1948*. Toronto: Osgoode Hall, 1997.

Brown, Atholl Sutherland. *Silently into the Midst of Things*. Lewis, UK: The Book Guild, 1997.

Brown, Gordon and Terry Copp. *Look to Your Front ... Regina Rifles: A Regiment at War, 1944–1945*. Waterloo: Laurier Centre for Military Strategic and Disarmament Studies, 2001.

Browning, C.R. *The Origins of the Final Solution: The Evolution of Nazi Jewish Policy, September 1939–March 1942*. Lincoln: University of Nebraska Press, 2004.

Bryce, Robert. *Canada and the Cost of World War II: The International Operations of Canada's Department of Finance, 1939–1947*. Montreal: McGill-Queen's University Press, 2005.

Buckley, John. *Monty's Men: The British Army and the Liberation of Europe*. New Haven: Yale University Press, 2013.

Buckley, John. *The RAF and Trade Defence, 1919–1945*. Keele: Ryburn Publishing, 1995.

Burdick, Charles and Hans-Adolf Jacobsen (eds.). *The Halder War Diary, 1939–1942*. Novato: Presidio, 1988.

Burrin, Philippe. *Hitler and the Jews: The Genesis of the Holocaust*. London: Edward Arnold, 1994.

Burrow, Len, and Emile Beaudoin. *Unlucky Lady: The Life & Death of HMCS Athabaskan, 1940–44*. Toronto: McClelland & Stewart, 1987.

Campion, Garry. *The Good Fight: Battle of Britain Propaganda and the Few*. Basingstoke: Palgrave, 2009.

Casey, Steven. *Cautious Crusade: Franklin D. Roosevelt, American Public Opinion, and the War against Nazi Germany*. Oxford: Oxford University Press, 2001.

Chickering, Roger, Stig Förster and Bernd Greiner (eds.). *A World at Total War: Global Conflict and the Politics of Destruction, 1937–1945*. Cambridge: Cambridge University Press, 2005.

Churchill, Winston. *The Second World War, Volume III: The Grand Alliance*. London, Houghton Mifflin, 1950.

Churchill, Winston. *The Second World War, Volume IV: The Hinge of Fate*. London: Houghton Mifflin, 1950.

Citino, Robert. *The Wehrmacht Retreats: Fighting a Lost War, 1943*. Lawrence: University Press of Kansas, 2012.

Cohen, Deborah. *The War Come Home: Disabled Veterans in Britain and Germany, 1914–1939*. Berkeley: University of California Press, 2001.

Collier, Richard. *Eagle Day: The Battle of Britain*. London: Macmillan, 1981.

Cook, Tim. *Clio's Warriors: Canadian Historians and the Writing of the World Wars*. Vancouver: UBC Press, 2006.

Cook, Tim. *Shock Troops: Canadians Fighting the Great War, 1917–1918, volume II* . Toronto: Viking, 2008.

Cook, Tim. *Warlords: Borden, Mackenzie King, and Canada's World Wars*. Toronto: Allan Lane, 2012.

Comfort, Charles. *Artist at War*. Toronto: Ryerson, 1956.

Copp, Terry. *Fields of Fire: The Canadians in Normandy*. Toronto: University of Toronto Press, 2003.

Copp, Terry. *No Price Too High*: *Canadians and the Second World War*. Toronto: McGraw-Hill Ryerson, 1996.

Copp, Terry and Bill McAndrew. *Battle Exhaustion*: *Soldiers and Psychiatrists in the Canadian Army, 1939–1945*. Montreal: McGill-Queen's University Press, 1990.

Cormier, Ronald (ed.). *The Forgotten Soldiers: Stories from Acadian Veterans of the Second World War*. Fredericton, NB: New Ireland, 1992.

Corum, James S. *The Roots of Blitzkrieg: Hans von Seeckt and German Military Reform*. Lawrence: Kansas, 1992.

Craven, W.F. and James Lea Cate. *The Army Air Forces in World War II*, volume 3. Chicago: University of Chicago Press, 1958.

Crickard, Fred W., Michael L. Hadley and Robert N. Huebert (eds.). *A Nation's Navy: In Quest of Canadian Naval Identity*. Montreal: McGill-Queen's University Press, 1996.

Cumming, Anthony J. *The Royal Navy and the Battle of Britain*. Annapolis, MD: Naval Institute Press, 2010.

Dancocks, Daniel. *The D-Day Dodgers: The Canadians in Italy, 1943–1945*. Toronto: McClelland & Stewart, 1991.

Dancocks, Daniel. *In Enemy Hands: Canadian Prisoners of War, 1939–45*. Edmonton: Hurtig, 1983.

Danson, Barney. *Not Bad for a Sergeant: The Memoirs of Barney Danson*. Toronto: Dundurn, 2002.

Darlington, Robert A. and Fraser McKee. *The Canadian Naval Chronicle, 1939–1945: The Successes and Losses of the Canadian Navy in World War II*. Rev. ed. St. Catharines: Vanwell, 1998.

Delaney, Doug. *The Soldiers' General: Bert Hoffmeister at War*. Vancouver: UBC Press, 2005.

D'Este, Carlo. *Eisenhower: A Soldier's Life*. New York: Henry Holt and Company, 2002.

D'Este, Carlo. *Patton: A Genius for War*. New York: Harper, 1995.

Dickson, Paul. *A Thoroughly Canadian General: A Biography of General H.D.G. Crerar*. Toronto: University of Toronto Press, 2007.

DiNardo, R.L. *Mechanized Juggernaut or Military Anachronism? Horses and the German Army of World War II*. New York: Greenwood,1991.

Donitz, Karl. *Memoirs: Ten Years and Twenty Days*. London: Weidenfeld and Nicolson, 1959.

Doughty, Robert. *The Seeds of Disaster: The Development of French Army Doctrine, 1919–1939*. Hamden: Archon Books, 1985.

Douglas, W.A.B., et al. *A Blue Water Navy: The Official Operational History of the Royal Canadian Navy in the Second World War, 1943–1945, volume II, part 2*. St. Catharines: Vanwell, 2007.

Douglas, W.A.B. *The Creation of a National Air Force: The Official History of the Royal Canadian Air Force, volume II*. Toronto: University of Toronto Press and the Department of National Defence, 1986.

Douglas, W.A.B., et al. *No Higher Purpose: The Official Operational History of the Royal Canadian Navy in the Second World War, 1939–1943, volume II, part 1*. St. Catharines: Vanwell, 2002.

Douglas, W.A.B. *The RCN in Transition, 1910–1985*. Vancouver: UBC Press, 1988.

Dover, John. *War without Mercy: Race and Power in the Pacific War*. New York: Pantheon, 1986.

Dundas, Barbara. *A History of Women in the Canadian Military*. Montreal: Art Global, 2000.

Dziuban, S.W. *The Military Relations between the United States and Canada, 1939–1945*. Washington: United States Army in the World War II, Special Studies, 1959.

Edgerton, David. *Britain's War Machine: Weapons, Resources, and Experts in the Second World War*. London: Allan Lane, 2011.

Edwards, Bernard. *Attack and Sink!: The Battle for Convoy SC 42*. Dorset: New Era Writer's Guild, 1995.

English, John A. *Failure in High Command : The Canadian Army and the Normandy Campaign*. Ottawa: Golden Dog, 1995.

Erickson, John. *The Soviet High Command: A Military-Political History, 1918–1941*. London: Macmillan, 1962.

Evans, Richard J. *The Third Reich at War*. New York: Penguin, 2009.

Evans, Richard J. *The Third Reich in Power*. London: Penguin, 2005.

Farrell, Brian and Sandy Hunter (eds.). *Singapore, Sixty Years On*. Singapore: Eastern Universities Press, 2002.

Feasby, W.R. *Official History of the Canadian Medical Services, 1939–1945, volume I*. Ottawa: E. Cloutier, Queen's Printer, 1953.

Ferguson, Bernard. *The Watery Maze: The Story of Combined Operations*. London: Collins, 1961.

Francis, Martin. *The Flyer: British Culture and the Royal Air Force, 1939–1945*. Oxford: Oxford University Press, 2008.

Franks, Norman. *The Greatest Air Battle: Dieppe, 19 August, 1942*. London: W. Kimber, 1979.

Fraser, Doug. *Postwar Casualty: Canada's Merchant Navy*. Nova Scotia: Pottersfield, 1997.

Frieser, Karl-Heinz (with J.T. Greenwood). *The Blitzkrieg Legend: The 1940 Campaign in the West*. Annapolis, MD: Naval Institute Press, 2005.

Fritz, Stephen G. *Ostkrieg: Hitler's War of Extermination in the East*. Lexington: University Press of Kentucky, 2011.

Fochuk, Steven. *Metal Canvas: Canadians and World War II Aircraft Nose Art*. St. Catharines: Vanwell, 2000.

Fowler, Will. *The Commandos at Dieppe: Rehearsal for D-Day*. London: Collins, 2002.

Gardner, Juliet. *The Blitz: The British under Attack*. London: Harper, 2012.

Gardner, W.J.R. *Decoding History: The Battle of the Atlantic and Ultra*. London: Macmillan, 1999.

Gardner, W.J.R. (ed.). *The Evacuation from Dunkirk: Operation Dynamo, 26 May–4 June 1940*. London: Frank Cass, 2000.

Gelb, Norman. *Dunkirk*. New York: William Morrow and Company, 1989.

German, Tony. *The Sea Is At Our Gates: A History of the Canadian Navy*. Toronto: McClelland & Stewart, 1990.

Gilbert, Sir Martin. *Finest Hour—Winston Churchill, 1939–1941*. London: Heinemann, 1983.

Gimblett, Richard H. (ed.). *The Naval Service of Canada, 1910–2010: The Centennial Story*. Toronto: Dundurn, 2009.

Gimblett, Richard H., Peter T. Haydon, and Michael J. Whitby (eds.). *The Admirals: Canada's Senior Naval Leadership in the Twentieth Century*. Toronto: Dundurn, 2008.

Glantz, D.M. and J.M. House. *When Titans Clashed: How the Red Army Stopped Hitler*. Lawrence: University Press of Kansas, 1995.

Gooderson, Ian. *Air Power at the Battlefront: Allied Close Air Support in Europe 1943–45*. London: Routledge, 1998.

Gooderson, Ian. *A Hard Way to Make War: The Italian Campaign in the Second World War*. London: Conway, 2008.

Goodhart, Philip. *Fifty Ships that Saved the World*. London: Heinemann, 1966.

Goodwin, James. *"Our Gallant Doctor": Enigma and Tragedy: Surgeon Lieutenant George Hendry and HMCS* Ottawa, *1942*. Toronto: Dundurn, 2007.

Gough, Barry M. *HMCS Haida: Anatomy of a Destroyer*. St. Catharines: Looking Back Press, 2007.

Granatstein, J.L. *Canada's Army: Waging War and Keeping the Peace*. Toronto: University of Toronto Press, 2002.

Granatstein, J.L. *Canada's War: The Politics of the Mackenzie King Government, 1939–1945*. Toronto: Oxford University Press, 1975.

Granatstein, J.L. *The Last Good War: An Illustrated History of Canada in the Second World War, 1939–1945*. Vancouver: Douglas & McIntyre, 2005.

Granatstein, J.L. and J.M. Hitsman, *Broken Promises: A History of Conscription in Canada*. Toronto: Oxford University Press, 1977.

Granatstein, J.L. and Dean F. Oliver. *The Oxford Companion to Canadian Military History*. Toronto: Oxford University Press, 2011.

Graves, Donald E. and L.B. Jenson. *In Peril on the Sea: The Royal Canadian Navy and the Battle of the Atlantic*. Toronto: Published for the Canadian Naval Memorial Trust by Robin Brass Studio, 2003.

Greenfield, Nathan M. *The Battle of the St. Lawrence: The Second World War in Canada*. Toronto: HarperCollins Publishers, 2004.

Greenfield, Nathan M. *The Damned: Canadians at the Battle of Hong Kong and the POW Experience, 1941–45*. Toronto: HarperCollins, 2010.

Greenfield, Kent Roberts (ed.). *Command Decisions*. New York: Harcourt, Brace & Company, 1959.

Greenhous, Brereton. *"C" Force to Hong Kong: A Canadian Catastrophe, 1941–1945*. Toronto: Dundurn, 1997.

Greenhous, Brereton. *Dieppe, Dieppe*. Montreal: Art Global, 1992.

Greenhous, Brereton and W.A.B. Douglas. *Out of the Shadows: Canada in the Second World War*. Toronto: Dundurn, 1995.

Greenhous, Brereton and Hugh A. Halliday. *Canada's Air Forces, 1914–1999*. Montreal: Art Global, 1999.

Grove, Eric J. *Defeat of the Enemy Attack on Shipping, 1939–1945*. Aldershot: Ashgate, 1997.

Gruhzit-Hoyt, Olga. *They Also Served: American Women in World War II*. New York: Birch Lane, 1995.

Hadley, Michael L. *U-boats Against Canada: German Submarines in Canadian Waters*. Kingston: McGill-Queens University Press, 1985.

Hadley, Michael L. and Roger Sarty. *Tin-Pots and Pirate Ships: Canadian Naval Forces and German Sea Raiders, 1880–1918*. Montreal: McGill-Queens University Press, 1991.

Hague, Arnold. *The Allied Convoy System, 1939–1945: Its Organization, Defence, and Operation.* St. Catharines: Vanwell, 2000.

Halford, Robert G. *The Unknown Navy: Canada's World War Two Merchant Navy.* St. Catharines: Vanwell, 1995.

Hall, David Ian. *Strategy for Victory: The Development of British Tactical Air Power, 1919–1943.* Westport, CT: Praeger Security International, 2008.

Halliday, Hugh. *No. 242 Squadron: The Canadian Years.* Stittsville: Canada's Wings, 1981.

Halliday, Hugh and Brereton Greenhous. *Canada's Air Forces, 1914–1999.* Montreal: Art Global, 1999.

Hansen, Randall. *Fire and Fury: The Allied Bombing of Germany 1942–1945.* Toronto: Doubleday Canada, 2008.

Harmon, Christopher. *"Are We Beasts?" Churchill and the Moral Question of World War II "Area Bombing."* Newport: Naval War College, 1991.

Harris, Sir Arthur. *Bomber Offensive.* Toronto: Stoddart, 1990 [1947].

Harris, Sheldon H. *Factories of Death: Japanese Biological Warfare 1932–45 and the American Cover-Up.* Northridge: California State University, 1994.

Harris, Stephen J. *Canadian Brass: The Making of a Professional Army, 1860–1939.* Toronto: University of Toronto Press, 1998.

Hartcup, Guy. *The Effect of Science on the Second World War.* Basingstoke: St. Martin's, 2000.

Hastings, Max. *All Hell Let Loose: The World at War (1939–45).* London: HarperCollins, 2012.

Hatch, F.J. *Aerodrome of Democracy: Canada and the British Commonwealth Air Training Plan.* Ottawa: Directorate of History, 1983.

Heathcote, Blake. *Testaments of Honour: Personal Histories from Canada's War Veterans.* Toronto: Doubleday, 2002.

Henry, Hugh. *Dieppe through the Lens of the German War Photographer.* London: After the Battle, 1993.

Higgins, Trumbull. *Soft Underbelly: The Anglo-American Controversy Over the Italian Campaign, 1939–1945.* New York: The Macmillan Company, 1968.

High, Steven (ed.). *Occupied St. John's: A Social History of a City at War, 1939–1945.* Montreal and Kingston: McGill-Queen's University Press, 2010.

Hinsley, Frances H. *British Intelligence in the Second World War,* volume II. London: Her Majesty's Stationary Office, 1979–1988.

Historica-Dominion Institute. *We Were Freedom: Canadian Stories of the Second World War.* Toronto: Key Porter, 2010.

Horrocks, William (ed.). *In Their Own Words.* Ottawa: Rideau Veterans Home Residents Council, 1993.

How, Douglas. *Night of the Caribou.* Hantsport, NS: Lancelot, 1988.

Howard, Michael. *British Intelligence in the Second World War, Volume V: Strategic Deception.* London: HMSO, 1990.

Hunter, T. Murray. *Canada at Dieppe*. Ottawa: Canadian War Museum Historical Publication No. 17, 1982.

Jackson, Ashley. *The British Empire and the Second World War*. New York: Hambledon Continuum, 2006.

Jackson, Julian. *The Fall of France: The Nazi Invasion of 1940*. Oxford: Oxford University Press, 2003.

Jackson, Robert. *Before the Storm: The Story of Bomber Command, 1939–1942*. London: Cassell & Co., 2001 [original 1972].

Jarratt, Melynda. *War Brides: The Stories of the Women Who Left Everything Behind to Follow the Men They Loved*. Toronto: Dundurn, 2009.

Johnston, Mac. *Corvettes Canada: Convoy Veterans of WWII Tell Their True Stories*. Toronto: McGraw-Hill Ryerson, 1994.

Kahn, David. *Seizing the Enigma: The Race to Break the German U-boat Codes, 1939–1943*. Boston: Houghton Mifflin, 1991.

Keegan, John. *The Second World War*. London: Penguin, 1989.

Kennedy, J. De N. *History of the Department of Munitions and Supply: Canada in the Second World War, volume I*. Ottawa: King's Printer, 1950.

Kennedy, Paul. *Engineers of Victory: The Problem Solvers Who Turned the Tide in the Second World War*. Toronto: HarperCollins, 2013.

Kerry, A.J. and W.A. McDill. *The History of the Corps of the Royal Canadian Engineers, Volume 2: 1936–1946*. Ottawa: Military Engineers Association of Canada, 1966.

Kershaw, Ian. *Hitler: A Biography*. New York: W.W. Norton, 2010.

Kershaw, Ian. *The "Hitler Myth": Image and Reality in the Third Reich*. Oxford: Oxford University Press, 1987.

Keshen, Jeffrey. *Saints, Sinners, Soldiers: Canada's Second World War*. Vancouver: UBC Press, 2004.

Kesselring, Albert. *Kesselring: A Soldier's Record*. New York: William Morrow, 1954.

Kiesling, Eugenia C. *Arming Against Hitler: France and Limits of Military Planning*. Lawrence: University Press of Kansas, 1996.

Kingsley, F.A. (ed.). *The Development of Radar Equipment for the Royal Navy, 1935–1945*. London: Macmillan, 1995.

Kirby, S.W. *The War against Japan, Volume 1: The Loss of Singapore*. London: HMSO, 1957.

Knox, MacGregor. *Hitler's Italian Allies: Royal Armed Forces, Fascist Regime, and the War of 1940–1943*. Cambridge: Cambridge University Press, 2000.

Kochanski, Halik. *The Eagle Unbowed: Poland and the Poles in the Second World War*. London: Allen Lane, 2012.

Lamb, James. *The Corvette Navy: True Stories from Canada's Atlantic War*. Toronto: Macmillan of Canada, 1977.

Lee, Bruce. *Marching Orders*. New York: Crown Publishers, 1995.

Levine, Alan J. *The War against Rommel's Supply Lines, 1942–1943*. Westport: Praeger, 1999.

Lewis, Peter. *The British Bomber since 1914: Fifty Years of Design and Development*. London, 1967.

Liddel Hart, Sir Basil. *History of the Second World War*. London: Pan, 1977.

Linderman, Gerald F. *The World within War: American Soldiers' Combat Experience in World War II*. New York: Free Press, 1997.

Lindsay, Oliver. *At the Going Down of the Sun: Hong Kong and South-East Asia, 1941–1945*. London: Hamish Hamilton, 1981.

Lindsay, Oliver. *The Lasting Honour: The Fall of Hong Kong, 1941*. London: Hamilton, 1978.

Lowe, Keith. *Inferno: The Fiery Destruction of Hamburg, 1943*. New York: Scribner, 2007.

Lynch, Mack (ed.). *Salty Dips*, volume 1. Ottawa: Ottawa Branch, Naval Officers' Associations of Canada, 1983.

Lynch, Mack (ed.). *Salty Dips*, volume 2. Ottawa: Ottawa Branch, Naval Officers' Associations of Canada, 1984.

Lynch, Thomas. *Canadian Flowers: History of the Corvettes, 1939–1945*. Halifax: Nimbus Publishing, 1983.

Lynch, Thomas J. (ed.). *Fading Memories: Canadian Sailors and the Battle of the Atlantic*. Halifax: The Atlantic Chief and Petty Officers Association, 1993.

Lynch, Thomas G. and James B. Lamb. *Gunshield Graffiti: Unofficial Badges of Canada's Wartime Navy*. Halifax: Nimbus, 1984.

MacFarlane, John. *Triquet's Cross: A Study of Military Heroism*. Montreal: McGill-Queen's University Press, 2009.

MacMillan, Margaret. *Paris 1919*. New York: Random House, 2002.

Macpherson, Ken and Marc Milner. *Corvettes of the Royal Canadian Navy, 1939–1945*. St. Catharines: Vanwell, 1993.

Macri, David. *Clash of Empires in South China: The Allied Nations' Proxy War with Japan, 1935–1941*. Lawrence: University Press of Kansas, 2012.

Magenheimer, Heinz. *Hitler's War: Germany's Key Strategic Decisions, 1940–1945*. New York: Barnes & Noble, 1997.

Malone, Dick. *Missing from the Record*. Toronto: William Collins Ltd, 1946.

Marteinson, John (ed.). *We Stand on Guard: An Illustrated History of the Canadian Army*. Montreal: Ovale Publications, 1992.

Marteinson, John and Michael McNorgan. *The Royal Canadian Armoured Corps: An Illustrated History*. Toronto: Robin Brass Studio, 2000.

Mason, David. *U-Boat: The Secret Menace* (Ballantine's Illustrated History of World War II). New York: Ballantine, 1986.

Matlof, Maurice. *Strategic Planning for Coalition Warfare: 1941–1942*. Washington: 1959.

Mayne, Richard O. *Betrayed: Scandal, Politics, and Canadian Naval Leadership*. Vancouver: UBC Press, 2006.

McAndrew, Bill. *Canadians and the Italian Campaign, 1943–1945*. Montreal: Art Global, 1996.

McCaffery, Dan. *Hell Island: Canadian Pilots and the 1942 Air Battle for Malta*. Toronto: James Lorimer, 1998.

McGeer, Eric, Terry Copp, with Matt Symes. *The Canadian Battlefields in Italy: Sicily and Southern Italy*. Waterloo: Canadian Battlefields Foundation, 2008.

McKee, Fraser M. *"Sink All the Shipping There": The Loss of Canada's Wartime Merchant Ships and Fishing Schooners*. St. Catharines: Vanwell, 2004.

McNab, Chris. *Hitler's Armies: A History of the German War Machine, 1939–45*. Oxford: Ospery, 2011.

McNeil, Bill. *Voices of a War Remembered: An Oral History of Canadians in World War Two*. Toronto: Doubleday Canada, 1991.

McNeill, William Hardy. *American, Britain and Russia: Their Cooperation and Conflict, 1941–1946*. London: Oxford University Press, 1952.

Megargee, Geoffrey P. *Inside Hitler's High Command*. Lawrence: University Press of Kansas, 2000.

Melnyk, T.W. *Canadian Flying Operations in South East Asia, 1941–1945*. Ottawa: Department of National Defence, 1976.

Memories on Parade: Aircrew Recollections of World War II. Winnipeg: Wartime Pilots' and Observations' Association, 1995.

Middlebrook, Martin. *The Battle of Hamburg: Allied Bomber Forces against a German City in 1943*. London: Allen Lane, 1980.

Mierzejewski, Alfred C. *The Collapse of the German War Economy, 1944–1945*. Chapel Hill: University of North Carolina Press, 1988.

Millberry, Larry and Hugh Halliday. *The Royal Canadian Air Force at War, 1939–1945*. Toronto: Canav Books, 1990.

Miller, Nathan. *War at Sea: A Naval History of World War II*. Oxford: Oxford University Press, 1995.

Milner, Marc. *Battle of the Atlantic*. St. Catharines: Vanwell, 2003.

Milner, Marc. *Canada's Navy: The First Century*. Toronto: University of Toronto Press, 1999. 2nd ed., 2010.

Milner, Marc. *North Atlantic Run: The Royal Canadian Navy and the Battle for the Convoys*. Toronto: University of Toronto Press, 1985.

Milner, Marc. *The U-boat Hunters: The Royal Canadian Navy and the Offensive against Germany's Submarines*. Toronto: University of Toronto Press, 1994.

Mitchell, George Duncan. *RCHA—Right of the Line: An Anecdotal History of the Royal Canadian Horse Artillery from 1871*. Ottawa: RCHA History Committee, 1986.

Molony, Brigadier C.J.C. *The Mediterranean and the Middle East*, volume V. London: HMSO, 1973.

Munro, Ross. *Gauntlet to Overlord*. Toronto: Macmillan, 1945.

Murray, Williamson. *Strategy for Defeat: The Luftwaffe, 1933–1945*. Maxwell Air Force Base, AL: Air University Press, 1983.

Murray, Williamson and Allan R. Millett. *A War to Be Won: Fighting the Second World War*. Cambridge: Harvard University Press, 2000.

Neiberg, Michael. *Fighting the Great War: A Global History*. Cambridge: Harvard University Press, 2005.

Neillands, Robin. *The Dieppe Raid: The Story of the Disastrous 1942 Expedition*. London: Aurum, 2005.

Nicholson, G.W.L. *Canada's Nursing Sisters*. Toronto: A.M. Hakkert, 1975.

Nicholson, G.W.L. *The Canadians in Italy, 1943–1945*. Ottawa: Queen's Printer, 1955.

Nicholson, G.W.L. *The Gunners of Canada: The History of the Royal Regiment of Canadian Artillery*, volume II. Toronto: McClelland & Stewart, 1967.

Nicholson, G.W.L. *Seventy Years of Service*. Ottawa: Borealis, 1977.

Nolan, Brian. *Hero: The Buzz Beurling Story*. Toronto: Lester & Orpen, 1981.

O'Connor, Edward. *The Corvette Years: The Lower Deck Story*. Vancouver: Cordillera, 1995.

O'Keefe, David. *One Day in August: The Untold Story behind Canada's Tragedy at Dieppe*. Toronto: Knopf Canada, 2013.

Oliver, Dean F. and Laura Brandon. *Canvas of War: Painting the Canadian Experience, 1914 to 1945*. Vancouver: Douglas & McIntyre, 2000.

Overy, Richard J. *Bomber Command, 1939–1945*. London: HarperCollins, 1997.

Overy, Richard. *The Bombing War: Europe, 1939–1945*. Penguin: Allan Lane, 2013.

Overy, Richard J. *Russia's War: A History of the Soviet War Effort, 1941–1945*. London: Penguin, 1997.

Overy, Richard. *Why the Allies Won*. London: Pimlico, 1995.

Parker, Mike. *Running the Gauntlet: An Oral History of Canadian Merchant Seamen in World War II*. Halifax: Nimbus, 2003.

Paris, Michael. *From the Wright Brothers to Top Gun: Aviation, Nationalism and Popular Cinema*. Manchester: Manchester University Press, 1995.

Paterson, Lawrence. *The First U-boat Flotilla*. London: Leo Cooper, 2002.

Peattie, Mark R., Edward J. Drea, and Hans J. van de Ven (eds.). *The Battle for China: Essays on the Military History of the Sino-Japanese War of 1937–1945*. Stanford: Stanford University Press, 2010.

Perkins, Les. *Flight into Yesterday: A Memory or Two from Members of the Wartime Aircrew Club of Kelowna*. Victoria: Trafford, 2002.

Perras, Galen. *Franklin Roosevelt and the Origins of the Canadian–American Security Alliance, 1933–1945*. Westport: Greenwood, 1998.

Perry, Mark. *Partners in Command: George Marshall and Dwight Eisenhower in War and Peace*. New York: Penguin, 2007.

Pierson, Ruth Roach. *They're Still Women after All: Canadian Women and the Second World War*. Toronto: McClelland & Stewart, 1986.

Place, Timothy Harrison. *Military Training in the British Army, 1940–1944: From Dunkirk to D-Day*. London: Frank Cass, 2000.

Porch, Douglas. *The Path to Victory: The Mediterranean Theatre in World War II*. New York: 2004.

Portugal, Jean. *We Were There: A Record for Canada*, volume 7. Toronto: The Royal Canadian Military Institute Heritage Society, 1998.

Powley, A.E. *Broadcast from the Front: Canadian Radio Overseas in the Second World War*. Toronto: Hakkert, 1975.

Probert, Henry. *Bomber Harris: His Life and Times*. London: Greenhill Books, 2003.

Raddall, Thomas. *West Novas: A History of the West Nova Scotia Regiment*. Liverpool, NS: no publisher listed, 1947.

Rawling, Bill. *Death Their Enemy: Canadian Medical Practitioners and War*. Self-published, 2001.

Reader's Digest, *The Canadians at War, 1939/45*. Montreal: Reader's Digest Association, 1986.

Reid, Max. *DEMS at War! Defensively Equipped Merchants Ships and the Battle of the Atlantic, 1939–1945*. Ottawa: Commoners' Publishing Society, 1990.

Rein, Christopher M. *The North African Air Campaign: U.S. Army Air Forces from El Alamein to Salerno*. Lawrence: University Press of Kansas, 2012.

Reinhardt, Klaus. *Moscow—The Turning Point: The Failure of Hitler's Strategy in the Winter of 1941–42*. Oxford: Berg, 1992.

Richard, Béatrice. *La mémoire de Dieppe: Radioscopie d'un mythe*. Montreal: VLB Éditeur, 2002.

Richards, Denis. *Portal of Hungerford*. London: Heinemann, 1977.

Rickard, John. *The Politics of Command: Lieutenant-General A.G.L. McNaughton and the Canadian Army 1939–1943*. Toronto: University of Toronto Press, 2010.

Rohwer, Jürgen. *Axis Submarine Successes of World War Two: German, Italian, and Japanese Submarine Successes, 1939–1945*. Annapolis, MD: Naval Institute Press, 1999.

Rolf, David. *The Bloody Road to Tunis: Destruction of the Axis Forces in North Africa. November 1942–May 1943*. London: Greenhill, 2001.

Roskill, S.W. *The War At Sea, 1939–1945*, volume II. London: HMSO, 1956.

Ross, Richard M. *The History of the 1st Battalion Cameron Highlanders of Ottawa (MG)*. Ottawa: published by the regiment, 1948.

Rossino, Alex B. *Hitler Strikes Poland: Blitzkrieg, Ideology, and Atrocity*. Lawrence: University Press of Kansas, 2003.

Roy, Patricia, et al. *Mutual Hostages: Canadians and Japanese during the Second World War*. Toronto: University of Toronto Press, 1990.

Roy, R.H. *The Seaforth Highlanders of Canada, 1919–1965*. Vancouver: The Seaforth Highlanders of Canada, 1969.

Russell, Ruth Weber. *Proudly She Marched: Training Canada's World War II Women in Waterloo County, Volume 2: Women's Royal Canadian Naval Service.* Waterloo: Canadian Federation of University Women, Kitchener-Waterloo, 2006.

Sarty, Roger. *Canada and the Battle of the Atlantic.* Montreal: Art Global, 1998.

Sarty, Roger. *The Maritime Defence of Canada.* Toronto: Canadian Institute of Strategic Studies, 1996.

Sarty, Roger. *War in the St. Lawrence: The Forgotten U-boat Battles on Canada's Shores.* Toronto: Allen Lane, 2012.

Schull, John Joseph. *The Far Distant Ships: An Official Account of Canadian Naval Operations in the Second World War.* Ottawa: King's Printer, 1950.

Smith, Colin. *Singapore Burning: Heroism and Surrender in World War II.* London: Penguin, 2006.

Smith, Kenneth B. *Duffy's Regiment.* Don Mills: T.H. Best, 1983.

Smith, Wilfred I. *Code Word: Canloan.* Toronto: Dundurn, 1992.

Snyder, Timothy. *Bloodlands: Europe between Hitler and Stalin.* New York: Basic Books, 2010.

Stacey, C.P. *Arms, Men and Governments: The War Policies of Canada, 1939–1945.* Ottawa: Queen's Printer, 1970.

Stacey, C.P. *A Date with History: Memoirs of a Canadian Historian.* Ottawa: Deneau, 1983.

Stacey, C.P. *Six Years of War: The Army in Canada, Britain and the Pacific.* Ottawa: Queen's Printer, 1955.

Stacey C.P. and Barbara Wilson. *The Half Million: The Canadians in Britain, 1939–1946.* Toronto: University of Toronto Press, 1987.

Stahel, David. *Operation Typhoon: Hitler's March on Moscow, October 1941.* Cambridge: Cambridge University Press, 2013.

Stevens, G.R. *The Royal Canadian Regiment, volume II (1933–1966)* London: London Printing, 1967.

Stoakes, Geoffrey. *Hitler and the Quest for World Domination.* Leamington Spa: Berg, 1986.

Suvorov, Viktor. *The Chief Culprit: Stalin's Grand Design to Start World War II.* Annapolis: Naval Institute Press, 2008.

Syrett, David. *The Defeat of the German U-boats: The Battle of the Atlantic.* (Columbia: University of South Carolina Press, 1994.

Tennyson, B.D. and Roger Sarty. *Guardian of the Gulf: Sydney, Cape Breton, and the Atlantic Wars.* Toronto: University of Toronto Press, 2000.

Terraine, John. *The Right of the Line: The Royal Air Force in the European War, 1939–1945.* London: Hodder and Stoughton, 1985.

Torontow, Cy (ed.). *There I Was: A Collection of Reminiscences by Members of the Ottawa Jewish Community Who Served in World War II.* Ottawa: Jewish War Veterans and the Ottawa Jewish Historical Society, 1999.

Tooze, Adam. *The Wages of Destruction: The Making and Breaking of the Nazi Economy*. London: Allen Lane, 2006.

Trotter, William R. *A Frozen Hell: the Russo-Finnish Winter War of 1939–1940*. Chapel Hill, NC: Algonquin Books of Chapel Hill, 1991.

Tucker, Gilbert Norman. *The Naval Service of Canada: Its Official History, Volume 2: Activities on Shore during the Second World War*. Ottawa: King's Printer, 1952.

Wakelam, Randall T. *The Science of Bombing: Operational Research in RAF Bomber Command*. Toronto: University of Toronto Press, 2009.

Webster, Sir Charles and Noble Frankland. *The Strategic Air Offensive against Germany*, volume I. London: HMSO, 1961.

Whitby, Michael (ed.). *The Admirals: Canada's Senior Naval Leadership in the Twentieth Century*. Toronto: Dundurn, 2006.

Wilford, Timothy. *Canada's Road to the Pacific War: Intelligence, Strategy, and the Far East Crisis*. Vancouver: UBC Press, 2011.

Vance, Jonathan. *High Flight: Aviation and the Canadian Imagination*. Toronto: Penguin, 2002.

Vance, Jonathan. *Maple Leaf Empire: Britain, Canada, and the Two World Wars*. Don Mills: Oxford University Press, 2011.

Villa, Brian. *Unauthorized Action: Mountbatten and the Dieppe Raid*. Toronto: Oxford University Press, 1989.

Vincent, Carl. *No Reason Why: The Canadian Hong Kong Tragedy—An Examination*. Stittsville: Canada's Wings, 1981.

Wallace, Robert. *The Italian Campaign*. Alexandria: Time-Life, 1981.

Watt, Frederic B. *In All Respects Ready: The Merchant Navy and the Battle of the Atlantic, 1940–1945*. Scarborough: Prentice-Hall Canada, 1985.

Weinberg, Gerhard L. *Germany, Hitler, and World War II*. Cambridge: Cambridge University Press, 1995.

Whealey, Robert H. *Hitler and Spain: The Nazi Role in the Spanish Civil War, 1936–1939*. Lexington: University Press of Kentucky, 1989.

Wheeler, William J. *Flying Under Fire: Canadian Fliers Recall the Second World War*. Calgary: Fifth House, 2001.

Whitaker, Denis and Shelagh Whitaker. *Dieppe: Tragedy to Triumph: A Firsthand and Revealing Critical Account of the Most Controversial Battle of World War II*. Whitby: McGraw-Hill Ryerson, 1992.

Wieviorka, Olivier. *Normandy: The Landings to the Liberation of Paris*. Cambridge: Belknap Press of Harvard University Press, 2008.

Wyatt, Bernie. *Maximum Effort: The Big Bombing Raids*. Erin, ON: Boston Mills, 1986.

Wyatt, Bernie. *Two Wings and a Prayer*. Erin, ON: Boston Mills, 1984.

Yeide, Harry. *Fighting Patton: George S. Patton Jr. through the Eyes of His Enemies*. Minneapolis: Zenith, 2011.

Zimm, Alan D. *Attack on Pearl Harbor: Strategy, Combat, Myths, Deceptions*. Philadelphia: Casement, 2011.

Zimmerman, David. *The Great Naval Battle of Ottawa*. Toronto: University of Toronto Press, 1988.

Zuehlke, Mark. *Operation Husky: The Canadian Invasion of Sicily, July 10–August 7, 1943*. Vancouver: Douglas & McIntyre, 2008.

Zuehlke, Mark. *Ortona Street Fight*. Victoria: Raven Books, 2011.

Zuehlke, Mark. *Tragedy at Dieppe: Operation Jubilee, August 19, 1942*. Vancouver: Douglas & McIntyre, 2012.

DISSERTATIONS AND THESES

Cessford, Michael Pearson. "Hard in the Attack: The Canadian Army in Sicily and Italy, July 1943–June 1944." Ph.D. dissertation, Carleton University, 1996.

Dubord, Denis. "Unseen Enemies: An Examination of Infectious Diseases and Their Influence upon the Canadian Army in Two Major Campaigns during the First and Second World Wars." Ph.D. dissertation, University of Victoria, 2009.

Field, Vincenzo. "Explaining Armageddon: Popular Perceptions of Air Power in Canada and Britain and the Destruction of Germany, 1939–45." MA thesis, University of New Brunswick, 2003.

Gann, Emily. "Correspondence, Camaraderie, and Community: The Second World War for a Mother and Son." MA thesis, Carleton University, 2012.

Maker, John. "Home Away from Home: Citizenship and National Identity in the Canadian Army Overseas, 1939–1943." Ph.D. dissertation, University of Ottawa, 2010.

Pletsch, Mary C. "The Guardian Angels of this Flying Business: RCAF Ground Crew in 6 Group." MA thesis, Royal Military College of Canada, 2002.

Windsor, Lee. "Anatomy of Victory: Allied Containment Strategy and the Battle for the Gothic Line." Ph.D. dissertation, University of New Brunswick, 2006.

CANADIAN SERVICE PERSONNEL MEMOIRS, PUBLISHED AND SELF-PUBLISHED

Baird, Major Kenneth G. *Letters to Harvelyn: From Japanese POW Camps: A Father's Letters to His Young Daughter during World War II*. Toronto: HarperCollins, 2002.

Barrett, Harry B. *The Navy & Me* . Self-published, 2003.

Bennett, Air Vice-Marshal D.C.T. *Pathfinder: A War Autobiography*. Manchester: Crecy, 1983.

Berard, Leo Paul. *17 Days until Christmas*. Self-published, 1997.

Bishop, Murray Winston and Arthur Adelbert Bishop. *The Bishop Brothers of New Minas in World War Two*. Self-published, 2003.

Bourassa, Rollie (ed.). *One Family's War: The Wartime Letters of Clarence Bourassa, 1940–1944*. Regina: Canadian Plains Research Centre, 2010.

Brock, Jeffrey. *The Dark Broad Seas: Memoirs of a Sailor*. Toronto: McClelland & Stewart, 1981.

Chapman, J.K. *River Boy at War*. Fredericton: Goose Lane, 1985.

Coldridge, Stan. *Recollections of Stan Coldridge (Halifax Pilot)*. Self-published, 2008.

Corrigan, Leonard. *A Hong Kong Diary Revisited: The Family Remembers*. Baltimore, ON: Frei, 2008.

Crozier, Robert. *Looking Backward: A Memoir*. Self-published, 1998.

Culley, Ray. *His Memories Can Survive*. Self-published, 2003.

Curry, Frank. *War at Sea: A Canadian Seaman on the North Atlantic*. Toronto: Lugus, 1990.

Cybulski-Ross, Martin. "Wanderers by Night," *CAHS Journal* 25.2 (1987) 45–57.

Clark, John Irwin. *My Memoirs of the War Years*. Self-published, 2005.

Davis, Eldon S. *An Awesome Silence*: *A Gunner Padre's Journey through the Valley of the Shadow*. Carp, ON: Creative Bound, 1991.

Easton, Alan. *50 North: An Atlantic Battleground*. Toronto: Ryerson, 1963.

Frost, C. Sydney. *Once a Patricia*. St. Catharines: Vanwell, 1988.

Galloway, Strome. *Some Died at Ortona: The Royal Canadian Regiment in Action in Italy*. Royal Canadian Regiment, 1983.

Gossage, Carolyn. *Greatcoats and Glamour Boots: Canadian Women at War, 1939–1945*. Toronto: Dundurn, 2008.

Greer, Fiddy. *The Girls of the King's Navy*. Victoria, BC: Sono Nis Press, 1983.

Hamilton, Nigel. *Monty: Master of the Battlefield*. London: Hodder & Stoughton, 1985.

Hancock, Glen. *Charley Goes to War*: *A Memoir*. Kentville: Gaspereau, 2004.

Harvey, J. Douglas. *Boys, Bombs, and Brussels Sprouts*: *A Knees-up, Wheels-up Chronicle of World War II*. Toronto: McClelland & Stewart, 1981.

Hewer, Howard. *In for a Penny, in for a Pound: The Adventures and Misadventures of a Wireless Operator in Bomber Command*. Toronto: Anchor Canada, 2004.

Irwin, Walter. *World War II Memoirs*. Self-published, 1998.

Jackson, W.G.F. *Alexander of Tunis as Military Commander*. London: Batsford, 1971.

Jenson, Latham B. *Tin Hats, Oilskins & Seaboots: A Naval Journey, 1938–1945*. Toronto: Robin Brass Studio, 2000.

Jones, Harlo. *Bomber Pilot: A Canadian Youth's War*. Toronto: Vanwell, 2001.

Kensett, Robert C. *A Walk in the Valley*. Burnstown: General Store, 2002.

King, Captain Dudley. *Reminiscences*. Self-published, 1999.

Kutyn, George. *Diary of R.C.A.F. Serviceman Michael Kutyn*. Self-published, 2nd ed., 2010.

Lamont, A.G.W. *Guns Above, Steam Below in Canada's Navy of WW II*. Ely: Melrose, 2006.

Law, C. Anthony. *White Plumes Astern: The Short, Daring Life of Canada's MTB Flotilla*. Halifax: Nimbus, 1989.

Lawrence, Hal. *A Bloody War: One Man's Memories of the Canadian Navy, 1939–45*. Toronto: Macmillan of Canada, 1979.

Lay, H. Nelson. *Memoirs of a Mariner*. Stittsville: Canada's Wings, 1982.

Layard, A.F.C. *Commanding Canadians: the Second World War Diaries of A.F.C. Layard*. Michael Whitby, ed. Vancouver: UBC Press, 2005.

MacDonell, George S. *One Soldier's Story (1939–1945): From the Fall of Hong Kong to the Defeat of Japan*. Toronto: Dundurn, 2002.

Mackereth, Ben. *To Do or Die*. Self-published, 1993.

Margison, John. *H.M.C.S. Sackville, 1942–1943: Memoirs of a Gunnery Officer*. Cobalt: Highway Book Shop, 1998.

Matthews, Georgina (ed.). *Wartime Letters of Flt. Lieut. D.J. Matthews to His Wife 1943–1945*. Guelph: Georgina H. Matthews, 2003.

McDonald, B. Graham. *Have No Fear. "B.G." Is Here*. Self-published, 2007.

McDougall, Robert L. *A Narrative of War: From the Beaches of Sicily to the Hitler Line with the Seaforth Highlanders of Canada, 10 July, 1943–8 June 1944*. Kemptville: Golden Dog, 1996.

McIntosh, Dave. *Terror in the Starboard Seat*. Don Mills: General, 1980.

Miseferi, Frank. *I Never Forget: Memoirs of Frank Miseferi, World War 2 Heavy Bomber Air Gunner*. Self-published, 2006.

Mitchell, Howard. *My War*. Self-published, n.d.

Morrison, Les. *Of Luck and War: From Squeegee Kid to Bomber Pilot in World War II*. Burnstown: General Store, 1999.

Mowat, Farley. *And No Birds Sang*. Toronto: McClelland & Stewart, 1979.

Nixon, Charles Patrick. *A River in September: HMCS Chaudière, 1943–1945*. Montreal: John Mappin, 1995.

O'Brien, John. *Through the Gates of Hell and Back: The Private War of a Footslogger from "The Avenue."* Halifax: New World, 2010.

Patterson, John. *World War II: An Airman Remembers*. Burnstown: General Store, 2000.

Peden, Murray. *A Thousand Shall Fall*. Stittsville: Canada's Wings, 1979.

Peel, Ron. *My Time at War ... and a Little Bit More*. Self-published, 2004.

"Pooch" [C.E. Corrigan]. *Tales of a Forgotten Theatre*. Winnipeg: D-Day Publishers, 1969.

Pugsley, William Howard. *Saints, Devils and Ordinary Seamen: Life on the Royal Canadian Navy's Lower Deck*. Toronto: Collins, 1945.

Pullen, T.C. "Convoy O.N. 127 & the Loss of HMCS *Ottawa*, 13 September 1942: A Personal Reminiscence," *The Northern Mariner* 2.2 (April 1992) 1–27.

Reid, George A. *Speed's War: A Canadian Soldier's Memoir of World War II.* Royston: Madrona, 2007.

Riley, Alan. *A Sparker's War.* Self-published, 2005.

Scislowski, Stanley. *Not All of Us Were Brave.* Toronto: Dundurn, 1997.

Silver, L. Ray. *Last of the Gladiators: A World War II Bomber Navigator's Story.* Shrewsbury, UK: Airlife, 1995.

Smith, Sydney Percival with David Scott Smith. *Lifting the Silence: A World War II RCAF Bomber Pilot Reunites with His Past.* Toronto: Dundurn, 2010.

Stevens, Allan W. *Glory of Youth.* Self-published, 1995.

Stewart, George. "I'll Never Forget ...," *CAHS Journal* 12.4 (1974) 116–19.

Thompson, Walter R. *Lancaster to Berlin.* London: Goodall, 1985.

Turnbull, Fred. *The Invasion Diaries.* Kemptville: Veterans Publications, 2007.

Wahlroth, Arthur B. "Wellington Pilot," *CAHS* 19.2 (1981) 49–60.

Wallace, Jack. "Shermans in Sicily: The Diary of a Young Soldier, Summer 1943," *Canadian Military History* 7.4 (Autumn 1998) 63–8.

Whitby, Michael. "The Strain of the Bridge: The Second World War Diaries of Commander A.F.C. Layard, RN," in Colonel Bernd Horn (ed.) *Intrepid Warriors: Perspectives on Canadian Military Leaders* (Toronto: Dundurn, 2007) 75–94.

Wilkinson, Alta R. (ed.). *Ottawa to Caen: Letters from Arthur Campbell Wilkinson.* Ottawa: Tower Books, 1947.

Zarn, George. *Prairie Boys Afloat.* Self-published, 1979.

INDEX

Able Company, 267, 347, 366, 367

Ableson, George, 361

Acheson, William, 122

Admiral Graf Spee, 96

Advanced Flying Unit (AFU), 167–69

aerial bombardment, 55–58, 155–59. *See also* Bomber Command
  1940–1941 Allied campaign, 156–59
  1942 Allied campaign, 217–21
  1943 Allied campaign, 309, 314–16, 319–22
  area bombing, 201, 314–16
  Blitz, 55–58
  bombs, 220, 240
  and civilian morale, 221
  civilian targets, 157–59, 204–5, 241, 314–16, 320–22
  German defence, 205–6
  German industry, 220, 319–20
  Second Front strategy, 420–21

Afrika Korps, 63–64, 329

Air Gap, 110–13

airmen
  Canadian identity, 310–12
  chances of survival, 316–17
  culture, 163, 170, 227
  morale, 322–28
  public image, 160–61

slang, 170–71

strain of war, 223, 225–26, 230, 231, 249–50

superstitions, 228, 231–32, 246

Alexander, Harold, 343, 344, 379

Allen, Ralph, 413

Allister, William, 72

Amy, Ned, 398

Annis, Clare, 175

anti-colonial attitude, 168, 182, 302, 311–12. *See also* inter-nation tensions

anti-semitism, 15, 16–17. *See also* racism

Anti-Submarine Detection Investigation Committee. *See* asdic

anti-tank guns, 339–40, 353, 381

anti-war sentiments, 23

Appeasement, 18–19

Arcadia (conference), 174

area bombing, 201, 314–16

Armstrong Whitworth Whitley bomber, 153, 169

artists, war, 397

asdic, 121, 124, 144–45

Ashton, Clifford, 138

Athenia, 20–21

atrocities, war, 31, 65–66, 67, 83–84, 86, 87–90, 209

Audette, Louis, 105

Avant, Alan, 163
Avro Lancaster, 202–3, 233–34, 313

Babin, Alfred, 74, 86
Bader, Douglas, 54
Baird, Douglas, 192, 225
Baird, Kenneth, 79, 91
Baker Company, 366, 367
Baker, James, 316
barbiturates, 229
Baroni, Ross, 226, 228
Barrett, Harry, 138, 142, 294
Barrymore, Lionel, 207
Bartley, Hugh, 204
battle exhaustion, 416–17
battlefield experiences, 4–6, 9–10
Battle for Western Europe, 37–48
Battle of Britain, 49–55
    German strategy, 50–51
    No. 1 Squadron, 51–53, 54
    radar, 49
    RAF, 49
Battle of Britain Sunday, 54
Battle of Malta, 213–17
Battle of Ortona, 389–417
    Canadian casualties, 415
    Casa Beradi, 404
    Gully, the, 398
    Ortona (town), 405–6
    Pescara, 395
    Point 59, 415
    San Leonardo, 392–98
    Santa Maria di Constantinopoli, 414
    urban warfare, 407–15
    Villa Rogatti, 392
Battle of Second Ypres, 284
Battle of the Atlantic. *See* convoy escort
Battle of the St. Lawrence, 186–89

Bayerlein, Carl, 408
Befehlshaber der Unterseeboote (BdU),
    126, 127
Bell, Bill, 4–5
Bell, William, 90
Bender, Paul, 195
Bennett, Donald, 323
Bennett, Edwin, 274
Bennett, E.I., 79
Benzedrine ("bennies"), 230
Berard, Leo, 77, 87, 88
Bernays, Max, 290
Betcher, Bruce, 247
Beurling. George, 215–16
Birchall, Leonard, 209
Bishop, Arthur, 230
Bishop, Billy, 21, 161, 167
Bishop, W.A., 79
Bismarck, 96, 126
Black Pit. *See* Air Gap
Black Watch (Royal Highland Regiment),
    258, 263, 265, 267
Blitz, 55, 58
blitzkrieg, 31, 37
Boforce, 383
Bogert, M.P. "Pat," 383, 401
Bomber Command, 153–72
    accidents, 165, 169, 172
    bomb aimer, 162, 170, 225, 233–34, 240
    Canadian recruits, 162
    civilian targets, 157–59, 204–5, 241,
        314–16, 320–22
    enemy fighters, 157, 243–44, 245,
        247–48
    established, 153
    flight engineer, 162, 170, 233
    four-engine planes, 201–3
    ground crew, 227

gunners, 162, 235, 244–45
intelligence officer, 225
Lübeck operation, 208
meteorological officer, 225
navigational aids, 217–18
navigator, 162, 225, 234
night raids, 156
pilot, 162, 233
responsibilities of aircrew, 169–70
specific-target strategy, 155–57
training, 162–72
"turn back rate," 317–19
two-engine planes, 153–54
wireless operator, 162, 169, 170, 234,
    235, 237
bomber stream, 235–37
bombing operation, 223–50
    aerial photographs, 241, 243
    aircrew, 230
    bomber stream, 235–37
    "bombing up," 227
    bomb run, 237–41
    briefing, 223–26
    crippled aircraft, 248–49
    debriefing, 249–50
    fatigue, 229–30, 249
    pre-flight preparation, 230
    searchlights, 237–38
    shellfire, 236, 237, 238–39, 240
    spare time, 224–27
Bonner, Al, 138, 146
Boston, social life, 296
Bourassa, Clarence, 270
Bowen, Gerald, 133, 142, 143, 145, 147
Boyd, Harry, 197
Boyd, Roy, 408
Bren gun, 335
Bretagne, 49

Brick, Paul, 116, 295
Bridgwater, Al, 227
Bristol Blenheim bomber, 153
British Commonwealth Air Training Plan
    (BCATP), 161–67, 309
British Eighth Army, 329, 343, 350, 352,
    377, 378, 379, 389
British First Army, 332
British Fourteenth Army, 209
Brittain, Miller, 165, 238
Brock, Jeffry, 141, 147, 197
Brodeur, Louis-Philippe, 308
Brooke, Sir Alan, 319, 332
Brookes, George, 312, 318
Brown, Atholl Sutherland, 210
Brown, George, 168, 314
Brown, W.I., 131
B-17 Flying Fortress, 316
Buchan, John, 358
Burbridge, Ralph, 115, 151
Burnett, Wilf, 210
Butt, D.M., 201

Cagney, James, 161
Calder, Vince, 71, 89
Calgary Regiment. *See* 14th Canadian Army
    Tank Battalion
Cameron Highlanders of Ottawa, 114, 258,
    267, 268, 269–70
Campbell, Alex, 236, 350, 357, 358
Campbell, W.R., 361
Campobasso, 387–88
Canada
    economic conditions, 59
    enlistment, 25–28, 29
    national identity, 168, 182–84, 422–23
    national unity, 21–23
    outbreak of war, 20–30

rearmament, 23–24

trade imbalance, 61–62

Canadian Active Service Force. *See*
    Canadian Army Overseas

Canadian army
    in 1939, 28–30
    British images of, 36
    demographic profile, 35
    French Canadians, 29
    social life, 37

Canadian Army Film, 412

Canadian Army Overseas, 29

Canadian Defence Quarterly, 340

Canadianization policy, 309–14

Canadian National Steamships Ltd, 197

Canadian Women's Army Corps, 7

Canso. *See* Consolidated Catalina flying
    boat

Captains of the Clouds (film), 161

cargo ships, 190, 192. *See also* convoy escort

Carleton and York Regiment, 339, 356,
    378, 384, 401, 404–5, 415

Carley float, 194

carpet bombing, 56, 220

Carrière, Felix, 36

Carswell, Andy, 172

Casablanca Conference, 230, 309

Cassels, Bon, 327

Catto, Douglas, 266

C Force, 72

Chamberlain, Neville, 18, 43, 49

Chance, David, 235, 243

Chapman, J.K., 26, 323

Char B (French tank), 39

Charlie Company, 267

Chatham, 187

Cheney, Donald, 160, 237, 241

Chequer, George Joseph, 327

Chiang Kai-Shek, 69

China, Japanese atrocities in, 67

Christie, Kay, 86

Churchill tanks, 273–74

Churchill, Winston, 43, 55, 68, 84, 94,
    107, 110, 153, 156, 174, 178, 204,
    209, 256, 283, 303–4, 315, 330–31

"circus" operation, 210

Clark, John, 246

Clark, Mark, 378–79

Clayton, Bob, 75

Clever, W.H., 162

Cockin, Battle, 358

Coldridge, Stan, 171, 237

Coles, George, 108

Collins, Robert, 162–63

Cologne, bombing, 208 of

Colville, Alex, 397

Combined Bomber Offensive, 309, 314–
    16, 319–22

Comfort, Charles, 397

conscription, 21, 22, 23, 24, 188

Consolidated Catalina flying boat, 175,
    177–78, 189, 308

Conspicuous Gallantry Medal, 292

Convoy
    ON 127, 297–302
    HX-1, 98
    HX 133, 126–28
    OB 336, 127
    SC 42, 128–31
    SC 58, 116
    SC 94, 287–88
    SC 95, 293

convoy code, 114–15

convoy escort, 124–31, 422. *See also*
    Newfoundland Escort Force (NEF)
    air protection, 110–14, 179, 308

anti-submarine weapons and technology,
    120–24
C groups, 307
collisions, 116
corvettes, 103–7, 109, 122–24
depth charges, 122–24
destroyers, 108–9
escort tactics, 115–18
inshore convoy, 180–81
insufficient resources, 174, 178, 297,
    304–5
losses, 302–4
oil tanker, 184–85
ramming the enemy, 120, 291, 292
Triangle Run, 181
U-boat attacks, 126–31, 287–93,
    297–302
UK-to-Gibraltar route, 304
convoy formation, 114–18
"cookie" (bomb), 220
Co-operative Commonwealth Federation
    (CCF), 34
corkscrew dive, 245
Cormier, Rudy, 356
Corrigan, C.E., 388
Corrigan, Leonard, 90
Corvette K-225 (film), 181
corvettes, 103–7, 109, 122–24, 133–52
    food, 138–39
    living conditions, 135–38
    morale, 145–50
    rough seas, 133–34
    seasickness, 137–38
    strain of war, 141, 144–45, 150–52
    winter conditions, 141, 142–44
    work routines, 139–42
Cousins, Howard, 133
Cousins, S.J., 361

Coventry, bombing of, 57
Crawford, J.N., 90
Crerar, Harry, 70, 71, 92, 253, 256, 283
"crewing up," 171–72
Crozier, Robert, 26
Culley, Ray, 137, 149–50
Currie, Sir Arthur, 21, 331
Curry, Frank, 124, 138, 144, 148, 152,
    293, 295
Cybulski-Ross, Martin, 167

Danson, Barney, 4
Davis, Eldon, 416
death, dying, 193–200, 422
debriefing, 249
deflection shooting, 53
DeMone, Edison, 239
Dempsey, Joseph, 192
DEMS (Defensively Equipped Merchant
    Ship), 192–93
Denmark, German invasion of, 37
depth charges, 122–24
Desert Air Force (DAF), 363, 394
"destroyers for bases" deal, 107–8
Deutscher, Joseph, 158
Deutschland, 96
DeWolf, Harry, 40
Dicks, Bud, 83–84
Dieppe raid, 251–85
    air battle, 274–76
    Berneval, 260, 262
    Canadian casualties, 282
    deficient planning., 256–59
    German casualties, 282
    German defence, 260
    lessons learned, 283–85
    Pourville beaches, 267–70
    Puys, 263–67

RAF Fighter Command, 257
  strategic goal, 259
  tactical goals, 258–59
  tanks, 258, 273–74
  whitewashed, 282–83
Dobing, Sid, 299
Dobson, Andrew "Dobby," 297
Dog Company, 267, 394
dogfight, 47, 53, 211–13
Dönitz, Karl, 20, 110, 119, 179, 194, 287
Donnelly, Howard, 88
Dorion, Aimé, 290
Dornier 17, 50, 276
Dornier 217, 276
Douglas C-47 Dakotas, 209
drinking, 145–46, 293–94, 323–24
Duffy, Warren, 204
Dumais, Lucien, 278
Dunkirk, retreat from, 41
Dunlap, Larry, 346
Duplessis, Maurice, 33–34

Eastern Air Command, 110, 125, 175,
  177–78, 186, 308
Eastern Front, 62–67, 251
  Battle of Stalingrad, 330
  German atrocities, 65–66
  resilience of Soviet soldiers, 63
  winter conditions, 66–67
Easton, Alan, 121, 135, 192
Eddy, Roy Ernest, 192
Edmonton Regiment, 338, 359, 367, 398,
  400, 407, 408, 409, 413, 414, later
  Loyal Edmonton Regiment
Edwards, R.L., 53
Eisenhower, Dwight D., 342–43, 346
Elliot, Elwyn, 194
Elliot, Raymond, 85

Ellis, L.G., 264
Enigma naval codes, 126, 254
Essen, terorized, 322
Essex Scottish, 258, 271
Eves, R.W., 209

Farquharson, Bob, 209–10
federal-provincial relations, 33–34
5th British Division, 378
Fighter Command, 210–16, 257. See also
  Battle of Britain
Final Solution, 66, 315
Finland, war with Soviet Union, 63
Finnie, Jim, 245
First Canadian Army, 253
1st Canadian Army Tank Brigade, 334, 340
1st Canadian Infantry Brigade, 42, 331,
  338, 357, 390, 415
1st Canadian Infantry Division, 29, 43,
  251, 331, 334, 338–40, 377
1st Middlesex, 73
First Nations soldiers, 27
First World War
  Canada and, 21
  trench warfare, 15–16
Fishpond radar, 235
Fitz, H.C., 302
5/7 Rajputs, 73, 76 77, 79
flak gun, 205–6
Fleming, Margaret, 8
Foch, Ferdinand, 360
Focke-Wulf Fw 190, 212, 275
Forin, J.D., 370
Forster, Hugo, 130
Forsyth, Tom, 85
48th Highlanders of Canada, 338, 394,
  395, 415
44th Royal Tank Regiment, 393

4 Group, 200

14th Canadian Army Tank Battalion, 258, 273–74, 340, 383, 397

4th Princess Louise Dragoon Guards, 339

France
British retreat, 41
defeat of, 38–44
evacuation at Dunkirk, 41
German strategy, 38–40
southern campaign, 41–42

Freya radar stations, 205

Fulton, John "The Moose," 207

Funkmessbeobachtung 1 radar detector, 186

Fusiliers Mont-Royal (FMR), 258, 277–78

Galloway, James, 141

Galloway, Jim, 106

Galloway, Strome, 356, 367, 417

Gee, John, 201

Gee, navigational aid, 217

Geraghty, Donald, 89

German
1st Parachute Division, 406–7, 410
15th Panzer Grenadier Division, 354, 358, 359
90th Panzer Grenadier Division, 390
302nd Infantry Division, 260

Germany, 13–30
Allied bombing, impact, 319–22
defeat in North Africa, 329–30
rearmament, 15, 18
Soviet campaign, 64–67
territorial expansion, 17–19
trench warfare, 15–16
war production, 220, 319–20

Girouard, Pius, 383, 404

Godefroy, Hugh, 212–13

Goebbels, Joseph, 319–20

Gostling, Alfred, 269

Gouk, George, 269

Graham, Howard, 338

Gray, Robert Hampton, 292

Great Terror, 62

gremlins, 246

Gresham, A.B., 80, 81

Griffin, Anthony, 120

Grubb, Freddy, 130

Haggard, W.A., 267–68

Halifax (city), reputation of, 295

Halton, Matthew, 413

Hamburg, bombing of, 320–22

Hamilton, H.S., 24

Hancock, Charlie, 170, 199

Handley Page Halifax, 202–3, 233–34, 313

Handley Page Hampden bomber, 153

Harrington, Mike, 230, 243

Harris, Sir Arthur, 203–4, 208, 218, 257, 309

Harris, Lawren P., 397

Harrison, Eric, 397

Harrison, Joseph, 168

Harvey, Douglas, 226, 229, 245, 324

Hastings and Prince Edward Regiment, 35, 338, 350, 352–54, 354, 358–59, 358–60, 366–67, 369, 387, 393, 398, 415

Hawker Hurricanes, 45, 212, 213, 275

Hawker, Kitty, 8

Heavy Conversion Unit, 172

Heflin, Van, 207

Heinkel 111, 50

Hennessy, R.L., 290

Hepburn, Mitchell, 34

Hermann Göring Division, 354, 369

Hewer, Howard, 166, 199, 323

HF/DF ("Huff-Duff"), high-frequency
    direction finder, 296
Hibbard, Jimmy, 129
Hickson, George, 276–77
Hill, A.C., 277
Hill, Audrey, 6
historical officers, 396–97
Hitler, Adolf, 13, 14–15, 31, 96, 380, 383
    rise to power, 13–14
    Roosevelt, Hitler's opinion of, 62
    Soviet Union, attack on, 62
    two-front war, creation of, 94
HMCS Agassiz, 106, 141, 296
HMCS Alberni, 150
HMCS Algoma, 133
HMCS Annapolis, 108
HMCS Arvida, 139, 295, 301
HMCS Assiniboine, 95, 288–92
HMCS Athabaskan, 292
HMCS Calgary, 184
HMCS Capilano, 147
HMCS Celandine, 297, 301
HMCS Chambly, 130
HMCS Charlottetown, 187–88
HMCS Chaudière, 115
HMCS Columbia, 108
HMCS Dauphin, 152
HMCS Drumheller, 308
HMCS Dunver, 183
HMCS Fraser, 95, 98, 109
HMCS Galt, 293
HMCS Kamsack, 293
HMCS Kenogami, 129
HMCS Lachine, 196
HMCS Margaree, 109
HMCS Midland, 146
HMCS Mimico, 149
HMCS Montcalm, 181

HMCS Moose Jaw, 116, 130, 184
HMCS Niagara, 108, 133
HMCS Oakville, 184–85
HMCS Ottawa, 95, 122, 126, 127, 183,
    297, 299–300
HMCS Outremont, 192
HMCS Prince Robert, 150
HMCS Quesnel, 183
HMCS Regina, 122
HMCS Restigouche, 95
HMCS Rimouski, 106
HMCS Sackville, 135
HMCS Saguenay, 95, 294
HMCS Skeena, 95, 129–30
HMCS Spikenard, 294
HMCS St. Clair, 108
HMCS St. Croix, 108, 297
HMCS St. Francis, 108
HMCS St. Laurent, 40, 95, 98
HMCS Summerside, 137
HMCS Wetaskiwin, 184
HMCS Windflower, 116
HMS Buttercup, 183
HMS Calcutta, 109
HMS Roberts, 347
Hoffmeister, Bert, 407
Home, W.J., 84, 85
Hong Kong
    battle, 74–85
    blame for defeat, 90–93
    Canadian army, 70–73
    defence of, 68–70
    Japanese army, 73
    King government and, 70, 92, 93
    opening attack, 74–75
    prisoners of war, 87–90, 91
Hong Kong Defence Corps, 73
Hornsey, Denis, 317

Howard, Don, 171
Howe, C.D., 32, 59
Hughes, Sam, 397
Hughson, Geoffrey, 133, 139, 145
Humphreys, Douglas, 160, 323
Hurst, Allen, 124

Iceland, reputation of, 295–96
IFF (Identification Friend or Foe) signal, 247
Ilsley, J.L., 32, 61
infantry
    battalion, 335–36
    brigades, 338–39
    Canadian, 335–40
    rifle companies, 335
    support company, 335–36
    training, 33–338
Inouye, Kanao, 90
inter-nation tensions, 168, 182, 294–95,
    302, 311–12
Irish Regiment of Canada, 26
Irwin, Walter, 171, 238, 249
Italian campaign, 377–88. *See also* Battle of
    Ortona
    Allied landing, 377–79
    compo rations, 386–87
    German defence, 378–79, 380, 383,
        388–89
    Gustav Line, 389
    invasion strategy, 379
    local conditions, 380–81, 384, 388
    local residents, 382–83
    morale, 385–88
    Potenza, 383
    RCAF, 379
    Reggio di Calabria, 377
    Salerno, 378–79
    Winter Line (German), 390

Italy
    declaration of war, 63
    surrender, 377

Japan
    expansionism, 67–70
    Pacific war, 67–94
Japanese Canadians, evacuation of, 92–93
Jasperson, Fred, 272–73
Jefferson, Jim, 360, 400, 409
Jenson, L.B., 147, 182, 295, 297, 299, 300
Jenson, L.B. "Yogi," 133
Jewish refugees, 25–26
Johnston, Joseph, 271
Johnston, R.R., 416
Jones, G.C., 306
Jones, Harlo, 167, 171, 245, 324
Jukes, Yvonne, 7
Junkers Ju 88, 50, 205, 276

Kammhuber Line, 205
Kassel, bombing, 322
Keelan, Larry, 243
Kensett, Robert, 169, 231, 235, 247
Kesselring, Albert, 350, 380, 383
Kimber, Jack, 108
King, Dudley, 121, 295–96, 301–2
King, George, 171
King's Regulations for the Canadian Navy,
    306
King, William Lyon Mackenzie, 21–24,
    59–62, 70, 92, 421–22
    cabinet, 32–33
    Canadianization policy, 309–10
    and Churchill, 303–4
    conscription, 21, 22, 23, 24, 188
    federal-provincial relations, 33–34
    "limited liability" war, 22, 161

and Sicily campaign, 331–32
United States, strengthened ties with, 59–62
Kowloon, 75
Kriegsmarine, 37, 96–97
Kutyn, Michael, 232
kye, 142

Labatt, Robert, 277
Lady Hawkins, 197–98
Lamb, James, 101, 105, 117, 137, 142, 150, 179
Lamont, A.G.W., 142
Lapointe, Ernest, 24, 33
Law, A.T., 270
Lawrence, Hal, 107, 117, 144, 145, 145 146, 146, 151, 185, 293, 295
Lawson, J.L., 72, 76, 80, 82
Lay, Horatio Nelson, 99
League of Nations, 17
Lee-Enfield rifle, 335
Lee, Norma Etta, 327
Leese, Sir Oliver, 366
Lemcke, Rudolph, 288, 291
Les Fusiliers Mont-Royal, 114
Levitin, Nat, 163
Lewis, Mike, 157
Liberator aircraft, 308
life jackets, 144, 194, 228
Lindsay, Douglas, 213
Lockheed Hudson, 174, 177
Logos, Steve, 298
Londonderry, social life, 296
Lovat, Lord, 262
Luftwaffe, 41, 49
    Battle of Britain, 50–51
    bombing Blitz, 55–58

Macdonald, Angus, 32, 70, 305
Macdonald, B.G., 295
MacDonell, George, 72
Macdonell, Sergeant, 82
Macleod, Peter, 264
MacQueen, John, 334–35
Maffre, Jim, 275
Maffre, John, 275
Maginot Line, 31–32, 38, 39
malaria, 370–71, 384
Malkin, Ben, 334
Malone, Richard, 338
Maltby, Christopher, 73, 75–76, 77, 84, 86, 90–91
Manstein, Erich von, 39
Margison, John, 135
Marshall, George, 342
Marsh, Tom, 79
Massey, Vincent, 292
Matthews, D.J., 326
Matthews, Jack, 193
Mazerolle, Henri, 384
McCaig, Leslie, 227, 229, 232, 243, 322, 323
McCann, Don, 246
McDonald, Angus, 192
McDonald, B.G., 223, 239, 312, 325
McElroy, John, 215
McIntosh, Jack, 227
McKnight, William, 46
McNab, Ernie, 52, 53
McNair, R.W. "Buck," 215
McNaughton, Andrew, 29–30, 41, 253, 256, 283, 331–32, 374–75
McRae, Bill, 162
Medd, Bruce, 395
Menard, Dollard, 277– 278
merchant navy, 189–93

Merritt, Cecil, 269
mess, 323–27
Messerschmitt Bf 109, 45, 50, 51, 205, 275
Messerschmitt Bf 110, 50, 205, 211–12, 243
MGM, 207
MG-42 machine gun, 392, 400
Mid-Ocean Escort Force (MOEF), 179–81
Miller, Erle "Dusty," 172
mines, 381
Mitchell, Howard, 359–60, 381, 405, 411
Mk XIV, bombsight, 240
Molson, Hartland, 54
Montgomery, Bernard, 254, 329–30, 343–44, 351, 375, 379, 389
Moody, Alfred, 263–64
Morey, Mike, 124
Morrison, Les, 238, 241, 245–46, 311
Mountbatten, Louis, 252–53, 256, 283, 284
Mowat, Farley, 285, 342, 356–57, 358, 385, 388, 394
Muir, Fraser, 235, 241
Munro, Ross, 255, 265, 413
Murch, Doug, 296
Murray, Leonard W., 125, 173, 189, 306
music, 146–47, 183, 293–94, 324–25, 388
Mussolini, Benito, 63
   removed from power, 372

Nailsea Moor, 195
National Nationalist Party, 14
National Resources Mobilization Act, 43
Nelles, Percy, 107, 122, 184, 305
Nelligan, Bill, 118
Nelson, Patrick, 139
Nethery, Alex, 318, 327

Newfoundland Escort Force (NEF), 125–26, 150, 173–98. See also convoy escort
   American cooperation, 175–76
   insufficient resources, 174, 178
New York, social life, 296
Nixon, Charles "Pat," 115
Nixon, Patrick, 40
North African campaign, 63–64, 329–30
Norway, German invasion of, 37
nose art, 227

Oboe, navigational aid, 218
O'Brien, John, 401
Ogilvie, Keith, 51
104th Panzer Grenadier Regiment, 263, 356
Operation Husky, 343. See also Sicily campaign
Operation Rutter, 255
Operation Torch, 188, 330
Osborn, John, 80–82

Pacific war, 67–94, 251, 329
   American commitment to, 174
   Canadian squadrons in, 209–10
   Philippines, 68
   Singapore, 68, 94
Panzer tanks, 397
Pariseault, M., 387
Parker, B.G., 342
Parker, Maurice, 73, 77, 84
Park Steamship Company, 190
pathfinders, 218–19
Patterson, John, 217, 236, 243, 246
Patton, George, 343, 344, 351–52, 371, 378
Payne, John Oliver, 88
Pearce, Richard, 139

Pearl Harbor, attack on, 74, 94

Peden, Murray, 223, 249

Peel, Ron, 159, 170, 206, 326, 328

Penhale, M.H.S., 339

Permanent Joint Board on Defence (PJBD), 61

Perry, Bill, 150

Perth Regiment, 9

Peters, Jim, 122

Peterson, John, 137, 146, 149

Phoney War, 31–37

photographers, combat, 412–13

PIAT, anti-tank weapon, 381, 402, 409

Pickard, Charles, 161

Pickford, R.J., 106

Pitcher, Paul, 54

P-51 Mustang, 275

Poland, invasion of, 19, 26

Policy Directive Number 22, 204

Portal, Sir Charles, 155, 204, 218, 257

Powell, A.J., 185

Power, Charles "Chubby," 32, 33, 70, 313

Powers, T.M., 347

Price, Albert, 155

Prince of Wales, 69, 75

Princess Louise Dragoon Guards, 381

Princess Patricia's Canadian Light Infantry (PPCLI), 35, 36, 338, 360, 367, 392, 393, 401

Prince, Tommy, 27

Proudly She Marches (film), 8

pub, 327–28

Pugsley, William, 101

Pullen, Thomas, 178, 299, 300–301, 302

racism, 15, 27, 73–74

radar, 49, 121–22, 205, 302

radar detection, 186–87

Raeder, Erich, 96

Ralston, J.L., 29, 32, 70, 92, 188, 331

Ramsay, Sir Bertram, 283

RCAF Women's Division (WD), 7, 228

RCN officers, 107

RCNR (Royal Canadian Navy Reserve), 100, 102, 107

RCNVR (Volunteer Reserve), 101–2, 105, 107

rear gunner, 244–45

Reid, George, 347, 359, 384

Reid, Max, 135, 193

Reid, Thomas, 165, 217

Repulse, 69, 75

rescue, of survivors, 193–98

"rhubarb" operation, 210

Richardson, Ray, 149

Richmond, George, 137

Riley, Allan, 288

Roberts, J. Hamilton, 254, 277, 282–83

"rodeo" operation, 210

Rogers, Norman, 32

Rommel, Erwin, 39, 63–64, 329, 380

Roosevelt, Franklin, 23, 60–62, 68, 107, 315, 330–31

Rose, H.B., 77

Rotterdam, aerial bombardment of, 55, 155

Rousseau, J.P., 402

Royal Air Force (RAF), 49, 110, 213. *See also* Battle of Britain; Bomber Command; Fighter Command

Royal Canadian Air Force (RCAF), 45, 49–50, 110, 309–10, 379

Royal Canadian Army Medical Corps, 344

Royal Canadian Army Service Corps, 381

Royal Canadian Artillery, 269, 358–59

Royal Canadian Engineers, 274, 276, 360

Royal Canadian Horse Artillery, 41

Royal Canadian Navy (RCN), 23, 95–96, 98–102. *See also* convoy escort

Royal Canadian Regiment (RCR), 35, 102, 338, 347, 365–67, 369, 394, 395

Royal Hamilton Light Infantry, 271, 276–77

Royal Naval College of Canada, 125

Royal Navy, 37, 48, 292–93

Royal Regiment of Canada, 114, 258, 263–67

Royal Rifles of Canada, 70, 76, 77, 79, 82, 86, 89, 91

Royal 22e Régiment, 35, 339, 378, 387, 402–4, 415

Rudd, A.J., 408

Rundstedt, Gerd von, 39

Russel, Blair, 53–54

Salmon, H.L., 338, 340

Sansom, E.W., 37

Saskatoon Light Infantry (SLI), 339, 359, 381, 411

Schayler, Ed, 80

Schellin, Martin, 323

Schlieffen Plan, 38

Scislowski, Stanley, 9

Scott, Dennis, 274

Scott, F.R., 23

Scott, Randolph, 181

Seaforth Highlanders, 35, 338, 347, 359, 367, 392, 397–98, 407, 410, 413

2nd Canadian Infantry Brigade, 338, 356, 357, 407

2nd Canadian Infantry Division, 43, 254

Second Front, 252, 319

2nd Royal Scots, 73

Second Tactical Air Force (RAF), 215

Second World War, 1–11

"good war," 10–11

Western Allied strategy, 419–21

78th British Division, 390

sexism, 6, 8

Sharpe, Harold, 171

Sharpe, Jim, 116–17

Shepherd, Jack, 387

Sherman tanks, 340, 361

Short Stirling, 202, 203

Shufelt, Keith, 196

Sicily campaign, 329–75

    Agira, 363–67

    air support, 346–47, 363

    Allied strategic goal, 330–31

    assault landing, 344–48

    Assoro, 358–59

    Axis defenders, 333, 346

    Canadian forces, 352, 355–61, 363–71, 373–74

    casualties, 372

    Catania, 346–47, 351–52

    friendly fire casualties, 348

    geography, 332–33

    German forces, 333, 350–51, 354, 356, 363

    German withdrawal, 371–72

    Grammichele, 352, 354

    Italian forces, 347–48, 350, 354

    Leonforte, 354, 359–61

    local conditions, 348–50, 370–71

    Nissoria, 363–67

    Palermo, 352, 362

    Regalbuto, 369–70

    transport ships, 340–42

    Valguarnera, 354, 356, 357

Silver, Ray, 208

Simonds, Guy, 340, 368–69, 374, 390

Singer, Jack, 232

6 Group (Canada), 312–14, 317

Small, Jack, 326

Small, Norville, 177

Smith, Jack, 193

Smith, Rod, 215

smoking, 145, 387

Soløy, 127

songs. *See* music

South Saskatchewan Regiment, 258, 267, 269, 270

Soviet Union

  Baltic states, occupation of, 63

  Finland, attack on, 63

  and Nazi aggression, 16–17

  non-aggression pact, 19, 31

  occupation of Poland, 31

Spanish Civil War, 18

Speer, Albert, 220, 321

Spitfire, 50, 212, 213, 275

Squadron

  No. 9 (RAF), 159

  No. 57 (RAF), 204

  No. 109 (RAF), 326

  No. 110 (RAF), 46, 49

  No. 113 (RAF), 177

  No. 128 (RAF), 204

  No. 158 (RAF), 231

  No. 165 (RAF), 275

  No. 214 (RAF), 249

  No. 218 (RAF), 199

  No. 235 (RAF), 52–53

  No. 242 (RAF), 45–46, 48, 54

  No. 303 (RAF), 54

  No. 1 (RCAF), 49–50, 51–53, later 401 Squadron

  No. 5 (RCAF), 112, 308

  No. 10 (RCAF), 112, 125, 177

  No. 11 (RCAF), 112

  No. 401 (RCAF), 212, 275

  No. 403 (RCAF), 213, 216

  No. 405 (RCAF), 157, 200, 207, 311, 318

  No. 407 (RCAF), 323

  No. 408 (RCAF), 199, 200, 207, 210, 225, 226

  No. 413 (RCAF), 209

  No. 415 (RCAF), 207

  No. 416 (RCAF), 275

  No. 418 (RCAF), 210

  No. 419 (RCAF), 207, 227, 247

  No. 420 (RCAF), 200, 346

  No. 424 (RCAF), 245, 324, 346

  No. 425 (RCAF), 207, 346

  No. 426 (RCAF), 207, 232

  No. 427 (RCAF), 207, 318

  No. 428 (RCAF), 327

  No. 429 (RCAF), 207

  No. 432 (RCAF), 207

  No. 433 (RCAF), 207

  No. 434 (RCAF), 207

  No. 435 (RCAF), 209

  No. 516 (RCAF), 213

Squires, Ray, 85, 87

SS *Caribou,* 188–89

SS *Coamo,* 197

SS *Muneric,* 129

Stalin, Joseph, 31, 62–63, 256

Stapleton, Cornelius, 273

Statute of Westminster, 24

St. Elmo's fire, 245–46

Stevens, Allan, 121, 134, 197

Stevens, E.B.K., 150, 173

Stewart, Alastair, 124

Stewart, George, 249

St. John's, social life, 293–95

Stollery, Jack, 413

Stone, Jim, 413

Stubbs, John, 288, 290, 291, 292
Sudetenland, 18
Sutcliffe, Bruce, 358
SW1C (Surface Warning—One Canadian)
    device, 121. *See also* radar
Syer, Ralph, 171

tail gunner, 235
Thexton, Robert, 354, 378
3rd Canadian Infantry Brigade, 339, 357
3rd Field Company, 360
Thompson, Alfred, 155
Thompson, F.D., 37
Thompson submachine gun, 335
Thompson, Walter, 236
Three Rivers Regiment, 340, 352, 360, 361,
    407, 409, 413
331 Wing, 346–47
"tip and run" raids, 167
toilet, aircraft, 246–47
Tojo, Hideki, 68
torpedo, 118
Tracy, Spencer, 207
Treaty of Versailles, 13–14, 15
trench warfare, 15–16
Tripartite Pact, 67
Triquet, Paul, 404
Trist, George, 91
Triton, 307
Tucker, Gilbert, 290
Tunisia. *See* Operation Torch
Turnbull, Fred, 347
Turner, Lana, 207
Turner, Stan, 48
Tweedsmuir Lord, 358, 366, 367
2/14th Punjabis, 73
231st Malta Brigade, 357
Type VIIC U-boats, 118

U-66, 197
U-69, 188–89
U-91, 299–300, 302
U-94, 185
U-132, 186
U-203, 127
U-210, 288–92
U-371, 127
U-454, 288
U-501, 130–31
U-517, 187
U-553, 186
U-652, 129–30
U-753, 308
U-754, 177
U-boat-hunting formations, 307–8
U-boats, 96, 97, 99, 100, 117–20, 124–31,
    176–78, 184–89, 194, 287–93, 295
Ultra, 126, 178, 383
United States
    defence of Canada, 23, 60–61
    isolationism, 17, 43
    and Japanese expansionism, 68
    Pacific War, 74, 94, 174
    support for Britain, 55, 60
    trade with Canada, 61–62
United States Army Air Force (USAAF), 316
United States Fifth Army, 378, 379, 389
United States Seventh Army, 343
Universal Carriers, 381–82
Untamed (film), 311
Urwin, Harry, 114

Vale, Sid, 86
Vaughan, W.E., 223, 231, 241
venereal disease, 166, 167, 388
Verreault, Georges, 82
Vicker bomber, 153

Vickers Wellingtons, 200, 312–13

Victoria Cross, 292–93

Vokes, Christopher, 338, 390, 392, 400, 401, 402, 404, 405, 415

Vradenburg, William P., 147, 194

Wagner, Earl, 190, 191

Wahlroth, Arthur, 157, 159, 169, 230, 240, 311

Wallace, Bob, 327

Wallace, Jack, 367

Wallis, Cedric, 76, 84, 85, 91

Wannsee Conference, 66

Ware, Cameron, 393

Warren, Bruce, 275

Warren, Douglas, 275–76

Watson, Kenneth, 290

Weimar Republic, 13, 14

Weir, John, 159

Welsh, D.L., 89

Westland Lysander aircraft, 49

West Nova Scotia Regiment, 35, 339, 354, 378, 399, 401, 404

Whitaker, Denis, 271

White, Maurice, 414–15

Wiens, R.H., 46–47

Wilkinson, Arthur, 42, 311

Williams, George, 232

Willson, W.H., 130

Wilson, Frederick, 213

"Window" (aluminum foil strips), 320

Wings on Her Shoulders (film), 8

Winnipeg Grenadiers, 70, 79–82, 88, 90

Winter War, 63

Women's Royal Canadian Naval Service, 6

women, wartime work, 6–9

Wrens. *See* Women's Royal Canadian Naval Service

Würzburg radar system, 205

Young, Sir Mark, 84

Zarn, George, 150, 295

Z Force, 113–14

Zinkhan, John, 225–26, 245, 325

Zyphenberg, 116

CREDITS

All attempts have been made to track down copyright. All photographs are held by the author unless otherwise stated. Permission to reproduce the following copyrighted works is gratefully acknowledged.

Page 33: Library Archives of Canada, PA-104216

Page 56: Laurier Centre for Military Strategic and Disarmament Studies

Page 71: Laurier Centre for Military Strategic and Disarmament Studies

Page 76: Laurier Centre for Military Strategic and Disarmament Studies

Page 81: Library Archives of Canada, PA-37483

Page 89: Laurier Centre for Military Strategic and Disarmament Studies

Page 92: Imperial War Museum, A 30523

Page 99: Library Archives of Canada, PA-112993

Page 104: Laurier Centre for Military Strategic and Disarmament Studies

Page 136: Library Archives of Canada, PA-170292

Page 148: Library Archives of Canada, PA-188786

Page 154: Laurier Centre for Military Strategic and Disarmament Studies

Page 158: Laurier Centre for Military Strategic and Disarmament Studies

Page 166: Laurier Centre for Military Strategic and Disarmament Studies

Page 175: Library Archives of Canada, PA-134171

Page 183: Laurier Centre for Military Strategic and Disarmament Studies

Page 185: Laurier Centre for Military Strategic and Disarmament Studies

Page 187: Laurier Centre for Military Strategic and Disarmament Studies

Page 195: Library Archives of Canada, PA-134432

Page 202: Library Archives of Canada, C-004713

Page 211: Library Archives of Canada, PA-115117

Page 224: Laurier Centre for Military Strategic and Disarmament Studies

Page 239: PL-144258
Page 248: Imperial War Museum, CH 6627
Page 262: Library Archives of Canada, PA-113246
Page 268: Library Archives of Canada, PA-183772
Page 272: C.P. Stacey, *The Canadian Army, 1939-1945* (Ottawa, 1948) 77
Page 279: Library Archives of Canada, C-017294
Page 281: Library Archives of Canada, C-017293
Page 289: Library Archives of Canada, PA-037443
Page 291: Library Archives of Canada, PA-037444
Page 303: Library Archives of Canada, C-54474
Page 310: Laurier Centre for Military Strategic and Disarmament Studies
Page 315: Laurier Centre for Military Strategic and Disarmament Studies
Page 317: Laurier Centre for Military Strategic and Disarmament Studies
Page 323: Laurier Centre for Military Strategic and Disarmament Studies
Page 349: Library Archives of Canada, PA-193883
Page 355: Library Archives of Canada, PA-151798
Page 362: Library Archives of Canada, PA-136216
Page 365: Library Archives of Canada, PA-134527
Page 368: Library Archives of Canada, PA-166750
Page 373: Library Archives of Canada, PA-130249
Page 374: Library Archives of Canada, PA-130215
Page 382: Library Archives of Canada, PA-129763
Page 385: Library Archives of Canada, PA-163928
Page 386: Library Archives of Canada, PA-032222
Page 392: Laurier Centre for Military Strategic and Disarmament Studies
Page 396: Library Archives of Canada, PA-141867
Page 403: Library Archives of Canada, PA-153181
Page 406: Library Archives of Canada, PA- PA114487
Page 409: Laurier Centre for Military Strategic and Disarmament Studies
Page 410: Laurier Centre for Military Strategic and Disarmament Studies
Page 412: Library Archives of Canada, PA-136198
Page 414: Library Archives of Canada, PA-147111
Page 416: Library Archives of Canada, PA-193909